The Golden Gate, with the steamship *John L. Stephens* and the clipper ship *Flying Cloud* at entrance. Lithograph by Kuchel and Dresel, 1855.

IN PURSUIT
OF THE GOLDEN DREAM

*Reminiscences of San Francisco and the Northern
and Southern Mines, 1849-1857
By Howard C. Gardiner*

EDITED BY DALE L. MORGAN

WESTERN HEMISPHERE, INC.
STOUGHTON, MASSACHUSETTS
MCMLXX

DESIGNED AND PRINTED BY LAWTON AND ALFRED KENNEDY
SAN FRANCISCO

TABLE OF CONTENTS

LIST OF ILLUSTRATIONS

MAPS

To

HELEN HARDING BRETNOR

AND

JULIA HAMILTON MACLEOD

who welcomed me to the Bancroft Library in 1954

and have dwelt with me since, stimulatingly, companionably,

and amusingly, in that wide world between

Benvenue and La Loma.

DALE L. MORGAN

THROUGH THE HAZE OF TIME
The California Gold Rush in Retrospect

Personal narratives of the California Gold Rush fall into three broad categories. First are the starkly contemporary records, the diaries and letters written en route to or after reaching the Golden Shore, and while toiling in the mines. Second are the travel narratives written and published soon after the event. And, finally, we have the often richly-colored reminiscences which look back down the years.

These categories shade off into one another. Diaries kept on the trail or on the high seas, even when preserved in the form of manuscripts, sometimes prove to be versions rewritten from pocket memoranda, with full benefit of hindsight; and letters describing the journey or voyage to California may sum up the experiences of many months of travel. In turn, the travel narratives may be generalized, but as often are faithful to the day-to-day memoranda on which they are based, deliberately keeping within the framework, the imposed limitations, of actual diaries. And for their part, the reminiscences may lean upon memoranda preserved down through the years.

Recent scholarship in Gold Rush history has been primarily concerned with the diaries and letters of the Forty-niners, especially those which have survived in manuscript, and those petrified (as we may say) in the columns of contemporary newspapers. This preoccupation has been a healthy one, and there is still a vast labor to be done, scarcely a beginning made in digging out the history of the Gold Rush, in broad outline and in minute detail. One need only examine a map of Gold Rush California and turn to the available county histories to realize how little is known about the origins and evolution of mining in most areas, who the first miners were, or even how the places received their names. Some of these names are remarkably picturesque, and their precise origins may forever escape us; thus far, placename studies have leaned somewhat helplessly on the county histories, very few of which date back of 1875. If this local history is to be recovered, we are going to require some mighty aid from the still largely buried literature to which I have alluded. (In editing this book, for example, I found no trustworthy source for the origins of even such famous names of the Tuolumne area as Hawkins' Bar, Swett's Bar, and Wood's Diggings; yet men who were mining there in the spring of 1849 may have recorded all we need to know in letters written to the folks at home in New Jersey, Indiana, or South Carolina.)

The contemporary narratives of travel to and within Gold Rush California commenced as early as 1849, when Theodore T. Johnson got home to publish his *Sights in the Gold Region, and Scenes by the Way* (New York, 1849). They continued all through the 1850's; one calls to mind such works as *G.S.Isham's Guide to California and the Mines* (New York, 1850) or Alonzo Delano's *Life on the Plains and among the Diggings* (Auburn, N.Y., 1854) among the narratives of overland travel; Bayard Taylor's *El Dorado* (New York, 1850) or John S. Letts's *California Illustrated* (New York, 1852) among the narratives of those who chose the Panama route; and George G. Webster's *Journal of the Hartford Union Mining and Trading Company* (Printed by J. L. Hall aboard the *Henry Lee* en route, 1849) among those who voyaged the whole way to California by sea.

Our present interest, however, is the literature of reminiscence, relatively neglected by scholars in recent years, and less abundant than is generally supposed. Howard C. Gardiner's recollections stand in the very front rank of this literature, and it seems worth while to review the principal narratives by which his must be judged.

The literature of recollection began early; if one were so minded, he could trace its beginnings to J. H. Carson's *Early Recollections of the Mines, and a description of the Great Tulare Valley* (Stockton, 1852), for the point of view is what counts, and at the very outset Carson says, "To the 'good old times' now past, when each day was big with the wonders and discoveries of rich diggings [that is, in 1848–1849], I would like to principally confine my observations. . . ." However, we must establish some standards involving a longer perspective, so we arbitrarily decide that nothing published earlier than 1860, twelve years after the gold discovery, meets our requirements.

On this basis, we look first at L. M. Schaeffer's *Sketches of Travels in South America, Mexico and California* (New York, 1860). In his preface Schaeffer relates that he kept a daily record of "what I saw and did" while pursuing a journey to and from California some years since. On his return, he contributed reminiscences of a life among the miners to a religious paper, under the signature of "Quartz," and now publishes them in book form; "while they may possess no literary merit, still a full and correct history of events which came under my own observation, will, it is hoped, compensate for other deficiencies." Schaeffer's narrative covers the period from March 24, 1849, when he sailed from New York aboard the ship *Flavius*, to June 4, 1852, when he returned via Panama. His is an excellent and veracious account, sensible, uninflated, and informative.

With periodically dated entries, Schaeffer describes the passage around the Horn and arrival at San Francisco on September 17, 1849. After a look at San Francisco and its gambling establishments, he went on to Stockton by schooner in a party of 14. He tells of journeying on to Hawkins' Bar, afterward dignified as Hawkinsville, his membership in the Tuolumne River Mining Company, and his departure November 20 for San Francisco, which he found much improved. He also tells of life in a boarding house, the fire of December 24, and a visit to Mission Dolores; and he remarks generally on the disregard of the Sabbath, women, the numerously arriving Chinese, and French people. On March 27, 1850, he left San Francisco for Sacramento in the schooner *Susan Farnham*, making his way to Nevada Dry Diggings via Nicolaus, Rough and Ready, and Grass Valley. He gives us an account of the Gold Lake expedition of June, 1850, with daily entries, describes Downieville, and tells of successful mining on Gold Run. In late July he returned to San Francisco, and on August 3 sailed for Panama aboard the brig *Ann and Julia*, voyaging for the sake of his health and not caring where they stopped en route. He was back in San Francisco from Leon by December 13, and a week later took the sternwheel steamer *Jenny Lind* to Nicolaus. With attention to the road houses along the way,

A Road Scene in California
By G. Nahl, *del.*

Chinese Camp in the Mines
From James Borthwick, *Three Years in California* (1857)

he reached Grass Valley December 29, 1850, to remain until his final departure on April 25, 1852. He sailed for Panama on the *Winfield Scott*, arriving May 22, and for New York from Aspinwall on May 25 aboard the *Crescent City*.

Next in line is a work by Lawson B. Patterson, *Twelve Years in the Mines of California; embracing a general view of the gold region, with practical observations on hill, placer, and quartz diggings; and notes on the origin of gold deposits* (Cambridge, 1862). Patterson reached California by a route across Mexico to Mazatlan, thence by sailing ships to San Francisco, where he arrived July 20, 1849. He mined during the summer at Mormon Island, on the South Fork of the American River, but in November made his way to the Georgetown area, where he labored until he left California in September, 1861. At the time of his departure, the *Alta California* printed some remarks about Patterson which are incorporated into the book: "He is one of the few *Forty-niners* who have remained faithful to the business of mining, and kept steady. In the summer of 1850, about one-fourth of the miners worked in the beds and bars of rivers; the other three-fourths in cañons and gulleys. The diggings were then all shallow. Two years later, tunneling for hill diggings commenced, and in 1855 quartz mines became a regular branch of mining in that county. About one-tenth of the miners are now engaged in quartz, which pays more in proportion to the number of men engaged, than any other branch of labor, and is looked upon as the only kind of mining that can be considered as permanent in El Dorado County." Patterson has more to say about his experiences down to 1851 than in later years, and much of his book is given over to theories of various authorities on the geology of the gold region; it is also noteworthy that as late as 1862 he should be offering a chapter of "Advice to New Beginners in Mining."

Not a Forty-niner's narrative as such but an autobiography is Stephen C. Massett's *"Drifting About,"* or what *"Jeems Pipes of Pipesville"* saw–and did (New York, 1863). Back of the rather unpromising façade of this title is an entertaining record of personal experience. Massett had had extensive experience on the stage before he was swept up in the Gold Rush, and he is a hundred pages into his narrative before he takes us aboard the schooner *Sovereign* at Baltimore in January, 1849. The vessel was bound for Vera Cruz but ended up at Chagres instead. After crossing the Isthmus, Massett sailed for San Francisco in the English bark *John Ritson;* thus in both vessels he was a fellow-passenger of James L. Tyson, whose *Diary of a Physician in California,* published in 1850, gives May 18 as the date of arrival in San Francisco. Col. J. D. Stevenson gave him a job, which afforded an advantageous point of view on the inrushing goldseekers. Presently Massett was giving concerts and installed as alcalde of New York of the Pacific, but he went to Sacramento as an auctioneer for Sam Brannan, soon started his own auction house there, embarked anew upon the theatrical life, endured the Sacramento flood of January, 1850, and after a visit to the Hawaiian Islands, became a co-proprietor of the Marysville *Herald*. Massett was of a roving disposition, and in March, 1852, left for New York and Europe via Panama. After extensive travels, described at some length, he returned to California in December, 1853. He bought a lot out Mission Street which he denominated Pipesville, and after two eventful years set sail for Australia and points west. He revisited California briefly in 1859 but does not go into detail on his experiences. If Massett ever spent much time in the mines, he neglects to say so. Carl Wheat has well summed up Massett as a man "who knew everyone and saw everything during those first frantic years of the Gold Rush."

J. Ross Browne's *Crusoe's Island: A Ramble in the footsteps of Alexander Selkirk. With sketches of adventure in California and Washoe* (New York, 1864) has only an incidental bearing on the Gold Rush. Browne took passage around the Horn early in 1849, he says, in the ship *Anteus*. He gives only a brief account of the voyage, prefatory to his visit to Juan Fernandez Island in May, 1849, an episode which provides a title for the book. The ship *Brooklyn* was anchored at the island, and figures in the action. Browne quotes a passage from the journal of his fellow-passenger, Dr. J. B. D. Stillman, who in his own narrative (published in 1877, as seen below) more correctly names the vessel as the *Pacific*. In a later section of his book, Browne describes "A Dangerous Journey" from San Francisco to San Luis Obispo in the summer of 1849, an interesting contribution to Californiana, but not greatly concerned with the Gold Rush. He also furnishes a chapter on the Indians of California, and a long account of a visit to Washoe after the silver discoveries there.

A captain in the Danish merchant service, Peter Justesen, makes the next contribution to our record. The Bancroft Library has his 78-page *Two Years' Adventures of a Dane in the California Gold Mines* (Gloucester: Translated and printed for the Author by John Bellows, 1865). Presumably this was originally first printed in Denmark; Yale has a 62-page second edition, published in Kjobenhavn, 1867, with the title, *En dansk manda haendeler i Californien og en sandfaerdig beskrivelse of hans toarige ophold i minerene*. In this modest narrative Justesen relates how he sailed the schooner *Civilian* from Boston to San Francisco, leaving November 12, 1849, and entering the Golden Gate 144 days later. He sold the ship on arrival, worked in San Francisco, went to Sonora in June, 1850, and mined on Woods Creek. (Perhaps by a quirk of translation, he employs the word "Gulf" in place of Gulch, as "Woods Gulf," "Mormon Gulf.") Justesen spent his last evening in the mines May 31, 1852, then went by stage from Campo Seco to Stockton, on to San Francisco, and via Nicaragua, New York, and Liverpool to Copenhagen. In an appendix he gives further attention to Campo Seco. Not a major contribution to Gold Rush history, Justesen's book is still noteworthy for many of its details.

Another work emanating from an unexpected place is that by the Abbe Henry J. A. Alric, *Dix Ans de Résidence d'un Missionaire dans deux Californies, et un épisode guerre civile dans le district du nord de la Basse Californie* (México, 1866). Father Alric sailed from Havre for San Francisco on September 9, 1850, as chaplain to a "compagnie californienne, *La Ruche d'or*," aboard the bark *L'Anne Louise*. Via Cape Horn he reached San Francisco April 26, 1851. He gives only a brief account of the voyage, and a still shorter narrative of his experiences in the Southern Mines, ecclesiastically based on Sonora, to which he immediately repaired; 21 pages suffice to detail his experiences to February, 1856, when he sailed for Lower California (to which most of this 53-page work is devoted). Father

Alric offers some comment on prevailing social conditions and the harsh treatment of Mexicans in the Tuolumne County area, but does not say a great deal about the mines. In the title he identifies himself as an ex-missionary, and chaplain to the military hospitals (of the Maximilian regime). Subsequently he accompanied the French troops when they evacuated Mexico, and by April, 1867, had reached Toulon. Dr. Doyce B. Nunis advises me that later that year he published at Paris, in 71 pages, another version of his experiences, *Esquisses d'un voyage autour de monde et un épisode de guerre civil dans le district du nord de la Basse-Californie;* and two years later he got out a still more extensive version in 144 pages, also at Paris, *Esquisses d'un voyage sur les deux océans et a l'intérieur de l'Amérique et d'une guerre civile au nord de la Basse-Californie.* (Dr. Nunis is publishing a translation and collation of these several versions.)

The last title I shall cite from this decade is Edward E. Dunbar's *The Romance of the Age: or, the Discovery of Gold in California* (New York, 1867). Dunbar's is more a history (with major attention to pre-Gold Rush events) than a personal narrative, but does offer reminiscences of travel to Chagres by the first voyage of the *Crescent City,* December 23, 1848–January 2, 1849, the crossing of the Isthmus, and the further voyage to San Francisco by the first sailing of the *California,* January 31–February 28, 1849.

The 1870's brought varied additions to the literature, of which the earliest are rather marginal in character. *Men and Memories of 1850* (San Francisco, 1873) was written by T. A. Barry and B. A. Patten, owners of a famous San Francisco bar, and though extraordinarily revealing of the San Francisco scene—a minor classic, almost—has little to say about the gold region. One point of interest is that the authors discuss "What Makes a Pioneer?"—a live question for many decades, since by fiat of the Society of California Pioneers a man must have reached California prior to January 1, 1850, to be a "pioneer." Also peripheral is a work published in San Francisco in 1874, *First Steamship Pioneers,* edited by a Committee of the Steamship Pioneers to commemorate the silver anniversary of their arrival aboard the *California.* This book contains much useful information on the Panama route of 1849, besides a number of biographical sketches of steamship pioneers. Among these are two first-person sketches by Edwin L. Morgan and Rodman M. Price, received too late to be rewritten like the others.

An event of 1875 was the *Memoirs of General William T. Sherman,* published at New York in two volumes. This work deals mainly with Sherman's Civil War experiences, but the first five chapters concern his "Early Recollections of California," 1846–1850, and some experiences of 1853–1857. Sherman came to California with the New York Regiment of Volunteers, and was stationed at Monterey at the time of the gold discovery. In an official capacity, he twice visited the gold region in 1848, and his recollections of this period have great interest and charm, like his account of experiences surveying townsites in the boom era that followed. Sherman also made profitable use of his time during leaves of absence, surveying some of the California land grants, before returning East in 1850. He came back to California on a banking enterprise in 1853, traveling by way of Nicaragua, and he gives us a lively account of the bank crisis in San Francisco in

February, 1855, and of the vigilance committee activities of 1856. Sherman terminated his banking enterprise in May, 1857, and though he revisited California on business next year, his future was bound up with the looming Civil War. Sherman's is not a Gold Rush memoir as such, but will always be read with fascination by those attracted to the turbulent history of California during that era.

J. B. D. Stillman's *Seeking the Golden Fleece; a record of pioneer life in California . . .* (San Francisco and New York, 1877) is dedicated to "the Argonauts of California . . . as a memorial of experiences which, with slight variations, were common to you all," and in his preface Stillman says that to some his words "will restore the rapidly fading recollection of events in which they bore their part, and faces of companions who, one by one, have dropped into the Lethean stream. The reader will find little to found a claim for the writer to anything above the average experience of his fellow pioneers; but it was his fortune to have his letters and journal preserved through all the disasters by flood and fire that proved so destructive to manuscript records of that eventful year in California. The return from San Francisco, by the way of Central America, was written out at the end of the journey from notes kept by the way, but the first portion of the book is made up from letters written to friends at home. . . ." [Stillman published a preliminary version of his experiences in *Overland Monthly,* "Seeking the Golden Fleece" (September, 1873–March, 1874), and "From Colchis back to Argos" (April–August, 1874).] He narrates a voyage around the Horn in the ship *Pacific,* leaving New York January 23 and reaching San Francisco August 5, 1849. The doctor's subsequent experiences were at Sacramento, primarily. He sailed from San Francisco for Nicaragua in the ship *Plymouth* October 24, 1850, and eventually reached Baltimore February 10, 1851. Like Howard Gardiner, he visited Old Providence Island in the Caribbean when homeward bound. In an appendix he tells of Argonauts who sailed the schooner *Dolphin* north from Panama, and had to abandon the vessel and foot it up to San Diego through Lower California.

From our point of view, the most that can be said of the Rev. J. L. Ver Mehr's *Checkered Life: In the Old and New World* (San Francisco, 1877) is that it deals with California during the Gold Rush era. (Ver Mehr published a book with the same title in 1864, dealing with Old World experiences; he continued his story in Part II of the present work.) An Episcopal minister, he sailed from New York in the *George Washington* in February, 1849, but on reaching Valparaiso, transshipped in the *Hebe,* to enter the Golden Gate the second week of September. Thereafter his narrative is an account of ecclesiastical labors in San Francisco and elsewhere in northern California—but not, it would seem, in the mines.

Jessie Benton Frémont's *A Year of American Travel* (New York, 1878) is a small pocket volume written for Harper's "Half Hour Series." Chance alone, the discovery of gold in California, made an Argonaut of her, for she and her husband, John Charles Frémont, had decided that she would join him in California prior to his departure from the Missouri frontier in the fall of 1848 on his disastrous Fourth Expedition. Her book tells of the poignant parting, the voyage to Panama (on the same steamship with Gardiner, as we shall see), her stay on the Isthmus and further voyage to San Francisco on the steamship *Panama*, life in San Francisco and Monterey, and her eventual return to New York with her husband, again by the Panama route. (They left San Francisco January 1, 1850.) All these experiences are engagingly recorded, but except that she was borne along in the flood tide of the Gold Rush, Jessie's is not a chronicle of the Argonauts. Neither does she have much to say about Frémont's Mariposa grant and the mining in progress there, though in her usual felicitous style she described the Mariposa of the 1850's in a series of articles contributed to *Wide Awake* in 1888–1889, gathered up as *Far-West Sketches* (Boston, 1890). Jessie's *Souvenirs of My Time* (Boston, 1887) retells the story of her visit to California in 1849, but in very sketchy fashion.

We return to the mainstream with Samuel C. Upham's *Notes of a Voyage to California via Cape Horn, together with Scenes in El Dorado, in the years 1849-'50 . . .* (Philadelphia: Published by the Author, 1878), characteristically dedicated to "the Pioneers of California, who encountered dangers by flood and field, and whose brave hearts and willing hands have caused the arid plain and the wilderness to 'blossom as the rose.'" Upham sailed from Philadelphia in the brig *Osceola* on January 15, 1849, arriving at San Francisco on August 5. About two-thirds of his book is devoted to the voyage. He describes San Francisco, life on the Bay shore in Happy Valley, and the gambling saloons which impressed all comers. By September he was ready to go on to Stockton and the Calaveras mines, but ill-health soon brought him back to the Bay. Upham became a carrier for the *Pacific News*, then its bookkeeper; and early in 1850 he established himself in Sacramento as a co-proprietor of the Sacramento *Transcript*. However, he sold out his interest the following July, and next month sailed to Panama on the *Columbus*. His book is more especially interesting for its viewpoint on San Francisco, Stockton, and Sacramento, and for its information on California's evolving newspapers; he added an appendix on "Pioneer Journalism in California." Later on, Upham interested himself in the affairs of "The Associated Pioneers of the Territorial Days of California," about which his book has a good deal to say.

A third work of 1878, published in New Haven, was Charles F. Hotchkiss' *On the Ebb: A Few Log-Lines from an Old Salt*. About a fifth of this book is concerned with California in the Gold Rush era. Hotchkiss relates that he fitted out his sons Henry and Charles, and that they left New York via the Isthmus on the *Crescent City*, December 23, 1848. He consigned goods to them by the ship *Orpheus*, from New Haven, then himself sailed for Chagres on the *Crescent City*, September 15, 1849. Hotchkiss describes "Crusus," Panama, the 21-day voyage to San Francisco on the *Panama*, and Happy Valley on arrival, with miners coming in from the gold fields to recruit. After the *Orpheus* landed, he sold the cargo to advantage, then visited Stockton aboard the steamer *Sutter*. Hotchkiss winds up his narrative by saying: "The writer was satisfied that chronic diarrhoea was no respecter of persons, and if life was worth more than gold, it was time for him to nurse his health, and with his son, Henry, after closing up our business, took steamer for home. We had a beautiful run down the coast; crossed the Isthmus, joined the steamer for New

York, and arrived safe at New Haven, August 7th, 1850, with two good-sized bags of gold, showing a balance against the enterprize of $23,000." As a speculator, Hotchkiss made out better than most, without ever turning a shovelful of earth.

Another chronicle by a sailor, rather more prominent in his time, is Captain Edgar Wakeman's *The Log of an Ancient Mariner*, edited by his daughter (San Francisco, 1878). Wakeman was a true character, and a striking figure of the California scene in the 1850's and 1860's, but his book resembles that of Jessie Frémont somewhat, in that he was never himself a goldseeker, simply caught up in the turbulent California milieu resulting from the Gold Rush. He first came out to the Golden Shore in 1850 as captain of the steamer *New World,* touching en route at Pernambuco, Rio de Janeiro, Valparaiso, Callao, Lima, Panama, and southern California ports. After reaching San Francisco on July 11, he operated the *New World* as a river steamer to Sacramento. In February and March, 1852, the Captain visited the mines in the vicinity of Murphy's Diggings, Gold Hill, Sullivan's Flat, and Coyote Diggings. Mining was not for him, however. He was the acting sheriff for the first San Francisco Vigilance Committee of 1851, and a prominent San Franciscan generally, sailing in and out of the port in command of many different vessels. In later years, Mark Twain made his first visit to the Hawaiian Islands on one of his ships, further contributing to the Captain's celebrity. Wakeman's is an eminently readable book, but we must content ourselves with this notice of it.

The year 1879 added to the literature a varied collection of books which entertainingly illuminate the California scene, but in most instances are only peripherally related to the Gold Rush. The first of these, O. P. Fitzgerald's *California Sketches* (Nashville, Tenn., 1879), was written by a Methodist minister, and deals with a time so late as to be almost beyond the pale. Its opening sentence reads, "Sonora, in 1855, was an exciting, wild, wicked, fascinating place," and here he experienced his first Sunday in the mines. Many of the sketches deal with people and events of the Sonora area, but also reflect his experiences in Stockton, San Francisco, and Santa Rosa. Four editions of this book were printed by 1880. Next year, Bishop Fitzgerald published *California Sketches, New Series;* and in 1895 he got out a "new and consolidated edition in a single volume, in which some new Sketches are introduced and some of the older ones are omitted," with the title, *California Sketches, New and Old.*

Another divine, earlier on the scene, was the Presbyterian minister, Albert Williams, with his *A Pioneer Pastorate and Times embodying contemporary local transactions and events* (San Francisco, 1879). Williams first went out to California amid the hurly-burly of the Gold Rush, taking the *Crescent City* on her second voyage to Chagres in February, 1849, and the *Oregon* on her first voyage from Panama. His account of the city by the Golden Gate from 1849 to 1854 is a lively one, if dominated by his ecclesiastical interests and values, and with a blind eye for the mining activities in the hinterland, notwithstanding one notable visit to Sacramento.

There must have been "something in the air" for men of the cloth in 1879—Samuel H. Willey was also moved to publish his recollections, *Thirty Years in California. A contribu-*

tion to the history of the State, from 1849 to 1879 (San Francisco, 1879). This modest 76-page pamphlet devotes almost a third of its space to California's pre-Gold Rush history, then tells how the author, as a young Congregational minister, was sent out to the Golden Shore by his church in the first floodtide of the Gold Rush, taking the *Falcon* on its first voyage to Chagres, and the *California* on its first voyage from Panama, so as to land at Monterey on February 23, 1849. The Reverend Willey gives an interesting account of his labors in California over the next thirty years, but has only incidental references to miners or the mines—an encounter with trains of Sonoranians; and manners and morals (especially in San Francisco).

George D. Dornin's modest *Thirty Years Ago, 1849-1879* was apparently printed for the author in Berkeley. Dornin sailed from New York February 3, 1849, in the ship *Panama* (not the steamboat of the same name), and reached San Francisco August 8. He describes San Francisco and Happy Valley, and the bizarre destiny of the ship, which ended up as a church. After working in San Francisco that fall and winter (one of his jobs being a contract "to put together a number of ready-made zinc, or corrugated iron houses, imported from some Eastern city, packed and numbered, really requiring but little mechanical skill to erect"), he paid a visit to Sacramento in March, 1850, but returned to San Francisco, first opening a restaurant, then entering the general merchandising business, which was ravaged by the great fire of May 4, 1851. A year later Dornin went to Nevada City. What was intended to be a brief visit became a stay of 15 years as merchant, daguerreotyper, member of the legislature, express agent, and successful insurance agent. Later he lived at San Jose and Berkeley. Although his narrative is comparatively short and not much concerned with mining, the story it tells is in many ways characteristic of the Gold Rush and its aftermath.

A fourth title of 1879 is W. Jackson Barry's *Up and Down; or, Fifty Years' Colonial Experiences in Australia, California, New Zealand, India, China, and the South Pacific . . .* (London, 1879). (Barry republished essentially the same story as *Past & Present, and Men of the Times* [Wellington, N.Z., 1897].) The author voyaged to California in the *Eleanor Lancaster*, first vessel to leave Sydney for the Golden Shore in 1849, and about a tenth of his book is devoted to life in California. He tells of San Francisco, Happy Valley, Sacramento, and Hangtown; the flood of January, 1850; the Sacramento Vigilance Committee of that year; Sydney emigrants; a quick voyage to Sydney and back in the summer of 1851 (bringing livestock which sold well); further experiences in San Francisco and in "Reddon's [Reading's] diggings" on the upper Sacramento; troubles with the Indians; a meat contract for "Fort Reddon" in the fall of 1852; a severe winter which almost put a stop to mining throughout the country; a cattle-buying trip to "Napier" (Napa) Valley; the swindling effect of the Adams Bank, which cost himself and party, he says, some £12,000; and the arrival of Kit Carson with sheep in the summer of 1853. By that time, Barry says, the antipathy to "Sydney Ducks" was dying out. He shipped for Sydney in the *Kit Carson* later in 1853. Both the point of view and the experiences are unusual.

The year 1880 is notable for the reminiscences of Peter H. Burnett and Stephen J. Field.

Burnett's *Recollections and Opinions of an Old Pioneer* (New York, 1880) was commenced, he says, in October, 1860, broken off a month later, and only resumed in March, 1878, after H. H. Bancroft called on him and asked for such historical data as he possessed. Burnett's is a genuinely eventful autobiography, describing his early life in Tennessee and Missouri, his relations with the Mormons in the 1830's, his migration to Oregon in 1843, and life there over the next five years. He journeyed down from Oregon in the fall of 1848, his party guided by Thomas McKay, and relates some experiences in the Northern Mines. Not for him the life of a miner, and in December, 1848, he set out for Sutter's, where he became the agent of John A. Sutter, Jr. Burnett describes the evolution of Sacramento in January, 1849, a visit to San Francisco two months later, the inrush of gold-seekers by sea, and the unsatisfactory condition of affairs, leading to the formation of a provisional government and his own election as governor (he served until January, 1851, when he resigned in consequence of the pressure of private business). Burnett has much to say about some of the eccentric characters of the period, including Judge Almond, Chinese exclusion, California in the 1850's, his law practice, especially in San Jose, experiences as justice of the California Supreme Court, 1857–1858, and banking experiences of the 1860's and 1870's, the whole adding up to a highly readable, always interesting, frequently valuable memoir—marred, from our present viewpoint, only by the fact that it has very little to say about the Gold Rush in general and the evolution of the mines.

Stephen J. Field's *Personal Reminiscences of Early Days in California with other sketches. Printed for a few friends. Not Published* (San Francisco, 1880) is noted to have been taken down by a stenographer in the summer of 1877, at San Francisco. Field made his way to California via Panama late in 1849. He describes his first experiences in the city by the Golden Gate, Judge Almond's remarkable court, an encounter with Jonathan D. Stevenson, from whom amusingly he collected a note for $440, and hanging out his shingle as attorney and counselor-at-law. He went on to Sacramento while the great flood of January, 1850, was in progress, and established himself at Yubaville (later renamed Marysville), where he made fortunate investments in real estate. Field was elected alcalde, an office on which he interestingly remarks, and subsequently was elected to the legislature. In 1857 he was nominated Judge of the California Supreme Court, became Chief Justice, and in 1863 was appointed to the U.S. Supreme Court. Like Burnett, Field was not largely concerned with the Gold Rush as such. (Another edition of his reminiscences appeared in 1893.)

Two works published in 1881 are clearly peripheral to the Gold Rush. Major Horace Bell's *Reminiscences of a Ranger; or, Early Times in Southern California* (Los Angeles, 1881) begins with his arrival at San Pedro in the *Sea Bird* in October, 1852, and mainly describes life in southern California, with only incidental remarks on the Gold Rush aspect of California history. William F. White, writing under the pseudonym William Gray, brought forth in San Francisco *A Picture of Pioneer Times in California illustrated with anecdotes and stories taken from real life*, which is essentially an anecdotal history, using Frank Soulé's *Annals* of 1855 as a jumping-off point; the latter part of the book is made up of three short novels oriented toward children. Although the main text is recurrently written in the first person, it does not have the structure of a personal memoir, and the book is mainly relevant to Gold Rush history in that Chapters VI–VII describe the voyage of the White family in the ship *South Carolina* (arriving June 30, 1849), and in that Chapter VIII records first impressions of San Francisco—all without disclosing the identity of the author as White.

In 1882 Ludvig Verner Helms added to the record a work published in London, *Pioneering in the Far East, and journeys to California in 1849 and to the White Sea in 1878*. Helms left his native Denmark in 1846, and after adventures in the Far East sailed from Singapore on a mercantile venture on June 7, 1850, to enter the Golden Gate after a voyage of 67 days. (Hence the title is less than accurate.) Helms describes San Francisco on arrival, the gambling hells, and a fearful fire; he also notes that this was an unfavorable time for a mercantile adventure, the first rush having passed, and supplies overcrowding both the market and storage capacity. He visited Mission Dolores and "Flag-staff Hill," the view from which he sketched. In mid-September he sailed for Hong Kong and Singapore with a scant crew in an unnamed vessel; and California saw him no more until 1872, when he revisited the Bay region before taking the train for New York. In this book, again, we have a peripheral title.

The year 1884 brought Henry DeGroot's *Recollections of California Mining Life*, printed at San Francisco as a slight sketch of 16 pages, which does not live up to the promise of its title. No personal memoir, this pamphlet barely mentions arriving at San Francisco in February, 1849, and finding the places crowded with miners who at the commencement of the rainy season had come in to pass the winter. DeGroot had done much better in the way of personal reminiscences of the Gold Rush with two sketches printed in *Overland Monthly*, September, 1874, April, 1875. Henry DeGroot had an extraordinarily varied life, and we may regret that he never addressed himself to a full-scale autobiography; see the notes on his career provided by Carl I. Wheat, *Mapping the Transmississippi West* (San Francisco, 1963), vol. V, pp. 17–18.

A relative late-comer was Mrs. Mallie Stafford, whose story is told in *The March of Empire through three decades. Embracing sketches of California history; early times and scenes; life in the mines; travels by land and sea before the era of railroads; the East during the years of the Civil War; life in the border states; crossing the plains with ox teams; crossing the plains on the transcontinental railway; progress and improvement of the Golden State; resources; etc., etc.* (San Francisco, 1884). After such a title, it seems necessary only to add that Mrs. Stafford came out to California via Panama in October, 1854, her husband having preceded her by that route amid the heavy emigration of 1852. She lived for a while at Nevada City, then at Chipps Flat in Sierra County, finally at Marysville on a farm. Her husband went to Washoe in 1860 while she went east. She started back to California in 1864, but ended up in Colorado, and finally made it to the Golden Shore again after the Pacific Railroad was completed; she lived in Napa County for a time but moved to San Francisco in 1884.

This general pattern, autobiography by Californians not primarily centered upon the

Gold Rush or life in the mines, is found in yet another title of 1884, E. D. Keyes' *Fifty Years Observation of Men and Events,* which was printed in New York. Keyes came to California via Panama, arriving with a contingent of troops on the *Oregon* April 1, 1849. As he reflects, "All the men who lived in California in the year 1849 arrogate to themselves a special glory," and he himself had particular status, being commander of San Francisco at the head of his artillery company. Keyes tells of the City, the Hounds, the labors of the Indian commission of 1851, for which he provided a military escort, and the San Joaquin Valley that year. He also describes the assassination of James King of William in 1856, though at second hand, since he himself was then fighting Indians in Washington Territory. Having returned to the San Francisco Presidio in October, 1856, Keyes was well situated to comment on military affairs in California and the Pacific Northwest in the later Fifties. He also reflects on San Francisco, its law firms, and the California judiciary, without having much to say about miners or mines; he does note that gold production fell off annually after 1853, and that general prosperity also declined, so that in 1857 and 1858 there was a vast shrinkage in the value of real estate.

John H. Brown's *Reminiscences and Incidents, of "The Early Days" of San Francisco, . . . actual experiences of an eye-witness, from 1845 to 1850* (San Francisco, 1886) is mainly concerned with the period before 1849, and has only glancing reference to the Gold Rush era.

We reach slightly more solid ground with A. Hersey Dexter's *Early Days in California* (Denver, 1886), "a simple memory of men and days long since departed." Dexter left New York for San Francisco September 22, 1849, in the ship *Susan Drew.* He briefly describes the 150-day voyage and the visionary schemes and fate of the owners. "I stayed a year in 'Frisco,' going into the pilot boats, which were then as good as a paying gold mine; then I started to try my fortunes in the mines." Dexter engaged with an uncle to operate a ferry on the American River at Sacramento, but a disastrous law suit broke up the venture. He then went to Grass Valley, where he fell in with the crew of the *Susan Drew,* wandered around and located a claim on the Yuba, and was summoned back to Sacramento to testify in the lawsuit. The winter of 1853, he says, was the most severe he ever experienced in the mines. He had been mining on the Calaveras with a partner named Crouse, and went to the little mining town of San Antonio to winter. He describes the deluges, a prospecting tour in the spring of 1854, and going with Crouse to Murphy's Camp, where he bought a claim on the flat; he also tells of the salting of a mining claim, the treatment of Chinese, and a stay in Tuolumne County. On the whole, Dexter's is a rather disorganized book, anecdotal about individuals. Some 50 pages at the end are given over to his own poetry.

The year 1887 brings us the *Life and Adventures of Col. L. A. Norton. Written by Himself,* and published in Oakland. Norton says at the first possible moment, "In unveiling my life to the public gaze, I am not actuated by any eulogistic or mercenary motives. Nor do I think that the life of any man in the ordinary walks of life is going to electrify the world, or even be extensively circulated or generally read, in this day and age when so many are rushing into print." So a thousand copies of his book seemed to him sufficient.

After experiences in the Mexican War described at considerable length, Norton made his way to California in 1850. He passes over the events of that journey as having no interest, but in rather more detail tells of a second journey overland in 1852. He mined profitlessly on the South Fork of the American River, then began buying and selling claims. Next winter he worked a claim at Prospect Flat, but after a fight embarked upon the study of law and began to practice at Placerville, described with considerable verve. He also tells of a trip to Monterey County, and has much to say about Carson Valley, especially after the Mormons organized Carson County there; he served as district attorney in the area. In 1857, convinced that mining had seen its best days and that the future lay with agriculture, he moved to Healdsburg. Most of the rest of his life was spent in this northern area, with occasional trips east and to various California points. His is a lively, anecdotal account, if not very largely concerned with the Gold Rush and the mines.

Jacob Wright Harlan's *California '46 to '88* (Oakland, 1888) is the story of an overland emigrant of 1846 who served in Frémont's California Battalion. Harlan narrates the gold discovery in 1848, his own experiences at Coloma and mining on the Middle Fork of the American River, as also subsequently wintering in what became Santa Clara County. In March, 1849, he set out for Sonora; after mining there for a time, he purchased lots in Stockton. Soon we find him describing life at Mission San José and at San Francisco from 1849–1850, farming ventures in Alameda County, a second overland journey of 1853, and ranching in the Cholame Valley, San Luis Obispo County, with a sketchy account of experiences through the 1860's. In 1896 Harlan got out a second edition of this work with a rather sad preface; his health had deteriorated, and he had had some disagreeable experiences at the Soldiers' Home in Napa, which made him happier to be in the Alameda County Infirmary.

More characteristic as a contribution to the record of the Gold Rush is Charles D. Ferguson's *The Experiences of a Forty-niner during thirty-four years' residence in California and Australia* (Cleveland, 1888). An Ohioan, Ferguson describes his overland journey in 1850 with a company from Ottawa, Illinois. He gives a less than credible account of Jim Bridger, then describes Salt Lake City, beyond which he seems to have taken the Lassen Cutoff, unusual in this year. Ferguson first mined at Reece's Bar on Butte Creek. After various wanderings in the Northern Mines, he describes Marysville in 1850–1851, and life at Nevada City and Grass Valley to 1852, after which he went to San Francisco and sailed to Australia. Chapters XIV–XXXI describe his experiences in Australia until 1883, when he came back to the States, then crossing the country by train to Cleveland. The volume is noted to have been edited by Frederick T. Wallace. In 1924 Ferguson published at Chico, California, a "pamphlet edition" of his book, *The Experiences of a Forty-niner during A Third of a Century in the Gold Fields*. This edition omits the Australian experiences, and a few pages at the end tell of his life from 1888 to 1923. Near the close Ferguson says, "Although I still retain all my mental faculties to their fullest extent, my physical strength is nearly exhausted, and I have been compelled to resort to the publishing of this pamphlet to secure funds enough to carry me through my last remaining days." There had been three printings of the 1888 edition, 10,000 copies having been sold at $5 each. We fear he did less well in 1924.

At the close of the decade James Steele published *Old Californian Days* (Chicago, 1889), primarily a collection of essays. In Chapter IX Steele discusses the Argonauts as a type, in rather critical vein. He recounts a visit to the missions, and travels in southern California, but does not appear in the light of a miner.

Another title doubtfully included in this survey is William Heath Davis' *Sixty Years in California, a history of events and life in California; personal, political and military, under the Mexican regime; during the quasi-military government of the territory by the United States, and after the admission of the State into the Union being a compilation by a witness of the events described* (San Francisco, 1889). Davis reached California early enough, in the 1830's, and was soon assimilated into the mercantile culture. But he is primarily concerned with events before the Gold Rush, or with parts of California distant from the mines. His narrative will always be found possessed of great verve and charm, but not integrally of Gold Rush interest. After his death, a revised edition was printed at San Francisco in 1921 with the title, *Seventy-five Years in California*, and that title again served for another revised edition printed at San Francisco in 1967, each a book of large appeal.

To wind up the decade comes *Prentice Mulford's Story: Life by Land and Sea* (New York, 1889), technically not a Gold Rush narrative. Mulford came out to the mines from Howard Gardiner's home town just as the latter was preparing to return to Long Island in 1857, as we shall see, and the picture he presents is less the Gold Rush than its after-glow. As a seafarer, he first reached San Francisco, and gives an interesting account of The City in that year. After another whaling cruise, Mulford came back to San Francisco in 1857, and only then went on to the Tuolumne County area. His experiences until 1866, when he went to San Francisco to write for the *Golden Era*, have a rare charm, and his book has acquired the status of a minor classic. From this time forward, it will also have a special interest for its relationship to the experiences and the scenes described in Howard Gardiner's reminiscences.

One of the better-known books written by a Forty-niner inaugurates our record for the 1890's, C.W. Haskins' *The Argonauts of California, being the reminiscences of scenes and incidents that occurred in California in early mining days by a Pioneer. And believing that it will be of some historical value as well of interest generally to know the names of those who were the first to venture forth in the search of gold, and by whose energy and labor the foundations of a great state were laid, and also a general prosperity created throughout the entire country, I have therefore prefixed to the work the names of those that I have been able to obtain, numbering about 35,000, and including among them the names of several thousand who are now living in the various States of the Union . . .* (New York, Published for the Author, 1890). I am uncertain whether this book has ever before been cited by its full title, and if so, the reason is not far to seek! The particular importance of Haskins' work is indicated by its self-description, deriving from the mass of names. (To make these more accessible, the work was at one time indexed by WPA; copies of that index are in the Bancroft Library and the California Historical Society library.) Haskins also provides a list of vessels that sailed from the Atlantic States for California in 1849, organized by ports (but not distinguishing ports of destination—Chagres, San Francisco, etc.).

Aside from the reference materials, Haskins' book is more an anecdotal history of the California gold region from a miner's point of view than a personal memoir, though having occasional first person episodes and with a retrospective account of a late visit made to the Hangtown area. From the preface, the book was written while winterbound at Kingston, Idaho, on the Coeur d'Alene River, in 1887–1888, set down entirely from memory. Haskins sailed from New Bedford in the clipper ship *America* April 1, 1849, and reached San Francisco September 20. He went on to Sacramento and Hangtown, and began mining at Oregon Ravine. Much of the latter part of the narrative is developed in dialogue, fictitious or otherwise, and it is difficult to make out a connected record of the author's life. At least once, he seems to have returned east via Panama.

The Reverend Stewart Sheldon, in *Gleanings by the Way, from '36 to '89* (Topeka, 1890), devotes a chapter to a California visit, supposedly in 1849–1850, though dated only in the Preface. He reached San Francisco from Valparaiso in the ship *Lyon*, the supercargo of which was A. A. Sargent, later U.S. minister to Berlin. After the inevitable description of San Francisco and its gambling resorts, Sheldon says he spent the winter largely in "surveying, laying out many of the lots of San Francisco, cutting through the brush, sighting the first chain, and sticking the first stakes that were made in preparation for that now wonderful city." He gives us an anecdote of the pugilist Tom Hyer, arrested for riding his horse into saloons and restaurants, tells of the ravages of poison oak, then says that early in February his party left for Sacramento on the *Golden Gate*. A small steamer took them to Marysville, after which he recounts a visit to Nevada City (then called Deer Creek), excitement of mining on the Yuba, rude mining law, a visit to Concord Bar, and his return to Sacramento. How or when he left California is unexplained, except that in the next chapter he is "Again on the deep, bound for old Mexico."

W. F. Swasey, *The Early Days and Men of California* (San Francisco, 1891) barely places within our canon by including two dozen sketches of "Argonauts" in his book, to supplement 61 sketches of "Pioneers" and a comparatively brief autobiography which tells of his coming to California in 1845 and events of the next two years; Swasey's book is more a history than a memoir, occasionally in rebuttal to H. H. Bancroft's histories.

We feel more comfortable with John Carr's *Pioneer Days in California: Historical and Personal Sketches* (Eureka, Calif., 1891), based on a series of sketches published in the *Humboldt Daily Mail*. Carr came overland in 1850 by way of Salt Lake City and the Carson River. He mined on Hangtown Creek, then on Webber (Weaver) Creek, at Georgetown and Missouri Gulch, and finally on Sutter Creek. Late in 1850 he went on to San Francisco, just in time to be swept up by the Gold Bluff excitement of January, 1851. After sailing to Trinidad Bay in the *Minerva*, he wandered between Trinidad and Weaverville, where at length he settled down as a blacksmith. In 1866 he moved to Humboldt

County, and in 1880 went to Tombstone, Arizona, where he was twice elected mayor. He came back to Eureka, however, and closes his narrative with an account of that town in 1890. Carr's is an often lively account of the more northerly mines; and in a concluding chapter he provides a number of brief biographies of pioneers who established themselves in Humboldt and Trinity counties.

A work more commonly thought of as a diary than as a reminiscence is *Experiences of a Forty-Niner, by Wm. G. Johnston, a member of the wagon train first to enter California in the memorable year 1849* (Pittsburgh, 1892). Nevertheless, Johnston remarks in his preface, "Whilst adhering to the diary form in which the notes were originally made, this has not curbed a desire manifested in a number of instances, to take the wings of time to fly to periods even remotely in advance. . . ." Although he traveled overland via Salt Lake and the Carson River route with some fellow Pittsburghers, Johnston also prints the record of his unavailing effort, as early as December, 1848, to buy a ticket on one of the Chagres steamers. His is an interesting and valuable chronicle of the overland trail, though he was not so close to the very fore-front of the emigration as he seems to have recalled. Nevertheless, he reached Sacramento by July 29, 1849. The daily record kept while traveling overland becomes a more general chronicle thereafter; he visited San Francisco, came back to Sacramento in early September, and until the onset of the rainy season, mined on the North Fork of the American River. He then sailed in the barque *Glenmore* for Panama, leaving San Francisco December 5, and reaching New Orleans on February 6, 1850. Thirteen days later he was back in Pittsburgh.

Supposedly written by Major William Downie is *Hunting for Gold. Reminis[c]ences of personal experiences and research in the early days of the Pacific Coast from Alaska to Panama* (San Francisco, 1893), though we are informed that material provided by Major Downie was compiled and revised by Chris M. Waage, "a journalist and literateur of some note" —presumably the book was ghost-written. Downie's work is dedicated "To the surviving members of the advance guard of gold hunters, the California pioneers and their descendants, who are now living throughout the United States." Downie came from New Orleans as a hand aboard the clipper *Architect,* thus reaching San Francisco June 27, 1849. He gives a brief account of "The City" on arrival and of embarking for Sacramento July 5 in the schooner *Milwaukee,* a vessel turned back at Benicia until clearance papers could be obtained from the port of San Francisco, so that it took 11 days to reach Sacramento. Thence he went to Vernon's, on to Nye's Ranch (subsequently Marysville), Rose's Bar, and Bullard's Bar on the Yuba, where he has much to say about anti-foreignism, Kanakas, and Negroes. He tells of the first discovery of gold at the forks of the Yuba, which became Downieville, and recounts the Gold Lake excitement of 1850. After some years at Downieville, Downie joined in the Fraser River rush of 1858, and has much of interest to say about his northern experiences. He also relates some adventures in Panama in 1874, and a brief visit to Alaska.

The year 1894 stands out above all others in this chronicle, with no less than five additions to the literature of reminiscence. First and foremost, one of the classic accounts, is

William Lewis Manly's *Death Valley in '49. Important chapter of California pioneer history. The autobiography of a pioneer, detailing his life from a humble home in the Green Mountains to the gold mines of California; and particularly reciting the sufferings of the band of men, women and children who gave "Death Valley" its name.* Published at San Jose, this long narrative is principally renowned for its first fourteen chapters, which tell of Manly's early life in Vermont, Ohio, Wisconsin, and Michigan, his overland journey to Salt Lake in 1849, and experiences of the Death Valley party that fall and winter. The other four chapters are of great interest also, relating travels up through California from Los Angeles in 1850; San Jose; the Mariposa mines; Big Oak Flat and Garota; the attraction of the Gold Lake affair; Coloma; mining at Georgetown; and voyage from San Francisco to Panama on the *Northerner,* leaving November 29, 1850; and further travels to Wisconsin via Havana and New Orleans. He came back to California through Panama in July, 1851, mining for a time on the Yuba, traveling about California, and settling finally in the San Jose area, all this told in unpretentious but compelling fashion. Manly also published a number of articles, many of which have been gathered up by Arthur Woodward as *The Jayhawkers' Oath and other sketches* (Los Angeles, 1949).

Published at Albany, N.Y., was Daniel Knower's *The Adventures of a Forty-Niner. An historic description of California, with events and ideas of San Francisco and its people in those early days.* Shortly after the news of the gold discovery, Knower organized a company to go out to El Dorado, he himself writing up its by-laws and system of government. This company sailed from New York in the ship *Tarolinta* January 13, 1849. Subsequently Knower lost confidence in the certainty of a fortune from his interest in the company, and conceived the project of shipping out prefabricated houses made of wood. He had twelve constructed, and arranged to ship them in a Havre packet ship, the *Prince de Joinville,* while he himself set out for California via the Isthmus. He sailed from New York on the steamer *Georgia* July 1, and subsequently reached San Francisco aboard the *Panama,* arriving August 18, 1849. His house speculation, which could have been very profitable, because of deliberate delays by the captain (or so he thought) arrived during a glut, so that he was hard put to it finally to break even. Knower made a trip to Coloma, thence to Dutch Bar on the South Fork of the American River, where a party from Albany was working. When the rainy season set in, he returned to San Francisco. Thereafter he engaged in a mercantile venture to Stockton, as also, to his regret, in "Towalma City" speculation. After revisiting Dutch Bar, from which his friends had removed to the Middle Fork of the American, he started home on the steamer *Ecuador,* going first to Nicaragua, thence to Panama, and back to New York late in the fall, again on the *Georgia.* Knower has much to say about the state of morals, gambling, San Francisco generally, lack of prejudice against the Chinese as of 1849, and experiences with speculators and sundry rascals. He intended to return to California but never did. A nephew, Abraham Schell, who went out in the *Tarolinta* in 1849, died at Knight's Ferry in 1893, owner of a notable vineyard.

David Rohrer Leeper's *The Argonauts of 'Forty-Nine. Some recollections of the plains and the diggings* (South Bend, 1894) despite its imprint may not have appeared until the following year, for it was copyrighted by Leeper "1894 and 1895." He was one of a party of six who set out from South Bend, Indiana, February 22, 1849. Over half his book describes the overland journey, which was via the Lassen Cutoff. He gives an account of Sacramento and Sutter's Fort, as also a visit to Coloma (in this connection quoting from a letter written him by Henry W. Bigler from St. George, May 31, 1894, respecting the gold discovery). Thereafter he mined on Hangtown Creek and in nearby Kelsey's Canyon, and later in the Trinity diggings, especially at Reading's Bar, where he found himself in the spring of 1850. He served in Indian campaigns, was stationed at Uniontown (later Arcata) on Humboldt Bay, and engaged in redwood logging before returning east via Nicaragua in April and May, 1854. Leeper's narrative is interesting and displays a historian's critical sense.

The fourth of our titles for 1894 is John G. Williams' *The Adventures of a Seventeen-Year-Old Lad and the fortunes he might have won*, printed in Boston for the author. He says in his preface, "The first chapters relate the first seven years' experience as a sailor on board a whaler, and adventures while travelling in foreign lands and dwelling with cannibals and other savages. The later chapters contain the gold-mining experiences of the author in California, Australia, and British Columbia, commencing in the early days of 1849 and continuing until 1858. . . . The story has been written from memory forty years after. . . ." Williams left his home in the backwoods of Canada at the age of 17, in 1841. He gets around to his California experiences only in the latter half of his book, and his narrative is generalized, the chronology hard to follow when not repetitive, the approach anecdotal. He sailed from Boston in the brig *Attila* January 12, 1849. The captain sailed around the Horn, changing his mind about tackling the Straits of Magellan, and reached San Francisco July 6, 1849. The city is described, its monte games and the Parker House; but Williams set out next day for the mines, going by way of "McKnight's Ferry on the Stanislaus River" to Wood's Diggings. He soon went on to Big Bar on the Mokelumne, thence back to the Stanislaus, where he mined on a bar below Coyote Creek. He set out for Australia in the early spring of 1852, and after a year there, returned home via South America. Williams then came back to California with a brother, going to Angel's Camp, Murphy's Camp, and subsequently Coulterville. He joined in the Fraser River rush of 1858. With all this roving, luck tended to elude him.

Somewhat less confusing is Daniel Cooledge Fletcher's *Reminiscences of California and the Civil War*, published at Ayer, Mass. Fletcher's brother Theodore had hoped to go to California in 1849, but his father objected, especially because of the dangers of Panama fever. When, for business reasons, Theodore bought a ticket for California in January, 1852, their father insisted that Daniel go along; neither was an experienced traveler. He tells of their voyage to the Isthmus, and deck passage to San Francisco, from which they went on to "the City of Nevada, in Nevada County, as we had read in the papers that it was a good mining locality." They stopped at Grass Valley, where another brother joined them overland in 1853. He left for home in December of that year, going via Nicaragua in the fast time of 23 days, and a year later came back to California on an unsuccessful apple tree speculation. He recounts more Grass Valley experiences, and tells of the fire at Nevada City in July, 1856, in which a fourth brother lost his life. Eventually he came back to the States in 1859.

The record for 1895 opens with something of an oddity, *Voyages of Nicholas Ball, from 1838 to 1853. In tabulated form, with notes. Together with a summary of a trip to Europe in 1888.* Printed at Boston, this 38-page work has a preface dated Block Island, R.I., January 1, 1895. The tabular information shows that he left New York for California as first mate in the brig *General Cobb,* October 24, 1849, and reached San Francisco April 27, 1850. He went home via Panama in June and July, 1851, and returned to California at two later times, but we will not follow his "tabular travels" in detail. More useful to us are some preliminary remarks, from which we learn that he mostly mined in 1850–1851 on the North Fork of the American River at Rattlesnake Bar; detailed results of the digging, on a daily basis, are supplied. Also included is a letter written to his brother-in-law from Rattlesnake Bar on January 19, 1851. Ball was a member of the Society of California Pioneers of New England, and also published a narrative of the excursion made by that Society to California in 1890.

A memorial volume is *To the Golden Gate and other sketches* (San Francisco, 1895); the preface, dated in June, says, "This volume contains selections of personal reminiscences and sketches by Dr. J. C. Tucker, now published by his wife with the hope that they may prove interesting to his family and friends." The doctor sailed from New York January 13, 1849, as surgeon of the ship *Tarolinta,* which we encountered in Daniel Knower's work of 1894. The vessel arrived at San Francisco July 6, after a voyage described at some length, and nine days later, he says, the New York and California Mining and Trading Company for the last time flew its flag above its great tent in Happy Valley. With three others, Dr. Tucker took passage to Sutter's in the schooner *Olivia.* He describes Sacramento, tells of buying mules from Stewart's fast mule train, "the first across the plains," which had just arrived at Sutter's (for this company, see William G. Johnston's work of 1892), and of going on from Sacramento to Coloma. He thereafter tells of the great flood of January, 1850, and its aftermath, and of becoming involved in an offshoot of the Gold Lake excitement. Dr. Tucker devotes a chapter to Sacramento in the fall and winter of 1850, and others to adventures in Nicaragua and Guatemala as a filibusterer. He came back to California in 1859 by the Butterfield Overland Stage Line. The book closes with some sketches of literary character relating to northern California.

The year 1896 is launched with Oliver Goldsmith's *Overland in Forty-Nine. The Recollections of a Wolverine Ranger after a lapse of forty-seven years. Exclusively for my family and friends,* published by the author at Detroit. Goldsmith set out for California from Marshall, Michigan, and about two-thirds of his book describes the overland journey via the Lassen Cutoff. After arrival, he went to San Francisco, worked there for a time, and after a fire (probably that of May, 1850) made his way to the Middle Fork of the American River. Late in the year he sailed for Panama in the ship *Montezuma,* but left this vessel at

Realejo, Nicaragua, and from Greytown took passage to Havana and New York, where he arrived in March. Goldsmith mentions revisiting San Francisco in 1889, where he encountered another survivor of the Rangers, W. W. Hobart, whose story he gives at some length.

Another overland narrative is R. C. Shaw's *Across the Plains in Forty-Nine* (Farmland, Indiana, 1896), originally published in 1895 as a series of articles in the Farmland *Enterprise*. Shaw traveled in the same company with Kimball Webster (see below), but his narrative is not comparable in accuracy; also it ends shortly after arrival at Sacramento, without having much to say about California.

A notably rare work is *Personal Recollections of Harvey Wood,* printed by the Mountain Echo Job Printing Office, Angels Camp, Calaveras County, California, in 1896. Twelve copies only are understood to have been printed for Wood's son in the year after his father's death; the manuscript was written in 1878. Wood sailed from New York February 13, 1849, in the ship *William B. Travis,* as a member of the Kit Carson Association of New York. From Galveston he went to Corpus Christi, Chihuahua, and Janos, thence to Tucson and Warner's Ranch, and on to the Merced River, where on July 30 he mined his first gold. He moved over to the Stanislaus River at McLean's Ferry, then to the area later called Robinson's Ferry, now Melones, where he settled permanently, having acquired an interest in the ferry. He closes in rather melancholy vein: "As the seasons come and go many changes have taken place, many once prosperous mining camps have now become almost deserted. An occasional 49er can be seen, generally poor, grey-headed, broken down specimen of humanity."

Austin S. Clark is a relative late-comer with his 54-page *1852-1865. Reminiscences of Travel* (Middletown, Conn., 1897?), and his personal record is not very extended. He sailed from New York for Nicaragua in the *Daniel Webster,* March 20, 1852. Briefly he describes San Francisco, Sacramento, and mining 6 miles from Coloma, with comment on mining techniques, hill diggings, etc., and a chapter on the Digger Indians. In 1865 he traveled from Placerville to Idaho; he taught the first public school in Owyhee County, and acted as county superintendent of schools.

Another relative late-comer was R. N. Willcox, as set forth in his *Reminiscences of California life, being an abridged description of scenes which the author has passed through in California, and other lands. With quotations from other authors. A short lecture on psychic science. An article on Church and State: written by his son; R. P. Willcox* (Avery, Ohio, 1897). Willcox relates that returned Californians began wishing "for the old California prices" for labor, so in the fall of 1851 a company of twelve concluded to make the trip via Panama, he one of their number. They set out in January, 1852. He describes the Isthmus and the voyage on to San Francisco, where the gambling palaces could still shock onlookers; pleasing impressions of Sacramento; carpentering at Uniontown in the Georgetown area; the Sacramento flood next winter; the Cosumnes Valley; the Big Tree cut down in 1854; and California crops, economy, society, etc. After extended "meanderings," he returns to his own experiences, and especially his journey home via Panama after some six years in

California. Willcox thrice revisited California in later years, but had to leave on grounds of health.

One of the most notable of all these reminiscences by the Argonauts is Jean-Nicolas Nicolet's *Vie et aventures d'un enfant de l'Ardennes* (Arlon, Belgium, 1897), a substantial work of 545 pages. As a record of experience in the California mines over an extended period, only Howard C. Gardiner's account compares with it; and unlike Gardiner, Perlot stuck strictly to gold mining. Despite the imprint, the book is dated at the end Janvier, 1898. Perlot briefly recounts his early life in Belgium and France, then in unhurried manner addresses himself to his California experiences. With a company of French gold-seekers he sailed around the Horn in the *Courrier de Cherbourg*, departing Havre October 3, 1850, and reaching Monterey April 6, 1851. From this point he made for the mines, going via San Juan, Pacheco, San Luis, Round Tent, and Wood's Ferry on the San Joaquin, thence to Griffine on the Merced River, and on to Hornitos, Bear Valley, and Mariposa. In the fall he worked a claim on Agua Fria Creek but settled in for the winter near Mariposa. In the spring and summer of 1852 he tried the country farther south, Coarse Gold Gulch and the Fresno River, but that fall settled on a claim in Bear Valley. Over the next few years, he spent most of his time at Spring Gulch, near Big Oak Flat, at Marble Spring, and at nearby Bull Creek. He saw much of the Yosemite Indians, and has much to say of them. In the spring of 1857 he visited Yosemite Valley. By this time the placers seemed played out. At a loss what to do, Perlot drifted to San Francisco, then took ship to Portland. Chance turned him into a landscape and truck gardener, the first in Portland. In 1867 he revisited his homeland, also acquiring a wife whom he brought back to Oregon with him in March, 1868. Land increased in value, gardening became more difficult, so he sold out in 1871, and next spring traveled by railroad from San Francisco to New York, and so on to Belgium, where a modest fortune enabled him to spend his declining days in comfort. In the mines and elsewhere in the West, birds of a feather tended to flock together, so Perlot is especially interesting for his viewpoint on French and Belgian adventurers.

Another title out of Europe close on the heels of Perlot's is Heinrich Lienhard's *Californien unmittelbar vor und nach der entdeckung des goldes. Bilder aus dem leben des Heinrich Lienhard von Bilten, Kanton Glarus in Nauvoo, Nordamerika. Ein beitrag zur jubiläumsfeier der goldentdeckung und zur kulturgeschichte Californiens* (Zurich, 1898). This account of California "immediately before and after the discovery of gold" is a condensation of Lienhard's massive manuscript which later come into the possession of the Bancroft Library, and his experiences are better discussed with an eye on translations of extensive portions of the original manuscript. His account of his overland journey in 1846 was published in translation by Erwin and Elisabeth Gudde in 1961; what is here relevant is the California section, most of which was translated by Marguerite Eyer Wilbur as *A Pioneer at Sutter's Fort, 1846–1850: The adventures of Heinrich Lienhard* (Los Angeles, 1941). After he reached New Helvetia in 1846, Lienhard was employed by Captain Sutter as a gardener and overseer. He tells how the news of the gold discovery broke upon them, and of his labors in the mines in the summer of 1848. Next year Sutter sent him to Switzerland via Panama to bring Sutter's family to California, and he did not return until January, 1850. Having prospered, he went back to Switzerland in 1852, but subsequently he returned to America and settled at Nauvoo, Illinois, as a farmer. His is a garrulous, even gossipy narrative, and not the less interesting for his prolixity.

The experiences of one who must have met Lienhard are detailed in *Life of a Pioneer. Being the autobiography of James S. Brown* (Salt Lake City, 1900). A Mormon Battalion member, Brown was working at Sutter's Mill when gold was discovered in January, 1848, so that he is one of the standard sources on this event and subsequent happenings till he departed for Salt Lake in June following. He returned to California by the southern route in the fall and winter of 1849–1850, bound for the Society Islands as a missionary. To raise a stake, he and his brethren worked for a time at Burns' Diggings on the Merced River. Soon, however, he went on to San Francisco via Stockton, and two weeks later was on the bounding main. He had a long and varied life as a Mormon pioneer, and we shall not attempt to describe it here, except to note that while on a visit to California in 1894 he wrote a pamphlet version of his recollections of the gold discovery, thus foreshadowing his eventual autobiography.

In D. A. Shaw's *Eldorado or California as seen by a pioneer, 1850–1900* (Los Angeles, 1900), we have much reminiscent material frequently correct and often interesting, but marred by interpolation of doubtful historical data beyond the range of his own experience, dealing with such personalities as Jedediah Smith, William Bent, and Kit Carson. Shaw set out from Marengo, Illinois, in April, 1850, with four others, going via Council Bluffs, where they joined with others from Illinois and Wisconsin as the Wild Rovers. Beyond Fort Laramie, the company broke up into smaller segments. He supplies doubtful recollections of various Indians, and tells of going via Salt Lake, where he breaks the chain of his narrative to tell of a second overland journey of 1853, when he went via the Salt Lake Cutoff and the Carson route. In 1850 he took instead the Hastings Cutoff, across the Salt Desert, which adds novelty to his narrative. He remarks on Ragtown, Reese's Mormon trading post on the Carson River, and his experiences in the mines around Hangtown, Coloma, and on the Cosumnes River over a period of some five years. He also devotes a chapter to "An account of the sufferings of a party of Argonauts who were compelled to abandon their vessel *The Dolphin* on the peninsula of Lower California, and make their way on foot to San Diego"—this account "obtained from various authentic sources."

A notable addition to the record made in 1901 is Nicholas Dawson's *California in '41. Texas in '51. Memoirs*, privately printed in Texas. Dawson is above all notable as a member of the Bartleson Party, but after a year's stay in California, he returned east in 1842. After a period in which he occupied himself teaching school in Arkansas, gold fever took him, and Dawson set out for California again, starting from Sherman, Texas, about March 1, 1849, and traveling the southern route. After reaching Los Angeles, he turned north to reach the Mariposa diggings about November 1. He describes his experiences through the rainy winter that followed, the cordial reception given him at Stockton by his fellow traveler of 1841, Charles M. Weber, his slow accumulation of a modest stake, and eventual return east via Panama in the spring of 1851. That same year he visited Texas, and was so much delighted with the country that he settled there permanently, in the vicinity of Austin, where "my experiences were those of any pioneer farmer."

John Steele's *In Camp and Cabin. Mining life and adventure, during 1850 and later* (Lodi, Wis., 1901) presents a few complications, in that it was written as a sequel to his *Across the Plains in 1850,* though the latter work was not separately published until 1930; in each case, the text was first published in the *Lodi Valley News,* commencing in 1899. The overland narrative adheres so rigidly to the diary format that it will not be given further attention here, but the California reminiscences are more than eligible for inclusion in these notes, even though written with reference to a diary. Steele tells of reaching Nevada City September 23, 1850, and of mining there and at Jefferson on the Yuba River. He subsequently visited Washington, a then-deserted village higher up, and mined at Nelson Creek and other localities. In March, 1851, he started for the Klamath mines, but next month came back to the South Fork of the American River near Mormon Island. He gives a considerable account of Coloma and vicinity. While mining at Texas Bar, also on the South Fork, between June and November, 1852, he encountered Pegleg Smith, then living at nearby Kelsey. After further mining in the Coloma area, he set out for home in the summer of 1853, going via Nicaragua. The Reverend Steele (he became a minister) was an acute observer who wrote well concerning interesting experiences.

Francis Whiting Halsey's *The Pioneers of Unadilla Village, 1784–1840 . . . Reminiscences of Village Life and of Panama and California from 1840 to 1850 by Gaius Leonard Halsey M.D.* (Unadilla, N.Y., 1902) is primarily important to us for the second half of the book, made up of reminiscences by Dr. Halsey originally published in the Unadilla *Times,* 1890, republished by his son after his death in 1891. Francis Halsey also included his father's brief diary, February 12–November 11, 1849, describing the same experiences. Dr. Halsey sailed from New York for Chagres February 23, 1849, as one of the "Bristol and California Company" in the brig *Abrasia.* He gives an interesting account of the Isthmus and the further voyage to San Francisco on the *Panama.* After arrival, June 4, he went on to Sacramento in a sloop loaded with freight (and considered afterward that he would have done better investing in Sacramento real estate than in going on to the mines). He made his way to Big Bar on the Middle Fork of the American River, and mined with some success. In October he returned to Sacramento, intending to open an office and practice his profession, "but on looking over the ground I was simply amazed to see the number of doctors' shingles hanging out." Accordingly he went on to San Francisco in what he describes as the first down trip of the first steamboat. Despite the marvelous changes in San Francisco, he decided to go on home via Panama, and reached New York on Christmas Day. (His diary says he made up his mind to return because in San Francisco he found more doctors than patients—a commentary on the times!)

Another work dating from 1902 is Obed G. Wilson's *My Adventures in the Sierras,* printed at Franklin, Ohio. Wilson was a late-comer, who from his Maine home traveled to California via Nicaragua late in 1854. After a siege of illness in San Francisco, he made his way to Marysville, then to Camp Warren, a mining town between the Yuba and Feather rivers. Here (with occasional visits to nearby LaPorte, Downieville, Secret Diggings, and Goodyear's Bar) and at Whiskey Diggings, with forays into other areas, he sought the yellow metal until his eventual return home, in the summer of 1859. There is much of interest in this modest narrative, including an early account of skiing, a visit with Jim Beckwourth, and the warm feeling that existed among Down-Easters.

A slender 27-page pamphlet is George S. McKnight's *California 49er. Travels from Perrysburg to California* (Perrysburg, Ohio, 1903). McKnight went to New Orleans, by steamer to Galveston, thence across Mexico as a member of the Defiance Company. He relates that he reached Mazatlan August 1, was shipwrecked on the French ship *Rolland,* and started on August 31 in the schooner "*Dose Meyus,* meaning three friends in Spanish." He reached San Francisco after a 36-day voyage, got acquainted with "Subtits [Andrew Sublette] the sheriff," and worked for him for a time. McKnight says that he went to the mines then, and stayed till he came home in June, 1864, mostly on the Yuba and in dry diggings near Bear River. We would have more faith in McKnight's recollections had he not told of a visit from "Old Kit Carson," then over 80, who came with his boys but not to work, "one of the finest old gentlemen I ever saw."

G.W.Thissell's *Crossing the Plains in '49* (Oakland, 1903) has a misleading title in that the author only *started* for California in 1849. He fell ill on the frontier, spent nine months working as a carriage-maker in the interior of Iowa, and started again in 1850 from Bellefontaine, Iowa. His story is presented in the form of a journal, March 6–September 16, 1850 (when he arrived at Hangtown having traveled via Salt Lake), but with much correlative and reminiscent material woven in, from other years and other men's experiences. Very briefly at the end he says that he began mining on the north fork of Weaver Creek, 25 miles east of Hangtown, and after four years of toil in the mines, settled in Pleasant Valley.

Privately printed at San Francisco in 1904 was Edward Bosqui's *Memoirs,* said to have been limited to an edition of 50 copies for his friends and family. In his brief preface, Bosqui said: "These recollections of my early life and pioneer experiences in California were jotted down from time to time at the earnest request of members of my family. Although reluctantly commenced, the work, as it progressed, became absorbing; memories of almost forgotten incidents were revived; and a project which began as a task, developed into a pleasing recreation. What I have written will at least serve to keep green the memories of old friends and fellow-pioneers, to whom, and to the dear companions of my youth, these memoirs are inscribed with affection and gratitude."

The Montreal-born Bosqui made his way to New York in February, 1850, took ship on March 26 for Brazos Santiago, at the mouth of the Rio Grande, and in a party of nine crossed Mexico to Mazatlan, via Camargo, Monterrey, and Durango. Aboard the French ship *Camilla,* he then sailed for San Francisco June 16 and reached his destination on his eighteenth birthday, July 23. Entertainingly he describes life in San Francisco, a visit to the Mariposa mines in the winter of 1850–1851, and his return to San Francisco next May after getting a good look at "the elephant." For some time he worked for the bank of Palmer, Cook & Co., occasionally involved with Frémont's affairs at Mariposa; later he became interested in real estate, worked in the Custom House, and established a very successful bookbinding, engraving, and printing business. His narrative is highly informative, enlivened by many interesting anecdotes, especially with regard to life in the San Francisco Bay region, and if not much preoccupied with mining, not untypical of the Gold Rush experience of 1849–1850.

Despite its promising title, Thomas Edwin Farish's *The Gold Hunters of California* (Chicago, 1904) is a very slight addition to the gold chronicle. Farish's father, a Tennessee merchant, went to California by the Gila route in 1849, did well, and sent for his family. They set out via Panama in January, 1852, eventually reaching San Francisco on the *Northerner* April 11. He describes San Francisco at the time, with a mistaken recollection of the *Niantic* (burned the previous year), and tells how he went to work for Cooke & Lecount. In 1854 Farish went to Marysville (and mentions various rushes, some misdated). By 1856 he and his partner were the owners of a rough wooden building on the Feather River which had been used as a boarding house; they got an interest in a mining company in exchange for the house, made money rapidly that fall, then lost heavily when the dam washed out. Following some disjointed remarks on mining and mining men, he says that placer and river mining were exhausted in California in 1857, after which attention was directed to hydraulic and vein mining, which required large capital investment to be successful. "From this time on California was no longer the poor man's paradise, where he could get gold without the outlay of money." Most of the last 200 pages of this 246-page book deal with noted personalities and incidents of California history, some within Farish's personal notice.

A. A. Enos, *Across the Plains in 1850* (n. p., 1905) is made up of 22 reminiscent letters written for his son's newspaper, the *Stanton Pickett*. They describe a journey from Laporte County, Indiana, to Hangtown, March 18–July 25, 1850, via Council Bluffs, Salt Lake City, and the Carson River. After reaching California, Enos tells of mining near Hangtown, an epidemic in Sacramento, mining on the American River; Coloma; a miner's trial; further mining on "Antewine [Antoine]" Creek; exaggerated reports of rich strikes; and his return home via Nicaragua, having been gone 21 months.

We must begin the chronicle for 1906 by dismissing *The Diary of a Forty-Niner. Edited by Chauncey L. Canfield,* which is fictional, a made-up diary for one "Alfred T. Jackson" on Rock Creek, Nevada County, 1850–1852. More factual, if perhaps less well written, is W. J. Pleasants, *Twice across the Plains 1849 . . . 1856* (San Francisco, 1906). Pleasants set out from Pleasant Hill, Cass County, Missouri, and went via the Lassen Cutoff. He mined at Bidwell's Bar, Oregon Flat, and South Fork (presumably, of the Yuba), visited Sacramento late in 1850, then settled near Winters in the valley subsequently named for his family. In 1856 his father sent him east via Panama to bring out their family. He started from Big Creek, Johnson County, Missouri, May 6, 1856, and went via the Carson River; his narrative ends on arrival in Pleasants Valley. His preface is dated in that valley September 12, 1905.

The year 1908 added five more chronicles to the literature. The one with the most rambling title is *Recollections of a '49er. A quaint and thrilling narrative of a trip a[c]ross the plains, and life in the California gold fields during the stirring days following the discovery of gold in the Far West. By Edward Washington McIlhany "one of the Last of the Old Boys"* (Kansas City, Mo., 1908). McIlhany wrote these recollections in his 81st year. He set out from Charleston, (West) Virginia, describing the overland journey only briefly. After reaching Johnson's Ranch, he went north to Shasta City but soon came back to Bidwell's Bar on the Feather River. Subsequently he had a store at Onion Valley. After other experiences in the Northern Mines and at Marysville, he sailed from San Francisco for the Isthmus November 24, 1856. The latter part of the book describes experiences in the East, in the Pikes Peak rush, in Missouri, and cattle trading in New Mexico and Colorado. The whole is not so weighty as might be wished.

Of more solid character is George Coffin's *A Pioneer Voyage to California and Round the World, 1849 to 1852, Ship Alhambra* (Chicago, 1908). Coffin captained the *Alhambra* in her voyage around the Horn from New Orleans to San Francisco, which she reached October 12, 1849. Coffin describes San Francisco and Happy Valley, tells how he finished clearing cargo on December 27 and sold the vessel to the Pacific Steamship Company on January 30, 1850, with a comment on the swindling San Francisco courts. He bought a sloop, the *Sophronia,* and voyaged to Marysville, Sacramento, and other river ports; but he was back in San Francisco, broke and sick, by the summer of 1851. In August of that year he arranged the purchase of the ship *Arco Iris,* and sailed her to Honolulu, thence on around the world; he finally reached New York November 1, 1852.

Another substantial work is *Memoirs of Cornelius Cole, ex-Senator of the United States from California* (New York, 1908). Cole traveled overland in 1849 via Independence, Salt Lake, and the Carson River, reaching Sutter's July 24 as one of the earliest overland arrivals. He describes Coloma and Greenwood Valley, "where the old mountaineer Greenwood and his son John, with his Indian wife, were camping," as also Georgetown and Oregon Gulch. Cole left the mines, successful, in the spring of 1850. After picturing Sacramento and San Francisco, he relates how he entered into a law partnership with James Pratt of Michigan. He removed in 1851 to Sacramento, where he practiced for 10 years, meanwhile traveling generally in California. The public events of the period he remarks upon, politics in particular, leading to his election as U.S. Senator in December, 1865. The narrative more or less ends with his defeat for reelection six years later.

One of Cole's Washington colleagues published his recollections in the same year: *Reminiscences of Senator William M. Stewart of Nevada,* edited by George Rothwell Brown (New York and Washington, 1908). Remembered as one of the forceful political figures of his age, Stewart set out for California in January, 1850, taking a shaky old steamer, the *Philadelphia,* to Chagres, and a little propeller, the *Carolina,* on to San Francisco, not without misadventures along the way. He went to Marysville and then to Deer Creek, where he commenced mining, with some success. According to his story, he first crossed the Sierra while on a prospecting tour that fall, visiting the ruins of the Donner cabins en route. After engaging in a ditch-digging enterprise on the waters of the Yuba, in the spring of 1852 he began reading law at Nevada City, and was made district attorney the ensuing November. From this time until he left California for the embryo Nevada in the spring of 1860 law and politics in Nevada County largely engaged him. Afterward he became a celebrated lawyer on the Comstock Lode, and was elected to the Senate when Nevada was admitted to the Union in 1864, serving as a member of that body until 1905, except for the period 1875–1887. His recital is richly adorned with anecdotes and continuously interesting, if perhaps a bit overblown with that egotism so often accompanying the holding of public office.

To us, only the first quarter is very interesting of *Life and times of S. H. West. With an appendix on evolution, religion, and spiritual phenomena* (Leroy, Ill., 1908). West came out to California in 1852 via New Orleans, Vera Cruz, Mexico City, and Acapulco. From San Francisco he made his way to Sacramento, then to Elizabethtown in Placer County; he fell ill, and on recovery located claims in Indian Canyon nearby, this in June, 1852. He tells of the fire in Sacramento that fall, and of wintering at Jamestown. In the summer of 1853 West moved to Sullivan Creek, at the mouth of Curtis Creek, from whence he set out via Nicaragua for his Illinois home in February, 1854, first commenting on "Sydney ducks," the mines around Sonora, and Table Mountain. West returned to California in 1859 via the Butterfield Overland Stage, only to find conditions much changed, the best of the placer mines worked out, the fast and exciting spirit of the early days gone, and a dullness settled on the country, distressing to an old timer. He went to Big Oak Flat and remained there until his return to Illinois via Panama in August, 1861, not omitting to visit Yosemite Valley before his departure.

The fifth title dating from 1908, published at Shenandoah, Iowa, is a slim pamphlet not personally examined: *Autobiography of George Meyer Oregon, Missouri Across the plains with an ox team in 1849.* It is described by T. W. Streeter, in the catalogue of the fifth Streeter sale, October, 1968, as the tale of one who did well as a miner, kept his money, and returned East when he had made his little pile; "though these are the recollections of an old man . . . dates are from time to time given so exactly as to indicate that written memoranda had been preserved. Meyers left the Indian Mission on May 3, 1849 and reached the summit of the Sierras on August 3 and Hangtown on August 19th."

Julius Howard Pratt's *Reminiscences Personal and Otherwise* (n. p., 1910) was privately printed by his children in the year after his death, but had been a part of the Gold Rush chronicle since three chapters appeared in *Century Magazine,* April, 1891, under the title, "To California by Panama in '49." Pratt sailed from New York in the brig *Mayflower* March 22, 1849, arrived at Chagres April 13, and took passage for San Francisco in the ship *Humboldt.* A 48-day passage got them as far as Acapulco on July 7, and here Pratt and others left, rather than endure the "prison ship" further. Eventually they reached San

Francisco on the steamship *California*, all of this entertainingly described. The company made its way to Sacramento and then to Stockton, mined for three months, and finally broke up amicably, eight months from the time of its inception. He had a store at Stockton for a year, and gives us good descriptions of San Francisco in November, 1849, and of some incidents at Sonora and in the Mariposa area. Pratt left San Francisco by steamboat in February, 1851, going via Panama, and on to New York on the *North America*. His later life we shall pass over.

After the lapse of two years, we have another title for our list, J. W. Gibson's *Recollections of a Pioneer* (St. Joseph, Mo., 1912). Gibson set out for California in 1849 from Buchanan County, Missouri, with his brothers William and James, a returned Oregonian, Robert Gilmore, and others, including "old man Greenwood and his two sons" (which I take to be a confused recollection of 1848). They took the Carson route and saw their first gold on Weaver Creek in August. He went to Sacramento, not then much of a place, thence to the American River, and after a few weeks, on to Shasta City. Presently he came back to Salmon Falls on the American River, where various Buchanan County goldseekers had congregated. The five Gibson brothers started a ranching enterprise on "Cash Creek," and by 1851 were doing well. They went out to meet the emigration in the expectation of replenishing their herds, but found few trains, and no cattle to be had. Accordingly, with two other brothers Gibson set out for Missouri, going via Salt Lake (at a time when eastbound travel overland from California was still very uncommon). They got home about the middle of September, and next May he set out again for California with some 550 head of cattle. Gibson did the same thing in 1853 and 1854, though each year he went home via Panama. Eventually he sold out in California and returned to Missouri in the spring of 1860. His later adventures, though interesting, need not be described.

Not the less interesting for their brevity are the *Memoirs of John Marshall Newton* (n. p., 1913), written between 1867 and 1894, with a concluding note by Ellen Huldah Newton telling of his last years and death in 1897. Newton, who was from Section Ten, Ohio, set out from Independence in April, 1850, with a party from Mansfield, Ohio, reaching Hangtown via the Carson River route in September. He comments on Sacramento, Stockton, Mokelumne Hill, and on Rich Gulch in detail, including the "French war" there. Much of the time he was troubled by illness; he went to San Francisco, and a sea voyage to San Pedro and back cured him. He now established himself in Tuolumne County near the confluence of Woods and Stone creeks. He got on well with Chinese miners, befriended them, and finally sold out to them. After returning to San Francisco, he offers some excellent remarks on the character of Californians in 1850–1852. Newton left California for good in the latter year, eventually getting home by working as a coal heaver on the U.S. steamer *Massachusetts* from Valparaiso. The memoirs extend only to the spring of 1861.

Another posthumous work is *The Autobiography of Theodore Edgar Potter*, published at Concord, N.H., in 1913, three years after the author's death. George C. Sprague, who copyrighted the work, also wrote a preface for it. Potter offers a detailed account of an overland journey of 1852 via the Sublette and Hudspeth cutoffs, the Truckee River, and Beckwourth Pass. For some time he mined in the area east of Marysville—Onion Valley, Poor Man's Creek, Nelson Creek, and Forbestown. By 1855 he was working claims at Jacksonville and Columbia, in Tuolumne County. In 1856, when he decided to return home, he found San Francisco buzzing with excitement over vigilance committee activities. He became one of Walker's filibusterers in Nicaragua, but after brief service took ship to New York, then went on to his Michigan home. Although he once started for California again, he changed his mind. He was in Minnesota in the late 1850's and early 1860's, participated in the Sioux campaign of 1863, and eventually returned permanently to Michigan, to engage in farming and lumbering.

Commenced about 1893 and carried to a conclusion twenty years later was *California 1849–1913, or The Rambling Sketches and Experiences of Sixty-four Years' Residence in that State* by Lell Hawley Woolley, "Member of the Society of California Pioneers and of the Vigilance Committee of 1856" (Oakland, 1913). Hawley set out for California from Independence in the first mule train of Turner, Allen & Co.'s Pioneer Line (which was a remarkable effort to set up a stage line to California amid the turmoil of the Gold Rush). He gives a lively account of the troubles encountered on the overland journey, a useful supplement to Niles Searls' published *Diary*. On arriving at Weaverville, he found himself too worn out for mining, so he went to Sacramento and to Grass Valley. Woolley got a small stake and started a hotel in Grass Valley, but was soon "busted." In the winter of 1849–1850 he went from Sacramento to Beal's Bar near the junction of the North and South Forks of the American River, did fairly well by spring, but an effort, with thirty others, to turn the South Fork of the American River into the North Fork and thus gain access to the river bed turned out none too well. Woolley went to Mokelumne Hill, realizing just enough there to pay the debts he had incurred in Vermont to set out for California. He returned home via Nicaragua in the spring of 1852, but two years later, having meanwhile married, returned permanently to San Francisco. Most of the rest of his story has to do with his experiences there, and with the Vigilance Committee of 1856, and offers much information of antiquarian interest respecting the sites, personalities, and development of San Francisco. For many years he was a merchant, and for two decades (until his retirement in 1904) associated with the Southern Pacific.

We assign tentatively to the year 1914 *Echoes of the Past about California by the late General John Bidwell* (Chico, Calif., n. d.), a pamphlet made up of three articles contributed to *Century Magazine* in 1890–1891, and some further reminiscences printed in *Out West*, 1904. Bidwell traveled overland to California in the Bartleson Party of 1841, and principally recounts the experiences of that party and his adventures in California afterward, with supplementary remarks on "Fremont in the Conquest of California." He has very little to say about Marshall's gold discovery and subsequent events, content to remark: "Time does not permit me to relate how I carried the news of the discovery to San Francisco; how the same year I discovered gold on the Feather river and worked it; how I made the first weights and scales to weigh the first gold for Sam Brannan; how the richest of the mines became known by the Mormons who were employed by Sutter to work at the sawmill, working about on Sundays and finding it in the crevices along the stream and taking it to Brannan's store at the fort, and how Brannan kept the gold a secret as long as he could till the excitement burst out all at once like wildfire."

More centrally concerned with the Gold Rush is the *Autobiography of Isaac Jones Wistar 1827–1905 Half a Century in war and peace* (Philadelphia, 1914). In his preface, dated Philadelphia, 1892, Wistar says his narrative is written almost entirely from recollection, but it includes two diaries, one of May 3–August 26, 1849, recording his overland journey from Independence to the Yuba River. Wistar tells of experiences in the Northern Mines, and of illness which persuaded him to go to the Sandwich Islands or some other mild climate to winter; finally he went to Panama by a sailing vessel. After a side trip to Nicaragua, he came back to San Francisco with mules. Subsequently he went to Trinidad Bay and began trading in a hostile Indian country, the more northerly mining area. He hunted and trapped in the Northwest, came back to northern California, spent some time in Scotts Valley, then embarked on a trading venture to the Northwest Coast (with a diary of December 30, 1852–January 8, 1853, while so engaged). After another voyage up the coast, he began to practice law in San Francisco. He departed San Francisco at last September 5, 1856, on the steamer *California*. Later he visited Missouri, served in the Civil War, and had a highly successful law practice in Pennsylvania.

Issued in modest paper covers at Sacramento in 1915 was *The Autobiography of Charles Peters In 1915 the oldest pioneer living in California who mined in "The Days of Old, The Days of Gold, The Days of '49." Also historical happenings, interesting incidents and illustrations of the old mining towns in the good luck era, the placer mining days of the '50s.* The author was a Portuguese whose proper name was Carlo Pedro Deogo Laudier de Andriado. He came to California from New York, evidently in 1849, in the ship *Elfa*. He went to Sacramento, then to Dry Creek, and soon to Jackson, which he reached in the latter part of 1850. He mined on the Mokelumne River, but stopped placer mining late in the 1850's and took up a ranch. This slender autobiography, chiefly of interest for the Amador County area, is succeeded by extended remarks on "the good luck era,' much anecdotal information but not a personal memoir. Peters was in his 91st year when he published this work.

L. Dow Stephens' *Life Sketches of a Jayhawker of '49* (n. p., 1916) is chiefly remembered as a 68-page footnote to Manly's book of 1894, but it has independent interest. Like Manly, Stephens tells of the overland journey to Salt Lake and Los Angeles in 1849–1850 as one of the Death Valley party. Afterward he made his way to the mines by the coastal route to San Jose, thence to the Merced River and Hurts (Hart's?) Bar on the Tuolumne. He mined at Chinese Camp and Fine Gold Gulch after the rains came. Later he visited southern California several times on cattle-buying ventures, sailed to the Sandwich Islands and back, went to Nevada in 1861–1862, and joined in the Cariboo rush to British Columbia in 1862, spent some time in Arizona, the Owens Valley, and Idaho, and even joined in the Klondike rush of 1898. He closes his narrative with some miscellaneous recollections of experiences in the mines in the 1850's, and notes on the fate of individual Jayhawkers.

Despite his title, Carlisle S. Abbott, in *Recollections of a California Pioneer* (New York, 1917) notes that he doesn't fully qualify as a "California Pioneer," being an arrival of 1850. His Recollections were "entirely written after I had passed my eighty-eighth birthday, the chief inducement to the undertaking being a desire on my part to leave to my children, my grandchildren, and their posterity a story of my long life." Abbott traveled overland from Wisconsin via Salt Lake and the Carson route; some of his companions attempted the Hastings Cutoff west of Salt Lake, and he has an amusing anecdote of their tribulations. Abbott began his gold digging at Missouri Canyon, then moved on to Volcano Bar, Mud Spring, Yankee Slide, and Sandy Bar, which he had reached by the summer of 1851. He then went on to San Francisco, and home via Panama and New York, where he arrived January 20, 1852. Within two months he was off for California again, but has little to say of the journey beyond the Pawnee country. He lived in Sacramento and Nevada City, took up dairying at Point Reyes in Marin County in 1858, moved to the Salinas Valley in 1865, occupying himself with ranching, building, and wheat farming; in 1879 shifted to Tombstone, Arizona, and eventually returned to the Salinas Valley. Abbott's is a livelier narrative than many.

One who did not survive to see his book in print, having died in 1916, was Kimball Webster, *The Gold Seekers of '49. A personal narrative of the overland trail and adventures in California and Oregon from 1849 to 1854* (Manchester, N.H., 1917). His narrative is preceded by an introduction and biographical sketch by George Waldo Browne. Webster traveled overland in the same company with R. C. Shaw. He gives us an actual diary, April 17–October 19, 1849, of the overland journey via the Lassen Cutoff, then relates more generally his experiences in California to June, 1851, and in Oregon to July, 1854. The company having broken up soon after reaching the mines, Webster dug for gold at Bidwell's Bar on the Feather River, then labored on the ranch of Charles H. Burch. He also tells of the Sacramento flood, January, 1850. Thus far his account was based on contemporary memoranda; he resumed the narrative in 1894, having made only scanty notes after 1850, which he undertook to flesh out from memory. Webster went to Yuba City, engaged in woodcutting, mined on the Middle Fork of the Feather River, and did surveying for what proved a paper city at Burch's Ranch. He gives us a chapter on "The Illusion of Gold Lake," a by-product being the discovery of the Nelson Creek mines, on a tributary of the Feather's Middle Fork. He tells of labors there, and some murders, then of mining on the Yuba to March, 1851. After that, he went to San Francisco and to Oregon. He came home in the summer of 1854.

By 1921 practically all the Forty-niners were dead; from this point on, their experiences come to us through publication of memoirs written earlier. A rare exception is *Recollections of John McWilliams. His youth, experiences in California and the Civil War* (Princeton, 1921). McWilliams at the age of 17 set out for California in 1849 with three other boys from Griggsville, Ill., going via Fort Hall. At the junction of the Oregon and California trails in the Snake Valley, their train split, 16 wagons heading for California, while nine made for Oregon; McWilliams accompanied the latter group. After reaching the Willamette Valley, he and one other continued on to California overland, thus reaching Shasta City in October. He tells of experiences in that locality, and adds, "We were the first party that ever mined on the South Fork of the Salmon River with any moderate success." They moved on to new diggings afterward known as "Scotch [Scott?] River mines," and had further adventures in the more northerly mines through 1850–1851. Via Panama and New Orleans, he got back to his Griggsville home about the last of January, 1853. Subsequent Civil War experiences we shall pass over.

James J. Ayers enlarged the chronicle with *Gold and Sunshine, Reminiscences of Early California* (Boston, 1922), which was based, as he says in his preface, dated in Los Angeles County, 1896, on a continuous residence of 47 years. Ayers set out for California from St. Louis in February, 1849. He took passage from New Orleans on the Chagres-bound steamer, *Galveston,* which had an explosion en route, and had to make for Belize, British Honduras. While others went on to Chagres, he and 16 others sailed in a small schooner to Omoa, at the head of the Gulf of Honduras, then traveled by land across the mountains to Puerto la Union, in San Salvador. Failing to obtain passage there, he journeyed to Realejo in Nicaragua, and after a long wait there, embarked in the brig *Laura Anne* for San Francisco. Thus he had a most varied and adventurous passage to the Golden Shore, arriving October 5, 1849.

After seeing the sights, he sailed for Stockton in the *José Castro,* and then spent a year mining on the Calaveras and the Mokelumne, experiences briefly but entertainingly described. In October, 1851, Ayers became one of the co-founders of the *Calaveras Chronicle* at Mokelumne Hill, and he has much of interest to say about early journalism, politics, and the theatre in California. He made a visit east in 1853, and subsequently established himself in the newspaper business in San Francisco, being there at the time of the Vigilance Committee violence of 1856. Soon after, he founded the San Francisco *Call.* We shall not attempt to describe his life thereafter in any detail; Ayers was a characteristic Californian of his age, managed to get mixed up in everything (including a tour of duty as editor of the *Territorial Enterprise* at Virginia City, and publisher of a paper at Hamilton, Nevada, during the White Pine excitement of 1868). From 1872 he lived mainly in southern California. Ayers knew interesting people in a lively era, and wrote about them well, while carefully avoiding, as he says, "the meretricious custom, which has too largely prevailed among those who have written about pioneer times, of degrading their publications . . . by praising the successful survivors of the pioneers beyond their merit and exalting the names of some who were entitled to but scant recognition. Indeed, my general plan has been to let the living round out their career to the end unemblazoned, but to carefully rescue, as far as I could, from oblivion many who have gone over in undeserved obscurity to the majority." We are not enlightened how Ayers' reminiscences came to be published, more than a quarter of a century after they were written.

Our next title was written in 1922–1923 by Mrs. Lee Whipple-Haslam, *Early Days in California. Scenes and events of the '50s as I remember them* (Jamestown, Calif. [1925?], a 34-page pamphlet in double columns. Her father, Franklin Summers, reached California around the Horn in 1850, mined successfully at Shaws Flat near Sonora, went back around Cape Horn for his family, and brought wife and daughter overland in 1852 via the Carson River. They established themselves near Shaws Flat, but in the fall of 1854 moved to the site of Tuolumne, ten miles from Sonora. Diggings were found in the fall of 1855 near their place by the Scott brothers, half breed Cherokees, so that the locality became known as Cherokee. The father was shot to death in June, 1856 at French Bar (now LaGrange), after which the mother opened a boarding house on Turnback Creek. The writer tells of violence in the mines, the attitude toward Chinese labor, Indians, pioneer physicians and lawyers, Mark Twain, and life at Summersville from 1859.

Another woman who came overland in 1852 was Mary E. Ackley, *Crossing the Plains and early days in California. Memories of girlhood days in California's golden age* (San Francisco, privately printed for the author, 1928), a 68-page reminiscence. Her overland journey at the age of 20 was via Salt Lake and the Carson River. Principally she recounts her life in Sacramento, with 6½ years in Aurora (from 1864), and intermittent visits to San Francisco, to which she moved in 1891.

A full-scale reminiscence, edited by Anna Paschall Hannum, and with a foreword by John Bach McMaster, is *A Quaker Forty-niner. The adventures of Charles Edward Pancoast on the American frontier* (Philadelphia, 1930). Pancoast was born in 1818 and died in 1906; he seems to have finished his recollections in May, 1890. He tells of his early life in the East, removal to St. Louis in 1840, visit to Nauvoo in the winter of 1841–1842, and varied experiences in Missouri, especially at Warsaw. Infected with gold fever, he set out from Fort Leavenworth on April 29, 1849, accompanying a party from Peoria. They took the Santa Fe Trail to Bent's Fort, then continued on to Pueblo and the Greenhorn, and finally, via San Miguel, to Galisteo. Some of the party visited Santa Fe, but he did not. He kept on to California by the Gila route, then made for the mines by way of Los Angeles, Santa Barbara, and San Luis Obispo. After reaching Mariposa, he tried Sonora, Chinese Diggings, Moccasin Creek Diggings, Big Oak Flat, and a bar on the Tuolumne River, then after a visit to the Merced River, went on to San Francisco. He was soon on his way to the Trinity Mines, finally reaching Humboldt Bay by sea. After a season of woodsplitting at Uniontown, he went on to the mines in April, 1851. He spent some time at Weaverville and Shasta City, came back to San Francisco by way of Sacramento early in 1853, apparently, and returned to Philadelphia via Nicaragua in April, 1854.

Sarah Royce's reminiscences, eventually published under the title *A Frontier Lady, Recollections of the Gold Rush and Early California,* edited by Ralph Henry Gabriel (New Haven, 1932), were originally written in the early 1880's for the use of her son Josiah, then engaged in writing a volume on frontier California. The narrative is one of great charm, describing her overland journey via Salt Lake City in 1849, experiences for a few months at Weaverville, then at Sacramento during the flood of January, 1850, afterward at San Francisco, and eventually in a mining town she does not name, apparently in the Grass Valley area.

Doubtfully included in our list is Erwin G. Gudde's *Sutter's Own Story. The life of General John Augustus Sutter and the history of New Helvetia in the Sacramento Valley* (New York, 1936). This is a biography of Sutter largely based upon, and with extended quotations from, the manuscript reminiscences in the Bancroft Library dictated to H. H. Bancroft in 1876. Gudde frankly says: "A publication of the original would have not even academic interest; it presents only in a very limited sense Sutter's own words. Therefore, I have rewritten the entire story, correcting the numerous errors, inserting the necessary dates and names, supplying connecting passages wherever advisable, and arranging it in chronological order as far as possible. In cases where it rises to a dramatic climax, I have endeavored to retain his own words as much as possible." In view of all this, we shall be content to observe that three chapters are titled, "The Discovery of Gold," "The Argonaut Invasion," and "The Aftermath," and that very little is said of events after 1848.

A slender work of 61 pages is *Luzena Stanley Wilson '49er. Memories recalled years later for her daughter Correnah Wilson Wright. Introduction by Francis P. Farquhar* (Oakland, 1937). Mrs. Wilson dictated these reminiscences to her daughter in April, 1881. She came overland, not giving much detail on the route, but via the Carson River. She tells principally of life in Sacramento, Nevada City, and in the Vaca Valley.

Oddly complicated in its history is a book printed at Buenos Aires in 1937 with an introduction by Hector Pedro Blomberg, William Perkins' *El Campo de los Sonoraenses. Tres años de residencia en California 1849–1851.* The Spanish title is Perkins' own, but his original manuscript, written about 1862 after he settled in Argentina, was composed in English; consequently it had to be translated into Spanish for this first appearance in print. The work is more accessible as edited by Dale L. Morgan and James R. Scobie under the title, *Three Years in California. William Perkins' Journal of life at Sonora, 1849–1852* (Berkeley and Los Angeles, 1964). For this new edition a fresh transcription was made of Perkins' original English version of the manuscript, which had been condensed somewhat in Spanish translation. The last few pages of the manuscript having disappeared, the loss was rectified by retranslating the Spanish version of this part of the text. Morgan and Scobie also added three letters contributed by Perkins to California newspapers in 1850–1851 over the nom-de-plume "Leo." Perkins was a young Canadian who was living in Cincinnati when the Gold Rush began. He traveled by steamboat to New Orleans and Punta Isabel, at the mouth of the Rio Grande, thence across Mexico to Mazatlan, and on to San Francisco in the Danish brig *Johanna and Oluffa,* arriving June 9, 1849. He soon made his way to Sullivan's Diggings, then to Sonora, where he gave up mining for merchandising. His is an extraordinary account of life in Sonora, the heart of the Southern Mines, with a society wholly different from any seen elsewhere in California during this decade; the foreign element and the larger number of women among the population gave Sonora a quality all its own. He sailed from San Francisco in May, 1852, and via Panama and Havana reached New Orleans on June 16, his narrative ending there. Down to the present, Pancoast and Perkins are the only Argonauts whose reminiscences have been edited by modern scholars.

A troublesome addition to this list of reminiscences is a *Biography and Early Life Sketch of the late Abram Sortore including his trip to California and back*. This pamphlet of 10 pages, in double columns, appears to have been printed from newspaper type. It is dated at the beginning, and on the title page, Alexandria, Missouri, March 25, 1909, but that is the date it was written to his niece, Jennie Thomas. A concluding note says only: "The foregoing was dedicated by Mr. Sortore to his niece, Miss Almena Osborn and written by her, for him. Mr. Sortore's home was south and east of Wayland, now owned by Chas. Neumann. He was the father of the late Mrs. Ora Nelson and grandfather of Russell Nelson." The Bancroft Library seems to have acquired its copy of the pamphlet in 1954; how much earlier it might have been printed, I do not know.

What is immediately to the point, Sortore came overland to Hangtown via Council Bluffs and Salt Lake in 1850. He first went to Louisville, on the South Fork of the American River, then to Oregon Bar on the North Fork—this in the spring of 1851—and then, after some two months, to the mouth of the South Fork of the Yuba, where he mined till October, 1857. He then went home via Nicaragua and New York. With his pile of California gold dust, he bought a little farm in Clark County, Missouri, where he spent the rest of his life. Sortore's reminiscences are interesting for his journeys going and returning, but starved for detail in California.

Although in form a journal, *Bigler's Chronicle of the West: The conquest of California, discovery of gold, and Mormon settlement as reflected in Henry William Bigler's diaries*, edited by Erwin G. Gudde (Berkeley and Los Angeles, 1962) is in effect a reminiscence. The text of the Bigler diaries utilized for this book is that especially written for H. H. Bancroft's use by Henry W. Bigler in 1872, and he permitted himself many asides and extensions of remarks in preference to making a literal copy of his original diaries. Bigler came to California in 1846–1847 as a member of the Mormon Battalion, and was working at Sutter's Mill when gold was discovered; it is his diary that fixes the date, January 24, 1848. He went on to Salt Lake in the summer of 1848, and this book ends with his arrival there.

So concludes our survey of all the Gold Rush reminiscences of any moment published from 1860 to the present day. Our concern has been not so much with the literary quality of these reminiscences as with their content, their values as historical record, particular attention having been directed to where these Argonauts spent their time while in California. That has seemed a necessary contribution to scholarship, helping to bring their experience to bear upon the broad canvas of Gold Rush activity, and thereby extending the record for personal accounts by goldseekers to be dealt with by scholars in time to come.

Even with the inclusion of many peripheral accounts, it will be seen, as remarked at the outset of this survey, that the literature of reminiscence is not nearly so extensive as has been supposed. It would be passing strange if I have not overlooked some narratives, perhaps even some of major importance; nevertheless I have staked off for closer examination one whole area of Gold Rush literature, and now we can view it as a whole.

Some men who set down accounts of their participation in the Gold Rush did so with the frank hope of making some money out of their books, and a few even did so. It is clear, however, that the large majority had other ends in view, the desire to fend off the annihilating impact of time by recording their experiences—sometimes for their own satisfaction, sometimes for the pleasure of their family and friends. The interest of the writers, or those close to them, was the most powerful force operating in the conversion of these reminiscent narratives into books; nothing makes this clearer than the virtual dying out of the reminiscent books as the Argonauts themselves passed from the scene.

The existence of manuscripts like Howard Gardiner's, however, suggests that scholars must raise their sights, focusing less narrowly upon the exactly contemporary records, the letters, diaries, and travel narratives. We have been missing something in the loss of the wide-angle view. If there are many more such Forty-niner records like Gardiner's, we need to have them brought out fully into the light, their unique values appreciated, and their shortcomings properly estimated.

If those who read Howard Gardiner's account of his experiences in California between 1849 and 1857 will thereafter return to this summary survey, they will be impressed with the immense solidity of his narrative, and the large extent of the canvas on which he has worked. I think it is quite clear that nothing in the existing literature compares with his reminiscences, unless it be Perlot's account, published in 1897–1898. Gardiner stayed in California long enough to have a far broader range of experiences than most, and he managed to tell his story with a minimum of involvement with his own ego. It is not the importance of Howard Gardiner, but the significance of the California experience that emerges finally from his story. That is an achievement for any man who writes an autobiography.

WANDERER OUT OF SAG HARBOR

Howard Calhoun Gardiner was born at Sag Harbor, Long Island, on September 17, 1826. For nearly two hundred years his family had been prominently identified with the history of the island, his being the seventh generation. The Gardiner family was established in America by Lion Gardiner (1599–1663), an Englishman who had served in the Low Countries as a military engineer under the Prince of Orange. Becoming interested in a Connecticut colonizing venture, Lion voyaged to Boston late in 1635, charged with the responsibility of designing and erecting defenses for the new settlements. He lived four years at the mouth of the Connecticut River, and figured prominently in the Pequot War of 1637.

Two children had been born by 1638, when Lion purchased from the Indians what was then called the Isle of Wight, but subsequently became known as Gardiner's Island, in Gardiner's Bay at the eastern end of Long Island. Afterward he obtained from the Connecticut colonizers a formal grant to the island, which became the first English settlement in what is now the State of New York. (In 1686, by which time the property had passed to his son, Gardiner's Island was converted into a manor, with full manorial rights.) In 1649 Lion Gardiner joined with others in purchasing a large tract on which Easthampton was founded, and four years later he established himself in that Long Island village, to dwell there peacefully the last ten years of his life.

These facts are set forth in a biographical sketch of Lion Gardiner in *Dictionary of American Biography*, as in such earlier works as Benjamin F. Thompson, *History of Long Island* (New York, 1839), and a genealogical study by Curtiss G. Gardiner, *Lion Gardiner and His Descendants* (St. Louis, 1890), to which we shall devote attention hereafter. Lion's son David died in 1689. To him were born two sons, John and Lion. Gardiner's Island passed to the first-born, John, and remained in the possession of his descendants. (For interesting modern accounts of the island, see the New York *Herald-Tribune*, October 9, 1932, March 21, 1937, *Saturday Evening Post*, October 11, 1952, and *Life* magazine, April 26, 1968. The pirate William Kidd buried a valuable treasure on Gardiner's Island in 1699.)

Our primary concern, however, lies with the other main branch of the Gardiner family. The second son of David, Lion, remained in Easthampton and died there in 1781 at the age of 93, a wealthy and respected farmer. He had three sons, John, Lion, and Jeremiah. John dwelt in Easthampton until his own death in 1780 at the age of 59, remembered as "a man of more than ordinary talents, much devoted to philosophy and the mathematics, for which he was distinguished." The quotation is from Benjamin F. Thompson, who adds that John had a son, also named John, "who hired the estate of his father, and followed the business of a farmer till a short time previous to his death. In 1795 he purchased a farm at Moriches, where he died, at the age of forty-eight, in the year 1800. He ['Deacon John'] left three sons, the Rev. John D. Gardiner, Abraham H. Gardiner, and Dr. Aaron F. Gardiner."

The eldest of these three sons, the Presbyterian minister John D. Gardiner, became

Howard Calhoun Gardiner's father. The second son, Abraham, was the father of six children, among whom the two youngest sons, Robert Emmet and Thomas Abraham, are particularly interesting to us because they were intimate associates of their first cousin, Howard C. Gardiner, in California. (Robert was born October 29, 1826, and died in California February 3, 1886; Thomas was born November 9, 1831, and died unmarried in California October 1, 1862.)

However indigestible at first glance, Curtiss C. Gardiner's 1890 genealogy must be quoted (pp. 154–156) respecting Howard's immediate family:

"John-David Gardiner (*John⁶, John⁵, Lion⁴, Lion³, David², Lion¹*), son of John⁶ and Esther (*Hedges-Fithian*) Gardiner, of East Hampton, was b. 2 Jan., 1781. He m. *first,* 18 Feb., 1800, Frances, b. 2 Aug., 1780, dau. of Abraham Mulford, of East Hampton. She d. at Sag Harbor, 23 March, 1814. He m. *second,* 20 Nov., 1814, Mary (*L'Hommedieu-Cook*), b. 8 April, 1791, dau. of Samuel L'Hommedieu and wid. Nathan Cook, both of Sag Harbor. [Nathan Cook died in November, 1811.] Samuel L'Hommedieu was a grandson on his mother's side of Nathaniel Sylvester, proprietor of the Sylvester Manor on Shelter Island, and grandson, on his father's side, of Benjamin L'Hommedieu, the Huguenot emigrant. Rev. JOHN D. GARDINER received his early education at Clinton Academy [in Easthampton], and was grad. at Yale in 1804. Among his classmates at Yale were John C. Calhoun, John S. Winthrop, Royal R. Hinman and David Gardiner. He early took rank as a scholar of fine literary attainments, and as an impressive public speaker. From 1805 to 1811 he was the principal of Chester Academy, in Morris County, N.J., and while at that place he began the study of theology, under the guidance of the pastor of the Presbyterian Church. Subsequently, he was licensed to preach by the Presbytery of New Jersey and New York, and, very soon thereafter, he accepted a call to be the pastor of the Presbyterian Church in Sag Harbor, where he was ordained and installed 2 Oct., 1812, and there he continued to discharge his pastoral duties with marked ability and usefulness for upwards of twenty years, when on 5 June, 1832, his pastorate was terminated. He remained at Sag Harbor to the end of his life, surrounded by his children and the people of his late charge, beloved and honored. He d. at Sag Harbor, 13 Sept., 1849, and his wid. d. at Milwaukee, Wis., 16 Nov., 1860. Children, by his first wife:

i. CHARLES-FOX , b. 10 Dec., 1801; m. 23 Sept., 1823, Eliza A., b. 5 March, 1802, dau. of Phineas F. and Nancy Corey. He was a farmer, and resided at Sag Harbor. He d. 12 Jan., 1840. His wid. d. 15 Feb., 1850. Children: 1. *Charles-Adrian⁹,* b. 21 July, 1824; m. 25 May, 1846, Caroline J. Cooper. Resides at Sag Harbor. Children: 1. Nettie-M.,¹⁰ b. 23 Jan., 1848; m. 2 Nov., 1887, Edgar Wade. 2. William-C., b. 29 Aug., 1852. 2. *Nancy-Maria,* b. 14 July, 1827; d. 9 March, 1845. 3. *James-Madison,* b. 5 Aug., 1829; m. 15 Oct., 1856, Mary Louise Sprague, of New York. She d. 1 May, 1879. He m. *second,* 15 March, 1884, Margaret Adair Bulkley, b. 16 July, 1858, of Memphis, Tenn., a descendant of the late Gov. John Adair, of Kentucky. He is a merchant in New York. Child, by first wife: Charles-Fox,¹⁰ b. 12 Oct., 1857; m. 20 Nov., 1884, Daisy Monteath, of New York. He is

HOWARD C. GARDINER
Courtesy of Mrs. John L. Gardiner

a physician, residing at Crested Butte, Col. Child, by second wife: Cara-Leslie,[10] b. 31 March, 1886. 4. *Fanny-Mulford,* b. 15 Sept., 1831; d. unm., 18 Oct., 1856. 5. *Henry-Havens,* b. 8 Aug., 1835; m. 17 June, 1867, Kate F. Shean, of Boston. Children: 1. Carrie-S.[10] 2. Charles-H. 3. Henry-H. 4. Fannie-A. 5. May-F. 6. Gertrude-P. 7. Milton-A. B. He resides at Sag Harbor. 6. *Caroline-Elizabeth,* b. 11 Nov., 1837; m. 6 July, 1859, Oscar F. Stanton, b. 18 July, 1834, Lieutenant in the U.S. Navy, son of Joseph Stanton and Eliza Havens Cooper Stanton, of North Stonington, Ct. Children: 1. Fanny-Gardiner,[10] b. 18 Oct., 1867. 2. Elizabeth, b. 3 Sept., 1875.

ii. CAROLINE-HUNT, b. 24 July, 1805; m. 1 March, 1832, Nathan H. Cook, of Sag Harbor. She d. 1 Feb., 1878. He d. 1 Dec., 1884. He was captain of a whaler. Children: The first four d. in infancy. Their dau., *Agnes*[9], d. 1851, and their son, *Sylvanus,* d. 1851. Their youngest child, *John-Gardiner-Cook,* was a Union soldier, and d. in hospital, Nashville, Tenn., 1865.

iii. JAMES-MADISON, b. 17 Feb., 1810; d. unm. 3 April, 1856.

Children, by his second wife:

iv. SAMUEL-L'H., b. 3 Sept., 1815; d. 25 Sept., 1815.

v. SAMUEL-L'H., b. 30 Aug., 1816; m. 1 Oct., 1842, Annie Shaler, of Kentucky. He grad. at Yale, 1835; lawyer. Resided at Sag Harbor. He d. 2 Aug., 1885. His wid. d. 3 May, 1886. Children: 1. *Geraldine-S.*[9] 2. *William-S.* 3. *Josephine-L'H.* 3. *John-H.*

vi. JOHN-D. b. 23 July, 1818; m. 17 Aug., 1846, Mary Starr, of Jewett City, Ct. He d. 14 Feb., 1875. He was a lumberman, and one of the pioneer lumber manufacturers in the North-West. His latest residence was at Chicago. He d. suddenly of heart disease, while in New York City. He had one child, *Charles-Starr*[9], b. 2 June, 1847, who resides at Chicago.

vii. FRANCES-M. S., b. 25 June, 1820; m. Henry L. Gardiner, her cousin, son of Abraham H. Gardiner. Children: 1. *Marcia-Ball*[9]. 2. *Elizabeth.*

viii. EZRA-L'H., b. 4 Sept., 1822; m. at Riverhead, 7 Oct., 1846, Ruth, b. 25 Nov., 1825, dau. of Elijah Terry, of Riverhead. Manufacturer. Resides at Chicago, Ills. Children: 1. *Mary-L'H.,* b. Perry, N.Y. 10 May ,1848. *Frank-H.,* b. Milwaukee, Wis., 11 Sept., 1850; d. 30 Aug., 1851. 3. *Frank-H.,* b. Milwaukee, Wis., 7 Jan., 1852; m. 13 June, 1883, Helen F., dau. of George F. Root, of Hyde Park, Ills. Children: 1. Lion,[10] b. 19 Nov., 1884. 2. Alexander-S., b. 9 Dec., 1886. 4. *Cornelius-S.,* b. Riverhead, 28 Dec., 1863.

ix. ALEXANDER-S., b. 19 July, 1824; m., New York City, 18 Dec., 1851, Caroline-Frances, b. 18 Dec., 1827, dau. of Roger and Maria Williams, of New York City. He entered school at Clinton Academy, New York; grad. at New York University in 1847; admitted to practice law at New York in 1848; removed to Milwaukee, Wis., in 1850; licensed and ordained to preach by the Presbytery of Milwaukee, in 1851, and entered upon his first pastorate at Greenport, L.I. His present charge is at Milford, Pa. Children: 1. *Maria-L'H*[9]., b. Greenport 29 Nov., 1852; m. 18 Oct., 1874, Charles H. Griffin, of New York, b. 12 Feb., 1835. Resides, St. Paul, Minn. Children: 1. Nellie,[10] b. 20 Jan., 1877. 2. Mabel, b. 23 Dec., 1879. 3. Edith-D., b. 7 March, 1882; d. 21 July, 1883. 4. Gertrude-F., b. 22 July, 1885. A dau. b. 4 Feb., 1888. 2. *Julia-Evangeline*, b. Cold Spring, N.Y., 18 Oct., 1860; d. Milford, Pa., 26 Aug., 1883. Buried in Oakland Cemetery, Sag Harbor. 3. *Irving-L'H.*, b. Cold Spring, N.Y., 29 Nov., 1863; d. Milford, Pa., 5 June, 1888. Buried in Oakland Cemetery, Sag Harbor.

x. HOWARD-C., b. 17 Sept., 1826; m. *first,* 22 Aug., 1866, Sarah Louise Crosby, of Essex, Ct. She d. 4 Aug., 1869. He m. *second,* 5 Sept., 1871, Sarah-Frances Urquhart, of Essex, Ct. Lumberman, and resides at Green Bay, Wis. Children, by first wife: 1. *Adelaide-Louise-Gettine*[9], b. 20 Nov., 1867. 2. *Ethel,* b. 1 Aug., 1869. Child, by second wife; *John-Urquhart,* b. 11 Sept., 1873.

xi. SARAH-E., b. 11 Oct., 1828; m. 1857, Chas. J. Carey. She d. 1857, Middletown, N.Y.

xii. HENRY-MARTIN, ⎫ Twins. ⎧ b. 7 Nov., 1830; d. 9 May, 1832.
xiii. THOMAS-SPENCER,⎭ ⎩ b. 7 Nov., 1830; d. 30 July, 1831.

xiv. EMILY-M., b. 18 April, 1833; d. 22 Aug., 1834.

This genealogical record tells us in small compass a great deal about Howard Calhoun Gardiner and the web of relationships which made up his world, as a child and later as an adult. He was the youngest of the Gardiner sons who lived to maturity, and the next-youngest of the children who survived the ills of infancy, so that the hold he had upon his mother's heart is evident. His next elder brother, born only two years before him, may well have been his particular boyhood chum, and clearly it was this brother, Alex, of whom Gardiner speaks in the opening chapter of his book. Whence came his middle name, reported in his narrative only as "Cal," is apparent when we recall that John C. Calhoun was his father's classmate at Yale.

Further enlightening information about the family comes from Franklin B. Dexter's *Biographical Sketches of the Graduates of Yale College* . . . (New York, 1885–1912), vol. 5, pp.660–662; the sketch of Gardiner's father notes that his mother, Sarah (White) L'Hommedieu Cook, "was a lady of considerable literary ability, and a *Collection* from her prose and poetical writings was published in 1843." Two of Howard Gardiner's brothers were college graduates, and though nothing is said with regard to his own education, it can be taken for granted (even without the evidence of his book) that, raised in such a household, his education progressed far beyond a mastery of reading, writing, and arithmetic.

Growing up in Sag Harbor must in itself have been a liberal education. Gardiner devotes a chapter to "Our Village," but with primary emphasis on the seafaring tradition of this town near the eastern tip of Long Island. Nathaniel S. Prime, in a *History of Long*

Island published at New York in 1845, just prior to the opening scenes of Gardiner's book, has this to say about Sag Harbor:

"This now important village is situated on the north shore of the south branch of the island, in the northeast corner of the township of Southampton, 5 miles north of Bridge-hampton. The dividing line between Southampton and Easthampton runs through the eastern main street, so that a part of the village . . . lies in the north-west corner of the latter town.

"The site of the village is a perfect sand-bed; and, consequently, agriculture presented no motive to the settlement of the place, which was commenced but a little more than 100 years ago. About the year 1730 a few fishermen's cottages were erected along the shore; but it was nearly 30 years afterwards, before any considerable accession was made to their number. Among the first settlers, the names of Hicks, Fordham and Conklin were found. The descendants of the two latter still remain; the first name does not now exist in the place.

"In 1760, a considerable addition was made to the population by the accession of several respectable families, whose enterprising spirit had marked the place as one possessing peculiar advantages for trade and fishing. Between 1760 and '70, while as yet the commerce of New York was carried on principally by schooners and sloops, this little retired port had opened a small trade with the West Indies in larger craft. Col. Gardiner, at that time, owned and employed two brigs in that business, while several smaller vessels were busily engaged in the fishing and coasting trade. At this early period, two or three sloops cruised in the Atlantic, a few degrees to the south, for whales, which were then so plenty, that more or less of them were taken every year, by boats, along the whole southern coast of the island.

"The war of the revolution, as a matter of course, completely interrupted the rising business of the place, which was not resumed till the return of peace. [During the Revolution, from 1776 to 1783, Long Island was more or less abandoned to the British; several British ships were stationed in the bay, and Sag Harbor was made not only a depot for military stores but the garrison for a considerable body of soldiers, as remarked by Benjamin F. Thompson.] At this time [1783], Dr. Nathaniel Gardiner and his brother sent out a ship called the *Hope* upon a whaling voyage, under the command of Capt. Ripley; and a brig of the first class was despatched upon the same business. These voyages proved entirely unsuccessful, and almost an entire loss to the owners—the ship returning with only 30 bbls of oil, and the brig with still less. In 1785, Col. Benjamin Huntting of Southampton, and Capt. Stephen Howell embarked in the same enterprise, and sent out vessels which gradually extended their voyages to the coast of Brazil, and usually returned deeply laden with the treasures of the deep. The embargo of 1806, with the troublesome times that succeeded, resulting in the war of 1812–15, necessarily checked, and for a while suspended the increasing enterprise of the place. And a most disastrous fire, which occurred May 26th, 1817, and laid in ruins the most valuable portion of the village, gave a tremendous blow to the energies of the place, which were just beginning to recover from another 7 years' suspension of trade, by virtual or actual warfare. But the enterprise of the people soon rose superior to all these untoward events; and, in a few years their exertions were not only crowned with success, but extended far beyond their most sanguine expectations, and at this moment are in the full tide of successful operation.

"By the vast extension of the whaling business in the United States, and other countries, and the consequent scarcity of whales in the Atlantic, the principal theatre of these operations is now on the bosom of the great Pacific. So that these voyages, which, 30 years ago, were of only 10 or 12 months' duration, are now necessarily extended to 2 and 3 years.

"In 1807, there were only 4 ships owned and fitted out from this port. Now (1845) there are 61 ships and barks engaged in the whaling business, besides a number of smaller vessels in the coasting trade; employing a capital of nearly $2,000,000. The village included within the Fire District, which is the only incorporation it enjoys, embraces a population, according to the recent State census, of 3,621 souls. Of these, 2,924 are within the town of Southampton, and 697 in the town of Easthampton. Between 300 and 400 of the inhabitants spend the principal part of their lives on the 'vasty deep.'

"It is worth while to mention, that as early as 1771, an officer was appointed 'to inspect the trade and navigation of the harbours, bays, and creeks,' on the east end of Long Island, which was considered as included in the District of New London. Shortly after the organization of the Federal Government, Sag Harbour was made a distinct port of entry, and the necessary Custom House officers appointed. Henry P. Dering was appointed Collector by President Washington, in 1790, and held the office till his death, which occurred April 30th, 1822—a period of 32 years."

Prime discusses two military episodes which have distinguished the history of Sag Harbor. The first was the "rapid and successful expedition of Lieut. Col. Meigs," who in May, 1777, mounted a raid upon the village from New Haven to destroy military stores collected by the British forces. Despite armed resistance, he succeeded in burning 12 brigs and sloops, one of which carried 12 guns, and with them 120 tons of hay, 10 hogsheads of rum, and a large quantity of grain and merchandise. Six of the enemy were killed, and 90 taken prisoners. The second notable event in Sag Harbor's military history came a generation later. "In June, 1813, while a British squadron, under Com. Hardy, lay in Gardiner's Bay, a launch and two barges, with 100 men, attempted to surprise this place, in the night. They landed on the wharf, but an alarm being quickly given, the guns of a small fort were opened upon them with such effect, that they had only time to set fire to a single sloop, and retreated with so much precipitation, as to leave a large quantity of guns, swords, and other arms behind them. The flames were speedily extinguished, and no other injury sustained. What a striking contrast, on the part of the assailants, between the result of this expedition, and that of Col. Meigs!"

Nathaniel Prime was a predecessor (1806–1809) of John D. Gardiner in the Presbyterian field at Sag Harbor, and accordingly he has much to say about churches, ministers, and revivals at Sag Harbor. We shall be content to note that there were memorable revivals in 1808–1809 and in 1816, before Howard Gardiner's birth; again in 1842; and during the winter of 1844–1845. "Besides these remarkable visitations, this place has enjoyed many precious 'seasons of refreshing from the presence of the Lord;' so that this tract of arid sand may, in a spiritual point of view, be regarded as one of the most favoured 'mountains of Zion,' on which 'the dew of Hermon [Heaven] hath oft descended,' and 'there the Lord hath commanded his blessing, even life for evermore.' The present number of church members is 360."

Among his papers Howard Gardiner preserved a few of his father's handwritten sermons. One, dated April 25, 1819, was on a theme suggested by Isaiah 1, 17: "Judge the fatherly, Plead for the Widow." Another, "The second coming of the Son of Man," served a number of times over the years, May 19, 1821, January 5 [?], 1822, August 30, 1829, and November, 1831. A third, suggested by Micah 2, 10, "Arise ye and depart, for this is not your vest," is dated Sag Harbor, June 26, 1840," and bears Howard C. Gardiner's notation, "Read to Louise Sunday evening, April 19th 1868." Also preserved is a funeral sermon, perhaps adapted to the last rites of many of his friends and fellow-church members, together with a "Retrospection Thoughts suggested by my 85th birthday anniversary," noted by Howard Gardiner to have been written by his father, though the Rev. John D. Gardiner did not survive his 69th year. The formal ecclesiastical language, the faded ink and aging paper, poignantly evoke the circumstances of Howard Gardiner's upbringing.

In his book Gardiner accounts rather fully for his life from the fall of 1848 to that of 1857, when he returned from California. It was his intention, he tells us, only to make a visit home at this time, but the Panic of 1857 had struck at the country by the time he reached New York, and circumstances determined that he should never go back to the Golden Shore.

Apparently in 1850, three of Gardiner's brothers, John, Ezra, and Alexander, moved to Milwaukee. John and Ezra established themselves in the lumber business, but Alexander decided to enter the ministry, and soon returned to a first pastorate on Long Island. Their mother also moved to Milwaukee, where she died in November, 1860.

A few family letters that have survived, principally between Howard C. Gardiner and his first wife, Sarah Louise Crosby, during the six years prior to their marriage, 1861–1866, form part of the Gardiner collection in the possession of the publisher. They are so revealing of the personalities of the writers, and afford such an insight into the times, that it is clearly desirable to print them here. The first letter that has been preserved, marked "No. 2," and addressed by the 17-year-old Lou, to Howard C. Gardiner at Milwaukee, is dated Cold Spring, N.Y., April 24, 1861:

Dear Howard.

You may imagine I was rather surprised to know that you had *volunteered*, although it had been the chief subject of my meditations for some time past, yet I always banished it from my mind, as quickly as possible, by trying to make myself believe, that it would be impossible for you to leave Mr. Ezra. Your letter of course, quite upset all my vain reasonings, and for a time, am sorry to say, made me very unhappy. I could not get to sleep last night until the "wee, small" hours, and then (Affing like) dreamed that you were in all kinds of danger. You need not denounce me as a weak-minded girl, for I have already bravely overcome those foolish fears. (?) There is considerable excitement even in the village. The "Kemble Guards" have received notice to be ready to start for Washington, twelve hours after receiving orders. They had a mass meeting opposite the Diamond house night before last, Mr. Gardiner made quite a "speech" I hear, and a very excellent one too, we were not there, staid at home to make a large flag, for our house. After Mr Gardiner had finished speaking up jumped Darius Truesdall on the *barrels*, erected for the occasion and being rather tipsy, nominated Mr Abram G, as captain of the "Guards," he had scarcely said the words, when someone accidentally hit the barrels, and down fell Darius, being much exasperated at such treatment, he "pitched in"—as you would say— to Gus Warren, and someone had to separate them. They raised fourteen hundred dollars in one day for the support of the families of volunteers, was not that doing nobly, for our little village.

Are you aware that you left your name engraved on everything in this house? Nearly every day I read that same word "Howard" over and over again. I go to the "extension table," and then you and glue-foot, immediately rise up before me, I never look toward the glass door, in the evening, but I seem to see you tapping, tapping for admittance; whatever dress I put on, calls to mind your criticism, "sur ma robe."

Now for an "N.B." I *am not* going to stand being imposed on, in this manner any longer, for I am not *unsophisticated,* and I will maintain my *dignity* if it must be by force of arms, so I challenge you, Mr. G, you can choose your second, and I will name the weapons with which, and the place where the duel shall be fought. After considerable deliberation, I conclude the weapons shall be *arms* on both sides, the rendezvous, down under the chestnut tree, will that suit your gentlemanship? You have no idea what a splendid *cook* I am getting to be, we had company the other day so I offered my services, to make some pies, my first was a custard, it really looked *splendid,* but on taking it out of the oven, I, unfortunately let it drop *on the floor,* so "settled my hash." The other one baked itself to death—now, will you let me go to Washington with you, as pastry cook? By the way, I will be eighteen years old in a week or so, will you not redeem your promise and send me your ambrotype, for a birth-day present? You know I wont ask you for any thing, very often, please send it by way of Mr Abram G. Is it possible that you are going to pass Cold Spring, without stopping? I think I prefer not to know when you go, it would be merely an aggravation. Our home is beginning to look very lovely now. I wish you were here to enjoy it with us, we would indeed enjoy a moonlight drive or walk. I went over to Stony Point the other day, and hunted all over for that tree where you carved your name, but could not find it. Every one in the house is a bed, and it is

high time I followed their example. I am going down to the post office Wednesday night.
Good night, Howard, ever think of me as your little schezicke

Louise

You certainly place me in a very ludicrous position, *on your knee,* and I seem to imagine
myself writing to you when you were so near me, that I could communicate my thoughts
in a far more agreeable manner, than by putting each one on paper. [*In pencil:*] Thursday
morn. I was looking at a vessel beating up the river, about two minutes ago, when she
careened and went over. I screamed at the top of my voice, and the whole school rushed
out on the piazza, but the men all got on the side of the boat, then she commenced to
sink, and they managed to cling to the rigging, until a small boat from Cold Spring
reached her. I never was so frightened in all my life, I tremble now. I can scarcely write
excuse a lead pencil.

Addie and I send love to Mr Ezra, *Addie,* to you likewise. Oh! I almost forgot to say, that
I think your last letter contained altogether too much euphuism would you ever have
forgiven me, if I had neglected such an important sentence?

Lou, again

The second of these letters, marked "No. 3," was dated Cold Spring, May 13, 1861,
again addressed to Howard at Milwaukee:

Dear Howard

Yours was received last Wednesday; while reading it, I could think of nothing but
"Hark! from the tomb a doleful sound," you certainly must have fallen into a *slough* of
some kind, "despond," or *blue dye,* I cannot determine which. Why not let the future
take care of itself, suppose the war does ruin business for a time, you can be no worse off
than a thousand others, and as long as all smash up together, one may as well laugh as cry.
I never saw any *good* come yet, from the "lowfer," and it always pains me to see any one
indulging in it, pardon, if I have expressed my views too freely.

We have not heard much about the hard times as yet, General Sherman is the principal
topic of conversation in the village, he has done more mischief there, than the war would
have brought about, for some time to come. Every one has endorsed for him, some
three, and some four hundred dollars, and after completely ruining Mr Lawson, he has
proved to be a real swindler, he is in Washington now, he dont even write to his wife,
his property is to be sold at sheriffs sale in a day or two. H. A. & E. A. will lose four hundred, probably. They have sent Darius T. on to Washington, to bring him home, dead
or alive.

The Kemble Guards have not gone away yet. Dont know whether Mr. Truesdall intended to insult the "Dominie" or not some thought he did, some thought otherwise,
perhaps if his speech had not come to an untimely end, he would have explained himself
more fully. Yes, I have heard from *Essex* lately, and was not surprised to learn that they
had a large standing army, consisting of fourteen men, beside a recruit just arrived from

Sag Harbor, of half that number, who went or were conveyed (more properly speaking) in a Sag Harbor fishing smack. The good people of Essex planted a tree, some eighteen years ago, on which to hang Jeff. Davis, as they were convinced, that no one else would be smart enough to catch him. I believe I have answered all your questions, *worthy of notice*. Uncle Mase arrived two weeks ago, from California, and spent a few days with us, I have barely recovered from the effects of laughing so much at his nonsense yet, he kept us on a broad grin continually, and he is so strong, he used to catch me up as if I were a feather and set me on his shoulder, and always insisted on carrying me down stairs, no matter how much resistance I made. He has commenced a law suit—oh dear, *against* Uncle Handy, and is "going in" for *ten thousand* dollars damages.

We all went to Baptist meeting last evening, and the church being full, they seated me in a chair, up by the pulpit, I came very near losing my equilibrium of mind, I assure you and laughing out loud, when a very illiterate man, made some lengthy remarks calling "height" *haith,* and repeated "Hush a by baby" verbatim, twice, and making several egregious blunders. We have no governess yet, Aunt Eliza has expended twenty dollars, in trying to procure one, but they all prove to be "maiden ladies," tomorrow we advertise again. George Keeler spent two or three days in the place, last week, came over to see us one evening. We acted a charade last week, that we had been preparing for some time, had a few friends together with the school girls for spectators, all pronounced it excellent, we have had several invitations *out,* to rehearse it. Perhaps you remember reading it, one day, over here, the word was "Drama-tic." How is Mr Ezra Gardiner, you never mention him. I sincerely trust you are in better spirits than when you last wrote, hope the air of "Green Bay" agrees with you. Aren't you glad that you have waded through this long letter, allow me to congratulate you, for I know I have wearied you. Adieu   Louise

I never made such work before, trying to write a letter, but can't spend time to write another, as I have ever so many music lessons to give.

We next find the pert Miss Crosby writing Howard C. Gardiner at Chicago, a letter endorsed "No. 7," and dated Cold Spring, October 17, 1861. The letter is filled with pleasant chitchat, but the only light it sheds upon Gardiner's affairs is that the envelope is addressed to a Post Office box in Chicago; and at one point she says, "It seems to me you must be lonely in Chicago, away from the friends with whom you have been living so long." Nothing but the envelope survives of "No. 38," postmarked New York, June 22, and addressed to Gardiner at Little Suamico, Oconto Co., Wisconsin (this being a village on the west shore of Green Bay). "No. 46," sent to the same address, and dated at Essex, Conn., September 4, 1864, shows that a crisis had arisen in their courtship:

Howard
I cannot forget you. I am going to San Francisco with my cousins, Capt. Williams and wife, in the ship "Herald of the Morning" which will sail from Boston, October tenth. I feel confident that you are not succeeding in your business, perhaps when I return in

eighteen months fortune will have favoured you again, and if so I shall expect to hear from you again. I am sorry if you have been too proud to tell me, it would have saved me a year of unhappiness, past, and God knows how many in the future. I trust you still. Good bye, a long, long farewell.

Louise.

Off she went to San Francisco, for we find her addressing "Mr E. L'H. Gardiner, Sonora, Tuolumne Co. California," from the Chincha Islands, June 8, 1865:

Dear Mr Ezra

Your kind, friendly letter is just received, dated some three months ago, mail arrangements on this side of the globe are rather in "*Essex*" style, dont you think so?

I assure you I was very sorry not to have seen you in San Francisco, although (to dash right into *the* subject) I think you could have had no influence, in regard to my returning home, I cannot comply with your or Howard's wishes in this respect, a single word would have detained me at home, whereas a thousand cannot call me back. Howard tried a dangerous experiment, and risked the chances of a failure; that he now sincerely regrets it, I cannot doubt, and that he made me miserable and unhappy for fifteen long months, I do not forget. He must now wait my return; I cannot tell how it will end, time will decide. My voyage thus far, has been a delightful one. I am a perfect sailer, and enjoy sea life above all things, have never had a single fear yet. We are having a merry time, here in the "guano" regions, there is a large fleet of American vessels here, and a number of ladies, and time passes very pleasantly. We will remain here six or seven weeks longer, and then proceed to Hamburg, which I anticipate "pretty much," and will probably be home again in eight months. Aunt Elizabeth speaks of your visiting them in Brooklyn, it must have seemed like good old Cold Spring times; we did enjoy ourselves, those long winter evenings when sitting around the *heater* with Howard for "fire tender," and I think we had many a sly joke when wise heads were unconscious of it, I wonder when we will all meet again. I hope you are not going to *settle* in California, but I am so glad that your troubles are past, and that you are again successful in business.

I am sorry that I cannot do as you wish, but I cannot think it would be best. With much love believe me

ever yours affectionately
Louise

This letter was postmarked at Panama June 19, and at San Francisco July 10. Soon after, beyond all doubt, it was sent on to Howard by his brother Ezra, so unexpectedly found in Howard's old haunts. All the rest of the surviving letters—ten of them; none with envelopes—are dated between the time of Louise's return home and their marriage on August 22, 1866. The first, written to "Mr. Gardiner" from Essex, March 29, 1866, by A. M. Pratt, advised: "Louise is absent from home on a visit to her sister Ada's at Eddington Penn. about seventy miles from N.Y. on the line of the N.Y. & Phil. rail road.Should you think it best to go there to see 'Lou' you will probably have no difficulty in finding the place." Instructions were given for reaching Col. R. Clay Crawford's place, "where you will probably find some one who will be glad to see you."

Howard Gardiner made the obligatory pilgrimage, and we next hear from him direct, in a letter to his Louise written at Chicago on June 3:

My Dear Louise—

Yours of 26th ultimo was received by me yesterday on my return from Rockford, where I had been to see the "Dominie" [his brother, now the Rev. Alexander S. Gardiner]. You say nothing about either *time* or *place* in your letter but seem to treat altogether on generalities.—Now Lou I want you to take a *"good big sober think"* on the subject & let me know the result of your cogitations—Tell me when you will be ready for me to come after you, & where to find you when I do come—I sometimes think that I shall loose you after all, & imagine you starting off on another voyage around the world—I am gratified to know that your mother is convinced that I do cherish *some* feelings of regard for Lou —I trust I shall be able to convince *you* that I do love you dearly, even if you are not already satisfied to that effect—Now please my dearest girl set my mind at ease and name some definate day when the parson shall be called upon to assist us in tying a knot with our tongues which we shall not be able to untie with our teeth—I am busily engaged at this time in settling up the affairs of the old firm, & trust by the latter end of August, I shall be again established in some business which will be permanent. I am of a restless disposition & if I had no business to employ my mind I think I should go crazy—It is possible I may locate at St Louis, though the probability is that I shall remain in Chicago—I sometimes think I missed it when I sold out my interest at the mills, as lumber never was in greater demand or commanded better prices than at present—We have about one million feet left over at the mills which we were not able to get forward last season, owing to scarcity of vessels—As soon as we get this forward and dispose of it we can close up our business—My brother J. D. G. will go to the water cure establishment at Cleveland this month, as close application to business has completely undermined his naturally strong constitution—His physician tells him he must give up business entirely, and allow himself three or four months time to recuperate—His wife will go with him & stay at Cleveland during his sojourn there—I hope he will be benefitted by the treatment at the water cure —I hear nothing from Ezra—I wrote him three months ago and it is time for me to receive an answer—The small space I have left on this sheet warns me to bring this to a close—Give my love to Sister Addie & tell her I have a picture hanging in my room which reminds me of her every time I chance to glance at it—I know not where this may reach you, whether in the shady precincts of "Hazel dell," the quiet & retired village of "Essex," or seated on the deck of the "Plover" initiating some neophyte in the mysteries of the game of "cribbage." Wherever it may be, that it may find you in the enjoyment of health and happiness is the wish of

Yours   Howard

Again he wrote from Chicago on June 14, 1866, tantalizing both Louise and us with some remarks on California:

Dear Lou—

Yours informing me that you were off for a cruise reached me in due time—As the time of your return to Eddington is rather uncertain I have decided to await an answer to this ere I write you again—I trust you will have a nice time on the yacht and return safely—I am progressing but slowly in winding up my affairs, for the reason that the last years stock has not yet all come forward—I am determined to have a full & final settlement of all old business, ere I make any arrangement for a new start—I am sorry now that I sold out, as contrary to all precedent, and against the vaticinations of experienced business men, lumber has ruled higher this season & the demand for it is greater than was ever before known—Now my dear "Baroness" (that might have been) I don't propose to bore you with a long homily on business matters, but as my mind is occupied with such things, it [is] but natural that my pen should "follow suit" & give the same expression— Yesterday I received a letter from E L'H G dated at Sonora, California, May 9th—He does not write in very good spirits, as he intended when he went away to return again inside of two years—Now however the time of his return has been indefinitely postponed & he may remain on the Pacific coast for years—I had some idea of visiting San Francisco during this Summer—J D G is anxious for me to go out & says that if I will consent to go, he will pay one half the expense—E has a good mine out there but has not the means of building a mill & putting up the necessary machinery for working it—He wishes us to assist him & take an interest with him—He will require about 25 or 30,000 dollars.— J. D. G. is willing to go in with me & furnish him the means to develope the claim provided he is satisfied that it is a good one—Therefore he is anxious that I should go out & see for myself how things are, as E is too sanguine oftentimes & his hopes are apt to warp his judgment—What do you think?— Is it best to go?—This is a great "Love" letter ain't it?—Well suppose I commence on this last page and address you as my beautiful, my own, my transcendental, preeminent, bewitching, lovely, *hifallutin* Lou—My darling girl "in esse" & my gentle, incomparable wife "in posse." Call you pet names dearest call you a *bird*—Suppose I mount my Pegasus & give vent to my feelings in a *poetic strain,* well here goes.

> "Oh Louy Crosby you are my darling
> My looking glass from night till morning
> I'd rather have you without a *farden*
> Than another girl with a *house & garden.*"

Now you've got it. Never hereafter dispute the correctness of that trite & venerable axiom "Poeta nascitur non fit"—Perhaps I had better hold up here as I want to ask you to give me the names of those who constitute your party on board the "Plover"—Please give us a full description of your trip where you went, who went with you what you saw, who you saw &c &c &c &c &c &c—Give my love to Addie & remember me to all who enquire—I shall await a letter from you ere I write again & close this by subscribing myself yours for 30 days Mr Gardiner—

Ten days later, on June 24, Howard wrote from Chicago:

Dear Louise—

I have not been to the office for the past two days, as Mary was in the city on her way to Rockford, for which place she left last evening—Your letter mailed at Phila consequent on my not going to the office did not reach me till last evening, when it was brought down by our book keeper who informed me that it had been received two days previous —Don't you fret about my going to California as I had but a remote idea of visiting that far off section, and even had I concluded to have gone I should have done so with the intention of returning again immediately—The chances are that I shall not visit the Pacific Coast very soon, but if I should go out there *Mrs H. C. G shall if she desires go along too—* As for engaging in any speculating operation in mining shares or stocks you can just set your mind at ease, for this individual has been there and to use a cant phrase "staid all night" and saw the elephant from tusks to tail—Now let me impress upon your mind one fact, & that is the first journey I intend making is one just sufficiently extended to find a young lady about your size, and to bring her home with me as my wife—Excepting of course little trips incident to business which I may make in the interval—I am sorry you took my going away so seriously, as your previous letter was written in such a happy joyous strain that it sounded like old times, and I read it & re-read it a dozen times— Write just such letters all the time & I shall be pretty certain to ascertain the contents—I hate to write a "blue" letter & awfully dislike to read one—Present my kind regards to "Madame" & acknowledge for me the receipt of her note from "Chesepeake City"— Tell her I will answer it ere long, and enclose in one to you—The weather here is very warm and the least exertion is a tax on a man's energies—Where are you going to spend the Fourth?—I would like to be with you on that day—We might in connection with the "Seven Sisters" get up a Picnic and have a nice time generally—Tell me the result of the boat race—I hope the "Ada" won the cup—That is the boat I have bet on in my own mind—Give us all the news local & otherwise & please discuss the "question"—"question"—

> And now in conclusion my dearest Louise
> Send no more *blue* letters this way if you please
> Epistles all full of "oh dears" & ah me's
> Expressions that make us feel ill at our ease,
> But let them be jolly and full of the—
> The contents don't matter so long as they're civil
> Quote Shakespeare & Milton & Mother *Goosee*
> And apply the quotations to *you* & to *me*
> Dont treat of any topics "a la Doctor Gardner
> For that's not the style which suits

>> Howard C Gardiner—

Fortunately, Louise's letter in reply to this one, dated "Hazel dell," June 28, 1866, has been preserved:

Dear Howard—

Your last witticism is in my bureau drawer, glad you have proved yourself a sensible man in not going to California yet awhile; the more I think of it—dont believe you meant to go, you thought perhaps it would be a pleasant little fright for me, thank you *sir!!*

I'll take up subjects now as they come along—I left you, or your letter (all the same) in Philadelphia, last, on my way to the regatta—the day was a *gal(e)a* one, we went down the river in the "Plover," were towed by a steamer during the festive scene, there were about two hundred boats entered for the race, and it was a fine sight to see them start off —but the wind blew furiously—and the smallest ones upset then and there, in the most inglorious manner, while the pen men were bobbing around in the water like so many small porpoises. We had our own peculiar trials, such as keeping our hats on our heads by main strength, and while our hands were thus engaged, witness our dresses ascending high in air, like young ballons, then, while being introduced to some fine gent—our dishevelled hair would completely conceal our features. Now came our great trial—we couldn't see our "Adda," the boats had all started and she was invisible, finally the young Captain boarded us foaming with rage, the *law* forbade "outriggers" and the crew refused to go without them—in such a heavy sea; and what made it more provoking the Adda beat the *winning boat* on the river, the night before, in a fair race. But we had a good dinner aboard the yacht—and enjoyed the day. General Pennrose came home with us and spent the night. P. The spell is broken now, I must say good bye to Hazel dell Ma has sent for me to be home on the "Fourth." The "Congregational Society" are to have a *fair,* whether I am to represent the "goddess of Liberty" with a grab-bag and a fortune wheel in hand, and a silver dart in the hair, I know not—but Monday morning I leave, Robert & Addie will go to New York with me. Aunty sends love to you and says to tell you that she has pitched her *tent* and is going to try gipsying this Summer—that is the trysting place for us, and we were anticipating many a sly lunch out there, Robert is going to photograph us today out there.

Now Mr G, I demand attention. I am going to discuss *the* subject—*the question,* so open your eyes wide, and I will first take away your breath by saying that I propose your coming East by the first of August—romance aside—my wardrobe is nearly ready for a summer campaign, in the Fall it would be much more trouble *to get it up.* I am going now into minutiae—The "noces" will take place in Essex, Conn. (I will name the County, if you wish I know it) Wednesday has always been a favorite day with me, as the old rhyme says "*it is* the best day of all" so note Wednesday) in the evening, I can't say how many friends will be present,—on my side the number is illimitable—perhaps *you are not* a general favorite—but you have the privilege of course of bringing along any friends that you like—I dare say "Mary Plevin" would be happy to be one of the sleighing party. Please say the Rev Mr G, that nothing would gratify me more than to have him *and Mrs G* officiate at my wedding. Fannie Urquhart and cousin Julie have had for many years the *refusal* of being my bridesmaids—will that be too much display for a gentleman of your quiet tastes? I cannot help it—and do not mind if it is, you must pick up some nice SUITABLE groomsmen, aged and infirm, so Fannie & Julie wont fall in love at first sight. Now my extreme diffidence, will not permit me to say, that from my youth up I have always had an ardent desire to visit "Catskill Mountain House" and to go from there to Niagara—and from there to any quarter of the globe that may be suggested— but now I have said it—I will defend it to the last inch of tongue in my mouth. Let me see, is there aught else to be said? You have the floor now brother Gardiner—put your stamp of approval or non-ap—on the foregoing.

I will be in Essex when you receive this—so write me immediately—you are getting on the old track—a letter a fortnight. Addie has just come in—in her robe of night—you can imagine what time of morn it is, and she advises me to prepare for breakfast—then we will have a fine ride this bright morning—have our photographs taken some few dozens of times, which will leave me but little time for literary pursuits before Thomas goes to the office, and I will now try and put these few words as far apart as possible, and cheat you into the idea that you have a very long letter (there has been one fly on my cheek five minutes and I cant get him off) *That* filled up the page beyond my most sanguine expectations, and contrary to the *vaticinations* of exper- ienced men. Good bye Addie sends love. Hazel dell says good bye too. So does

yours affection
Lou.

This letter went astray, and plans for the wedding remained in limbo. Louise and Howard wrote each other again in mid-July, the letters crossing in the mails. Hers was first, dated at Essex July 14, 1866:

Dear Howard.

I have been home ten days: Aunty & self left Eddington the day before the "Fourth," & she would not leave me short of my mother's door, the cars were crowded, and the heat insupportable, every body seemed going abroad, to spend "Fourth" and I think if it had not been for a dime fan, that I plied most vigorously, you would never have heard aught of me again. It makes it rather pleasant, to write you a long letter, and tell you most confidentially that I would be pleased to see you, the first of August, and then not hear a word from kith or kin for several hundred weeks—it seems to me a kind of a "reckon without your host" affair. I guess, between "posts" I will have time to take an- other short circumnavigating trip. I tell you Howard, let's arrange that I go around the "horn" & you cross the isthmus, and we will chance together in San Francisco, six years from next January; thirty first day. We had rather of a merry time at the "Fair" here, Fannie & I tended the flower stand, and we were so engrossed in each other, we forgot to sell our flowers and customers had to knock us on the shoulder, and ask us how much we taxed for *them air posies*—before we paid any attention to their requests—

Fannie thought one woman's dress was cut decidedly low in the corsages for the fash- ion—and I knew another stood before a mirror full an hour to get her hair scalloped so high on her forehead Fannie did not know that I was in the place, until I appeared before her there; she does not know either that I have seen you—she asked me if I ever had the heart-ache now-a-days—and I said oh dear No!! I have quite recovered from it.

> Woman is changeable
> Light as a feather
> Fickle as fancy—

I decided before leaving Eddington that I did not care for a *wedding*, there would be no certainty of Addie's being with me, and without *her*, I would prefer to be married in the morning, and leave home immediately.

Aunty returned to Eddington Tuesday—brother Robert and Addie were very sorry to have me leave them, and I can't say but that I miss yachting and horseback riding. We have a horse & carriage here and I sally out quite often, I am learning to harness—yesterday I unharnessed but couldn't get the halter on the horse, although I tried fifty different arrangements of the buckles—the "General" finally got discouraged with me, and rushed to the oat-barrel, and I had to toll him out by slow degrees and much coaxing.

We live near the "Point" now, the house is very pleasant—and I quite enjoy being home, we expect my cousins, Capt. Williams & wife home to night—

> Good bye
> Yours aff
> Lou Crosby.

It seems to me that was rather of an abrupt termination and as a small space remains, I will add, that I am well & hope you are too; that the mercury stands about 99° in the shade, and that the heat renders patent leather shoes a trifle disagreeable to the feet.

> Now I sign myself again
> Yours truly
> Lou.

Chicago July 15/66

My dear Louise—

It is so hot to day that I had made up my mind to defer writing you, but as you will probably be expecting a few lines from this vicinity during the coming week I dislike to have you disappointed—Your last letter written about the 30th ultimo has never been recd by me—It came forward to Chicago, & as I was absent from the city our bookkeeper thinking that I would be glad to have it as soon as possible, forwarded it to me at Rockford—I have written twice for it but as yet have heard nothing from it, or rather *of* it.

I was expecting a letter from you yesterday, but none came—It is now nearly a month since I last heard from you, at which time you were about starting for Phila to witness a regatta—I am not positive but I think I am about half a dozen letters ahead of you—On the receipt of this you will please hurry up & let us hear from you *just a little oftener*—The weather here for the past week has been "perfectly awful"—The thermometer has stood at 98° in the shade nearly every day, and at no time less than 90° between the hours of 11 A.m. & 4 P M—It is laughable to see how the big fat portly fellows wilt under the effect of the heat—I was in at the Gas Cos office yesterday and saw one of the directors, a man weighing somewhere in the vicinity of 300″—He sat in an arm chair with his coat off, vest & "what do you call ems" all unbuttoned, his boots laying on the carpet by his side, his shirt unfastened in front, while in one hand he held his hdkf—with which he wiped the perspiration from his face, & with the other wielded an enormous fan—He put me in mind of Sir John Falstaff, "larding the lean earth" & I thanked God that I was not fat— The time is rapidly approaching when I shall be ready to leave for the East—I shall try and be with you in the latter part of August or by 1st of Sept *sure* unless I shall hear something from you to cause me to postpone my visit—I shall have no business to attend to at the East aside from the matrimonial business, and shall try & make the hours pass pleasantly for both you and me after I shall have joined you—I will leave it for you to imagine all I should and would say were it not so almighty hot, but as it is I shall cut the string off right straight here Please present my kind regards to Madame Crawford, and your Aunt Eliza—I shall expect to see you personally pretty soon and in the meanwhile accept renewed assurance of esteem and *so forth* from   Howard

                                                        Chicago July 22d 1866

My Dear Louise—
    Your letter of June 28th came to hand day before yesterday, & the same day I received yours of 14th instant written in Essex. These letters gave me the first intimation I have received that you had left Eddington and gone back to Connecticut—I have written you several letters since your last written at Eddington was mailed but not being posted in regard to your whereabouts I directed them to the care of Colonel Crawford—You have probably received them ere now & hereafter I shall direct to Essex, Middlesex County, State of Connecticut—I agree to the programme as laid down by you so far as concerns the places to be visited, but would a great deal rather have the ceremony performed in the morning & start immediately thereafter off on a *regular toot*—I cannot arrange conveniently to come on as soon as the first of August but will try and see you if possible by the middle of the month—It is my present intention to leave here for N Y. by the 15th of next month—I shall stay in N. Y one day and go on to Essex the following day—Stay with you for two or three days return to N York for a day and then go back again after my *wife*—I am glad you changed your mind about the wedding as I perfectly detest these country gatherings & would sooner have the affair pass off quietly and get away on our journey as soon as possible—However all details can be arranged by us when I come to Essex for the two or three days as laid down heretofore in this document—The time is near at hand—Have your lamp trimmed and burning—I don't think I shall bring the "dominie" on with me—We shall have to depend on a *Yankee* divine to perform the ceremony—Should the parsons all be away we can find a *Justice of the Peace,* Quien Sabe? Give my love to Fanny Urquhart & tell her I shall take her in my lap when I come to see her—She is such a little bit of a thing she won't mind it, & besides I can tell her some nice stories—I'm done Good bye Lou
                                                        Yours
                                                        Howard

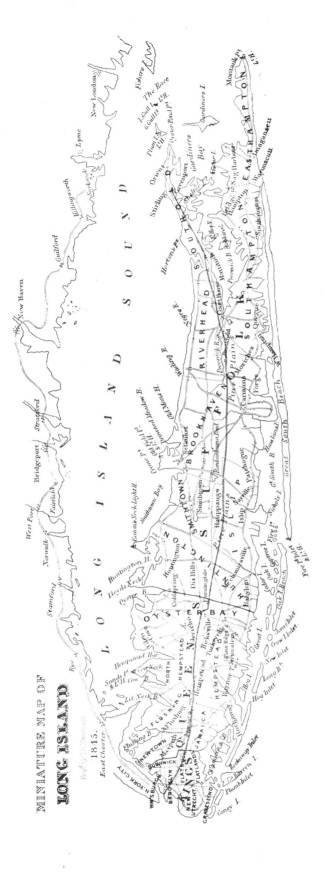

Map of Long Island illustrating Nathaniel S. Prime's *History of Long Island* (1845). "Gardiner Territory," was, above all, the eastern end of the island.

Chicago Aug 7th 1866—

My Dear Louise—

Yesterday evening I returned from Milwaukee where I was called suddenly on acct of business affairs—I intended to have written you on Sunday but was too busily engaged otherwise—I saw Marcia while at Milwaukee & she and all are disposed to welcome you on your arrival at the West—It will be but a few days ere I shall see you & you need not write any more letters, as I shall probably be with you by the 15th instant—The 22d comes on Wednesday & that is the day for the ceremony to come off, at least so the *ring says*—However we can arrange all about that next week—I am merely writing now to tell you when you may expect me—It is not because I have nothing to say that my letter is so brief, but because I shall be with you "D V" in propria personae nearly as soon as you will get this—

Yours

Howard

Chicago August 8th 1866

My Dear Louise—

I wrote you yesterday, but I will risk the chance of any suspicion being aroused that I am afflicted with the "cacoethes scribendi" and fill this page at any rate—This is probably the last letter which Louise Crosby will ever receive from me—(or any other man) & as brevity is the soul of wit, and as your time is so occupied &c &c I will try and have it as short as possible—If nothing happens to prevent you may expect me in Essex by Thursday the 16th *sure* If there is any boat running I shall probably come that way otherwise to Westbrook by cars—I hope to be able to stay with you over Sunday, when I must return to New York & be back in time for the "knot to be tied" on Wednesday, the 22d and, and, that's what's the matter—

Yours

Cal

P. S.

Sweet flower, Good Night

On this appealing note, just before the time set for the wedding, Howard C. Gardiner closed his correspondence with the lively girl he had courted so long, and who on August 22, 1866, became his bride. He was just short of his fortieth birthday, she twenty-two. They went out to Wisconsin, where their first child, Adelaide, was born November 20, 1867. A second daughter, Ethel, came along August 1, 1869, apparently at the cost of her mother's life, for Louise died three days later. Two years after that, on September 5, 1871, Gardiner took as his second wife Sarah Frances Urquhart, she who had figured so playfully in his correspondence with Louise during the two months preceding their wedding. Fannie bore him one son, John Urquhart Gardiner, on September 11, 1873.

The elder daughter, Adelaide, was married to Daniel E. McKercher at Green Bay, Wis., in November, 1919. He died in California in the 1930's, and she at Meriden, Conn., February 12, 1859. They had no children.

The younger daughter, Ethel, was married to Albert Lemuel Judd at Green Bay October 17, 1894. Born December 23, 1864, he died August 7, 1944, and she December 8,

1953, both at Wallingford, Conn. They had three children, the first of whom, Gardiner Wells Judd (October 17, 1896–October 10, 1899), died of typhoid fever. The youngest child, Howard C. Gardiner's only granddaughter, Lucelia Wells Judd, was born August 18, 1905, and was married April 7, 1956, to Harley C. Warner, born May 6, 1907. Both were born at Wallingford, where they reside.

The second of Ethel's sons, Howard Stanley Judd, was born June 26, 1898, and died February 20, 1956, at Cranbury, N.J.; he is buried at Arlington National Cemetery. He was first married October 30, 1925, to Martha Marvin, of Pittsburgh, Pa.; she died June 21, 1930, ten days after the birth of their second child. Their first daughter, Nancy, born October 20, 1927, died seven days later. Their second daughter, Susanna, born June 11, 1930, was married August 23, 1953, to John Van Kirk Silcox, Jr., who was born January 23, 1928. The latter's children are John Van Kirk Silcox III, born December 21, 1955, at Fayetteville, N.C.; Martha Silcox, born May 20, 1958, at Raleigh, N.C.; and James Edgerton Silcox, born November 23, 1959, at Dover, Dela. The Silcoxes live at Glen Falls, N.Y.

After the death of his first wife, Howard Stanley Judd was married to Gladys (Hudson) Gregory, February 8, 1933. Born in October, 1908, Gladys survived him and is now married to Walter Johnson, living at Cranbury, N.J., and New York City. By a prior marriage she had a daughter, Ethel Gregory, born May 17, 1927, who was subsequently adopted by Mr. Judd. Ethel was married January 8, 1953, to Dorman McFaddin, Jr., and they have two children, John Dorman McFaddin, born January 7, 1954, and Marjorie McFaddin, born May 27, 1956, both at Long Branch, N.J.

Two sons were the issue of Howard Stanley Judd's second marriage. The elder son, Howard Stanley Judd, Jr., born August 11, 1936, was married to Ingrid Mueller June 23, 1962. They live at Palo Alto, Calif. The younger son, Rodney Layton Judd, born November 20, 1940, was married to Dorsett Montelius December 21, 1963, at Cranbury, N.J. Their children are Amanda Clark Judd, born May 21, 1965, in California; Melanie Clark Judd, born October 2, 1967, also in California; and Rodney Layton Judd, Jr., born December 2, 1968, in Morton, Pa.

Howard Calhoun Gardiner's second wife, Sarah Frances Urquhart, died at Green Bay July 7, 1919. Their only child, John Urquhart Gardiner, in August, 1907, was married to Louise Mayer, born at Washington, D.C., October 1, 1876. She now lives in Hyattsville, Md.; her husband died in Prince Georges County, Md., September 2, 1965. Their only son, John Lion Gardiner, was born October 14, 1908, at Washington, D.C., and died June 14, 1965, at Takoma Park, Md. He married Elizabeth Simonds in 1930, but they were divorced in 1936. On September 16, 1939, he was married to Lois LaBruce Lott, born December 19, 1912, at Robinwood, Miss., and she survives him, living at Arlington, Va. No children were born of either marriage.

How it happened that Gardiner was impelled, in the 1890's, to write a detailed account of his experiences in California, he explains hereafter. The only other writing he is known to have done was an article on "The Past, Present and Future of the Democratic Party," intended to have been published in the *Arena Magazine*, and written in February, 1897. The article was accepted and highly praised by the magazine's editors, but through the mischance of accidental delay, "the proper time of publication" passed, and in the end it did not appear, as Gardiner explains in a note dated July, 1898, accompanying the copy of this article recorded in the same ledger in which he wrote his book.

As for the book itself, there are two versions, each handwritten in ledger volumes, only one of these being a complete manuscript. The version transcribed for printing consists of 392 numbered pages (followed, pp. 393–428, by the article referred to above). The manuscript book is beginning to crumble, the pages separating from the binding, and the spine deteriorating, so it is just as well that something is now being done to realize Gardiner's dream of publication.

That he had very definite ideas of publication is shown by the fact that a printed prospectus has been preserved with the manuscript for *The Story of a California Pioneer by Howard C. Gardiner*, designed to have been printed in Chicago by Donohue & Henneberry, Publishers, 1896, copyrighted in that year by Gardiner himself. The Preface which he published in the prospectus, dated Green Bay, Wisconsin, February, 1896, has been incorporated into the present volume. Also printed in the 8-page prospectus was Chapter I, First News of the Gold Discovery, with a note at end: "The Title Page, Preface and Initial Chapter attached hereto, show the style and size of pages in the proposed book, the manuscript of which is now ready for the press. The volume will be a 12 mo. of 500 pages, S. & S. C. tint, bound in cloth, No. 40 board, head banded, plain edges lithograph end sheets, one leaf XX gold stamped on side and back." The work was to have been sold by subscription, apparently, and that may have been the reef on which the project foundered. It is disappointing in one sense that Gardiner's dream could not have been realized in his lifetime, but we had better mince no words: The book now published is a generally more useful and far handsomer production than could have been conceived in 1896.

Howard C. Gardiner survived into his 91st year, dying at Green Bay, Wisconsin, on February 22, 1917. His obituary, as printed that afternoon in the Green Bay *Press-Gazette*, had this to say:

"H. C. Gardiner, 'forty-niner' and pioneer resident of this region, died at his home, 1038 South Jackson street, at 6:45 a.m. today. He was 90 years old, and death was caused by old age and general debility. Up to a year ago Mr. Gardiner was hale and hearty, but last Easter he fell, injuring himself. He failed since that time.

"Born in Sag Harbor, Long Island, Mr. Gardiner was the seventh generation of Gardiners in this country. He came to the county shortly before the Civil war, after having gone to California with the gold seekers in 1849. He was one of the few survivors of the gold discovery period of California.

"When he came here, Mr. Gardiner engaged in the lumber business, a line he followed many years. He lived at one time in Little Suamico, where he was in business with his brother. He was postmaster there. About 25 years ago Mr. Gardiner retired from business.

"He moved to Green Bay more than 36 years ago, and for a quarter of a century lived on Webster avenue, in the Gardiner home. Up to the last he was deeply interested in politics. He cast his first vote for Polk, and his last presidential vote for Wilson, last Fall. He was a life-long democrat.

"At the time of the Civil war, in which Mr. Gardiner was incapacitated from serving because of deafness, he brought a number of negroes to this region to work in his mill. Survivors of these negroes still live in this [Brown] county.

"He is survived by a widow and three children. The children are Mrs. A. L. Judd of Wallingford, Conn.; John U. Gardiner of Washington, D.C., and Miss Adeline [Adelaide] L. Gardiner of this city. Funeral arrangements have not yet been made."

Gardiner's death certificate, the only source found which gives his full name, notes the immediate cause of death to have been "Arterio Sclerosis," and his place of burial Woodlawn Cemetery in Green Bay. The county has no record of a will, or probate of an estate; and at the time of his death nothing was said about the reminiscences he had written twenty-one years earlier. That wonderfully vivid account of experiences in California now triumphantly bursts the bonds of time, as that old-young man, "Cal" Gardiner, draws us into the circle of intimate acquaintance to talk about the years which glowed in his memory.

PREFACE

In the following story of a "Forty Niner," the writer tells of his adventures in California, and explains why he went there, how he went, how long it took him to go there, what he did when he got there, and how, after a sojourn of nine years in the Golden State, he returned to New York with less wealth, but a vast deal more experience than he counted on when he left his home on Long Island in the spring of 1849.

Every incident in the narrative is related just as it occurred, and every character referred to is a real one. The full names are suppressed in some instances, but when given are the true ones. Though nearly half a century has elapsed since the events transpired, every detail is as distinctly remembered as if it were an occurrence of yesterday.

There was no occasion to draw on the imagination, as nine years' experience during the early days of California afforded ample material. The great difficulty was to condense, as events crowded so thick and fast on the mind, that elimination became a necessity.

The story was written at the request of my children, for their children, and if it shall afford them one-half the enjoyment in reading that I have experienced in writing it, my object will have been fully accomplished.

The common remark that youth lives on anticipation, old age on memory, is a plain statement of an indubitable truth. Why it is I am unable to explain, nevertheless, the fact exists, that in the evening of life, the most trivial events of its morning are readily recalled, while others of its meridian, of far greater importance, are entirely forgotten.

At three score years and ten, when near the close of a checquered life, and one has retired from its active pursuits and entered upon the last stage of its eventual history, his mind, divested of business cares, seeks other food for reflection, and his thoughts revert to scenes of by-gone days.

Memory, long dormant, awakes from her slumbers, unbars the portals of her treasure house, and bids him enter in.

Upon its walls are hanging the portraits of old familiar friends, against whose names the "fatal asterisk of death has long been set."

Its corridors re-echo the sweet sound of voices that have long been silent.

The panorama of his life is spread out before him, and as he gazes through the far-reaching vista of departed years, he recognizes every landmark he has passed, every mile-stone on the road.

Far away in the distance he beholds the home of his childhood, and fancy's pinions bear him swiftly to its threshold.

Nothing is changed. He sees his gray-haired father sitting in his accustomed place by the fireside, his mother greets him smiling as of yore, his brothers and sisters come and go, the tall clock ticks a friendly welcome from its corner, and where'er his casual eyes are cast, they fall on some familiar object.

Thus it is, that in the great gallery of retrospection, in what Ingersoll calls the "Dark Continent of the Brain," old age clasps hands with infancy.

Green Bay, Wisconsin, February, 1896.   HOWARD C. GARDINER

FIRST NEWS OF THE GOLD DISCOVERY

The discovery of gold in California marked an era in the history of the world, and caused an excitement throughout the land unparalleled in the annals of civilization. When the news of Marshall's find on the American river came to be disseminated, it created a sort of furor among the people, and seemed to awaken the "auri sacra fames" in every breast.[1] The farmer forsook his plow, the merchant his counting room, the mechanic his workshop, the doctor his patients, the lawyer his clients, the minister his pulpit, and all, with one accord, joined in the general rush for the gold fields.

The newspapers eagerly seized on every scrap of intelligence calculated to fan the flame, and from day to day gave such information regarding that hitherto "terra incognita" as they were able to gleam from existing authorities. Even the better-informed people had but a vague idea of California, and thought of it only in connection with hides and tallow. The principal textbooks we had to consult were Dana's *Two Years Before The Mast,* Wilkes' *Exploring Expedition,* and Frémont's *Journal of His Trip To Oregon and California.*[2] These authorities were earnestly studied whenever they could be procured, by those intending to try their fortune in the newly discovered mining regions; but so far as the gold fields were concerned, all were silent. The various routes were discussed, and early in the day the steam ships *Oregon, California,* and *Panama* were dispatched around Cape Horn, preparatory to the establishment of a line of steamers via the Isthmus to San Francisco; Chagres being the port of entry on the Atlantic side.[3]

The Panama Railroad Co. was organized, and during the winter of 1849 work was begun and pushed vigorously to completion; but the nature of the country presented many obstacles, which at times seemed almost insurmountable. It was very difficult in many places along the line of survey to secure a proper foundation for the roadway, owing to the swampy character of the soil adjacent to the Chagres River. The writer has seen piles thirty feet long sink into the black ooze, the mere weight of the hammer being sufficient to force them down. These were split, and others driven above them, till solid bottom was reached. Fever lurked in the jungle, and a very large percentage of those employed in building the road died from exposure to the infected atmosphere. It has been estimated that every rail in the road from Aspinwall to Panama, represents a human life sacrificed in the construction.[4]

Under such circumstances the completion of the railway was retarded much beyond the time originally fixed, and in the meanwhile passengers for Panama were compelled to ascend the Chagres River in "bungoes" as far as Gorgona, and thence, either on mules or on foot, finish the journey across the Isthmus.[5] Many, especially from the Southern States, chose the route through Mexico to the Pacific Coast, taking the chances of finding transportation to San Francisco on their arrival.[6] From the far West, the overland journey was occasioned by the ignorance of the pioneers of the proper route across the plains, and the almost constant harassment they were subjected to by hostile Indians.[7]

But, after all, the voyage around Cape Horn was chosen by a majority of the Argonauts, especially the large mining companies, many of which owned the vessels in which they sailed. These companies were formed mostly on the eastern seaboard, by men accustomed to a seafaring life, many of whom had in pursuit of their calling been 'round Cape Horn time and again, and were supposed to know the ropes thoroughly. Such associations were generally organized with the understanding that they were to continue for five years, as it was estimated that in that time every man would have accumulated sufficient wealth to enable him to "take things easy" for the balance of his life. Constitutions were adopted, by-laws were formulated, officers were chosen whose functions were duly set forth, and the members were all pledged to a strict observance of the rules and regulations of the company.

These organizations, however, proved to be short-lived, as in almost every instance, on their arrival in San Francisco, they found such conditions prevailing as rendered all their schemes for co-operation ineffective. They found that their "Great Centrifugal Hydropital" gold washers, which had been selected after so much discussion, and in which they had placed such implicit reliance, were but waste lumber, and entirely worthless for the purpose intended. They found that in ignorance of the state of affairs existing in California, they had from the outset reasoned from false premises, and as a result had drawn erroneous conclusions.

The mechanics soon learned that their services were more valuable than those of the other members, and the carpenter who could earn $16 per day by plying his trade in San Francisco became dissatisfied, and expressed his desire to retire from the combination; the result of all which was, that the constitution, and by-laws, which had been originally adopted with such formality, became inoperative, and were abrogated by mutual consent. The assets of the company were either sold or divided among its members, and thereafter it was every man for himself.[8]

It is not to be understood that the great exodus of gold-seekers followed "immediately" upon the first reports, as the discovery of the precious metal was for a while mere rumor, and could not be traced to any reliable source; hence, many were skeptical regarding its existence in paying quantities, and it was not till the fall of 1848, after the arrival of parties that had come direct from the new "El Dorado," and had brought with them evidence indisputable, in the shape of buckskin bags filled with yellow specimens which they had dug with their own hands, that all doubt was dispelled.[9]

This was indeed conclusive, and the "gold fever" which had up to that time been merely sporadic, became at once epidemic, and soon raged unchecked throughout all Christendom. The columns of the daily papers teemed with advertisements of vessels up for Vera Cruz, Nicaragua, Chagres, and San Francisco direct, via Cape Horn, setting forth the advantages of the several routes. The latter was, however, the favorite, not so much because it was cheaper, but that it enabled the passenger to carry with him stores and provisions that could not be transported without great expense by the others. Moreover, the uncertainty of finding transportation on the Pacific Coast caused many to choose the longer route, rather than take the chance of vexatious delay on the Isthmus, or in some obscure Mexican seaport.

The wharves of New York were lined with vessels, displaying large placards in the rigging stating that they would sail for San Francisco on the day specified, and that it was expected to make the passage inside of four months. This expectation, however, was never realized, as the first vessels that sailed for California were, as a class, dull sailers, and the average passage was six months.[10]

Many of these ships were undesirable, and ill-fitted for carrying passengers. Some of them were old whalers, that on the collapse of the whale fishing a few years previous, had been dismantled and consigned to "rotten row" in New Bedford, Sag Harbor, and other whaling ports. These had been purchased by speculators, and such temporary repairs as the exigency required were hurriedly made. They were "hove down," and the worm holes in their bottoms plugged, the decks and top sides, which had long been exposed to the weather, were caulked, the hulls were treated to a fresh coat of paint, the standing rigging was "set up," and "tarred down," the sails and running rigging were brought from the sail loft where they had long been stored, and in a very short space of time they were made ready for sea. As a general thing their timbers were sound, and so far as making the voyage was concerned, they were considered to be perfectly seaworthy; but all of them lacked the great requisite of speed, as in the whale fishery storage capacity was the main consideration. Nevertheless, all of the "old hookers" reached San Francisco; the time occupied in making the passage varying from six to nine months.

I remember going on board the good ship *Balance* as she lay at her pier in the East River, and listening to the encomiums passed upon her by the agent. This old vessel was captured from the British in the War of 1812. Her strength was her only recommendation. Her timbers were of teak wood, and as sound as when she was launched. Whatever her other qualities, there was no doubt in the minds of the Argonauts regarding her "strength," and as a result she even secured her complement of passengers, and started on her voyage. Nine months afterwards, her arrival was reported in San Francisco.[11] The old *Brooklyn* was another specimen of naval architecture that early in the day left New York for San Francisco, crowded with passengers, and sorely tried their patience ere she reached her destination.[12]

This condition of affairs, however, soon changed, as quick transportation was a desideratum, and the necessities of trade called into existence a class of ships renowned for speed, and known as "California Clippers," one of which, the *Flying Cloud,* in 1851 made the passage from New York to San Francisco, 14,000 miles, in 89 days; her logbook showing one day's run of 374 miles. Another ship of her class, the *Trade Wind,* in 1853 made the return passage from San Francisco to New York in 75 days.[13]

During the year 1850, and afterwards, these clippers were no novelty in San Francisco harbor. I remember seeing at anchor there at one time the *Greyhound, Grey Eagle, Contest* and *Mechanic's Own*,[14] all unable to secure a crew for the return voyage. As high as $1,000 was offered for the run to New York, without any takers, as under such circumstances the ships were liable to sail "short handed," and no sailor relished the idea of being deproved of his watch below by the call of "all hands," every time it became necessary to reduce sails. Furthermore, the clippers were what are called "wet ships," and at times made Jack's life a burden, which once rid of, he was in no haste to resume.

Competition between the shipmasters was another cause of discomfort among the foremast hands, as in his endeavor to "break the record," the captain would sometimes "carry on" longer than with a proper regard for the safety of his crew was justifiable, and at the last minute, everything was "let go," all hands were called, and the ship presented a scene of "confusion worse confounded." "What she can't carry, let her drag," was the motto of these reckless skippers, and sometimes by hanging on too long, a spar was lost, and it even happened that sailors' lives were sacrificed through sheer foolhardiness. It was in 1852, I think, that the ship *Challenge* lost six or eight men from the yard, while reefing topsails off Cape Horn, owing, it was alleged, to criminal recklessness on the part of the captain, who was notorious for his habitual disregard of all obligations for the safety of his crew.[15]

The day of California clippers is now long past. They served the purpose for a few years, but the completion of the Pacific railroad turned the carrying trade overland, and the class of merchandise that went to make up their cargoes is now sent by rail. Built on lines which curtailed their storage capacity, they were unable to compete profitably for the ocean traffic, and after their withdrawal from the California trade, they were stripped of their sails and rigging at the home ports, and laid up in ordinary.

The foregoing sketch is, however, a matter of history. It is written with the design of giving the reader an idea of the conditions prevailing during the early days of California, and serves as a prelude to the personal narrative which follows.

II

A WINTER IN THE SOUTH

OCTOBER, 1848–FEBRUARY, 1849

It was in the early fall of 1848 that I left home for the South with the purpose of disposing of a stock of dry goods, the property of a local merchant, who was closing up his business preparatory to removal to the then frontier city of Milwaukee.

I had but just reached my majority, and up to that time had never been farther away from home than New York City, a distance of 100 miles. Of course I was enchanted at the prospects of an outing, which would give me the opportunity so long desired of seeing something of the world, which so far as my own experience was concerned was virtually a sealed book. Having shipped my merchandise, I took the train for New York, and on my arrival registered at Lovejoy's Hotel, in Park Row, then the chief rendezvous for visitors from the east end of Long Island.[1]

As I had no particular point in view when I left home, I consulted the columns of the *Herald* and *Journal of Commerce* to ascertain what vessels were up for southern ports. The schooner *Ann D*, Captain Bedell, was advertised to sail for Norfolk, Va., with good accommodations for freight and passengers, for which, according to the advertisement, application should be made to the captain on board the vessel at Peak Slip.[2]

Having seen the captain and arranged for my passage and transportation of the goods, he informed me that he expected to get away the next day, and had he done so, it would have saved me no little mortification as the sequel will show. Unfortunately, freights were slow, and it was more than a week after the time set before the schooner was ready to depart. In the meanwhile I had been "seeing the elephant" from every conceivable point of view.[3]

Falling in with John H[ildreth], an old schoolmate and congenial companion, we made the rounds together.[4] John was a sailor boy, and was learning the duties of his profession under the tuition of his uncle, Captain B., who was master of a brig plying between New York and Savannah. There was nothing in his appearance, however, that indicated the nature of his calling, for immediately on reaching port he put off his marine garb, and assumed the habiliments of a Broadway dandy. He was a congenital dude, and Beau Brummel himself was not more particular regarding the set of his collar, or cravat, than was this salt water neophyte.

It was something to see his shipmates gather about him while making his toilet, and question him as to the use of this or that article of apparel, and watch his motions during the transition period; and when, after the transformation, having emerged from the chrysalis, he stood forth the gorgeous butterfly of fashion, a feeling of awe seemed to creep over them, a sort of physical metempsychosis seemed to have taken place, and in lieu of their whilom messmate they beheld a demigod.

Charles Kean was at that time playing at the old Park Theatre, with Ellen Tree as

5

"Ion." "Old" Placide, and George Barrett in "Speed The Plow," were the attraction at the Olympic; Chanfrau in the character of "Mose" was the idol of the Bowery boys, and night after night the little Chatham theatre was crowded from pit to dome with the representatives of the proletariat.[5]

We took in all these sights, and it goes without saying that we enjoyed them thoroughly. We ate porterhouse steak at Windust's in Park Row, whose motto, "*nunquam non paratus*," emblazoned in gilt letters above his door, was familiar to every New Yorker. We played billiards at Pintoux's, and from time to time dropped in at Florence's for an oyster stew. We ordered Welch rabbits [rarebits] at the Grapes in Chambers Street, and drank the red wine at the Arbor on Broadway.

It is astonishing what a faculty for enjoyment a youngster of 20 years develops when the opportunity occurs, and in how many different phases it displays itself. As for us, we drank, and were merry for a week, at the end of which time the flaccidity of our purses became so apparent, that we were compelled to hold up through sheer financial exhaustion.

Meanwhile, the *Ann D* had been slowly receiving cargo, and one morning the captain called at the hotel and notified me that he would probably get away that evening. My money was about exhausted; in fact, a deficit existed in the shape of the hotel bill. Moreover, provision had to be made for current expenses until such time as I could realize something from the sale of goods. As there was no other way to replenish the exchequer, I was reluctantly compelled to draw on home. A friend in Wall Street readily consented to cash my modest draft, and thereby relieved me of all apprehensions regarding the immediate future. New York had proved my Capua, and fearful of further temptations, I hastened to settle my hotel bill, and leave them behind.

Having seen my baggage sent forward, I took my way to the vessel, where I found my friend of the commercial marine waiting to see me off, and bidding him goodbye, I went on board. Shortly afterward, the foresail was hoisted, the lines were cast off, and as the schooner shot out from her berth, a strong ebb tide caught her and speedily swept her out of the East River into the bay, when all sail was made. A fresh N.W. breeze soon brought us up with Sandy Hook, and ere night had fallen, the *Ann D* had passed the light ship, and was standing southward along the New Jersey coast.

During the trip no incident worthy of note occurred outside the regular routine, and in due time we entered Hampton Roads, passed Fortress Monroe, then in an inchoate condition,[6] and tied up alongside the wharf at Norfolk. Calling a Negro hackman, I pointed out my baggage, which he placed on his vehicle, when I was driven to the National Hotel, where for the first time in my life, I sat down to a public table d'hote. The living at the National was excellent, and with oysters ad libitum it did not take long to recuperate after the quasi fast I had endured on board the *Ann D*, whose cook was by no means a first-class artist.

Having arranged with the master of a small vessel which was bound for Winton, North Carolina, via the Dismal Swamp canal, to land my goods at Edenton, where I had decided to "open up," I took the stage for Elizabeth City, and on the evening of the third day reached Edenton and registered at Bond's Hotel.[7] By this time my finances had again become depleted, to an extent that left but a single five-franc piece to represent my entire cash capital.

Having found a suitable building not far from the hotel, I agreed with the owner for a lease from month to month, and engaged carpenters to fit it with shelves and counters. This was a shore job, but as the vessel with my goods had not reported, I had no money to pay them off, so kept them at work till she came, which fortunately was not long. My bales and boxes were landed, the skipper sending word that as the wind was fair, he would go on to Winton[8] and collect his freight on his return. The five-franc piece sufficed for the drayman's charges, the boxes were quickly opened, the sales were satisfactory, the joiners were paid and discharged, and when the skipper called for his freight I was in a condition to meet all demands.

Edenton in North Carolina is situated near the mouth of the Chervan [Chowan] River which flows into Albemarle Sound. Located in the midst of a flourishing agricultural district, it was, at the time I write of, the principal depot of supplies, and all the farmers living within a radius of 20 miles came there to do their trading. As my stock consisted mainly of staple goods, the sales were fair, and I had no reason to complain of my treatment.

Soon after my arrival in Edenton, news came confirming previous reports from California, and the fact that gold in any quantity might be had for the digging, was established beyond a doubt. The whole community was in a condition of abnormal excitement, and in January, 1849, the grand exodus commenced. Even in that quiet southern village, the news from the gold fields was the principal subject of discussion.

Doctor N., the resident physician, had his office near my quarters, and it was there that the staid citizens were accustomed to meet and talk over current events. The stirring news from the Pacific Coast afforded an interesting topic of conversation, and the desire for further information respecting our newly acquired territory was universal.

Although the little coterie which met daily at the doctor's office was composed of men of more than average intelligence, they found themselves at fault when the topography of California came in question, and it became necessary for them to "read up" and gain some more definite knowledge regarding its surface, soil, and climate.

In some way they had become possessed of a copy of Dana's *Two Years Before the Mast*, and while one read aloud, the others would listen, and from time to time make appropriate comments. That under the circumstances the narrative proved interesting may be taken for granted, and though the description of the country was necessarily vague, still, much valuable information was gained by its perusal. The book, as its name implies, treats largely of matters nautical, and those simple planters, none of whom could tell the difference between a "bunt gasket" and a "back-stay," were puzzled by the technical phrases; and having learned that I was raised in an "amphibious" community, I was often called on to explain, and participate in their discussions.

Meanwhile I received letters from home advising me that the exodus from that vicinity seemed likely to depopulate the village, as almost all the able-bodied men had either gone or were preparing to go and reap the golden harvest which they had no doubt awaited them in the streams and gulches of the Sierra Nevada. A large company had been organized, and a ship purchased for the voyage around Cape Horn, and among its members were a half-dozen young fellows with whom I had grown up from boyhood.[9]

The thought of being left behind was so depressing that I resolved, if possible, to join them. Circumstances, however, forbade my departure till after I had disposed of my merchandise, and as that would require several months, I decided to meet them in San Francisco, as I would be able to make up for lost time by taking the shorter route across the Isthmus of Panama. Having made up my mind to this effect, I devoted all my energies to the disposition of my goods, so when trade became slack, after the Christmas holidays, I determined to seek a new field.

Plymouth, a small town on the Roanoke River, was some 25 miles distant on the opposite side of the Sound, and as it seemed to be the most eligible point, as well as the most convenient, I decided to go there.[10] The trip from Edenton to Plymouth was a memorable one. The wind failed us soon after leaving port, and instead of making the passage in a few hours, as we anticipated, we were nearly two days in crossing the Sound.

There were no provisions on board, and as a result we were compelled to go hungry and whistle for a breeze. The skipper got out his sweeps, called "all hands," which consisted of a solitary Negro boy, and while I held the tiller, they pulled the oars. It was on the evening of the second day that we reached the mouth of the river, a black, turgid stream with an impenetrable forest on either side. This was my first sight of a cypress swamp, which under the circumstances was a forbidding one.

As darkness settled on all around, it brought with it a feeling of home-sickness that I had never before experienced, and as I was nearly driven wild with hunger while the town was yet several miles distant, I suggested to the captain, that as the snags and sawgrass in the river prevented the use of sweeps, the boat (a small dinghy which we carried on deck) should be launched and manned by himself and the boy, with a view to towing the vessel to Plymouth. This was done, and though our progress was slow, by taking advantage of the eddies we made some headway, and about midnight caught sight of the lights in the town, and soon after tied up at the landing.

Once more on terra firma, it is perhaps unnecessary to state that I sought the hotel without delay, where I found the table already spread for the passengers by the mail stage which had just arrived. Without waiting for an introduction, I was the first one seated at the table, and regardless of conventionalities, at once proceeded to "fill up." Beefsteak, cold turkey, hot biscuits, and coffee disappeared to an extent that surprised the Negro waiter who officiated as purveyor. For an hour I kept him and my knife and fork in a constant state of activity, and when at length the vacuum was filled, I arose from the table with a feeling of regret that my storage capacity was so limited.

My sojourn in Plymouth was brief, as I found a schooner from New York there, with a cargo of dry goods, notions, hardware, etc., which the owner was disposing of in exchange for corn, shingles, and whatever else he could find a market for in the North. Under such conditions it seemed useless for me to compete, so after due consideration I decided to go elsewhere. Some 30 miles from Plymouth, on the Tar River, is a town called Washington, and after consulting the landlord, I fixed upon that as the most available point. There were no railroads in the South in those days, and transportation facilities were decidedly primitive. The road to Washington was through a dense swamp, which had been "corduroyed" so as to make it passable for teams, and was the only available means of communication between the two points.

Pettijohn, the landlord, had agreed to furnish transportation, and accordingly the merchandise was loaded on ox carts (vehicles with two large wheels, peculiar to that region), and on the second morning after my arrival in Plymouth, I made my exit, seated in a two-wheel sulky, followed by a procession of five carts in charge of one old Negro and four little darkies.

At that season of the year (January) the water was high; consequently many of the logs that formed the "corduroy" were afloat, and all unaccustomed to such roads, it was with no little trepidation that I assumed a driver's responsibility. The horse, however, was "native and to the manner born," and seemed to take it as a matter of course, as he picked his way over the floating logs, and the half-submerged bridges.

It was 4 o'clock when I reached the halfway house, where I was to stop overnight, and as my progress through the swamp was necessarily slow, the teams were not far behind. They came up soon after dark, and the cars were placed under shelter just in time to save the goods from a heavy shower of rain.

As the Negroes started before daybreak next morning, they had been gone several hours when I sat down to breakfast. The swamp ended at the halfway house, and the road for the rest of the way was high and dry, so I was able to drive faster than on the preceding day and reached Washington at noon. It did not take long to find suitable quarters, and when the goods arrived, I was ready to receive them.

Washington is, or was at that period, the chief outlet for the products of the Tar River district, which consisted mainly of cypress shingles, tar, pitch, and turpentine. It was an old-fashioned town, and the contrast between it and our busy northern seaports was decidedly striking.[11]

Its citizens, however, were kindly and sociable, and I still cherish pleasant recollections of my intercourse with them. The mayor, Isaiah Respass, was a genial gentleman, with whom I soon formed an acquaintance, and to whom I was indebted for many courtesies. Years afterward, during the War of Secession, he became quite conspicuous, as notwithstanding his surroundings, he was a staunch Union man, and stood by the old flag through "thick and thin."

It is not my purpose to give the details of my experience in the South; therefore it is sufficient to state that by the middle of February I had closed out my stock and started on the return journey northward. On my arrival at Baltimore I found the city all astir over the impending prize fight between Tom Hyer and Yankee Sullivan. The hotels were filled with sporting men from all over the country, and much interest was manifested in the result of the contest. As I had barely time to reach New York so as to take the Chagres steamer on the following day, I did not stop to see the fight, which came off the next morning on Pell's Island, a short distance from Baltimore.[12]

As the railroad was out of condition, passengers for the north were compelled to take the boat for Havre de Grace, and as we were unfortunately delayed on the route, it was midnight ere I reached Philadelphia, too late to take the train for New York. Consequently, I missed the steamer, which had sailed a few hours previous to my arrival there.

Much to my surprise, I found my brother awaiting me at the hotel. He had come to the city at the request of our mother, to induce me to wait over and take the next steamer for Chagres, and in the meanwhile go home and make proper preparations for my journey. As the steamer had gone, and the next would not sail till March 15, there was an interval of three weeks for me to spend at home.[13]

There was nothing to detain us in New York, so we took the train on the Long Island Railroad next morning, and soon after noon were driven from the station to the old homestead. The sound of the sleighbells called our mother to the door, and her anxious inquiry, "Have you got him?" showed what was uppermost in her mind. It is not necessary to state that my welcome was a warm one, and the weeks passed in the family circle were happy ones; nevertheless there was a constant yearning to be off, notwithstanding my pleasant surroundings.

III

OUR VILLAGE: SAG HARBOR

As before stated, I was raised in an amphibious community. Every boy in our village was an embryo Sinbad. He was as much at home in the water as on land, and learned to swim almost as soon as he knew how to walk. The ropes of a ship were as familiar to him as A B C, and when he reached the mature age of 15 years, he began to press his claim for recognition as a candidate for the forecastle. Every boy wanted to "go to sea." About half did go. Most of that half, however, were satisfied with one voyage, and on their return, unless a second was compulsory, were content to "tarry in Jericho till their beards were grown." The conversation was nautical. When a boy's mother urged him to immediate action, the command was, "Start your sheets." It is with our village, I think, that the following incident is connected:

A boy 10 years old rushes out at the front gate with a piece of pie in his hand, which he has just "hooked." Immediately after him follows his mother, in hot pursuit, with something in her hand for which the boy has no relish. The wind, which is blowing half a gale, catches the woman's wide skirt and propels her with a velocity that bodes ill for the youngster. An older boy, on the opposite side of the street, views the situation with interest, and seeing that capture is imminent, calls out sympathetically, "Try her on the wind, Jimmy, try her on the wind." Mindful of the suggestion, Jimmy "luffs" incontinently, and running directly in the "wind's eye," soon leaves the old lady astern, and for the time being "saves his bacon."

Up to 1846, the whale-fishing was the main dependence of our village.[1] A man's commercial rating was based on the amount of his "ship stock." The forehanded farmer invested his surplus in "ship stock." The widow's income was derived from "ship stock." The orphan's patrimony was represented by "ship stock." In fact, ship stock was the cornerstone of the commercial fabric. Thus it was that when the business failed to pay, the fabric fell, and buried local prosperity in its ruins.

In the palmy days of the whale-fishing, there were about sixty ships hailing from our village, and as nearly everybody was either a stockholder, or had some friend or relation on board, news from the fleet was a matter of paramount interest. The *Whaleman's Shipping List,* published in New Bedford, was the principal source of intelligence, and was a vade mecum with old and young. The latitude and longitude of each ship when last reported, and the quantity of oil and bone on board was an index, telling when to expect her return; hence every available means was resorted to to get the latest reports.

Some ships were known as "lucky ships" and invariably made profitable voyages. Others were classed as "unlucky," and though the masters were often changed, seldom paid remunerative dividends. A captain's social status depended on his success as a whaleman, and if fortunate he was apt to be lionized on his return home; but if unfortunate his reception was as cold as a stepmother's kiss. Every officer was graded according to his ability to throw a harpoon, or wield a lance. No matter what other qualifications he lacked or possessed, his dexterity as a harpooner was the main consideration.

Should an officer occasionally show the "white feather," and the rumor go out that he was "afraid of whales," he lost caste in the community. He might be a gentleman in deportment, well-read, and intelligent; in short, he might possess every virtue that the other lacked; yet, if it was well-known that he was "afraid of whales," he was damned in the estimation of the body politic.

The following conversation reported as having occurred between one who had just returned from an unsuccessful voyage and his faithless fiancée, shows the sentiment that prevailed in a whaling community:

"Susan, you promised fair and square to marry me."

"Yes, that's true."

"Then why do you refuse me now?"

"Do you remember when you missed that 60-barrel sperm whale last year, off the River La Plate?"

"Yes, I do—what of it?"

"Well, that's the time you missed me."

The arrivals each season comprised about one-half of the number of vessels belonging to the port, and during the summer the village streets were thronged with a miscellaneous multitude of sailors of almost every hue and nationality. Portuguese from the Azores, Spaniards from South America, Maoris from New Zealand, Kanakas from the Sandwich Islands, convicts who had stolen on board while the vessel was at anchor in some harbor of Van Dieman's Land, and even cannibals from the Fijis were included in the incongruous collection.

Yankee [James] Sullivan, who gained notoriety as a prizefighter, and who subsequently killed himself in San Francisco through fear of the Vigilance Committee, who were after him for some alleged crime, was brought from Botany Bay in the ship *Hamilton* of our village. He had managed to secrete himself on board, and was not discovered till after the vessel had sailed. He never tired of expressing his obligations to Captain Hand for his kind treatment, and years afterwards, when told of the latter's death in California, his tearful tribute to the memory of the man who had befriended him showed that one virtue still lingered in his breast, and though linked with a thousand crimes, the spark of gratitude was not extinguished.[2]

On the collapse of the whale-fishing, the coopers, calkers, riggers, sailmakers, blacksmiths, boatbuilders, stevedores, and all others who looked to it as a means of livelihood, were compelled to seek fresh fields, and pastures new. The tidings of the gold discovery came just in time to provide an outlet for their surplus energy, for though the whale-fishery was dead, the captains, coopers, and boat-steerers were very much alive, as events soon showed.

The spirit of adventure was rife in the community. Everybody was awake to the fact that gold was to be had in California for the digging, and nearly everybody proposed to go there and join in the work of excavation. The opportunity of a lifetime was before them, and they hastened to seize it—the tide of fortune was setting strongly in their favor, and they determined to take it at the flood.

A company was soon formed, a ship was purchased, and in a short time made ready for sea. The *Sabina* was an old whaler belonging to the port, and had gained quite a reputation as a fast sailer, and in fact did make an excellent passage for a ship of her class, landing her passengers in San Francisco in six months to a day from the time of sailing; but as she sprang a leak when only a few days out, and was compelled to put in at St. Catherines for repairs, where she was detained a month, her actual sailing time was only five months.[3]

Captain [Henry] Green, who was in command of the ship, had many able assistants among his passengers, about twenty of whom were retired sea captains. The high rocks of Tierra del Fuego were as familiar to them as their native hills. They had for years encountered all the perils incident to a seafaring life, and in the course of their experience had piloted their vessels safely amid the stormy waters of Cape Horn, had contended successfully with the cyclones of the tropics, and in pursuit of their calling had pushed their way through the straits of Bering, and chased leviathan among the icebergs of the Frozen Zone. With all those skillful mariners on board, the dangers of navigation were reduced to a minimum, as every indication of bad weather was promptly noted, and when it came, the vessel was prepared to meet it. The crew of the *Sabina* had an easy time, for their duties were by no means onerous. In rough weather they were relieved of extra exertion by the "ancient mariners" among the passengers, and whenever a "reefing match" occurred, it was generally one of these ex-captains whose cheery call, "Haul out to leeward," announced that he had taken the position of honor at the weather [b]earing.

Here we will leave the *Sabina* for the present, but before I take up the thread of my story, I will relate an incident that occurred in connection with the whale-fishing, which shows to what extent a man will sometimes go in order to gratify his taste for adventure.

It was, I think, in 1844 [1845] that the ship *Plymouth* sailed from our port bound for the North West coast. Among her crew was a young Scotchman named Alexander McDonald [*i.e.,* Ranald MacDonald], who was an expert boatsteerer; hence the desire to secure his services excited much competition between the shipmasters. He finally decided to join the *Plymouth*, and signed the shipping articles under the following conditions: McDonald was to stay with the ship until her cargo was completed and she was ready to leave the "whaling ground" on her homeward passage, after which time he was to receive his discharge, at any time he might desire. It was also agreed that the captain would furnish at a fair price, a boat and whatever provisions he might require. With this understanding McDonald entered upon the voyage, and during the time he was on board performed his duties to the satisfaction of all concerned. The *Plymouth* was absent three years, and after his return Captain Edwards told the following story:

"The ship was homeward bound, when one morning McDonald came aft and demanded his discharge. We were then in latitude 35° North and longitude 160° East. Of course, I was taken all aback at his request, as I had supposed that he would leave us at the Sandwich Islands where we were to touch on our way. He asked for a boat and provisions, and reminded me of our agreement, stating that he had performed his part in accordance with its terms, and insisted on a strict fulfilment on my part. I tried to dissuade him from his purpose of leaving the ship in mid-ocean, and entering on what I considered a wild and foolhardy expedition. All my arguments, however, were unavailing, and as he persisted in his determination to leave the ship then and there, I was constrained to comply with his demand, and very reluctantly proceeded to make preparations for his departure. The best boat we had was selected, and supplied with provisions and water sufficient for three months' consumption. I gave him a compass, fitted the boat with a sail, and made such other arrangements for his safety as my experience suggested. He had a gun with an ample supply of ammunition, fishing lines, etc. We placed a tub of sand in the boat, with a few cooking utensils and a quantity of fire wood. These together with his sea chest constituted his cargo. When the preparations were complete, I called McDonald into the cabin and paid him the balance due. All my endeavors to ascertain his motive in embarking in his reckless enterprise were futile, as he refused to explain, and during all the time he was with us, had never given the slightest intimation of his intention to leave the ship, until he came aft and asked to be discharged as stated. Going on deck, he bade goodbye to all hands, jumped into his boat, cast off the line, hoisted sail, and proceeded on his lonely voyage. We watched him awhile from the deck, when the order to put the helm up was given, and the ship kept away on her course."

Such was the captain's story. Now for the sequel: Years afterward, the United States cruiser *Preble* visited Japan and came to anchor in the harbor of Yeddo. One object of her visit was the rescue of certain American sailors, who had been shipwrecked on the coast, and having reached shore alive, were captured by the Japanese, and in accordance with the custom then prevailing, shut up in prison. News of their incarceration had in some way reached our Government, and measures were taken for their release.

In response to the peremptory demand of the Commander of the *Preble*, backed by a show of force that it was useless to resist, the shipwrecked seamen were released, and not only them, but many others who had from time to time fallen into the clutches of the barbarians, were also set free and delivered on board the man of war. Among these was Alexander McDonald. He had survived the perils of the ocean, but under what circumstances he had fallen into the hands of the Japanese, must still remain a subject of conjecture.

The episode is a romantic one, and a history of McDonald's adventures from the time he left the *Plymouth* till he was delivered to the commander of the *Preble* would no doubt prove highly interesting.[4]

IV

IN NEW YORK CITY

During the time passed at home, my outfit was prepared with a view to "roughing it" in the mines. Shirts and drawers of good, substantial, homespun flannel, trousers of Kentucky jean, stoga boots, and all such necessaries as the occasion seemed to require were amply provided; and when the time came for my departure, everything had been done that willing hands could do to insure my physical comfort.

As transportation across the Isthmus was expensive, my wardrobe was packed in as small a compass as was consistent with prudence. A medium-sized trunk, an india-rubber clothes bag, and a roll of blankets comprised all my baggage. I had also provided myself with a revolver—one of those newly patented pistols known as an "Allen," which for "comprehensive shooting" was truly a wonder, for no matter in what direction it was pointed, there was no telling where the bullet might strike. I took the pistol out in the yard one day for a little private practice, and to say that I was astonished at its performance conveys but a faint idea of my disgust over the result of my experiment.

Having been accustomed to the use of firearms from early boyhood, I considered myself a fair marksman, but my experience with that "pepper box" fairly surprised me. Setting up a target against the back fence, and assuming that twelve paces was a reasonable distance, I stepped off that number and blazed away; but when after firing six shots I proceeded to inspect the target, I was confounded to find that not only was the mark unscathed, but even the high board fence against which it was nailed, failed to show a single bullet hole. As it was evident that the bullets had gone wide of the mark, I decided to try a wider range, and accordingly turned the pistol toward the barn, aiming at a knot in the door about midway of the building, and not only failed to hit the knot, but came near missing the barn altogether, as the bullet struck just under the eaves, about two feet from the end of the building.

My brother, who had been an interested spectator of the performance, suggested that I should buy a "pocket compass," for, said he, "it is evident that the only way to get anything out of that pistol is to set it by compass, and as it seems to shoot about four points out of line, it would be necessary in case the object should bear, say southeast, to point your shooter due south, and thus stand some chance to hit your mark."

Though this advice seemed to be eminently sound, I failed to follow it, as that was my first, and also my last experience with the "old Allen," which before leaving home I deposited in my trunk, where it remained ever afterwards, till destroyed by fire in San Francisco.

It was on the morning of March 13 [1849] that I took my departure from the old homestead, across whose threshold I was not destined to pass again for long, long years. I will not dwell on the parting scene. My mother was spared to welcome me on my return, but my father, who was already near the age allotted to man, must have felt that in the course of nature he must soon be called from earth; and, as he clasped my hand in farewell, realized that in all probability it was goodbye forever. [The elder Gardiner died September 13, 1849.]

The following lines were published in the *New York Journal of Commerce* on the morning of my departure from home,[1] and are inserted as appropriate to the narrative:

A Father's Advice to His Son, Leaving His Home for California
By Rev. John D. Gardiner

Farewell my son, the hour has come,
The solemn hour when we must part;
The hour that bears thee from thy home,
With sorrow fills thy father's heart.

Farewell, my son, thou leav'st behind
Thy mother, brothers, sisters dear,
And goest the far-off land to find
Without one friend thy way to cheer.

Alone, thou leav'st thy vine-clad cot,
Thy childhood's lawn, thy natal bowers,
Sweet scenes that ne'er will be forgot,
Where life has passed its sunniest hours.

When far away in distant lands,
'Mid California's golden streams,
Where brightly shine those yellow sands,
Oft will "Sweet Home" come o'er thy dreams.

Thy father's counsels, prayers, and love
Pursue thee through thy dangerous way,
And at the mercy seat above,
Implore his son may never stray.

From that strait path where virtue guides
To purest, noblest joys on high,
Where God in holiness presides,
And springs perennial never dry.

Remember, His omniscient eye
Beholds each devious step you take,
That you can ne'er His presence fly
At home, abroad, asleep, awake.

On California's sea-beat shore,
Where the Pacific rolls his tide,
Where waves on waves eternal roar,
You cannot from His notice hide.

He holds you There upon His arm,
Encircles with His boundless might,
Preserves you safe from every harm,
'Mid brightest day and darkest night.

Let that great thought be deep impressed
Upon the tablets of thy heart,
Be cherished there within thy breast,
And from thy memory ne'er depart.

If strong temptations round you rise,
Where sin's deceitful smiles betray
This thought will prompt you to despise
The course that leads the downward way.

When Fascination spreads her charms
But to allure, betray, destroy,
Think then a father's faithful arms
Are thrown around his wandering boy.

So keep him from the fatal snare,
Sprung to entrap his youthful feet,
And lead his heedless footsteps where
Pale ruin holds its gloomy seat.

What pangs must rend thy father's soul,
To find his counsels all are crossed,
Are set at naught, without control,
And his beloved son is lost.

Oh! think what mourning, anguish, grief,
Would bathe thy kindred all in tears,
That one dear youth in life so brief
Should cloud in night their future years.

Should those bright hopes that gild thy sky,
And cast their splendors on the west,
Fade on thy sight, grow dim and die
And heart sink down with gloom oppressed.

Should sickness chain thee to thy bed
In California's distant land,
No brother there to hold thy head
Nor sister take thy trembling hand,

Trust then, my son, that Guardian Power
Whose eye beholds the sparrow's fall,
He'll watch thee in that lonely hour,
Whose gracious care is o'er us all.

Then, if beneath the evening star,
Beside the great Pacific's wave
Thou find'st an early tomb afar,
His grace will there thy spirit save.

Or, if upon thy safe return
Thou find'st no more thy father here,
Pay one sad visit to his urn,
Drop on his dust one filial tear.

May God's rich blessings on thy head,
Descend in showers of heavenly grace
And keep you safe where e'er you tread
As we here end this fond embrace.

So live, my son, while here you stand
On Time's bleak ever-changing shore,
That we may reach that better land
Where sons and fathers part no more.

The steamship *Crescent City*, Captain Stoddard, was advertised to sail for Chagres on the 15th, and my first business after reaching New York was to arrange for a passage. This was a matter, however, that required no little consideration, as it involved the necessity of choosing whether I should purchase a cabin ticket or take my chance in the steerage. Therefore I decided to go on board the steamer and see for myself what the accommodations were.

As is usually the case on the eve of sailing, the ship was in an unsettled condition, and what with the multitude of carpenters, calkers, painters, etc., it was difficult getting around. I managed, however, to find my way below, where everything was in a state of confusion, not at all calculated to impress one favorably.

The carpenters were busily engaged in putting up berths for the steerage passengers, and as the *Crescent City* was very high between decks, there were four tiers, one above the other, and each berth was intended to accommodate three occupants. These berths were constructed of undressed lumber, and occupied both sides of the steerage, midway of which, a rough table covered with oilcloth ran the whole length of the compartment.

That the surroundings were far from being attractive, may be taken for granted; nevertheless, as the voyage was like to be a short one, and as it was a question of dollars and cents with me, the difference in price between a cabin and steerage ticket being eighty dollars, I reasoned that I could not make ten dollars a day easier than by roughing it in the steerage for eight days, the time required for the trip from New York to Chagres. Having made up my mind to this effect, I returned to the agent's office and purchased a steerage ticket.

As the conditions were such as required each steerage passenger to furnish his own bedding, I invested $1.50 in a straw mattress, which was placed in the berth corresponding in number with that on my ticket, taking care that my bed should be on the front side. This arrangement was altered subsequently as will presently appear.

Having provided the furniture of my berth, my next move was to purchase mining utensils. These I procured in a shop in Maiden Lane, where I selected a short-handled shovel, also a pick, which, though polished "up to the nines" and apparently "O K," proved in the end to be a mighty poor investment; for, though it eventually reached the diggings, it went back on me the first time I had occasion to use it, as it lacked backbone, the main element of steel having been omitted in its composition; hence it doubled up like lead at the first blow I struck, and proved useless for all practical purposes. There is a tale connected with that pick, as will appear in the course of this narrative.

As I was informed by a friend that dimes would pass current on the Isthmus at the rate of eight for a dollar, I purchased $75 worth of a broker in Wall Street; for use during my sojourn in Panama, should I be detained there, and as events proved it was a precious investment. The balance of my money, which consisted of English sovereigns, I placed in a belt around my waist, the sum total amounting to $400, all of which was needed 'ere I reached San Francisco.

On the evening of the 14th I had arranged to meet several of my friends and enjoy with them a final symposium, and in accordance with this arrangement, they came around to the hotel for the purpose of carrying out the programme. My recollection is rather vague as to the details; nevertheless I remember that we visited the theatre, after which we adjourned to Florence's for refreshments, both solid and liquid, of which we partook to an extent that, to say the least, was rather indiscreet. The reader must remember, however, that this was fifty years ago, when such escapades were common, and viewed with a lenient eye. It was at a late, or perhaps more properly speaking an early hour, when the festivities broke up, and the last incident that I remember in connection therewith, was joining in the chorus of an old drinking song which Washington Irving has immortalized in his *Sketch Book:*

> Back and sides go bare, go bare,
> Both fool and brand go cold,
> But belly, God send you good ale enough,
> Whether it be new or old.

Good night: "Cras ingens iterabimus sequor."

V

ON BOARD THE *CRESCENT CITY*

MARCH, 1849

There were four of us piled on the bed when I was awakened by my brother the next morning. He was about to leave for the West and came to say goodbye. It goes without saying that the hair on our heads was pulling to an extent that made us feel decidedly antiquated, and the consensus of opinion seemed to be that we had rather "overdone it" the night previous. We turned out, however, as the nature of their occupation was such that dallying in bed after 8 o'clock was altogether out of the question so far as my friends were concerned; and as for myself, the steamer was to sail at noon, and there were several matters that required my attention before going on board. Making a hasty toilet, we sought the restaurant, where after partaking of a slight (very slight) refection, and bracing up on strong coffee, we shook hands and parted.

Many a time in after years the memory of the breakfast left untouched that morning recurred to my mind and furnished a sort of Barmecide feast, which though not exactly filling, afforded a pleasant contrast with the plain diet of pork and beans, which formed the staple dish of the miner's commissariat.

God forbid, however, that I should say anything in depreciation of pork and beans. They were the miner's standby, and eaten with a liberal supply of Spartan sauce, which was seldom lacking, were partaken of with a gusto which under other circumstances the famed ambrosia of the gods would have failed to excite, and Lucullus himself might have envied the enjoyment exhibited by the hardy Argonauts over their simple meals, where good digestion waited on appetite, and health on both.

At noon, the hour set for the departure of the steamer, accompanied by a few friends, I went on board the *Crescent City;* and shortly afterwards the drayman with my luggage made his appearance, when it was transferred to the vessel. The departure of the Chagres steamer was in those days a notable event, and caused no little excitement even in New York City, whose citizens were accustomed to the arrival and departure of vessels every day in the year; nevertheless the unique spectacle of a horde of gold-seekers, made up to a great extent of the flotsam and jetsam of humanity, and representing about every known trade and profession, possessed an irresistible attraction for the "quid nuncs" with whom the pier was invariably crowded on "steamer's day."

Notwithstanding the fact that it was a typical March day on which we sailed, the snowstorm that prevailed, failed to check the crowd which thronged the pier, and had assembled to "see us off."

Although the steamer was advertised to sail at noon, several hours elapsed ere the order was given to cast off the lines, and in the meanwhile I sat on deck watching the ever changing panorama.

There were at least 400 passengers, each of whom had one or more friends among the crowd on shore, who testified their good will by tossing apples, oranges, etc., to those on board. The fruit peddlers reaped a rich harvest, and had occasion to replenish their baskets several times during the afternoon.

One interesting feature of the exhibition was a man (I think it was Paul Boynton), who, dressed in a rubber suit, was floating in the water of the slip, displaying his "patent life preserver," apparently regardless of the danger he incurred from the falling rubbish which the sailors threw overboard while cleaning the deck.[1]

In addition to the sights, the sounds also had a peculiar interest; for what with the shouts of the teamsters as they dashed through the crowd, and up to the last minute tumbled their loads of bales and boxes on the wharf, the continuous roar of the steam escaping through the safety valve, the rumble of the trucks as they passed to and fro over the gangplanks, the hoarse tones of the mates as they gave their orders to the deck-hands, and the constant stream of conversation that was kept up by those on the ship with their friends on shore, it seemed as if pandemonium had broken loose, and all the devils were there.

It was past 3 o'clock when the rush ceased and the last package was brought on board, and although the ship was in a chaotic condition, that matter could be remedied later. The captain took his place on the bridge, a quartermaster held the wheel, the gangplank was hauled ashore, the hawsers were let go, when at a signal from the engineer the engines were started and amid the acclaim of the multitude of spectators the *Crescent City* proceeded on her voyage.[2]

Leaving the noise of the great city behind us, we soon passed the Romer buoy, and in due time came up with Sandy Hook, shortly after which our pilot left us, and the ship's officers assumed control.

Up to this time I had not realized my position, and the isolated condition in which I was placed. With the exception of a young man [William H. Allen] to whom I was introduced a few hours before sailing, I had not a single acquaintance among the passengers. Moreover, he was a cabin passenger, while my quarters were in the steerage, between which and the cabin the line of demarcation was likely to be soon drawn, and all intercourse shut off. This quasi-ostracism seemed to brand me as a social pariah; a feeling of homesickness crept over me, and for the first time I experienced a pang of regret at leaving home, and home associations.

Lonely and forlorn, I paced the deck, and at intervals leaned over the bulwarks and watched the shores of old Long Island, now grown dim in the distance; and as they receded, and were finally lost to sight, I turned my face inboard and quoted Childe Harold's apostrophe:

> Adieu, Adieu; my native shore
> Fades o'er the waters blue;
> The night winds sigh, the breakers roar,
> And shrieks the wild sea mew.
> Yon sun that sets upon the sea,

We follow in his flight;
Farewell awhile to him and thee,
My Native Land—Good night!

After remaining on deck for a while, I decided to go below and see what was going on in the steerage. I found matters there in a quiescent condition. The table was set, and the steward readily responded to my request for a cup of coffee, which was served in a tin pot holding about a pint. There was a good supply of salt beef and pilot bread on the table, neither of which had any attraction for me. The coffee, however, wasn't bad, if it was served in a tin cup and sweetened with brown sugar without cream. Holding my cup in my hand, I sought my berth in which was deposited a box of cookies for private consumption.

As I approached the berth, I saw that it was occupied by two young fellows who had purchased the other two-thirds, and on taking possession, had removed my mattress to the back side. They had in short "jumped my claim," and that, too, in contravention of every principle of equity, as I was the first-comer and had metaphorically driven my stakes before either of them had put in an appearance. To my inquiry as to what they meant by usurping my place, in disregard of the distinction between meum and tuum, they had a ready reply.

The boys were a long way from being fools, and made a specious plea in justification of their action. They took the ground that we were "tenants in common," each owning one-third of the berth, and that as neither of us had purchased any particular third, the apportionment must necessarily be made by the joint owners, and as they constituted a majority, both in number and value, they had a perfect right to assign me the back side.

The colossal cheek of the youngsters, neither of whom was more than eighteen years old, fairly paralyzed me, and I was about to assert my prerogative in an emphatic manner, when they proceeded to explain that aside from all question of moral or legal obligation, I should give way on "humanitary" grounds—That they were both suffering from sea-sickness, and had already felt premonitory qualms, which had sent them to bed hoping to avoid further complications. That they were morally certain that they would have occasion to "throw up" during the night, in which case it would be a great convenience to be on the front side, and also save me from a good deal of annoyance.

The latter plea was a "clincher," so I consented to waive my rights, giving them to understand, however, that I did so on strictly "humanitary" grounds, and entirely through sympathy for their condition. This discussion ended, I fished out a few cookies from the box, and having eaten them and drank my coffee, I returned to the deck to enjoy a smoke.

The ship was still lumbered up to an extent that made locomotion very difficult. Moreover, it had "come on to blow" with the wind from the northeast, which kicked up quite a sea and caused the steamer to roll in a manner that was calculated to test the sea-going quality of the passengers, most of whom had already retired to their berths in an unenviable condition of discomposure, while to those who still kept the deck, the ocean began to assume the appearance of "one vast emetic." As for myself, having all my life been habituated to boats and boating, the motion of the vessel failed to affect me, hence I suffered no inconvenience from sea-sickness.

It is different with a steamer in a heavy sea-way, from what it is with a sailing vessel under like circumstances, as the former pursues her course regardless of the wind, and often follows the trough of the sea, when, having no sails to steady her, she rolls terribly, and makes it difficult for one to keep his feet, while a sailing vessel, having her canvas to counteract the weather roll, is far more comfortable in rough weather.

The *Crescent City* was a "side wheeler," and when there was a big sea on, she sometimes rolled so badly that her weather wheel would be almost clear of the water, and whenever this happened, it would whirl round like a buzz saw till checked by the governor valve. Then again it would bury itself so deep that it seemed impossible for wood and iron to stand the strain.

As the sky was overcast, and the wind chilly and disagreeable, there was not much comfort to be had on deck, so having finished my cigar, I concluded to go below and turn in. The steerage was lighted by several lanterns, that enabled me to find my sleeping quarters without difficulty. The boys were asleep, but the indications showed that they had not been disappointed in the matter of "throwing up." Divesting myself of coat and boots, I crawled to the back side of the berth without disturbing my companions, and as I had not slept much the night previous, I soon "dropped off."

I was awakened next morning by the voices of the boys, who were both sick and disgusted, and seemed inclined to take a pessimistic view of all things sublunary. They had passed a disagreeable night, and as a result were in a bad humor, and disposed to find fault with their surroundings. The violent tossing to which the ship had been subjected had stirred up the bilgewater in the hole, the smell of which by no means tended to relieve their nausea.

The condition of a man suffering from sea-sickness is truly a pitiable one. He feels no interest in anything, either in the heavens above or the earth beneath or the waters under the earth—he simply wants to lie down and die. His chief desire is to put off the garment of mortality and assume that of immortality, and he is inclined to exclaim with Job, "Let the day perish wherein I was born, and the night in which it was said, There is a man-child conceived."

As the boys' conversation in part, referred to me, I listened with some interest to what they said. My exemption from sea-sickness seemed to excite their envy. "Look at that fellow," said one, "I wish I could sleep as he does." "Yes, by George," was the reply, "here have you and I been mewling and puking like two blessed infants all night long, while he snoozed as comfortably as if he had been lying on a spring mattress at the Astor House. He's been reeling it off at a ten-mile gait ever since he struck the bed, and hasn't made a single break. God bless the man who invented sleep, as Sancho Panza says."

Just here I sat up, and announced my intention to turn out and have a cup of coffee, and advised the youngsters to do the same, and go on deck and get some fresh air, as that was the best remedy for their ailment. They rejected the coffee with scorn, but acknowledged that fresh air might prove a panacea. By this time, those of the steerage passengers who were in a condition to be about had made their appearance, and taken seats at the break-fast table. The bill of fare, however, proved far from acceptable, and there was much grumbling over the food provided. The dissatisfaction finally culminated in a general row, during which the steward's life was in repeated jeopardy, as he was made the scape-goat for the alleged sins of his employers.

I have somewhere read that whenever Dante made his appearance on the streets of Florence, people were accustomed to point him out, and remark, "There goes a man who was in Hell"—and it occurred to me that morning as I watched the proceedings in the steerage of the steamship *Crescent City,* that by changing the tense of the verb, a like ex-pression would be applicable to myself.

Man, under certain circumstances, is the most unreasonable animal in existence, and those fellows who were chiefly instrumental in kicking up the disturbance should have recognized the wide difference between the cuisine of a ship's steerage and that of Del-monico's, and instead of demanding soft bread, and milk for their coffee, would, had they stopped to consider, have realized the absurdity of their request, and contented themselves with what was set before them. They soon learned, however, that meals on shipboard

> Are not such things as can be fixed
> But must be taken as they're mixed

The truth of the matter is that the food provided for our consumption, though coarse, was good of its kind. The meat was sweet, and the biscuits fresh and free from weevils. The majority of those who were dissatisfied with the fare were compelled to partake of far worse ere they reached their destination, and not long afterwards it became a question with some of them, not of "what is it?" but "where is it?" that they found it hard to solve, and the tin cup, the iron spoon, and the two-tined fork were accepted as a matter of course.

Many a California pioneer, who has achieved the end he sought, and is today sur-rounded with all the luxuries that wealth can buy, now that age has overtaken him, and "turned to penance all the joys of youth"; when he is forbidden to participate in the pleasures of the table, and restricted to the meager diet of an anchorite; as he looks back to the time when with unimpaired digestion he hailed "duff day" on shipboard as a day of feasting, and swallowed with impunity a mixture which would have burdened the pancreas of an ostrich, will agree with me when I say that it [is] not so much the quality of the food, but the capacity to enjoy it that makes life worth living.

Having dispatched my breakfast, which consisted of a pot of coffee, and a second in-stallment of cookies, I went on deck and mingled with the crowd. A great improvement on the condition of the previous day was apparent at the first glance. The sky had cleared, the wind and sea had gone down, and the bright sunshine had the effect of raising the spirits of all. The sailors were busily engaged in relieving the deck of the accumulated rubbish and stowing it in the hold, while matters generally had assumed a more orderly appearance.

It was not long before I came across Mr. Allen, my new acquaintance of the day before, and was by him introduced to his three partners, James Merrihew, Henry Richmond, and Edward Pollard, all from Fair Haven, Mass., and like myself, belonged to the genus amphibia.[3] They were all good fellows, and immediately adopted me as a member of their mess, for which action I had every reason to be grateful. None of us had been troubled with sea-sickness, and our physical condition was superb. Young and unmarried, our responsibilities were light, and every symptom of nostalgia soon disappeared. We readily became reconciled to a life on shipboard, and when some one suggested that we should go below for a game of whist, the suggestion was at once adopted. Accordingly, we adjourned to the saloon, where we passed the hours till dinner time in making and counting points.

It goes without saying that the forenoon was passed pleasantly, so when I returned to the deck and found that during the interval the fence separating the steerage from the cabin passengers had been erected, it occurred to me that I was on the wrong side of it, and it fairly made the cold chills run down my spinal column when I realized the difference between where I was, and where I belonged, for the reader may rest assured, that after my experience at the breakfast table, I had no hankering after my legitimate quarters.

The boys, one and all, scouted the idea of my returning to the steerage; and when I urged the propriety of doing so on moral grounds, Jim, whom we soon learned to look upon as our oracle, proceeded to argue the case logically, taking his premises, and drawing his conclusions, to the entire satisfaction of all concerned. For, said he, "It is evident that you have been placed in this position by no act of your own, and since the officers of the ship have seen fit to build that fence without notifying you that they intended to do so, they have virtually corralled you, and placed it out of your power to return, and as there is nothing in the Koran, or the Ten Commandments, or the Sermon on the Mount, that required you to scale that fence, you can just put your morality in your pocket and stay where you are."

"But," said I, still hesitating, "you seem to forget that I must have something to sustain my corporeal system for the next week or ten days, and a meal ticket intended for the steerage, will hardly pass current at the cabin table."

"That objection is trivial and easily met," was the reply. "There are meal tickets lying around loose to feed you six months if you had as many stomachs as a camel; there is Worthington" (pointing to a young man apparently in the last stage of collapse, who, while leaning over the rail and feeding the sea birds that followed the ship, had heard the conversation), "take his, he's not likely to need it for some days to come."

"Yes," said Worthington,[4] straightening himself up and fishing in his vest pocket for his voucher, "take it and use it, for it is certain that I never shall, and the very thought of it, or anything else connected with eating is simply nauseating."

"Now," said Jim, as Worthington tendered me the ticket, "take the goods which the gods have provided, and since there is nothing to prevent you from standing up to the 'lick log,' and taking your salt with the rest of us, I propose that we go down and fill up."

We went down, and filled up, too, at least I did, before I left the table. The surroundings were rather different from those in the steerage, and I appreciated the change thoroughly. The table was spread with enticing dishes, which I disposed of in liberal quantities. My friend Worthington had no occasion to blush for his substitute, as I easily held my own with the crowd. Fairchild, the purser, vised my passport in due form, and all went well.

Though I represented Worthington at the table, he was in no condition to dispense with his "berth," hence I had to take my chance for sleeping accommodations. I suffered very little inconvenience in that respect, however, as the second night out we had made several hundred miles southing, and the weather was perceptibly milder, so I managed to sleep very comfortably on a settee in the cabin.

The weather was pleasant, the ocean quiet, and when we were three days out, with but few exceptions all whose who were sea-sick had recovered, and taken their places at the table. The evenings were passed in card-playing—whist, seven-up, euchre, and to a small extent poker were the prevailing games. As Pollard was ignorant of the game, his three partners and myself constituted a merry coterie, and enjoyed ourselves hugely at the whist table during the passage.

Everyone conversant with ocean travel must have noticed the invariable tendency to form cliques on shipboard. Thus the passengers are split up into groups of half a dozen, who sit together at a table, smoke and drink together, and seldom have any intercourse with those outside of their immediate circle. The passengers on the *Crescent City* were no exception to the rule, and we five (six including Worthington) were a community by ourselves, and made few acquaintances on board.

As one day's doings is an index to all the others, aside from special incidents, I forbear further details. It is sufficient to state that we ate well, slept well, and felt well during the whole passage. We noted the day's run at noon, and from time to time laid wagers on the number of revolutions the wheels were making. Worthington was on the sick list for a week, and by the time he recovered so as to take his place at the table, I had established such relations with the purser, that there was no further use for the meal ticket, so I returned it with thanks.

One morning, when we were four or five days out, word was passed to remove the rubber bags from the hold, as the captain feared that the odor there exhaled, might cause sickness. As my bag was stowed with the others, I took my place by the fore hatchway to claim it as it came out, for not having any stateroom I had been on short allowance to towels, and desired to procure some, of which there was a good supply in the bag. There were several hundreds of these rubber bags in the hold, as every passenger had one or more.

Before leaving home, I had encased mine in a stout canvas sack to prevent its getting torn. Between the bag and the canvas cover I had stowed the pick purchased in New York, which was sharp as a needle, but as it was securely wrapped in several thicknesses of heavy paper, there seemed to be no danger of its doing any harm. Every bag, as it came out, was shouldered by a sailor and carried aft to the quarterdeck where all were piled together.

After waiting a while, I spied my bag and was about to claim it when a sailor seized it and threw it on his shoulder. It did not remain there long. Giving a grunt, he dropped it incontinently, and stooping down, instituted an examination which resulted in the exposure of about two inches of the sharp end of the pick, and although the blood from his wounded shoulder had already stained his shirt, he neither swore, nor did he exhibit the least anger—he appeared to be simply disgusted, and remarked that "he wished he knew the man that owned that bag," he picked it up gingerly and carried it aft.

Of course, I kept shady in regard to the ownership, and though I sympathized with the sailor, had he been an ordinary baggage-smasher, I would have gloated over the episode.

Still keeping an eye on the sack, I walked aft to claim it, but Providence had so ordained that there were to be further complications ere I could safely do so, for no sooner had the sailor deposited it on the deck than a long, lank specimen of humanity, clad in a suit of brown jean, with a lugubrious expression, and having the appearance of an itinerant preacher, walked up to the bag and deliberately "got down on it." He did not maintain a recumbent posture for any great length of time, however, as the contact caused him to assume a perpendicular attitude without any unnecessary delay. There was no exhibition of stoicism so far as he was concerned—he did not, like the sailor under similar provocation, view the matter dispassionately. There was nothing in his deportment to remind one of the philosophic Zeno; and as he rubbed the injured part of his anatomy, he too expressed a desire to form the acquaintance of the owner of that bag, so that he might "wipe him off the face of the airth." The owner of the bag, however, was not courting publicity just then; he was quietly watching the proceedings, and wondering when, if ever, he would have an opportunity to secure those towels. The language of the irate Southerner—for such he evidently was—dissipated all my preconceived notions regarding his profession, and led me to believe that his accustomed vocation was that of a mule-driver.

Generally during the passage we had good weather; but one night in the Caribbean Sea, just after supper, the mate came below and directed that the "bull's eyes" in the staterooms should be closed, as it promised to be a "dirty night." After he left, in order to make assurance double sure, he sent one of the hands down to see that his instructions had been carried out. The man visited every stateroom and saw that all was secure, and so reported.

Along about 10 o'clock, while we were engaged playing cards in the saloon, and the ship was pitching and tossing like a cork in a kettle of boiling fluid, we were astonished by a deluge of water that entered the cabin through one of the stateroom doors, followed by an ear-piercing shriek that showed somebody was in trouble, and caused a general rush to the scene of the disaster, where we found poor Worthington in a deplorable condition and almost frightened out of his seven senses.

The day had been a warm one, and the heat in the staterooms so oppressive that most of them had been vacated by their occupants, who slept either on the settees in the cabin, or on the deck.

Worthington had, as it seemed, fallen asleep, so when the order was passed to close the ventilators, he had failed to hear it, and when subsequently the sailor had closed the "bull's eye," he did so without disturbing the sleeper, who when he awoke and found the ventilator shut, at once proceeded to open it in utter ignorance of the mate's warning.

As he found it impossible to rest comfortable in his berth, he withdrew the mattress therefrom, and placed it on the floor immediately beneath the open "bull's eye," when jaded, and worn out with retching, exhausted by his long fast, and entirely unconscious of the impending cataract, he laid him down, and sleep diffused its balmy arms over his weary limbs.

He was not destined, however, to enjoy an extended nap. Old Ocean was "laying for him," with an eye on the open porthole. The opportunity soon came, and as the Atlantic met the weather-roll of the steamer, it discharged a column of the "briny" through the six-inch ventilator that tore through the stateroom with the force of a catapult, and swept everything before it.

It is superfluous to state that we found W[orthington] wide awake when we reached his room. He was indeed very wide awake, and also very wet. Old Ocean had got in her work and it was plainly obvious that as an eye-opener and sleep-disturber the douche had proved a complete success.

The first thing in order was to close the "bull's eye," and having done that, we turned our attention to our frightened comrade. He had sustained no injury, however, and it is my belief that the fright cured his sea-sickness, as he made his appearance at the table next morning, and continued to take his meals regularly till we reached Chagres two days afterwards.

As we neared Chagres, the question of transportation across the Isthmus became the subject of discussion among the passengers. John Conness, who subsequently represented California in the United States Senate,[5] was a conspicuous character at the meetings and took a prominent part in the proceedings. Chagres was held to be a sort of death-trap, and the universal desire to avoid detention there, governed cabin and steerage passengers alike. Committees were appointed to act in the interest of all in securing "bungos" and arranging generally for the transit to Panama. In this way it was thought that competition would be avoided, and as a result, transportation charges would be reduced to a minimum.[6]

Jim, however, took exception to the manner of proceeding, and calling our little coterie aside, he advised us to go slow in the matter of delegating authority to any committee, as he considered that so far as our own interest was concerned, it was safer in our own hands than it would be in any other's, and that we were perfectly competent to look after our own affairs without the intervention of a committee. As we had the greatest respect for Jim's opinion, and were ready to defer to it in all important matters, we listened eagerly as he proceeded to explain as follows:

"Now, boys, speaking for myself, I can speak positively, and as for you, I am morally certain that none of you have any more in your pockets than the law allows you to carry; therefore, the main consideration with all of us should be to make our finances hold out long enough to enable us to reach our destination. To be sure, Chagres may not be a desirable place of residence for any considerable length of time; nevertheless, people do live there, and have lived there for years, and I can see no imperative reason why we should be in such a hurry to get away after we get there. We can stand the climate for a few days, at least, and I for one do not propose to pay an exorbitant price for transportation to Panama. This plan which we have seen adopted at the meeting may be all right in theory, but in my opinion it won't work, for just so soon as the four hundred passengers are landed, each will be distrustful of the others, and proceed to look out for himself. The natives will be sure to take advantage of the situation, and make prices accordingly.

"Under such circumstances, it would be folly for us to enter into competition with the crowd, and submit to the excessive demands of the boatmen. Moreover, so far as I can see, there is nothing to be gained by undue haste. The captain says we are likely to reach Chagres before morning, and we must decide what course to pursue now. My advice is to cut loose from the crowd on our arrival, and let it go ahead. Meanwhile, we will abide in our tent at Chagres for a few days, and await developments. Tomorrow there will be a grand rush, and you will see a dozen passengers after one boatman. A few days hence the rush will be over, and you will see a dozen boatmen after one passenger. Then we can make our own terms, and as there are but five of us, we shall be more comfortable in every respect, than we would be in a crowded boat."

The Oracle had spoken, so there was nothing for us but to accept the decree. Therefore we decided to pitch the tent and tarry in Chagres for a while.

The next morning [March 24] when I awoke, as I no longer felt the throbbing of the engines, I came to the conclusion that the ship was at anchor, and going on deck found that my surmise was correct. We were lying about two miles from shore, and the view from the vessel's deck was an attractive one. I do not recollect ever to have been impressed with higher admiration for a landscape than I was by the coast scene which greeted me that morning. The wildness and sublimity of the mountains, clothed from base to summit with tropical verdure, with its rich and varied colors; the luxuriance of the vegetation, which was not repelled by the salt air, but actually overhung the breakers, seemed more like a picture of fairy-land than a reality. No fancy sketch could surpass this scene as I gazed upon it from the deck of the *Crescent City,* and the magnificent picture still lingers in my memory.[7]

All was bustle and confusion on board that morning, while the passengers were getting their traps together preparatory to a landing. A small steamboat came alongside soon after breakfast, and about one-half of the people were transferred to her deck and safely landed.[8] By noon all the passengers had left the ship with the exception of our party, who had elected to remain on board till the rush was over, and it was not till the little steamer came back the third time, after some freight for the Panama R. R. Co., that we placed our belongings on board and went ashore.

VI

ON THE ISTHMUS OF PANAMA

MARCH–MAY, 1849

On reaching terra firma, we were astonished to learn that every passenger by the *Crescent City* had gone, bag and baggage. Not a single soul was left. They had disappeared as if by magic, and of all the busy throng that so lately peopled the steamer's deck, we were the sole representatives.

Opposite the village on the left bank of the river is a pretty flat several acres in area, and free from shrubbery, and it was there that we decided to pitch the tent and await events. This was quickly done, and within an hour our temporary quarters were ready for occupancy.

Having completed our camping arrangements, we got out pens and ink and proceeded to advise the folks at home of our safe arrival, intending to hand the letters to the captain when he came ashore to clear his vessel. It was hot as blazes in the tent, which afforded but slight protection from the rays of a vertical sun; moreover, the rank odor of the adjacent forest, was highly suggestive of yellow fever.[1] Nevertheless we took matters easy, and found much to interest us in our novel experience.

The most objectionable feature about an extended stay in Chagres was the quality of the water. Of this we had been advised; consequently we had arranged to qualify it, whenever we had occasion to quench our thirst, by the addition of a modicum of brandy, which we were told would neutralize the ill-effects produced by the natural element.

Having finished our correspondence [on Sunday, March 25], we were sitting like Aram in the door of our tent, smoking and chatting, when Captain Stoddard, who had just come from the Custom House caught sight of us, and turned out of his way to accost us.

Capt. S. "Boys, what the devil are you doing here? Do you propose to take up a ranch at the mouth of the Chagres River?"

Jim. "No; we don't propose to do that, but we do intend to remain here till some of the boats return, when we hope to get transportation at a more reason[able] rate than those fellows paid who went off this morning. We are told that some of them paid as high as thirty dollars for a passage to Gorgona."

Capt. S. "Well, if you take care of yourselves, I don't think that there is any great risk in stopping for a few days, and aside from that, there is no occasion for haste. I was told at the Custom House that neither the *Oregon* nor *California* has returned from San Francisco, and as the *Panama* has not yet reported on her way up, all their passengers are "hung up" in Panama, together with many others who have come by sailing vessels, expecting to catch those steamers. The collector says there are at least three thousand people in Panama, and the prospect of an early departure is by no means encouraging.[2] What have you got in that bottle?"

33

Jim. "Brandy—Have a drink? We can't give you any ice."

Capt. S. Pouring out a tooth full—"Well, boys, here's luck—By the bye, I'm going off in a shore boat, and as you are likely to have a long siege of it in Panama, one of you had better go off with me and get a barrel of bread."

Taking our letters, and saying "Goodbye," the captain left us, accompanied by Jim, who returned in about an hour with the barrel of bread, and a big pineapple cheese.

The cheese was something we had not expected, and we naturally asked how it came to be added. He explained that, going on board, the steward was ordered to pass a barrel of bread into the boat alongside. This was soon done, and as he still lingered, the captain asked him what he was waiting for; stating that the anchor was under foot, and the ship ready to start. "I know it," said Jim; "but the fact is, Captain Stoddard, you have given us a whole barrel of bread, and we haven't a d—m bit of cheese." "Well," said Capt. S., laughing at the young man's assurance, "we are pretty short of cheese, but I reckon we can spare one.—Steward, pass a pineapple cheese into that boat—Goodbye, Jim. Take care of yourself, and don't stay too long in Chagres—Get over on the Pacific side as soon as possible." With this parting suggestion, the captain turned away, and Jim followed the bread and cheese into the boat.[3]

We remained several days in Chagres, during which time we visited the village on the opposite side of the river, but found little there to interest us. There were forty or fifty houses, or rather huts of primitive construction, thatched with palm leaves. The men were away on the river, and with few exceptions only women and children remained at home. The women of Chagres cannot be charged with extravagance in the way of dress; their only garment being a cotton chemise, but low in the neck and falling to the knees. As for the children, they wore no clothing, and ran about naked. One peculiarity we noticed was the extraordinary abdominal development exhibited by the young ones. Little fellows of eight or ten years sported "corporations" of such huge proportions that they reminded us of Shakespeare's Justice, "with his fair round belly." This tendency to obesity may be accounted for by the fact that their diet is almost exclusively vegetable, and the gases generated thusly are the cause of the abnormal distention.

While in Chagres, Richmond and I took our guns one morning and started out in pursuit of game. His was a small rifle, mine a fowling piece. The woods were full of birds of gorgeous plumage, and we had not gone far ere R[ichmond] blazed away and brought down a small parrot. Several native boys had followed us, and their amazement at the result of R[ichmond]'s shot was comical—they had no idea of firearms, and were unable to account for the hole in the bird's head. They had heard the report of the gun, had seen the parrot fall, and assured themselves of its death, but what had caused it was a mystery. They peered into the muzzle of the gun, and failing to discover anything, became frightened and started for home incontinently.

In the course of our explorations we came across what I supposed was a young alligator, and at once proceeded to fill him with No. 4 shot, when he ceased his efforts to escape, stretched himself out, and gave up the ghost. The reptile was about fifteen inches long and weighed perhaps two pounds. As we were curious to know what it was, we decided to carry it to camp and throw it to the natives. Neither of us liked to handle it, so we attached a slip, cut from a climbing vine nearby, to its tail, and dragged it after us. We learned on our return that the reptile was an iguana, a species of gigantic lizard, highly valued by the natives as an article of food, and ours furnished half a dozen of them with a supper that night.

We left Chagres on the fourth day after our arrival [March 27?], as by that time quite a fleet of bungos had returned from above, and we had no difficulty in arranging for a passage on reasonable terms.[4] We chose a large canoe, manned by two stalwart Negroes, who agreed to carry us, with our traps, to Gorgona for forty dollars. Thus, by waiting a few days, we not only saved some twelve dollars each on transportation, but secured far better accommodations than would have been the case had we gone with the throng. After we had placed our baggage on board, the boatmen showed no disposition to hurry matters, and in response to our repeated solicitations to put out, the only reply was "poco tiempo, poco tiempo," which being interpreted means "a little while," and with which we were compelled to rest satisfied. It was several hours afterward that our "gondoliers" made their appearance and shoved off.

Our passage up the river was uneventful. The boat was provided with an awning of palm leaves, which shielded us in a measure from the sun's rays. Nevertheless, the heat was oppressive, and we were glad when night came, even if it did bring with it an unhealthy fog, which settled on the river, and enveloped us like a wet blanket.

Our first stopping place was Gatun,[5] where we had a chance to go ashore and stretch our limbs, which after a confinement of hours beneath the boat's awning was a great relief. It was midnight when we reached Gatun, where we secured quarters in an ancient hut near the river bank. Dry bullocks' hides stretched on poles formed our beds, which under the circumstances answered the purpose as well as a more luxurious couch would have done, for the surroundings were not at all conducive to sleep. Fleas innumerable were waiting for us, and as soon as we lay down, they began to get in their work with a unanimity that showed they were there for business. Moreover, the heat was intolerable, and the hut exhaled odors that have little semblance to either frankincense or myrrh. All these causes combined drove slumber from our eyelids, and not only that, but drove us from the house altogether, and we fled to the boat, where we passed the remainder of the most uncomfortable night we had ever experienced.

Morning [of March 28?] came at last, not so the Negroes; one of whom we had named "Palinurus," and the other who by his tendency to delay, and his eternal "poco tiempo," had so severely tried our patience at the start, we had christened "Procrastination." Presently, however, Palinurus "showed up" and intimated that Procrastination was not far behind, and when shortly afterwards he did come, we hustled on board and proceeded on our way.

A dense fog hung over the river and hid everything from view. This was soon dispelled by the rising sun, and within an hour from the time of starting the mist had entirely disappeared. For most of the way from Chagres to Gorgona, the river is bordered on both sides by an impenetrable swamp, and the malarious exhalations therefrom, fruitful of calentures and other kindred disorders, are to those unacclimated, dangerous in the extreme. Hence our desire to push forward and reach our destination as soon as possible.

The sun was hot, and the Negroes stripped of their clothing, toiled unremittingly at the oars. From time to time, as we came to a "ripple," they would jump overboard and pull the canoe as far as the shoal water extended, when they would resume their oars. Their black hides glistened with perspiration, yet the heat, which was so oppressive to us, did not seem to affect them. They were jovial and good-natured, and sang and shouted as they bent to their work. They were overjoyed when we, ignorant of its meaning, echoed their favorite expletive, "carrajo." I knew nothing of the Spanish language at that period; nevertheless, an expression that frequently occurred in one of their songs, "Yo que soy contrabandisti" is still remembered.

At noon we came to a bend in the river which was several miles around, but only a quarter of a mile across. Here our boatmen gave us to understand that we might cross over and meet them on the opposite side. As any change from our recumbent position beneath the awning was a relief, we gladly embraced the suggestion to walk, and jumping ashore, followed the trail which the Negroes pointed out. We soon struck the river again, but more than an hour elapsed 'ere the bungo made its appearance, and as the insects annoyed us terribly while waiting, we were content to take shelter under the thatch of palm leaves once more.

The country now began to assume a different aspect. The ground was higher and no longer swampy, and the indications were that we would soon reach the end of our journey. The signs of occupancy in the shape of houses and cattle showed that we were approaching a habitable locality. Just as the sun went down, the boatmen shouted, "Gorgona! Gorgona!" and the first stage of our passage across the Isthmus came to an end.[6]

We pitched the tent at the outskirts of the village, near the bank of the river, kindled a fire and prepared supper, which consisted of coffee, bread, and fried fish, the latter of which we purchased of a native peddler. After supper we had a smoke, and as we had slept but little the night before, we retired early and slept like tops.

The sun was high in the horizon when we awoke next morning [March 29?], much refreshed by our long sleep, and immediately after breakfast we proceeded to arrange for the trip to Panama. Accordingly we sought the office of the Alcalde, and through him arranged for the carriage of our goods and chattels. That official was a very accommodating gentleman, and readily acceded to our request that he would act for us in procuring transportation. Each of us had a trunk, clothes bag, and roll of blankets, and in addition to these were the tent, kit of cooking utensils, and the barrel of bread with the cheese given us by Captain Stoddard. A woman took charge of the bread and cheese, and carried them over the rough road to Panama for the insignificant consideration of two dollars.

We remained all day in Gorgona, recruiting our strength for the pedestrian trip on the morrow, which as we afterwards realized was a fatiguing one. After supper that evening, we all went for a swim in the river. The water was about four feet deep, with a fine, sandy bottom, which afforded an excellent opportunity for a good bath, which we were not slow to take advantage of.

It was dark when we undressed on the river bank, and I carelessly placed the belt which held my money in my hat; and throwing my shirt over it, plunged into the water. The bath was a delightful one, and I do not remember that I ever enjoyed a more agreeable sensation than that experienced as I entered the water that night. An hour passed ere we sought the bank and resumed our clothing. I had given no thought to my money belt while bathing, and it was not till after I was dressed that it occurred to me that I had forgotten to replace it on my person. Thinking it an oversight that was easily remedied, I stooped down to raise the belt from my hat, and received a mental shock such as I hope I may never again experience. The belt was gone! Too late I realized how thoughtless I had been, and was ready to exclaim like the Ass in the fable, "O, me miserum, O me stolidum." Hoping against hope, I immediately instituted a search for the missing treasure, but the quest was fruitless.

Here was a pretty kettle of fish. Aside from the $75 in dimes which I had purchased in New York for my expenses on the Isthmus, every dollar I had in the world was in the lost belt. Here I was, midway between the two oceans, practically penniless, virtually between the "devil and the deep sea"—"Dextrum Scylla latus, laevum implacata Charybdis obsidet." What was I to do? I could neither go ahead nor go back. All these thoughts crowded on my mind, and nearly drove me wild. I was ready to kick myself for my stupidity. The thought that I, a civilized American citizen, twenty-one years old and a free man, should be such an infernal fool, and so lost to all sense of prudence, as to leave that money lying around loose in the dark, while in utter forgetfulness of the risk of losing it I disported in the waters of the adjacent stream, was almost beyond endurance.

As yet I had said nothing of my loss, and by the time my search was ended, all hands had taken their departure. Going to my tent, I threw myself on my blankets in a state of mental, physical, and financial collapse. I tried to think the matter out and devise some plan of action, but my thoughts traveled in a circle, and invariably returned to the starting point.

As I lay thus meditating, the flap of the tent was pushed aside, and Jim [Merrihew] entered and threw down my money belt, at the sight of which the reaction in my mind was so great that it made me actually speechless. "There," said he, "your money is all right, and though you have been badly frightened, I think the lesson will do you good, and teach you to take care of it hereafter. I saw you place it in your hat, and also noticed that others saw you who might not be so honest as I am, so I took charge of it, and resolved to let you sweat for a while, before returning it. A half-hour, however, is an eternity under such circumstances, and though you said nothing, I could imagine the state of your feelings, and had not the heart to retain possession till morning, as I originally intended."

While Jim was speaking, I had in a measure recovered my wits, and realizing that the money was safe, hesitated whether to curse him for taking it, or thank him for returning it. My judgment told me that I had been guilty of gross carelessness, and that the lesson was a needed one; for had another captured the belt, it would have perhaps been lost beyond redemption; but as it was, however, I had sustained no loss, and aside from the fright, there was nothing to complain of. So I thanked him for looking after me, and promised that thenceforward I would never lose control of the belt so long as there was a sovereign in it. "And I never did."

The next morning [March 30?] the carriers took charge of our baggage, and we were early en route for Panama, following the same trail that Balboa traveled 350 years before.[7] The road was a rough one, and the traveling fatiguing. We suffered greatly from thirst, as, trusting to find plenty of water on the way, we did not take the precaution to carry any with us. Nevertheless, we managed to pull through, and at the end of the day's journey, found accommodations at the "half way house," in a tent which an enterprising Yankee had erected with a view to supplying passing travelers with food and lodging.[8]

The landlord had provided himself with a sheet-iron stove, in which he managed to bake passable biscuit, which, together with pork and beans and a cup of coffee, afforded an acceptable meal. Conscious that the most difficult part of our journey was over, we stretched ourselves on the floor of the tent with a degree of satisfaction that soon induced a sound and refreshing sleep.

We had passed our carriers the first day, so, when we started next morning [March 31?], we were under the impression that they were still behind, and walked leisurely, sitting down from time to time for a visit, hoping that they might overtake us, but somehow they failed to connect. Whether they took a different route or passed us in the night, we were unable to ascertain, but as it soon became evident that we had missed them, we proceeded on our way, trusting that they would report in Panama.

It was about noon when we first caught sight of the Pacific Ocean, and within a few hours we reached the paved road, said to have been constructed by Cortez,[9] which led us directly to Panama, where we arrived early in the morning, and decided to put up at the "American Hotel" till such time as we should find our baggage.[10] How to proceed in the premises was difficult to determine, as we were uncertain whether the carriers had preceded us or were behind on the road. The consensus of opinion inclined to the belief that the Negroes had come, and gone back again, so we decided to watch for their return.

Panama is, or rather once was, a walled city and all comers from Gorgona necessarily passed through the same gate when they entered the town.[11] Near the gates were two stone benches, so located as to command a view of all who came and went, and it was arranged that one or more of us should occupy one of the benches and keep an eye on the traveling public. Accordingly, at any time between daylight and dark, for several days, at least one of our crowd might be found seated at the gates, earnestly scrutinizing all comers and goers.

Meanwhile we remained at the hotel, which did a rushing business during the blockade at Panama, where before we got away, six thousand Argonauts were hung up, waiting for transportation to San Francisco.[12] The hotel was scantily furnished, and without either tables or carpets. Small cots, with canvas sacking, and without mattresses, served for sleeping, and the meals were carried to the guests, wherever they might be sitting about the premises. These meals consisted of light food, and were composed chiefly of canned meats and vegetables. The charge for subsistence was two dollars per day, which under the circumstances was very reasonable, yet it afforded a large profit to the enterprising proprietors.

On the evening of the fifth day [April 5?], Jim [Merrihew], who was on watch at the gates, recognized the head man of our carriers, just as he was about to leave the city, and nailed him incontinently. The recognition was mutual, and the carrier seemed as pleased to see us as we were to see him. He had made one trip since bringing our traps across, and was just about to return a second time when Jim recognized him. Having found our man, we at once proceeded to interrogate him as to the whereabouts of our lares and penates— Motioning for us to follow, he started off, and we "tailed on," determined not to lose sight of him a second time. Our guide led us to a vacant building not far away, where, in a large room on the ground floor, was piled indiscriminately a mass of merchandise of every description—trunks, clothes bags, boxes, bales, and all the varied insignia of a gold-seeker's outfit. There were at least two hundred large trunks in the room, whose owners were probably as anxious to recover them as we had been to find ours. The carriers had failed to meet them, and had deposited their loads in this place, which it seems was the common dumping ground for unclaimed baggage. How much of this was claimed eventually it would be hard to say, but it is fair to presume that a large proportion went to somebody as "treasure trove."

We had no difficulty in selecting our property from the mass, and it was soon transferred to a room we had rented in a large building outside the walls. We were, of course, jubilant over the recovery of our baggage, especially myself, as the bag of dimes was in my trunk, and I relied on them for current expenses.

After we had established ourselves in our new quarters, there was nothing for us to do except eat and sleep and figure on the chances of getting away from Panama. None of us had bought tickets further than Chagres, so we were free to embrace any opportunity that might occur. The steamer *Oregon* and *California* were tied up in San Francisco, their crews having deserted and gone to the mines, hence there was no telling when they might return. The *Panama,* though overdue, had not arrived, and grave doubts were entertained regarding her safety. With the exception of the old *Humboldt,* an English ship which lay at anchor in the bay, laden with coal for the Panama S. S. Co., there were no vessels in sight, and aside from the overdue steamship, none was expected.[13]

The crowd at Panama was daily augmented by the arrival of passengers from the Atlantic side, and the question "how to get away?" became a very serious one. One singular fact was that among the multitude of adventurers, there were no women. During the six weeks passed in Panama, I do not remember seeing one American woman.[14]

The detention at Panama at last became so irksome that it was decided to send down the coast and try to charter vessels at Callao and other southern ports, where whale ships were accustomed to put in for supplies.[15] A large metallic lifeboat was purchased from some vessel in Chagres, and taken to Gorgona, and from there transferred on men's shoulders to Panama. This boat was provisioned and manned, and dispatched southward in charge of one Captain Barry. Several large bungos were fixed up for the ocean voyage to California. These boats were merely canoes, dug out of the mahogany tree, and though some forty feet long and good enough for smooth sailing, were utterly unfit to encounter the rough seas of the Pacific. Nevertheless, there were among the crowd a few men who were willing to assume the risk, and venture their lives in the endeavor to reach the common goal. The sides of the bungos were raised by attaching stanchions, to which, in the absence of better material, raw hide was nailed, and such other devices resorted to, to make them sea-worthy, as the nature of the case suggested. At least three of these frail pirogues took their departure for San Francisco, but none reached their destination. One returned, after a few days, to Panama. Another was run ashore a few degrees to the northward, and those of his crew who survived experienced many hardships while trying to make their way on foot along the coast. A third was never heard of from the time she left Panama.[16]

It was during the Easter festivals that we were in Panama. Early every morning we were awakened by the chimes? of the cathedral bells, which fell on our ears with a dolorous sound. These bells were rung by a half-dozen young natives in each belfry, who used hammers in place of the missing tongues, and at times the discord was horrible, as may be imagined, since there were at least twenty of these cathedrals in and outside the city, each of which had its quota of bells, and not a sound one in the lot.[17] At a distance the steeples of these churches have the appearance of being covered with tiles of burnished silver as they glisten in the sun's rays. In order to gratify my curiosity respecting the material covering the steeple, I one day climbed to the roof and made a personal inspection, and ascertained that the tiling was composed of large pearl shells, and as all were loose and many of them had disappeared altogether, I felt no compunction in detaching one, which I carried away as a memento.

The Easter festivities continued for several days, during which time numerous processions thronged the streets, preceded by an image of the Virgin Mary or some other emblem of the Catholic faith. The whole wound up with the hanging of Judas Iscariot. A figure representing Judas, filled with firecrackers and other explosives, was suspended from a gibbet in the plaza, when after certain ceremonies the torch was applied and Judas was disposed of secundum artem to the great amusement of the multitude.[18]

During our sojourn in Panama, each of us in turn officiated as cook. Our breakfast usually consisted of fried fresh pork and fried plantains, which with fresh rolls and coffee furnished an acceptable meal. Fresh fish were also plentiful in the market. The barrel of bread which Captain Stoddard had given us was soon exhausted, and one day when it fell to me to do the cooking, it occurred to me that the crumbs left in the barrel would, if properly treated, furnish the material for an excellent pudding. As my stock of culinary information was at that time exceedingly limited, I had but a vague idea of what, aside from the crumbs, went to make up the constituents of a bread pudding. My judgment told me that the first move was to soak the crumbs, but what came next was a puzzle. It is astonishing what a helpless individual the average man is when it comes to preparing his own meals. During his whole life he has been accustomed to passing through the kitchen at home, but has never given a thought to the preparation of his food, and when the time comes that he is compelled to fall back on his own resources, he wonders why he did not take more notice of what was going on in the kitchen.

Had there been a public library in Panama in those days, it is highly probable that the cook book would have been in greatest demand, for unfortunately none had thought to provide such an indispensable adjunct to housekeeping. Among all that vast crowd of Argonauts, I do not believe a single cook book could have been found.

In the absence of any reliable information, I proceeded to concoct a pudding after my own ideas, and as eggs seemed necessary to give the mess stability, I started out to procure a half-dozen. Now, it may seem to the reader a very simple matter to purchase a half-dozen eggs, but I can assure him from my own experience that there is no simplicity about it, under such circumstances as prevailed when I went on my little shopping excursion that morning. My Spanish vocabulary was limited to a few words I had picked up in my intercourse with the natives, such as "carne," "pan," "piscao" [pescado], "cacao" and a few other nouns in common use,[19] but what the deuce "egg" was in Spanish was a sticker. When two individuals are unable to understand one another, the sign language is often successfully resorted to to explain their meaning, but so far as "eggs" were concerned I could think of no equivalent sign, so that when I reached the market place I was at a loss how to conduct the negotiations. The ancient dame with whom I usually did my trading was wholly unable to "catch on," and to my repeated attempts to make her understand, her sole response was "quien sabe?"

"Cock a doodle do," I shouted in desperation. Her eyes brightened, and saying "poco tiempo" she disappeared and presently returned with a game cock in her hands. This looked encouraging but was still far from satisfactory, so, changing the sex I cried, "Cut, cut ca darket." Again her eyes gleamed with intelligence; she exchanged the rooster, and in lieu thereof brought me a hen. Once more I shook my head negatively and the woman threw up her hands in despair. She was fertile in expedients, however, and meandered off a third time and returned with a pictorial primer. Eureka! A woman's wit had solved the problem. Opposite the letter "H" was the picture of an egg—"hueva" was the word, pronounced "wava." This was the "open sesame" to the egg basket, and my want was soon supplied, and another Spanish noun added to my vocabulary, never to be forgotten. I have taught it to my children, and should any of them ever be caught hungry in a Spanish community, they at least know enough of the language to call for eggs.

The pudding proved a success, and was about the only successful effort in the way of cooking that I accomplished while on the Isthmus.

Day after day passed, and though the accessions to the population of the overcrowded city were numerous, the departures were nil. Every day we visited the mole and cast longing glances seaward, but no vessel came. We watched the *Humboldt* as she lay at anchor near the coaling station at Tobago,[20] and were tempted to board her and take possession vi et armis. We respected the taboo however, and when afterwards we sailed out of the harbor we passed her still lying in her old berth. The *Humboldt* was subsequently chartered for San Francisco and had a gay old time in making her way up the coast, but after contending with adverse winds for nearly five months, finally reached San Diego, where her passengers, disgusted with a life on the ocean wave, abandoned the ship and made their way to their destination as best they could.[21]

As the weeks went by, the dimes in the shot bag gradually disappeared, until the sum in hand became so small that I feared I should be compelled to draw on the gold reserve in my belt to provide for current expenses, but ere that time came, matters took a different turn, as will presently appear.

One night, after we had retired to our hammocks, the boom of a cannon aroused us from sleep, when we at once turned out and, hastily dressing, started for the "mole." The streets were thronged with an excited multitude, all wondering what was about to happen. All had heard the report of the gun, but none knew what it imported. Speculation was rife—rumor with her hundred tongues found use for all of them. Some were convinced that the gun was that of a man-of-war sent by the Government to our relief. Others, that the *California* had returned from San Francisco.

The "mole" was alive with an expectant crowd, but what it was they expected none could say definitely. Those who had tickets for the *California* hoped that they had now become available. It was the same with others who were ticketed by the *Oregon*. As for the *Panama*, all expectation of her arrival had vanished, and tickets on her were held at a heavy discount, and comparatively unsalable.

In this condition of incertitude we remained till the splash of oars told us that a boat was approaching. Presently it made its appearance, and to the anxious inquiry "What vessel is it?" the response was "the steamer *Panama*." Then those who held tickets by the *Panama* were jubilant, while the others were correspondingly depressed.[22] It reminded one of the game of Keno as described by the inquiring Frenchman.

"Vot is that leetle game?" he asked, "vere all the peoples sit by von long table with leetle cards with feegers on dem, and von man takes the numbers out of a leetle box one at a time, and tells the others vot gay be, and by and bye somebody cries, "Keno," and all the others cry, "Oh h—ll?" It was the passengers by the *Panama* who cried "Keno" that night, and tickets by that vessel commanded fabulous prices. One Captain [Charles] Butler sold his ticket for $1,100 and afterwards took passage on the same vessel with us.

The *Panama* coaled and took her departure in due time, and we who watched her disappearance were left lamenting.[23] No tidings came from the boat dispatched weeks before for Callao, and as time passed a feeling of despondency crept over us, and the condition of suspense became almost insupportable. Many of those who had been long waiting, had dependent families, and the thought that expenses were running up at home, while they were spending money that had perhaps been borrowed on the security of their homesteads to support them in their compulsory idleness, was extremely depressing. Some who had not counted on the long delay had started with just sufficient means to pay their passage, and were compelled to use the money for expenses while detained in Panama.

One man, a Captain [George H.T.?] Cole, a good-natured, happy-go-lucky fellow, who reminded me of "Mark Tapley," came out strong under the adverse circumstances.[24] Meeting him one morning, he said to me, "I tell you what, if this state of affairs continues much longer I shall be cleaned out entirely; I hated to do it, but was compelled to make a draft on my wife yesterday for $60." "Will she pay it?" I asked. "Pay it! Why, man, she would sell the very shoes off her feet rather than have me come back again."

Day after day passed, and the condition remained unchanged. We watched the pelicans as they went out to sea in the morning, and saw them as they returned with full crops at evening. We witnessed the daily contest between the butcher and the buzzards for the possession of the hides, which the man was compelled to stake down to prevent the birds from carrying them off bodily. The question was seriously debated whether the buzzards could in case of emergency be utilized in the commissariat, and by some hitherto-hidden process be rendered palatable in the shape of a fricassee, when one morning [April 23] the news that there was a "ship in the bay" sent us all pell-mell to the "mole." Sure enough, there were the white sails of a vessel distinctly outlined against the horizon. There was very little wind, but the flood tide swept her slowly towards us, and enabled us to see by her rig that it was a ship, but where from or what she had come for was still a mystery.

Finally she reached her anchorage, the sails were clewed up and furled, and the Stars and Stripes flying at her spanker gaff showed that she was an American vessel. Presently a boat was lowered, and as it approached was hailed from the shore.

"What ship is that?"

"The *Sylph* of Fair Haven."

"Where are you from?"

"Last from Callao, where we were chartered for passengers from Panama to San Francisco."

"Oh," said Jim, as he recognized a townsman in the man who answered the hail. "Whatever happens, we are all right, boys, so you make up your minds to take passage on the *Sylph*."

The ship had been chartered by an enterprising Englishman, named Green. She was a new vessel, on her first voyage after spermaceti whales, and her cruising ground was in the low latitudes of the Pacific Ocean. She had not met with good success, so on her arrival at Callao, where she put in for supplies, her captain decided to abandon the voyage and accept the Englishman's offer to charter the vessel as stated. What little oil there was on board was shipped home, the try works were thrown overboard, and the vessel made ready for the passenger service. The false deck was torn up and everything put in a ship-shape condition. Being a new vessel, the *Sylph* was admirably suited for carrying passengers. The most objectionable feature about her was she was too low between decks, the height being only five feet. She registered 300 tons, and in an hour after the sale of tickets began, every berth was taken. The price of passage was fixed at $300, which under the circumstances was not excessive. So great was the demand for berths that in order to accommodate as many as possible, a house was built on deck in which some twenty passengers found quarters.[25]

There were when we sailed, including the crew, 328 souls on board, which for a vessel of 300 tons was an excessive number, and as the law allows but two passengers for every five tons, it will be seen that the ship was greatly overcrowded, as her legal quota was but 130.[26]

Owing to a misunderstanding regarding the time when the tickets were to be sold, I failed to put in an appearance in season, and as a result "got left" in the general scramble that ensued. Had the price of passage been fixed at $500, there is no doubt that every berth would have been taken within 24 hours.

I was rather frightened at the idea of being left behind, especially as the other boys had all secured berths, and for a while I was thoroughly demoralized. Jim, however, came to the rescue, as usual, and it was arranged that I should take his ticket, and as he stood in intimate relations with the powers on board, he would chance it without one.

VII

ON BOARD THE *SYLPH*

MAY–JULY, 1849

It was on the afternoon of the 8th[9th] of May that we took our departure from Panama.[1] As every passenger was expected to provide his own bed and table furniture, I had availed myself of the opportunity afforded in Panama of securing such articles as my experience in fitting out seamen for the whale-fishing had taught me were indispensable, and accordingly purchased a pot, pan, knife and fork, and spoon. The tin pot held a quart, and I had reason to congratulate myself on my forethought ere the voyage was ended.

Before leaving the *Crescent City*, I had emptied the straw out of my mattress, and brought the tick with me, but what to fill it with was a case of quien sabe? As there was not a pound of hay or straw to be had for love or money, had the forest trees been deciduous like those of our northern clime, I might have used leaves, but as there were no leaves to be had, I was compelled to leave the leaves out of the question. Sea weed would have made a good substitute for straw, but I searched the shore in vain, and had about concluded to accept the situation and content myself with the soft side of a plank, when one day, in passing a carpenter's shop, my eyes fell on a pile of shavings, and it occurred to me that they might be utilized to fill my bed sack, so I arranged with the owner to let me have them for a small consideration. In filling the sack, however, I grasped the shavings indiscriminately and the result was that numerous small blocks were introduced, which afterwards caused me no little discomfort. During the passage, these wooden cubes made themselves painfully manifest, though I eventually succeeded in collecting about a peck of them in one corner of the mattress, where they no longer disturbed me.

On the [third] morning following our departure, a meeting of the passengers was called for the purpose of systematizing matters in regard to eating arrangements. There were no tables on board outside the cabin, and every man had to provide for himself in that respect. As for myself, I usually ate my meals from the head of a big water cask which was lashed to the rail.

Of course, everybody was in attendance at the meeting and various suggestions were considered. Finally, however, it was decided to separate the passengers into two messes, to be called the starboard and larboard messes, those whose berths were on the starboard side to form one mess, and those on the port side the other. As there was only room on deck for one mess to eat, the question of precedence was settled by arranging that each mess should be called to meals first on alternate days. One of the passengers, Charles Mac[e]y, was chosen steward, and it became his duty to deal out the grub.[2]

It goes without saying that when the time for meals came, every man was on the qui vive, and when the order to form ranks was given, the response was general. Two long lines were formed, extending from the "galley" aft. The steward passed between the ranks and dealt out the victuals from an immense tin bucket as each passenger held out out his individual receptacle.

It was laughable to see the variety of dishes in the hands of the passengers, most of whom had neglected to provide themselves before going on board with the necessary utensils. Some had sardine boxes, others had coconut shells, while many had nothingbut simple pieces of board with cleats nailed to the edges. Every conceivable expedient was resorted to to supply substitutes for cups and plates.

As a rule had been adopted that no one should receive a second installment, which consisted of a big ladle full of whatever constituted the meal, those who had small vessels that would not hold one-half the allowance had good grounds for complaint when a second supply was refused; consequently Macy's position was not an enviable one during the first week out.

Notwithstanding the fact that the height between decks was but little over five feet, there were two tiers of berths on each side, and in addition to these, four hammocks were slung opposite every berth. Underneath these hammocks the passenger's baggage was stored, and as the space between the baggage and the hammock did not exceed two feet, it left but little room, so that we were compelled to get down on all fours and crawl to and fro whenever we went below.

The *Sylph* did not proceed direct to San Francisco, but ran down the coast [for two weeks] to a small port called Atecamus for the purpose of filling the water casks, of which fortunately there was no lack. The whole ground tier was composed of large cells entirely new, which were originally intended for oil. We remained one day [four days] at Atecamus, when, having secured an ample supply of water we proceeded on our voyage.[3]

As the wind was adverse, the captain decided to stand to the westward, hoping to catch the S.E. trades. A few days after leaving Atecamus, we fell in with a New Bedford whaler, and as she signaled a desire to speak to us, we hove to, when she lowered a boat and her captain came on board. With our skipper he retired to the cabin, where they had a long conference. I have forgotten the name of the vessel, but she was a fine-looking ship with bright sides, and I think considerably larger than the *Sylph*. We learned from the boat's crew that the vessel was a sperm whaler. She had been out many months and had seen but few whales. As a result, the crew had become dissatisfied and demanded a change of programme. They had spoken several vessels bound for San Francisco, and learned of the great gold discovery, and were anxious to go and try their luck in the mines.

When the captain of the whaler heard the condition of affairs in Panama, he immediately decided to abandon his voyage and go there for passengers. This he did, and found no difficulty on his arrival at Panama in securing a full complement at such rates as made the trip extremely profitable. With one exception, this was the only vessel we saw on the passage.[4]

We had not been out long before every man on board had found his place and become in a measure reconciled to his surroundings. The two messes, larboard and starboard, took their meals first in turn, and though the quality of the food was far below what we had been accustomed to, good appetites gave it a relish and we always came up hungry at meal time. The staple articles of diet were salt pork and beef, with bean soup one day in the week, and duff on Sundays. We had no soft bread, and aside from the beans, no vegetables. We received our regular allowance of tea and coffee, such as it was, and managed to keep body and soul together with what food was provided. The bread was not first-class, as it had been on board the ship some eighteen months and was alive with weevils. At first we demurred at eating it, and refrained from doing so, till after we had picked out the weevils, but in time we lost our fastidiousness, and bolted it as it came, weevils and all. In fact, the weevils were about all the fresh meat we had on the passage. As I was never a hearty eater, I generally found my allowance sufficient, but will confess I often yearned after the fleshpots of Egypt. My breakfast usually consisted of a pot of coffee in which I soaked my bread, and if the coffee was hot enough, cooked the weevils, which was preferable to swallowing them alive. Except on bean soup and duff days, I cared but little for dinner. There was a cask of molasses on deck to which all had free access, and with its help I concocted a mess every day which served me for supper. I used to crumble a couple of cakes of bread in my pan at noon, pour on what water it would absorb, and leave it till supper time when it would be well-soaked and soft, and with the addition of molasses, afforded quite a palatable meal.

One day when we had bean soup for dinner, I had just finished eating my allowance and was wishing for more when I saw a fellow turn up his nose and start for the rail with the evident intention of throwing his soup overboard, and caught his arm just as he was about to pour his oblation to Neptune.

"Hold on," I said, "don't throw that away."

"Why not?" he asked, "do you want it?"

"Yes, I do."

"Well, take it," he said, as he poured the contents of his dish into mine.

"What's the matter with the soup?" I asked him between spoonfuls.

"What's the matter; why d—n it are you blind?"

"Not when there is a pan full of good soup about to be wasted."

"Well," said he, "it is a mere matter of taste, I've got used to weevils, but by Christmas, when it comes to eating maggots, you can count me out; I haven't been educated up to that stage yet."

"Eating maggots, what the devil are you talking about?"

"What am I talking about? Don't you see that soup's full of maggots? and you are bolting them as if they were so many shrimps."

"No! I don't see anything of the kind."

"What do you call that?" pointing to the eye of a bean which remained at the bottom of my now-empty pan. "Well, my friend, I'm sorry you have lost your dinner, still you have the consolation of knowing that what was your loss was my gain. Those things are not maggots, they are the "eyes of the bean." The soup today was made of lima beans, one peculiarity of which is that when boiled the eyes come out and float on top. Nevertheless, they do look like maggots, and you were perhaps justified in taking them for such. You'll probably know better next time."

"I rather think I shall, I always was apt to jump to conclusions without due consideration. Don't say anything to the boys about it. I wonder if I'll get it if I strike Mac[e]y for a second installment?"

"You might try it."

"Well, I reckon I will."

With this remark he turned away, and shortly afterwards I saw him in earnest conversation with Mac[e]y, who was pointing to the empty bucket, from which I concluded that the day's allowance of soup was exhausted.

Day after day we continued standing to the westward, close-hauled on the starboard tack—hence our progress was necessarily slow. The first inquiry on coming on deck in the morning was "How does she head?" Panama lies in latitude 8° North and longitude 80° West—San Francisco lies in latitude 38° North and longitude 122° West, hence we had to make 30° latitude and 42° longitude to reach our destination. A straight course would be about northwest by north and a ship sailing within six points of her course, making no allowance for leeway, would gain about 38 miles for every 100 miles sailed, so that with a head wind a vessel must sail about three miles to gain one mile.[5]

As the days grew to weeks, the pessimists on board, who were constantly borrowing trouble, insisted that all hands should be put on an allowance of water and restricted to a pint a day, and in order to conciliate them, the captain consented. A lock was attached to the "scuttle butt" and the pint of water was served to each one of us daily. As we had previously been accustomed to help ourselves whenever we desired, this limitation to a pint a day was felt seriously by many, myself among the number, for though I was a light feeder, I was a great drinker, and the allowance of a pint a day was altogether insufficient for my wants, hence I suffered much inconvenience from thirst. I made no complaint; still I was satisfied that there was water enough on board to last us for months, and frequent conversations with Mr. [Samuel] Allen, the cooper, confirmed that opinion; therefore, though I said nothing, I was in a rebellious mood, and ready to "kick" on slight provocation. As it entailed considerable trouble to lock and unlock the "scuttle butt," whenever any one came for his allowance, it was arranged that the cask should be left open for a while every day and a guard maintained during the interval, after which the butt was locked and remained closed till the next morning.

It happened one Sunday that, having consumed my daily allowance, when I proceeded to make my weekly change of raiment and treat myself to a clean shave, there was no water to shave with, and though we used salt water for our daily ablutions, when it came to shaving, fresh water was an absolute necessity, so I made up my mind to procure some regardless of the arbitrary rule which had been in force about three weeks. Taking my tin cup, I went on deck, and proceeded at once to the water cask, and all unmindful of the guard helped myself to a sufficient quantity for shaving purposes, and walked aft. The guard immediately raised a "hue and cry," and ere I reached the main hatchway, I was surrounded by an excited crowd, to whom I explained matters, when the clamor ceased, and I was permitted to go below.

This quasi-attack was the culminating outrage; it was the last hair on the camel's back, and I determined at once to enter a vigorous protest. Having finished my toilet, I returned to the deck and proceeded without delay to interview the captain, who was standing on the quarterdeck near the wheel. Approaching him, I at once broached the question and asked him by what authority he acted in curtailing my allowance of water? He replied that he had acted at the request of certain passengers, and had not the least idea that his order had caused any inconvenience to anyone on board, and so far as he was concerned personally, a pint of water was sufficient, but that he spoke for himself alone. I said that men were differently constituted, and what might be sufficient for him would be altogether insufficient for another; that as for myself, I had suffered much inconvenience by being restricted to a pint of water daily, and even then would not complain had I not good reason to believe that his action was unwarranted by the facts, and that there was no necessity for putting us on such short allowance.

"You are right," said Captain G[ardner], "there was no necessity for curtailing the water supply, and I would never have given the order if I had thought for a moment that it would cause dissatisfaction. We are now six weeks out, and have 30,000 gallons on hand today, enough in my opinion to last us under any circumstances till we reach San Francisco."

"Then, Captain, since you are convinced that there is no necessity for enforcing the order, it would perhaps be well if you should rescind it at once."

"I will do so," he replied, and, calling the cooper, instructed him to remove the lock from the "scuttle butt" and pipe all hands to quench their thirst.

This ended the matter, and the water cask was no longer taboo. The order was ill-considered in the first place, and was only given at the instigation of a few croakers to whom the captain yielded against his own convictions.[6]

As time passed, the grumblers on board began to display their discontent in various ways. The ship was overcrowded, and the lawyers among us intimated that the vessel would be libeled on her arrival for carrying an excess of passengers. The captain was naturally annoyed at the prospect of a libel suit, as he had been guilty of an infraction of the law through sheer ignorance of its provisions, so sought some way in which he could evade it. As the restriction in number applied solely to passengers, and had no application to the crew, it was suggested that he might find among the former a sufficient number willing to sign shipping articles, and consent to class with the crew, in order to reduce the passenger list to its legal quota. This suggestion was adopted. Shipping articles were prepared for signature in the cabin, and within a few days enough had signed to relieve the captain of all apprehensions regarding a libel suit.[7]

Never before in the history of our commercial marine was there such a conglomeration of trades, professions, and pursuits of every description—except sailors—as was included in the list of names appended to the shipping articles on board the *Sylph*. There were ministers, doctors, lawyers, farmers, merchants, and mechanics, not a blessed one of whom would have ventured aloft as far as the maintop in any emergency, yet they legally belonged to the crew, and were as legally subject to the orders of the ship's officers as the old hands in the forecastle, since they had each agreed in consideration of the sum of one dollar, to perform a sailor's duty till the vessel arrived in San Francisco. Nevertheless, had an officer ordered any of them to do anything, there would have been music by the entire band. Think of a common sailor going to windward of the skipper on his own quarter-deck and addressing him familiarly as "Cap," apparently oblivious of the social void existing between the monarch of the quarterdeck and the helot of the forecastle.

It was evident that each and every one of the "new crew," as they were derisively called by the kickers, had signed the shipping articles with a mental reservation, hence their action in so doing entailed no sacrifice of self-respect, and they considered their social status unchanged. It was an anomaly, but it was a fact, nevertheless, and is perhaps the only case of the kind on record.

That life on shipboard after a few weeks becomes monotonous is the experience of every one who has taken a long ocean voyage, and it is especially so with those who have nothing to do, hence any changes from the usual routine is a relief.

One morning, while we were all watching a school of porpoises that were playing about the vessel, turning somersaults and sometimes breeching their whole length out of the water, Captain [Charles] Butler, who was an old whaleman, remarked that porpoise stew properly cooked was "mighty good eating." Now anything in the line of "good eating" possessed an interest that under the circumstances was not at all surprising, as everyone was longing for a change in the matter of diet, hence Capt B[utler]'s remark caused quite a sensation, and it was the universal opinion that a porpoise stew was the very thing needed to tone up our systems, and strengthen the relaxed fibres; moreover our bellies yearned for something in the way of fresh meat in lieu of weevils. Therefore, when the suggestion was made to forego our regular dinner, it was adopted unanimously

Accordingly Mr. [Thomas] Hussey, the [chief] mate, armed with a "grain" took his station on the martingale and watched his opportunity to capture a porpoise. As there were plenty just under the ship's "fore foot" it was not long ere he was fast to a whopping big fish, when we all "tailed on" to the warp and the porpoise was soon floundering on the deck. It was an enormous fish, some six or seven feet long, and had to me at least, an oily look that was suggestive of whale blubber; nevertheless, I entertained strong hopes that it might be properly cooked and furnish some "mighty good eating."

Under the supervision of Captain Butler, the cook proceeded to cut up the porpoise and prepare the stew. Meanwhile an expectant crowd looked on with watering mouths, and from time to time walked to leeward of the galley and regaled themselves with a sniff of the seething mass in the coppers.

It was sometime after the regular dinner hour ere the stew was done, and it goes without saying that when it was served we were ready for it. When ranks were formed, there were no delinquents. Every man was on hand hungry for the fray. The steward of the mess passed through the long lines and as each one's dish was filled, he sought some place where he could enjoy his meal in quiet.

It was not long, however, ere a reaction set in. There were no post-prandial rejoicings on that occasion. There were no eulogistic compliments wasted on Captain Butler. Grim disappointment had succeeded hopeful expectation. Every brow was clouded, and as the murmurings became more and more apparent, the climax was soon reached. There was nothing angelic about those Argonauts on board the ship *Sylph* of Fair Haven. No exemplification of Patience on a monument was shadowed forth in their actions. They had no smiles for grief in that exigency; they did not sit silent and brood over their disappointment—they gave free vent to their feelings, and ere long their fitful murmurings culminated in one universal howl of indignation. For a while it seemed

> As if the fiends from heaven that fell
> Had pealed the banner cry of hell

The air was filled with ejaculations of rage and disgust. They had been swindled and imposed upon, and their resentment was natural. They had borrowed a dinner of their vacuous stomachs and invested it in a "blind pool" which had failed to pan out in accordance with their expectations. The dish they hungered for had been provided, but their stomachs rejected it. An empty stomach is a merciless creditor. There were 300 of these empty stomachs, each clamoring for its own. Porpoise stew was repudiated by one and all—it was not "legal tender." The condition was serious; the margin was exhausted, yet the liability still existed. What could be done? Nothing, and the creditors were reluctantly compelled to grant an extension of 24 hours.

Captain Butler, whose suggestion regarding the palatable nature of porpoise stew, had sprung from the kindest motives, and who had done his best to verify his statement, was in disgrace, and found it expedient to seek seclusion between decks to avoid the consequence of what many considered a practical joke, and it was difficult to convince them that he had acted in good faith.

The storm soon blew itself out, however, and quiet was restored, so that within 24 hours matters returned [to] their normal condition; nevertheless, the episode was not forgotten, and the mere mention of porpoise stew at any subsequent period would call an execration to every lip, and awaken emotions of disgust and indignation in every heart.[8]

During the time I was on board the *Sylph,* the greater part of my waking hours was spent aloft. Before leaving home, I had placed a set of the Waverly novels in my clothes bag, but some vandal stole them while in the hotel in New York, and I did not discover my loss till it was too late to replace them; hence I was compelled to borrow from my fellow passengers what books I read, and as a result my reading was rather promiscuous. The intellectual food was a sort of olla podrida. Law, Physics, and Divinity, subjects political, historical, theological, and philosophical, were all included in the curriculum.

Every morning, immediately after breakfast, I used to resort to the maintop, where, snugly ensconsed, and free from interruption, I passed many pleasant hours. After a while, however, reading matter became scarce, and I found it very difficult to procure books. I ransacked both the cabin and forecastle, but the supply was limited, and soon exhausted. Under such circumstances time began to hang heavy on my hands, when one day, while I was longing for some congenial occupation, Tom Anthony, the captain's clerk, remarked that he had a book in his chest which he would get for me. He went below and presently returned and handed me a copy of Dumas' *Three Guardsmen* which, as I had never read it, I seized with avidity and started for my quarters in the maintop.

The book proved a perfect bonanza, and I often turned back and re-read parts of it to avoid reaching the end too quickly. Athos, Porthos, Aramis, and D'Artagnan were indeed interesting characters. They took my imagination captive, and I thoroughly enjoyed the story of their deeds, conspiracies, and hairbreadth escapes. It was not till after I had read it a third time that I returned the book to its owner.

Notwithstanding the fact that the Pacific Ocean was dotted with the white sails of vessels from every port in Christendom, with the exception of the whale ship spoken when we were few days out, we had not seen one, so one day in June when aloft, as usual I scanned the horizon, and far away in the distance discovered a sail, and when satisfied that my eyes had not deceived me shouted, "Sail ho."

"Where away?" asked the captain.

"Dead astern."

"What is it?"

"Can't say, she's hull-down and can see nothing but her upper sails."

By this time, everyone was on the qui vive trying to locate the stranger. The captain sent for his glass, but though he looked long and carefully in the direction indicated, he failed to discover anything, and thinking I had been deceived, remarked that it must have been a cloud that I had mistaken for a vessel, but as I still insisted that there was no deception, the mate came up and I pointed her out. He gazed for a while, but unable to see what I saw, returned to the deck and reported that there was "no sail in sight." Though all were on the lookout, not one besides myself could see any sign of the vessel, which to me was plainly distinguishable, and for a while my report was discredited, but as it was apparent that the stranger was coming up with us hand over hand, I bided my time and wondered at the shortsightedness of the others.

Presently, however, all doubt was dispelled when the captain caught sight of the approaching sail through his glass and corroborated my report. The vessel was too far away for us to make out her rig, but it was obvious that she would soon overhaul us, and by noon we could see that it was a full-rigged brig, close-hauled on the starboard tack, and evidently a clipper. The excitement among the passengers was intense, and the desire to speak the stranger was universal, but she laid two points nearer the wind than we did, and sailed two feet to our one, passing us about a mile to windward [leeward?] as if we had been at anchor. My!! but she was a beauty as she came up with everything set from her royals down, and careened to the breeze under a cloud of canvas that seemed disproportionate to the size of her hull. There is no prettier craft than a full-rigged brig with her graceful lines and tapering spars, and it was delightful to watch her as under full sail

> She walked the waters like a thing of life
> And seemed to dare the elements to strife.

Previous to encountering the brig, our passengers had no opportunity to judge the sailing qualities of the *Sylph,* but when they saw that vessel walk away from us at a rate that promised to soon leave us hull-down, they were disgusted, for California seemed further off than ever, and they longed for the wings of a dove to carry them to their destination.[9]

We were now nearly two months out, and during all that time our course had been "full and by," having contended against a head wind from the start. It really seemed as if the fates were against us, and the grumblers were in the majority. The same dull routine day after day became monotonous, and any change was hailed as a relief. Moreover, we wanted something to eat that would be an improvement on the daily bill of fare. We were hungry all the time; we went to bed hungry and got up hungry, for though our food was filling, it was not relished, and we often thought with regret of the home cuisine. Of course those in the cabin fared better than we of the proletariat, and we cast envious glances at the dishes carried aft by the steward.

There was a small pig on board which had been bought in Panama for the captain's table. The little fellow was killed and when dressed weighed about ten pounds. He was stuffed and roasted whole, and had not the steward kept vigilant watch, that pig would have been stolen from the stove oven by the hungry passengers. He managed to save it, however, and in due time it was carried aft for the delectation of the captain, his wife, and the ship's officers.

It was a tantalizing sight, that roast pig on the platter as it disappeared down the cabin stairs, and I made up my mind that if there was any left after the people aft had finished their dinner, I would make interest with the steward and secure a piece. I took my position near the companion way ready to interview him when he reappeared, which he presently did, carrying the platter with the pig thereon comparatively untouched, so when I asked for a piece and he presented me with one whole carcass I was as much astonished as if I had asked for an apple and the owner had given me the whole orchard, nevertheless, I seized the pig and bore it away, followed by a motley crowd all eager to share in my good fortune. My judgment however told me that there must be some cause for the steward's unwonted generosity, and the fact that the dish came back intact from the cabin excited suspicion and warned me that there was "something rotten in Denmark." A single smell confirmed my suspicion, and banished all desire for roast pork, so I resigned my claim in favor of a fellow passenger who, less squeamish, proceeded to devour the rejected meat, apparently regardless of the offensive odor which had disgusted me.

Men are differently constituted. I remember hearing a sea captain tell of an incident that occurred one day while he was walking on the beach at Cape Town. Having occasion to pass the carcass of a whale stranded on the shore, he walked well to windward in order to avoid the disagreeable smell, and when just opposite the body observed two "Tots" [Hottentots], as he called them, inside the whale busily engaged in making a meal off the putrid fish. This story was called to mind when I saw Jarvey [Peter Jarvis?] bolt that pork; and, reasoning by analogy, I was strongly inclined to the belief that he had been able to trace his lineage to some far-away period in the past, the chances were that somewhere among his remote progenitors he would have discovered a "Tot."

The passengers on the *Sylph* were as a class as regardful of the ethical code as any like number of men, but so far as it applied to delicacies in the way of food, the difference between meum and tuum was absolutely disregarded and ignored. "Wherever you see a head, hit it" is the motto that governs during a row at Donnybrook fair. "Wherever you see anything good to eat, steal it," was an unwritten provision of the code on board our vessel, which was obeyed to the letter, and in the matter of eatables the eighth was practically eliminated from the Decalogue.

The steward's pantry containing the cabin stores was located in the wake of the fore hatchway between decks, and separated from the passengers' quarters by a picket fence which allowed free ventilation, and through which we could see many articles of food taboo to the proletariat. One night the light in the pantry went out, and simultaneously the passengers "went in," and before the lamp was relighted got away with quite an amount of spoils. They had broken through the slight barricade and helped themselves, and when the steward took an inventory next morning, he reported "thirteen hams missing."

Although I took no part in the raid, I was benefited nevertheless, as somebody secreted a ham in my berth and forgot where he hid it, so I appropriated it, and it furnished me many a lunch afterward. It was a pork ham and proved a very acceptable addition to the commissariat even if it was eaten raw. Notwithstanding the fact that I took no part in the raid on the pantry, no exemption is claimed on the score of morality, as I was on deck at the time, otherwise I would have undoubtedly gone in with the others. Later on, however, an opportunity came for me to prove that when something good to eat was to be had, I was prepared to discard all moral scruples and gratify my longing for "soft tack" at the expense of a fellow passenger named [A.D.] Hatch,[10] who was one of those "Now I lay me down to sleep" kind of fellows for whom we had little sympathy; so when one day he prevailed with the captain and received an order for flour, with permission to use the galley stove to bake his bread, anxious eyes watched his proceedings and noticed every move he made.

Having procured the requisite flour and slush for shortening, he mixed the ingredients and therefrom produced two enormous "short cakes" at least a foot in diameter, which he placed in the oven, and in due time withdrew crisp, brown, and done to a turn. Carefully wrapping the loaves in a linen coat which he took off for the purpose so as to conceal them from view, he started for his quarters between decks, where I had preceded him in order to see what disposition he made of them, intending to capture them if possible, and provide myself with a square meal at all hazards. Managing to conceal myself where I could watch his motions, I kept a bright lookout.

Presently he made his appearance, and after carefully looking to see whether he was watched, proceeded to unlock his trunk. The clock of that lock fell on my ear like a death knell, and "Hope for a season bade the world farewell." My stomachic barometer fell several degrees lower than at any time since the porpoise stew episode, and the prospect of regaling myself on warm bread looked exceedingly blue. Fortunately, however, the box was too full to admit more than one loaf, so when he had stowed that away, he sought some place of concealment for the other. Above his hammock was a shelf nailed to the deck beams, where he kept his pot and pan and such articles as he required for daily use. These he removed, and breaking a small piece from the loaf, he placed it on the back side of the shelf and concealed it with his pot and pan. Then he went on deck, and I followed to see what disposition he made of himself after he got there.

Just as my head reached the coamings of the hatchway, George Batchelor [Batchelder], a fellow passenger, accosted me and confidentially informed me that "Old Stick in the Mud" had carried below "two almighty big short cakes," with an incidental suggestion that we should steal them.

"I'll keep watch," said he, "while you go below and find them."

"I know where they are, George, but one of them is locked in his trunk beyond reach, the other may be easily come at, and we will confiscate it as treasure trove."

Meanwhile, Hatch had established himself in one of the quarter boats, and together with a Mr. [David] Fairchild, a Methodist minister,[11] and several others, was chanting a Methodist hymn in blissful unconsciousness of the conspiracy we were hatching to deprive him of the fruits of his labor.

Having seen that all was secure, I dived below again and soon returned with the spoils, which I divided with George, and as I stowed my half inside my shirt-front, that line of Virgil:

Sic vos, non vobis mellificatis apes

was uppermost in my thoughts.

To use a New England expression, that warm bread was "beautiful," and as it was the first that passed my lips in nearly two months, it goes without saying that I enjoyed it hugely as I stood munching it, leaning over the rail and looking seaward to avoid observation, fearing that Hatch might see me eating and come to suspect me afterward.

While thus chewing and ruminating, Tom Anthony came along, and said the captain desired to see me in the cabin. Thinking that all had been discovered and complaint made at headquarters, my first impulse was to throw the bread overboard, and relieve myself of all evidence of an incriminating nature, but on second thought decided that it was just as well to be hung for an old sheep as a lamb, and concluded to hold on to my plunder. Hastily swallowing the victuals in my mouth, and brushing the crumbs from my whiskers and clothing, I proceeded to the cabin, where the captain greeted me so cordially that all suspicions regarding a criminal arraignment were at once dissipated. It was some matter connected with the "new crew" that he wished to discuss, so after a brief interview I returned to the deck.

Nothing occurred to disturb the harmony on board that afternoon, and it was not till late at night, when Hatch was about to turn in, that he discovered his loss, when he immediately charged Capt. K., an old man from Maine[12] who occupied the adjoining hammock, with "stealing his short cake." This was denied, and a war of words ensued, when the plaintiff appealed to me, who had just retired filled to repletion with the article in question, to say whether the presumption was strong enough to warrant the accusation. Knowing as I did that the charge was groundless, still, considering the defendant's antecedents, as it was undoubtedly he who had stolen the ham and secreted it in my berth and afterward forgotten where he put it, and also believing that had he known of the bread, he would have had no scruples about appropriating it to his own use, I deemed myself justified in holding that the probabilities were all in favor of the plaintiff, but as a man could not be convicted on mere probability, the defendant was entitled to the benefit of the doubt, and unless something more tangible than presumptive evidence was produced, the plaintiff must submit to a "non suit."

This ruling satisfied neither party. The one reiterated his charge, and the other affirmed his innocence with such vehemence that it really looked as if they would come to blows, when in the midst of the melee the lanyard on the Maine man's hammock parted and he came down by the run, striking his head against a trunk and was knocked senseless. He soon came to, however, when still unpacified and full of fight, he declared his neck was broken, and charged Hatch with cutting him down, but the fall had so jarred his nerves that he was in no condition to resume hostilities, and he finally subsided. We assisted in making temporary repairs, when he again turned in, and for the rest of the night, quiet reigned.

Thus ended the episode of the stolen short cake, but from that time out, a coolness existed between the loser and the man from Maine, and during the remainder of the passage their relations were strained and far from amicable.

As the Fourth of July approached, arrangements were made for an appropriate celebration. Meetings were held, committees appointed and a programme agreed upon, and it was decided to hail the anniversary of our country's independence with such demonstrations of joy and thanksgiving as our surroundings permitted. It was arranged that the Declaration of Independence should be read, an oration delivered, and a banquet provided from such materials as the ship's stores afforded.

The day before the Fourth, the "committee on doughnuts" took possession of the ship's galley and began operations.[13] Three men were engaged in mixing the dough, and three in shaping and frying the doughnuts, which as fast as cooked were deposited in a large cask guarded till the cask, which held five barrels, was full, when it was headed up by the cooper, and as it was necessary to have a vent to prevent the contents from sweating, the bung hole was left open, over which a strict watch was maintained during the night. Jim was one of the frying committee and took occasion to pass me several doughnuts surreptitiously, which was a treat I had not counted on, and of course appreciated thoroughly.

The morning of the Fourth dawned brightly, and every one was up betimes to meet the sun in his coming, the ship was gaily dressed with flags, and all hands were prepared to celebrate the national jubilee in a manner befitting the occasion, and in accordance with the following order of ceremonies:

Prayer
Rev Mr. [David] Fairchild
Song
The Star Spangled Banner, by the choir
Declaration of Independence
Doctor Hathaway [H. Ray Bowie]
Oration
Mr. Parbutt [George R. Parburt]

At the banquet which followed, the following was the Bill of Fare

Soup
Consomme de Frijoles

Entrees
Boiled Rice
Plum Duff
Honey

Interlude
Necessarily omitted

Dessert
Doughnuts
Raisins
Brazil Nuts

Potables
Agua Frio—Tea
Wines impossible
Whisky   Ditto

Individual contributions freely authorized

Taboo
Porpoise Stew

The above programme was carried out to the letter, Mr. Fairchild made an impressive prayer and prayed fervently for a fair wind. The "Star Spangled Banner" was rendered creditably by the choir, all hands joining in the chorus. The Declaration was read in a distinct voice and well read too, after which Mr. Parbutt took his station on the quarterdeck and reminded us that seventy-three years ago that day our fathers threw off the yoke and severed their connection with Great Britain. He made a stirring address. . . .[14]

The oration was well received, duly applauded, and then came the banquet. Belshazzar's feast was an everyday affair in comparison with that meal, and Lazarus himself would have turned away in disgust at the scarcity of crumbs which fell. The menu was followed to the letter, but the proper apportionment of the doughnuts was a serious question. The mathematicians had figured that nine doughnuts to each would about exhaust the supply, but when divided on that basis the cask was not half emptied, and everyone received a second installment of nine, after which, as there was still a remainder, a further dividend of three doughnuts was declared, which made each man's quota twenty-one.

Everybody was satisfied with the dinner, the stomachic vacuum was agreeably filled, and for a day or two afterward doughnuts were freely staked in games of cards. As for myself, I ate so heartily that I was constrained to go below and turn in, where I wrestled with indigestion and bad dreams till next morning. As my allowance of honey had been more than sufficient on the Fourth, the surplus was stowed away in anticipation of the next duff day, but when I sought it, I discovered that the cockroaches had forestalled me, and taken it all. There were about a thousand roaches in the cup, which I had the satisfaction of destroying, and thereby freed my berth of a disagreeable pest, and gave my toenails a chance to grow.

It was about the 10th of July [June 21], when we were in the latitude of Cape St. Lucas, that we encountered our first gale of wind.[15] Up to that time, though we had experienced squalls incidental to the low latitudes, we had met with no heavy weather. Aside from the continuous head wind, the voyage had been fairly prosperous, and though we had made slow progress, we began to feel that we would soon see the end of our pilgrimage. In the afternoon of that day the sky became overcast, and the general appearance indicated rough weather. The captain, noting that the barometer was falling, made preparations to meet what might occur. The light sails were furled, the boats secured by extra lashings, and such precautions taken as prudence seemed to require. Just after supper, the wind came in puffs from the northwest, and the mate's countenance showed that he expected a "dirty night." Lifelines were stretched along the deck, and the watch were on the qui vive to execute such orders as might be given. The weather rapidly became worse, all hands were called, sail was reduced, and at nine o'clock, when I went below, the ship was under double-reefed fore and main topsails and whole foresail.

As I had every confidence in the ability of the ship's officers, and knew the vessel was staunch and seaworthy, I did not worry over the circus on deck, but composed myself to sleep and soon dropped off. We had been on the starboard tack constantly since leaving port which, as my berth was on the larboard side, brought me to leeward. I was sleeping quietly, when about midnight I was suddenly awakened by a change of position, which almost threw me from my berth. My pot, pan, and other articles stowed on a shelf in the bunk "fetched away" and went down to leeward with a tremendous clatter, which so startled me that I thought for a minute that the ship was on her beam ends and we were all likely to go to Davy Jones together. But she soon assumed a more upright position and I knew the vessel had been brought to the wind on the port tack and was evidently "lying to." I could hear the tramp of the sailors overhead, the hoarse tones of the mate, the wind whistling through the rigging; and though feeling some curiosity to know what was going on, I was convinced that there was nothing very attractive to call me outside, so turned over, took a fresh start, and slept till morning, when I went on deck at the usual hour.

That old Boreas had not been idle during the night was plainly visible as soon as I reached the upper air. The ship was lying to under a close-reefed main topsail and fore topmast staysail, and the wind was blowing great guns. Sometime in the night the jib boom had broken in the cap and gone off to leeward, carrying away the fore top gallant mast. The boom was hanging by the gear, and from time to time collided with the vessel in a way that threatened to stave a hole in her bows. The mate was busy with a gang forward, trying to clear the wreck, and relieve us of the danger from the pounding spar. This he finally succeeded in doing, but the stick was lost with the gear attached. The top gallant mast hanging by the rigging was swinging to and fro aloft, the port quarter boat was smashed, one-half gone entirely, and the other hanging by the crane. The wind howled through the rigging and blew so fiercely that with what little sail we had the ship was at times beaten down so that her lee scuppers were under water; but lively, and in good ballast trim, she quickly recovered, and rode the waters like a duck. Captain G[ardner] said that he had doubled Cape Horn ten times and in all his experience had never encountered so fierce a gale.

As it was a task of great difficulty to clear away and send down the broken top gallant mast, the captain hesitated about giving a peremptory order and called for volunteers, but there was no ready response, as the crew were young men and were completely demoralized. Presently, however, the carpenter, an old English sailor, the most indefatigable grumbler on the ship, constantly complaining of his grub and ready to kick at the slightest provocation, very much to the surprise of his officers and shipmates jumped into the rigging and went aloft. It was with no little trepidation that we watched him as he climbed from ratlin to ratlin, passed the futtock shrouds, dodging the spar as it careened from starboard to port, and finally installed himself at the fore topmast crosstrees, where, above and clear of danger from the broken mast, he proceeded to attend to the business before him. The man seemed perfectly devoid of fear, and as he set about his task, it was evident to all who watched him that he was a thorough sailor, and one to be depended on in a case of emergency at sea. In less than half an hour he disengaged the spar from the rigging that held it and sent it down secundum artem, and it was afterward utilized as a stump topgallant mast. That sailor was a brave man, but when I subsequently complimented him on his pluck and seamanship, he laughed as though the episode was a matter of course, and deserving of no special notice. I afterward talked with the carpenter, who told me much of his varied experience on shipboard, especially of a reefing match in a gale off Cape Horn, where he with forty others on the yard struggled with a frozen main topsail in a snowstorm at night.

The appearance of the ocean was similar to that presented on our western prairies during a winter blizzard. The sea was not so very rough, as the tremendous force of the wind flattened the waves, but the general outlook was dreary enough, and a change from the vessel's deck to terra firma would have been hailed by all hands with gratitude. We had no regular meals that day, as the ship laid over so the cook could keep no water in the coppers. It was 36 hours before the gale broke, and though at times the sky to windward seemed to indicate a change for the better, when I made a remark to Mr. Hussey, the mate, to that effect, he said, "We must look to leeward for signs of the gale breaking, as those in the weather horizon are no criterion."

It was not till some hours after the wind moderated that our captain considered it safe to make sail and proceed on our course, but when we discovered a vessel far to leeward under sail our topsails were again loosed.[16] For a day or two after the gale the crew were busy repairing damages. The broken top gallant mast was sent up again, a new jib boom was made from a spare spar, and matters began to assume a more orderly aspect.

We learned after our arrival in San Francisco that two other ships, the *Capitol* and *Pharsalia* of Boston, were caught in the same gale with us, and sustained far more serious damage, the one having lost all her topmasts, and the other all her boats.[17]

From the time of the gale we had pleasant weather, though the wind was still adverse, and on the morning of July 24 [21] we made the land off Monterey, some 80 miles south of the Golden Gate, and coasted along the shore till our captain decided we were far enough to the northward, when we dropped the anchor about three miles from land.[18]

It was on the night of the 25th that we came to an anchor, and next morning all hands were jubilant over the prospect of soon landing in San Francisco. It was a relief after our long voyage to behold the land once more, and all watched the bold coast with much interest, and wondered where the entrance to the harbor might be.[19]

It must be remembered that at that period the chart of the coast was very imperfect. We knew nothing of the Farallon Islands only a few miles from the Golden Gate, where there is now a light house from which to take the bearings of the entrance to the harbor. We were close in, and the captain's observation told him we were in the right latitude; nevertheless there was no indication of an opening in the coast.

Taking a copy of *Wilkes' Exploring Expedition* and a spy glass, Capt G[ardner] ascended to the foretop and I followed him to investigate. "Now," said he, reading from the book, "Wilkes described the landmark at the entrance to the harbor as a headland, with a white sand beach inside."[20] The captain was puzzled as he pointed his glass towards the shore, for though there were plenty of headlands in plain sight, there was nothing to show which if either was the proper one, as he could see no "white sand beach" or any sign whatever of an opening—and just as he had decided to lower a boat and explore closely, we saw the head sails of a schooner coming from behind a point of land.

"Eureka!" exclaimed the skipper. "If Wilkes had said a 'rugged' headland, we would have recognized it without difficulty, as that is the only rugged one in sight."

The reason why wc failed to see the white sand beach was because we were too far to the southward, and the point hid it from sight. Satisfied with our discovery, we proceeded to the deck, when the captain ordered a boat and boarded the schooner. She was bound for the Sandwich Islands, and when the captain returned he brought several New York newspapers, when we got the first intimation of the "Astor Place" riot in that city, said to have been incited by Forrest the tragedian in retaliation for some offence by Macready an English actor.²¹

We got up our anchor at the turn of the tide, made sail, and stood in for the Golden Gate. The entrance is quite narrow, and by the time we reached it, the young flood was running like a "mill tail" and swept us along at a tremendous rate. The most prominent object I remember was a large rock with a hole through it which we passed on the starboard hand.²² The current soon swept us past the Presidio into Washerwoman's Bay,²³ where we saw a large ship on shore, which as we approached it proved to be the *Thames* of Sag Harbor, and it really seemed like meeting an old friend.²⁴ The tide hustled us on, however; we soon left the *Thames* astern, and were swept round Telegraph Point into the bay and harbor of San Francisco.²⁵ The sight that met our eyes as we rounded the point filled us with astonishment, for never before in the world's history was collected such an incongruous assortment of marine craft as lay mingled together "heads and points" in the bay when we came to an anchor in the midst of the fleet on [Thursday] the 26th of July, 1849, 76 [78] days from Panama.²⁶ We had one death on board during the passage, but aside from that there was little sickness and every passenger was delivered in "good order" at the port of destination.²⁷

As we looked around us and saw the immense fleet lying at anchor, and the white sails of other vessels just entering the port, it seemed as if all Christendom had preceded us and taken possession of this modern Colchis. Steamers, ships, brigs, schooners, and even Chinese junks, had brought each its quota, and having performed their mission, now lay neglected and deserted. When I say deserted, I state a literal fact, for it was an exception in the general condition of affairs to find even one man as shipkeeper on many of these abandoned vessels. They were left to swing at their anchors, while captain, cook, and all hands sought fortune in the gold fields. The steamers *Oregon, California,* and *Panama,* for which so many anxious passengers waited on the Isthmus, had indeed been able by the payment of enormous wages to get away on their return trips, but aside from them, with the exception perhaps of a few small schooners owned by their masters and manned chiefly by Kanakas, every vessel in port was as effectually tied up as if it had been frozen in. The constant accessions to the fleet by the daily arrivals went on for months, but the departures were few and far between.²⁸ At that period the owners who saw their property lying idle and neglected, without any prospect of an early release or of collecting demur-rage, might well have looked at the Golden Gate as did Dante at that of the infernal re-gions and with a like feeling of repulsion might have considered the motto "Who enters here leaves hope behind" as appropriate for the one as for the other.

Speaking of the forlorn condition of the shipping in San Francisco harbor in 1849 and '50, I will recite one incident that happened under my own eye. Under ordinary circum-stances the bay is a safe anchorage, but during the prevalence of strong southwest winds, the shipping is very much exposed, and serious accidents occur. It was during one of those strong southwest gales that I saw a fine ship under the influence of the wind, combined with a strong ebb tide, part her cables and drift down on another vessel, against which the force of wind and tide threatened to sweep her with an almost irresistible momentum; but fortunately the second vessel was a late arrival and had part of her crew on board, and as the derelict approached, preparations were made to avoid the shock. The fore topsail was loosed, and the helm so changed that the ship swung round, and the drifting vessel surged by without doing any material damage and was swept out of the harbor by the receding current. I watched her till she passed behind Telegraph Hill, and afterward learned that she struck the rocks in the vicinity of the Golden Gate and sank.

Many instances of his kind occurred with no one to record them. Sometimes deserted vessels were found to be leaking, and as there was danger of their sinking in the harbor, their cables were surreptitiously slipped, and they were started seaward on the ebb tide. The man who acted as harbor master in those days was probably cognizant of many such cases.

From this digression we will return to the *Sylph,* which with anchors down and sails furled had joined the fleet of immovables. All was bustle on board, and the passengers were busily engaged in transferring their traps to the shore boats that had come off for fares. It was about noon when we dropped anchor, and by night all had left and were ensconced beneath the shelter of their tents in Happy Valley, the camping place for most newcomers, who there made arrangements to proceed to the diggings.[29] Of all those who made the passage with me from Panama, with perhaps two or three exceptions, I have never met one since we parted on the vessel that day. Most of them had one or more partners with tent and camp equipage provided before they left home, and were prepared to set up housekeeping in primitive style.

I was alone and "flocked by myself." "The world was all before me where to choose my place of rest, and Providence my guide." The whole extent of my pecuniary re-sources was six dollars, and the eminent necessity that I should at once "get up and get" was too apparent to be ignored. As I had neither tent nor other conveniences for camp-ing, I decided to go ashore and spy out the land, meanwhile leaving my effects on board, and as the captain was about to visit the Custom House and enter his vessel, I went ashore in his boat.

The first acquaintance I met after climbing the bank at Clark's Point was Captain Erastus Cartwright, who had left Sag Harbor in command of the bark *Romulus* which had been condemned in Honolulu, and he had drifted to San Francisco.[30] He appeared very much disheartened, and seemed to have lost all his courage. He told me that Captain Payne was camped on the shore at Washerwoman's Bay looking after his ship, the *Thames*, before mentioned as being ashore at that point. As I desired to prospect further, I made my way uptown to investigate. There were not to exceed a dozen frame buildings. It was a city of "tents," pitched without regard to regularity, and the thoroughfares were a succession of trails or footpaths leading to the most important points. At the post office, a little one-story building painted white, I found several letters from home assuring me that all were well.[31]

As I passed along, a gentleman hailed me and asked me to test a sample of brandy which he had purchased from a French ship. He had a proof glass in his hand, which he dipped into one of a number of barrels among which he stood. "Isn't it oily?" he asked after I had drank to his success and good health. I readily admitted the "oiliness," and so sincere was I in my admission that a second glass was disposed of before we parted. I judged by his accent that he was a Southerner, and he had a genial manner calculated to win friends anywhere.

The two drinks acted as a sort of appetizer, and seeing "Restaurant" in big letters on a tent nearby, I decided to refresh my inner man with a square meal. That square meal consisted of hot pork and beans, hot biscuit, and hot coffee, which, though coarsely served, filled the vacuum and reduced my capital two dollars. When I asked for lodging, the man replied that he was not exactly fixed for lodgers, but if I would bring my blankets, I might sleep on the floor for a dollar. As I had but four dollars left, and knew that I could occupy my old berth on board the *Sylph* and "ring in" for breakfast next morning, I concluded to return to the ship that night, So when evening came, I paid a boatman two dollars to take me off, and I slept in my old quarters. The next day [July 28] was Saturday,[32] and after breakfast I again went ashore with the captain, perfectly convinced that the two dollars still left would not suffice for a very extensive picnic. Under such circumstances it was obvious that I must seek employment at once, and I proceeded to do so; with what success will be revealed in the next chapter.

VIII

IN SAN FRANCISCO

JULY–AUGUST, 1849

When my memory reverts to that Saturday morning when I landed in San Francisco with but two dollars in my scrip, and no provisions for the future, every incident of the day is as easily recalled as if it occurred but yesterday. The old saying, "Root, hog or die," was thoroughly exemplified in my case; and with a disposition to accept any honest employment that would enable me to procure the means to reach the gold fields, I started to find work.

Such work as presented itself in those days was no holiday employment, and whoever procured a job was required to pitch in for all he was worth. Many of the young men had never been accustomed to manual labor, and the nature of the work demanded taxed their endurance to the utmost, but when it came to a choice between physical exertion and starvation, they were compelled to take off their coats and buckle to in earnest. As for myself, I had never done any work that required more effort than occasionally to split oven wood for my mother, or perhaps dig a post hole when my father was repairing the fences about the homestead. It was not long, however, before I found a job and at the same time found a friend.

As I strolled along what is now called Sansome Street, I noticed a pile of lumber which had been placed preparatory to the erection of a building. The timbers were already framed, and I saw they had been prepared for shipment ready to be put together when landed from the vessel. A mechanic was engaged in pegging out the site of the structure, and as I glanced at him, I recognized one who had formerly plied his vocation in my native village.

Satisfied regarding his identity, I hailed him with "Good morning, Mr. Hudson."[1] He looked up, returned my greeting, and, when asked for a job, inquired whether I was a carpenter. Now, though I knew him, he had no idea who I was, so I had no hesitation in replying affirmatively, for it was evident that if he put me to work, he would soon learn that my knowledge in that line was very limited. Nevertheless, my mind was in that condition that prepared to do or die; had I been required to preach a sermon, I would not have hesitated to choose a text and extemporize a discourse that would have at least convinced him of my theological orthodoxy.

When the question of wages was broached, he said, "Come on Monday and I will pay you $12 a day." "That's satisfactory," I replied, "but this is Saturday, and Sunday intervenes between now and then; meanwhile, though the foxes have holes and the birds of the air have nests, I have nowhere to lay my head." Then I explained who I was, and where I had known him; that I had just landed, and having come from home alone, had no acquaintances, and aside from those who were passengers on the ship with me, knew absolutely nobody.

65

"Well," he said, "I have an abiding place down in Happy Valley; go there with me to-night and we will camp together." This suggestion suited me perfectly, so I thanked him and fell into the plan without further discussion. As he had to go off to the vessel and attend to the discharge of the balance of the material for the building, I left him, promising to meet him at 6 o'clock and take supper in Happy Valley.

A visit to the Custom House to ascertain whether the *Sabina* had arrived satisfied me that she had not yet reported. This was gratifying, as many of my old friends were on board, and I feared the long passage from Panama had so delayed me that they had reached San Francisco and departed before my arrival. Now, however, there was a chance to earn some money before they came, and go with them to the mines.

That evening I went with Mr. Hudson to his quarters. He informed me that just previous to his embarkation for California, he was on the point of emigrating from New York to a western State, and had made all his arrangements to do so, but the startling news from the gold fields caused a change of plan.

As a part of his outfit for the west, he had provided a large covered wagon to transport his household goods, and as the change of route seemed to make a superfluity of the wagon, he was at a loss what to do with it. He had taken passage on the ship *Daniel Webster* of New York,[2] and being unable to dispose of the wagon at a fair price, decided to ship it with the rest of his traps; so when it was discharged from the vessel at San Francisco, it was taken to Happy Valley and used as a homestead. The vehicle contained two mattresses, one at each end, and afforded excellent sleeping quarters.

Mr. Hudson had brought his two sons, George and Henry, with him from New York, and we found them preparing supper when we reached camp. The young fellows, aged respectively 16 and 18 years, welcomed me cordially, and sans ceremony adopted me as a member of the family. There was another young man, Edward Howell, who had come out in the ship with the Hudsons, and made his home with them. Having known him from childhood, and his mother before him, I was pleased to meet him.[3]

As supper was ready, we squatted around the campfire and partook of our rations with good appetites. There was no table, so each held his plate in his lap and fed himself in primitive style. After the meal was ended, we washed the dishes, put things to rights, filled our pipes, and sat down for a comfortable chat.

Having no small vices, neither addicted to the use of tobacco or whiskey, the old gentleman left us to enjoy our smoke and turned in, as he had been hard at work all day, and felt the need of repose. He was an intelligent, wide-awake, energetic man, and no grass grew beneath his feet during the early days in San Francisco.

After the "old man" retired, we sat by the campfire and discussed matters personal and impersonal for an hour or two. We talked of home, recounted incidents of our experience on shipboard, wondered when the *Sabina* would report, and formed plans for proceeding to the mines as soon as the boys on board of her made their appearance. As she was then nearly six months out, it was reasonable to look for her arrival every day.

George, who was a good singer, piped up and gave us the "Canadian Boat Song," and about 10 o'clock we sought our beds in the wagon and lay down to pleasant dreams.

Notwithstanding the next day was Sunday, the head of the family was up before daylight, and roused us out before sunrise. He had much to do, many schemes in view, and could not afford to take time even on Sunday. After breakfast, the boys volunteered to go with me and bring my baggage from the *Sylph,* so we took Mr. Hudson's rowboat and started out. She pulled four oars, and being all accustomed to rowing, we made her hum. The last of the ebb was running, and as was usually the case in the morning, the waters of the bay were smooth. We soon reached the vessel, where I found but one man on board, acting as shipkeeper. He told me the captain was living on shore, and all the crew had skedaddled for the diggings.

It did not take long to move my effects from between decks, and after placing them in the boat, we pushed off and left the *Sylph* behind us. From that day I never saw her, and how long she remained in San Francisco Bay, or what became of her after she got away, I cannot say, having seen no one connected with the vessel or heard of any of them since. Trusting that good luck followed her, we will now leave her, as she will appear no more in this narrative. Captain G[ardner] was a genial fellow who did all he could to promote the comfort of his passengers, and though we were a long time on the voyage from Panama, there were others that were longer and suffered far more hardships than we did.[4]

After landing my baggage, I decided to go over to "Washerwoman's Bay," call on Captain Payne, and ascertain how it happened that the old *Thames* was piled up in the sand at that point. A walk of about three miles brought me to where he was encamped on the shore near his vessel. He greeted me cordially, brought out his bottle, and after a social glass talked confidentially—told me how he came to be in San Francisco, what he had done since he left the home port, and what he proposed doing.

It was evident that he was living economically and using every effort to release his ship and conserve the interest of his owners. It seemed that the vessel under the influence of a strong gale and a flood tide had dragged her anchors and taken the ground. She was lying on a sandy bottom, resting easily and not likely to sustain any serious damage. "Now," said Captain Payne, "if I was like some skippers, I would take rooms at the Parker House and live in style, but having the interest of my owners at heart, and remembering that Thomas Brown trusted me with the ship when others were afraid of me, I brought some sails ashore, pitched my tent on the beach, and here you find me keeping "bachelor's hall." As I glanced at a Spanish girl sitting in the tent, he smiled and added, "Well, so d—d near to it there's no fun in it."

He told me that he had put in at Talcuhana [southern Chile] for supplies, and on his arrival found the whole country in a state of wildest excitement over the news recently received of the discovery of gold in California. He had not met with much success during the season on the whaling ground, and felt greatly disappointed at the outlook. His crew were dissatisfied, and in a humor to desert. This, together with the effect produced by the

California news, convinced him that they would run away rather than resume the whaling voyage. He considered the pros and cons, and after weighing matters in his mind, finally concluded to accept an advantageous charter to carry passengers to San Francisco, and was now figuring how to get his ship away. There was no crew on board, and he was under little expense. He had hired a few men by the hour when the tide made and conditions were favorable, and had managed to move the ship some fathoms nearer deep water, and had no doubt that at the next spring tide he would be able to heave her off uninjured. He then proceeded to formulate a programme for future operations. He proposed to ship a few men to work the vessel to a southern port, where he could complete his crew, cruise for a while in the Pacific Ocean, double Cape Horn, take a season off the Rio de la Plata, and then sail for home. If he had been let alone, there is no question in the writer's mind that his intentions would have been carried out. His sympathies all seemed to be with Thomas Brown, the ship's agent, who, despite his dissipated antecedents and irrascible temper, had trusted him; and he was determined to prove worthy of the trust.

Such was the condition of affairs when some mischievous intermeddler wrote home that Captain Payne was in a bad way and the ship in bad shape. This frightened the stockholders, a meeting was called, and against the remonstrance of agent Brown, Captain Payne was suspended and another sent out to take his place. When these proceedings were imparted to Payne, all his latent passions broke forth, and the sleeping devil within him was aroused. His friend Brown had been overruled, and it was only for him he cared; the others "might go to Hades." He was a passionate man, but was inclined to act honestly, and if the stockholders had continued him in command, it is very probable there would have been a dividend instead of a deficit. After his suspension, he removed to Angel Island, where a few years later he died a violent death.[5]

On Monday morning I went to work. The first thing in order was to grade a place for the foundation, as the lot was on a hillside. Mr. Hudson gave instructions, provided picks and shovels, and told us to "pitch in." There were, besides myself, the two Hudson boys and a young man named Brown, just about as well-qualified for the work as I was. It was in the midst of the dry season, and the ground was so hard the stroke of a pick made but little impression. The weather was hot, and we found nothing attractive in the task of grading. Our hands were soon blistered with the friction of the pick helves, and when the blisters broke and the red earth intruded on the raw spots, the pain was exasperating. Nevertheless, we did the best we could, and after a couple of days, the ground was leveled, and we began putting the sills and sleepers in place. The pieces being all framed and numbered, there was no difficulty in arranging them. The building was for one Wardell, and was, I think, the first frame structure on Sansome Street.

Mr. Hudson was a driver, and kept us busy. At noon, after taking lunch, there was no chance for a siesta, for as soon as it was dispatched, it was "Hurrah, boys, man the boat and take me to the vessel, there are some materials lacking that we must have immediately." Ordinarily, a boating excursion would have been a pleasant break in the day's work, but with blistered hands, festered with splinters from the timber, pulling an oar was not altogether agreeable.

After a week, Brown struck work and sought some more congenial employment, as the dust caused by the high wind that prevailed every afternoon so affected his eyes that it nearly blinded him. I continued for a while longer but was compelled to "lay off." That endemic disease, the dysentery, which proved fatal to so many of the pioneers, attacked me, and though for a few days I endeavored to stave it off by a large absorption of brandy, it grew worse and compelled me to succumb and quit work.[6]

Mr. Hudson was not disposed to be hypercritical, and when I explained my condition, instead of discharging me, as I expected, he said, "Now, Cal, you go home and lay off for a while, I'll keep your name on the time book, and you can do the cooking and marketing till you get better." This was very generous treatment, yet, though appreciating his kindly sympathy, I felt thoroughly dejected, conscious that my disorder was likely to prove serious, and that absolute rest and freedom from physical exertion was imperative. Following his advice, however, I returned to camp, and for a while attended to matters there and did what light work I could.

As my bag was full of soiled clothing, none having been washed since leaving Panama, there was, of course, a large accumulation of shirts, drawers, and socks that required cleansing, and having had but little experience in that line, I am willing to admit that as a laundryman I was by no means a success. Nevertheless, after the application of much soap and vigorous rubbing, most of the dirt was removed, and the garments were certainly clean "in spots," but it was long before I became sufficiently expert to wash a shirt so that it presented a uniform color. If, as is often asserted, "cleanliness is next to godliness," there was little to prove the connection between the two in the habits of the pioneers, since it was generally customary to wear a shirt till it "dropped off," and then replace it with a new one which was subjected to the same process. Cooking was disagreeable, but washing clothing was absolutely detestable to the majority.

One day, while occupied with my culinary duties in camp, Will Allen, with whom I had made the passage from New York, came and excitedly advised me that the *Sabina* had just arrived.[7] This was indeed glad news, so after arranging for a substitute at the campfire, we procured a boat and proceeded to board the vessel where, it goes without saying, we met with a royal reception.

The boys were all well, all expectant, and all anxious for information regarding the status quo, as the immense fleet in the harbor impressed them with the idea that the whole world had preceded them, and the gold fields were already pre-empted. Allen, who was a [fellow] townsman of many of the old skippers who were passengers, retired with them to the cabin, where they pumped him effectually, and thoroughly confused him with their multifarious queries. I affiliated with the boys, many of whom had officiated during the voyage as "gentlemen rope-haulers," and whose quarters were legitimately in the forecastle, though I do not believe there was ever a vessel that sailed the seas where the crew consorted with the officers on such terms of social equality. The fact is, the crew was composed of young men, among whom were some from the best families in the village, and though they had accepted and performed the duties of foremast hands, they did not consider they had sacrificed a particle of self-respect in so doing, and conducted themselves accordingly. They even hail-fellowed with all the prominent stockholders on board; and even the officers, though debarred by custom from associating freely with the crew, relaxed the reins when off duty, and Mr. Warren, the second mate, was generally addressed as "Tom." So it happened that when the interview with Mr. Allen was ended, and Captain [Henry] Green gave the order to "man the boat," the response was so general that at least thirty jumped in as soon as she struck the water, and became inextricably mixed, "heads and points," like so many angleworms. This proceeding so roused the ire of Mr. Rhodes, the mate, that he called out, "Come out of that boat, all but six, or I'll find a way to help you out." The tone of the mate's voice convinced those who heard it that he was in earnest, and a majority returned to the vessel. Nevertheless, when the boat pushed off, there were still thirteen on board.

Meanwhile, the boys and myself were in close communion between decks, and I gave what information I could regarding the prospect ahead, but as my knowledge was slight respecting the conditions at the mines, I could not say what luck might await us in the mountains. They were thoroughly prepared for camp life, so far as the usual accompaniments went, and had brought a tent and provisions sufficient for a half-dozen for at least a twelve-month. There were two barrels of clear and one of mess pork, a barrel of beef with a good assortment of cooking utensils, also a medicine chest, which had been put up by a skillful physician. The tent was an excellent one, not made of flimsy cotton jean, but of good, substantial Methuen duck that could shed water and keep its occupants dry, a thing we learned to appreciate when the rainy season came. In fact, the boys had provided everything in the way of food and shelter.

There was not much sleeping on board the *Sabina* that night, as everybody was too much excited to think of bed. The captain's boat returned about midnight, and brought encouraging reports to the expectant Argonauts. There were about sixty in the company proper, and as there were, of course, diverse views as to the mode of procedure, nothing was decided that night, as further information was desirable before taking any decisive step, but the consensus of opinion inclined to an immediate departure for the mines, as soon as a proper locality could be agreed upon.

I remained on board and took breakfast with the boys next morning, which John Hull, the steward, supplemented with a mince pie concocted from salt beef, dried apples, etc., which was really very good. John was famous for his mince pie, and how he managed to furnish such palatable fare from the means at hand was a mystery.

After breakfast, the boys got their traps together and we took departure in one of the ship's boats, landing at Happy Valley and pitching the tent in close proximity to the wagon. When everything was made snug, the newcomers started for the post office, where they found a multiplicity of letters awaiting them with all the home news. That night a council was held, and as they were desirous of reaching the diggings as soon as practicable, and as money was a a sine qua non, it had to be earned before starting. Henry Mott, a fellow townsman, who was engaged in lightering, offered them employment in his line which they accepted, though fully aware of the intense muscular exertion necessary to perform the work, as in the absence of proper appliances, they were compelled to handle and stow the heavy packages by main strength. This was terribly wearing labor, and only the toughest could stand it. After a few days, they resigned and sought an easier job. There was no lack of work, and they early found employment, and after a fortnight on shore, had accumulated sufficient capital to warrant them in striking out for the diggings.

Meanwhile, I had continued with Mr. Hudson, but though able to be up and around, my complaint unfitted me for great physical exertion, and seemed to have become chronic. The fact that for eighteen months after the first attack I was never entirely free from it, shows with what tenacity the disease held on. I had to be very careful of my diet and confine myself to certain simple articles of food. Sometimes the pain was excessive—I found more relief in "Perry Davis' Pain Killer" than anything else. A little sweetened water, with a spoonful of pain killer, always relieved me, and dozens of bottles were consumed before I was entirely restored to health. Moreover, the disorder was very weakening; thus I, who had always been strong and robust, was unable to withstand fatigue that others made nothing of. Hence it was that I was handicapped the first year and a half spent in California.

By the time the boys saw their way clear to leave for the mines, I was sufficiently ahead to warrant my joining them. Mr. Hudson had paid us off every Saturday night, and it was laughable to see the kinds of currency tendered and accepted as a matter of course. He would come with a bag filled with roleaus [?] of silver coin, foreign coins of every description, simple slugs of gold stamped with their weight and value, Miner's Bank coins, etc. Everything went in those days, and in whatever shape wages came, there was no grumbling, as there was not sufficient coin in circulation to supply the demand.

Mr. Hudson was a speculative genius, constantly on the lookout for bargains, and kept his employes busy at noon and on Sundays, too, pulling to the various vessels as they arrived to see what he could pick up and dispose of at a profit. As a result of his financing, he was always short of money, and accustomed to borrow on Sunday what he had paid us on Saturday, so as he had borrowed all my wages, when I decided to leave with the others, I went to him and asked for a settlement.

"What," he said, "are you going to leave us, Cal?"

"Yes, if I remain here with these disagreeable winds, and daily afternoon fogs, and continue to drink the water, I believe it will kill me, and a change is necessary, else I may soon be one of Peter Smith's patients and eventually carried to Campo Santo,[8] where I have no desire to go. You know very well what my ailment is, and there are scores dying all round us every day of the same complaint, so I have concluded that the sooner I get away, the better it will be for me. The other boys will leave in a day or two, and I have determined to go with them."

"Well, I suppose you have thought the matter over, and as you do not seem to get any better here, I am inclined to think it will be a beneficial change if you go to the mountains; there are no fogs there, the air is pure, and the river water must be pure also."

"Thank you. Are you ready to settle with me now?"

"No, I am not, but I tell you what; I want to put up a brush shanty for a blacksmith shop, and if you will get the boys to help build it tomorrow, I will pay you off next day sure."

"All right, I'll speak to them when they come home tonight and reckon they will be willing to turn on in the morning."

That night I mentioned the matter to the boys, who readily assented to my request that they would lend a hand, as the proposed shanty would be a rude structure, only calculated to shield its occupant from the sun's rays, and but a short and easy job, anyway.

The next morning Mr. Hudson pointed out the site and dimensions of the shanty, and left the rest to our judgment. The first thing in order was to secure poles for the frame, and while one dug holes in the sand to receive the posts, the others went to procure them. There were some scattering trees growing on the hillside not far away, where it was thought the proper sticks might be found. It was towards there that the choppers directed their way, and soon afterward the ring of the axe notified us that business had commenced.

It proved, however, a more serious matter to one of the boys than he counted on when he started out, for we were presently startled by a piercing shriek that denoted trouble of some kind, and looking up, saw Ed H[owell] hatless and hurried, flying down the hillside, waving his arms, executing a series of jumps and covering a space at every leap that would have taxed the muscles of a kangaroo. He was yet too far away for us to ascertain what caused his surprising stampede, but it was evident he was making for camp at the best gait he could command, while his arms never ceased their rotary motion. As he came nearer, we could hear his voice, and when he burst into camp, saw that he was attended by a swarm of insects that seemed to disturb his equanimity beyond measure.

Shouting, "Take 'em off, take 'em off," he made straight for Will H[untting], who was digging post holes, who when he saw Ed approaching with that halo of hornets in attendance, utterly refused to consider the proposition to "take 'em off," but dropping his spade, "put out" to avoid his pursuer, and though a heavy weight, made most remarkable time in his effort to shun closer proximity, till Ed, despairing of assistance, rushed into the tent, wrapped himself in a blanket, and subsided; when Will, who had been terribly frightened returned to his labor, exhibiting no curiosity to ascertain the condition of the young man in the tent.

About a half-hour afterward when Ed reappeared, his face was a sight to behold. It looked like a map of the Southern Confederacy. With both eyes closed, and his features swollen and inflamed, he was a forlorn and pitiable object as he explained the cause of his trouble.

It seemed that in his peregrination through the wood, he had inadvertently stepped on a hornet's nest, and the insects were not slow to resent the intrusion, as we had seen. They surrounded him by hundreds, and in the attempt to drive them off with his hat, he unfortunately dropped it. The pursuit was so hot he could not spare time to pick it up, so sought safety in flight, with the result as stated. The whole episode was a ludicrous exhibition, and notwithstanding the fact that we sympathized with the victim and did what we could to relieve him "after the hornets were gone," it was impossible to restrain our laughter over his curious antics. Ed was what is called a "mother's boy"; he had been tenderly reared, and his experience in California taught him that there were many things between heaven and earth never dreamed of in his philosophy.

The blacksmith shop was completed that day, and when Mr. Hudson returned that night, he pronounced it "good," and accepted the structure complacently. The next morning he paid me off, and I have always remembered my association with him and his sons kindly. He was a good friend to me while we lived together, and though afterward we had a dispute that was settled by litigation, I have never borne ill-will on that account. He was a man past middle age when he reached San Francisco, and has probably long since joined the great majority. May the clods of the valley lie lightly on his bosom.

It was to the Northern Mines that a great proportion of the Argonauts bent their steps, and we after canvassing the matter thoroughly, decided to try our fortunes in the Southern Mines.⁹ There were seven of us in the party that departed from Happy Valley one August day bound for Stockton.

We had purchased a whaleboat of Captain Payne of the *Thames,* which, though old, was sound, tight, and seaworthy, and freighted her with such of our lares and penates as were indispensable, placing our trunks with our good clothes in store at San Francisco, where they were kept at the rate of a dollar per month till burned in the great fire that occurred in 1850.¹⁰

IX

FROM SAN FRANCISCO TO STOCKTON

AUGUST, 1849

Before leaving San Francisco, we shipped one barrel of pork to Stockton on the small schooner *Favorite*,[1] took a part of the barrel in the boat with us and buried the barrel of beef in the sand at Happy Valley. When, six months afterward, I looked for it, it was gone. I learned, however, that a teamster built a stable over the spot, and one day his horse, in stamping, struck the head of the cask and put his foot through it. The teamster made an examination, discovered the beef, found it sweet, and confiscated it to his own use.

With our clothing, blankets, camp equipage, cradle, gold pans, picks and shovels, provisions, etc., the boat was pretty well loaded when we got under way. The crew consisted of Robert E. Gardiner, Stephen B. French, William F. Huntting, Napoleon Griffing, Absalom Griffing, Edward Howell, and the writer—familiarly called Bob, Steve, Will, Griff, Absy, Ned and Cal; and when we started on our trip, we little knew the trials and vexations the future held in store for us.

It was the latter part of August when we one morning pulled out on the bay in the direction of Saucilito [Sausalito], but as the wind was fresh and favorable, we soon dispensed with the oars and extemporized a sail by attaching a blanket to an oar stepped as a mast. The tide was running flood as we passed the Sister Islands and entered San Pablo Bay.[2] The water was full of seals and I took a shot at one, but never knew whether I hit him or not, as he went down and did not reappear. We crossed San Pablo Bay, steering for the Straits of Carquinez, and passing through, entered Suisun Bay, and at evening tied up at Martinez opposite Benicia, a young settlement which its projectors hoped would one day rival San Francisco.[3] After supper we spread our blankets, and pillowing our heads on the roots of a tree, slept comfortably till morning, when after breakfast we resumed our voyage.

Early in the evening we reached the *Sabina*, which had been brought up from San Francisco and was lying at anchor off Stevenson's embryo city, rather inaptly named "New York of the Pacific," which like many another speculative town "died a-bornin'" and is now forgotten except by old settlers.[4]

The vessel had been brought up so as to furnish a convenient base of supplies to the company, which when we arrived had departed for the mines with Captain Green, the president in command. As was universally the case in such combinations, it soon broke up, and as a company accomplished nothing. Jealousies were manifested, charges and recriminations were bandied, the members generally were disaffected and disappointed, and anarchy reigned supreme. The result was disbandment before a stroke was made at mining, and the members scattered to follow their individual fortunes. There was much sickness and an undue proportion of deaths, especially among the old shipmasters. Those

75

who recovered were so wasted by sickness and exposure to conditions foreign to their habits that they were utterly unfit for business, and whoever could afford the expense returned home, mere wrecks of their former selves. After disbandment, the company went into liquidation, the ship was sold, and the final dividend was broken hopes and grievous disappointment.

Folios might be written descriptive of scenes and incidents connected with the *Sabina*, but it is impracticable, as the story of the writer's experience requires so large a space that the omission of a thousand interesting details is compulsory, and in the effort to confine it within reasonable limits I must cling in my recital to those persons and incidents most directly concerned with my individual career.

Captains James Parker and Albert Payne greeted us as we boarded the ship. They were both invalids, and not long afterward bade goodbye to earth, shuffled off the mortal coil, and departed to solve the dread mystery of the hereafter.

We staid on the ship that night, and it really seemed that if ever hell existed on earth, the *Sabina* had found it and anchored right in the middle of it. When the shades of evening closed around us, the mosquitoes closed in on us, and made things exceedingly lively. The day had been sultry, and they had been lying off in the shade, but after sunset they came out strong. It was a sort of insectorial convention, where every delegate was present, bent on vivisection. The air was actually black with them, and they formed a perfect wall above and around us. As it was impossible to remain on deck and live, we retired to the forecastle, started a smudge, and remained there during the night, inhaling the fumes of smoking oakum and well-nigh stifled with the exhalation; nevertheless, the mosquitoes despite the atmospheric conditions made themselves painfully manifest, and we got but little sleep.[5]

We were away early next morning after breakfast on board, but not so early as to prevent someone of the party from inspecting the coppers in the galley and capturing a piece of boiled salt beef, which afforded the groundwork for lunch and supper that day.

It was not far from the ship to the mouth of the San Joaquin River, a sluggish stream covered with leaves of aquatic plants and as yet unvexed by steamboat wheels. The appearance of the river was so similar to that of the sloughs branching from it, we found it difficult at times to decide which was the main stream.[6] We had received general instructions to "keep the starboard hand aboard" whenever we were in doubt, and progressed favorably till about noon, as the breeze was fresh and fair, but at that hour came to a place where there were three openings and were undecided which to take. We held up to discuss the question, and were about to take the starboard hand, when we discovered a boat coming from that direction, and as it neared us, hailed it. Three Irishmen composed its crew, who informed us they had pulled several miles, when they came to the end of navigation in that branch and were now in search of the main river. There were two other openings, and after some talk the Irishmen chose that on the port side and pulled away. Of course we did not know whether they were right or wrong, but as the writer suggested that wherever there was a chance for a blunder those fellows were pretty sure to take it, and advised that we should choose the third, we did so; and events proved that we were right.

We continued on and met with no further difficulty. When night came, as there were no banks to the river, which ran through an immense marsh and nothing to tie up to, we hauled up close to the flags, made the boat's warp fast to a big iron pot, and threw it overboard for an anchor. The mosquitoes were plentiful, but not near so annoying as the night before. After taking a bite of cold beef and pilot bread, though there was little danger of being run down, we arranged to keep anchor watch, and all except one turned in.

It was my watch from 8 to 10 o'clock, and while the others were sleeping, I smoked my pipe, fought mosquitoes and moralized on things in esse and in posse. When my watch was up, I called Stephen, and after much shaking partially awoke him, when he stood up, and to my surprise and consternation "walked overboard." I grabbed him as he came up, and he climbed into the boat very wet, and also very wide-awake. We overhauled the luggage, found his bag, and he proceeded to don dry raiment.

Everything went well during the rest of the night; we managed to make some hot coffee for breakfast, and got up the anchor. When we pulled the pot on board, it was filled with sand which glistened with particles of what we afterward learned were "iron pyrites," but which we in our ignorance took for gold, and were strongly tempted to stay where we were and dredge a fortune from the river bottom with the pot. Closer investigation showed the worthlessness of the dross, and we proceeded upstream.

Aside from its extreme crookedness, there is nothing about the San Joaquin River below Stockton worthy of comment. The "tuleys" [tules] extend to the horizon on either side, and there is little or no timber. As we had good luck in keeping the proper course, and made rapid progress, we hoped by nightfall to reach Stockton. There were no milestones to consult, nor had we met a boat except that of the "lost Irishmen" since we entered the river. Along in the afternoon, Ed shinned up the mast to explore, but to the question, "what do you see?" his reply was, "nothing but tuleys." Nevertheless, about 5 o'clock we came to a slough which put out on the port side, and as we glanced up it, caught sight of a vessel's mast a mile or two away, and turned into the slough. We soon came to the vessel, which was lying by the river bank in Stockton, which is not on the main stream, but at the head of what is now known as Stockton Slough.[7]

Our effects were landed, the tent was pitched, supper prepared; and while we were eating, a man came who desired to purchase the boat, which having served our purpose, we had no further use for. The price named was $200, which proved satisfactory, and the transfer was made. The purchaser had just come from the mines, bound for San Francisco, and one of us went with him to the store, where the merchant weighed out 13 oz. 6 dwt. and 16 grains of dust, which at $15 per ounce made up the purchase price. We were a little shy of the gold dust, but as the trader assured us it was all right, did not demur. We were fortunate selling the boat so soon, as we had anticipated some delay in finding a customer. The barrel of pork shipped on the *Favorite* was stored on board the

Mazeppa subject to order by our friend John Mills, who had taken passage on the schooner.[8] He enclosed the warehouse receipt in a letter, advising us he had gone to Hawkins' Bar on the Tuolumne River, and we decided to follow him.

It was late when we retired, and as our rest had been broken the two previous nights, it is perhaps superfluous to state that we slept well.

FROM STOCKTON TO HAWKINS' BAR

AUGUST, 1849

Stockton at that period was only a collection of a few trading tents, but its location was such that it was evident it must soon become an important point as a shipping place for the Southern Mines. A young man named Weber owned all the land thereabout, and its sale subsequently made him very wealthy. There was little about the town to interest us, as it was in an inchoate condition and not at all attractive.[1] It was here that we first witnessed the dexterity of the Mexican vaquero in handling a riata. There was a herd of cattle grazing near our tent owned by a city butcher, and we one day watched a cowboy as he proceeded to rope one for the slaughterhouse.

Mounted on a wiry mustang, with his riata hanging to the horn of his saddle, he rode into the herd to select a victim for the shambles, and having made choice of a big steer, pursued him for a while before he had a chance to make a cast, but eventually the coil was swung above his head and flew out, lighting on the bullock's neck, at which the animal gave a bellow and set off at tremendous speed, the horseman being unable to pull him up, as unfortunately the folds of the riata had encircled a calf beside the steer, and the latter was towing it along at a breakneck gait. It was here that the marvelous expertness of the rider came in play, as he so manipulated the rope that he succeeded in releasing the calf while the steer was still retained in custody, thrown down, secured, and dragged to the slaughterhouse. The poor calf was a dejected-looking specimen after its disengagement from the toils, and giving a lugubrious ba-a-a as if to say, "excuse me please," sought the shade of the willows on the river bank and lay down, perhaps to weep its sad bosom empty.

We remained in Stockton one day and secured transportation for our traps at the rate of $20 per hundred lbs., which under the circumstances was not unreasonable for a distance of 120 miles. Before starting, we boiled a lot of salt beef tongue for use on the road, as our cooking utensils, once stowed in the wagon, would not be available in transitu. The food was left in the pot, which was slung to the rear axle, and had the journey lasted a month, there would have been enough to carry us through, for though palatable for a few meals, we soon tired of it; moreover, it was so salty, our thirst was aggravated by eating it, and after the second day no one hankered for tongue, which was ever afterward eliminated from our bill of fare.

It was a jovial party that followed the wagon, that August morning when it left Stockton en route for the mountains. The day was awfully hot, the ground was parched, and for twenty feet down was dry as an ash pan, while the soil was so shrunken that large crevices six or eight feet deep were of frequent occurrence. There was but little water on the road, and the extreme heat in connection with the salt tongue, generated such abnormal thirst that what we carried was soon exhausted, and by noon the air of joviality

79

had entirely disappeared. Peck, our teamster,[2] encouraged us by saying there was a well a few miles further where we might perhaps find water, and as we plodded along, anxious to assuage our thirst, we kept a bright lookout for the aqueous reservoir.

Neither Peck nor his team seemed to be discommoded by the lack of water, as they were accustomed to it; but for us, who were unacclimated, the deprivation was serious, and when we neared the locality of the well, all rushed ahead to discover whether it would yield anything of a potable nature. The well itself, about eight feet deep, was at the bottom of a natural fissure some fifteen feet deep, and as we peered into the depths, we were gratified to see the sheen of water at the bottom. There was not more than a gallon or two, at most, and it was difficult to get at, but by tying our belts and handkerchiefs together, and attaching a tin cup thereto, we managed to draw up sufficient to slake our thirst, and whoever has panted after water in the desert, can imagine our relief.

That night we camped near what was called the "Lone Tree," the only one on the route between French Camp and the Stanislaus River, which in its isolation formed a prominent landmark in the arid plain.[3] There we found water for the team, got supper, and turned in, thoroughly exhausted with the day's travel.

The second day was a duplicate of the first; we suffered the same pangs of thirst, but fortunately met Col. Jackson, a trader for whom Jacksonville on the Tuolumne was named, who gave each a drink from a large canteen slung to his saddle, and encouraged us with a good account of the prospect at the diggings.[4] We afterward met several young fellows returning from the mines, bound for San Francisco after a short and unsuccessful campaign in the gold fields. From their point of view, the mines were a humbug, and they advised us to turn back, as there was nothing ahead but hard work and disappointment. Though this advice was rather dispiriting, we took their statement cum grano salis and continued our journey.

We made camp at Knight's Ferry on the Stanislaus River[5] that night, where after supper we took a bath in the stream, washed away the accumulated dust of the journey, and much refreshed by the ablution spread our blankets, laid down, and slept the dreamless sleep of exhaustion.

On the evening of the third day we reached Green Springs,[6] within about six miles of our destination, where we camped for the night, and early next morning started on the last stage of our journey, much pleased with the thought that our pilgrimage was so nearly ended. Soon after we started, the teamster pointed to an Indian trail, which he said was shorter than the wagon road; and as anything that would tend to shorten the route was considered a sort of godsend, we followed the trail, and a half-hour's travel brought us to Red Mountain Bar, about a mile above Hawkins' by the rough path along the river bank.

It was about 10 o'clock when we reached Hawkins', where we proceeded to select a site for our permanent camp. We soon found an eligible location between two evergreen [live] oaks, beneath which we seated ourselves to enjoy a rest while we watched the unique picture presented by the camp, and waited for the wagon.

XI

LIFE AT HAWKINS' BAR

SEPTEMBER, 1849

At the time of our arrival, there were probably two hundred men congregated on the flat adjoining the bar, and their white tents pitched promiscuously among the trees presented a fascinating and picturesque appearance. The flat proper, which extended from the river back to the base of the mountain, occupied about five acres, and looked like a vast orchard that had been carefully tended. The clean, smooth sod, free from underbrush, the beautiful evergreen oaks scattered at intervals on its surface, and the magnificent natural framework of chaparral, chamisal, and manzanita on the mountainside, all combined to please the eye, and we were gratified to know that our lines [*i.e.,* lives?] had fallen in such an alluring locality.[1] At that period the flat, yet-unscarred by pick and shovel, retained all its pristine beauty; and the river, yet-undefiled by slum and tailings, flowed clear as crystal over its rocky bed, unimpeded by dams, and unvexed by waterwheels. Mining was still in its primitive stage, and the pan and cradle were the sole dependence of the miner. The "Long Tom" sluice box and hydraulic pipe had not yet been introduced.

The camp was peopled with young men from 18 to 35 years old, and but few exceeded the latter age. Old men were scarce in California in those days, and as for women and children, except Indians there were none; and it was not till the immigrants with their families crossed the plains that our eyes were gladdened with the sight of either.[2] It was an anomalous condition of affairs, and altogether an unnatural state of existence; nevertheless, there was a friendly affiliation among the populace, and each was disposed to assist the others and give a newcomer the benefit of his advice and experience. Of course, it was an incongruous community, made up of all classes and nationalities, drawn there by the magnetic influence of gold, and each came cherishing a latent hope that his most sanguine expectations might be realized, only, however, to be disappointed in the end; and with some it eventually became a question of mere bread and butter.

As was always the case, some made good wages, while others who failed to "strike it" went about prospecting, rather than rest satisfied with six or eight dollars a day and working steadily. The fact was, gold-digging was very hard work, and as a great majority of the young Argonauts had never been accustomed to bone labor they were easily discouraged and pronounced the mines a delusion and a snare. Any man at that time by working ten hours a day could have taken out from six to ten dollars daily, but that sum did not accord with their preconceived ideas, and was considered too little. Every few days, reports would come in of "big strikes," when a general stampede occurred, and away they would go in pursuit of what usually proved an ignis fatuus. It was the reckless, "happy-go-lucky" ones who were generally the most fortunate, but their good fortune did not avail them, as they were very apt to "blow in" their dust at the monte bank and

81

celebrate Sunday with a big drunk. While such fellows were taking out gold dust hand over hand, and squandering it in dissipation, others who perhaps had wives and families anxiously waiting for a remittance, failed to earn more than sufficient for necessary current expenses, and one would often hear the remark from such, "I guess I'll go and get drunk and see if it will change my luck."

It was about noon when the team came with our traps, and we immediately unloaded them and set about preparing a local habitation. The tent was pitched beneath the shade of the two trees, the ridgepole running from one to the other, and securely fastened to the ground with wooden pins.

Leaving the others to arrange the camp and prepare food, Will H[untting], Griff [Napoleon Griffing], and myself carried the cradle and tools to the river where, after selecting a claim, we placed our rocker and commenced operations in an awkward fashion.[3] We chose a little rocky point covered with grass and jutting into the river, which had till then been neglected by everybody. The soil near the water was shallow, and the roots of the grass extended to the rock, which as we pulled them up and deposited them in the hopper, were actually alive with flakes of gold; but, unable to judge, we were not particularly struck with the prospect, and simply considered it a matter of course. After working for two or three hours and washing perhaps twenty buckets of dirt, we were called to supper, when taking our tools and cradle to camp, we deposited the pan in the tent, and like infernal fools sat down to eat and deferred panning-out till morning.

The next morning we panned out the proceeds of our experiment of the previous day, dried the dust at the fire, and took it to the store, where, after blowing out the black sand, the grocer weighed it and told us there was something over $20. We were speechless and dumbfounded, as we had no idea there was to exceed two or three dollars at most. Of course, we hurried at once to the claim, but alas! too late. We had removed the tools and left nothing to hold it, and it had been "jumped." There was no use crying over spilt milk; we had forfeited the claim through sheer ignorance and colossal stupidity, and it goes without saying we were ready to howl with vexation. That claim, afterward known as the "Gauly claim," was the richest spot ever struck on Hawkins' Bar, and yielded thousands of dollars before it was exhausted.[4]

From that time on, our luck was by no means phenomenal, though we managed to pay expenses and keep a small sum in the treasury. Our deposit safe was an ordinary glass bottle, which by looking at, we were able to judge pretty accurately the condition of the finances. We gauged it as one would a thermometer, and expressed its indications by like terms. When, say, half-full, it was considered to be at a temperate stage, and so long as it stood between that and freezing, matters went smoothly; but when it got below freezing point, the bottle was contemplated with wrinkled brows and anxious eyes, and as it was generally lying around loose in the tent handy for inspection, the boys as they from time to time picked it up and glanced at it were exhilarated or depressed by the result of their investigation. Some one of the crowd had pasted narrow strips of writing paper across the bottle at regular intervals, after the manner of a thermometer. These points ran from zero to the apex, and were marked as follows: The lowest strip read, "half-rations," next in succession came "pork stew," "pork and beans," "roast beef and potatoes," "plum duff," "canned turkey with fixings," and at the very summit and culminating point, "oysters with ale and Porter—ad libitum." The receptacle when full held about 30 ounces, but its capacity was never fairly tested. It was our spiritual thermometer, and as its contents increased or decreased, our hopes rose or fell accordingly. The line of dust seldom rose above "plum duff," and never actually receded to half rations. The average height was at pork and beans, which formed the main constituent in the bill of fare. None of us had been habituated to strict economy in the matter of diet, and after five or six weeks of plenty of hard work with insufficient remuneration, during which time we had just about managed to pay the grocery bills, the chance of becoming millionaires seemed to grow small by degrees, and beautifully less. Hence the financial horizon presented no roseate hues; and, unknown to us, a change was impending, destined eventually to separate us and knock our combination into a "cocked hat."

One Sunday morning, when the gang just after breakfast were standing about the camp fire smoking their pipes and discussing matters political, philosophical, and theological, Bob [Robert Gardiner] came from the store where he had been to settle the weekly bill. Holding the mustard bottle in his hand, he inaugurated a conversation, which may be summarized as follows. First, however, it may be well to give the reader an idea what were his peculiar characteristics. He was a little fellow weighing about 120 lbs., and had officiated as cook that week. Well-liked by his chums, generous as a prince, and tender-hearted and sympathetic as a woman, he was a confirmed pessimist, always looking at the dark side and never considering that the cloud which temporarily overshadowed him could by any possibility possess a silver lining. Constantly prophesying evil, he was subject to periodical outbreaks, when he would come down on his fellows like an avalanche, any one of whom could have picked him up and thrown him over his head with ease, but when he opened on them with his mouth, they would shrink and cower like whipped children or criminals receiving sentence for some awful misdemeanor; not that Bob was quarrelsome or disposed to back his words by an appeal to force, but he had a "wicked tongue" and when aroused by opposition was apt to use it in such a way that it cut like a two-edged sword. He had a knack of dropping hints, of firing from behind a masked battery of smiles, and might[il]y rubbing "raw spots," which was a vast deal more effective than outright blows. Smooth words dropping from his tongue, although apparently harmless, had the effect of tearing and wounding, and would send limping to the rear any unlucky wight who had the temerity to oppose him. All these characteristics were well-known to the boys, none of whom ever dreamt of resorting to the lex talionis, but waited patiently and silently till the storm blew over, for all knew that, having "said his say," he would afterward tone down and perhaps be the first to propose some extravagance in direct conflict with his uttered speech.

Such was Bob, who had just come from the store and was exhibiting to his colleagues a round of pork which he had purchased and from which he proceeded to cut a piece to season the beans then in process of cooking. He was pointing to the pork that hung on a branch of the tree which shaded the camp, and declaiming on the extravagance of certain members of the party in the consumption ot food, the excessive cost of keeping body and soul together, and the utter impossibility of even doing that without a change in the habits of certain individuals whom he proceeded to name seriatim, while he expatiated on the urgent necessity of economy in the matter of grub.

"Now, boys, have you any idea what I paid for that pork? Have you the slightest inkling of the expense of housekeeping? I just paid Jim Hall $11.50 for that miserable belly piece, and I wish to impress it upon you that with pork at $1.50 per lb., and everything else in proportion, you have got to get up and get, and be on hand early and late if you ever expect to see old Long Island again. You cannot afford to lie in bed mornings till the sun burns a hole in your shirt tails. I've been cook for the past week, and know about what it costs to feed you, and by Jove there is not one of the lot that I would not rather board a week than a fortnight. There's Will H., he'll eat more at one meal than his whole day's wages will pay for."

"A man can't work unless he eats," growled Will, goaded beyond endurance by the personal allusion.

"Very true, I admit all that, but there is no necessity for a man to gorge himself like an Esquimaux; overeating is as bad as starvation, and you don't seem to observe the happy medium. If, instead of filling your pan a half-dozen times, you would content yourself with a reasonable allowance, you would work all the better and enjoy your next meal better, also."

"There's Cal, he goes in for luxuries, sugar is his strong point; he'll put more sugar into one pot of coffee than would suffice an ordinary man for a week. Not satisfied with one or two spoonfuls, he fairly thickens his coffee with sugar at $2 a pound, and the worst of it is, the coffee can't absorb it all, and there is about an inch of sugar left in his pot at every meal.

"Then again, it was only last night that Steve [French] suggested 'fried pies' as something which all would appreciate. Fried pies at a dollar apiece might prove a palatable morsel to Stephen, but as for me, I can't see it. Look at that bottle—Does that look like fried pies? Talking about fried pies with the thermometer at zero; it looks to me more like half-rations.

"I had a talk with Jim Hall this morning when I paid our bill, and Jim says that from today he is going to shut down on the credit system, as the population of Hawkins' Bar is getting too d—d 'circumforaneous' to meet his views, and hereafter 'money' has got to do the talking. How loud do you imagine our money can talk? Look at that bottle, not an ounce in the pot."

"I move," said Cal, "that we give it to Steve for a poker stake, and let him go over and sit in with the boys at the store tonight; it might prove a fortunate investment."

"You move, do you? You had better move down to the river and wash that shirt, or take a dose of castor oil and work it off, you have worn it six weeks to my certain knowledge."

"Ah, Robert, my Christian friend, you are away off. Just allow me to observe in the most delicate way in the world that you are entirely mistaken; I bent this shirt last Sunday. Will washed it, thinking it was his own, and when I saw it spick and span hanging on a bush, I recognized it and claimed it as a matter of course. Ask Will if it isn't just as I say."

"Look at the back of it, the dirt is an inch thick."

"That's where Steve used it for a towel; I told him he was raising thunder with my clean raiment."

"Well, that's neither here nor there; it was the financial question I was discussing, and in view of the condition of the treasury, I really think we should make up our minds to curtail expenses to the minimum, and begin by cutting off luxuries. The first thing to go must be sugar."

"What!!" exclaimed Cal impulsively, but he took a sober second thought and subsided.

Ed H[owell] suggested that the balance be invested in dried apples.

"Good idea," remarked Stephen, "there's the river handy."

"Oh, you can sneer, but I'm giving you cold facts. There's nothing theoretical in what I say, as a glance at the bottle will prove. We must cut the coat according to the cloth. The condition is serious, and we must meet it by reducing expenses. We know more than we did when we came here some weeks ago, and I have been studying the situation while you were at work.

"The truth is, there are too many in the crowd; we have but one cradle, and there are six to feed it, when three at most could attend to it and give it all the dirt it can wash. I have watched you the past week, and at every 'wash-down,' all hands drop their tools and run to the rocker to see the 'clean-up.' It reminds me of a parcel of old women watching a sick baby, and the only remedy I can devise is for us to separate and not waste the energies of the whole crowd over one cradle; the work is too easy and induces laziness.

"There were Will, Steve, and Cal off all yesterday afternoon on what they call a 'prospecting expedition' across the river, but what they expected to find in that sand bank the good Lord only knows. They came home to dinner, and when they left they took both trowels and the crowbar, and what was the result of their afternoon's work? I saw the whole thing from camp. Steve and Cal crossed over and Steve returned for Will. Now, I know as well as if I were in the secret that it was a put up job between Steve and Cal to dump Will in the river, for as soon as the dugout reached mid-stream, over it went and out rolled Will with a trowel in each hand. Steve, knowing of course what was to happen, had his eye on the crowbar and managed by great exertion to save it, but Will, taken by surprise, was less fortunate. He sounded once and came up with one trowel, he went down a second time and lost the other, when, having recovered his wits, he struck out for shore. They came home at night having accomplished nothing except losing two trowels worth $10 apiece, and half-day's time for three men, but they came home hungry as we can all attest, and got away with more victuals than usual."

Having listened patiently to Bob's lecture, a general council was held. Matters were talked over, the situation was discussed, and the consensus of opinion seemed to favor his suggestion to separate and divide the chances, and it was agreed that Will, Griff, and myself should seek some other field.

XII

THE TRIP TO SULLIVAN'S CREEK

OCTOBER, 1849

Reports had lately come of big strikes at Sullivan's Creek, some 20 miles away,[1] and that one eighteen-pound nugget had been taken out. As it was comparatively a new field, we resolved to try our fortunes there, and immediately began preparation for departure.

As our blankets, tools, and cooking utensils were no light weight, and the road a rough one, we hesitated at assuming their carriage on our own shoulders; nevertheless, there seemed no way to avoid it, and we had about made up our minds to accept the inevitable, when a suggestion was made which was readily adopted, as it would, if carried out, relieve us of the disagreeable necessity of making pack animals of ourselves.

There was a jackass roaming about the camp which no one claimed, and as it had no owner to dispute our right, we resolved to use it, not doubting that we would receive the thanks of the community for removing what had become a public nuisance, as the jack had made frequent raids on the miners' provisions and almost every camp had suffered from his depredations. Before deciding, we consulted with one and another of our neighbors, and the general opinion was that the removal of the jack would be a good riddance, for, as nobody claimed ownership, none could be held liable for its inroads. When thoroughly satisfied that there would be no hue and cry over its disappearance, we decided to claim the jack as a "maverick" and use him to transport our goods to Sullivan's; so after due inquiry we located the donkey, led it to camp, and picketed it near the tent.

Early on the following day, the resounding bray of the ass awoke us from slumber, and after a hasty breakfast, we proceeded to pack him with what was indispensable for our trip. Without a pack-saddle it was difficult to adjust the load securely, but we managed so to arrange it that on level ground it would maintain a proper equilibrium, and when all was ready, bade goodbye to the fellows and started on our journey, utterly oblivious of the difficulties we were to encounter ere it was completed.

The jack was a docile animal, and as we drove it before us, we congratulated ourselves that we traveled light-footed, as the day promised to be sultry, and our way ran over steep hills and beside wild gorges that made locomotion exceedingly tiresome and difficult. Moreover, on rough ground we had to be very watchful of the pack, as it slipped forward and aft on the jack's back, and required frequent adjustment. Nevertheless, we progressed very well till we came to the Red Mountain, up which the trail ran in a zigzag course, and it was there that our troubles began, for during the rest of the way our patience and inventive facilities were thoroughly tested, and we were several times compelled to repack the whole load, which for want of a saddle it was impossible to make permanently secure.

Although we carried no burden, the ascent of the mountain tested our endurance, as the pack required vigilant supervision to prevent its slipping over the jack's hindquarters, and as we scaled the steep, beneath the sun's burning rays, it became a question whether under such circumstances life was worth living.

At length, however, we reached the summit and sat down in the shade of a friendly tree to recover breath. As we sat there, we heard the sound of a horse's feet in our rear, and presently the horseman came up and excitedly hailed us with the curt question, "What do you mean by carrying off my jackass without leave or license?"

"Your jackass? Well, that's news, as it appears to be our jackass at present, and as we are three to one, we think you will have some difficulty in establishing your right of possession."

"I tell you, the jack belongs to me, and I intend to take him back with me."

"Hell, they say, is paved with good intentions, but as to taking the animal back with you, we reckon if you go back at all, you'll certainly go without the jackass."

"I tell you, the jack is mine, I bought him and paid for him, and have the bill of sale in my pocket."

"You say you bought him; now, it takes two to make a bargain, and as it was notorious in camp that the animal had no resident owner, it is difficult to conceive how you acquired title. At all events, we've got him, and as possession is nine points of the law, we propose to hold him unless you are able to convince us that your title is better than ours."

"If you are reasonable men, I think I can easily do that—I am willing to admit that up to yesterday the jack had no recognizable owner, but since then the condition has changed, and he now belongs to me."

"Prove it, then, and if we consider your title better than ours, we will surrender the jack on certain conditions to be arranged after you have established your ownership."

The man, whose name was Pine and who kept a small store on the Bar, exhibited a bill of sale with several names attached which were familiar to us, and proceeded to explain that the jack had ravaged a number of camps and got away with edibles cooked and uncooked to an extent that exhausted the forbearance of the victims, who called a meeting at which it was resolved to sell the ass and appropriate the proceeds of sale pro rata among the losers by his depredations; and in accordance with that resolution, the jack was put up at auction, and he, Pine, bought him and thereby became responsible for his future thefts. This occurred on the morning of the previous day, which was Sunday, and as it was not till evening that we captured the donkey, it was evident that the title had already passed to Pine, and as the fiat of a meeting of the Bar was final and conclusive,[2] it was useless to kick. This was so apparent that we decided to temporize with him and make the best terms we could.

It was some five or six miles to Wood's Creek,[3] where it was possible for us to procure another animal, and we suggested to him that if he would go that far with us we would surrender the jack. He demurred, and swore he would not go a foot further, but finally consented with an ill-grace when informed that the proposition was our ultimatum, and that whether he went or not, the jack would go with us to the creek.

The descent of the mountain was nearly as steep as the ascent. The donkey carried his pack most of the way on the back of his neck, and it was only his tremendous ears that prevented it from sliding off altogether. After reaching the base of the mountain, it was comparatively easy traveling till we came to the hill at Wood's Creek, which was a "holy terror," as all will admit who have ever climbed or gone down it.

Here we overtook an ox team, and the wagon, loaded with supplies for some trader, was about to start on its perilous descent as we came up with it. The teamster had adopted every possible precaution against accidents. The wheels were all locked, and a big tree was attached to the rear axle as a drag. All these preparations, however, proved ineffective, for no sooner did the wagon reach the declivity than it began to slide forward with increasing velocity, which, despite the efforts of the wheel oxen to hold it, soon brought it upon them, and as they sheered out to avoid the collision, the vehicles was brought crosswise of the road, and over it went, rolling down the hill one indiscriminate conglomeration of oxen, wagon, dry goods, groceries, clothing, beans, rice, pork, bacon, hams, flour, picks, pans, shovels, and dust "hell bent for destruction," as the teamster remarked sententiously. It was the most perfect wreck imaginable, and as everything was smashed and mixed with the red soil, there was but little salvage.

Though we sympathized with the teamster, we could not render any material assistance, and as the owner of the merchandise was with him to assist in relieving the unfortunate cattle of their yokes, we continued on our way, and finally after many a tussle with the impracticable pack reached camp at the creek, where we unloaded the jack and surrendered him to Pine, who immediately took the back track for home.

It was about three o'clock when we arrived at Wood's Creek, and as we were tired and needed time to look for another pack animal, it was decided to stop overnight and resume our journey next morning; but though we made earnest endeavor, we were unable to hire an animal or procure transportation of any kind; and as it was desirable to get on as fast as possible, we very reluctantly concluded to carry our luggage on our own shoulders.

The sun never shone on a more dejected trio than ourselves as we prepared next morning to pursue our pilgrimage to the Shrine of Sullivan, which was still about ten miles distant, every furlong of which seemed equal to a degree of longitude, nor was such dejection to be wondered at when it is considered that each was handicapped with a burden weighing about seventy pounds. Fortunately, there were no mountains to scale, and our way was for the most part over a good trail, but the heat was almost unsupportable, and it soon became evident that in assuming our packs, we had undertaken a task far beyond our strength, as we were utterly exhausted before we had proceeded two miles on our journey.

Of the three, the writer was least able to cope with the difficulties of the road; and as the complaint contracted in San Francisco still held on, and had weakened him to an extent that forbade extra exertion, he was, much against his will, constrained to succumb to circumstances, "throw up the sponge," and declare himself out of the race. Though Will and Griff each volunteered to relieve me of a portion of my load, I refused to listen to the suggestion, knowing that their own burdens were already greater than they could bear.

While we were discussing the situation, a drove of horses made its appearance over a ridge not far distant, and it occurred to us that we might possibly catch one and press him into service temporarily as a common carrier, turning him loose at the end of the journey, when we would undoubtedly find his way back to the herd. Acting on this idea, we determined to make a "rodeo"[4] then and there; and though there was not much prospect of success, we were encouraged by the sight of some dead trees nearby, which had fallen in such a position that they enclosed a triangular space that we hoped might be utilized as a corral, into which we proposed to drive the animals.

Taking one of the ropes that bound our packs, we approached the drove, and as we came nearer, discovered it was composed of used-up pack horses that had been turned out to recruit. They all had sore backs, which in an ordinary case would have excited compassion and induced us to spare them, but as we, too, had sore backs, selfishness prevailed over humanity and hardened our hearts. There was not much life in the poor creatures, and we found no difficulty in driving them towards the corral, where we succeeded in capturing an iron-gray mustang, which seemed to have less spirit and a sorer back than any of the others. Could we have chosen, we would have selected another, but it was a case of "Hobson's choice" and we had no option. Having secured the horse, we proceeded to pack our effects without delay. The mustang stood quietly while we arranged the load and packed it the best we could, but it was a bad job, after all, as we had no saddle and but a scant supply of rope.

We christened the horse "Uriah Heep." Griff led him, and Will and I walked on either side to keep the pack in place. All went well for about two miles, when unfortunately a loose tin cup collided with a pick, and "woke the mustang up." At the noise of collision between cup and pick, his deportment changed instanter; he was no longer the patient pack horse that had submitted so quietly to the imposition of his load, he no longer exhibited any of the characteristics of Uriah Heep, but threw off all semblance to humbleness and developed into a perfect terror. Giving one ear-piercing shriek, he let fly both hind feet, and we witnessed a specimen of ground and lofty tumbling that would have astonished a cowboy. He bucked, grunted, snorted, and cried "ha-ha" like Job's war horse until finally, breaking the cord which bound him, he fled into the wilderness and left us disconsolate and forlorn.

All our household goods were carried off when the mustang stampeded, but before he had gone eighty rods, he managed to relieve himself of his load, which was scattered promiscuously in his track; hence we were enabled to collect our effects without much effort and put them in shape for transportation; then, having gone over the field and assured ourselves that we had recovered everything, we lit our pipes and sat down for consultation—at least Will and I did, but Griff shouldered his pack and started out alone.

He had not been gone ten minutes, however, when we saw him returning, leading a little sorrel pony by the forelock that he had picked up in the next valley, where he discovered it grazing alone, and it made no effort to avoid him as he walked up and caught it. It will be easily understood that we considered the pony a godsend, as we threw our traps on its back and started afresh on our journey. The little mare walked along willingly, and really seemed to enjoy our society, but though honors appeared to be easy, there were other complications in store for us, as we shall presently see.

Just before we reached Curtis' Creek,⁵ we noticed three men coming from that direc-tion. They were on foot, and as they neared us, their appearance indicated that they were rough customers. Each carried a rifle, a big revolver, and a bowie knife, and they really looked as if they were on the warpath. They saluted us as they came up, and asked if we had seen any horses on the road. We told them we had seen what appeared to be a drove of pack horses a few miles back, and they passed on without further questions.

They had not gone far, however, when one called to another "Oh, Joe! that looks like your mare those fellows have got, I know her by her crooked tail."

Joe looked back, scrutinized the pony, and having recognized it, exclaimed "By G—d, it *is* my mare."

This assertion took us all aback and placed us in a terrible quandary, and as we had been caught in flagrante delicto, it looked like a short shrift. Horse-stealing was considered worse than murder, as a horse thief usually had a quick and speedy trial, and summary punishment if convicted.⁶ We had taken the pony without weighing the consequences if detected, and of course had no idea of keeping it after it had served our purpose, but the fates were against us, and the mare's owner confronted us with scowling brow and loaded rifle. Had we had time to consider, we would have shouldered the responsibility and made a plain statement of facts as they existed, for we could have proved our res-pectability and undoubtedly convinced its owner that we had taken the pony for tem-porary use, without the slightest idea of retaining possession.

But we were confused, obliged to think quickly, and there was no chance to weigh the pros and cons. The angry mien of the strangers showed that they were ready to proceed to extremities, and as they were heavily armed, while we were comparatively defenseless, there was no room for doubt that in case of a collision, we would stand a very poor chance. Quick as lightning these thoughts rushed through our minds, and though it is humiliating to confess, we foolishly suppressed the truth and sheered off into the Ser-bonian bog of mendacity, and in explanation avowed we had "hired the pony at Wood's Creek."

"Who did you hire it of? What's the man's name?"

"He said his name was Peters."

"What kind of a looking man is he?"

"He is a tall, slim man, about 30 years old, sandy hair and beard, and talks with a drawl, like a Down-east Yankee."

"What part of the camp does he live in?"

"We do not know, we met him near the store, he was leading the pony at the time and we hired it for six dollars."

"Will he come after it?"

"No, we agreed to turn it loose this evening, he said it would find its way home."

After some further conversation, it was arranged that we should give the mare a feed of barley and leave her in the corral at Curtis' Creek.

With this understanding, the strangers with blood in their eyes started for Wood's Creek in pursuit of Peters, while we, who by our misrepresentation had dispatched them in search of that mythical individual, were but ill at ease, conscious that we would inevitably be caught in the tangled web of deception woven by ourselves. We had sacrificed self-respect as a mere temporary expedient, for we were satisfied that when the strangers failed to discover their man, they would conclude that we had deceived them and sent them on a fool's errand, and as a result would concentrate their anger on us.

Taken altogether, the outlook was not at all encouraging, hence we were in a despondent mood when we reached Curtis' Creek. We felt that Nemesis was close at our heels, and the thought was far from agreeable. Nevertheless, we yarded and fed the pony, and prepared supper, resolving to make an early start next morning and reach Sullivan's as soon as possible, for we had friends there, who in a case of emergency would stand by us.

Before leaving Hawkins' Bar, we had wrapped twenty dollars in a handkerchief for current expenses. This was rolled up in a shirt and packed with the rest of our traps, but when we sought it that night to pay for the barley and provisions consumed at supper, we were unable to find it. Our belongings had been subjected to pretty rough usage when the mustang stampeded, and it was evident that the package of money had escaped observation in the general wreck. We explained matters to the grocer, and when Griff and myself passed that way six weeks later, we settled with him.

Completely used up both physically and financially, we spread our blankets and lay down to rest with heavy hearts and sad forebodings, and when morning came, it found me with a splitting headache and in no condition to resume the journey. Nevertheless, it was plainly apparent that we must put out at once and get over the three miles to Sullivan's without delay, as the three strangers were likely to return at any time, and if there was to be a fuss, we preferred it should occur where we had friends to back us up. Thus reasoning, we swallowed a hasty breakfast, and before sunrise started up the creek for our destination.

We will not dwell over the incidents of that three-mile tramp; it is sufficient to say that it was a memorable one, and though we started early, it was noon ere it was ended; but I wish to record it right here, that I swore that day never again under any circumstances to make a pack animal of myself, and I never did—That oath was kept religiously.

When we deposited our packs in front of the store at Sullivan's and walked inside to interview Bruce F., the merchant, an old acquaintance and fellow-townsman, he failed to recognize us, which was no wonder, for three more dilapidated specimens of the genus homo are seldom seen, and it was difficult to convince him that we, whom he had last met in all the glory of fashionable attire, had been transformed into the miserable tramps who greeted him so familiarly. He welcomed us cordially, however, and as dinner was just ready, we joined him in the meal without change of toilet.

We soon enlightened our friend in regard to what had transpired on the way from Hawkins', and he, like us, believed we were likely to hear more from the men whom we had dispatched on a wild-goose chase after the non-existent Peters. We had no time, however, to brood over our troubles, as we were dead broke, and it was necessary to get work without delay. The merchant had a small tent, which he kindly loaned us, and we proceeded to pitch it on a neighboring hillside. Leaving the others to grade a level place for our domicile, I went prospecting for tent poles.

Shortly afterward, Will came up in a state of great excitement, and while I trimmed the poles, advised me that the owner of the pony and his two companions were at the store, were half-drunk and in an ugly mood; they were inquiring for us, and seemed anxious for an interview. We canvassed the matter hurriedly, and as there was no escape, decided to face the music and make the best settlement we could. Picking up Griff on the way, we proceeded to the store, where we met the strangers, who informed us that they had made due inquiry at Wood's Creek, but had failed in their search for Peters, and wanted one of us to go there with them and identify the man.

Knowing that Peters was a nonentity, we recognized the absurdity of any attempt to find him, and though the strangers made the proposition in apparent good faith, we demurred, assigning as a reason that we were strapped, and must at once try to earn a grub-stake, and could not afford to go meandering about the country in pursuit of a man whom we had seen but once, and of whom we knew no more than we had already told them. Acknowledging that our statement was reasonable, as we had no direct interest in the search, they proposed that one of us should go, and in the event of success in locating the man, they would pay an ounce a day for the time spent. As the bonus was contingent on finding Peters, we could not see any money in that proposition, and refused to consider it, for reasons satisfactory to ourselves, at least.

During the dispute, drinks intervened at short intervals, and as the strangers imbibed, they grew excited, and the interview became stormy, and at one time it looked as if it would end in a free fight all round. The excitement ran so high that finally the strangers asserted their total disbelief in our story, and plumply charged us with stealing the pony. This charge came near precipitating a row at once, but the merchant interposed and succeeded in reducing matters to a more amicable basis. The strangers complained that they had each lost two days in pursuit of Peters, and that we could do no less than remunerate them for the time so spent, and demanded a hundred dollars; else, as we had been found in possession of the horse, they would call a meeting, charge us with stealing it, and compel us to prove a negative. It was vain to plead poverty, for the more they drank, the uglier they became, and refused to compromise for less than the sum demanded. Things looked serious, but through the intermediation of the merchant and a few outsiders, it was finally arranged that we should pay them forty dollars, which sum we borrowed of the trader and the affair was settled. It was unfortunate and humiliating for us all through. We had acted inconsiderately in taking the pony in the first place, and the fact that the owner found his horse in our possession militated against us, and placed us in a bad position. It was a good lesson, however, for none of us ever troubled other people's quadrupeds after that, which may perhaps be accounted for by the fact that temptation under like circumstances never again occurred.

AT SULLIVAN'S CREEK

OCTOBER–NOVEMBER, 1849

The next day we commenced housekeeping under such strict economical conditions that for a while we lived more like pigs than human beings. Our food was of the cheapest and coarsest description, and consisted mainly of "pinoche," a Mexican preparation of parched corn pounded in a mortar, and fried pork with Chili [Chile?] hard bread, which required a half hour's boiling to render it masticable. The water in which the bread was boiled was sweetened with coarse Mexican sugar and used instead of tea and coffee at meals. The pinoche was made into mush over which we poured pork gravy after frying it. This diet, though not attractive, was sustaining, and enabled us to reduce living expenses to the minimum; nevertheless, the cost of such food was about a dollar a day for each. That debt to the grocer hung over us like an incubus, and we vowed to indulge in no luxuries till it was paid.

The gold at Sullivan's was coarse, and as is generally the case in the dry diggings, not distributed so uniformly as on the river bars, but when one did strike it, he was apt to strike it rich, and recover for many previous fruitless days' work. The most desirable part of the creek was occupied when we reached there, mainly by English sailors, who seemed to have the best claims. Their luck was phenomenal, and it was one of them who had taken out the eighteen-pound lump the week before. There was one happy-go-lucky crowd of six or eight, always in a condition of semi-intoxication, whose daily average was ten pounds, about two thousand dollars, for days together. They would kick up a row among themselves frequently, stop work, climb out of their hole, and organize a fight between two of their comrades, while every minute thus wasted was worth dollars. Paradoxical as it may seem, this was all done good-naturedly and without malice. The ring was prepared, seconds, bottle [stake] holders, and referee chosen, the men stripped for the fight, and everything conducted according to the rules of the prize ring, and when time was called, the principals responded promptly, and went in for all they were worth. The damage sustained by the gladiators was not very serious, however, as they were usually too drunk to make their blows effective, and occasionally missing each other, would fall headlong in the ring, where they were suffered to lie till time was called, and in case either failed to get up and respond, he was counted out and lost the fight. Such encounters seldom lasted long, and when all was over, the men would resume their clothing and return to work as if such an episode was a matter of course and not at all calculated to disturb their friendly relations.

The sojourn of those fellows at Sullivan's was one constant carnival of whiskey. They were drunk all the time, and seemed to experience no ill-effects from their excesses, for they were present every day, working their claim and taking out gold galore. Nothing appeared to hurt them. One of them fell into a shaft twenty feet deep, which had been used as a catch hole by the grocer, into which he threw broken bottles, tin cans, etc., the fellow landed right in the midst of the debris, but when his mates fished him out, aside from a few cuts by the broken glass, he was uninjured. He was drunk, of course, and limber as an eel. If he had been sober, the fall would have killed him sure. The gamblers had a picnic off that crowd, for what gold they got by day was blown in at night, either at the faro or monte tables, and it is doubtful whether any of them were richer at the month's end for all their fabulous luck.

Our own success, however, was by no means encouraging, for though we prospected industriously, the result was not remunerative. The first shaft we sunk yielded about twenty dollars the first day, but as we went down, the returns were smaller, until finally we struck blue clay, beneath which it was useless to dig, as no gold settles below that strata. After prospecting industriously for a fortnight, we discovered that despite our frugal diet we were running behind at the grocery, when an opportunity occurred to work for a company which was opening a ditch to drain its claim. The wages were eight dollars per day, and the job lasted a week, at the end of which we had earned $150, sufficient to pay the grocery bill and stake us for a few days' search on our own hook.

Having selected what we considered an eligible claim in the bed of the creek not far from that of the Englishmen, we commenced work there with strong hopes of retrieving our fortunes, and though the indications soon made us suspicious that we were working old ground, we were unable to determine, as it was a wet claim, and the water percolating through it naturally loosened the gravel. Nevertheless, we would have abandoned the claim had not a prospector one day imparted a piece of news that fairly made our hair stand on end, and so frightened us that we determined to stick and see the bottom if it took us a month. The purport of his story was that he discovered the shaft we had sunk and left when down to the clay, and noticing that there were no tools in it, took possession to try his luck. Seeing it was useless to go deeper, he struck his pick into the side and opened a pocket at the first blow. He stated that the first pan of dirt yielded about $300, and that he took out over $1,000 ere the deposit was exhausted, all within the space of a couple of days. Thus we learned that a second time, here as at Hawkins', we had beaten the bush and another had caught the bird.

This story settled the matter, and despite our conviction that we were "threshing old straw," we continued work, fearful of being euchred a third time. As the water bothered us a good deal, we took a partner, and bought a wooden bucket, for which we paid eight dollars, to bail with. This, however, proved insufficient and we hired a pump at six dollars a day. We worked like beavers, but the gravel was so loose and water came in so fast, we made slow progress. Though we took out some gold, it was nothing to brag of, and the main hope was in getting to the bedrock, as it is there the deposit is usually found. We never got down to the rock, however, for after two weeks' work we came upon an empty whiskey bottle which dissipated all doubt, and was proof conclusive that somebody had been there before us, so we threw up the sponge and quit incontinently, with just enough in the treasury to pay for the use of the pump by throwing in the bucket.

Though by restricting ourselves to the plainest food, and in other ways practising the strictest economy, we had managed to reimburse the merchant for his loan of $40 and pay current expenses, that was about all we had done, and the outcome after six weeks' hard work was far from satisfactory. The next move after abandoning the wet claim was discussed seriously, and canvassed at meal times in a spirit of despondence. Nor were we alone among the disappointed ones, as there were many others who had met with no better success than ourselves. Some whose reputation for sobriety and correct deportment had never been questioned, became disgusted and got drunk. Others assumed a spirit of recklessness, tackled the monte banks, and lost what little money they did have. As for us, we were discouraged and had but little heart for prospecting. The writer was taken down with fever and confined to the blankets for a week. It was a dreary experience. For hours I would lie with my eyes fixed on a hole in the tent-cloth, and so long as I gazed steadily, there seemed to be a relaxation of the violent headache, but the instant my eye was turned from a fixed point, the aching returned. Some parties were blasting rocks not far away, and at intervals the air was filled with debris from the explosions. Once a small fragment came through the tent and landed but short distance from my head, and from that time I trembled with apprehension at the sound of every shot.

One day I observed two prospectors, evidently strangers, walking along the gulch in close proximity to the blasters, when suddenly without notice an explosion occurred, and a ton or two of rock shot upwards but a short distance from where they stood. They, of course, realized their danger, but too late to avoid it, and prompted by the same instinctive impulse fell flat on their faces and shielded their heads with their hands, while for a few seconds it actually rained rocks all round them. Fortunately, both escaped injury and hastened, thoroughly demoralized, to remove from the dangerous vicinity.

After a week's confinement, during which I eschewed pinoche and fed almost exclusively on quinine, the fever abated and I was able to walk down to the store. The merchant had been very kind during my illness, often came to see me, and prepared many delicacies to tempt my appetite, but though there was no desire for food, my thirst was excessive, and the consumption of lemonade, which he concocted daily from lime juice, was enormous. Meanwhile Will and Griff were at work on wages and managed to keep the pot boiling, but day by day the conditions grew more dispiriting. I was so weakened by sickness that there was little probability of my resuming work for days to come, and all were dissatisfied over our ill-success, the food was coarse and unattractive, and discontent prevailed throughout the ranks.

Moreover, the rainy season was approaching,[1] and in a few days, unless prepared with winter quarters, we would be out in the wet, as our tent, though well enough for dry weather, would not shed rain. We had no money, and in view of past experience, the prospect of earning more than a bare subsistence seemed slight. If we went into winter quarters, it was necessary to build a log cabin, and we could not see our way clear even to provide supplies, as we would have to lie by much of the time on account of rain. Furthermore, I was unfit for work and anxious to relieve the others from providing for me, though no complaint was made, and no exceptions taken on that score. Finally, it was resolved that Griff and myself should return to Hawkins' as soon as I was strong enough to endure the journey, while Will [Huntting], who had a proposition from the merchant to assist him, would remain at Sullivan's.

It was early in November when we started on our return to the river, and though still far from strong, I hoped to get through. I had no weight to carry, as a "sport" who was going over to open a Sunday game at Hawkins', kindly volunteered to carry my traps strapped to his saddle. We started at early dawn, intending if possible to make the journey in one day. Griff carried nothing but his blankets, and we pushed on bravely to Curtis' Creek, where we rested for a few minutes and embraced the opportunity to pay the trader the debt incurred on our outward journey. The day was fine and the heat less oppressive than on our previous jaunt, hence we meandered along cheerfully and reached the foot of the hill at Wood's at noon, where we partook of a slight lunch and after a brief rest breasted the mountain with untired spirits.

We had not gone far, however, before I was exhausted, and discovered that though the spirit was willing, the flesh was weak. In fact, I feared that in attempting to make the river in one continuous journey I had figuratively "bitten off more than I could chew," for though matters went well so long as the road was comparatively level, when it came to climbing, it soon tired me. Griff, who was stronger, did not mind the effort so much, and went on, promising to wait for me at the summit, but even he wilted before he reached it, as he acknowledged afterward, alleging that his blankets seemed to weigh a ton. I continued to climb by short stages, and when about half-way up met a party going down, who asked how far it was to the base. I replied it was about a mile, but to judge by my feelings, it was a hundred miles, and requested them to inform me how far it was to the top, and from what they said, I judged there was a longer stretch ahead than I had already passed. Summoning all my resolution, I continued to climb. The mountain was not a single hill, but a succession of hills piled "Ossa on Pelion," and it seemed as if I would never reach the summit. I did, however, at last, and found Griff, who had been some time waiting, reclining beneath a tree.

As the trail to Red Mountain was unobstructed by hills, we made pretty good time that far, but when we came to the mountain itself, I kicked, and refused to climb it, as I had experience in that line at Wood's. As the mountain was isolated, I determined to go around it, arguing that the bale of a pot was no longer lying down than standing up.[2] It was impossible to convince Griff, who preferred to stick to the trail, and deprecated the idea of wandering off into the wilderness to survey a new route, with the chance of getting lost and staying out all night. So we parted; he faced the mountain and I turned southward along its base. It was then about five o'clock, and there was not much time for new discoveries before dark; yet confident that I could find my way out, I continued on till I came to a gulch which evidently debouched into the river and concluded to follow it. There was not much water in the creek, but what there was ran clear as crystal, which assured me that whatever happened I was not likely to suffer from thirst. The sides of the canon, which was afterward known as "Six Bit Gulch," were precipitous and composed of black flint rocks. A succession of waterfalls at short intervals made the walking rather tedious, but far preferable to the steep mountain trail. I eventually reached the river just above Red Mountain Bar, and believe mine was the first trip of a white man along that gulch. It was in the dusk of the evening when I greeted the boys at Hawkins', who were expecting me, as Griff had arrived a few minutes before and advised them of my coming.

BACK AT HAWKINS' BAR

NOVEMBER–DECEMBER, 1849

The reader will readily understand that I was exhausted by the day's tramp, and it was evident that my looks showed it, for as soon as I made my appearance, there was a general exclamation of surprise. My hair, which had not been cut for months, hung down to my shoulders, my beard was tangled and unkempt, my whole person was covered with the accumulated red dust of the road, my countenance was attenuated and cadaverous from the effects of the fever; and, taken altogether, there was but little resemblance between myself and the robust youngster who landed in San Francisco a few months before.

"My stars and garters," exclaimed Tribbe, an old acquaintance who had joined the crowd during my absence, "can that be Cal? Sit right down here on this log; Steve, get the scissors and let me shear him right away, he looks too much like a digger Indian to associate with this company."

I sat down quiescent, while Tribbe proceeded to ply the scissors and denude me of my "ambrosial locks," which fell like Samson's at the feet of Delilah. After this operation, a bath in the river refreshed me, and without waiting for supper I turned in for rest and recuperation of my wasted forces. As might have been foreseen, the undue exertion, following so soon after my previous illness, brought on a relapse, and it was many days ere I was up and about again.

During the time we were away, we had heard nothing from our friends at Hawkins', and learned on our return that Ed H[owell] had been seriously ill, and only a few days before had departed for San Francisco in charge of Peck, our old teamster, as far as Stockton. The boys had met with no better luck than ourselves, and though they had worked diligently and lived economically, fortune had eluded them, and as a general thing their condition had been that of impecuniosity. At several times they had been subjected to severe straits, and resorted to every device to save expense, as the following incident will show:

There was a butcher in camp who bought cattle on the foot and killed them as occasion required. It was customary with him to dress the carcass on the hide, which being worthless was left on the ground. Tribbe, who was older than the others and had in the course of this experience gained a good deal of knowledge regarding the physical structure of the bovine species, noticed this fact, and suggested skinning the tails and utilizing the bones for soup. His hint was taken, and thereafter, for a while, whenever a bullock was slaughtered, the boys invariably had oxtail soup next day for dinner. By and bye, however, the butcher noticed that the tails had been skinned, and aware that he was being euchered by somebody, skinned them himself, sold them to a negro who had started a restaurant in camp, and thereby cut off the supply. There were many instances of sharp practice in the commissariat department, both instructive and amusing, but of a rather too personal character to be recorded here.

The rains came in November, and as the [Tuolumne] river rose, mining operations were virtually suspended. The "Turner Company," consisting of about forty members, [which] had been working two months on a canal into which it was intended to turn the river and thereby drain its bed for some five hundred feet, where it was expected rich ground would be developed, was driven out by the high water. The company struggled against great natural difficulties, as the route of the canal for part of the way was through solid black flint rock hard to drill and difficult to blast, and as a result the work was never properly completed. The impending advent of the rainy season hurried matters so that, when the stream was dammed and the water turned into the raceway, the canal could not carry it, as it was impossible to make it run up hill, hence when half-way through, the upper end of the ditch was full and the water ran over the side. Further excavation was necessary, but there was no time for that; as the rains came, the river rose, the dam was swept away, and the projectors of the enterprise were compelled to abandon the work.[1]

As the rise in the river laid an embargo on further operations along its bar, a general exodus succeeded, and the miners sought other localities. Some went to Sonora, Shaw's Flat, and elsewhere in the dry diggings;[2] others, disgusted with their luck, left the mines altogether and tried for more congenial occupations.

There was much sickness at Hawkins' after the rains came, and it was no uncommon sight to behold several burials in one day. Little sympathy was evinced for sick men, and if one was taken ill, unless he had an old and familiar friend to look after him, he was left to die or recover as heaven might please, and oftentimes there was no reliance to be placed on partners. The fact was, the heterogeneous population had drifted there from all quarters, made acquaintances after their arrival, and formed alliances for selfish ends. Such incongruous partnerships often developed cruel and unfeeling natures, as was exemplified in the case of one Brown, whose mate, Bert Phillips, was taken sick and most outrageously neglected. Their tent was near ours, and as Bert was from our town, Bob [Gardiner] interested himself and remonstrated with Brown, condemning his negligence and unchristian conduct, but the appeal had no effect, as Brown brutally replied that he "must look after his own bread and butter and had no time to attend Bert who must take his chances." Bob made it a point to look after Phillips, who eventually recovered. Brown himself was taken down shortly afterward and died neglected and unattended. Hastily wrapped in his blanket, he was buried on the hillside. No mourners followed his remains to the grave, no tears were shed over his departure, no funeral service was read. A simple unit among the multitude, his death was a mere episode and soon forgotten.

After December came in, there was not much work done in camp. A majority had gone elsewhere, and those who remained stood in danger of starvation. The roads were impassable for teams, and all communication with Stockton was cut off so far as freight was concerned. All sorts of devices were resorted to, to overcome the difficulties of the mud. One inventive genius secured a large puncheon, filled it with clear pork, had it strongly bound, and attached steel gudgeons to the heads, which revolved in the eyes of a split tongue. A scraper to clear the cask of mud at every revolution was provided, and the outfit was complete. To this he hitched on a couple of yoke of cattle and wherever the oxen could wallow through, the cask would follow.

My own condition at this time was far from comfortable, and the outlook almost drove me demented. For many days I had been confined to the tent, which, though impervious to rain, was by no means a desirable residence for a sick man. The water with which the ground was saturated oozed up inside, and from time to time pine branches were thrown down to raise our blankets above the wet earth. Frequent trampling over these had pressed them into the mud and given our domicile the appearance of a hog sty. The rain fell constantly, and though I passed many subsequent winters in California none could compare with that of '49 and '50 for moisture.

One afternoon, while the boys were all at the store, an old gentleman whom we called the 'Squire' came in to see me, and while he busied himself in cleaning and oiling his six-shooter, we discussed my feverous symptoms diagnostically, and I appealed to him for advice, for though he made no pretensions as a medical expert, he was a man of intelligence and wide experience, and we placed much reliance on his counsel.

"Well," he said, after some consideration, "I do not know how it would affect you, but if your case were mine I would take a little brandy with some peppermint in it, and some sugar with a little absinthe and try and break that fever, but mind you, I do not wish to interfere with your doctor, I merely state what I would do, were I in your condition."

Shortly after this conversation, when the Squire had gone, I considered the advisability of adopting his suggestion and doing as he said he would do in my place. After debating the question thoroughly in my mind and calculating the chances, the "ayes had it," and I decided to act in accordance with his prescription.

Throwing off the blankets, I pulled on my boots, invested myself in a coat, seized my hat, and proceeded to the store, where I invited the boys to join me in a drink. They at first thought me crazy, and tried to persuade me to return to the tent, considering I was risking my life by my imprudence. All their arguments, however, were unavailing, as I was determined to follow the Squire's advice, and follow it I did, despite their remonstrance. I took my brandy with the sugar and other condiments as recommended and sat down at the table for a game of cards, called at intervals for more brandy, peppermint, etc., and remained at the store till bed-time, when I went home in a condition sometimes defined as "half mops and brooms," wrapped the draping of my couch about me and lay down to sleep.

When I awoke next morning, I felt like a new man, and for the first time since my return from Sullivan's, joined the crowd at breakfast, who were as much delighted as myself at the result of my experiment. When the doctor came and found me up and dressed, he was dumbfounded, for though the fever had gone, he could not account for its sudden departure, and, when told of my heroic treatment, threw up his hands in amazement.

"Nine times out of ten," said he, "yes, ninety-nine times in a hundred, your reckless course would have killed you, but you fortunately caught the single chance and it has cured you. There is no further present need for me, the fever is broken, and all that is necessary now is proper care and food to build up your system."

Thankful that I was no longer an invalid, I participated to the extent of my ability in the avocations of camp, and while convalescent developed an abnormal appetite and gained strength rapidly. Our table, however, was provided with no luxuries, and we tried to content ourselves with the substantials. Deer were quite plentiful in the hills; the hunters frequently brought in a carcass, and we were sometimes remembered in its distribution.

When sufficiently recovered to endure the fatigue, it occurred to me that I might possibly add something to the larder in the way of venison, and accordingly arranged with a young man named Velsor to try our luck in deer hunting, So, one wet and misty morning in December, we started out on our expedition. With the exception of a buck and doe, which sprang from a bunch of chaparral too far off to shoot, we saw no game. We followed the tracks of the deer until convinced it was useless to pursue them further, and along in the afternoon, when some distance from camp, started homeward. After traveling for an hour or so, a disagreement arose as to the proper route. The weather was rainy, there was no sun to guide us, nor any trail or known landmark, and we could not tell north from south. Each was confident he was right, and both obstinate, so we separated, he going in one direction and I in another. The event proved that Velsor was right. As for myself, I soon got bewildered and lost all idea of the proper course, but believing that camp could not be more than five miles distant, I continued traveling, hoping to strike the river somewhere.

Coming to a gulch, which satisfied [me that] it found an outlet in the river, I followed [it], and struck the Tuolumne about dusk. Discovering a man cooking supper not far away, I hailed him and asked where I was. He informed me that it was Morgan's Bar, about seven miles below Hawkins',[3] and pointed to a trail, which he said led up the river. I had become distrustful of trails, however, and resolved to stick to the stream. He said it was impossible to follow the river, as there was a canyon a few miles above. To my query how far it was to the next camp, he replied two miles would take me to Texas Bar, and I could follow the river that far without difficulty. As I had an old acquaintance at Texas Bar, I concluded to go there and pass the night with John Mills, who had come out in the *Sabina*,[4] so I started upstream and soon reached the camp.

John was not at home, but Weekes, his partner, told me he would soon come, as he had only stopped to pan out the day's work. I seated myself and presently "John, the son of Drake," as he sometimes styled himself, made his appearance with spectacles on nose and his pan beneath his arm. He greeted me cordially, and we all sat down to supper. John was nearsighted, and this defect of vision proved very embarrassing at times, as I will proceed to narrate.

A Texas steer[5] had escaped from the corral at Hawkins', and though often pursued had managed to elude capture. In one of the raids, the animal had been struck in the nose by a rifle bullet. The flies settled in the wound and generated maggots, which so annoyed the steer that it drove him wild, and he would charge on anybody or anything that happened to cross his path. Several wayfarers had been held up by the vicious brute, and though none were hurt, all were terribly frightened, hence everybody who had occasion to use the river trail invariably kept a bright look out for the bullock, which grazed on the mountainside nearby.

John had come up for his weekly supplies, and as he listened to the awful predictions of what might happen in case the steer was encountered, his imagination was so wrought upon that, when he started for home, his nerves were all unstrung. Conscious of his visual disability, he was exceedingly cautious as he proceeded, for it was impossible for him to distinguish an object more than a rod away. Having responded freely to more than one invitation to "take something" during the afternoon, he was more than ordinarily excited when he shouldered his pack and took the trail for Texas Bar, full of apprehension and bad whiskey.

All went well, however, till he was far advanced on his way home, and having passed Indian Bar,[6] he came to the last hill that intervened between him and his camp, when an incident occurred that made him the laughing stock of the community for many a day afterward. The shades of evening were just closing as he toiled up the ascent, congratulating himself that he would make the transit safely, when he caught sight of the dreaded horns waving to and fro on the trail before him, and without stopping to investigate, dropped his pack and fled like a scared dog.

> Speed, Malise, speed, such cause of haste
> Thine active sinews never braced

Such was undoubtedly John's conviction as he skipped hastily along the backward track and burst into the store at Indian Bar breathless and demoralized, where he recounted his experience with the crazy steer, and took "four fingers" to steady his nerves as he told his story to the gaping crowd. Just here, however, a man came in and interrupted the thrilling tale, stating that he had killed the animal a few hours previous and had part of the remains outside packed on a jackass, and in order to show what torture the poor beast must have suffered, had cut off his head, which was on the ass now standing at the door. It was the jackass which John had encountered, as any other man would have seen distinctly, but he, poor fellow, with his defective sight and his brains and belly full of "horns," had mistaken those on the pack saddle for the bullock itself, hence his incontinent fright and harrowing tale of danger and disaster.

I do not know whether John is still living, but if he is, he is now like the writer, an old man, and should the above meet his eye, he will, let us trust, take it kindly, as it was only one of the many moving incidents by flood and field encountered during his sojourn in the Golden State.

I stayed with the boys that night, and next morning, just as I was about to depart, after

John had gone to his work, having left Weekes to pick over some beans for dinner, a Texan came along and stopped at the water pail for a drink. The bucket stood on a pine tree that had been felled, and the upper surface sawed off for a table where the cooking utensils were kept. The man had been out in search of some mules which had strayed off, and, vexed at his failure to find them, was in a quarrelsome humor. As he held the drinking cup, he scrutinized it closely and remarked, "Weekes, that is my cup."

Weekes, who was kneeling by the campfire, about to put the beans in the pot, said in reply, "I don't know where it came from; John brought it home, and when he comes, I will ask him about it, and if it is yours will hand it to you."

"I don't care a d—n what John says, the cup is mine and I shall take it."

"I have already told you I know nothing about it, but I must see my partner before I surrender it, so it is unnecessary to kick up a fuss now, for I assure you I shall defend my property."

The claimant, who was apparently spoiling for a fight, called out to his brother to bring his double-barrel gun, who refused, saying "What do you want of a gun? The cup is not worth two-bits anyway, certainly not worth quarreling about."

Regardless of his brother's protest, he started after the gun himself; meanwhile, Weekes, who was a splendid shot, took his rifle from beneath the blankets in the tent, cocked it, set the trigger, and laid it beside him as he returned to the fire and proceeded to place the kettle thereon.

Presently the Texan came from his tent, gun in hand, and approaching within about forty yards pulled up and let fly with the first barrel. There was no time for him to get in a second shot, for quick as a flash, Weekes ducked his head below the fallen tree, grabbed his rifle and returned the fire. The bullet found its billet, the Texan threw up his hands and fell prone on his face. He lived just long enough to acknowledge that he was the aggressor, ere his life went out and his soul departed for Kingdom Come.

The Texan shot left-handed; Weekes' bullet struck the trigger hand, passed through the wrist and upper arm, and entered the body, passing completely through the chest. The distance was so short that the impact of the bullet was resistless.

It was evident to all who had witnessed the fracas that Weekes had acted strictly in self-defense, and that the homicide was justifiable. We prepared a sort of proces verbal reciting the details of the transaction, and all who were present signed it.

California, which was then a territory, was still under Mexican law,[7] and the Alcalde, whose powers were about equivalent to those of a justice of the peace, resided at Hawkins' Bar, then the most populous camp on the river. Weekes took the exculpatory document, and together we departed to interview the Alcalde. Miller, who held that office, had but one leg, and when we discovered him on the river bank, he was securely anchored by his wooden pin, which was wedged between two stones which held him fast. After extricating him, we explained the object of our call and presented the written statement, which he proceeded to read, and having perused it, remarked that it was "evidently a case of justifiable homicide" and wanted to know "what we expected him to do about [it]?" He refused point-blank to consider the case judicially; said that "the dead man had instituted the quarrel, taken the chances and got wiped out, and no jury would ever correct the wiper," then, having delivered himself to this effect, he handed the paper to Weekes and advised him to go home without giving the matter further consideration.

Human life was held cheaply in those days, and when a man was killed in a fight, it excited but little comment. Legal proceedings were seldom resorted to. If one carried a civil tongue and kept sober, he could mix safely with the multitude, but if he [was] so disposed, he could easily inaugurate a quarrel; and where every man went armed, it was apt to end in bloodshed. There were no thieves in the mining camps, and the miner's treasure, if he had the good fortune to possess such, was freely exposed to the common eye. The difference between meum and tuum was rigidly observed, and private rights generally respected.

Velsor had returned home the evening before and reported our disagreement regarding the route. My absence during the night had somewhat worried the boys, who feared I was still wandering in the wilderness, hence they were relieved when I made my appearance. My story of my experience and the shooting scrape at Texas Bar caused but little comment, as such incidents were too frequent to excite much of a sensation.

Though now and then we had fair days in December, the weather gradually grew worse, until at length it rained almost continuously six days in the week. Supplies of all kinds were nearly exhausted, and it became necessary to get away to avoid actual starvation. A general exodus was unavoidable. We boys held a consultation, and there was a division of opinion regarding our future course, but all realized that a move of some kind was inevitable; finally, however, it was decided to separate, and thereafter each would paddle his own canoe.

Bob [Gardiner] engaged with Col. Jackson as clerk in the store. The two Griffs [Napoleon and Absalom Griffing] stuck together, and Stephen [French] and myself arranged to leave the diggings and take our chances in San Francisco. Before leaving, however, we determined to have a square meal, if such a thing were possible. Steve, who was constantly "pirouetting" about, had discovered a negro whom he pronounced a "dabster at cooking" and proposed that we should test his qualifications in that line, which I readily agreed to. As the dried apples still held out at the store, it was arranged to top off with fried pies. The meal, though expensive, was a success, and the fried pies capped the climax as a dessert.

XV

EN ROUTE TO SAN FRANCISCO

December, 1849

There were half a dozen of us who left Hawkins' next day.[1] Besides Steve [French] and myself, there were Charley S., usually called "Adam," Messick, a Texan, and two others whose names I have forgotten. The ground was soft, and as the mud clung to our feet, the walking was tedious and exhaustive [exhausting]. We reached Green Springs that evening, about seven miles from Hawkins', and as we were pretty tired, decided to pass the night there. The day had been clear, hence our blankets and clothing were dry, and we were soon comfortably asleep; but after a few hours' rest, the floodgates were opened and the rain came down in torrents, soaking our blankets and making matters so disagreeable that we got up and resumed our journey in the dark. It was about midnight when we turned out, and the downpour was so continuous our clothing was soon saturated. It was too dark to see the inequalities in the road, hence falls were frequent and we were soon covered with mud from head to foot. The water absorbed by our blankets doubled their weight and thus made traveling more difficult. We plodded on, however, all night, and considering the circumstances made fair progress, for when daylight came, we were only some six miles from Knight's Ferry.

The rain had fallen ceaselessly after midnight, nor did it hold up during the day. It accomplished one good end, however, as it washed the accumulated mud from our persons and lightened us to that extent. The majority were well-shod, but Messick was in a bad plight, as he wore cloth gaiters which had suffered from the night's tramp and seemed to have an affinity for the mud in which they stuck, and from time to time he had to fish them out and replace them. At intervals we met equestrians whom Messick invariably hailed with an offer to buy their animal, but his offer was unheeded, as the riders knew when they had a good thing and were disposed to hold on to it.

As it was desirable to reach Knight's as soon as possible, we tramped onwards, encouraged with the prospect of a good breakfast on our arrival, and as we had eaten nothing since the previous morning except a slight lunch, we were, of course, hungry. It was about eleven o'clock when we reached the ferry, and as the boat was about to cross, the others went over, leaving me to dicker with an Indian for the purchase of a salmon which we had seen him capture a few minutes previous. The native soon came with the fish which must have weighed twenty-five pounds. After some bargaining, I bought the salmon for eight dollars and, hailing the boat, crossed to the other side where the boys, who had already started a fire, were negotiating with the trader for the necessary groceries, and arranging for the loan of cooking utensils.

Knight, the proprietor of the ferry and trading post, had died a few hours previous to our arrival.[2] The man in charge requested us to be quiet and decorous in respect to his

109

family, which was sorely stricken at his loss. Though so far as we were concerned there seemed no necessity for such a request, we took it in good part and readily assented.

There was plenty of food at the crossing, and a great deal cheaper than at Hawkins', as the transportation charges were much less; hence there was no difficulty in satisfying our wants. We had borrowed a skillet or "Dutch oven," and Adam was manipulating a batch of biscuits. Another roasted the coffee, and a third attended the fire and did the shopping and borrowing. The salmon was consigned to me, who having been accustomed to pis-catorial dissection, soon dressed it secundum artem and prepared it for the frying pan. Within an hour, breakfast was ready, and we attacked it with ravenous appetites, plying our knives and fingers industriously. The biscuit were light and done to a turn, the fish was excellent, the pork gravy answered for butter, and the strong hot coffee thoroughly warmed the cockles of our hearts and comforted us exceedingly. We made a splendid meal, notwithstanding the fact that all were soaking wet; and as for myself, I do not think I ever enjoyed one more thoroughly.

Breakfast over, we filled our pipes, and after returning the borrowed utensils, sat down for a smoke regardless of the rain, which was still falling. Somebody brought on a bottle of whiskey, a luxury which under the circumstances was perhaps excusable. We all par-took more or less, and Adam, who became quite exhilarated, volunteered a song. He gave us "The Banks of Brandywine," an old-time farmhouse ditty now obsolete; and though a good singer, his peculiar manner of pronunciation excited our mirth. Although I had never before heard the song, nor have I heard it since, it was so strongly impressed on my memory that I still remember the opening lines which are:

> One morning very ear-ly in the pleasant month of May,
> I walk-ed forth to take the air, all nature being gay.

The heroine was a fair maid who resided on the river bank, and was betrayed by her lover. According to the song, various untoward and malignant influences were brought to bear, which

> Did cruel-ly combine
> To win this maid's affections on the banks of Brandywine—

We all enjoyed Adam's effort, especially his pronunciation, and applauded to the echo.

After a good rest at Knight's, we bade goodbye to the Stanislaus River, expecting to find quarters for the night at a roadside hotel some ten miles away. It was something of a climb up the hill at the crossing, and we rested several times to gain breath ere we reached the summit. Adam, whose frequent potations had somewhat affected his head, was a genial companion and the life of the company. At one of these stops, he met with a mis-hap that excited our laughter. He carried his blankets slung by a strap across his breast, and in an attempt to back against a tree to relieve the weight while he slipped the strap over his head, he unfortunately missed the tree, fell backwards, and rolled fifty feet down the declivity ere he recovered his equilibrium. No harm was sustained, however, and he soon rallied from the shock. No further incident occurred to interrupt our ceaseless tramp, tramp, tramp, except when Messick, who was now virtually barefooted, hailed some rider with a proposition to buy his horse, which was as often rejected.

Despite all our efforts, we were not destined to reach the roadhouse that night, as I gave out, and the others were nearly used up, when at dark we came to a clump of willows and decided to camp, as it had stopped raining and promised to be a clear night. Someone had brought the surplus coffee provided for breakfast, and as there was a tin pot attached to Adam's belt, we resolved to utilize it and have something hot before turning in. It was difficult to make a fire, but by chopping down a dead willow with bowie knives and splitting it for dry kindling, we eventually succeeded in starting a blaze. The cup was boiled three times before all had a drink, but the coffee warmed and refreshed us so that, wet as we were, we wrapped our saturated blankets around us and slept till daylight.

The reader may perhaps wonder that we did not take cold. Colds in the mountains were unknown, and though we suffered all sorts of exposure, no one was seen sniveling and complaining that he had "caught cold." Men would go into the river and work in water four feet deep for an hour or two and then resume their occupation on the bank without thinking of taking cold. Fevers and dysentery were endemic, rheumatism was not uncommon, but fear of catching cold worried nobody.

We were up betimes that morning, and on our way to the roadhouse for breakfast. We had not gone far when we discovered a "prairie schooner" standing by the highway, which, when we came to it, we found empty, and judging it was bound for Stockton, concluded to pile in our traps and send them by wagon. The boys divested themselves of every pound of encumbrance except their clothing, even leaving their revolvers and gold dust, and there were some twelve or fifteen pounds of the latter placed in my charge. It was understood that I should ride, as they intended to rush things and go right through to Stockton.

The teamster was away searching for his cattle, and after the foregoing arrangement was made, we took a survey of the premises. The campfire was smoking, and a coffee pot nearby, the contents of which were still warm, notified us that the teamster had breakfasted. There was dry wood in the wagon. Instituting a search, we discovered a mammoth loaf of brown bread, also a round of pork, and a package of ground coffee. Satisfied that the teamster had eaten before he went out, we had no hesitation in taking the viands. The fire was renewed, coffee made, pork fried, and together with the huge loaf, were deposited where they would do the most good. Having satisfied their hunger, my comrades bade me goodbye and left me to face the man whose larder we had despoiled.

Seating myself on the wagon tongue, I awaited the teamster's return with some trepidation, not knowing how he might conduct himself when he discovered the raid on his provisions. He soon made his appearance, driving six oxen before him. He made no demonstration, however, when he came up, and simply nodding in response to my salutation, proceeded to yoke his cattle without evincing the least sign of discomposure while he listened to my explanation. I told him the circumstances under which we acted, promised to defray his expenses on the road and pay freight on the luggage we had so unceremoniously piled into his wagon, as well as my own passage, should he permit me to ride, but got no word in reply, nor any acknowledgment that he heard what I said.

This irresponsive deportment rather provoked me, and I resolved to wait until he felt inclined to talk. It was impossible to tell whether he was angry or not. He had the most inexpressive countenance imaginable, and as I silently watched his immobile features and speculated regarding his thoughts, it occurred to me what a wonderful success he would be as a poker player, for there was no more to be gained by studying his face than if he had been a wooden Indian. Lanator himself could have made nothing of it. As for me, I gave up guessing whether he held a pair of deuces or a straight flush, and concluded to await the outcome, so when the team started I bundled into the vehicle and proceeded to make myself as comfortable as possible.

Our progress was necessarily slow, as the oxen were tired and weak for want of proper nourishment. They had evidently lately finished the long overland trip, and should have had a chance to rest and recuperate after their toilsome journey. The abnormal rate of freight probably excited the cupidity of their owner and induced him against his better judgment to disregard all considerations of humanity and keep them at work despite their obvious unfitness.

The rain was again falling; and, reclining beneath the shelter of the wagon cover, I watched the teamster as he plodded along beside his cattle, and wondered at his reticence. Had he become disgusted with a cruel and unsympathetic world and foresworn communication with his kind? Was he under a vow that constrained silence? Not so far as his oxen were concerned, for he spoke to them quietly from time to time, so the restriction if any, must apply to mankind alone.

Certainly, during the two days we traveled together, he spoke no word to me nor to anyone else in my presence. As we neared Stockton, the stopping places became more numerous, and we found no difficulty in getting meals, which I paid for. Only one incident out of the regular course occurred, worthy of note. One of the oxen on the second day was taken sick and exhibited signs of distress, unnoticed by me but familiar to the teamster, who came to the wagon and cut a piece of pork from the round, which he proceeded to thrust down the bovine's throat. Whether it acted as a cathartic, a tonic, or an astringent is still a mystery, but such a commingling of pork and beef was foreign to all my ideas of veterinary practice.

We met many teams on the road, but their loads were necessarily light, as in some places the weight of the wagon alone was sufficient to test the strength of the mules, six or eight of which constituted a team. Three or four teamsters usually traveled in company, so that in case of emergency they could assist one another, and it was an ordinary occurrence to see from sixteen to twenty-four mules hitched to one wagon in the attempt to release it from a mud hole. At such times the position of mule-driver was no sinecure, and in the way of profanity they could have discounted the army in Flanders.

We reached French Camp in the evening of the second day, where we found the boys awaiting our arrival. I paid the unloquacious teamster what I considered was a fair price for transportation, which he received without a word. To my parting salutation, he responded with a nod, which, though hardly in accordance with the conventional code, was accepted in lieu of speech.

Stockton was about two miles from French Camp.³ We soon covered that distance, when we sought a restaurant where we had supper *a la* Chinese, after which we sought lodgings, which we finally secured in the hold of the brig *Mazeppa* at a dollar each. As there was nothing attractive about the muddy thoroughfares in the city, we repaired to our sleeping quarters, which we found packed from stern to stern with recumbent humanity lying with feet to the keelson. After some persuasion, we induced them to move up, took our places among the crowd, and were lulled to sleep by the squealing of rats, with which the place abounded.

The next morning Stephen and I sold the barrel of pork stored on the brig when we departed for the mountains, to Mr. [Harvey H.] Spencer,⁴ one of the owners, for eighty dollars free of storage, and as it was "prime pork," it was a good sale. An opportunity soon after occurred to secure passage on a sailboat to San Francisco, which we embraced with avidity. The incidents of that trip would alone fill a volume, but I must forbear details and simply state that the passengers were a promiscuous crowd, all jolly good fellows, and of course whiskey was abundant. There were about a dozen on board, the fare was thirty dollars, and it required three days for the trip.

ONCE MORE IN SAN FRANCISCO

DECEMBER, 1849–MARCH, 1850

It was during the Christmas holidays that we returned to the city of tents and canvas avenues. Though we had been gone only four months, a great change had taken place. Many buildings had been completed and many more [were] in process of erection. The immense flood of immigration continued unabated, and the opportunities for profitable investments were unprecedented. Had the writer possessed more wisdom and more experience, he would have engaged in some legitimate mercantile pursuit, instead of attempting labor for which he was unfitted and competing with those who were inured to toil. But the overruling idea was that nothing could be done without capital, and in order to secure that, it must be gained in the gold fields. This method of reasoning was to a certain extent sound provided there was no other way of effecting the desired end. One aged relative—God bless him! He has long since gone to his silent home—repeatedly offered pecuniary assistance which inexperience and false pride prompted me to reject rather than incur what might be considered an obligation. This rejection resulted in many a subsequent humiliation, and necessitated a long struggle ere the goal was won.

Gold dust was at that period selling for $15 per ounce in San Francisco, and commanded $20 per ounce at the mints. Of course many took advantage of that fact, and every pioneer will remember the multiplicity of signs bearing the legend "se compra oro en polvo" which met the eye on every street. Gold dust was the only crop produced, and the receipts in the city were enormous. One with capital to purchase could ship the dust by steamer monthly and realize the difference between fifteen and twenty dollars an ounce, less freight and insurance, every sixty days.[1]

There were thousands of chances for the capitalist to invest with quick returns and large profits, and it was comparatively easy to engineer a "corner" in certain articles of daily use and absolute necessity.

Ordinary cut tacks were consumed largely in the construction of stores and dwellings to fasten the canvas to the studding. Lumber was not to be had, and, moreover, was too expensive, as what little there was in market readily commanded $500 per thousand feet. Some man of perspicacity saw an impending scarcity of tacks, bought all to be had in the city, held them for a while till the price advanced to "sixteen dollars a paper," then sold out and realized a fortune. Such instances of successful speculation were by no means rare, as will appear in the course of this narrative.

Little has been said heretofore regarding San Francisco and the conditions then prevailing, and it may interest the reader to know something more definite in that respect: matters were, however, in such a chaotic state that it is difficult to give a connected description. At that period, January, 1850, the harbor was crowded with shipping, and few facilities attended the discharge of cargoes. There were no wharves for the accommodation of vessels, and merchandise was transferred from ship to shore at enormous expense. It actually cost more to land the goods after arrival, than for freight around Cape Horn. When the consignors received notice that their goods were ready for delivery on payment of freight, they settled for the same, [and] received their orders, which were handed to the lighterman, who of course charged for the transfer all the traffic would bear, and such charges were by no means uniform. In the absence of warehouses, merchandise was often left exposed, unsheltered from the rain, or dispatched to the auction rooms, where it was disposed of at less than the cost of freight and charges. Shipments were made without proper discrimination in many instances, as when news was received in the East of exorbitant prices paid for certain articles, everybody went in to supply the demand, and as a result the market was glutted, the goods were unsalable, and left lying around promiscuously. There were at one time heavy shipments of tobacco which it was absolutely impossible to sell, and as the mud was some four feet deep on Montgomery Street, cases of tobacco were used for stepping blocks at the crossings. These cases were also used as foundations for buildings, and the piers of a small wharf built in the winter of '49 and '50 were tobacco cases piled one upon another. Tobacco being a staple article, it may seem strange that no one bought and held it for an advance, which must inevitably occur when shipments stopped, as they were sure to do. This may be accounted for by the fact that there was no place to store it on shore. This state of affairs was remedied, however, as the merchants purchased old vessels and moved them at convenient points for store-ships. The old whaler *Niantic* of Sag Harbor was hauled up in the mud at the foot of Commercial Street; a big opening was cut in her side, a staging erected from shore to ship, and thus the "*Niantic* Warehouse" was inaugurated, which afterward became so well-known to citizens of California. The old vessel had a roof built over her and was a prominent landmark in the city. Years subsequent, when the bay all about her had been filled in and she was encircled with towering buildings, the old ship whose bottom was tight, having been relieved of merchandise so that she was nearly empty, suddenly rose in their midst and created a tremendous sensation, as many thought an earthquake had happened. The cause of the disturbance was soon discovered, however, when the vessel was scuttled and settled down in her mud bed once more, and it may be that long years hence, when the early history of San Francisco shall have been forgotten, some future generation will unearth her timbers and the archaeologists vainly endeavor to form a reasonable hypothesis to account for their presence.[2]

San Francisco was cosmopolitan, and its mercantile community, speaking different languages and governed by different customs, was rather incongruous. Its members affiliated readily, nevertheless, as all were alike attracted by the desire of gain. They did not as a general thing "put on airs," but were unostentatious and democratic in their intercourse. The writer was present one day when two merchants were engaged in a big trade involving some thousands of dollars, when one suddenly remarked, "I've got a bite," stooped, rolled up his trousers, and wetting his finger came down on something. To the query of his companion whether it was a "quick" or a "slow," his reply was, "a quick." "Roll him, then, roll him, or you will lose him, sure." The rolling was duly performed, the insect captured and killed, and the conversation resumed without the incident exciting further comment.

Fleas were a great annoyance, as they were indigenous, and the ground was full of them, and they were called "quicks" to distinguish them from another parasite [lice] which pulled twelve oars on a side and was known under the generic appellation of "slow," the very thought of which causes a shiver even now. Every old pioneer will understand the allusion in the foregoing sentence, for all alike were subjected to the same annoyance.[3]

There was much litigation in the early days, and the court calendar was crowded with cases. Mexican law prevailed, and the Court of First Instance, in which Judge Almond presided, was in daily session, where suits were quickly tried and summarily decided.[4]

The firm of Coghill & Arrington purchased 150 barrels of pork with the understanding that they should be allowed the "longest possible time" to take it away, and when afterward demanded, they were unable to get it, as it was stored in the ground tier and would have necessitated breaking out the whole cargo to deliver it, so the firm had to carry it. Meanwhile, the price of pork depreciated and the owners were subjected to great loss. They brought suit to recover damages for non-delivery, but as there was no saving clause in the agreement, which only called for the "longest possible time," and there was no question that the defendants had failed to give it, the plaintiffs failed to recover.

Another case that excited a good deal of comment, was that of Peter Smith vs. the City. Smith built a hospital and made a contract with the Ayuntamiento, a corporate body equivalent to our Common Council, to care for the indigent sick, but when he presented his bill, it was considered exorbitant and rejected. As the city refused to pay, Smith brought suit and recovered the full amount claimed. In due time, execution was issued, under which a number of lots belonging to the city were sold for mere nominal prices, as the attorney Heydenfeldt assured the city fathers that the sale was illegal, and would be upset in the Supreme Court. Nevertheless, the city was beaten in the appeal, and the sale was confirmed, much to the chagrin of the community. Those lots subsequently became very valuable, and the Peter Smith titles, as they are called, are today considered the best on record. That there was a colossal nigger in the fence in connection with that transaction, and that the city had been deliberately swindled, by the very men paid to protect its interest, was universally conceded.[5]

The city fathers in those days were much the same as at present, and every man played for his own hand. They voted themselves gold medals at the expense of the city, but the populace and the newspapers kicked up such a disturbance that every member was compelled to pay for his own.[6]

There were but two daily papers, the *Alta California* published by [Edward C.] Gilbert, who was subsequently killed in a duel, and the *Pacific News* by Buckelew, which was discontinued after a few months. Sam Brannan also issued a publication called *The Hombre*, but it was short-lived.[7]

There were no churches,[8] but the gambling houses ran wide-open, and were a general resort for everybody, especially at night. Chief among these establishments were El Dorado on the corner of Kearney and Washington, Dennison's Exchange, a few doors south, and Bella Union, on the corner diagonally across the street from the first named.[9] All these institutions occupied prominent sites fronting the Plaza, now called Portsmouth Square.[10]

These establishments were gorgeously fitted, with resplendent bars glittering with cut glass, silver pitchers, gold spoons, and magnificent mirrors. Flaming chandeliers hung from the ceiling, and the walls were decorated with meretricious pictures. Brass bands discoursed sweet music, and no expense was spared to make the rooms attractive to the multitude. The gambling tables, covered with expensive cloths, were piled high with coin and large nuggets of gold, and behind each sat the suave sport manipulating the cards and soliciting customers. At least a half-dozen barkeepers, with helpers to wash tumblers, were kept busy, and from time to time the tinkling of the dealer's golden bell announced that the crowd at his table were thirsty and about to imbibe at the expense of the bank. Every game was liberally patronized, and banker's winnings were satisfactory. Inspired by the unholy thirst for gold, and a latent hope that they could beat the game, bettors waged unsuccessful war against the tiger and bearded him in his very den, but it was seldom that the outsider got the better of the dealer.

Every game known to the gambling fraternity was represented, faro, monte, roulette, rondo, keno, chucker luck, rouge et noir, lansquenet, tub and ball, vingt et un, thimble rig, three-card monte, strap and pin, and other devices to skin the public were in full blast, and each had its patrons, though as a general thing, "the more they put down, the less they took up." The dealers paid from sixteen to twenty dollars a day for table room, and probably twice as much for liquid refreshments.

These places had a peculiar attraction for all, and were constantly crowded, as they were far more comfortable than the chill, damp tents in which the majority resided. The crowds were a motley mixture of classes, colors, nationalities, and conditions. The Mexican in his dirty serape jostled the preacher with his soiled white necktie, and the lawyer touched glasses at the bar with his red-shirted client from the mines. They were a convivial set; everybody drank and exchanged courtesies with everybody else. Nobody put on style, and one man was as good as another.[11]

The fascination of the gambling rooms for the young man who had been brought up strictly was wonderful. He was now for the first time removed beyond the restraint of home influences, and brought in contact with vicious surroundings. Such scenes, even on a limited scale, he had never before beheld, and he was drawn insensibly from the rigid path of morality and in too many instances given over to dissipation and destruction through sheer inability to withstand temptation; while on the other hand, the tough boy, who had early learned the mysteries of euchre and seven-up, had run away from school to attend horse races, had stolen watermelons and robbed orchards, and in his limited sphere had participated in all the deviltry that was going on and rubbed against the rough edges of wickedness in his youth, was proof against the temptations of cards, wine, and women, and their evil influences fell away from him like water from a duck's back.

Had I a dozen boys, I would never curb them too tightly, but reason with and advise them carefully, and give them full swing while young, for such is the innate "cussedness" of mankind that what it is forcibly debarred from it will invariably hanker after. Take, for instance, a guileless baby a year old, sitting on the carpet beside you. You may coax that baby for an hour, using all the endearing words in the vocabulary, and you cannot induce it to put its toe in its mouth; but if, when all your coaxing proves unavailing you raise your finger and sternly forbid it to do so, then up goes baby's toe. This is simply an illustration of what may be called innate "cussedness," as natural to humanity as the act of breathing; therefore, I hold that it is an error to restrain a boy too rigidly, but give him plenty of good advice and a long rope with an opportunity to learn that

> Vice is a monster of such hideous mien
> That to be hated needs but to be seen

and if there is any moral force in him, he will come out all right, but if he lacks that moral force, he is pretty sure to go to the bad anyway.

Before leaving, we will take a paseo around the room, stopping first at a long table about which are seated some twenty players, each with a card before him containing pictures of birds, beasts, and other things animate and inanimate. The tall Spaniard standing at the head of the table twirling a box held between two standards is the banker and caller. The box holds a number of blocks on which are pictures corresponding with those on the players' cards. No two of the cards have the same arrangement of pictures, for though all have the same figures, there is not the same relation between them on any two cards. These cards have been purchased of the banker at a dollar each, and as he twirls the box, he takes out a block and calls, "Now, listen." Round goes the box, and out comes a block with, say, an elephant depicted, and the caller shouts "Una Elephanta," when every player covers the elephant on his card with a chip taken from the table. Next a horse is drawn, and the call is "Una Caballo," and the horse is covered. Next call is "Una Hombre," and a man is covered, and so it goes on indefinitely until someone has covered a line of figures straight across his card, when he cries, "Keno," and rakes in the money deposited for all the cards, less say 10 per cent for the bank. This is a simple game of chance and seems to be a fair one, provided there is no collusion between the caller and some card holder.

"Come, gentlemen, 'pungle,'" says a seductive voice nearby, and we turn to the monte table, around which a group is collected. The dealer holds a monte deck from which he has drawn two cards, a queen and an ace, which he lays face upwards on the table, and the betting begins by guessing which of the two cards will be drawn first. Should one of them be in the door, that is the first one when the deck is turned face upwards, it is an advantage to the bank, but should a player desire, he may "bar the port" and perhaps save himself by placing his stake on the corner of his chosen card. When the betting ceases, the deck is turned up and if neither of the two cards on the table appears, it is again reversed, and two more cards drawn for a second "lay out," and the betting proceeds as before. Then the dealer turns up the deck and draws the cards off carefully one by one. If the card chosen by the bettor comes first, he wins; if not, he loses. This game is a general favorite; nevertheless, there are many tricks by which the players are defrauded, such as waxing the cards, which enables an unscrupulous dealer to draw two cards as one. The cards are also "clipped," and one end made a shade wider than the other and so arranged as to give the bank a great advantage.

There is a big crowd gathered at a neighboring table, the bell is ringing for drinks, and the spectators seem in a state of unwonted excitement. There is evidently heavy betting— Let us go and see. Our surmise is correct. A young man in a miner's garb, apparently fresh from the mountains, is wagering largely, and the numerous buckskin bags already corralled by the dealer show that the bettor is in bad luck. One by one, the player takes the plethoric little sacks, each containing about $500, from a pouch hanging at his side and deposits them on his favorite card. The game is monte. The miner has already lost a dozen bets, as is evidenced by that number of packages piled on the banker's side. They represent at least $6,000. Fortune has favored the young man in his researches at the gold fields and he has probably come to the city with the intention of taking the steamer for home. Home is a good deal farther away now than it was an hour ago. Will he stop, or will he try to recover and perhaps lose all? The miner was the only player, the others had withdrawn from the game and were watching him with bated breath. The dealer, cool and level-headed, held the cards and waited impassively. "Facilis descensus Averni." Experience had taught the gambler the truth of that axiom, and he was evidently satisfied that the young man would decide to either "win the horse or lose the saddle." Here comes the waiter with the drinks, the dealer passes them round, touches his lips to a glass of sherry, and replaces it on the tray. The miner, who has already had too much, swallows his whiskey at a gulp and calls for a layout. The cards are shuffled, a layout dealt, another bag of dust is withdrawn from the pouch and staked; a second layout, and a like sum is placed on that. The cards are drawn and both sacks deposited with their predecessors in the bank. Again and again the miner bets and loses, until without winning a single stake he draws the last bag of dust from the pouch, deposits it, and demands the privilege of drawing the cards himself. This is accorded, the deck is passed over, he pulls the cards, beats himself, and is "bursted." No, not quite; he has a valuable watch and chain which he takes off and stakes at his own appraisement. Once more he draws the cards and the bank wins. The play is played-out, the miner has lost $10,000 in gold dust and his watch and chain. No home for him this time, his itinerary is changed, he must go back to the mountains and begin again. The dealer hands him a hundred dollars for a grubstake, the curtain falls, and the unfortunate actor retires from the scene, having afforded an object lesson to the onlookers which perhaps saved some of them from a like experience.

The above is no fancy sketch; the incident actually occurred precisely as stated under the writer's own eye, and is but one of hundreds of like character that happened in the early days of California.

We will now leave the gambling room for the present, as space forbids further comment thereon. This narrative has already grown to the dimensions of a respectable volume, though there are still eight years of California life to be accounted for, hence it is absolutely necessary to stick to my individual record and to a great extent avoid collateral details, else this book would inevitably attain the proportions of Josephus' *History of the Jews.*

On our return to the city, Stephen [French] and myself made our way to the Long Island House, a hostelry located on Broadway a short distance south of Battery Street, where in consideration of $25 per week each, we were accommodated with board and lodging. The building was a coarse structure flimsily built of undressed lumber, about 20 x 40 feet, two stories, and a lean-to attachment which served for a kitchen. The office and dining room occupied the whole lower floor. A pine table covered with oil cloth extended the whole length of the room, on either side of which were rough wooden benches for the guests. The upper floor was fitted with bunks, a row on each side, and a double row in the middle, each of which was furnished with a straw mattress, the occupants being expected to provide their own blankets. This caravansary was the rendezvous for many Long Islanders, with some of whom we were previously acquainted.

With no definite plan of proceedings, having left that matter in abeyance to be governed by circumstances after our arrival in San Francisco, and with board at $25 per week, we could not afford to remain idle, so lost no time before seeking a means of livelihood. In conversation with Capt. Dennison one day, he remarked that fuel was very scarce and hard to procure, and that if we could find some wood fit to burn, he would take fifty cords at his Exchange and pay us $2,500 therefor. Now, $50 a cord for wood was decidedly remunerative, provided we could find a supply within reasonable distance, so we resolved to prospect and ascertain what could be done in the line of combustibles. Such fuel as was to be had in the city was brought by Mexicans in the shape of fagots bound together and packed on donkeys, which was of course very expensive, as the sticks were dry and soon consumed.

In traveling to and fro in the vicinity, we had seen a patch of scrub wood on the sand hills near the Mission Dolores,[12] which we decided to inspect closely and find out whether we could glean sufficient therefrom to fill Capt. D.'s order. The wood was only some three miles from town, and as the road was sandy, the wet weather improved it. We went over the ground and discovered that the timber was a sort of scrubby beech, crooked and dwarfed, averaging six or eight inches trunk-diameter, and though not what might be considered merchantable, we thought it would answer the purpose. There were, we estimated, about fifty cords in the tract, and [we] resolved to chop it. We felt no hesitation in appropriating the wood, as we neither knew nor cared who owned it, presuming that the proprietor would never fret over its disappearance.[13]

On our return to the city, we reported to Capt. D. the result of our examination, and our willingness to deliver the wood, provided some arrangement could be made to secure an outfit, as we would need a team, the expense of which was beyond our means. He told us to go ahead and he would furnish the money.

A few days before this, however, we had come into possession of a boat under the following circumstances: One night, while downtown, the writer drifted into a gambling room where he met Jetur Bishop, a townsman whom he had long known, who desired to sell him a boat which he and Captain Woolley had purchased that week for some purpose not now remembered. Since the purchase Capt.W. had accepted a position as master of a ship, which acceptance had dissolved their connection, and the boat was for sale, which he informed me was in excellent condition, about thirty feet long, sails, oars, etc., all nearly new. The boat with furniture had cost them $200, and they would sell for the price paid.

Knowing Bishop to be a reliable man, and having full confidence in his statement, I bought the boat on his representation, taking his story for granted, without going to inspect the craft, as I considered there was a chance for speculation, convinced that she could be disposed of at an advance of at least $100. The next morning Bishop went with me to Clark's Point and delivered the boat, which was really a bargain, nicely painted, nearly new, tight as a bottle, and must have cost originally with her outfit more than we paid.

As soon as the ways and means were provided, seeing our way clear to proceed with the wood business, we started at once to procure oxen. There were no American cattle in San Francisco, but learning that we could find Spanish oxen at the Mission Dolores, we decided to look at them and see if they would answer our purpose. The boat was put into commission and we sailed down, reaching Mission Creek at dead low water, where we threw the killick [small anchor], waded ashore, and went up to the ranch.

The old adobe buildings presented a forlorn and dilapidated appearance, not at all in consonance with what they must have shown a century previous, when the Catholic fathers ruled sovereigns of the region, with their Indian retainers, vast herds, and golden grain fields.[14] The cession of the territory to the United States, and the advent of gold-seekers, had worked a wonderful transformation. The fathers had departed, and their former quarters were occupied by a semi-civilized community of Greasers and half-breeds, some of whom we found engaged in a drunken quarrel with an ex-member of Stevenson's Regiment,[15] who was reviling them in broken Spanish as he careened around riding a half-trained and vicious mustang. What the dispute was about, we were unable to understand, but judged it was in reference to some woman whom the ex-soldier had insulted, and as he started to ride away, the coils of a riata in the hands of a Mexican flew out, caught him by the neck, and wrenched him violently from the saddle. This was probably considered sufficient punishment, as he received no further hurt, remounted and rode away.

Going to the corral, we were shown some cattle, which our attendant assured us were well-broken and accustomed to the yoke, but as their horns exhibited no sign of chafing, we were suspicious, and so said. He explained, however, that the oxen had never worn an American yoke, as the Mexican method was to secure a tough, straight stick to the horns, and it was by the horns they pulled instead of the shoulders, as with us. It was impossible to get near the cattle, which were wild as hawks, and the only way to catch them was with a riata. Moreover, it required two men to drive them when yoked, as they knew nothing about "gee" and "hoy," and could not be guided by the voice. The Mexican manner of driving is with a long quad in the end of which a sharp brad is affixed, to prod the cattle on the off or near side and so guide them. Though we wanted oxen badly, we did not care to experiment with those wild, long-horned Mexican steers, and concluded to ask the advice of an expert before purchasing.

When we returned to the boat, the tide had risen so that she was a dozen rods from the shore, riding at anchor in eight feet of water, and as she was beyond reach, we were compelled to leave her and go home on foot. Early next morning we started for the Mission to recover the boat, but when we reached there, discovered we had miscalculated regarding the tide, as it was about half-flood and rising fast. This was provoking, as it was raining like Sam Hill, and we were disinclined to wait for the ebb. Seeing a drove of mules grazing in a meadow nearby, it occurred to us to catch one and use him for a temporary ferryboat. The suggestion was no sooner made than acted on, and fortunately we caught a mule without difficulty. Using a black silk handkerchief for a halter, we led the animal to the shore, Stephen mounted as ferryman, while I with a piece of drift wood urged his steed forward. The mule took to the water like a sea lion, as it was just at the mouth of Mission Creek,[16] which it had probably been accustomed to cross. Steve headed for the boat, but the water was deeper than we bargained for, and before he was half-way out, the mule was swimming and the rider submerged to his arm pits. The animal was game, however, and minded his helm beautifully, landing his passenger alongside the boat, who grasped the gunwale and climbed aboard. The mule swam ashore and ran off to the drove, taking the halter with him, which was sufficient to remunerate his owner for his temporary use.

Stephen lost no time in getting the anchor and sculling ashore, for he was wet and cold, as a sea bath in January is by no means a pleasant affair even in California. The tide was still running strong flood, and as we had to stern it, we took to the oars and pulled vigorously. Steve's teeth chattered like castanets, but the extraordinary exertion necessitated by the adverse current kept his blood circulating, and after a tough pull we reached Clark's Point, secured the boat, and hastened to our quarters for dry raiment.

The next day was Saturday, and I again walked to the Mission accompanied by a western man who had driven an ox team across the plains and was supposed to know all about oxen. He had become so accustomed to the slow progress of an ox team that his gait did not exceed two miles an hour, and as it was useless to hurry him, it was difficult to accommodate my speed to his, so that I was frequently compelled to turn back, and in making that journey of three miles must have walked at least ten. We reached the Mission finally, however, when the cattle were duly inspected by the expert, who shook his head and ruled against them.

"The fact is," he said, "them are Spanish cattle, they don't sabe English, it takes two Greasers to drive 'em and a half-dozen to yoke 'em. They are wild as zebras and you couldn't do anything with 'em. What you want is American cattle that a white man can manage. You don't want to fool round with them plugs. Suppose they got away from you, all hell couldn't catch 'em, they would run away to this ranch or some other god-forsaken place, where it would take a month to find 'em, and even if you should find 'em, it would take a regiment of soldiers all day to catch 'em, and when they are caught, they ain't worth a d—n for any purpose whatever except beef."

This verdict was final and conclusive; the result was reported to Stephen, and we held a consultation, when it was arranged that he should go to Stockton and, if possible, buy a yoke of civilized oxen.

As the weather was fair next morning and the boat for Stockton did not leave till evening, we went for a sail on the bay, and in the afternoon landed at Happy Valley, where, as it was Sunday, we found Mr. Hudson at home. As we had not seen him since our return from the mountains, he was curious to know our experience, of which we gave him some details, and incidentally referred to the enterprise then in hand, which seemed to strike him favorably. He had an eye to business, however, for as soon as he learned our intention, he suggested that he might assist us in completing an outfit.

"Boys," said he, "you will certainly need a vehicle of some kind to haul your wood in, and I have just what you need, come and see."

We went with him, and he exhibited for our inspection an immense dray, which he had purchased on speculation from some vessel from Australia. It was fitted with shafts, and must have required a mighty horse to draw it.[17]

"Now," said he, "I can take those shafts out and put in a good substantial tongue, and there you are, all fixed for business."

Acknowledging that the cart would answer the purpose admirably, we reminded him that as yet we had no oxen, but in case we secured a pair, [we] would talk about buying and perhaps arrange to sell him the boat, taking the cart as part-payment. He evidently wanted the boat, and had several times during the afternoon expressed a desire to buy it. He was also anxious to dispose of the cart, and wished to consummate a trade at once, but we declined, preferring to wait the result of Stephen's mission to Stockton.

As both wind and tide were ahead, we left the boat in Hudson's charge, who promised to look after it. Mr. Hudson, however, went off half-cocked, assuming that we would get the oxen; he removed the shafts and put a tongue in the cart, as he had proposed. This procedure was afterward the cause of serious trouble, as we shall see by and by.

Stephen went off that night, and the next day I walked out to the wood with a chopper, who offered to cut and cord it for seven dollars a cord. A provisional agreement was made, dependent on our getting the cattle. At the expiration of ten days, Stephen returned without having accomplished his object, and reported substantially as follows:

There were but few oxen for sale, as the abnormal rates of freight gave profitable employment to their owners, who were earning fabulous sums in transporting merchandise to the mines. Some few cattle that he saw had lately crossed the plains, were worn-out, poor in flesh, full of alkali, and needed a year to recruit ere they were fit for service.

Some of the cattle that came overland were subsequently fatted and killed, and their livers were found to be actually honeycombed from the effects of the alkaline waters drunk on the route. Oxen were subjected to a terrible ordeal during that long journey, and only the most vigorous survived the trip. It was pitiful to watch the immigrant trains in the last stages of their pilgrimage, as they passed from the mountains to the plains. Four or five miles a day were all they could accomplish, and the oxen, so tired that they could hardly raise their feet, moved so slowly that it was difficult to decide whether they made any progress at all, and it was only by looking at the wheels that one could tell that the wagon was in motion.

The women, gaunt and travel-worn, the children, listless and exhausted, excited sympathy as they sat in the wagons behind the weary cattle. Since leaving their homes on the eastern frontier, they had encountered many dangers and privations. The husbands and fathers who guided the teams were typical frontiersmen, brave, indomitable, and indefatigable, quick to act in time of emergency, fertile in expedients, and when occasion required, could look danger and death in the face in defence of their wives and little ones.

In their long and toilsome transit they had been subjected to many hardships, and had contended against unexampled difficulties. They had defended themselves successfully from the assaults of hostile Indians, had crossed rugged mountains and brawling rivers, had sweltered beneath the scorching heat of the arid plains, and suffered the appalling pangs of thirst in the waterless deserts, had passed uncounted graves of those who had preceded them, had seen wagons abandoned, household goods scattered by the wayside, and still undaunted had pushed onward amid the wreck of matter, until at length their own cattle, overcome by excessive toil, poisoned by the caustic waters, weakened for want of proper sustenance, succumbed to the inevitable, lay down and died.

Deprived of means to transport them further, the wagons with their contents were necessarily left behind, all the surviving cattle were hitched to a single vehicle containing the children and only sufficient food to carry them through, and it became a race for life. The women trudged on bravely beside husbands, fathers, and brothers, until at last the snow-clad Sierras were passed and the goal was won.[18]

Few realize the trials and sufferings encountered by the caravans that made the overland journey to California in 1849 and 1850. The necrological list of those sacrificed in the pursuit of gold is amazing to such as now make the transit from Chicago to San Francisco in four or five days over the Pacific railway.

But in the farm houses of the Sacramento, San Joaquin, Merced, and Tulare valleys there are still living gray-haired pioneers who buried friends and kindred on the march, and the involuntary tear moistens their eyelids whenever they recount their experience and refer to their companions who

By the wayside fell and perished
Weary with the march of life.

From this digression we will return to Stephen and complete his report:

Out of such cattle as were offered for sale, there was but one yoke fit for service. These were thin in flesh but young, healthy, and good feeders, and would improve, it was thought, on light work, short hauls, and plenty to eat. For this yoke there were several competitors, who raised the bids until Stephen offered $1,100, and when he was in turn raised he drew out and permitted the others to do the bidding. The price was advanced $50 at a time until it reached $1,400, when the cattle were knocked down to Alonzo McCloud who ran a stage line between Stockton and the mines, and was also engaged in freighting.

We subsequently learned that those same oxen were hitched as leaders to two other yoke, and hauled 2,200 pounds to Don Pedro's Bar[19] on the Tuolumne River, had good luck, made the round trip in ten days and earned $3,300 freight. Though the load seems a light one for six oxen, it was as much as was safe to put on in the then-condition of the roads, and the recompense was certainly ample.

The inability to procure cattle defeated the wood scheme and drew us into an arrangement we both had reason to be sorry for a few weeks afterward. Circumstances beyond my control induced me to acquiesce, though my better judgment opposed it. What those circumstances were, was known to but one other besides myself. My lips were sealed and have so remained in regard to the subject till the present day, but my silence alienated more than one friend at that period. Sick, disappointed and disgusted, I lost all energy and ambition and the overruling desire was to sleep, for with sleep came forgetfulness, and forgetfulness seemed a blessing. During that winter, and for months afterward, I was not my natural self.

The arrangement above alluded to was the purchase of the fixtures and good will of the Long Island House. When the trade was consummated, with one exception the old proprietors stepped out and T. P. R.,[20] Stephen, and myself stepped in. What we stepped into will appear presently.

The building, owned by one [John F.?] Pope, was a coarse, rickety affair, which any contractor at the present time would put up and furnish all materials for about $200, commanded a monthly rental of $500. The butcher's, baker's, and grocer's bills and all other expenses were proportionate, making the monthly outlay some $1,500, which had to be met by cash at the end of every month. Though the place was generally full of boarders, all their pockets were by no means full of money, as many were dead broke, some sick and out of employment. Some of them had come from the mines, and many were old acquaintances whom we had not the heart to press. With expenses forty dollars a day, and receipts not much over half that amount, we soon saw that it was impossible to meet the monthly bills, as we had no capital to fall back on, and unless paid, the supplies would be cut off. The bunks in the loft had in many instances sick occupants, and the neglect they suffered is a harrowing remembrance even to this day. One poor fellow lay dead for several days before it was discovered that he had passed away. When it became known, report was made to Peter Smith's hospital, a vehicle was sent, and the remains carried to the burying place. Who he was, or what his name, no one knew. Friendless and forsaken, he suffered and died, unattended and unknelled, uncoffined and unknown, and was buried in a pauper's grave. This was but one of a thousand like instances which were so common they excited no comment.

Samuel F., a well-known personage among Long Island people, constituted himself majordomo of the establishment, where he flourished like a green bay tree. He attended the tables, washed the dishes, made out the bill of fare, hustled the cook, stove off importunate creditors, and loaned his boots to such as had none and were necessitated to go downtown. He was the first up in the morning and the last to retire at night, had a smile and pleasant word for everybody, and was generally popular. He is still living, and though nearly four-score years of age, engaged in active business. From all accounts he is as self-complacent and genial as ever.

A letter lately received from a mutual friend, an old California pioneer, tells of a visit made not long ago to our village, where among others he called on Samuel F. at his grocery, and in that connection related the following incident:

A little girl came in for a quart of molasses. Taking the receptacle, with smiling visage the proprietor proceeded to fill the order, and while so engaged conversed with his customer.

"Yes, my dear, your mother knows what's what, and where to send when she wants a good article in molasses. This is genuine Neuvitas, imported expressly for me, and I can recommend it. First rate for gingerbread, excellent for cookies, and when mixed with butter on your buckwheat griddle cakes, will make your hair curl. Is there anything else you want?"

"No, sir," replies the girl as she starts to go.

"Wait a minute, young lady, you have not paid me."

"Mother says you must charge it."

"Not by a d— sight," exclaims the irascible merchant, who seizes the pail, inverts it, and pours back its contents, and as he does so remarks sententiously, "My child, this is a cash store."

Such a mixture of the suaviter in mode, with the fortiter in re, is one of our friend's peculiar characteristics.

"Business is not very brisk," sighs Mr. F., as he seats himself on a soap box, "I think I'll shut up shop tomorrow and go eeling. My grandfather," he remarked in a reminiscent mood, "kept a store during the Embargo times and the War of 1812 when, I have heard him say, trade was at a standstill. As an exemplification of the prevailing dullness, he used laughingly to recount an incident that occurred at that period. He had come down one morning, swept out and put things to rights, spent the forenoon reading his weekly paper, when about eleven o'clock a little girl came for a penny's worth of snuff, which he did up and handed to his customer, the only one he had seen that morning, and shortly afterward went to dinner. He came down after dinner, discussed matters local and general with visitors, when just as he was about to go to supper, the child returned and handed the snuff back, saying, 'Grandmother says it ain't good, and wants her penny.'"

Though the Long Island House was fairly patronized, the business was not remunerative. At the end of the first month, when the other bills were paid, there was no money for the rent. We managed, however, to get a month's extension from the landlord. When the second month had passed, it was plainly evident that the concern could not be successfully conducted as an eleemosynary institution, and we were compelled to wind up, as we had neither means nor credit. It was reported that when, during the last week, someone called for meat, he was met with the reply, "We do not furnish meat at this establishment." If such was the case, it is probable that credit at the butcher's was exhausted. It is certain, however, that the whole thing fizzled out ingloriously and the hotel business ended in humiliation and disaster.

Meanwhile, the boat which we had left in Mr. Hudson's charge was still in his possession, and when one day two young men came with a desire to purchase it, we sent them to the custodian to ascertain its whereabouts. That evening they reported as having seen the boat and were prepared to buy it at the price named, $300, but at the same time informed us that Mr. Hudson claimed ownership, saying there was no boat that belonged to us but he had a cart subject to our order, insisting that the boat was his property, and the cart ours.

This was a specimen of injustice and sharp practice for which we were utterly unprepared, so we resolved to interview the claimant forthwith, and bade the would-be purchasers await the result. As the boat was certainly worth five times as much as the cart, the claim that we had made an even exchange seemed too absurd for consideration.

Though we no longer had any possessory rights in the hotel building, as it was still vacant, we slept there on the dining table. That night, before retiring, we canvassed Hudson's preposterous claim and decided to arrange the matter amicably if possible rather than take the property forcibly as he would undoubtedly replevy it. Early next morning, we proceeded to Happy Valley so as to meet Hudson before he went to his work, and ascertain what he meant by his conversation with the young men the day before.

Our amicable intentions were frustrated at the start, as Providence had ordained that the interview should be a stormy one. We found Hudson at breakfast, who from the first was unconciliatory, and showed fight. His bellicose attitude naturally excited our anger, and the discussion was acrimonious and unsatisfactory. He boldly claimed the boat, and asserted that the trade was a fair one, and had been fully consummated as was evidenced by the alteration of the cart in accordance with its terms.

We pronounced his assertion false and without any reasonable foundation, admitted we had talked of an exchange, but the whole thing was made expressly contingent on our purchase of oxen, which we had failed to secure; moreover, supposing we had bought the cattle and wanted the cart, did he consider us such infernal idiots as to imagine we would in any event have made an even trade and given property worth five times its value for his dray?

He was obstinate, however, refused to listen to reason, and affirmed "that if it came to litigation he reckoned he had as much money to spend in that way as his neighbors," which caused Stephen [French] to remark, "You wouldn't have if you paid your debts."

With this parting shot we left for town, where we met the parties who proposed buying the boat, and explained our inability to deliver it, as its recovery would involve litigation.

Naturally dreading the expense, and to a limited extent aware of its traps, pitfalls, delays, and uncertainties, we were indisposed to resort to the law and also unwilling to incur the cost of consulting an attorney. We hardly knew what course to pursue, as we had but little money, were out of employment, and needed our means for current expenses till we could find something to do. Finally, however, we resolved to consult Judge Almond of the Court of First Instance, tell him a plain, unvarnished story, give him a clear statement of facts just as they occurred, and ask his advice.

Accordingly, next morning we called on the judge before court opened. He listened patiently and courteously to our statement, and at its conclusion remarked: "Young men, as the judge before whom this case will probably be tried, I cannot consistently act as your legal adviser, but I will say this much for your guidance. Go home and make out a bill for the value of the boat in question, ascertain from some competent person what such a boat is worth per day for its use, and add the per diem value for every day the property has been detained, hand the bill to me and I will consider it as a declaration and issue a summons for the defendant to appear."

Thanking the Judge for his kindness, we left the courtroom resolved to act on his suggestion. Putting the value of the boat at $300, which we could have sold it for, as already stated, we consulted boatmen who plied their vocation in the harbor, who agreed that the use of such craft as ours was worth at least eight dollars per day, and declared they were ready to swear to it whenever requested. We could not consistently make any charge for per diem previous to the time we had demanded possession, as we had voluntarily placed the boat in Hudson's charge, so we claimed for use only from the date of demand to the time when final judgment should be rendered.

We handed our bill to Judge Almond, who filled out a summons, called an officer and gave it to him for service. I went with Powers, a deputy sheriff, to where Hudson was at work, and on the way we chatted sociably. He told me he was a brother of the sculptor Powers, who was lost on the steamer *President*, and I think said he was from Ohio.[21] We found the defendant, whom I pointed out, and the summons was duly served. Subsequent to the service, I talked with Hudson, and it was agreed that neither party would employ counsel, but appear in court, state their case, substantiate it with what evidence they had, and have it decided upon its merits.

This arrangement to dispense with counsel suited Stephen and myself exactly, as attorneys were too costly for our pockets, so after noting its place on the calendar and ascertaining it would be a month or six weeks before the case was called, we rested easy. During the interval, we managed to make expenses by attending the auction rooms, buying in job lots and selling at retail about the city, usually spending the evenings at the gambling rooms, as they were the most comfortable resorts, where we met acquaintances and enjoyed gossip.

One night, as I was watching a monte game in Dennison's Exchange, the proprietor, who was a fellow townsman and had known me from boyhood, clapped his hand on my shoulder and said, "Boy, are you betting on this game?"

"No," I replied, "I have no money to lose in that way."

"Right you are, take the advice of an old stager who has sounded all the depths and shallows of dissipation, and never bet against the bank. These fellows pay me from sixteen to twenty dollars a day for table room, and spend as much at the bar, so you see they cannot afford to give an outsider any show. If you ever decide to take to gambling, get a table and sit behind it, or hire somebody to do it for you, then you will have the inside track."

It was Sunday. "How much do you suppose we have taken in at the bar today?" he asked. "We have just counted the money."

Glancing at the bar, where half a dozen barkeepers were busily manipulating bottles and glasses, I replied that I could not estimate the receipts, though they had evidently been heavy.

"How much have you taken?" I asked.

"$3,200 since morning; it is not yet ten o'clock and the day is about half-gone."

Here Captain D. was called away, and the conversation ended. He was wild, but was one of nature's noblemen, nevertheless, and made all with whom he associated his friends. He was a fine-looking man, a great favorite with women, generous and perhaps lavish in his expenditures. From boyhood he had been accustomed to the sea, was rapidly promoted and had command of a ship at an early age. While his vessel was refitting at the home port, he and his contemporaries, with sailors' characteristic disregard for money, made things lively in the community. After the decline of the whale-fishing he was in command of a vessel trading among the islands of the Pacific and Indian oceans and was one of the very first American citizens who located in San Francisco. Though long years have passed since he was called from earth, his memory is embalmed in the hearts of many gray-haired pioneers, and if generosity and good deeds in this world count for anything in the next, let us hope they outweighed his errors, trusting that they were regarded with a lenient eye, and [that] like Abou Ben Adhem's his name is written in the "book of gold" and classed with those "who loved their fellow men."[22]

The chief among those who presided at the bar of the Exchange was one who had known its proprietor in youth, and though a scion of an exclusive family not overburdened with wealth, he had joined the innumerable caravan and sought the new El Dorado to mend his fortunes. Like thousands of others whose antecedents were such as warranted association with the beau monde, he had accepted his position because it served his purpose and afforded generous remuneration for his services. Nevertheless, he was high-strung and proud-spirited, and sometimes felt that his occupation entailed a sacrifice of self-respect, as it brought him in contact with a class towards whom he cherished a congenital antagonism, and he would sit up nights to curse a certain element that by reason of his calling presumed on a familiarity to which his every feeling was repugnant. His was by no means an isolated instance. Professional men were often reduced to great extremities in California. Lawyers peddled matches, merchants waited in restaurants, doctors drove express wagons, and clergymen were compelled to pick up a living as best they could. The latter sometimes went to the mines. One meek and lowly follower of the cross located at Hawkins' Bar. One day he accosted Old Man Martin, a Texan, and showing a prospect he had just panned out asked "if it would pay?" Martin took the pan, shook it, saw the prospect, handed it back, and quietly remarked, "It will pay to h—l." The dominie, puzzled at the comment, and undecided whether the verdict was one of approval or condemnation, withdrew without stopping for further question.

Despite his surroundings at the bar, our supercilious dispenser of "cocktails" managed his imperturbability, had the same smile for his old associates, and when occasionally the writer went up with a friend or two whom he had invited to participate, he was invariably "dead headed," and in return for his money received its full equivalent in change.

Having often witnessed the experience of others, and mindful of the advice of Captain D., I refrained from trying my luck at the gambling tables, and was a mere "looker-on in Vienna," but my comrade [Stephen French] was differently constituted. Excitement was the very breath of his nostrils. He would fight the tiger in a small way at every opportunity. It was not the love of money that impelled him, for I never saw one who cared less for it or spent it more freely when he had it, but though he knew there was not one chance in a hundred to win, he would at times go in as recklessly on that one as if the conditions had been reversed. He had, however, sufficient self-control to restrain himself, and seldom lost any considerable amount. If the luck was against him, as it usually was, he would quit after losing a few dollars. A man of exuberant spirits, life was for him one continuous round of excitement, and I have seen him as much exhilarated after drinking a bottle of pop as if it had been so much whiskey. He had not, like most men, any favorite game; his taste was omnivorous, and he bucked at everything from chucker luck to faro.

One night he stopped at a roulette table and placed what he thought was a quarter on the corners of four squares. The chances were enormously against him; indeed, they were so much so that in the event of winning he stood to recover six times the amount of his stake. Not one in a thousand would have wagered so recklessly, but as it was only a quarter, it was not important whether he won or lost. The ball was set twirling around the wheel, and when it finally rested, it was on one of the four numbers bet on. The dealer threw out six quarters, but Stephen, who had meanwhile discovered that what he had wagered was a ten guilder piece, was almost frightened out of his boots. He was naturally relieved at the result, and when the banker tendered the six quarters, refused to receive them and demanded twenty-four dollars.

The banker, who was a little curly-haired Jew, was dumbfounded when closer scrutiny revealed the size of the bet, and refused to pay.

"You bet that for a quarter, and by G—d, I'll pay no more. No sane man would ever venture ten guilders on four corners, and you know it."

"It makes no difference what I know or what I don't know, I made the bet, and if I had lost you would have raked in the piece; fortunately, I won, so you just fork over twenty-four dollars and be d—d quick about it if you wish to save trouble."

The Jew, seeing that he had no case, and that persistence in his refusal to pay would inaugurate a row, weakened, and reluctantly passed over the proper amount.

Discretion was the better part of valor in this instance, for had a shindy ensued, the crowd would have undoubtedly taken part, in which event the bank might have been looted, the wheel destroyed, and the Jew himself, if not killed outright, might have sustained serious injury.

It goes without saying that we were both jubilant over the fortunate result of Stephen's error, and resolving to celebrate the event, adjourned to Crockford's Restaurant, where we partook of a bountiful repast and finished off with a chasse cafe and cigars.

As we passed out of the restaurant on our way home, we saw two men, well-dressed, whom from their appearance we took to be sporting men, engaged in an altercation in front of the Bella Union Saloon. Suddenly, one of them, who was a man of commanding figure, threw up his hands and grasped the door post. Running across, we reached him just after he fell, and helped to carry him inside, where it was discovered he had been stabbed through the heart and was in articulo mortos. His assailant had immediately entered the gambling room and mingled with the throng, and as his victim died within five minutes, there was no clue to the murderer, neither was he ever traced or any knowledge gained of the cause of the homicide.

There were many of my fellow townsmen in the city whom I met frequently. It came to pass that on one Sunday morning James Erastus, an old acquaintance, in the course of a casual conversation, informed me he had tackled a tub and ball game the night previous, and broken the bank after winning $800. He claimed to have a sure thing, and proposed that I should go with him that evening, as he intended to have another "set to" with the same banker.

Astonished at his good fortune, I vainly tried to dissuade him from his purpose, for of all the cut-throat games then in vogue, the tub and ball was the meanest. The game is played with a ball some four or five inches in diameter, which is rolled in a tub lined with velvet. The ball is covered with different-colored spots about the size of a silver quarter, and whichever is uppermost when it comes to a rest, that color wins, and the payment in proportion to the number of like spots on the ball. My friend had, it seemed, bet solely on the red, for which I think the payment was two for one, and as he stated, had won almost every bet. It was evident from what he said that there was something wrong with the ball, for though these spheres present a fair outside, the interior is a mysterious combination of springs, etc., only known to experts, and the manipulator may so handle one as to give the advantage to any color he chooses. Hence an outsider stands no better chance than he would against loaded dice.

Heedless of cautionary advice, and confident of the correctness of his theory, my friend insisted on following his own program. Accordingly, we went together that night, he carrying all his winnings, prepared to venture them and either break the bank or get broken himself. The proprietor greeted the young man who had beaten him so badly the night before, with a grim, suave smile, and James E. took his stand by the table and wagered five dollars on his favorite color. The bank won. A second bet of ten dollars was lost. A third wager of twenty dollars was absorbed by the bank, but the attempt to double again was vetoed. The bank had won three straight bets, and it was obvious the machinery was in good working condition. Twenty-five dollars was the limit, hence, my friend's idea of advancing his bets in geometrical progression was defeated. The game proceeded, but as might have been expected, the bank won four times out of five, with such a result that inside of an hour James E. was "scooped," and his name was added to the long catalogue of victims to youthful indiscretion.

As in the above instance, the disposition to follow one's luck is often the salvation of the bank and the ruination of the bettor. The experienced gambler knows this, and when he sees the lucky winner depart, he feels an instinctive confidence that he will return and eventually leave his winnings, and all he has besides, in the clutches of the dealer.

The recital of the above incident recalls another, illustrative of the danger attendant on a conflict with the tiger as exemplified in the experience of Fred S. from our village, who had lately arrived, and like many another young fellow, was wise in his own conceit, and ready to back his faith with his works.

"Three-card monte" is essentially a sharper's game, and at that time was played indoors and out all over the city. As its name indicates, the game is played with three cards, which are manipulated with skilful fingers, accompanied with offers to bet that no man can pick up the winning card. The formula is somewhat as follows: The sharper establishes himself beside a dry goods box or some other convenient substitute for a table with three cards in his hand, say the jack, queen, and ten. These cards he throws on the table, at the same time indulging in a monologue to the following effect:

"Gentlemen, here are, as you see, three cards, the jack, queen, and ten. The jack is the winning card, which falls in the middle every time, as you may easily perceive. Nevertheless, I am willing to bet that after I have thrown them no man can pick up the jack."

Here he proceeds to distribute the cards in a bungling way, and it seems so simple to designate the jack, that one not conversant with the wiles of the swindler is very apt to be deceived when he sees one outsider after another pick up the card which in his own mind he has chosen. No bets have yet been made, but presently a man in the rough garb of a miner wagers $100 and picks up the card which every onlooker has seen is the winning one. He is paid by the dealer, who seems much surprised, and curses his bad luck. Though the simple ones are not aware of it, the winner is a "capper," that is, a stool-pigeon who acts in concert with the other rogue and assists him in the slaughter of the innocents.

Presently, when the sharper's attention is momentarily diverted, the capper reaches forward, turns up the jack, again places it face-downward, and turns up one corner so as to make it plainly recognizable. Fred sees all this, and when apparently unconscious of the marked card, the swindler redistributes the three, inviting some one to accept his wager regarding the jack, our young man, with his eyes still on the upturned corner, considers he has a dead-sure thing, planks down his $100, reaches forward, picks up the marked card, when lo and behold! it is a ten-spot. Hastily grabbing the stake, the rogue seeks fresh fields, and leaves his victim to mourn his loss and moralize on the depravity of his species.

As the time drew near when our case was likely to be called, we arranged that one of us should be constantly in the courtroom prepared to respond when necessary. As before stated, it was agreed that neither party would employ counsel, but simply state the facts, produce the witnesses, and submit the matter to the court to decide the equities. So when Stephen saw the defendant enter the courtroom one morning attended by Ned Marshall, a prominent attorney,[23] he was greatly discomposed. There was no time to notify me, nor opportunity for consultation, as Hudson had evidently waited till the last minute before he made his appearance, so as to surprise us and hold us at a disadvantage, for he had not been in the courtroom five minutes before our case was called.

Forgetting that he is "thrice armed who hath his quarrel just," and that all the special pleading of the lawyer would have no effect on the judge who was sworn to decide according to the law and the evidence, Stephen lost his head, and seeing no other way out of the dilemma, asked for a continuance, stating that he was not prepared for trial owing to the absence of certain important witnesses. The court granted his request, and our case was continued indefinitely.

This was very unsatisfactory, as we had already waited nearly two months, and it was now likely that the trial would be deferred months longer. As Hudson had gone back on his word, we resolved to fight him with his own weapons and secure legal advice. We accordingly called on Jesse B. Hart, who was Col. Stevenson's attorney, at a salary of $10,000 a year.[24] Mr. Hart, whose time was too valuable to spend in consideration of a case like ours, referred us to one of the young lawyers in his office, and said that he would look after our interest.

It was now May,[25] and as I desired to leave the city and return to the mountains as soon as possible, an early settlement with Mr. Hudson was imperative. When the young lawyer, whose name has passed from memory, had heard our story and learned the status of the case, he suggested that it be withdrawn from court and submitted to a referee for decision.

This suggestion was adopted, and John R. Satterlee, who was afterward Judge of the Superior Court in San Francisco, was appointed referee.[26] The young lawyer who advised us was a fine fellow, with whom we soon established friendly social relations, meeting almost every evening and discussing matters pertaining to our suit. He hurried things, and in a few days announced that the referee would hear the evidence at his office on the succeeding evening, so we made due preparations for trial.

There would have been no difficulty in establishing our claim for per diem detention had not Jim Hall, the waterman on whom we relied, unfortunately got drunk. Jim was a New York City boy, given to periodic sprees, and he had been bred a sailor, but when, after a long search, we found him, he was so tight that it was evident he was in no condition to take the witness stand. He was a good-natured fellow, who, when we aroused him from his stupor by pouring cold water down his shirt sleeves and explained what we wanted, readily consented to testify provided we could get him to the courtroom, which, though doubting his capacity as a witness, we decided to do. He had been off on a "target excursion," was chock-full of whiskey, limber as an eel, and perfectly incompetent to help himself. Nevertheless, we managed to drag him to the Bella Union, where our attorney was waiting, who when he saw Jim's condition shook his head and pronounced him non compos mentis and unfit to testify.

This was a grievous disappointment, as the per diem claimed exceeded the value put on the boat itself. It was already late, the referee was waiting, and as there was no time to look up another witness, even had we known where to find one at that hour, we were compelled to go unprepared with the most important evidence and submit our case for decision. Unable to prove our claim for detention, it was thrown out, and judgment rendered for $300 with costs against the defendant, who paid the amount and was discharged.[27] The loss of the per diem claim was a bad scald, but later developments proved that Hudson had euchered us in the final settlement by paying in liquidation of the judgment gold coins of the "Miner's Bank," which had previously passed current, but had that day been thrown out and were only receivable for eighty per cent, of their face value.[28] Our attorney, however, charged us nothing, as we had from first acquaintance sustained toward each other not the ordinary relations of lawyer and client, but rather those of familiar friends, enjoying frequent intercourse, drinking, smoking, and conversing together as young men of our age were accustomed to do when brought in contact with congenial spirits.

Despite the fact that we had failed to recover half the amount claimed, it was some consolation to know that Hudson had paid pretty dear for his whistle. In addition to the judgment and costs, his attorney's fees were no inconsiderable item, so that altogether he would have gained by an amicable settlement in the first place.

XVII

A SECOND TRIP TO THE MINES

APRIL, 1850

The climate of San Francisco, especially in summer, was so disagreeable that I determined to get away from the prevailing fogs and high winds, and seek a more genial atmosphere in the mountains. Stephen [French] decided differently, and concluded to remain in the city, so we parted for a while, and I started for Stockton, undecided where to go from that point.[1]

As I had heard of a party about to start for the San Joaquin, I took occasion to see them, and finding they had never been up the river, offered to pilot them. They cheerfully gave me a passage, and in due time we reached Stockton, where I met Bob [Gardiner], who had come down from the mountains and taken charge of Colonel Jackson's warehouse in the city.

My stay in Stockton was brief, as there were some young men who were to leave next day in a boat for the mouth of the Merced River en route for Mariposa, and I decided to go with them, so that Bob and myself had but a short time to swap news and post each other in regard to matters generally. He told of Griff's death in the mines, which rather shocked me, as the young man was the very picture of good health when I last saw him; rugged and strong, he seemed able to stand any amount of hardship and exposure, as was evidenced by our trip to and from Sullivan's Creek the year before. Though I had never known him till we met in San Francisco, we had been much together during the succeeding six [five] months, and our relations were always of the most friendly character.

That day and night I passed with Bob. We sat up late, discussing ancient history and the varied incidents of our experiences since we separated at Hawkins' Bar the previous December. Neither had grown rich, but he was in better shape financially than myself, had steady employment, was in receipt of a regular monthly salary, had no expensive habits, and saved his earnings, which in a few months enabled him to start merchandising for himself.

The next morning we parted, not to meet again for many months. My companions on the trip up the San Joaquin were from Oswego, New York. Their names were Randolph Loomis, George Hale, Charley Judd, and one other whose name I cannot recall. Messick, who came down with me from Hawkins' Bar, was also with us. The trip was by boat to the Merced, thence to Mariposa.[2] The country for the first day resembled that on the lower river, and we made our way through a succession of tulies [tules] that lined both banks. At night we camped in the tulies, where we managed to raise a field bed with willow boughs, on which we spread our blankets, but our weight sunk the boughs in the mud, so that when we awoke we were half-submerged. Breakfast with a cup of hot coffee refreshed us, and the exertion of pulling an oar set our blood circulating rapidly, so that we soon freed ourselves of the chill incident to our damp bivouac.

137

The second day, we left the marsh behind us and passed many beautiful farm sites as yet unoccupied. We camped at night on a pretty bluff where we found no difficulty in securing an excellent supper from the ducks, which were plentiful in the neighboring pond holes. It was a splendid country. The seemingly interminable plain stretching from the river bank was virgin soil that had never known the plow, but so great an extent was covered by Spanish grants that much litigation ensued between subsequent squatters and claimants under Mexican titles.[3]

Time has wrought great changes in that vicinity, and what was then an unbroken wilderness given over to the grizzly bear, elk, wild horse, and coyote, is now dotted with farmhouses. Children gather bouquets from the flowery meads, the busy housewife plies her daily care, the husbandman follows his team afield, and the eye is greeted with blooming orchards, waving grain fields, and domestic herds. The golden era has been superseded by the agricultural age, and the annual exports of farm produce now far exceed in value the product of her pactolian streams in California's palmiest days.

With a single exception, we saw no sign of human occupancy in our trip from Stockton to the Merced. On the third day, we passed a high bluff on the left bank of the river, where, nailed to a tree, a sign bearing the word "Grayson" was conspicuously displayed; but whether it indicated the site of a proposed town, or was merely the name of the claimant of the land, we were unable to determine.[4] So far as we could judge, the left bank of the river was far more eligible for farming purposes than the opposite side, which seemed to be traversed by sloughs and presented generally a moist and swampy appearance.

The fourth day was Sunday. The wind was fresh and adverse, the current grew stronger as we proceeded upstream, and combined with the wind militated against rapid progress. There being no necessity for undue exertion, we concluded to lie over till next day and treat ourselves to a good dinner, for which the abundance of game afforded ample material. From a contiguous sand bar we collected a supply of wild mustard, which, boiled for greens and served with fricasseed mallard, together with coffee and warm biscuit, furnished an excellent repast.

In the afternoon, taking a gun, I sauntered away, hoping to get a shot at some sand hill cranes that were feeding in close proximity to camp. They were shy, however, and baffled all my attempts to get near them, so I lay down among some tall weeds, thinking they might fly within range and give me a chance to bag one.

Meanwhile, one of the boys who had been out on the prairie caught sight of my gray shirt in the tall grass, and hastened to camp shouting, "bear, bear." This alarm created a big excitement, and the boys resolved to add bear meat if possible to the cuisine. There was no weapon, however, more formidable than a revolver in the party, which came within about a hundred yards of me, and halted for consultation. Though I saw the group, no suspicion of their intention crossed my mind, as I lay quietly unconscious of danger. Twice, as I afterward learned, Messick brought his pistol to bear, yet failed to shoot, knowing that the odds were a thousand to one against inflicting any serious injury. It was finally decided to send a messenger after the man who was out with the only rifle in camp.

Soon after the messenger's departure, I arose from my recumbent position and approached the boys, who, astonished at their ludicrous mistake, explained matters and congratulated themselves on Messick's caution.

The next day's pull brought us to New York Camp near the mouth of the Merced River,[5] where we found a small collection of tents, and a party of some twenty men bound for Mariposa. As the waters in the streams were still high, there was no occasion for haste, so we remained at the camp a few days, where with plenty of game we lived high. Some who had acquired a certain degree of expertness with a riata pursued the elk on horseback, and captured them by throwing the coil over their vast antlers.

Pursuant to a promise made to my friend Miller in San Francisco, of whom we shall speak hereafter, I desired to procure a pair of green elk horns, and took some pains to examine those about the camp, but found none that suited. Learning what I wanted, one of the hunters advised me that he had killed an enormous elk the day before, and left the horns where he had dressed the carcass, a few miles away. At my request he went with me, and I secured the antlers, which were indeed a noble pair and in perfect condition. An acquaintance who was going below agreed to carry the horns in his boat and deliver them to Captain House, who ran a small schooner between Stockton and San Francisco. They eventually reached the consignee, who forwarded them by the ship *Senator* to New York, whence Captain Coffin sent them to Miller's friend Snedacor, who kept a hotel, I think, at Babylon, Long Island, which was a popular resort for sportsmen.[6]

An incident that happened while in camp on the Merced is perhaps worthy of relation, as it ultimately eventuated in the violent death of one of the parties thereto.

Messick, who was about to start on an elk chase one morning, deposited his saddlebags in the hollow of an ancient tree, where he considered they would be safe, as he told no one where he put them. On his return at noon, he discovered that the bags had been rifled and $600 in gold dust taken therefrom. Of course he was incensed at the robbery, and as it was the second time he had been victimized in the same way, he determined, if possible, to "smoke out" the thief. Among a promiscuous crowd where all were comparative strangers to each other, and whose antecedents were unknown, it was exceedingly difficult to detect the criminal. Nevertheless, by persistent inquiry Messick got hold of a clue which led him to suspect a young man named Marcy, who on the day of the robbery had gone down the river en route for San Francisco. Marcy had been a soldier in the Mexican War, and had, it was alleged, left a bad record in the army, more than one of his comrades it was said, having suffered from his peculations.

Messick talked confidentially with me in regard to his loss, told what he had learned respecting Marcy's reputation in the army, and how by putting this and that together he had reached the conclusion that Marcy had stolen his money, and he was resolved to kill him on sight. He stated that he had been robbed once before of $700 that he had worked hard for, and this second misfortune nearly discouraged him, for it really seemed that he individually had been selected as a victim of persecution.

Though agreeing with him in the main, I advised him to go slow and ascertain something more definite before proceeding to extremity, for though he had perhaps good reasons to suspect his man, they were, after all, mere presumptions, and Marcy might be guiltless of the offense. It was a serious thing to take human life on mere suspicion, and it would be better to wait for some more tangible evidence ere he carried out his purpose, which, in the event of future disclosures establishing the dead man's innocence, might jeopardize his own safety.

The consensus of opinion in camp, however, appeared to sustain Messick's views, but as the accused was beyond present reach, delay was unavoidable. Hence nothing was done at that time further than to comment on the transaction and speculate on the outcome.[7]

After a week in camp, the Oswego boys, who in addition to their boat owned eight or ten pack mules and did a small freighting business, decided to leave for Mariposa, as the mud had dried up and their animals were no longer liable to mire in the low grounds. Accordingly, one bright May [April] morning we made up the train and started for the mountains. The journey was a short one; the roads were good, and our progress satisfactory. At night we camped in a valley where the grass was luxuriant, and the mules soon filled their bellies with the nutritious fodder.

In the interval between supper and bed-time, Randolph, who was a good singer, tuned up and woke the echoes with his vocal melodies. There was a chorus appended to his favorite song, and I have only to close my eyes to see the group as it sat beside the camp fire and listen to the words,

There's a good time coming, boys, a good time coming; wait a little longer.
The clock of the world goes back fifty years when that scene recurs to memory, and the prophetic tenor of the chorus, in which all joined, had such an exhilarating influence, and so renewed our courage, that we gained strength and confidence at every repetition. It seemed to dispel the cloud of uncertainty and despondence, and disclose the sun of prosperity shining brightly behind it. We were all young, each had only his individual self to care for; and though none had as yet realized his golden dream, the possibility of so doing still existed, and we could afford to "wait a little longer."

That night, after all hands had turned in, just as I reached that semi-unconscious state between sleep and wakefulness, I was aroused by the distant baying of a hound. Thinking it belonged to some belated traveler, I closed my eyes, turned over for a fresh start, and soon fell asleep. The nap was a short one, however, for presently the deep "bow wow wow" of a dog, apparently in our very midst, frightened Morpheus away. I sprang up, alarmed at the contiguity, and shouted, "Get out," for all I was worth—much to the amusement of the others, who, it seemed, had put up a game to scare me.

There was no dog, as the rest well knew. George Hale was an expert ventriloquist, and it was he who had caused my fright. Before going to sleep again, George gave an exhibition of his imitative powers, and for a while the camp was alive with the voices of birds and beasts of almost every description. It goes without saying that I was provoked at the disturbance of my slumbers and the laugh against me, but all was taken in good part, with a determination to get even should the opportunity occur.

We reached Mariposa the next day, and after helping the boys to unpack the mules, I remained with them till they started to return an hour or two later. George had collected his freight and carelessly dropped the bag of gold dust into the pocket of his overalls. Watching my chance, I successfully abstracted the bag and handed it to Charley Judd, enjoining him to keep shady and see how George took it when he discovered his loss. Charley readily cooperated in my attempt to repay George for the dog scare, and promised secrecy.

Two weeks later I learned from Charley the result of my pocket-picking experiment and its effect on George. Charley said everything went well till they had made about six miles on the return journey, when George put his hand in his pocket and discovered his loss. Without saying a word, he wheeled his mule and, socking the spurs into its flanks, started on the back-track at a tremendous gait. The suddenness of his action took Charley by surprise, and George was a quarter of a mile away before he started in pursuit. Though George had the fastest mule, Charley was the lightest rider, but it was not till after a chase of a couple of miles that he was able to warn his fleeing comrade that the money was safe. When George turned his pale face and realized the true state of affairs, he was so overcome that he had to dismount and sit down on the grass, when Charley proceeded to explain matters. George was soon made acquainted with the whole transaction, and when he learned to whom he was indebted for the practical joke, was compelled to acknowledge that "he laughs best who laughs last."

When the boys had gone, I gathered my traps, which consisted of blankets, cradle, mining and cooking utensils, together, and prepared to camp that night beneath a tree. I had come all the way from San Francisco to Mariposa without expense, had enjoyed the trip, and had as much money as when I left the city. I got my own supper that evening, wrapped my blankets around me and lay down to sleep.

XVIII

MINING AT MARIPOSA

April–July, 1850

Mariposa in 1850 was by no means an attractive settlement. The creek was similar to that at Sullivan's, and the diggings were of the same character, the gold being coarse and unevenly distributed. As at Sullivan's, one might work a week without finding anything, and then pick up a nugget that would pay for all the labor expended. The creek was bordered by mountains on the right bank, and the camp was located on the flat opposite, where saloons, stores, gambling establishments, and miners' tents were scattered promiscuously.[1] The population was cosmopolitan, and the proportion of monte dealers and poker sharps above the average. These fellows, who sat up all night plying their vocation, did their sleeping in the daytime, and turned out late in the afternoon. It was their delight to play rigs on passing travelers, and though those who were accustomed to such exhibitions of humor generally escaped, a stranger was apt to catch it, especially if he seemed to be in a hurry. For instance, a horseman was passing swiftly through camp one day, evidently on some important mission, as his animal showed signs of hard riding, when the rider's ears were greeted with the shout, "Oh, say!" which caused him to pull up suddenly and turn to the speaker, who, apparently unconscious of having attracted his notice, continued, "Can you see by the dawn's early light?" as if he was merely singing "The Star Spangled Banner" for his own amusement. The broad smiles on the faces of the bystanders convinced the stranger that he had been wantonly delayed and made a butt of by the man who so nonchalantly continued to hum his song; yet though it was obviously the singer's intention to make him a laughing stock, there was nothing to prove it, as anyone has an unquestioned right to sing our national anthem, so making the best of it, the stranger remarked that though perfectly familiar with the song, he had never before heard it rendered with such extraordinary stress on the opening words, and resumed his journey.

Indians, especially the squaws, were compelled to run the gauntlet and were subjected to many jokes and indignities as they passed through camp. Three squaws who came along one day, unaccompanied by bucks, were so bedeviled and tormented that they were almost frightened out of their wits. In fact, their treatment aroused the sympathies of the editor of the *Mariposa Gazette* to such an extent that he made it the subject of a leader in his next issue,[2] denouncing such practices as contra bonos mores, while a local bard in an adjoining column stigmatized such proceedings, and boldly declared he

> Had rather be an innocent lamb between two grizzlies' paws
> Than take the desperate chances of three unprotected squaws.

Soon after my arrival in Mariposa, I met Messick, who said he had learned that Marcy, whom he accused of stealing his money, had bought two mules in Stockton, which fact, as it was notorious that Marcy had no means, was conclusive evidence in his mind that they were purchased with the stolen money, and he was "resolved to kill him on sight."

A few days afterward, someone told Messick that Marcy was coming and would probably reach camp that afternoon. On the receipt of this intelligence, Messick prepared himself and laid for his man armed with a doublebarrel gun loaded with buck shot. About three o'clock Marcy made his appearance, when Messick stepped out of a Dutch restaurant, gun in hand, and confronted him.

"Marcy, if you are armed, defend yourself," was Messick's salutation, but before the former could pull his pistol, Messick, who had the drop, let go, and as Marcy whirled round he gave him the second barrel in the back. Only one word, "Mother," passed Marcy's lips as he fell dead. "Take him, take him," exclaimed the bystanders, but Messick threw away the gun, and drawing his big Texan sixshooter with a barrel some eighteen inches long, marched through the crowd, which had hastily collected, untouched. He presented a repulsive sight, for owing to excessive excitement or some other cause, the blood gushed from his nostrils and covered the whole front of his person. He was never called to account for the homicide, as after the affair was explained, public opinion justified the act.[3]

My experience in Mariposa was far from satisfactory. When I first came there, I met a casual acquaintance whom I had seen in San Francisco, who invited me to share his quarters, but the crowd he trained with were such a dissolute set, so addicted to whiskey, and so uncongenial in every respect, that I was soon disgusted, and after a sojourn of two or three days, resolved to cut loose and seek another abiding place.

Not far away lived a quiet, intelligent fellow named Long, who worked alone, so I made his acquaintance and proposed a partnership, which he agreed to. Having concluded this arrangement, I returned to my former quarters, tendered what was a fair equivalent for my share of living expenses, which was accepted. and I removed my traps to Long's tent. Long was a sober, industrious man, not given to dissipation, avoided roistering companions, and attended strictly to his own concerns. He was a newcomer, however, who had no cradle, but as I had a good one, the union of forces promised to work beneficially.

The next day I went for my cradle, which had been left at my previous quarters, but learned it had been taken away by my late messmates and carried to their claim some three miles distant. Ascertaining its locality, I walked over there, and when I reached the spot, was so provoked at their unceremonious appropriation of my property that without offering any explanation I seized the hopper, threw out the contents, reversed the cradle, picked it up together with its bed, and started homeward, while the fellow who was operating it stared open-mouthed and made no comment.

My proceeding of course ended their operations and they went off and got drunk. As for us, not dreaming of further complications, we used the rocker that afternoon, and when we quit work, carried it to the tent for safety.

Early next morning, while we were at breakfast, a man came and, pointing to the cradle, asked if I owned it. Receiving an affirmative reply, he stated that he was a constable, and produced a writ of attachment about which he professed to know nothing, referring me to the Alcalde, who had issued the writ. Conscious of no indebtedness of any kind, and altogether puzzled by the proceeding, I started immediately to interview the Alcalde and ascertain what it meant.[4]

The Alcalde explained that the San Francisco man, who was a consummate scoundrel as well as a drunken rascal, had filed a bill against me for board, despite the fact that he had been paid, and himself had received the money. Nevertheless, there was the bill for $25, which provided I had paid nothing, was greatly steep for three days' board.

Having learned the true inwardness of the matter, I returned to Long and we canvassed the situation. From observation, I judged that the Alcalde, who was a saloonkeeper, was as unscrupulous as the plaintiff, and in my opinion they were evidently both blackguards. The amount of the bill with probable accruing costs exceeded the value of the property attached, and as I had taken no receipt, neither could I prove payment, while the balance of his crowd would undoubtedly support the plaintiff's claim; there seemed really no show for justice, so it was decided to let the case go by default and lose the cradle, which it would be difficult to replace.

My sojourn in Mariposa was less than two months, and I will not dwell on my experience there. It is sufficient to state that it was a disagreeable one, and there are many unpleasant recollections connected therewith. After looking around the neighborhood and prospecting at Agua Frio, Hornetas [Hornitos], and Sherlock's Creek with but indifferent success, my patience was exhausted.[5] Moreover, I had come in contact with a shrub indigenous to California called "poison oak," the virus of which attacked my legs and ankles, and the itching was so intolerable, especially at night, that it made life a burden.[6] Disheartened and disgusted with the surroundings, I resolved to shake the dust from my feet and leave the diggings.

As I had quite a lot of culinary and mining utensils, I could not afford to throw them away, neither could I sell them; yet I hit on a scheme that enabled me to dispose of them at a fair price. The boys in camp, though they would not buy, were always ready to play cards, and put up everything from a penny whistle to a second-hand pulpit. Well aware of this idiosyncrasy, I decided to take advantage of it and stake my household lares at "seven-up." Pursuant to this idea, I provided a deck of cards; and, considering myself no slouch at the game, bantered those who passed to play me after fixing a price on an article, whether they should take it for nothing or pay double. The scheme took. I seldom challenged one who refused to accept, and as a result soon disposed of my traps, which, though I lost some games, realized enough in the aggregate to make me whole.

Having got rid of all my effects except my blankets, which I chucked into a wagon bound down, I started afoot for Stockton with no definite prospect in view after reaching that point. I carried a tin cup, a package of coffee, and food sufficient for the journey. The nights were warm, and I could well dispense with blankets. Though otherwise all right, my ankles were badly ulcerated from the effects of the poison oak and seemed to defy every effort to heal them. Nevertheless, I made rapid progress, and so managed that at the day's end I camped contiguous to water, prepared a cup of coffee, ate a lunch; and throwing myself on the ground without other covering than the clothes I wore, slept the dreamless sleep of the wearied wayfarer.

On the second evening I was rather disconcerted to find that three Mexicans in charge of a pack train had preceded me at the watering place, where their mules were grazing in an adjacent valley. Perplexed at the presence of the Greasers, and dreading their propinquity, I hesitated at passing the night in their neighborhood, but as there was no other spring nearby, was compelled to accept what was unavoidable. After eating my frugal supper, I lit my pipe and resolved to cultivate the friendship of the muleteers and ventilate my limited knowledge of the Spanish language. They proved to be simple, inoffensive fellows, whose evident satisfaction when I addressed them, and ready replies to my questions, soon convinced me that they were harmless, and that there was no cause to fear their proximity. Satisfied in that respect, I laid down and slept undisturbed till morning.[7]

On the evening of the third day, I reached Stockton and learned that Bob [Gardiner] had left Col. Jackson's employ, having taken a partner and gone to the mountains, where he opened a store at Rattlesnake Creek, near Big Oak Flat in Tuolumne County.[8] Missing Bob was a great disappointment, as I had counted certainly on seeing him and counseling on future proceedings, as we could talk freely and I had no hesitation in confiding to him what I would not perhaps have told to another.

My trip from Mariposa was a speedy one. Entirely unencumbered, I had made a forced march, and having become in a great measure acclimated, did not suffer from thirst as on previous occasions. It was the last pedestrian journey of any account I made in California. I visited Mariposa several times in after years, but always had a good horse under me, and sufficient money to pay my way, which was certainly a vast deal pleasanter than my first experience in that camp.

I made my quarters that night with William Trembly, whom I had known in Panama. He with his brother David had a store in Stockton and were apparently doing a successful business. After breakfast next morning, I walked down to the landing, undecided what course to pursue, as I had not intended to return to San Francisco when I left the mountains, but circumstances had so shaped themselves that I was all abroad concerning the future. Finally, however, after thoroughly weighing the pros and cons, and seeing no way out of it, I resolved to go down.

As I passed along the bank of the slough, a man hailed me, stating that he was about to leave for San Francisco, and if I desired to go down, he would carry me for eight dollars rather than go alone. He had a nice sailboat, and as the fare was very reasonable, I decided to go with him. Going up town for my blankets, I soon returned, jumped aboard, and we shoved off.

The trip passed without incident worth recording, except a shortage of provisions, the last of which were eaten on the third day at Sausalito, where we were detained by a head tide. The next morning we got under way, but the wind failed us, and the tide turned before we reached the city. It was only by the most strenuous exertions that we managed to catch the mizzen chains of the English ship *Vicar of Bray,*[9] to which we made fast, and climbed on board. The captain and steward were the only occupants of the vessel. The latter brought us a lunch, which we were sadly in need of, and when presently the breeze came, we cast off, hoisted sail, and were soon wafted to the shore.

It was the last week in July when I landed, and I had been a year in California without having improved my financial condition. I had grown a year older, and perhaps wiser, though I am not sure of it. Without any definite line of procedure, I left my blankets in the boat and sought the place where my trunk was stored for a change of apparel, which was eminently desirable, as my rough mining rig was soiled and dilapidated from hard usage. The trunk, which had been left in the loft of a store on Battery Street, contained what was necessary to enable me to present a respectable appearance and mingle with the crowd without exciting marked comment.

LIFE IN SAN FRANCISCO

AUGUST, 1850–MAY ? 1851

Miller's "ranch," as it was called, was the first building erected on Battery Street. Built in the summer of 1849, it was located just north of Broadway, and the site was chosen, as the proprietor explained, "because it was near deep water." The locality was generally known as "Clark's Point," about which the boatmen congregated, as the shore was bold, with plenty of water at the landing regardless of the state of the tide. Mr. Miller was himself a Long Islander, and his place was the main resort of people from that quarter. A thorough business man, he possessed a genial disposition, which made him universally popular. He was the central sun around which we all revolved, and shed his sympathetic and inspiring rays on rich and poor indiscriminately.[1]

Captains, cooks, and foremast hands alike made the ranch a rendezvous, and confided fully in its proprietor, who was eminently worthy of confidence. Many a poor devil who sought Miller discouraged and disheartened, retired from the interview with lightened spirits, prepared to renew courageously the battle of life, and struggle persistently to reach the goal of his hopes. My associations with Mr. Miller during my sojourn in San Francisco were such as will cause frequent allusion to him in the course of this narrative.

There was no one present when I entered the store that morning with whom I was acquainted, so I proceeded immediately to the loft, found my trunk, and divesting myself of my travel-worn garb, for the first time in sixteen months put on a white shirt with proper accompaniments, and as I had taken a bath in Sausalito, I was clean from top to toe. The transformation relieved me, and feeling like a new man, I went downstairs, where I met Miller, who after a brief salutation hailed me as I was about to pass out, saying, "Cal, where are you going?" I replied, "To get something to eat." "Have you anything particular to do?" he asked. When I gave a negative response, he said, "Joe's got the jaundice and has gone off to recruit; I wish you would tend shop for a while."

Of course, I assented joyfully, considering the proposition a godsend, as I was out of work and almost out of money. So after a visit to "Lovejoy's Restaurant," kept by one George [i.e., J.H.] Brown, who had been an employe at the hotel of that name in New York City,[2] I returned prepared to assume the duties of clericus magister during Joe's absence.

Except as an office, and for the purchase of gold dust, the business of the store proper was a secondary consideration, as the transactions were of a wholesale character, goods being received and delivered on the store ship Huron, which had come from Sag Harbor with a cargo of lumber.[3] After she was discharged, Miller had purchased her, and she was moved near the foot of the hill, a short distance from his store close by [Charles] Minturn's steamboat wharf, where there was safe anchorage and plenty of water. The space between the wharf and ship was only a few rods, and I often had occasion to go on board to receive and deliver merchandise.

One morning [in 1851?], having some mission requiring a visit to the vessel, I reached the wharf at dead low water and the yawl was some six or eight feet below the cap timbers. As it was inconvenient to climb down, I jumped, expecting to light on the boat's gunwale, but unfortunately my feet slipped off, and I was treated to an unceremonious bath, much to the delectation of Mr. Rhodes, the ship-keeper, who was watching me as he leaned on the vessel's rail. It was not so much for the bath, but because my clothes were saturated that I was provoked, as I had but few changes of raiment, and a change just then must necessarily be for the worse.

I hastened back, however, procured dry clothing, and returned just in time to see the hilarious ship-keeper take a dose of the same medicine. He had crossed to the ship *Haidee* which lay beside the wharf,[4] and grasping a rope, proceeded to climb up. He didn't get there, however, for the rope, which had been made fast with a slippery hitch, fetched away with him, and down he went, "ker souse." It was some little time ere he regained his dinghy; meanwhile I had reached the store-ship prepared to welcome him when he came on board. The rainbow of smiles had entirely disappeared from his visage, and he was much disgruntled because I had witnessed his mishap, for it was evident that the wind was taken out of his sails thereby, as his sole object in going ashore was to report my ducking.

Miller bought considerable gold dust, which was shipped by the Panama steamers to meet his drafts. The dust was packed in square tin cans each holding about $2,000. These cans when filled were hermetically soldered, and placed four in a box in wooden cases strongly nailed, and bound with iron, on each of which the name and address of the consignee was cut with a knife in plain letters.

It was part of my duty to attend to these shipments, which were usually held back till the afternoon of steamer day. The office of the S.S. company was at the foot of Leidesdorff Street, about half a mile from the store.[5] On one occasion I had $3,200, which I placed in a wheelbarrow and with Samuel Oakley, a young man from our village, as body guard, conveyed the treasure to the shipping office, where, after it was weighed and checked, it was necessary to wait while the clerk was preparing bills of lading.

Taking advantage of the delay, I stepped out to look up the boat where I had left my blankets, but found her deserted and a board nailed to the mast stating that she was for sale. The blankets had been brought from home and had accompanied me in all my wanderings. I was sorry to lose them but they were gone, however, and as it proved irrecoverably.

It was only a few weeks before Joe, whom Miller had brought with him from the East, returned prepared to resume his duties, and my occupation was gone. Thereafter, except at short intervals, I was a loose fish ready to snap at any bait. The annoyance caused by the poison oak had been abated in the simplest manner. Having tried many remedies suggested by one and another without relief, I incidentally referred to the affliction when writing home. One day a letter came from my uncle stating that he had heard that "hot water" was a panacea in such cases, and advised me to try it, which I did, and it proved efficacious, two or three applications curing me entirely. I make this note thinking it may meet the eye of some one suffering as I suffered, and enable him to rid himself of the scourge.

Miller, who was constantly on the qui vive, watched the market closely, and from time to time ordered from the East such articles as were likely to be in demand, and as a general thing ordered wisely. To show the nature of his transactions, a single instance which happened will suffice. He came into the office one morning from downtown and remarked casually,

"Cal, I have made $3,000 since breakfast."

"Is that so? How did you do it?"

"Sold 150 barrels of mess pork."

When he relied on his own judgment, the outcome was usually in accordance with his predictions, but on one occasion he was victimized by his "wicked partner," who unfortunately made a shipment without having previously consulted Miller. The notice was received too late to countermand the order, and when the mail brought advices that the ships *John* and *Edward* had cleared from Liverpool with cargoes of iron houses consigned to him, he was in a devil of a stew, and could not see his way out of the dilemma, as there was absolutely no sale for such buildings in San Francisco. Had it been possible, he would have stopped the vessels in transitu and sent them back, but as he could not do that, he held his breath and waited their arrival, making no comment, but probably thinking "d—n it" very often during the interval.

In due time both vessels reported, though I do not believe the consignee would have been inconsolable had both been wrecked on the passage, provided there had been no loss of life, as the cargoes were fully insured. With the exception of one warehouse sold to Minturn, both ships returned to Liverpool without breaking bulk.[6]

The fatuous ventures of consignors was illustrated in the case of the ship *Caroline Reed* of Philadelphia [New York?] in 1850. At one time there was a scarcity of corn brooms, which commanded amazing prices, even as high as $75 a dozen. The news of this advance reached Philadelphia while the *Reed* was loading, and a merchant named Howell, who happened to be in the city at that time, bought fifty dozen and shipped them on the *Reed* consigned to Miller, who when the vessel reported, paid the freight, handed the order to his lighterman, and instructed him to deliver the brooms at Middleton and Hood's auction room. A day or two after, while I was in the store, the lighterman came in, returned the order, and stated that the brooms were not in bundles but stowed singly and promiscuously among the cargo between decks. That it would cost more to pick them out and get them together than they were worth, and he would not bother with them. When informed that the expense of lighterage was a dollar a dozen, it occurred to me that as my time was less valuable than the lighterman's, who had a gang under pay, I could well afford to get the brooms and deliver them at the price named. So I took the order, borrowed the *Huron's* yawl, and at the last of the flood tide next morning, sculled off to the *Caroline Reed*.[7]

Going on board, I presented the order to the clerk, who informed [me] that the vessel had 2,800 dozen brooms in her manifest. He gave me a man to assist, and I proceeded between decks to begin the search. The brooms, [as] already stated, were stowed promiscuously, but as they were all marked on the handles there was no difficulty in distinguishing my lot. Wherever we found one, we found others in close proximity, so that in a few hours the quota was complete. We roused the brooms on deck and I went into the boat to stow them, as my assistant passed them down. Though my cargo was not heavy, it was bulky, and when all were on board, the brooms loomed up like a haystack. Every inch of room, except a small space in the stern, reserved for a standing place, was occupied for stowage, which having completed, I returned to the vessel and signed a receipt.

As ill-luck would have it, just after casting off, a smart breeze sprang up, which overcame the strength of the ebb tide, and drove me to leeward despite all my exertions, as the brooms caught as much wind as a sail would have done, and it was impossible to stem it. So I squared away and finally fetched up at Rincon Point, where I laid till evening. When the wind died away, I managed to get up to the auction room, where I found a dozen lighters ahead of me waiting to be discharged. Arranging with the man in charge of the next boat to watch my cargo, I proceeded to get something to eat, as it was then nine o'clock, and I had fasted since breakfast.

Fish balls were my diet for several months, as I had never fully recovered from the dysentery that attacked me a year previous. Though the disorder was not constant it was intermittent and required abstention from animal food. It was fish balls for breakfast, fish balls for dinner, and fish balls for supper. So accustomed was the waiter to my order, that as soon as I entered the restaurant, he would call "codfish balls" without consulting me in the premises, taking it as a matter of course that such would be called for.

After supper I returned to the boat, and seeing no probability of reaching the auction room in some hours, resolved to go to the theatre. [D.G.] Robinson and [James] Evrard were the proprietors of what was known as the "Dramatic Museum," which was well-patronized by the general public.[8] Though the actors were a curious agglomeration of incongruities, mostly unaccustomed to the stage, they had been pretty well drilled, while the play was usually of such a cast that the performance passed muster.

Doctor Robinson generally introduced an original song containing hits of a local character, which were easily understood by the audience. The city fathers, especially one Alderman [A.A.] Selover, were made the butt of many a joke in these screeds, which were always enjoyed and taken in good part. The play on the night in question was Goldsmith's comedy, "She Stoops To Conquer," the rendition of which would have surely mortified the author, had he been out on a ghostly tour of inspection and dropped in at the Dramatic Museum. Doctor Robinson, as usual, though not much of a vocalist, introduced an original song, and in the midst of it stopped to reprove the orchestra, saying,

"You must either stop playing or I must stop singing, for we cannot possibly go on together," at which rebuff the musicians dried up incontinently and the Doctor finished without accompaniment.

Evrard of the Museum was a great joker and jolly companion. I happened in one night at a Sans Souci [informal assembly] on Pacific Street, where there was quite a crowd. Evrard was also present. The purpose of the assemblage was fun and frolic, and whoever was called on was required to sing a song, spin a yarn, or treat. Someone in the room, probably unaware of his peculiarities, called on Evrard, who was not slow in responding. First explaining that it was obligatory on all to follow his motions on penalty of the usual forfeit, he commenced:

"One finger, one thumb, keep moving, one finger, one thumb, keep moving,
One finger, one thumb, keep moving, and all of you do the same."

As he was a man of commanding presence and towered among the company like a colossus, his movements could be easily seen by all. While he continued singing, he moved more fingers till the numbers of digits was exhausted, then he moved one arm, then two arms, the legs followed suit, and finally the head, when he had eight fingers, two thumbs, two arms, two legs, and his head all moving in rhythmic accord. It was a grotesque exhibition to see that vast audience follow the singer's whimsical movements, who without a smile on his countenance kept them going till they were thoroughly exhausted.

It was Saturday night, and when, after the play, I returned to my boat, which was the last in the line, there was but one ahead of me and my turn soon came. As I passed up the brooms, the receiving clerk proceeded to stow them away without counting them. I objected, stating that I had receipted for 50 dozen and desired a receipt for a like number as a voucher for my lighterage. As he still refused my request to count, we got into a wrangle and the loud talk called Mr. [John M.] Hood, one of the firm, to the scene, who when he heard the nature of the dispute decided in my favor. After he retired, the clerk, who was angry, declared that I was hypercritical, as the goods would be sold on Monday and I could collect my lighterage from the account of sales. This led to more loud talk, when Mr. [John] Middleton, the senior partner, put in an appearance and decided against me, saying it was nearly two o'clock Sunday morning, and all hands were tired out. So the brooms were not counted, but when the account of sales came in, they were all there. They sold for about enough to pay freight and charges, and the consignor was out for the original cost.

There were great sacrifices of staple commodities during the summer and fall of 1850, as the San Francisco market was glutted by eastern speculators, who took the chances and shipped recklessly. They soon learned the folly of such proceedings, however, and after sustaining some heavy losses, became more conservative. Moreover, the clipper ships had been put on, and the voyage around Cape Horn was performed in about half the time previously required.

The rush of immigration still continued; every clipper ship brought more or less passengers, and the Panama steamers came crowded every trip. The plains from Fort Independence[9] to the Sierras were dotted with the white covers of "prairie schooners" driven by sturdy immigrants who were destined to make California a great agricultural state.

The new arrivals hastened at once to the mines, confident of success, and on their way met many who had preceded them with like confidence and, having seen the elephant, had become disgusted and were either bound home, or to seek an asylum in San Francisco. Thus they went and came. The city was full of disappointed Argonauts, to whom the very mention of the mines was suggestive of an emetic. Bustle, bustle, speculation and confusion, exhilaration and disappointment, were mingled together like sunshine and rain.

During the summer of 1850, Captain Barney G.[reen], who had come out with other stockholders in the *Sabina*, having turned his attention to a more congenial occupation than gold-digging, and accepted a position as master of the ship *Deucalion*, came in from Australia.[10] He was very fond of pets, and while in the whaling service invariably brought home some strange bird or beast that he had picked up among the islands of the Pacific and Indian oceans. On one occasion he brought home an emu, a mammoth fowl similar to an ostrich, which he had procured in New Zealand. The biped created a big sensation in our village as the captain's steward led it along the street.

On this voyage he had brought a private venture as a matter of speculation. There were two dogs, a mastiff and a bulldog, to represent the livestock, several hundred bushels of potatoes; and among other things a large cask of small fruit trees of different varieties. Everything except the latter was soon disposed of. The potatoes were sold to an Englishman, and careless of collecting his pay, the captain delayed presenting his bill till he accidentally heard that the English merchant had failed and was trying to compromise for a mere nominal pro rata.

This news awakened the easy-going skipper, who, scouting the suggestion of a compromise, proceeded to collect his bill in a characteristic manner. All unused to law courts and the tergiversations of trade, he consulted no one, but evolved from his own inner consciousness a method of procedure which, backed with his native courage and nearly three hundred pounds of personal avoirdupois, promised a successful issue.

He bought a rawhide.

Armed with that instrument, he sought the quarters of the delinquent debtor, whom he found alone in his office. Entering the room, he closed the door, locked it, and the two were isolated from the outside world. Captain Barney presented his bill and demanded payment. The Englishman saw the bill and also observed the rawhide. A rawhide in the hand of a competent party who evinces a disposition to use it is a powerful argument in behalf of the holder. A rawhide in the hand of the relentless captain exerted such a controlling influence on the recalcitrant debtor that he was reluctantly compelled to acknowledge that in that special instance Britannia did not rule the wave. Realizing the futility of any attempt at compromise, the bill was paid in full without the slightest sug-

CHAGRES FROM THE ANCHORAGE
From John M. Letts, *California Illustrated* (1852)

PANORAMA OF SAN FRANCISCO
Sold by Charles Magnus, New York.

gestion of abatement. Capt. Barney was probably the only creditor who received one hundred cents on the dollar.

Though our doughty skipper succeeded in making a satisfactory settlement with the Englishman, he was less fortunate in the disposition of his fruit trees, which were really a treasure, being of choice varieties and invaluable to any man who had the sagacity to look forward a few years for their fruition. Nevertheless, Capt. Barney was unable to sell them, and after several days' unsuccessful effort, he came into the store and admitted his inability to find a purchaser.

Mr. Miller turned to me and requested that I would go down on the street and see what I could do. I went, with but little hope of effecting a sale, and in fact canvassed the city for half a day without finding a customer. Everybody repudiated the idea of buying fruit trees. They had not come to California to plant trees and await the slow process of growth. Mere adventurers for a temporary sojourn, their hearts were in their eastern homes, and they had no intention of making a permanent residence on the Pacific Coast. In response to my solicitations, I had but one offer, which a Jew made, of $20. This was so small that I refused to consider it, but as it was the only one I had, I so reported when I returned to the store.

The next time Capt. Barney called, I told him of my ill-success and the sole offer received, but though the custom duty amounted to $19, he advised me to accept the Jew's proposition, as he was convinced there was no sale for the trees in the San Francisco market.

There were a thousand choice trees in that cask which I sold for $20, and it has often occurred to me since that, had I possessed the perspicacity to see it, there was a fortune for me had I bought them myself. Had I done so, and gone to San Jose, where I could have purchased a few acres at a reasonable price and set an orchard, which I could have attended myself, in four or five years the returns would have come in the shape of luscious fruit salable at an enormous profit in the city [San Francisco]. While the trees were growing, I could have raised garden truck for current expenses. I can now see no reason why the enterprise would not have succeeded, but like most others among the earlier pioneers, I was possessed of what the lawyers call the animus revertendi, and any investment that required years to materialize had no attraction sufficient to induce me to engage in it. But "man proposes, and God disposes," and as things eventuated, it was years afterward before I saw my way clear to return to the East.

During the fall of 1850, Miller conceived the idea of buying up all the nails in the market and holding them for an advance, but after he had purchased extensively, he discovered that [F.W.] Macondry & Co. had an immense supply, which constrained him to abandon the project and forbear further purchases.

He gave me the contract to deliver the nails on board the *Huron* for a dollar a ton. There was a small lighter of about ten tons' capacity, which I think belonged to the ship. By taking advantage of the tide, I could handle it alone. The nails were stored on different vessels in the harbor. I would run alongside, present my order, receive my cargo, and when the fair tide made, scull back to the *Huron* and hire a man for a dollar an hour to assist in hoisting the nails on deck and stowing them below. In this manner I earned about eight dollars a day while the job lasted.

Thus I managed to earn sufficient to keep body and soul together, but the mode of existence was precarious. Sometimes I was a few dollars ahead, and at others it was a question where the next meal would come from. Fortunately, my credit was good at the restaurant, and in seasons of impecuniosity I could avail myself of it till a job of some kind turned up.

Jim Hedges of our village secured occupation on a whale ship that some Nantucket people were fitting for a voyage to the North West Coast. He was a cooper, and had engaged to overhaul the oil casks and put them in shape. Jim chose me for his helper, and for a fortnight I assisted him in his work, but in the meantime a native Nantucketer had been employed, who seemed to expect that I would serve him also. He was a morose, disagreeable fellow to whom I took an instinctive dislike, for though perfectly willing to work with Jim, I would not collaborate with the Nantucketer. Hence we quarreled; he reported me to the agent for insubordination, and I was discharged.

There were numerous Long Islanders in San Francisco in the fall of 1850 who had come down from the mines disgusted with their ill-fortune, some of whom returned home. Others that would have gone were compelled to remain, as they had not sufficient money to pay their passage.[11] They had been long enough in the mines to know that the work there was no child's play. The food was worse, the associations were rough, and the labor was rough also. Life in the mountains had not proved what they anticipated, and it was only by the greatest exertion that some were enabled to gain a mere living. The daily exercise they were subjected to was something they had not bargained for, and the remuneration was entirely inadequate to meet preconceived expectations.

Of the thousands in the mines, but a small proportion was sufficiently rewarded for the time and labor expended. Taking the Argonauts on an average, it was estimated that about two-fifths made from five to ten dollars a day, two-fifths from three to five dollars, and the remainder earned nothing above mere living expenses. There were certainly some big strikes, but these were exceptional cases that were bruited abroad, while no mention was made of the unsuccessful toilers.

Among those who located in San Francisco in 1850, were Bruce and Will H.[untting], whom I had left at Sullivan's a year previous. They leased a lot on Clark's Point near the foot of Broadway and built a restaurant which was subsequently inaugurated as the Commercial. Some of us who were disengaged volunteered our assistance in constructing the building, which was situated on the bay shore. A steep declivity in the rear was graded and leveled for a basement, intended for a kitchen. The structure was a story-and-a-half building, about 40 x 20 feet. On the ground floor was the dining room, and above were bunks for lodgers. The entrance from the kitchen was through a trap door in the floor, which Will H., who officiated as assistant cook and waiter at table, used to open with his head as he came up from the lower regions with both hands full of dishes.

The Commercial soon became a favorite resort for Long Islanders, who were sufficient in numbers to form a full quota of guests. The quality of board furnished compared favorably with the price charged, but unless on hand promptly at meals, one had sometimes to content himself with what he could catch, as what remained after those at the first table had eaten was apt to be a conglomeration of odds and ends far from satisfactory to a dainty feeder. One day in particular there was a great scarcity, when Captain Charles Howell, one of the *Sabina's* company, came late and found some difficulty in satisfying his hunger. After calling for one dish and another, only to meet a negative response from Will, who acted as purveyor, the man's patience was exhausted and he exclaimed irascibly, "What's the matter, is there a famine in the land?" Will never tired of relating that incident in after days, whenever he alluded to his experience as a publican.

One favorite amusement in the kitchen of the Commercial was killing rats. San Francisco in 1850 was overrun with rats; the streets were full of them, and Clark's Point was their headquarters. We became so accustomed to their presence that we minded them no more than so many chickens. I slept in a hammock, and one night a rat more audacious than his fellows caught me by the ear and awoke me. The clews of the hammock were full of rats, and as I struck a blow to dislodge them, a dozen or more tumbled to the floor. Miller had a squirrel rifle with which he used to amuse himself by shooting rats from his back door. Will H., however, reduced the slaughter to a system, and as his kitchen furnished an inexhaustible preserve, he never lacked game whenever inclined to try his hand.

His weapon was a dart, such as schoolboys use, tipped with paper and pointed with a big sail needle. So expert did he become by constant practice that he seldom failed to transfix a rodent when he made a cast. Their cries as they hung impaled by the needle touched no sympathetic chord in Will's bosom; their pathetic squeals were music in his ears as he gloated over their sufferings. Nothing in the kitchen was exempt from their inroads, and revenge was sweet to the assistant cook.

In the spring of 1850, bills had been introduced in Congress providing for territorial governments in Utah, New Mexico, and California, and the admission of the latter as a State. These bills were subjected to a long debate, acrimonious in character, and unsatisfactory in result. While the politicians in Washington were quarreling over the slavery question, discussing the omnibus bill, the Wilmot proviso, the abolition or extension of the compromise line of 1820 and agreeing on none, the people of California chose delegates to a constitutional convention, which assembled at Monterey and formulated an organic law excluding slavery, which was submitted to the people and adopted. This instrument was forwarded to Washington as conclusive proof that the sense of the community was opposed to slavery, or rather to its extension to free soil, and in August the bill admitting California passed the Senate. In September the House of Representatives took favorable action and the Golden State became a full-fledged member of the Union.[12]

News traveled slower in those days than now, and it was not till October that the Panama steamer which brought the tidings entered the harbor with colors flying and cannons booming, announcing by the display that she brought good news. I watched her as she steamed up to her anchorage with no little interest, and instinctively divined the cause of the feu de joie. The intelligence of our admission as a State, though joyfully received, failed to create any extraordinary excitement, as politics was not extensively discussed at that period, when the almighty dollar reigned supreme. Of course, there were some politicians who had axes to grind that were rejoiced at the outcome; these, however, were but an infinitesimal faction.[13]

One morning—I think it was in the fall of 1850—some Spaniards rushed along Battery Street about 4 o'clock shouting "Fuego, fuego" and roused Miller from slumber, who having more interest in such matters than his lodgers, turned out to investigate. The fire was in the downtown district, where, as the structures were principally of canvas, it did not take long to sweep off a considerable section of the town and do considerable damage. Our immediate vicinity escaped, but my recollection of the affair is vague and indistinct.[14]

During the summer and fall of 1850, interested parties got up quite an excitement regarding alleged extensive gold fields at Gold Bluff and Humboldt on the coast north of San Francisco. Many credulous individuals were beguiled by these false reports. There were lots of "Micawbers" in the city constantly on the lookout for such chances, and there were also those who, having some interest in coasting vessels, were contemptible enough to fan these false flames and induce many a poor devil to spend his last dollar in pursuit of what they well knew was an ignis fatuus. Hundreds went to Gold Bluff and elsewhere, only to find themselves victimized on their arrival, and left without means of support till they could find their way elsewhere.[15]

The fact is, San Francisco was full of impecunious specimens of humanity ready to jump at any means of subsistence, and these were constantly increased in number by accessions of disappointed gold-seekers. Miller had a rope suspended from a beam in rear of his premises with a hangman's noose surmounted by the legend, "This or Humboldt," which had a painfully suggestive meaning for a man dead broke.

One poor fellow named Blanchard, from a western State, whose parents were in good circumstances and would have doubtless responded with material aid had he so requested, was on Long Wharf [16] one day, "slinking," as Mark Twain has it, when he was accosted by a man who asked if he "wanted a job." Now, a job was just what he did want, and he answered accordingly.

"Go aboard that vessel then, and shovel coal. I will pay you a dollar an hour."

Blanchard went aboard and was put to work trimming coal. It was about 2 o'clock, P.M. He shoveled away till it began to grow dark, when, feeling a queer sensation, he climbed to the deck and discovered that the steamer was outside the heads. Perfectly paralyzed to find himself at sea, and disliking the idea of being kidnaped, he remonstrated emphatically against such a course of proceeding. His outcry brought the captain on deck, who, when the matter was explained, stated that he had brought him off inadvertently and could see no alternative but to make the voyage. Blanchard, who was by this time terribly sea-sick, and, having crossed the plains, was never before on salt water, was unable to continue the discussion, so he was passed below, where a berth was provided. There he lay for several days disgorging chyme and chyle, and in the intervals between throes cursed the hour that introduced him to existence on this sublunary sphere.

The steamer was bound to Portland, Oregon, and when Blanchard recovered from his sea-sickness, he was employed in the engineer's department. The trip occupied some thirty days, and when our involuntary sailor again landed in San Francisco, he made his way to the office of the agent who had employed him, where he found his man and demanded a settlement, claiming a dollar an hour for the time he was destined on the vessel. Though surprised at the unexpected occurrence, the agent did not kick, but decided to make the best of a bad bargain by an offer to compromise on the basis of two hours per day, which Blanchard accepted.[17]

It was now the winter of 1851. Many of my townsmen had returned home months before. Captain Henry Green, who came out master of the *Sabina,* with his brother, Captain Barney, had left for the East in the fall of 1850. The former invited me to take dinner with him the day previous to his departure, and we dined in state at a prominent restaurant. Though he had been disappointed in the result of his gold-mining enterprise, he was by no means cast down, as he had a sufficiency of this world's goods to carry him through safely. For many years he had been prominent in the whale-fishing and as master had invariably made successful voyages. He was already advanced in years, and survived but a few months after his reunion with his family.

In the fall of 1850, Captain Enoch Ryder, who was about to sail in command of a ship for China, offered me a berth as clerk on board his vessel with quarters in the cabin. He was an old acquaintance, and had I felt a predilection for a sea voyage, would have doubtless have been an agreeable companion. But my mind was fixed on a return to the mines as soon as circumstances would warrant, therefore I thanked him for his offer, though constrained to decline it.[18]

There are many interesting incidents connected with my life in San Francisco, which I would like to record, some pleasant, and some otherwise, but I must hurry up and avoid details, as there are still six years of an adventurous experience to narrate, which necessitates condensation and avoidance of much that might properly be introduced in connection with my story.

In March, 1851, Captain George W. Clapp, whom I had known at home, came down from the mountains to purchase a small steam engine. He was a genial, fine-hearted fellow, in whose judgment I placed implicit reliance. As my health was perfectly restored and I was thoroughly acclimated, I consulted him as to the probability of success should I decide to try my luck a third time in the diggings. Though he held out no inducements in the way of strikes, he gave me such encouragement that I resolved to cut loose from San Francisco, where I had steady employment, and try once more to wring subsistence from the auriferous streams and gulches in the mountains. For eight months I had been bumming round the city, where, though I had managed to pick up a living, my pockets were frequently empty, and never overburdened with a surplus.

My experience had been such that it entailed many a struggle with a deficit and humiliated me to an extent that is painful to recall even at the present time. Though I could look around me and see many others whose financial condition was perhaps no better than my own, it afforded no consolation. For nearly two years my time had been virtually wasted by reason of my inability to undergo the hardships of gold-digging, handicapped as I was with a chronic complaint, which so weakened me that it forbade any continuous attempt at hard labor. Now, however, it was different. My health was fully re-established, I was no longer restricted to a diet of fish balls, and felt confident that the future had better luck in store for me.

After my interview with Captain Clapp, who remained only one day in San Francisco, I determined to join him, and accordingly made preparations to that end. He was located at Horse Shoe Bar, on the North Fork of the American River, some seventy miles from Sacramento City. Having no business to detain me, and no loose ends to pick up, it did not require long to prepare for my exodus.

Going to Mr. Miller, who had been a constant friend and had given me many a job that enabled me to steer my way through dark thoroughfares, and who had always been kind and considerate in his intercourse with me, I told him of my design to leave the city and once more try my fortune in the mining region. He, as well as myself, knew that the prospect for accumulation under prevailing auspices was slight indeed, but my chance in the diggings was as good as another's. So he agreed with me in regard to the course proposed. He was owing me a small sum, which he paid, and bidding me godspeed, we shook hands and parted.

After saying goodbye to a few friends in the neighborhood, I took my way to the steamer *Senator* and was soon en route for Sacramento. Traveling facilities had improved, and means of communication with the interior were very convenient. The *Senator* and *Confidence* plied on the Sacramento, and the stern-wheel steamer *Fashion* on the San Joaquin. They had reduced the time between San Francisco, Sacramento, and Stockton very materially, as the trip which formerly required several days could now be performed in a few hours.[19]

It was on a May evening that I boarded the *Senator*, and as the *Confidence*, a competing boat, left at the same time, there was a trial of speed between the two. Captain [John] Van Pelt frequently interviewed the engineer, advising him to "throw in the bacon sides and make the old gal hump herself." The latter, who was as much interested in the race as the skipper, crowded the fuel into the furnaces until the steam escaped from the safety valve, and the boat shook from stem to stern under the vibrations of the engine. The passengers were also excited, as is invariably the case on such occasions, and did not seem to care whether the boilers were in danger of bursting or not, so long as our boat maintained the lead, which she did till we reached our destination next morning.

This was my first visit to Sacramento, where on my arrival I was in a strange latitude. I managed, however, to find a restaurant on J Street, where I got breakfast and afterward wandered out in quest of transportation to Horse Shoe Bar.

Sacramento, which is situated at the junction of the American and Sacramento rivers, was like all other towns of that day, in an inchoate condition, being composed mainly of tents and canvas buildings.[20] The city was the depot of supplies for the numerous mining camps, and did an immense business. Teams innumerable continually came and departed for the mountains.

As I walked along the street, someone saluted me and called my name, who, when I turned at the sound of his voice, proved to be Fred Tryon, a cooper from our village, who was plying his calling in Sacramento. He informed me that his shop was located on the road leading to the ferry on the American River, which all teams bound for the North Fork necessarily followed, and invited me to go and take dinner with him, as we could hail from his door every driver that passed till we found one bound for Horse Shoe Bar. Accepting his invitation, I went with him to his shop, where he manufactured kegs for the transportation of liquids in small quantities. He had plenty of orders from the merchants, at prices so remunerative that he considered he could do better at his trade than in the mines, which he like many others, had tried unsuccessfully. He was probably right; moreover, the labor was more congenial than handling the pick and shovel on mere speculation.

Fred made my visit the occasion for a holiday. He got up a good dinner, after which we took position at the door where we could watch the teams, and sat down in the sunshine to discuss matters generally. It was not till the middle of the afternoon that we struck a team bound my way. The driver was a clever fellow, who readily agreed to take me as passenger. The roads were good, the load was light, the weather was fine, and when I bade goodbye to Fred and seated myself beside the teamster, I did so with an exuberance of spirits to which I had long been a stranger.

A mile or so from the city, we passed Sutter's Fort,[21] and soon after crossed at the ferry. The appearance of the country was far more attractive than in the vicinity of Stockton. Instead of an arid, treeless plain, the road wound through oak openings. At that season, the grass was fresh and luxuriant, wild flowers sprang up on every side, and we seemed to be traveling through a vast floral conservatory. We camped that night in the neighborhood of what is now Folsom. The country thereabouts, which was then a wilderness, is probably now covered with farms and vineyards. It was a beautiful spot, the land high and dry, and the surface rolling. There must be some pleasant homes in that vicinity now, as Folsom is, I understand, a railroad station. It is probably at this day a suburb of Sacramento, and being beyond the reach of river floods, is utilized by the merchants of the city for residence purposes.[22]

On the evening of the second day, we reached our destination, where I met Captain Clapp, who took me across the river to his tent, where we had supper, and after a little while, as I was somewhat tired, turned in for a night's rest.

I was now about to begin a new life. My previous experience in the mines had been that of disappointment. Compelled by sickness to lie idle for a great part of the time, I had accomplished nothing. Now, blessed with health, I was determined to give the diggings a fair trial, and so long as I could make expenses, stick to them, buoyed by the hope that under Providence I might eventually strike something worthwhile. I had bidden farewell to San Francisco, resolved never to return there, unless business should call me temporarily, till I passed through on my homeward journey. And I never did. So long as my health was spared, I was confident that I could make a living, with a constant prospect of doing better as I became accustomed to the work. Others had wrought successfully, why should not I? Mining is at best a lottery, and a mere simpleton is as likely to strike it rich, as one of conceded intelligence and perspicacity. Ask any old miner, and he will tell you that as a general thing, the ignorant and improvident, who squandered their gains at the gambling tables and indulged in reckless dissipation of every description, were the lucky ones. In most cases, these men were workers, who had been accustomed to toil all their lives, and perhaps for the first time beheld themselves in possession of ample means to gratify their peculiar tastes. They could not bear prosperity. They seemed to consider their claims as a sort of Fortunatus purse which would supply them indefinitely. Some of these same profligates, who are still living, may be seen today picking a scanty subsistence from the abandoned gulches of the Sierras. Old, gray-haired, poor, and perhaps dependent on public charity, they delight to recount the incidents of the "good old times," and refer exultingly

> To the days of old
> The days of gold,
> The days of '49.[23]

Poor old fellows, they were young then. Dame Fortune smiled on them and filled their cups to overflowing. They drained them, however, and whose business was it if they did? They earned their money, and spent it to suit themselves. They had a good time while their means lasted, and the memory of those days perhaps repays them in a measure for the poverty of the present. Quien sabe?

In the morning Captain Clapp, who was engaged with a company on the opposite side of the river, which proposed to turn the stream into a canal, loaned me his cradle and mining utensils, pointed out what he considered an eligible place to commence work, and proceeded to Horse Shoe Bar to attend to his own interests.

My own locality was known as Whiskey Bar,[24] but I will reserve my experience there for another chapter, closing this with the simple remark that I that morning turned over a new leaf, resolved to work steadily, sail alone, and "salt down."

XX

HORSE SHOE BAR, AMERICAN RIVER

MAY ?–SEPTEMBER, 1851

The principal mining camps on the North Fork of the American River were at Mormon, Rattlesnake, Dead Man's, Horse Shoe, Long, and Murderer's bars.[1] The character of the population differed materially from that of the Southern Mines. There were but few gambling houses and few Greasers. Nearly all the miners were native Americans, chiefly from New England and the Middle States. They were as a general thing intelligent, industrious, and not given to dissipation. The two stores at Horse Shoe Bar were those of Abraham and John Bronk and the French brothers [Henry and   ]. The former included a boarding house, which was well-maintained and well-patronized. The most prominent residents, some of whose names are still familiar to my mind, were Esquire [Samuel] Carey and his son Will, Captain Thompson, William Kidd, Captain [George W.] Clapp, Holbrook, Charley Lay, Raynor Holcomb, Joseph Eustis, Sam Coffey, Charlie Hardenburgh, Merrick Moore, Jacob Collamor, Tom Haines, George Kelsey, the Bronk brothers, French brothers, and a Mr. French, who was a master mechanic.[2]

At the time of my arrival, a company known as the "Coffey Point Co." were excavating a canal on the right bank of the stream intended to drain some 1,500 feet of the river bed. There were about thirty men engaged in the enterprise, which entailed a vast amount of labor, and corresponding expense. We will not anticipate, however, as most of those named above will appear in the course of this narrative, and their present mention is merely preliminary.

After Captain Clapp left me the first morning, I proceeded to set my cradle and commence operations in good earnest. My claim was about 125 feet from the river, and the dirt was carried to the cradle in buckets. The manner of proceeding was to dig and free from large boulders some twenty-five buckets at a time, throwing out all stones as large as a hen's egg. The gravel was transported as stated, and washed in a cradle similar to an old-fashioned baby rocker. The machine, which is usually about four feet long, is set at a slight angle sufficient to cause a current when the water is poured in. The bed on which the cradle rests is made of two pieces of scantling with cross-pieces at each end, the space between which corresponds with that between the rockers attached to the cradle. These cross-pieces have each a small iron spindle that penetrates the rockers, which are shod with hoop-iron. A V-shaped notch is cut in the bottom of each rocker, and a hole drilled through the shoe immediately below it. The spindles pass through these holes, and the shape of the notch gives free play when the cradle is oscillated, while it is held firmly in place by the spindles.

The "hopper" is a square box with sides some four or five inches high, to the bottom of which is affixed a sheet-iron screen punched with holes about a half-inch in diameter, at intervals of three inches. The hopper fits the head of the cradle and sits perfectly level, the pitch of the machine being counteracted by dressing off an inch or two at the sides and head. The "apron" is a slight wooden frame covered with cotton cloth fitted to the inside of the cradle, immediately below the hopper, and inclines at an angle of forty-five degrees towards the head of the cradle. The machine has a slat across the lower end or foot, and another midway. These are called "riffles." They are about an inch high and catch the gold, which sinks to the bottom as it passes through, while the dirt runs off and forms what is called "tailings."

A bucket of dirt is deposited in the hopper, when the miner proceeds to rock the cradle, giving it a peculiar shake impossible to describe, while he continues to dip water from the river and pour it over the contents of the hopper till all the dirt has passed through the screen, leaving nothing but the clean stones, which he inspects carefully to see if there is a chispa among them, and then throws out. These stones are called "screenings."

Unless the dirt is extraordinarily rich, the usual run is ten buckets, after which the cradle is washed down carefully until nothing remains but the gold and black sand caught on the apron and by the riffles, which are removed with the "scraper" and placed in the pan for further manipulation at the end of the day's work. The quantity of dirt washed depends on its distance from the cradle and the difficulty of procuring it. After I became accustomed to the work, my "stint" was 150 buckets daily, and sometimes it required extra exertion to perform it; nevertheless, I never failed, even if compelled to work till starlight.

The first day's work yielded about four dollars, but from then on I did better, and my average earnings were about $50 per week. This was not extravagant, but a vast deal better than I had been accustomed to. There is an excitement in gold-digging which tends to reconcile one to the hard work, as he looks forward to the "wash-down" at the end of each run with a good deal of interest; moreover, the few minutes' relaxation afforded by the process is a period of comparative rest. A miner soon learns to judge by the clean-up at the end of the run what his dirt is paying, and can tell pretty near what will be the result of his day's work, as the gravel on the river bars is very uniform in its yield, especially when taken in the aggregate without stripping for certain rich streaks. Sometimes it is necessary to throw off several feet of the surface, leaving perhaps a couple of feet to be washed, in which case the stripping occupies so much time that one has to hustle to put through 150 buckets.

It was at Whiskey Bar that I first undertook systematic housekeeping. I lived alone, as Captain Clapp boarded with the Bronks on Horse Shoe Bar, where his work was. The greatest difficulty was making bread. The rest was comparatively easy, and except in bread-making, I soon became expert in the cuisine department. I could cook pork and beans, fry ham, boil potatoes, manufacture a pork stew, concoct coffee, and toss slap-jacks secundum artem, but bread was for a long time beyond my capacity. Simple as it seems, the preparation and baking [of] a batch of bread is no easy matter. Time after time, after mixing the ingredients with the utmost care, kneading the dough and setting it to rise till it reached a proper state of fermentation, then placing the loaf in the Dutch oven with glowing coals beneath and on the lid, I would watch it carefully, and at intervals probe it with a stick to see if it was done; yet, when the loaf was turned out upon the table, it invariably proved a "lap stone," heavy and indigestible. Finally, however, when I caught the knack, my previous failures were incomprehensible. My bread was excellent. The loaf when placed in the oven would gradually rise up, up, up, till it fairly raised the cover, and when taken out was light as a feather. Sourdough, left in the pan at the previous baking, was used for years, and after I once got the hang of it, I always had good bread.[3]

Sunday was the day for baking, washing, and wood chopping. On that day everything was prepared as far as possible for the succeeding week. The laundering was an easy matter, as one hickory shirt constituted the "wash." The mountain oak makes excellent firewood, and that was about all it is fit for. It splits easily and burns freely without seasoning. An hour sufficed to draw a week's supply from the hill, chop, and split it. In the afternoon I visited the store, bought my groceries, and after my return home, the balance of the day was devoted to letter-writing or reading.

A fifty-pound sack of flour lasted five weeks, hence my consumption of bread and slap-jack required ten pounds a week. Provisions were sold at reasonable rates, and I lived well, far better than at any previous period in California. Never a hearty eater, my wants were easily satisfied. Coffee, fried ham, fried sweet potatoes, with bread and butter, usually constituted my breakfast. Dinner was a pick-up meal, but supper was more elaborate. Salmon were then caught in the river,[4] and fried salmon was no uncommon dish. Taken all in all, my life at Horse Shoe Bar was a pleasant one.

One thing, however, annoyed me. That was my failure to get letters from home, two-thirds of which went astray, and it was not until my return to the East that I discovered the reason. Postal facilities were few, San Francisco, Sacramento, and Stockton having about the only post offices. The letters for the mining camps were collected at those offices by letter-carriers who were delegated for that purpose. It was their custom to circulate orders for signatures, directing the postmaster to deliver letters addressed to the parties signing it to the carrier. This was a lucrative business to the express man, who received from one to two dollars each for all letters delivered, and naturally corralled all he could, regardless, so long as his list contained the name, where the proper owner resided.[5]

It seems there was a man in Nevada County whose initials and surname were the same as mine, who was contemptible enough to take my letters, for though our initials were alike, there was no similarity between our full names. He was a lawyer, who must have discovered at a glance that the letters which were addressed in full and bore neither his name nor residence, were not intended for him, and had he acted as he should have done, would have returned them to the post office unopened. This he omitted to do, violating every rule of decency by appropriating as his own communications confidently addressed by mother to son, and brother to brother. John B. Smith may be excusable for opening letters addressed to J. B. Smith, but if he violated the sanctity of a document addressed to Jeremiah B. Smith, he commits an outrage altogether indefensible, unwarranted, and deserving of the severest reprobation.

So far as labor was concerned, one day was an index to the others. Up by starlight and at work at dawn was the unvarying rule. From time to time, I changed my claim for what I considered a better one, but spent little time in what is called prospecting, as that is often the bane of a miner's life, and sometimes resorted to as a reasonable excuse for idleness. I was doing fairly, and resolved to be content and work steadily so long as I could make "Congressman's wages." There was a Chinaman who had a claim not far from mine. He put in fewer hours than I did, and sometimes when delayed at my work, when I went home, I found that the Celestial had preceded me and prepared supper. At other times, when after a hard day's work I returned to my tent, [I was] so tired that when I laid down on the bed for a temporary rest, I involuntarily dropped asleep and slept soundly till morning. Rest on such occasions was more necessary than food.

Thus steadily digging, at the end of two months I had accumulated about four hundred dollars, which I resolved to use to better advantage than to hoard it. "Long Toms" had been lately introduced, and as one of my neighbors was operating one with apparent success, I decided to invest my little capital in a long tom, which required several men to work it. A horse and cart were also indispensable. My means were about sufficient to purchase the machine, horse, cart, and harness.[6]

There were four Vermonters camped near me who had lately arrived. They seemed to be honest, steady fellows, and I made them a proposition to work on shares, I to provide the outfit, which should count as one share, making six in all, of which myself and outfit represented two shares, and they one share each, they to pay two-thirds, and I one-third of the expenses of keeping the horse. This they agreed to, and I proceeded to make ready for work.

A carpenter at Horse Shoe Bar furnished the tom and "riffle box." I purchased a cart and harness at Long Bar, and a horse of Walter Goss, a Cherokee, who assured me the animal would work in harness. The horse was a big, powerful fellow, cream-colored, with a black mane and tail, and weighed about 1,100 pounds. As the bar was stony, it was necessary to have the animal shod. The shoeing cost me $16, and I helped with the striking. The shoes were made of scrap iron picked up here and there, and the nails were also of domestic manufacture. These preparations required several days.

Meanwhile the Vermonters had constructed a little dam on the ripple opposite Whiskey Bar, where there was a good fall in the river, and we set the long tom. The construction of the dam made it necessary to build a road to the machine, which was some fifteen feet from the shore. Here the horse and cart were first brought in requisition, and up to that time everything had worked serenely. The horse, which had probably never before been in harness, submitted quietly when hitched up, and though he worked awkwardly, drew two or three loads without any display of ugliness.

Had the road been good, with a secure footing, it is probable there would have been no difficulty, as the horse was naturally kind and tractable, but the nature of the work required that the loads should be delivered where the water was about two feet deep. The big boulders on the river bottom, together with the swaying of the cart, the attempts to turn him round and back him, combined with the difficulty of preserving his equilibrium so bothered the horse that it drove him wild, and he seemed possessed of the very devil.

Open-mouthed, he chased Aaron, his driver, into the river, who barely escaped with his life. In one of the horse's tantrums the axle of the cart was broken, and that ended the matter, as it was evident the animal would not answer our purpose.

I cut a tree on the hill, [and] made a new axle, after which I bought another horse. Bronk, the merchant, had one, but on trial he proved unfit and was returned to his owner. Captain Clapp ascertained in some way that Holcomb had a mule out at his ranch some three miles away. I interviewed Holcomb and proposed an exchange, my horse for his mule. Holcomb considered that the difference in value between the animals was $50 in his favor. I acquiesced, and the exchange was made. As I was bursted financially, I borrowed the boot money of Will Carey, and one Saturday rode the mule home. On trial, the animal proved satisfactory, and the next thing in order was to have it shod.

The next day—Sunday—I got an early breakfast and started for the blacksmith's shop at Salmon Falls. In my hurry I forgot my pistol and did not miss it till after reaching the top of the mountain several miles away, when I indiscreetly resolved to go without it.

The trail was full of Indians bound for some "powwow" on the river.[7] No one minded Indians, and I apprehended no danger from them. Having occasion to tighten the saddle cinch, which was loosened in the ascent of the mountain, I did so, and started on forgetful of the blanket, which had covered the saddletree, but soon missed it and returned for it. Two Indians had just picked it up as I reached the spot, and evinced a disposition to retain it. This of course did not accord with my ideas, but willing to conciliate, I offered them a piece of tobacco, which they rejected, demanding "plata" [silver], a Spanish word equivalent to money. Forgetting that I was unarmed, and accustomed to the Diggers, whom I considered of no account, I was vexed at their importunities, so giving one a shove and snatching the blanket from the other, I began folding it up. Instantly I realized that I had acted hastily. The Indians, who evidently noted the absence of my pistol, showed fight. Quick as a flash, one of them strung his bow, whipped an arrow from his quiver, and it really looked like a "long good night to Marmion," when casting a glance backward on the trail I perceived an acquaintance to whom I shouted, "Hackett, Hackett, come quick, for God's sake." The Indians stood back to him, and as he came bounding in with his six-shooter in his hand, they fled incontinently. It was indeed a narrow escape, as I would doubtless have been assassinated had not Providence so ordered that help was close at hand. Hackett censured me for traveling unarmed, and the incident taught me a lesson that was never forgotten.

The mule was put to work next day, the road was soon finished, and we began washing. All went well, the mule worked nicely, and after a few days traveled to and fro over the route without a driver. The claim did not pay, however; the men became dissatisfied, and after a fortnight's trial quit work. This proceeding, which was perhaps warranted by the circumstances, left me in the lurch. I was in the same fix that Robinson Crusoe was, when after finishing his big canoe, he was unable to launch it. I could not work the long tom alone, the proceeds of the dirt would not pay wages, and I was satisfied it would be difficult to get labor on shares.

After weighing the chances, I resolved to abandon the enterprise and go back to the cradle, where I could be president, vice-president, and general manager of my own business. Aside from about a week's time, I did not lose in the long tom fiasco, as while it was operated, my two shares paid wages. The outfit, except the mule, was sold without loss, and the animal grazed in the vicinity without expense till disposed of.

The most unpleasant feature of the transaction was the refusal of the Vermonters to pay their share of the expenses as originally agreed. It was but a small sum, about $25, but it was justly due, and I determined to collect it. So a meeting of the bar was called, and the delinquents summoned to appear. In due time the meeting convened, was organized by the appointment of a chairman, and a jury was impaneled. I stated my case, and as the defendants did not dispute the agreement but merely pleaded loss of time while engaged in the enterprise, the plea was disallowed and a verdict rendered in my favor. After the verdict, the defendants refused to recognize it, and declared they would pay nothing. I stated as much to the chairman, who decided that the "money must be paid then and there" or the defendants "must take the consequences." They were in a corner from which there was no escape, so rather than "take the consequences," they very reluctantly settled the account.[8]

About this time, the first political convention in Placer County for the nomination of members of the Legislature and County officers was held at Auburn, the county seat.[9] One morning, while at work in my claim, I was notified that I had been elected as a delegate from the Horse Shoe Bar precinct on the previous evening, and was expected to go with the others that day. At first I demurred, as I had no clothes fit to appear in at a public convention, but the demurrer was overruled, so I went to Bronk's store, purchased a decent rig, and in less than an hour was en route for Auburn.

Party lines were drawn at the first State election, and conventions were held in every county by both Democrats and Whigs. Abraham Bronk, Captain George W. Clapp, William Kidd, Captain Thompson, Henry French, and myself constituted the delegation from our precinct to the Democratic Convention at Auburn in the summer of 1851. The county seat was about eight miles from our Bar. We reached Auburn and participated in the proceedings of the convention, which was called to order just after dinner by a young lawyer named Thomas, who was, I think, a Southerner.

Mr. Thomas was chosen chairman, and, on assuming the position, explained the object of the meeting. He suggested the order of proceedings. Committees on credentials and resolutions were appointed, and matters were conducted in accordance with the rules generally observed on such occasions. There was a full attendance from every precinct in the county. Appropriate resolutions were adopted, and a full ticket was nominated. Abraham Bronk was nominated for county clerk and subsequently elected. The delegates were mostly strangers to each other, and aside from Bronk, I remember no county nominee. Everything passed off quietly; the convention adjourned with three cheers for the Democratic ticket, which at the ensuing election was successful.[10]

Though I returned to the cradle after the failure of the long tom scheme, I worked alone only a short time. One day Squire Carey, who was interested in the Coffey Point Company whose canal was nearly completed, came over to see me. He had been long on the Bar, and was a man of sagacity in whose opinion I had great faith.

He suggested the formation of a small company to drain a portion of the stream by cutting a race through a point just below the Coffey Point Company's claim. The canal would be only some three hundred feet long, and as the river doubled at the bend, it would drain five hundred feet of the bed of the stream. He thought eight members would be sufficient to do the work, and the indications were that the bed of the river was rich and would pay well. He proposed to take a share himself, offered me one, and mentioned six other first-class men who were ready to engage. Relying on his judgment, I declared my willingness to take hold, and we set about forming a company.

The members were William Kidd, Samuel Carey, George W. Clapp, Raynor Holcomb, Henry French, John Smith, myself, and one other whose name I cannot recall. Kidd, who was a professional engineer, was president, and I was secretary. The river had a good fall, and as there were no rocks to blast, the work was prosecuted rapidly. Our company was called the "Suffolk Co." Between the head of our canal and the foot of that of the Coffey Point Co., there was a space of 150 feet of river bed belonging to the latter. A dam to turn the river into our race would so back up the water as to impede the flow from that of the upper company, and as the intervening space was still water, and deep, the two companies resolved to join hands and flume that part by tailing on to the upper canal and conducting the water into ours. So a third company was formed under the name of the "Forlorn Hope Co.," in which both of the others were interested.

The construction of the flume necessitated the purchase of lumber for the sides and bottom. The conduit was sixteen feet wide, and as lumber was expensive, we decided to put only one tier of boards on the sides, as the lateral pressure was not great, and tack canvas above them, as there was a good fall to the flume and the water was not likely to be deep. The timber was procured on the adjacent mountain, hewed, hauled to the river, and floated down. It was good sport during those warm summer days to drive those timbers downstream, and all hands enjoyed it, as it was an agreeable change from the toilsome labor of digging the canal, which was faced with a stone wall on either side, and the exertion of raising the heavy stones to place was tiresome in the extreme.

From time to time we were called from work in the race to assist in placing the timbers for the flume. We would wade in, all standing, and after working for an hour or so, return to our digging soaking wet. This used to happen several times in the course of the day, yet we experienced no ill-effect from the frequent immersions. The long sills of the flume were too heavy to handle without some sort of mechanical appliance to raise them. One day six of us were standing on a stringer heaving away to lift it in the center so that a support could be placed under it, when the strap which held the four-fold tackle to the derrick parted, and we all tumbled into the deep hole beside the flume, much to the amusement of the spectators.

Such laughable accidents frequently occurred. Mr. Holcomb, who had conceived the idea of constructing a fish trap in the race, had occasion to go on the mountain for some poles, which after much labor he transported to the river bank. He was two days getting those poles down. There were six of them, about the size of an ordinary fence post, eight feet long. I happened [to be] near him when he launched them, preparatory to floating them to their destination. The water was deep where he rolled the sticks in, one after the other, and "every blessed one of them sank to the bottom."

"My stars," ejaculated Holcomb, as he took off his hat and wiped his steaming forehead. "Who would have thought it? They are all gone!! Now, if I had rolled one in first, I could have saved the others, but the idea of their sinking never crossed my mind." Holcomb was an intelligent, well-educated man from Granby, Connecticut, but was compelled to admit that he "didn't know it all" after he rolled those sticks in the river.

Under Kidd's wise management, the Suffolk and Forlorn Hope companies completed their works and were ready when the Coffey Point dam was finished and the water turned into the canal.

There was much standing water in the Coffey Point claim after the river was turned, and there was much discussion regarding the cheapest and quickest way to get rid of it. Charley Lay, one of that company, possessed a copy of Ewbank's *Hydraulics*,[11] from which he derived the idea of an "Archimedean screw" which he thought would, in connection with a water-wheel, quickly free the claims and keep it free. He brought out his book, exhibited an illustration of the screw, and explained its construction and manner of operation. His suggestion to build a screw was adopted, and a water-wheel was provided.

The machine, some fourteen feet long and four feet in diameter, was set in a frame and placed in the deepest hole, standing at an inclination of about fifty degrees. Connection was made with the water-wheel by means of a rope band. Though the screw made a few revolutions and vomited water amazingly, the strain was so great that it twisted off the shaft of the water-wheel like a pipe stem. Another shaft was fitted and the wheel set up again, but the screw was discarded and replaced with rotary pumps.

Few are aware of the difficulties that pioneer miners had to contend with when engaged in extensive operations. Far away from manufacturers and the source of supplies, they had to rely on their own ingenuity to overcome many serious obstacles. The wisest calculations were often rendered nugatory by unforeseen accidents and complications. Time was precious, as the period of working in the river bed was limited, so that delays on account of breakdowns or non-receipt of some indispensable article were apt to prove costly as well as disastrous. Everything was expensive, and transportation necessarily slow. Under such circumstances the wonder is, not that they failed in their operations, but that they succeeded as well as they did. After a company had managed under great difficulties to accomplish its work, expended months of time and hard labor, while many

Mormon Bar on the North Fork, American River
From John M. Letts, *California Illustrated* (1852)
Courtesy of Warren R. Howell

SONORA FROM THE NORTH

Published by G. S. Wells, Sonora, May, 1853. C H Goddard, *del.*

of its members had risked their last dollar in the enterprise, it was discouraging to have an early freshet overtake them and sweep dam, machinery, and everything to destruction. All these misfortunes were encountered time and again, and were the source of sad losses, not only to the operatives but to the merchants who had trusted them for supplies.

The fall in the river at our claim was so great that it nearly drained itself. What astonished us was the weight of water in the flume. The cross-ties, eighteen feet long, were placed two feet apart, and none flatted less than nine inches, but though only some sixteen inches deep, the weight so sprung them that we had to shore the flume with a girder along the center.

Kidd owned a small steam engine, which he attached to a rotary pump and soon drained the standing water from the holes, after which the pump, worked by a water-wheel in the flume, kept our claim entirely dry.

Our company being small, the dividends were very satisfactory. Some days we took out from six to eight hundred dollars. The dirt was not deep, but as a general thing paid well. So dry did we drain the river bed that we were able to brush the bedrock clean with a hair brush.

The Forlorn Hope claim was a deep hole, which we tapped with a ditch cut through the soft granite from the foot of our claim. This ditch was about three feet deep, and the work of excavation was not difficult, as the granite was easily pierced with a pick. The effect of the ditch was to lower the water in the hole three feet and expose a considerable area. This, however, did not pay satisfactorily, so the company disbanded and the ground was allotted in severalty to the individual members.

I was fortunate, through the interest of a friend, in securing an excellent spot. He had worked the adjoining ground as far as low-water mark, which paid better as he neared the river. Following his directions, I chose the locality, and it paid me from $16 to $20 a day.

Thus far I have said nothing about our manner of living while engaged in working the river. Up to the time when we began to take gold from our river claim, I kept bachelor's hall, and with the exception of dinner, which was taken at Bronk's, provided my own meals. After that time, I took all my meals at Bronk's, using my tent only as a sleeping place. There were about thirty boarders, and the conversation at meal times embraced almost every conceivable subject; arguments were rife, and differences common.

One day while at dinner, the question of fishing came up, and Captain Clapp in the course of conversation, spoke of the enormous quantities of "menhaden," or what was locally known as "moss bunkers," [that] were caught in the seines on Long Island, stating that as many as 250,000 had been taken at one haul of the seine. This statement was received with derisive shouts by those present, who pronounced it a "fish story," which the captain took as an imputation on his veracity. The guests were mostly from the interior, and had no idea of the immense piscatory product of the Long Island waters. Captain Clapp did not attempt to verify his statement, but suggested that I should be questioned when I came in, as I was "native there and to the manner born."

This suggestion was agreed to, and Captain Thompson was appointed inquisitor, with the understanding that the others should keep silence. Presently, when I appeared and took my seat at the table, Captain Thompson said he wished to ask me a question, and desired an answer to settle a dispute.

"Very well, I have no objection, provided the question is a proper one and I am able to answer it. What is it?"

"How many fish called bunkers have you ever seen caught at one haul of the seine?"

"Fifteen hundred thousand."

"What?"

"I said a million and a half."

At this reply, a shout of incredulity was raised that threatened to take the roof off the building. Somewhat provoked at the expressions of unbelief, and ignorant of the previous conversation, I proceeded to explain:

"Your refusal to credit my assertion shows plainly that you know nothing of the subject. Bunkers, like herrings, are gregarious and swim in immense 'schools,' which are often acres and acres in extent. They are used by our Long Island farmers as a fertilizer. The fishing companies are stock corporations, and the stockholders are farmers, who at the proper season make their headquarters at the fish houses on the beach and engage in fishing. The seines are five miles long, and when a school of bunkers is descried, the boats put out and the school is surrounded with a net, which when drawn in contains not bunkers alone, but vast numbers of other fish, among which are quantities of the finest eating fish in the world; in fact, every description of fish natural to that latitude. I have seen dogfish, skates, striped bass, chequit, mackerel, bluefish, sheep's head, porgies, blackfish, and other kinds, caught in one haul of the seine.

"When a school boy, I used during the fishing season, to visit Long Beach at Peconic Bay and watch the fishermen drain seine. Fish in those days were as free as air, and one could select the choicest to carry home, if he desired. When I say that I have seen 1,500,000 caught at one haul, I do not want you to understand that they were actually counted. I have seen a stack of fish as high as this building piled for a furlong on the bay shore. Every stockholder's allotment is in proportion to the number of his shares. Scores of teams are engaged in hauling the fish away. One wagon-load is counted, the others are tallied on that average. On the occasion referred to, the haul when all was carted away was estimated at 1,500,000."

The doubters were silenced; nevertheless, there were some who despite my explanation remained skeptical. After my return to the East, I one day asked an old fisherman how many bunkers he had ever known caught at one haul. He replied that he was present on the beach near Riverhead, L.I., when 2,700,000 bunkers were taken from Peconic Bay at one draft of the seine.

There was an itinerant preacher who sometimes visited the bar and held service. Among others who attended, one Sunday, was Raynor Holcomb. His was an argumentative disposition, and when he came to supper, the minister's discourse was the subject of discussion. Holcomb acknowledged that as far as the sermon was concerned, he had no fault to find, but there was one hymn given out that was altogether "too nonsensical and paradoxical to suit his views."

"What's the matter with the hymn?" was asked.

"Well, this is the stanza I take exception to:

> When we've been there ten thousand years
> Bright, shining as the sun,
> We've no less days to sing God's praise
> Than when we first begun.

"Now, I say that's nonsense."

"Where does the nonsense come in?"

"Why, can't you see? Suppose I should die today and be lucky enough to pass muster and get inside the ring. Once inside, I join the heavenly choir in singing God's praise. Two years hence you pass in your checks and follow suit, do you mean to say that you have no less days to sing God's praise than I had when I first started in?"

"That's not the question; you seem to be in a sort of intellectual fog. The hymn merely says that after you have been there so many years, you have no less time to stay than when you first 'started in,' as you phrase it. Now, I'll prove that the hymn is all right and neither 'nonsensical nor paradoxical.'"

Taking a pencil and paper from his pocket, he makes a circle.

"Now, we will assume that circle is a race track one mile in circumference, and that you have been walking two years when I take the track. How much nearer are you to the end of that circle than I am?"

"Why, there is no end to it."

"Ah! my friend, that is just it. Eternity has no end, and after your two years you are no nearer than when you began."

Compelled to acknowledge the point, Holcomb still contended that he would have sung two years the longest, which his opponent readily admitted.

Charley Hardenburgh called time for the miners with a small cannon that stood in front of his tent. During the hot days in summer, we took an hour and a half for nooning, which gave us nearly an hour for a siesta. The ground in front of Charley's quarters was literally crowded with sleeping humanity after dinner, who, when startled from slumber by the report of the gun, would have much preferred to retain a recumbent position.

Instead of resorting to cards and dissipation at night, as was customary in many camps, the boys organized a "glee club," which was very popular and thoroughly appreciated. Merrick Moore, Sam Messerne, "Little Bob," and Scotch Jack were the star performers. The latter was a fine singer. His favorite was Charles Dickens' "Ivy Green," and his rendition of the song was the best I have ever heard.

There was a burlesque society called the E. R. D.'s, which being interpreted means "Economical rum drinkers." This society, in which Squire Carey and Jake Collamer were conspicuous, had for its ostensible object economy in the matter of drinks. No member was allowed to treat at a public bar. Every member, however, could drink at an outsider's expense. If liquor was purchased at a bar, the minimum quantity was a bottle full. The purchaser of the bottle could dispense its contents to the bystanders, using the bar's tumblers for that purpose, but in no other manner publicly. There were many other preposterous and confusing provisions in the bylaws which eventually caused lots of trouble. The barkeepers kicked, and swore they would not wash glasses for men too mean to buy their whiskey at retail. The society boycotted the kicking barkeepers and carried its patronage elsewhere. This was all done in a good-humored way, excited some laughter, and relieved the participants of the monotony of camp life. The society after a few weeks died from exhaustion.

These incidents may seem trivial, and are introduced merely to show how the miners passed their idle hours.

About this time, the courts were instituted at the county seat and assumed jurisdiction in cases that had been previously controlled by the miners themselves at meetings of the Bar. This course of proceeding was resented by the mining community, which claimed the right to manage its own internal affairs in accordance with local rules and regulations, hence it was difficult for the courts to enforce process.

A company called the "Cherokee boys" were at work on the river a mile or two below our Bar. They had some dispute with another party over a claim, which was decided at a Bar meeting in their favor. The contestant refused compliance with the decision and appealed to the court at Auburn, where he got judgment of restitution, and the sheriff was sent to enforce it. He came alone at first, but after reconnoitering, returned home. The second time he came with a posse comitatus, prepared to place his man in possession vi et armis and arrest all who opposed him.

A runner brought the news to our Bar one afternoon, and an appeal from the Cherokee boys for assistance. Immediately every man laid down his tools and a universal stampede ensued for the Cherokee camp. Kidd, the president of our company, had acted as chairman of the meeting of the Bar when the decision was given, and was determined to uphold it by force, if necessary. The miners rallied like the Alpine [Highland] clans to the support of Roderick Dhu, and the sheriff was soon surrounded by a force of excited men outnumbering his posse ten to one. Like a wise man, he submitted to the inevitable and went home.[12] There was no attempt thereafter by the courts to overrule the fiat of the miners in our district respecting the administration of affairs in the settlement of mining disputes, which were always decided with due regard to the equities and in accordance with the unwritten law of the district.

It came to pass one day, while I was at work on my claim in the territory of the Forlorn Hope Co., that Tom Coffey paid me a visit. He stated that his company desired to make some repairs which would necessitate turning the river into its original bed. The work, he said, would require not to exceed ten days, and that all my neighbors had consented to step out and permit the Coffey Point Co. to flood their claims—temporarily. Though I disliked to take the chance, as my claim was paying over an ounce a day, nevertheless, as other interested parties made no serious objection, I reluctantly consented to step out also. As matters eventuated, I was afterward sorry that I did not ask for one day's delay and put on a dozen extra cradles, as the time would doubtless have been granted.

Having worked steadily all summer, I resolved to take a holiday and visit Bob [Gardiner], who had removed from Rattlesnake Creek to Swett's Bar on the Tuolumne River. Without stopping for details, it is sufficient to state that on the fourth day I pulled up in front of the "Grizzly Bear Pavilion."[13] Bob was surprised to see me, and as eighteen months had passed since our last meeting, there was naturally much news to receive and impart. After a three-day's sojourn at Swett's where I saw several old acquaintances and enjoyed the reunion thoroughly, I took my departure for home.

My mule, which a three-days' rest had invigorated, was in excellent form, and carried me along bravely. The roads were good, and as I proceeded, I thought of my previous trip over the same route in December, 1849. The remembrance of the toilsome tramp through the mud when we left Green Springs at midnight and blundered along in the dark, packed like jackasses, gave cause for congratulation over the changed conditions.

On my return to Horse Shoe Bar, I found things very different from what they were twelve days before. My fears when I abandoned my claim, as I hoped temporarily, had been more than realized. During my absence, rains in the mountains had caused a freshet that swept away dams and machinery and put an end to operations on the river for that season. Everybody was blue. The Coffey Point claim was not half worked out; moreover, what had been worked had not paid so well as was anticipated. The expenses were heavy, hence the dividends were light. Many became discouraged and left the Bar. Bronk sold his store to Sam Merchant and removed to Auburn, where he assumed the duties of county clerk, to which office he had been elected. Squire Carey, Captain Thompson, and Kidd remained. The latter, who had his family with him, owned a substantial log dwelling, and was there to stay. Captain Clapp left the Bar, but whether he resumed a seafaring life, tried his fortunes elsewhere in the mines, or returned home, I never learned. I have tried lately to discover his whereabouts, but without avail. As he was some years my senior, it is questionable whether he is still living. A great majority of the pioneers of '49 have already passed away, and those who are left, weary and old with service, are standing, as it were, on the very verge of dark eternity. My remembrances of Captain Clapp are all pleasant ones. The welcome he accorded me on my arrival at Horse Shoe Bar gave earnest of the firm friendship that existed between us ever afterward.

Resolved to change my vocation for a while, I arranged with George Kelsey to buy cattle and sell to the butchers. We had heard of a drove for sale on the Rio Chico some distance above Colusa,[14] and decided to go and inspect them. George bought a horse, and one morning we started for Sacramento.

From Sacramento we proceeded to Marysville, thence to Colusa. It was Sunday when we approached the town, but before we reached it, I encountered an accident that taught me a lesson that I have never forgotten, and since then, when in a strange locality, I have invariably followed the main thoroughfare without prospecting for a better one.

Just outside the town, the road crossed a slough, and was so cut up with wagon tracks that I hesitated about crossing, and sought what I conceived was a better place. The branch, though narrow, was deep; and before we reached the further side, the mule actually disappeared beneath the mud. Throwing myself off, I managed to gain the bank minus one boot, when the mule, relieved of my weight, made a desperate effort and with some assistance effected a landing. Both the animal and myself were completely enveloped in a black, glutinous covering of mud, which, as the sun dried it, presented a pachydermous aspect not pleasant to contemplate. Kelsey, who had kept the road, crossed all right.

Without attempting to cleanse myself, I rode into town and consigned the mule to a hostler at the hotel for ablution. A convenient clothing store supplied me with a new shirt and pair of boots, which were donned after I had taken a bath and rinsed the mud from my trousers.

At Colusa we learned that the cattle we were in pursuit of had been sold. As this intelligence made it unnecessary to go further, we decided to return home, not very sorry, however, as the difficulties attending so long a drive, the danger of losses on the way, and our inexperience as herdsmen, rendered the enterprise a risky one. So we resolved to abandon the cattle project and resume work in the gold fields.

At that period, the country west of the upper Sacramento was unsettled, perhaps for the reason that the land was low and liable to overflow. Among other trees in the river bottom we recognized the familiar sycamore so common on the eastern seaboard. Game was plentiful. We saw hundreds of deer and antelope, and many signs of bear, on our route. We rode through acres of wild geese feeding on the plain, which were not at all discomposed by our presence, and had we desired, could have killed dozens with our pistols. I must forego further details, as it would require a volume to record the incidents of that expedition.

After our return to the river, we prospected for a while at Mormon Bar, but made no camp there, as we boarded at the hotel. The landlord was an Englishman, a strapping fellow, and most of the guests were English seamen. The landlady was a pretty little woman and the proud mother of a six-months-old baby. At times she would come into the barroom, where she was always treated courteously by the occupants. The rough sailors who occupied the bench in front of the big fireplace would close up when she came in and provide an extra seat, where in response to the hearty invitation, "Shove in, mistress," she would establish herself and converse freely with the company.

On one occasion she came in with her baby in her arms, which I took, and as I held it, tried to make it stand on my knee. "It cannot do it," she said. "The child is very weak in the legs, very weak indeed," and casting a roguish glance at her stalwart husband, she added, "A little bandy, I believe."

"Bandy be d—d," ejaculated the irate father, who resented the innuendo, as he glanced proudly at his son and heir.

XXI

AT SECRET RAVINE

October, 1851–June? 1852

As our prospecting at Mormon Bar was not encouraging, Kelsey and I separated, he choosing to remain. I resolved to locate for the winter at Secret Ravine, some four or five miles from Horse Shoe Bar.[1] Accordingly, I went over one day to spy out the land and prepare an abiding place. Very fortunately I discovered and pre-empted an abandoned log cabin eligibly located on a small mound contiguous to a spring of water. The cabin was about 10 x 12 feet and had evidently been built by expert woodsmen. It had an excellent fireplace and chimney. The door and canvas roof had been carried away; otherwise the building was intact, even to the rafters and ridgepole.

Much pleased with my prospective habitation, I returned to my old quarters at Whiskey Bar with the intention of immediate removal to Secret Ravine. The cloth of my old tent was much worn and unfit to turn rain, so I decided to reinforce it with a "fly" or second roof, which would render the cabin impervious to water. Procuring a bolt of canvas at the store, and being an expert in the use of a palm and needle, I soon completed an excellent fly, which together with the old tent-cover, household goods, and mining utensils, were packed on the mule and conveyed to the new residence.

As everything was ready for the cover, it did not require much time to make the cabin habitable. The roof was soon placed in position, and by night a new door was hung, a bedstead made, the place thoroughly swept, and my traps moved in. Auger holes were bored in the logs and wooden pins driven, which afforded support for shelves on which were placed dishes, books, and papers. When all was arranged, I felt proud of my new dwelling, wherein I was ensconced as snug as a bug in a rug.

The fireplace was spacious, and took in sticks four feet long; moreover there was an excellent draft to the chimney, and no trouble from smoke. The cabin was isolated, being over a mile from the nearest habitation. Firewood was plenty and conveniently handy, so that with a riata hitched to the horn of the saddle, I drew in one day an immense pile of dead wood, and as there was no need of economy in fuel, a good fire was kept burning continually, which soon dried the damp earth of the floor and made the place comfortable.

In the ravine, about twenty rods away, I discovered a deserted claim which had probably been worked by the former occupants of the cabin. There I set my cradle and began work. The gold was very fine, almost impalpable dust, but was heavy and easily saved. The claim, which was in the center of the ravine, was wet. It filled up every night and required half my time during the day to keep it free of water; nevertheless, up to the time when steady rains came, I made fair wages. It was lonesome, to be sure, as sometimes days passed without my seeing a human being.

Hawes's ranch was about three miles from the cabin, and I occasionally went over to call on the brothers Tom and Elisha, whom I knew well. They kept a store, also a boarding house, as theirs was the changing station for the Sacramento line of stages to Auburn and other mountain towns. The ranch was also the site of the postoffice for Secret Ravine.[2]

Though my claim was difficult to work, it paid pretty well, and I stuck to it till driven out by the rains. Thereafter I was idle a good part of the time, and passed the hours in reading, writing, and eating, when not sleeping. Once a fortnight I ran up and passed a few hours with county clerk Bronk at Auburn, which was only five miles distant. His office was the rendezvous for the lawyers at the county seat, and whenever I visited him, I always carried home a supply of books and periodicals that had accumulated in his quarters. These were very acceptable, as they served to interest me during the long winter evenings. Occasionally my friends at Horse Shoe Bar called on me, especially Squire Carey and Captain Thompson, whom I was pleased to entertain.

There is a species of rat indigenous to California, known as the "kangaroo rat." It has long hind legs, short fore ones, and a bushy tail like that of a gray squirrel.[3] These rodents were a great nuisance in my cabin and made frequent raids on the provisions. I euchred them finally, however, by suspending a shelf from the ridgepole beyond their reach, on which the bread, meat, butter, flour, etc., were placed for security.

Wolves and coyotes also abounded, and frequently made night hideous with their howlings. They assembled in packs, and seemed to make my cabin a central point for their nocturnal serenades. I veritably believe there were at least a hundred at times, barking and snarling in my immediate vicinity, as if they had been called thither by a requisition for a general muster. It has since occurred to me that my mule might have been the attraction.

The grocer, located a couple of miles below me on the ravine, had an old white mare, which grazed with her colt in a valley near his place. One night a pack of wolves attacked the colt, and though the dam managed to beat them off, she was terribly bitten during the struggle. The most remarkable thing about the affair was the subsequent action of the mare, which went off next day and at night returned to her range in the valley accompanied by two horses, which afterward kept her company. As this is an actual fact, the wonder is, how that old mare made the horses understand what she wanted.

Indians were also a great annoyance, as they would steal at every opportunity. Though none lived in my vicinity, they passed by frequently, and when occasion offered, raided my cabin and stole my victuals. Coming home one evening after two days' absence, I dismounted at the cabin door, unsaddled my mule, and went in for supper, hungry as a bear. Conceive my disgust when I found the larder empty. Just before leaving home, I had baked bread and boiled a piece of corned beef, which with a pan of potatoes were deposited on the hanging shelf at my departure. Of course I was provoked, as I was hungry and tired. Without lighting a candle, I sat down to consider, when suddenly the door was opened and a squaw with two papooses came in for forage.

The poker, a small, green stick which I held in my hand, was temporarily diverted from its legitimate use and applied to that squaw's shoulders with an utter disregard of the conventionalities in favor of the sex feminine. The intruder was inside the door when the whack of the stick notified her of my presence. The door opened inwards, and for a while her efforts to unclose it were unavailing. During the interval the interior of the cabin did not present the slightest resemblance to a Sunday school. Finally, however, she managed to get out, and fled shrieking into the wilderness. Trusting that the castigation would cure the squaw of her thievish propensities, I lighted a fire, prepared supper, and went to bed.

After retiring, it occurred to me that the squaw might cherish revengeful feelings and attempt to get even for the flagellation, as there were probably bucks in the near vicinity who might come in the night and "wipe me out" while sleeping. This thought made me nervous, so I barricaded the door with a nail keg, soap box, and other loose articles, which if thrown down would awaken me, placed my pistol under the pillow and went to sleep. Nothing happened, however, and I rested undisturbed till morning.

The lack of society so depressed me at times that I was led to exclaim with Robinson Crusoe,

> Oh, solitude, solitude, where are the charms
> That Sages have seen in thy fall?

From Christmas to New Year's Day it rained constantly. During the whole time I was alone in my cabin, and did not see a human face. At intervals, when it held up, I would bring in a supply of wood and keep the ruddy flame glowing in the fireplace. On Christmas Eve, mindful of the occasion, with thoughts busy with home and home associations, I resolved, though alone, to enjoy the festival day.

"It is Christmastide, my boy! Let's you and myself enjoy it. Let us eat, drink, and be merry. Tomorrow Lucullus shall dine with Lucullus—

> Pile on more wood, the wind is chill
> But let it whistle as it will
> We'll keep our Christmas merry still,
> And hail with uncontrolled delight,
> And gladsome voice the happy night,
> That to the cabin, as the crown
> Brought tidings of salvation down."

Though prepared by myself, it is perhaps a pardonable pride that impels me to extol that Christmas dinner. Taking the surroundings into consideration, it was indeed a grand spread-out. I had procured a tin of canned turkey and a couple of bottles of Bass's ale. The turkey, with boiled sweet potatoes, good light bread and butter, doughnuts of home manufacture, strong black coffee, and the ale, with a post-prandial pipe at the finish, formed a dinner fit for the gods, at least I thought so, and enjoyed it accordingly.

The winter of 1852 passed away, but most of the time I was compulsively idle. My claim was under water, and I was unsuccessful in prospecting for a dry one. When spring came, weary of my long isolation, I resolved to pay Bob [Gardiner] a second visit, so closed up my cabin, leaving all my effects therein, and started out.

The season previous, I had cached a quantity of gold dust at my old quarters on Whiskey Bar, and not knowing what might happen, decided to recover it and take it with me. So I saddled my mule and rode over to the river. A young Englishman had appropriated my tent frame and fireplace and was inside when I came. Entering without ceremony, I introduced myself and asked him if he believed in dreams. Rather surprised at the abruptness of my question, he was at a loss for an answer. Explaining, I said that as a general thing I was skeptical regarding the fulfilment of dreams, but for months past had been under the influence of a sort of phantasmagoria which had so impressed my mind that I was unable to shake it off, and had come to satisfy myself whether the impression was based on truth or was a mere mental illusion.

Asking the loan of a shovel, I proceeded to clear away the ashes in the fireplace, and began digging, while the young man looked on in astonishment and evidently considered me insane. I kept on digging, however, and soon struck the buried treasure. The dust was in a tin can wrapped in a newspaper. When the can was uncovered and its contents exposed, the look on that young Briton's face was wonderful to behold, and he had no idea who I was, or that I had previously owned the fireplace. There was about $1,000 in the can, and when, having enjoyed his amazement at my—to him—strange performance, I told him that I had occupied the place the year before and buried the gold for safety, he began to understand that my proceeding was not induced by a mere dream, as I had led him to believe.

The next morning, after an early breakfast, I was en route for Sacramento, and at evening rode into the city. Here I met Jim Bassett, an old friend and former schoolmate, who was employed in the office of the steamboat company. I was glad to meet Bassett, as I had not seen him since his arrival in California some months before. We attended the theatre, and after the play sat up late, discussing ancient history, recounting schoolboy escapades, and commenting on the good or ill fortune of former companions. When we parted, it was for a long time, as I saw him no more till years afterward, when we had both returned to the East.

The road for a great part of the distance between Sacramento and Stockton was under water. Though I had been over the route before, I was not sufficiently familiar with it to find my way without a road to guide me, so decided to follow the stage that plied between the two cities. That decision was a mistake, as I soon learned. Had I known what was before me, I would not have started, but when, after proceeding a few miles, I repented and would have returned, it was too late. Though the water was not deep, it covered the track and deprived me of guidance; therefore I was reluctantly constrained to go on.

The stage had eight horses, which were changed for fresh ones every ten miles. Wherever practicable, the stage traveled rapidly, and it taxed my mule's endurance to keep up. The only chance for rest was at the change stations, and the time there was necessarily short; nevertheless, I managed to follow close behind, but it was rough on the mule.

Just before dinner we came to a branch, which though narrow was deep. The long string of stage horses reached across the slough, so that some part of the team was pulling all the time, for when the wheelers were swimming, the leaders were on the further side. The water came into the stage so that the passengers had to stand on the seats.

As I was behind, all this was hidden from view, so that when I approached the crossing, not considering it much of an impediment, I rode in carelessly, and down went the mule under water to the ears, while I was submerged to the waist, very much to the amusement of the passengers, who were expecting the catastrophe. Had I imagined the branch was so deep, I could have easily crossed on a fallen tree nearby and escaped a wetting.

Taking my animal to the barn for a feed, I joined the party at the dinner table and refreshed myself with a good meal. The mule had not finished eating when the stage was ready and the driver shouting, "Hurrah, boys," to the passengers. The ferry over the Mokelumne River was close by, but when the stage was on the boat, the ferryman objected to taking me, as he said there was no room. I insisted, however, and assuming all risks of navigation, managed to get my animal on the "flap" of the boat behind the stage, where there was about two feet [of] space. Had the stage backed, the mule would have inevitably been forced overboard. We crossed safely, the stage proceeded, and I followed. At the next changing-place we came to higher ground, so I let the vehicle go ahead and rode leisurely.

About 10 o'clock, P.M., I came to the Elk Horn Inn, seven miles from Stockton.[4] The people had all gone to bed, so I hailed the house, when presently the landlord replied from an upper window, telling me to lead my animal to the stock yard, and he would come down and open the door. I started as directed, when the clank of a chain frightened the mule, which jumped and pulled me along just in time to escape the clutches of an enormous grizzly bear chained close to the trail. Then the landlord hailed again, warning me "to look out for the bear." Replying that "I had found him," I proceeded to the stock yard, provided for the mule and returned by a circuitous route to the house, where I gave the publican a blessing for his carelessness in subjecting me to the danger of being eaten alive. He acknowledged his thoughtlessness, and said that he was half-asleep when he spoke to me first, and the bear never crossed his mind till he hailed me a second time.

After "taking a bite," I was shown to a room, where I passed the night in company with a hen and chickens, which the good wife apologized for next morning, stating that she had put them there to save them from the coyotes.

Before leaving the inn, I took occasion to inspect the grizzly. He was a formidable-looking beast, and must have weighed nearly 1,200 pounds. Ugly and untamable, had I given him a chance, he would have made mincemeat of me in short order. He was secured to a stump by a stout chain attached to a heavy iron collar riveted about his neck, and as I watched him and thought of my close call the night before, I thanked Providence that the chain was no longer. The landlord informed me he was keeping the bear for a "bull and bear fight" on the ensuing Fourth of July.[5]

When I took my departure that morning, the mule showed the efforts of the exhaustive [exhausting] journey of the preceding day, so I favored the animal and traveled slowly, passing through Stockton without stopping. Near French Camp, a few miles from the city, I overtook a teamster whose heavily loaded wagon was stuck in a small slough which crossed the road.

Reader: Did you ever see a mule teamster in a tight place and note how philosophically he regards the situation, and how quietly and deliberately, without a shadow of excitement, he proceeds to extricate himself from the dilemma?

I don't mean an ordinary "mule whacker," such as we see every day in the year, but a genuine, thoroughbred "Pike" who identifies himself with his team and reduces the profession to a science. Such a man is sui generis, and seldom encountered. He is generally quiet, not at all inclined to loquacity, and it is only under certain conditions that his wonderful command of language is exhibited. At such times he affords an object lesson that is both interesting and instructive. On this occasion I met the most unique specimen of the genus ever encountered in all my wide experience.

His name was Peck; and being an old acquaintance who hauled our traps to Hawkins' Bar in August, 1849, when I noticed his position, I volunteered to assist him. As before stated, he had got "stalled" in a small slough; the wagon had sunk to the axles in the soft mud, which as Peck remarked, "would mire a snipe."

After a half-hour's labor, we had dug out the wheels and completed a trench in front of them, leading on an inclined plane to the higher ground, and when that was done, Peck proceeded to straighten out his team, which consisted of six noble mules that with characteristic humor he had christened after the several religious denominations. The wheelers were called "Catholic" and "Episcopalian," the swing mules "Methodist" and "Baptist," and the leaders responded to the name "Mormon" and "Presbyterian."

Beginning with the saddle mule, he made a circuit of the team, giving each animal a slap and calling it by name as he administered the hand stroke. It was evident that a perfect understanding existed between the man and his team, and the light tap seemed to have the effect of hypnotizing each mule and placing it in strict accord with its driver. This proceeding, however, was but preliminary. It served as a sort of prologue to the play, and though I had watched his maneuvers, I saw nothing in either Peck's actions or utterance to excite any suspicion that he was mad "all through."

The mules knew better, however; they had "been there before," and were perfectly cognizant of the fact that the quiet words of the teamster were but mutterings indicative of the impending storm. Consequently there were no malingerers in that team when Peck took the lines. No schismatic differences interfered to prevent unity of action between Catholic and Episcopalian, no discord existed between the disciple of John Wesley and his brother of the aqueous faith, and the passionate ardor of the Mormon and his

Gentile mate was wonderful to behold. Every mule was on the qui vive, every chain was taut.

Then, after casting a glance around to see that everything was ready, Peck's countenance suddenly lost its placidity and became demoniac. Shouting, "Pull, you long-eared devils, pull," he raised his voice, and gave utterance to a yell so wild, so shrill, so piercing and prolonged, that it would have excited a feeling of envy in the breast of a Comanche Indian; simultaneously the crack of the whip awoke the echoes, and he plied the "buckskin" with an energy and assiduity that left no room for a doubt that his whole heart and soul were in the business before him. Then followed such a tirade of blasphemy, such a deluge of profanity, such an avalanche of oaths and imprecations, that I was appalled at the power of invective displayed by this unhallowed Jehu.

Its effect on the mules, however, was obvious; they were simply terror-stricken, as they writhed in their collars, and with straining muscles buckled to their work, and ere his vocabulary of malediction was exhausted, Peck had the satisfaction of beholding his wagon rescued from the slough, while the team with trembling limbs and quivering flanks rested from its labors in blissful consciousness of duty performed.

Mr. Peck was not habitually profane. In fact, he was as mild a mannered man as ever buckled strap or greased a wheel, and seldom used expletives in ordinary conversation. So when I expressed my surprise at the prodigious fertility of his imagination in the way of "cuss words," his reply was, "Oh, that was only mule talk," and with that simple explanation dismissed the subject.

Continuing my journey, I traveled slowly, and at night put up at the "Cottage Home." This was decidedly the most comfortable hostelry I had seen in California. Everything about the establishment was clean and home-like. The table was covered with snow-white damask, the cooking excellent, and the viands superb. Fresh yellow home-made butter, light hot biscuit, milk and cream ad libitum, vegetables from the home garden, boiled chickens, veal cutlets, together with cakes and cookies no end, demonstrated that there was a woman in the house that knew how to keep a hotel. I remained over one day to rest my animal and enjoy the good living. Everything showed care. The waiter girls were dressed as neatly as Vassar students. My sleeping apartment with its clean white sheets and pillow slips, was neatly carpeted and furnished, and was in fact the *ne plus ultra* of dormitories, very attractive to me, who had roughed it for three years in those wild regions.

In due time I reached my destination, where I was welcomed by Bob [Gardiner], who introduced me to Mike [Keogh], his partner, whom I had not met during my former visit.[6]

XXII

AT SWETT'S BAR

JUNE ? 1852–AUGUST ? 1854

More than three years had now elapsed since my departure from home, and that constant yearning to return, which had for a while oppressed me, had in a great measure subsided. I began to look upon California as my future residence. As the months passed, I had acquired a liking for the free and easy manner of living to which I had become accustomed. The fact is, man's natural condition is that of barbarism. One who has for years led a nomadic life, unrestrained by the conventionalities of society, will after a return to the business world invariably feel a hankering for the unlimited freedom of the plains and mountains.

We see evidence of this congenital disposition for a life of adventure every day. Give a man all that wealth can buy; unless he has some business that requires his undivided attention, his time hangs heavily on his hands. The ordinary pleasures of social life eventually lose their attraction. He seeks relief from the palling routine, and wanders forth to shoot tigers in the Asiatic jungles, or in pursuit of the buffalo on the far western prairies. Doctor Livingstone preferred the African wilds to the gilded salon, and Stanley, who was sent out to find him, became infatuated with the adventurous pursuit, and returned repeatedly to encounter all the hardships and perils incident to an exploitation of the mysteries of the "Dark Continent."

After a sojourn of a few days at Swett's Bar, it seemed so pleasant to be among old friends that I resolved to remain there. This resolution necessitated the abandonment of the traps in my cabin at Secret Ravine, which were not very valuable, however, and I preferred to lose them rather than again travel the disagreeable road between Stockton and Sacramento. I had my old letters forwarded to me, but the balance of the property went I know not where.

After deciding to take up my residence at Swett's, the first thing in order was to build a cradle. This accomplished, I proceeded to prospect the bar thoroughly, but with very indifferent success. The Bar, never very extensive, had been practically worked out. Those who had claims realized insufficient to pay them for the labor expended. The average returns did not exceed three or four dollars a day, and as that amount failed to satisfy me, I resolved to pull up stakes and go elsewhere.

Stephen [French], whom I had not seen or heard of since we parted in San Francisco in the spring of '50, made his appearance about this time. He had been for two years cruising in the Northern Mines, but like the rest of us had not made his fortune.[1] He was somewhere in the vicinity of Marysville the year before, and had I known it, I would have sought him out when there the fall previous on my cattle expedition.

He gave me full details of his wanderings, which proved that he had been a "rolling

185

stone." Always excitable, he had been victimized several times by his credulity. He had gone with a party in search of the famous "Gold Lake," which though it proved a myth, had for a while created a tremendous sensation throughout the State. Hundreds were deceived by the false reports and went in pursuit of the mystic locality, which really had no existence. These pilgrims returned, if not wiser, certainly poorer for their faith in unsubstantiated rumor.[2]

Jim Hedges, to whom I had sustained the relation of "cooper's mate" in San Francisco in '50, had found his way to the diggings. He, together with Stephen and myself, joined in an expedition to Moccasin Creek, some five miles distant from Swett's Bar. The creek had been worked in a superficial manner, chiefly by Mexicans; nevertheless, we thought we might find pay dirt there, and resolved to try it.[3]

Accordingly my saddle mule was brought into requisition and packed with what was necessary for a week's prospecting. The [Tuolumne] river was high for fording, so we proceeded to Don Pedro's Bar, five or six miles below, where there was a ferryboat. The trail followed the river, and between Morgan's and Don Pedro's bars ran close to the edge of a deep canyon, where extra care was advisable, as the mule was not accustomed to carrying a pack. Mindful of this, when we came to the place, I went ahead to lead, but as soon as I put my hand on the bit the animal reared, the weight of the pack carried her backward, and she disappeared in the canyon.

Though the side was not perpendicular, it was so steep that it was impossible for us to follow, so we were compelled to descend by the trail to the base of the mountain, where we struck the river and climbed along till we came to the scene of the disaster. We had no expectation of finding the mule alive after a sheer descent of more than seven hundred feet, as was subsequently established, but we had strong hopes of saving the pack, or what was left of it, at least. Imagine our surprise, then, when we found the mule alive. She had landed on a large flat rock, around which the angry waters were boiling, where, divested of pack, saddle, and every particle of harness, she was leisurely "cropping" the grass that grew in the crevices. A space of perhaps three feet intervened between the rock and terra firma, and as the animal was bleeding freely from its wounds, fearing that she might be weakened by loss of blood, I hastened to hurry her across the chasm to the mainland. That the animal was seriously injured was apparent, as her head was already so swollen that her ears looked really diminutive.

Leaving the mule to look after itself, we proceeded to climb the wall of the canyon to look after the merchandise. As the track was plainly perceptible, there was no difficulty in following the animal's course. Though it may sound incredible, it is nevertheless true as Holy Writ that in her unpremeditated flight from summit to base, she dislodged rocks weighing six or eight hundred pounds. The cans, cooking utensils, and smaller articles were thoroughly spoiled, but the sack of flour that formed the basis of the pack was unimpaired. We found it, together with the saddle, in the crotch of a tree five feet from the ground. The mule must have gone over that tree, and how the devil she ever reached bottom without breaking every bone in her body, has always been a mystery to me.

Stephen, in after years, informed me that he had told of the above incident, and declared that he would never tell it again, as he had found no one who believed it.

Three weeks after the accident, I visited the Golden ranch where the mule had been in the habit of running, and asked Colson, the proprietor, if he had seen it. He replied that he had seen it that morning. When asked how the mule was looking, he said she was all right, and had not observed that anything was the matter with her. That mule carried me many a mile afterward, and seemed none the worse for the terrible experience in the canyon.

After gathering up what was left of the pack, we left the mule on the mountainside and returned to Morgan's Bar, where we procured another animal, replenished our stock, and started afresh. A week's work at Moccasin Creek satisfied us that there was nothing to warrant our remaining longer. The place was absolutely deserted. Even the Chinamen passed it by. So we returned to Swett's Bar.

We formed a company to drain the river just below camp, where it was reputed to be rich. The place was known as the "Kensett claim." We worked faithfully there all summer, dug a canal, built a dam, and turned the river successfully, but we lost our time and threw our paint away, as there was very little gold in the stream at that point.

So it went. The harder I worked, the poorer I grew, till at last I became disgusted, foreswore gold-digging till I could find something to pay me, and took life easy.

In the fall of '52 I bought a cow. I had raised forty chickens, which I traded off to old man Kerrick for a black cow and calf. Angelina, as I christened her, was brought to camp, and with her calf, Oliver Twist, grazed on the flat opposite the Bar. I procured a big cowbell, strung it about the cow's neck, and let her run. The calf, Oliver, was about six months old, and had never been weaned. He was accustomed to absorb what lacteal fluid his dam secreted, which, as I was also fond of milk, did not accord with my idea of justice. The cow was poor in flesh, having crossed the plains that season, and gave but little milk, not to exceed three quarts a day, which I resolved to appropriate to my own consumption. Therefore I determined to wean Oliver.

Though it is a very simple matter to wean a calf a week old, it is a very different thing when you come to experiment with one six months old, as I soon discovered. My first thought was to separate cow and calf, so I placed one on each side [of] the river. That night, when I went to milk her, the cow's udder was empty. Thinking perhaps some of the boys had taken the milk for a lark, I started homeward, but had not gone far when I stumbled over Oliver lying perdu among the bushes. He had swum the river.

Thus the first experiment failed. Then I adopted the suggestion of a farmer and made a muzzle with long iron spikes sharpened at the ends. That too was a failure. Next I attached a light board to the calf's nostrils which hung down and covered his mouth. That answered for a day or two, but Oliver soon got the hang of it, and when occasion required would flip it up and proceed to business. Several other devices were tried, but all proved ineffectual. Oliver got the milk and I got left.

Determined to beat that calf, I set my wits to work to devise some plan to prevent him from sucking. Finally I hit on an idea which was certainly original, and proceeded to put it in practice. I arrayed Oliver in a standing martingale, and from that time the battle was won. Though the calf could graze and drink easily, the martingale held his nose within a foot of the ground. Thenceforward there was no further trouble. I had the inside track, and the milk reached its proper destination.

As it was necessary to cross the river morning and evening to milk the cow, it was sometimes extremely perilous, especially in the spring, when the water was at a booming stage. Accidents often happened during times of freshet. One day three of the boys started to cross the stream in the still water above the rapids, when the current proved too strong for them, and the boat, a good-sized scow, was swept downstream. Soon after it struck the rapids, it collided with a rock and capsized. Its occupants, Frank Casey, David Rivers, and a young fellow known as "Curley," managed to cling to the boat, which was swept onward by the raging torrent at a velocity of some twelve or fifteen miles an hour. At intervals the boat would strike a rock, when its position would be reversed, and those who clung to it would be thrown off. Three times Frank rescued Curley, who could not swim, from the angry flood, but all his brave efforts to save his comrade were futile. Curley, poor fellow, was drowned. Frank and Rivers managed to cling to the craft till it passed the rapids, when Frank jumped off in an eddy and swam to some willows which overhung the stream. Grasping a branch, he coolly proceeded to remove his heavy boots and save them by twining the twigs of the tree through the straps. Relieved of the weight of his boots, which he left hanging to the limb and afterward recovered, he struck out for the shore and landed safely.

Rivers, who was no swimmer, was also saved almost miraculously. Still clinging to the boat, he was swept along till, just before reaching the head of a raging canyon, the craft providentially struck an eddy and was carried near the shore, where he jumped off in shoal water and waded to land. Frank, who was one of the coolest men in danger I ever met, did not seem greatly impressed by the incident, but Rivers, who was a relic of the Mexican War, a poker sharp, and a devil-may-care fellow generally, wore a sober countenance for a month.

Stephen [French], who was an erratic, restless individual, sometimes drifted off, and after an absence of a month or two, would drift back again. On one occasion he came in excitedly from Sherlock's Creek,[4] where he had collaborated for a while with three other mutual acquaintances, Bliss, Bass, and Harwood. He had left Sherlock's hurriedly two days previous under the following circumstances, as he detailed them to me.

It seems that Stephen and his co-mates had on the preceding Saturday evening been sitting in front of their quarters engaged in a social game of "seven-up." The ante was a dollar. Stephen had been losing and Harwood winning till the former was reduced to his last dollar. Before staking that, he remarked, "Now, Harwood, if you win this dollar you must lend it to me, my washing is at the Spanish woman's, and I want the dollar to pay the laundry bill."

"All right," said Harwood, so Stephen staked his last dollar, lost it, and retained it as a loan.

The game ended, Stephen proceeded to the laundry, accompanied by his three friends. They reached the place, which was a sort of shebang where whiskey was sold. Stephen refrained, but the others took several drinks, which so excited them that they became hilarious and disorderly to an extent that offended the woman's husband, who remonstrated against their conduct and conversation. This remonstrance angered the visitors, and Harwood called out, "Bliss, what had we better do with this Greaser?"

"We'll hang him," replied Bliss, seizing a riata that lay in the corner of the room.

"It's a whack, by Jove; we'll string him up," exclaimed the reckless Harwood, as he gripped the Mexican by the neck.

The Greaser's shrift was indeed a short one. Despite the prayers, tears, and protestations of his hapless wife, the Spaniard's hands were bound, the rope placed about his neck, and in less time than it requires to tell it, the unfortunate man was strung up to a limb in front of his own door.

This summary execution staggered Stephen, who, dreading the consequences of such unwarranted proceedings, resolved to part company with his unscrupulous comrades, and accordingly went home, packed his traps and "lit out" the same night.

This is no imaginary story; it is a fact. Though the deed was known, fear kept the widow silent, and to all interrogatories respecting the perpetrators of the act, her invariable reply, as the tears rolled down her cheeks, was "quien sabe?"

In the spring of '53 Mike [Keogh] plowed the flat where the cow grazed, and sowed it with barley. I also took a horticultural turn and decided to plant a garden. Removing my quarters to the left bank of the river, I purchased a tent-house pleasantly located beneath an evergreen oak. There was a space covering about an acre on the bank of the stream immediately in front of my residence, which I spaded up. When the ground was dug, I caught five jackasses that were grazing nearby and hitched them after a fashion to an oak branch, with which I harrowed the garden thoroughly, broke all the clods, and prepared the soil for seed.

Having procured an assortment of seeds from Jacksonville, nine miles up the river, they were duly planted, and the next thing in order was a fence. Falling the trees, splitting the rails, chopping the posts, and snaking them to the garden was something of a job; nevertheless, it was all accomplished in about a fortnight, and in due time the garden plot was enclosed by a good post and rail fence. A small spring on the hillside nearby afforded sufficient water for irrigation, which was utilized when required.

About this time an event happened that I will stop to chronicle. Bob and I had been down at Don Pedro's Bar for some purpose, where we stopped overnight. In the morning on our return, as we approached home, we saw on the trail ahead a young man who was evidently a tenderfoot, as we judged by his dress and general appearance. As he came nearer, however, Bob recognized his brother Tom, who had reached Swett's the evening before, and being informed of our whereabouts, had started out to meet us. Of course, we were glad to see him, but I will say nothing further of him at present, as his name will come in incidentally later on.

The garden seeds germinated early, grew finely, and there was every indication of a good crop. There were watermelons, cantaloupes, cucumbers, beets, radishes, etc., which in California grow to perfection.

Confident that there was a gold deposit somewhere in the adjoining flat, I sunk hole after hole in attempts to find it. It was about eight feet to the bedrock, but though I prospected thoroughly, not even the color was found. Notwithstanding my ill-success, the conviction remained, and time after time I expressed my belief to Bob that some day it would be proved that my theory was correct. And I was right. Prentice Mulford, in his story of California life, tells us that rich diggings were discovered in that same flat farther back from the river than I had prospected. Mulford himself worked there years after I had returned to the East.[5]

Though the garden flourished like a green bay tree, unforeseen complications arose before the crop matured that came near upsetting all my calculations. Bob kept hogs, or rather, owned them, as the hogs kept themselves on acorns and whatever they could pick up in the mountains. They multiplied like strawberries in Bohemian forests, and wandered all over the township. For want of proper attention, they had inbred and deteriorated until they resembled peccaries. There were probably a hundred and fifty of them, and would have been twice that number had not the young ones been killed by unscrupulous hunters who had a taste for roast pig.

As the swine fed on the right bank of the river, it never occurred to me that they would cross the stream. I had always understood that if a hog ventured on an aquatic excursion, it would inevitably cut its throat with its fore feet. I was disabused of that fallacious idea in the summer of 1853.

The man who says a hog can't swim don't know anything about it. You can't drown a hog in a river. I have seen a sow with her litter of small pigs take to the water at a freshet stage and start right at the rapids where it would seem impossible for any living creature to cross. I have watched them as they were swept downstream by the resistless current, colliding with rocks and encountering perils innumerable, yet still floating like corks amid the troubled waters until, perhaps a mile or so below the starting point, all landed safely, when the old sow followed by her progeny would take a beeline for my garden.

I remonstrated with Bob against the incursions of the swine, who declared his inability to control them, and told me plainly that I "had no business to have a garden." I contended that my fence was a legal one, five rails high as defined by the statutes, in which there was no provision requiring me to fence against hogs, as such a requirement would be absurd. My remonstrance did not effect any good end, however, as neither Bob nor myself could control the intruders, so I concluded to be governed by circumstances and try to make my fence hog-proof.

There was an Indian loafing about the neighborhood with whom I arranged to weave chamisal bushes between the fence rails, securing the butts in a trench dug beneath and parallel with the bottom rails, intending to construct a sort of *chevaux de frise* all round the garden. The job was no inconsiderable one, and the Indian worked faithfully for ten days before he completed it to my satisfaction. Meanwhile I was compelled to keep a bright look out for hogs till the fence was made secure.

In some way I had become possessed of a big Allen's revolver which was of no earthly use, and had promised to give it to the Indian provided he made a good job of the wicker-work. All the six barrels were loaded, and fearing the aboriginal might injure himself with the weapon, I desired to discharge it before surrendering it.

Perfectly aware of the uncertainty of the old "pepper box," which had evidently been loaded for a long time, I feared to hold the pistol, so disconnected the barrel from the stock, tied a string to it and cautiously pulled it into a fire built for the occasion, myself standing some twenty feet away. Of course the string burnt off and when the barrel, which I had drawn into the fire with its muzzle from me, got hot, the first explosion occurred. The barrel jumped three feet into the air and fell back with the muzzle directly toward me. As there were five more charges to go off, either of which might hit me, I threw myself flat on the ground and counted with no ordinary anxiety the succeeding reports, and when the sixth charge went off, arose much relieved to find myself uninjured.

In the course of events it came to pass that Bob was subjected to the same annoyance that I had complained of. The barley patch, though surrounded by a brush fence, was frequently encroached on by a drove of jackasses, which broke through the obstruction and cropped the growing grain. When he requested me to keep an eye on the field and I humorously suggested that he "had no right to have a barley field," he did not seem to take the suggestion in good part. Nevertheless, I did keep watch, and from time to time ejected the donkeys.

One day Stephen discovered the drove in the barley field and crossed the river to drive it out. He had a gun in his hand and declared "he'd shoot 'em." He did let fly with both barrels at one jack, which merely shook its tail and continued browsing. This so angered Stephen that he clubbed his gun and struck the donkey across the back. The donkey sustained no injury, but the gun stock was broken short off. "What will Bob say?" ejaculated Steve, as he gazed lugubriously at the broken gun, for he, like all the rest of us, dreaded Bob's anger.

We held a council and decided to take the jacks across the river. There were a half-dozen of them, which we drove to the boat and swam over one by one. The last had a colt which we left on the shore, intending to return and carry it over in the boat, as it was not bigger than a Newfoundland dog. Much to our surprise, when we started to return, the colt was missing. Jackasses are poor swimmers, and if the water once gets in their ears, they are apt to drown.

Thinking that the colt had attempted to follow its dam, we concluded it was drowned, when suddenly in the eddy close by, up popped the infantile jack and walked ashore. We were dumbfounded. How the deuce that colt crossed the river, we were unable to divine.

He certainly never swam, or we would have seen him, and the only conceivable theory was that it had sunk, and walked across on the river bottom. Be that as it may, we congratulated ourselves on the colt's safety, as we had no right to remove the animals from their stamping ground.

That was an unfortunate week for Stephen. A day or two afterward, he met with a misfortune that almost broke his heart. Bob had occasion to go away, and left Steve in charge of the store. Before leaving, he advised Stephen that the team would be in that night, and as the barley was out, it would be necessary to procure a couple of sacks at Indian Bar, two miles below.

Sometime during the afternoon, Stephen captured a donkey and tied it in front of the Grizzly Bear Pavilion while he sought a pack saddle. Failing to find one, he concluded to use Bob's riding saddle, which was a very fine one and had cost $70 only a few weeks previous. Considering that contact with the grain bags would not injure it, he threw the saddle on the ass's back and went on his way rejoicing. Had the excursion eventuated as there was every reason to believe it would, there would have been no trouble, but unfortunately the saddle was placed upon a jackass, the very personification of "damfoolishness" and stupidity.

Stephen started for Indian Bar driving the animal before him, but when about halfway there, the donkey suddenly left the trail, proceeded to the river about a rod away, and plunged in—

The waters black closed o'er the jack,

And Steve was left lamenting.

Thoroughly demoralized by the unaccountable proceeding, which seemed to him a plain case of felo-de-se [one who kills himself], Stephen was for a while at a loss what to do. But the recollection of "Bob's saddle" quickened his thoughts; and, hoping to recover it, he hastened downstream. At Indian Bar he learned that the donkey had passed a few minutes before, floating with three legs out, or as he expressed it, "ship rigged." Following post-haste, when he reached Morgan's Bar, he was informed that the jack had preceded him. Still undiscouraged, he hastened onward to Don Pedro's, three miles below, where there was a ferryboat, by means of which he hoped to catch the carcass. But he arrived too late. Swept onward by the rapid current, the jack had already gone by ere Stephen came. Still buoyed by hope, though night was approaching, he followed the river trail till, sometime after dark, he reached French Bar,[6] where he stayed all night. He heard nothing more from the drowned donkey, however, and returned home.

When Mike came in with his team that evening, he was sadly nonplused by Stephen's unaccountable disappearance. He managed, however, after waiting several hours, to concoct some sort of mash from flour to feed his mules.

When Stephen came home next evening, before reporting to Bob, he sought my quarters and told the story of his mishap substantially as I have related it. What arrangement was made with Bob I never knew, nor did I care to inquire. It was a disagreeable affair all round. No blame attached to Stephen so far as I could discover, who had started in good faith to fulfill his mission, and was unfortunately euchred by the incomprehensible stupidity of a jackass.

The Indian's barricade proved a safeguard against further incursions of the hogs, and I managed to raise a fair crop. There were neither bugs nor parasites to destroy the plants, but gophers abounded. They interfered with nothing, however, except the watermelons, and in doing that, exercised a wonderful cunning. They would manage to have the outlet of their burrows immediately beneath a big melon, where, concealed from view and unsuspected, they would pierce a hole through the rind and completely gut the inside, leaving the fruit apparently intact.

It was at Big Oak Flat, ten miles away, that I found a market for my produce, which was transported in large gunny bags packed on mules. The trail was rough and tedious, and sometimes tried my patience sorely. At Moccasin Creek the path followed a ravine a mile or more, and was very steep. The trail was so narrow that, once on it, it was impossible to turn a loaded animal around, as the path was on a sort of shelf with a high bank on one side, and a precipitous declivity on the other.

On one occasion, when descending the trail, the pack saddle on one of the mules got loose and slipped forward, which brought a tremendous strain on the crupper, which cut the animal's tail half-off, as it was impracticable to relieve the mule till it reached the end of the shelf at the foot of the mountain. It was pitiful to witness the poor animal's contortions as it shuffled along, apparently conscious of the impossibility of relief till it reached the level ground. Ordinarily a pack mule will stop when its load becomes loose, and refuse to proceed till it is rearranged.

It is wonderful what intelligence these animals sometimes display, especially such as are accustomed to mountain travel. In certain districts wagon roads were impossible, and everything was transported by pack trains. I once saw a small mule carrying a large bureau along a trail on the Merced River, between what is known as Split Rock Ferry and Bear Valley.[7] A narrow path had been constructed by blasting the rock for a mile or so along the side of a canyon. The mule was on this path when unfortunately the bulky bureau struck the rock on the inside of the trail and threw the animal's hindquarters off the track. There was a sheer descent of five hundred feet to the stream below, and I trembled when I witnessed the accident. The mule, however, was self-possessed, and made no fuss. Luckily the load was light, so the animal was able to hang on by its fore feet till rescued by the muleteers.

When I reached the base of the mountain at Moccasin Creek, I adjusted the mule's saddle and eased up on the crupper, greatly to the animal's relief and my own satisfaction. Fortunately the trail ran uphill for the balance of the way, so the mule could travel more comfortably and give the sore tail a rest.

It is a stiff climb to ascend the mountain on the right bank of Moccasin Creek. The trail runs zigzag, after the manner of a vessel beating to windward, and is a succession of angles from base to summit. It was customary with me in making these trips to regale myself with a watermelon when I reached the top of the hill, and it is perhaps superfluous to state that the treat, under such circumstances, was duly appreciated, as the weather was intensely hot, and a short rest in the shade of a tree correspondingly alluring.

The market at Big Oak Flat was not a very extensive one, but was sufficient to absorb all my produce, which was disposed of at remunerative rates. On one occasion I took over an immense watermelon which I sold for six dollars. The boys chipped in and played cards for it. Captain Amyx, who was subsequently elected sheriff of the county,[8] won the melon, but of course all those who were interested in the game came in for a share. The garden, though it did not prove a bonanza, paid me for the labor expended in its cultivation; moreover, I enjoyed the work, and likewise lived well while the vegetables lasted.

During the season, I located claims along the river which I sold to the Chinese, immense hordes of whom came in day by day,[9] and in that way realized four times the money earned by those who plied the pick and shovel from morning to night. It was a case of head work against hard work, with the usual result.

When the barley was ripe, Mike found some difficulty in procuring harvesters. Those who were acquainted with the work declined one and all to participate in the "harvest home." On the principle that "fools rush in where angels fear to tread," Stephen and I volunteered our assistance to bind the barley and stack it. We had not worked long before we felt inclined to jump the job, and probably would have done so had our employers been any others but Bob and Mike. Binding that grain was a nasty undertaking, which we in our ignorance had failed to appreciate. When we grasped the sheaves to truss them, the sharp barbs penetrated the flesh, so that when our work was completed, we presented the appearance of animated pin-cushions. The barbs had pierced our bosoms, necks, and arms, where they festered and for several days made us very uncomfortable.

In the absence of proper facilities, Mike resolved to adopt the patriarchal custom of the Israelites and "tread out the corn" with his team. The sheaves were deposited in a circle, and the six heavy mules trod out the grain. The crop did not amount to much, however, for between the hogs and the donkeys, it was so depleted that what remained was hardly worth harvesting. Mike never tried a second experiment with the barley field.

Bob and myself were elected delegates to represent our precinct in the Democratic county convention, which met that year at Jamestown, on Wood's Creek, some twenty miles distant. The convention day came soon after we had harvested the barley, and as we felt a desire for some relaxation after that job, we were inclined to make the occasion a sort of holiday. Although Stephen held a different political faith, he went with us to enjoy the fun. Everybody who was anybody made it a point to attend these gatherings. The proceedings usually occupied two days. On these occasions men came from every part of the county, renewed old acquaintances and formed new ones.

Sonora, the county seat, was the headquarters of the lawyers and politicians, and was represented in convention by such men as Charles L. Scott, Henry I. Worthington, Leander Quint, Caleb Dorsey, P.W. [P.L.] Solomon, Charles H. Randall, A. N. Francisco, editor of the Sonora *Democrat*,[10] and others, all prominent in the political field.

The offices of sheriff and county clerk were the most important, and as Tuolumne County like most of the others in the State was strongly Democratic, a nomination by the democracy was equivalent to an election. Previous to the convention, the county was thoroughly canvassed by the competing candidates to win the support of the leading men in the various precincts.

On our way to the convention, we picked up many acquaintances who joined our crowd, so that by the time we reached Jamestown we formed quite a respectable caval-cade.

The convention was organized by the election of Paul K. Hubbs [*i.e.,* James W. Coff-roth] as chairman, who called the meeting to order, stated its object, and suggested the appointment of a committee on credentials. On motion, the suggestion was adopted, and the appointment of the committee delegated to the chairman. After this there were no further proceedings that day, as the delegates were in a hilarious mood, turbulent, and difficult to control. This was so apparent that some level-headed member moved to ad-journ to the following day and give the boys a chance to get sober.

After the adjournment, we passed the balance of the day in a convivial manner, and at night Stephen and I drifted off to a fandango house, where we danced with the maidens till the wee small hours. On our return to the hotel where we expected to lodge, we found it closed. The landlord turned a deaf ear to all our appeals for admission, said his beds were all full, the tables full, the floor full, and judging from our persistence in the face of repeated refusals, he rather thought we were full also.

Stephen remarked that the landlord evidently held a "full hand," and as we could not "call it," we meandered towards a light not far away, which proceeded from a gambling room, where four sports, whose faces reminded me of parrots, sat round a table playing poker. I stretched myself on a bench and tried to sleep, and did get into a doze, but woke suddenly with a feeling that my backbone was paralyzed. I had been lying on my pistol, which pressed against the base of the spinal column and probably stopped the circulation.

Stephen had in the interim taken a seat near the poker players, and was watching the game. Presently one who had been losing exclaimed abruptly, "Look here; you have no interest in this game, you have sat behind me half an hour, and I have not won a pot, I'm rather superstitious in such matters, and you would oblige me by removing your seat."

Stephen came over and sat down by me. I asked him if those men "reminded him of birds?" "By Jupiter," he replied, "that is the very question I was about to put to you, for they certainly resemble hawks." Singular, that we were both impressed with the same idea.

After a while, sitting on the bench in a semi-comatose condition became disagreeably monotonous, so I suggested that we should go to the stable where our animals were, and turn in on the hay. The barn man proved accommodating, and we climbed to the loft and lay down on the sweet fresh hay, which was a thousand times preferable to the best bed in the hotel, as it was clean, and there were neither fleas nor bugs to annoy us.

I slept soundly for the remainder of the night, but was somewhat startled when I awoke to find myself confronted with what resembled the bars of a prison. The mystery was soon solved, however, when I discovered that I was in a horse rack. I had lain down immediately above the hole in the floor of the loft over the rack, and the horse had eaten the hay from under me. The descent was so gradual that it had not disturbed me in the least. Consoling myself with the thought that better than I had once lain in a manger, I climbed out and awoke Stephen.

After a visit to the barber shop, where we had a bath, brushed our clothes, and combed the hayseed out of our hair, we sought a restaurant and got breakfast. By that time the hour for convening the delegates had arrived, and we proceeded to the hall.

It was a motley assemblage over which Paul K. Hubbs [i.e., James W. Coffroth] presided that day. Excluding the chairman and a few professional men, there was not a white shirt in the crowd. The delegates were nearly all young men whose average age did not exceed twenty-five years. Dressed in his mining rig, which consisted of shirt, trousers, and boots, a leather belt about the waist in lieu of suspenders, which supported the inevitable revolver, the hat being laid aside in deference to the occasion, you have a picture of each constituent member of that convention.

Every delegate was a man of some influence in his precinct, and many of them were known throughout the county. They were hale fellows, full of mirth and jollity, and though young in years were, as a general thing, men of more than average intelligence. Easily excited, sudden and quick in quarrel, it is true that collisions often happened, but so long as a man behaved himself and carried a civil tongue in his head, he could mix with the throng without apprehension of bodily harm.

Though the convention while in session bore little resemblance to a Methodist Conference, still the chairman easily controlled the delegates, who obeyed him without remonstrance. It was customary to require a pledge from every candidate, before his claim was considered, that whether he was the choice of the convention or otherwise, he would faithfully support the ticket and use his best efforts to secure its success. Thus it was a condition precedent that every man who sought public office should commit himself to the support of his more fortunate competitor in case he failed to receive the nomination. This was a good idea and prevented bolting. Every candidate was also required to define his position politically and express his views on questions local and general. There was no chance for tergiversation, as the candidate was compelled to come out "flat-footed" and tell just where he stood.

As a general thing, the delegates knew their men and made no mistake in the choice of a ticket. Ordinarily the members came pledged to the support of the different candidates, and made every effort to secure the nomination of their favorites, yet they yielded quietly to the voice of the majority.

At the convention in 1853, P.W. [P. L.] Solomon was named for sheriff, George S. Evans for county clerk, Henry P. Barber for county attorney, James W. Coffroth for State senator, and James W. Mandeville for the Assembly. The latter was a practical miner, and appeared before the audience in his red flannel shirt to make his maiden speech. He subsequently became quite a factor in State politics, as did his colleague, Coffroth. All the candidates were my personal friends, and all were duly chosen at the fall election.[11]

In the fall of 1853, Bob started a branch store near Campo Seco, a few miles from Jamestown, leaving Tom in charge at Swett's Bar. The branch at Campo Seco did not prove a success, and was removed to Santiago, near Columbia.[12] Many of Bob's satellites followed him to his new location, and made his place their headquarters. He suffered seriously from the multiplicity of his friends, some of whom incurred debts at the store and failed to pay them, not because of dishonesty, but because of their inability to do so. Many wandered away, promising to pay at some future time, but those promises were not always fulfilled. Bob lost much money in this way, but bore his losses with equanimity, and seldom referred to them.

On one occasion, however, when he heard that a young man had been shot, he turned to me and said, "That fellow owed me $50, and by Christmas, it seems as if the very fates were against me. Whenever a man is hung, shot, or drowned in the Southern Mines, he is sure to be one of my delinquent customers and dies owing me from $25 to $100." Despite his experience, he still continued to give credit, and when too late, discovered that the incapacity to say "No" had involved serious losses.

While Bob was at Santiago, Stephen and I drifted off to what is known as the Turnback, at the headwaters of the Tuolumne River.[13] A man named Smith had discovered a quartz vein in that vicinity that showed free gold, or at least his specimens did, which he declared had been taken from the vein. After some inquiry, we resolved to go with him and prospect the lead. Taking a young man named Henry Osborne, a Nantucket boy, with us, we packed my saddle mule, the same that had fallen into the canyon the year previous, and put out for the Turnback, some twenty miles from Sonora.

The vein was located beside a mountain valley where the grass grew luxuriantly and the mosquitoes also, as we found to our cost. The timber in the vicinity was truly magnificent. Tall sugar pines six or eight feet through at the butt towered up all around us to the height of more than two hundred feet. It was no fool of a job to fell one of those trees, yet I have seen axemen do it.

Attracted by the ring of an axe, I one day followed the sound, which conducted me to a huge sugar pine behind which I discovered two men chopping. The tree was at least six feet in diameter, and it was their intention to rive shakes from the trunk to cover a cabin they proposed building. They said they had begun that morning and expected to have the tree down next day. They worked three days, however, before the giant fell.

One of the men was the finest marksman I ever saw. He would bring down a bird with a bullet from the very top of a tall sugar pine. His occupation, he told me, had been creasing wild horses on the plains, which requires very accurate shooting.[14] I was walking with this man, whose name was Neely, one day when a small animal started from the trail and took to a tree trunk. "Hold on," said Neely, "don't stir. I want that for a purse." He fired, and the weasel, a beautiful little animal about the size of a chipmunk, dropped.

I was very much surprised to see no sign of a bullet, and so said. My companion smiled and pointed to the trunk of the tree. He had killed the weasel and yet the bullet had not touched it. "It is an old trick with hunters," he explained. "I shot at the bark between the weasel and the tree, and the bark flew off and killed it." That was the fact, as I soon discovered. Neely proceeded to skin the animal and did it without cutting the hide. In some mysterious way he turned the weasel inside out and preserved the skin intact. It was the prettiest piece of fur imaginable, and as I understood, very rare.

Let us return to the quartz vein. Though the specimens showed free gold, there was none to be seen in the ledge itself, which we inspected carefully with a magnifying glass. The rock was pure white quartz, hard as a flint, and we all pegged away on it for ten days with churn drills and from time to time put in a blast, but even with the aid of the glass we were unable to discover any encouraging sign. Both Stephen and myself doubted whether the specimens had been taken from that place.

Smith was a dogmatic, ignorant chap, whom we delighted to draw out, as his manner of expressing himself amused us exceedingly. There was another vein about a mile from ours, which was probably a continuation of the same lead. Smith was awful jealous of the neighboring vein, and anything commendatory thereof excited his anger. It is, I believe, generally conceded that the greater the angle, the better the show for a vein to pay. Ours stood at an angle of about 60 degrees.

One day, winking at Stephen, I remarked that I thought the neighboring vein "slanterner" than ours, using the comparative term purposely. This remark enraged Smith, who threw down his drill and declared emphatically that ours was the "slanternist." Stephen took his cue from me, and for half an hour the debate continued, during which time the comparative and superlative degrees of the adjective "slanting," were constantly reiterated. We were persistent in asserting the belief that the neighboring vein was "slanterner" than our own, while Smith maintained the contrary and called all the powers to witness that of the two our vein was the "slanternist."

At the expiration of ten days, the drills all needed sharpening and the provisions ran low, so we dispatched Ossy [Osborne] with the mule to town for a fresh supply. He departed, taking the drills with him, and we laid off, expecting he would return next day. Smith went hunting, and was fortunate enough to shoot a small doe. When he returned with the carcass, we pretended to doubt that he had killed the deer. He was an awful liar, and he knew it; nevertheless, any imputation cast upon his veracity made him raving. He could give Baron Munchausen points in the line of fiction, yet while it was evident to both of us that Smith was a liar from Liarville, we seldom contradicted him outright, though we sometimes endeavored to show the utter impossibility of his so-called facts.

On one occasion Stephen and I were discussing the practicability of making lumber of the immense pines in the neighborhood, when Smith interrupted and said we "didn't know what big trees were." Considering this a favorable opportunity to draw him out, we requested him to go ahead and explain himself.

"Well," he said, "I was over in Calaveras last summer hunting, and I came across some trees that *was* trees, these ere sugar pines ain't nothin more en currant bushes 'longside of 'em."

"How big were those trees, Smith?"

"How big? I thought some darn fool would ask that question sometime, so I jest spanned one of 'em and it spanned thirty fathoms."

"Thirty fathoms! Why, man, that is a hundred and eighty feet. Assuming the diameter to be one-third, a board from the center of that tree would floor a room sixty feet wide. Impossible. Smith, are you romancing?"

"What do you mean by that?"

"I mean that you are trying to play it on us."

"So you think I lie, do you? Well, seein' is believin'. You just go with me tomorrow and I'll show you the tree."

"How far is it from here?"

"About thirty miles, I reckon."

"Too far to go at present, but as it cannot be more than fifteen miles from Columbia, we will ride over when we go to town, and if the tree is as big as you say it is, I'll apologize for my incredulity, pay the expenses of the trip, and stand a bottle of whiskey in the bargain."

"It's a whack; we'll all three go. You'll lose the whiskey, sure pop."

This ended the matter, for events proved that once, at least, Smith had told the truth. He had in fact seen the big "redwoods" that afterward became famous and drew tourists from all parts of the world.[15]

Much to our surprise, Ossy failed to return. Flour, sugar, and coffee were all out, and but for Smith's doe, we should have been out of meat. We waited over one day, and then started for town on foot.

About noon we met a traveler who had dismounted from his horse and was eating lunch beneath the shade of a tree. He accosted us as we came up, and invited us to "pitch in," as he had a liberal supply of food.

While at lunch, the stranger told why he came to California. He had but lately arrived, was mighty homesick, and declared that as soon as he could raise $1,200 he would return to his family in old Missouri. His story was an affecting one, and is perhaps worth repeating.

The man was a farmer, about 35 years old. He had owned four Negroes, a man, his wife, and their two sons, 14 and 16 years old. The father of the boys had been raised on the farm, and the farmer had inherited him from his own father. The Negro, who had charge of all outside matters, was industrious, faithful, sober, and reliable. He took as much interest in the farm as the owner himself, and on one occasion informed his master that with one more hand he could increase the product very materially. The master pleaded poverty and declared his inability to buy another hand. The Negro insisted, and said he knew of a mighty likely boy that could be bought cheap, and would be willing to pay part of the purchase money himself, as he had "seven dollars" saved up.

The servant's pleadings were useless, however, as the farmer was already involved in debt far beyond his means to pay. He had unfortunately endorsed a note for a friend, who died suddenly and unexpectedly. Proceedings had been taken to collect the amount of the endorser. There was no defense, and judgment was sure to be entered, in which event, levy and sale under the execution were sure to follow.

In due time execution was issued. The sheriff notified the farmer that he held the writ, and unless the judgment was paid, he must make a levy. Consternation prevailed in the household. The mistress cried, the children cried, and the Negroes were inconsolable. Either the farm must be sold and the family left houseless and homeless, or the two Negro boys must be sacrificed on the altar of domestic affliction.

A family council was held, the Negroes were called in, and the situation explained. The boy's parents consented to their sale, with the provision that they should be re-purchased as soon as possible. This both master and mistress promised should be done. The two boys were sold to a neighbor with the privilege of redemption. The first consid-eration after the sale was how to get the boys back, and it was finally decided that the management of the farm should be confided to the black man, while his master sought the redemption money in the California gold fields. He had made the overland journey and had reached the mines only a few weeks before. The height of his ambition was to redeem those boys, and he declared that if he could accomplish that, it would be the happiest day of his life when the end was attained.

The Missourian told his story earnestly, and exhibited much feeling during its rehearsal. I never met him afterward, but he had my best wishes for his success. Whatever the event may have been, it was only a few years later that the black boys were released from serv-ice by the process of universal emancipation.

After an hour's rest, we continued our journey, but had not gone far when we met Osborne returning on foot.

"Ossy, where's the mule?" I asked.

"Stolen," he replied. "I have been looking for it for two days." This was cold comfort for me, but, hoping for the best, I refrained from scolding. Stephen and I had already decided that it was useless to prospect the quartz vein further, as we had found no indica-tion of gold, and believed Smith's samples were bogus. When we reached town, I im-mediately instituted proceedings to recover the lost mule. Advertisements were posted and a reward offered, but without avail. After considering the chances, we concluded that if the animal had been stolen, we might possibly gain some information by mingling with the laborers on a ditch then in process of construction, intended to convey water from the head of the Tuolumne River to the interior mining camps.[16]

So Stephen, Ossy, and I offered our services to the ditch company, which were ac-cepted, and we went to work on the line of survey. There were probably five hundred men at work on the ditch. The elements of the crowd were incongruous. There were lawyers, doctors, preachers, and almost every conceivable trade and profession employed there. It was the ultima ratio of men who were dead-broke. The wages were six dollars per day, payable in scrip, which was receivable at par for water rates.

It was not our intention to remain long when we engaged with the ditch company, our main object being to keep an eye for the lost mule. We did, however, remain for about a month, a week of which was spent on the Table Mountain, a mysterious sort of dike that runs for several miles parallel with the Stanislaus River. The top of the mountain, as its name implies, is level as a floor, and its height is perhaps five hundred feet. Though evidently the result of some volcanic disturbance, the mountain bears all the marks of primitive formation. Pines, apparently hundreds of years old, grow on the summit, and the immense rocks and boulders look as if they had lain there since creation.[17]

A company of miners, working what I think was the Raw Hide claim, followed the lead till it struck the base of Table Mountain, where they encountered solid rock. As the lead was a rich one, they determined to tunnel the rock and prospect beyond it. They found, however, that the contract was a bigger one than they anticipated; nevertheless, they stuck to it and continued work till, after tunneling eleven hundred feet, they pierced what is called the "skin" of the mountain and struck a subterranean river bed rich in gold. In the gravel of that stream they discovered bones of animals, ancient trees, and prehistoric relics innumerable.

Till I saw the California mountains, I was imbued with the stereotyped idea conveyed by Bible teachings, that our world was about 6,000 years old, but personal observation soon convinced me of the fallacy of that belief. I have seen the mountain torrents flowing hundreds of feet below me through canyons of black flint rock torn apart by some terrible convulsion, which, could the sides be brought together, would fit as accurately as a carpenter's dovetail.[18] I have seen and traced the beds of ancient rivers a hundred feet above the present streams.

What is known as the "Big Blue Lead" was once the bed of an enormous river, which flowed where mountain ranges now exist. It must have carried an immense body of water, and possessed a tremendous current, perhaps exceeding that of Niagara above the falls, if one can judge by the ponderous boulders excavated from the ground, which, worn perfectly round by attrition, show that they must have been tossed about by the resistless floods as if they had been so many marbles.

The bed of that ancient stream, which perhaps carried more water than the Mississippi, has been hoisted up by some awful convulsion of nature, and now, broken and detached, rests in the mountain peaks. It has been the source of an incalculable output of gold, and the miners are able, when the lead is broken, to relocate it in some adjacent valley or on some contiguous peak. I am no geologist—Hugh Miller[19] was a long ways ahead of me in that respect—but I have a theory which convinces me that what mining has been done in the California gold fields has been comparatively superficial, and that, some day, vast deposits will be discovered in the Golden State, to which those of the present and the past, are a mere bagatelle.[20]

The summit of Table Mountain is in places floored with boulders all worn by attrition as if they had formerly reposed in a river bed. At the time I speak of, there were huge banks of gravel on the mountain top, which, had water been obtainable at that height, would have paid fair wages for a long period.

The line of the ditch was marked by stakes driven a rod apart, and when a man finished his rod, he "fleeted" to the head of the column of workmen and began another. The foreman was a good-natured Irishman named O'Neill. He would walk to and fro on the works, and from time to time throw his measuring stick into the ditch to make sure that it was dug in accordance with the specifications. The conduit was about four feet on top, three at the bottom, and three feet deep. It may have been smaller, but such is my recollection. We three, Ossy, Stephen, and myself, tried to keep together, but it was "no go." One day, having completed my rod, I turned to assist Ossy, but O'Neill came along and hustled me to the front. The weather was excessively hot, and we worked all sorts of traverses to secure a rod in the shade of a tree, but others were on the lookout as well as we, and we did not often succeed.

O'Neill kept us on the full ten hours, and some days it seemed as if we were really working overtime. I extemporized a sort of ditty, which we sometimes sang. The chorus was—

> Oh, Mr. O'Neill, how tired we feel,
> It is six o'clock surely, now, Mr. O'Neill.

He took no offense at the improvisation; on the contrary, he seemed to enjoy it.

One day he put me in charge of a gang to roll rocks from the line of survey, which followed the mountainside. That was great fun, and we were as happy as schoolboys when we started the obstructive boulders and watched them go bounding and crashing to the valley below. Some of the rocks weighed at least ten tons, and when once started, rushed forward with the resistless impetuosity of an avalanche, sweeping trees and other rocks before them till they reached the bottom.

Though I heard nothing of the mule while working on the ditch, I did fortunately recover it in an unexpected way, which seemed at the time really Providential.

We were on our way one evening after supper to take in the sights at Shaw's Flat, which was at that time quite a camp, with all the usual accessories. It was Saturday. I had become habituated to keeping an eye on all stray mules, and as we walked along I discovered one grazing not far from the path, and remarked to Stephen that it looked like mine. A closer view and inspection of the brand proved that the mule was mine. It had grown fat and sleek during its six-weeks outing. Had it not been for the brand, I would have hardly identified the animal. The mule had grown wild, and as we could not catch it, we called to a Mexican who was riding by, to assist us. He threw his riata over the animal's neck, and I took possession.

The mule had not been stolen, after all. Its escape was simply the result of Osborne's carelessness. The fact that the halter was left behind, untied, gave us the impression that some thief had loosed it, whereas Ossy was alone responsible for the trouble that ensued.

The recovery of the mule changed our programme. There was no object to be gained by returning to the ditch, so we proceeded to the office of the company, handed in our time vouchers, and received our scrip, which we transferred to some friends who took water at Columbia, and in due time we received its par value. The next day we all put out for the river, where we remained permanently.

During the summer of 1853, I was elected Justice of the Peace for township number 5 in Tuolumne County. There were two tickets in the field, and had it not been for the exertions of Bob and Stephen, who worked for me at Don Pedro's, at that time the most populous Bar on the river, I think I would have been defeated. Stephen was constable. I wrote Jim Mandeville, our representative at Sacramento, who sent me a copy of the Statutes, and also bought a book of forms in Sonora. Thus heeled, I considered myself equipped for business.[21]

To be sure, I knew little about law; still I knew enough to fill out a summons, warrant or attachment, and was sufficiently mindful of my individual interest to collect my fees. That was all that seemed important. The lawyers did the rest. When called upon to decide a legal point, I avoided as far as possible assuming any responsibility. After listening to the arguments pro and con, the attorneys were reminded that the court was no Justice Mansfield, supposed to have all the fine points of law at his finger's end, and they were requested to produce their authorities.

The office of a Justice of the Peace in those days was quite an important position. The extent of his jurisdiction was $1,000. Some of the most eminent lawyers in the county practiced in my court. Judge Leander Quint, Henry P. Barber, Benjamin F. Moore, Charles L. Scott, Henry I. Worthington, E. F. Hunter, Green T. Martin, and other prominent attorneys often had cases in our justices' courts which were par excellence the miners' tribunals.

On the occasion of a law suit, not only the parties thereto but all their friends attended the trial. The trials were usually held at the store, to which the inevitable bar was an invariable adjunct, and at such seasons was well patronized. Plaintiff, defendant, witness, lawyers, and spectators were all armed, and at times the proceedings were exceedingly bellicose. It was customary with some attorneys, in examining a witness, to irritate and try to confuse him. It often occurred that a witness got angry at irrelevant questions and retorted sharply, sometimes coming down on the lawyer with a perfect torrent of abuse and profanity, altogether out of character in a court of justice.

"Very expressive language, very expressive indeed for a court of justice," remarked Henry P. Barber one day, as he appealed to the court, when after cross-questioning and badgering a witness for an hour, the latter, who was naturally good-natured, became excited and assailed Barber in language more forcible than polite.

"Very true, Mr. Barber," replied the justice, "but if you will insist on treating the witness discourteously, you do it at your peril, as the court will not attempt to protect you; therefore it is useless to appeal to me. Your method of examination has naturally angered the man, and it is very evident that such was your intention. You have sown the wind and reaped the whirlwind, and you must extricate yourself from the cyclone as best you can. In a case of this kind, the court will not interfere to protect a hectoring attorney."

And I was right. Over at San Andreas, in Calaveras County, only a few weeks before, a similar quarrel occurred between a lawyer and a witness whom he had wantonly insulted. The attorney appealed to the court, which attempted to enforce its authority. The result was that in less than two minutes there was a dead lawyer, a dead justice, and a general scrimmage in the courtroom.[22]

It looked at one time that day as if a like scene would be exhibited in my courtroom, but Stephen froze to a disturber in Israel, one Joe Derby, who had quite a reputation as a bad man, and ejected him without giving him a chance to draw his weapon, as both his arms were pinioned in the struggle. Joe's friends rallied around him and carried him off, as he was intoxicated and likely to cause trouble.

I might go on indefinitely with my judicial experience, cite cases and recapitulate arguments, but cui bono? There are still several years ahead of me that my story, which has already been drawn out to an unconscionable length, will necessarily include. I will, however, relate one incident that presents itself as I write, which was at the time rather amusing.

There was an old sailor on the Bar whom we called Barnacle, with whom I made an arrangement that promised to add something to my exchequer. A justice was ex officio coroner in his bailiwick, and the fee allowed was thirty dollars for each inquest. The justice in an adjoining township on the river below did quite an extensive business in the way of picking up cadavers that he drew from the river for inquisitorial purposes. There were dozens of people drowned every year in the Tuolumne River, most of whom were Chinamen, who to avoid ferriage, would often seize a boat and endeavor to cross surreptitiously. Being inexperienced, these fellows were sometimes carried away by the strong current, thrown into the river and drowned.

Barnacle, who operated a cradle on the river bank, told me he frequently saw a dead body float by, so one day I made a bargain with him, promising a bottle of whiskey for every subject for an inquest he could pick up. He took the proposition in good faith, and promised to "keep his eye skinned." Thinking no more of the matter, I was rather surprised when one morning he hailed me, saying,

"Squire, I want to tell you how I caught a couple of bodies for you today."

"You did! Let me hear all about it."

"Well, you see, I've been keeping a sharp lookout to earn that whiskey, so this morning when I caught sight of two Chinamen in the river some distance above me, for you see they were awfully swollen and loomed up like a cat's tail in a fog, I just dropped my dipper and ran for an eddy behind a point a little ways downstream. I waded out up to my breast and pretty soon they came along, two of 'em clasped in each other's arms. Just as I had figured, when they struck the eddy, they were swept upstream close to me. Their queues were floating out like boats' painters, and as they passed me, I reached out and grabbed a queue with each hand, and—"

"Have you got them safe where they won't float away?"

"I have not got them at all."

"Not got them at all! What's all this yarn you've been spinning me?"

"You didn't let me finish my yarn. You see I grabbed both tails and—"

"Well?"

"The tails came out, they didn't part, they just pulled out; you see the bodies were soft, and had been too long in the water, and when the tails came out the bodies got away from me. I've got both tails though, all safe."

"I don't see how I can hold an inquest on the tails."

"Nor I, either. I wonder, supposing those two bodies are caught down below, what the jury will think when they find the tails missing."

"We won't worry about that. They'll have the bodies with the tails gone and hold the inquest. We'll have the tails with the bodies gone and can't hold an inquest. You are out two bottles of whiskey, and I am out sixty dollars, all because the tails came out. As for the others, we will have the advantage of them in one respect. When we tell the story, we can say 'thereby hangs a tail,' and they can't."

The above incident recalls another connected with my administration. A miner named Hersey was sued for a debt and judgment was entered against him. He managed to scratch around and pay the debt, but could not raise the money for the costs, which were $30. Hersey, who lived at Morgan's Bar, was a clever fellow, whom I had long known, and I was disposed to accommodate him. He came to me one day and said he had a mule which had got mired in a bog, and in its efforts to extricate itself had strained its loin. He thought that after a while the animal would recover, and offered it to me as an equivalent for the costs.

Though disposed to make it easy as possible for him, I told him there was nothing in the statute that authorized a justice to take mules in satisfaction of a judgment, as I could not pay jurors and witnesses in that way. Nevertheless, I suggested that he should bring up the mule, and we would see what could be done. When the animal came, I discovered that it could not control its hind parts, which seemed to act independent of the rest of its body, so that when the mule walked, the hind legs at times started on their own hook and whirled the animal completely round. The mule was white, and when standing still, presented a very respectable appearance.

At my suggestion, Hersey put the quadruped up at a raffle. Thirty chances at a dollar each. The jurors and witnesses all took chances, and in a short time the required sum was made up. I took a chance, and won two more at seven-up, which I sold, retaining only my original chance. The dice were shaken, and "I won the mule," which I offered to sell at half-price; but as no one would buy it, I resolved to turn the animal out and let it run till it got better.

So I procured Bob's big branding iron, heated it red-hot, and branded the mule on its rear hind quarter. It so happened that just as the iron was applied, the hind legs got a move on and pressed forcibly against it. The brand was sunk half an inch deep in the mule's quarter, so that the letters K G were indelibly impressed on the white hide.

A year afterward, having occasion to go to the Black Springs some five miles distant, I could not find the animal, which had strayed off. It occurred to me that the "Spectre," as we called the white mule, might answer the purpose for so short a journey, and as it grazed in a neighboring valley, which it never left except when it went to the river to drink, I found it without difficulty. Leading the mule to the river, I swam it across. The bath removed all impurities from its hide, and it really looked fine, as during its long rest it had become fat and sleek. I roached its mane, combed out the tail, put on a nice Spanish saddle with a Mexican bridle having a wicked bit, and started off.

Ascending the mountain, I traveled slowly, and the mule went all right, but when, reaching the plain above, I tried to increase the speed, those infernal hind legs began to exercise their assumed prerogative and endeavored to get ahead of the fore legs. The result of this action of the posteriors was a circular motion, which neither proceeded nor retrograded, but just kept me whirling round in the road.

While the mule was in one of these tantrums, a horseman came along and stopped to watch the circus. He was evidently puzzled to account for the performance, as at every revolution the animal exhibited the big black brand on its hind quarter, his eyes seemed to be glued to that particular spot.

"I say, stranger," he asked, "what does K G stand for?" Provoked at my ludicrous position, and especially irritated by the question, I replied curtly: "K G stands for 'Keep Going.' If you are smart enough to take the hint, you had better shove, and leave me to manage my own business." He took the hint and proceeded on his way, probably impressed with the conviction that I was crazy.

Uncle Bob Stubblefield at the Black Springs was a western man who had crossed the plains the season before. He had two buxom daughters, on whom I was accustomed to call whenever business called me to the neighborhood. So I pulled up when I reached his residence, dismounted, and went in for a chat, leaving the mule standing in the road.

While I was inside, a stranger who had noticed the mule standing before the door, came in and expressed a desire to exchange with me for a horse he owned, which he said was picketed nearby. Telling him to bring his horse up, I went outside to await his coming. I had thrown the bridle over the horn of the saddle, and the mule did really look well as it stood with its head curbed in by the Mexican bit. Presently when the man came with his horse, I saw that he was very anxious for a trade. His animal was a "buckskin" with black points, apparently sound, and weighed about 950 pounds. After some discussion, I told the stranger that if he would pay me $15 I would take the saddle from my mule and place it on his horse. Without asking questions, the man agreed to my proposition, and the exchange was made.

Not long after the trade, I met Uncle Bob, who asked, "What kind of a mule was that you sold that fellow the other day?"

I had expected the question, and replied, "What's the matter with the mule?"

He explained that the hunter had packed it one morning with a load of venison and started for Sonora, but had gone only a short distance when the animal began to "cut up didos," and went round and round and round, and acted so queerly that the man returned and procured another animal.

"Ah!" I said, "that is one of the mule's confounded peculiarities; there seems to be an irrepressible struggle between the hind and fore quarters as to which shall take precedence." So Uncle Bob departed without any suspicion of the cause of the mule's gyrations.

There was a sort of political revolution in Tuolumne County in 1853. Bob and I were delegates to the convention, but the hand of the machine was so plainly apparent that many kicked over the traces and H. K. Swope was elected sheriff over the Democratic nominee.[23] Under the new regime Stephen was appointed collector of mining licenses in our district. Under the law, every foreigner was required to take out a license, paying six dollars a month therefor, but the statute was not rigidly enforced except in regard to the Chinese, who were bled freely.[24] The appointment gave Stephen regular employment for a while, but he resigned after a few months and left the mines.

Proceeding to San Francisco, he took passage for Honolulu, where he met his brother, who was master of the bark *Concordia*,[25] and returned in that vessel to his native village. In subsequent years he became quite prominent as a politician, was several times elected treasurer of Suffolk County, ran for Congress in the first district, but was defeated. President Grant appointed him to the Appraisership in New York City. He held that office only a few months, however. A year or two later, he was appointed to the Board of Police Commissioners, in New York City, and for several years was president of the Board. With Stephen's departure from California, our intimate social relations ceased. In after years we met from time to time, but our lives were cast in different places. Whenever we did meet, however, our adventures by flood and field in boyhood's days, and our subsequent experience in San Francisco and the gold fields, were the source of inspiration for many an hour's chat.

Though personally I did not engage in mining to any extent in 1853, I was interested in a company that dammed the river at a point just below where we worked the Kensett claim a year before. There were six or eight in the company, but as I could occupy my time to better advantage than in working with them, I sent a substitute to represent me. Though my man was reliable and industrious, the company refused to accept him, and advised me that they had hired a carpenter to represent my share. I took exception to this, as a carpenter commanded higher wages than an ordinary laborer, and there was no reason why I should be individually taxed to pay the mechanic. Therefore I kicked, contending that so long as I sent as good a man as any of them, they could not consistently require more, and if a carpenter was needed, let the company hire him, and I would pay my share of the expense.

My protestations were in vain, however, for though I sent several different men to represent me, all were rejected. The carpenter was retained, and his wages deducted from my dividends, which I declined to receive.

It came to pass, in the course of the summer, that another company commenced operations in the river below our claim and constructed a dam that backed up the water so as to interfere materially with our work.

A lawsuit was the result of this interference, and I was requested to manage the case. As the management, in case we recovered damages, seemed to afford an opportunity to recoup for my retained dividends, I accepted it, wrote the complaint and commenced an action for damages. Col. Benjamin F. Moore of Sonora was retained as counsel. As I was an interested party, the suit was brought before Justice [E.] Hillhouse [of Township 3] in Chinese Camp, where in due time the case was called.

The trial was a long one, many witnesses were sworn, and every point hotly contested. When, after an all-day's session, Col. Moore arose to address the jury, it was after 10 o'clock P. M. The jury were weary and half-asleep, and seemed to feel no interest in the proceedings.

Now, the attorney's plea is the very essence of the case in such instances, and when I noticed the listless and inattentive attitude of the jury, I resolved to wake the jurymen up. The court was held in a saloon, but when I suggested to E. F. Hunter, who was assistant counsel, the advisability of treating the jury, he objected. "No, no," he said, "it will not do; you will lose your case if you tamper with the jury."

"I don't care a continental," I replied, "the jury's asleep and I'm going to wake it up. If they ever did appreciate a drink, they'll do so now. Look at those fellows, and imagine yourself one of them, do you think you would refuse an 'eye opener' under such circumstances?"

Regardless of Hunter's warning, I proceeded to the bar and instructed "Tip" Douglass, the barkeeper, to mix a big pitcher of gin toddy and hand it to the jury, arguing that the Justice would think it was water and the treat would pass unnoticed except by the participants.

In accordance with my suggestion, Tip mixed a pitcher full and carried it with a glass to the jury. Filling a tumbler, he tendered it to the first man in line, who was about to reject it, but a wink and monitory kick induced him to put the glass to his lips, when back went his head and down went the toddy. The second juryman regarded the refilled glass scornfully; he also thought it was water, which he had no use for; a nudge from his colleague enlightened him, however, and he took his medicine kindly. Tip went the length of the jury, each of whom took his cue from his predecessor, and not one of the twelve refused.

It has always been my belief that the contents of the pitcher were a potent factor in our behalf. In fact, I was told as much by the foreman of the jury. The toddy actually revivified the jurymen, who during Col. Moore's plea, gave him their undivided attention. I can see him now as he stood before the jury and appealed to them individually and collectively. "Don't you see?" he would ask as he patted a juryman on the shoulder, and almost invariably got an affirmative nod in reply. He talked for an hour, and possessed a pleasing manner that seemed to captivate his auditors.

Col. Moore was a Southerner who occasionally imbibed too freely, when he was apt to express himself freely also. He often got into an altercation in the court room, when the Circuit Judge would fine him for contempt. He would never pay the fine, however, but preferred serving his time in jail, where I sometimes interviewed him on business matters.[26]

We won our lawsuit, and the jury gave us a verdict of $800. Lawyers, clients, and witnesses all got tight over the result. I strayed into a fandango house and tackled a one-horse monte bank presided over by a Mexican. There was not to exceed a hundred dollars in the bank. What prompted me I do not know, as I very seldom staked anything at the gambling table, and when I did, it was merely an insignificant sum. Here, however, I threw down a $20 gold piece and began betting a dollar at a time, and of course losing, for it was a "skin game."

Bill Saunders, the foreman of the jury that had tried our case, came along, saw what I was doing, took me aside and borrowed all my money. The Greaser was mad, but made no fuss as he was afraid of Saunders, who was "one of the boys" and well-known throughout the county. Bill took me to his cabin that night, and next morning returned my money, which he had borrowed to save it from the monte bank.

The above incident reminds me of another with which Saunders, who was an all-around good fellow, was connected. He had in some way offended Tip Douglass, who kept a saloon, and Tip, incited by Count Solinsky[27] of the Express office, sent Saunders a challenge. Everybody knew that the latter had sand, but whether Tip was game was an open question.

It was not intended by the seconds that either party should be injured, but they kept that fact from the principals, who anticipated a duel a la morte. This occurrence was before the introduction of cartridges, as in those days pistols were loaded with powder and ball. Count Solinski, who acted as Tip's second, had, in collusion with Saunders' friend, so arranged that the pistols could do no harm by placing nothing but powder therein. The powder was covered with a wad of "tin foil," which being pressed firmly with the old style ramrod, presented the appearance of a bullet, as the concavity in the end of the rod gave the wad a globular shape so that it would deceive anyone not in the secret.

When the hour set for the duel, news of which had been bruited abroad, arrived, all Chinese Camp[28] and all the surrounding camps were represented by a multitude of spectators, who like the principal actors, considered the affair a serious one, and came prepared to see either Tip or Saunders effectually wiped out. After the seconds had tossed for position, the principals took the places assigned them, received their pistols, and were instructed to withhold their fire till Count Solinsky gave the word.

All was quiet as the grave. A hush had fallen over the multitude that watched the proceedings, so that when Count Solinsky gave the words, "One—two—three—fire," his voice was distinctly audible throughout the whole of that vast assemblage.

At the word, both pistols were discharged, but though the men stood only twelve paces apart, neither was injured. Tip was nervous and excited, but Saunders seemed as unconcerned as if firing at a rabbit. Twice the shots rang out, still nobody was hurt. Tip declared the pistols were not loaded with bullets, but a sight of the four undischarged cylinders convinced him of his error. In the interval between the second and third shots, Saunders' second briefly explained to him that the whole affair was a "put up game," and advised him to drop at the next shot. Bill saw the point and proved himself equal to the occasion, for when his adversary blazed away the third time, Saunders dropped his weapon, threw up his hands, and fell forward with a dramatic effect that would have done credit to Edwin Forrest.

Thoroughly demoralized by the result of his third shot, Tip ran for the horse that had been prepared for the escape of the survivor, hastily mounted, and dashed through the crowd, waving his pistol and shouting as he fled, "Whoever attempts to stop me, is a dead man."

The crowd, who by this time suspected that the whole thing was a sham, made no effort to detain Tip, who got away unharmed. After Tip's flight, Saunders, who up to the third shot had been unaware of the collusion between the seconds, arose uninjured, and received the congratulations of his friends.

Tip, who was thoroughly frightened, sought seclusion in the cabin of a friend near Table Mountain, where he kept himself concealed for several days, when his mate, who thought the joke had gone far enough, relieved his anxiety by assuring him that Saunders was unharmed. So he returned to his old quarters, where he was subjected to many a jibe in connection with the duel, which so humiliated him that when I met him afterward, I had not the heart to mention the transaction.

There are doubtless men still living in the vicinity of Chinese Camp who remember the sham duel, and it is very possible that both the principals are still in the flesh, as both were young men. Should this ever meet their eye, they will, I trust, credit me with having related the facts just as they occurred. Should anyone question the correctness of my relation, I would refer to Alex Stair, John Payne, John Gashweiler, Count Solinsky, Miles Nesmith, Clark Reese, and Milton Graham, either of whom, if still surviving, will attest its truth.[29]

There was no execution issued for the collection of the judgment of $800 with the accruing costs, as the parties paid it before the sixty days were up. Meanwhile, the judgment creditors, knowing that in case I collected the money I would have the settlement of the dispute between myself and the others in my own hands, decided to have another collect the judgment. This caused an open rupture, and I determined, if possible, to euchre them and put them to the rowing oar.

The defendants, who knew of the quarrel between myself and the other members, sent me word privately that they intended to pay the judgment the following day. It was night when I received the message, the animals were all running at large, and it was impossible to find them, though I searched thoroughly. Conscious of the value of time, I started afoot for Chinese Camp and climbed the trail at Red Mountain, which was not such a terror to me as it had been years before. I reached the camp early in the morning, where I got breakfast and collected the money, after which I procured a horse from the livery stable and proceeded to Jamestown, where I had some business to attend to.

On my return in the afternoon, the Justice informed me that I had not been gone an hour before a man rode up post-haste and presented him an order signed by all the rest of the company to pay him the money, and in case the judgment was not yet settled, forbidding the Justice to pay me anything on account thereof. So it seemed the others had been on watch as well as myself, but as I had the money, I could afford to laugh. I was mad all through, however, and resolved that as I held the cards, to play them in my own interest for all they were worth.

I had served the company faithfully in the matter of the lawsuit, and had been put to considerable expense, for which under ordinary circumstances there would have been no charge. Now, however, it was different, and I determined to charge "all the traffic would bear." So, in accordance with that decision, I began to figure up what I was legitimately entitled to.

First was the matter of retained dividends. I was entitled to all those, and in addition the difference charged me between laborer's wages and carpenter's wages. So I put that down as a starter. Next, mindful of the axiom that the laborer is worthy of his hire, I considered that the time spent in conducting the lawsuit should be paid for, and I put that down. As horse hire was a legitimate charge, I added that to the bill. To be sure, I rode my own horse, but if I had owned none, would have had to hire one, and why were not my horse's services worth as much as another's? I had also written the Complaint, which was a long one, occupying nearly a dozen folios, had amended it, and added to it from time to time, so that it held water, and the opposing counsel were unable to find a flaw in it, so I charged for the Complaint. In fact I charged all I could do legally, even for the time spent in collecting the money. From the sum total of expenses I deducted my own pro rata share as a member of the company, and held the balance, a rather insignificant sum, subject to the order of its treasurer.

It was on a Saturday evening that the treasurer of the company called on me and requested that I would pay over the amount of the judgment. Presenting the bill I had made out, I tendered him the balance, provided he would give me a receipt in full. This he positively refused to do, and departed to consult with the others. Everybody in camp knew of the quarrel existing between me and the comapny. I had talked the matter over freely and openly, and the consensus of opinion sustained me.

Nothing further occurred till the following day, when in the afternoon I discovered the whole crowd approaching, led by one Sam McLean,[30] who had been their chief counselor and adviser, and to whom all the difficulty was due. Sam considered himself an erudite personage. It is Pope, I think, who says,

Where ignorance is bliss, 'tis folly to be wise

Sam knew just about enough to make his wisdom all folly on certain occasions.

When I saw them coming, I was standing in front of the tent talking desultorily with several friends. Though anticipating a row, I considered it would be nothing more than a war of words, and felt amply able to take care of myself. Sam was a heavy man and weighed probably 240 pounds, so when he came close and pulled a pistol from his shirt bosom and demanded the money, I was rather astonished, as I had no idea he would go to that extremity. My own pistol, which I never carried at home, was in the tent. When Sam so unexpectedly got the drop on me, the boys with whom I had been talking got out of range and cried, "Don't shoot, Sam, don't shoot." I tell you, reader, it does indeed have a "strange quick jar upon the ear, the cocking of a pistol," and for a moment I was paralyzed. Turning my right side towards him, I caught his eye, and something—it must have been intuition—told me he was not game to shoot.

Then I spoke, and offered to leave the question to any unprejudiced man in the camp. This he refused to do. I got angry and reproached him for threatening me with a pistol, spoke of the disparity in size between him and myself, who weighed about 150 pounds, and told him if the condition were changed, I would pick him up and throw him in the river, instead of assaulting him with a pistol, which he had meanwhile ceased to point at me but still held in his hand.

What frightened McL[ean]—I never learned till long afterward. It seems that Bob [Gardiner] had seen the party below and realized the imminent probability of trouble. Hastening to the store in a state of great excitement, he got his gun, but was so nervous that he called on Doctor Armstrong to load it. The doctor, who was an old hunter, charged the gun with thirty-two buckshot in each barrel. The store was not more than thirty or forty yards from where I stood. Just as soon as Sam got the drop on me, Bob covered him with his gun. I think McL[ean] saw the gun and weakened, as he was facing the store, while I stood back to it. Bob never mentioned the affair to me, and I only learned of it through Doctor Armstrong and others who saw the transaction. McL[ean] accomplished nothing by his cowardly demonstration, as the final outcome was a settlement on my own terms by the payment of the balance originally tendered to the treasurer.

That year the literary element in the community came to the fore, and a circulating library was established at Hawkins' Bar. This was done through the instrumentality of one Morgan Davis, who solicited subscriptions among the miners of Hawkins' and contiguous Bars. Davis selected the books, which though composed largely of fiction, were in the main very appropriate to the class of readers. Aside from the fictitious works, there were many standard publications, historical, biographical, and philosophical, so that all tastes were suited.[31]

In the long winter evenings, the boys would gather in some tent, appoint one of their number reader, while they sat by, smoked their pipes, and listened interestedly. Woe to the man who made a disturbance at these sessions; he was ejected summarily, sans ceremony. One group, reader and listeners, I remember specially. There were five of them. Munson Van Riper,[32] Henry Clendening of New York City, Jacob Yager of Philadelphia, and two English boys, Ned Coward and Hamer Metcalf.

Munsie and Clen, as we called them, had been raised in "Gotham," and had as boys seen about all that was worth seeing on Manhattan Island. Perfectly familiar with the inside of the Bowery and Chatham theatres, they could call every prominent actor by name and recite pages of *Coriolanus* and kindred plays. Shakespeare was with them a household word. Forrest, Booth, Charles Keen, Charlotte Cushman, Chanfrau, Placide, and Gentleman George Barrett were all familiar names, and they had often witnessed their performances on the theatrical stage. So when one day Munsie came from the library with a copy of *Nick of the Woods,* in which the "Jiboninesy" is a conspicuous character, and which had been dramatized and played years before to his delectation, all hands prepared for a feast of reason.

Munsie was the reader, and though no elocutionist, his familiarity with the play enabled him to follow the story without great effort. There was one word, however, that frequently occurred in the book that he was unable to articulate, neither could any of his audience render him any assistance. It was Greek to all of them, and hampered Munsie exceedingly, causing him, whenever he met with it, to slip an eccentric [gear] and slow up for repairs. This word was "aborigines." One day as I was passing his tent, Munsie came rushing out, book in hand, and pointing to the obstructive substantive, asked, "What is that word? It breaks me all up every time I come across it, and that happens on every page." Glancing at the printed expression which conveyed no idea to him, I pronounced the word. "I can't remember that," he said, "what does it mean anyway?"

"It means Indians as used here, so whenever you run against it, don't try to pronounce it, just read Indians, in place of it."

Munsie adopted my suggestion and thereafter eliminated the objectionable term, substituting "Indians" in place thereof, and by so doing glided over "aborigines" without slipping a cog.

Morgan Davis, who instituted the library, was a man of more than average intelligence. A graduate of Yale College, he was altogether out of place in the mines, where his devotion to study militated against his success as a miner. A few hours' work would realize sufficient to purchase provisions for a week, and so long as he had enough for present consumption, he seemed content. He showed no disposition to accumulate, and had apparently no ambition beyond a desire to live, move, and have a being. He was a modest, quiet, reticent man, ill-fitted for the life to which fate had consigned him. "Far from the madding crowd's ignoble strife," forsaken by the world, and forgotten of the world, he passed his remaining days at Hawkins' Bar. He had known the camp when it contained a thousand voters, had seen it gradually decline until a half-dozen constituted its whole population, and finally he, too, was called from earth and buried on the hillside where he had read the funeral service over so many departed companions.

Years afterward, Prentice Mulford in his story of his California life wrote, "Passing the deserted Bar I peeped in at Morgan's deserted cabin. An oak almost barred the door, part of the roof was gone, the bookshelves had vanished; naught remains but the old miner's stove and a few battered cooking utensils. I had thought at the time of camping for the night on the Bar, but this desolate cabin and its associations of former days contrasted with the loneliness and solitude of the present, proved too much for me; I feared the possible ghost of the dead librarian, and left for a populated camp."[33]

In the fall of 1853, I met with an adventure somewhat out of my former line of experience. My saddle mule disappeared, this time for good, and though I ransacked the country far and near, I never saw hide or hair of it again. It is in connection with my search for the animal that the following episode occurred.

Soon after missing the mule, which had unaccountably left the drove, I started out one morning hoping to find some trace that would lead to its recovery. It was a rainy day, and when I left home, a mule belonging to a gambler on the Bar followed the old white mare that I was riding. Not expecting to be gone long, I took no pains to drive the animal back, which I was confident would follow the mare.

A mile or two out, I struck the trail of several animals, and among the footprints imbedded in the soft soil discovered one that resembled my mule's. The trail was plainly defined, and there was no difficulty in following the tracks, which I continued to do until at evening I struck the bottom lands in the vicinity of French Bar. As darkness was so near I decided to abandon the pursuit and retrace my steps, as I had eaten nothing since morning and was some fifteen miles from home. Moreover, it would be impossible to follow the trail after night set in.

The mule, which had followed all day, had by this time got hungry, and often stopped to browse by the wayside. This necessitated driving it before me, which I did till it became so dark that I could no longer see it. Knowing that the owner would expect me to account for the animal on my return, I was sadly puzzled what course to pursue. There was no habitation that I knew of within miles, neither had I any means of building a fire. One thing, however, was indisputable; I must either take that mule home with me or chance a row with Williams, the gambler, who owned it, and had probably seen it follow me away.

The locality where night overtook me was a notorious resort for grizzlies, which I had no desire to encounter. I was wet all through, and decidedly uncomfortable, so that the prospect of passing the night there was extremely disagreeable. Nevertheless, there seemed no escape from the dilemma except to abandon the mule, which I was disinclined to do.

Without matches to kindle a fire, camping on the ground was not to be thought of, and the only alternative was to take to a tree. Dismounting beside an ancient pine, I managed to secure the mare by the bridle, took off the saddle, and climbed the tree. Fortunately the crotch was not far from the ground, so I was able to reach it without much exertion. The prospect of a ten hours' vigil was far from alluring, and my position in the tree was not exactly a terrestrial paradise. For an hour or two I sat like Zaccheus among the branches, till at last my position was so uncomfortable that I decided to improve matters by hoisting up the saddle for a seat. Moreover, I was very thirsty, and wanted a drink.

So I descended to Mother Earth, quenched my thirst at a little pool, and proceeded to elevate the saddle to the tree crotch. This was accomplished by tearing several strips from the saddle blanket, which were tied together and one end made fast to the girth. Taking the other end between my teeth, I made my way aloft, and, after reaching the fork, pulled the saddle up, which I adjusted astride a good-sized limb and seated myself with my feet in the stirrups and my back supported by the tree trunk. This was a great improvement, and enabled me to sit very comfortably. Time passed slowly, however; every minute seemed an hour, and every hour a calendar month.

Suddenly the old mare, which had lain down at the foot of the tree, snorted and arose to her feet, when I distinguished a dark form in the gloom which excited very unpleasant sensations. Thinking it was a grizzly, the idea of a circus performance beneath the tree was far from exhilarating. It proved a false alarm, however, as it was the mule which startled the mare, the discovery of which fact relieved me immensely.

When Robinson Crusoe slept in a tree, he tells us he made himself fast to prevent falling. I made no such provision, for I had no intention of taking any chance whatever, and resolved to keep wide-awake. Nevertheless, at some time during the "silent watches of the night" I did drop off, despite my good resolution. How long I slept, I have no means of knowing, but it must have been some hours, for when I awoke, every limb was benumbed, and the blood in my veins seemed to have stopped circulating. For a minute I was unable to move hand or foot, but brought common sense to my aid, which convinced me I was chilled through. After awhile I succeeded in restoring the circulation in my limbs so that movement was possible, and then instituted a series of gymnastics that would have done credit to a professional acrobat. Leaping from limb to limb, I explored every branch of that tree from fork to summit, taking chances that would have appalled a gray squirrel. For an hour this exercise continued, till every pore reeked with perspiration and warmth was restored to my whole system, so that when daylight soon after appeared, I was in a condition to proceed homeward. The mule had its belly full, and followed willingly. The eight miles between my roosting place and the Bar was soon passed over, and I reached home by breakfast-time.

As the river was high, the boys hesitated about coming for me. Bob, however, answered my hail and ferried me over. He was much amused when I recounted my night's adventure, and often referred to it in after years.

Bob went home that fall and was gone several months. He returned in the spring and was warmly welcomed by all. He had much home news to communicate, and I think would have enjoyed a longer visit, as there were many attractive ties he was compelled to sever when he came away. I remember he brought me a pound can of fine-cut tobacco, a present from J. M. G. [James Madison Gardiner?] in New York, which was duly appreciated.

During Bob's absence that winter, the Bar was almost deserted, the boys having transferred the scene of their labors to the dry diggings in the vicinity of Columbia. Tom [Gardiner] was in charge at the Grizzly Bear Pavilion, who with myself and two or three others were the only residents. The winter was uneventful, and we enjoyed ourselves as best we could.

Jack Tabor, an old friend and fellow-townsman who kept a store at Morgan's Bar, came up one day and in the course of conversation remarked that he had received some kiln-dried buckwheat flour the day before, so prepared that it was self-raising, and there was no reason why we could not have buckwheat griddlecakes. The mention of buckwheat cakes instantly suggested a thought of sausages as a proper accompaniment.

Buckwheat cakes and sausages! The very idea made our mouths water, and carried our minds to the breakfast table at home. We resolved to have some. "Sister" Stilwell, a smooth-faced, handsome youngster who had been thus christened by the boys on account of his fresh complexion, lack of beard, and effeminate appearance, was dispatched to Morgan's Bar for a package of flour. A pig was slaughtered, scalded, and properly dressed. Leaving Jack to cut up the pig and chop the sausage meat, I mounted my horse and set off in pursuit of sage and summer savory. Successful in my quest, I returned with the herbs, which with other condiments were mixed with the minced meat. "Sister" came soon after with the flour, the griddlecakes were prepared, the sausages fried, coffee made, and we all set down to enjoy the spread.

The meal was not an unqualified success, for though the sausages were excellent and finely flavored, the flour was musty, and had probably been spoiled in the long voyage around Cape Horn.

During the winter, I had heard of a Bar far up on the Merced River which I determined to prospect. So in the spring of 1854, after the rains were over, Frank Casey and myself started out to find the place and ascertain whether there was anything there in the shape of gold deposits.

I had become possessed of a mule called "Honest John," whose name belied his character, for though a good saddle animal, he had more mean tricks than any mule I ever saw. Unless hobbled when turned out, it was very difficult to catch him, and he would travel faster with his feet strapped together than other animals that ran free from restraint. He would untie a knot with his teeth, no matter how complex, and had all the obstinacy for which the species is proverbial. He was a good roadster, however, and tough as a pine knot, which qualities compensated in a measure for all his bad tricks.

We crossed the river at Don Pedro's Bar and reached Coulterville the same day, where we put up for the night. The next morning Honest John had disappeared. Knowing the unreliability of the animal, I had taken extra pains to secure him, but in some inexplicable way he had managed to free himself.

Borrowing Frank's mule, I started in pursuit of Honest John, hoping to catch him before he had gone far, and did indeed overtake him within a few miles of Coulterville. That confounded animal just played fast and loose with me for half a day. Though he was dragging his halter, it was impossible for me to get hold of it, as he had a mechanical eye which enabled him to judge when to start off and elude me. He was faster than my animal, which, handicapped with my weight, stood no chance whatever in a trial of speed.

Realizing the impossibility of catching him in the open, I resolved to race him to the ferry, and hurried him over the sixteen miles to Don Pedro's Bar where he boarded the ferryboat, ran to the outer end, and for a minute I feared he would jump overboard, but his courage failed him. Confined in the boat, it was an easy matter to catch him, when, shifting the saddle to his back, I returned to Coulterville leading Frank's mule.

It was too late to resume our journey when I reached Coulterville, where we remained till next day. Before retiring, I secured Honest John by hobbling both his fore and hind feet, and when morning came he was still safely moored.

When we proceeded on our way next day, we did not cross at Split Rock Ferry, the usual route, but followed the trail on the right bank of the river, for what reason I do not remember. In the afternoon we came to a ferry where there was a rawhide rope stretched across the stream, which at that point ran rapidly. A man soon appeared in answer to our hail, and crossed over in a "dugout," which was secured to the rope over which a tackle ran, and the boat was propelled by the current.

Frank swam his mule over first and returned for mine, leaving me with the saddles, etc., for a third trip. Midway of the stream, which ran like a mill tail, Honest John got into a flurry, went under, came up again with his ears full of water, kicked and splurged, and came near capsizing the dugout. Twice the halter threatened to slip over the mule's head, and twice Frank reached out and replaced it. Meanwhile, a knot in the rope got jammed in the block, and the ferryman, who was unable to disengage it, became alarmed and nearly lost his wits. I shouted to Frank to let the mule go and look out for himself. He hung on, however, and finally the ferryman succeeded in slipping the block past the knot so that they made the transit safely.

There was quite a fall in the river just below the ferry, which would have been sure death to the boat's occupants had the line parted. Nine men out of ten would have let go the halter, but he happened, luckily for me, to be the tenth man, and hung on to the mule, which would have doubtless been drowned had it been swept away at that point.

When I reproached Frank for risking his life by taking such desperate chances rather than let up on the mule, he remarked that he had his eyes on a place he thought he could fetch in case of emergency. The ferryman was so scared that he refused to return for me, so Frank took his place and ferried me over.

The ferry was a little below where Sherlock's Creek enters the Merced. That point was then the Ultima Thule of exploration along the river; all above was comparatively unknown.[34] The man who kept the store at the mouth of the creek advised against extending our journey into an unknown wilderness, but we pushed on and ascended the mountain by an Indian trail which left the river at that point.

Ere we had gone a mile, we met two demoralized Greasers, who had lost their bearings and requested us to direct them to the ferry. Pointing out the way, we left them and proceeded on our journey. The further we went, the wilder and more forbidding the aspect. So far as we could see was one wild waste of chamisal. From time to time we encountered bear signs, which made us feel rather uncomfortable about camping out. Moreover, there was no feed for our animals, and when finally we lost all signs of a trail and considered the uncertainty of finding our destination, we decided to turn back.

It was some hours after dark when we reached the store at Sherlock's Creek, to which we were guided by the instinct of the mules. The trail was so blind that, after night set in, we were all abroad as to our course, so we gave our animals their head, Frank leading and I following, as I had no confidence in the discretion of Honest John. We stopped at Sherlock's that night and returned home by the way of Split Rock Ferry.

Not satisfied with the result of our expedition, after gaining some more definite information regarding the locality we had failed to find, I resolved to try again. Securing the services of three Chinamen, as I desired to give the bar a thorough prospecting in case I found it, I set off a second time, accompanied by the three Celestials.

The journey was so timed that it was early in the day when we reached Sherlock's Creek, and so far as I had been able to ascertain, the Bar could be easily reached in five or six hours from that point. Where I led, the Chinese followed, apparently oblivious of where or how far they were going. As the Chinamen carried packs, we necessarily traveled slowly, so that it was late in the day when we struck the river and proceeded to descend the wild, rugged mountain from which we observed it. It must have been nearly two miles that we followed a gorge, ere we came to the base of the hill. A short distance below, we discovered the Bar we were in search of, which to all appearance had never been marked by pick or shovel.

Although not yet five o'clock, there was no prospecting done that day. The Chinese, who were wearied by their long tramp, disencumbered themselves of their burdens and proceeded to prepare supper, of which all were sadly in need. The grass grew rankly by the river where I picketed the mule, after hobbling both his fore and hind feet.

The locality was indeed a wild one. Although accustomed to mountain scenery, the view exceeded anything I had ever beheld in point of grandeur. Hill on hill, and mountain on mountain, Ossa on Pelion, piled on every side, gave an impression of God's illimitable power, which while life remains, will never be effaced. It seemed to me to be the chosen spot

> Where the proud Queen of Wilderness had placed
> By rock and cataract, her lonely throne

and as I gazed on pathless glens and lofty mountains, and listened to the voice of the torrents, which, falling from the cliffs, mingled their echoes with the murmurs of the rushing river, I was enraptured, and my soul was filled with a sublime but sad delight.

Meanwhile, Providence was preparing an exhibition such as human eye seldom beholds. The heavens were suddenly overcast with clouds, the thunder rumbled, and the indications gave promise of a coming storm. The terrified Chinamen grew pale and trembled, and the very mule knuckled in his tracks when Heaven's artillery opened and its reverberations were re-echoed from peak to peak.

> The sky was changed! and such a change! O night,
> And storm, and darkness, ye are wondrous strong,
> Yet lovely in your strength, as is the light
> Of a dark eye in woman! Far along
> From peak to peak, the rattling crags among
> Leaps the live thunder! Not from one lone cloud
> But every mountain now hath found a tongue,
> And Jura answers through her misty shroud,
> Back to the joyful Alps, who call to her aloud.

Yet the scene, though sublime, was sad. The savage grandeur oppressed my heart, and filled me with a stern sense of loneliness. I would have given anything for the sight of a familiar face, for I could hold no converse with my dusky companions. Though the storm was transitory, it was terrific and impressive while it lasted. Within the space of half an hour it passed away, leaving no trace of its presence, save the dead campfire, which had been extinguished by the hail that accompanied it.

The place where this scene occurred was in the immediate vicinity of the Yo Semite Falls, which have since attained a worldwide celebrity for the grandeur of the mountains, the immensity of the trees, and the sublimity of the cataracts. Then unknown except by the aboriginal tribes and perhaps a few venturesome prospectors, Yo Semite is now a famous resort for tourists. Government has reserved the spot for a public park, where hotels have been erected and improvements made for the accommodation of guests.[35]

Investigation showed that the Bar, which was but a small one, was not auriferous, for after prospecting it thoroughly, we found no show of gold. The place was far above where the river and its tributaries had been disturbed by miners, and the water was clear as crystal. Indeed, so pellucid was the stream that the strength of the current was imperceptible. Though the water was not deep, when I attempted to ford the river, my feet were swept from under me and I was carried downstream despite every attempt to regain my footing. Without trying to stem the current, I struck out downstream and swam diagonally. Fortunately I grasped a root projecting from the bank, otherwise I would have been swept into a nasty canyon a few rods below.

Stripping myself, the Chinamen wrung the water from my clothing, which soon dried, when we started on our return, having spent one day in prospecting.

This was but one of a hundred expeditions of the kind which had proved equally fruitless. Nevertheless, I made others subsequently, undiscouraged by previous failures. There is an excitement attending such adventures that no one who has not lived the careless, nomadic life of a prospector can realize.

After reaching Sherlock's Creek, I left the Chinese behind and traveled rapidly, but was destined to meet with another adventure ere reaching home. On my previous trip I had followed the trail from Split Rock Ferry, which crossed the summit of a point near the stream which ran through a canyon below. On my return I discovered another trail which led round the point. As a level road is always preferable to a hilly one, I took that which seemed the easiest. Before I had proceeded far, I noticed some miners on the opposite side of the river waving their hats and apparently trying to attract my attention. Though unable to hear them, their actions excited a suspicion that there was danger ahead, so I kept a bright lookout, and it was well I did, for presently I discovered that the trail, which overhung the canyon and was a mere shelf some twenty inches wide, was broken off, making further progress impossible.

The shelf was too narrow to turn around, and when I gazed into the canyon below, it seemed the wisest course to dismount without loss of time. Having no faith in the steadiness of Honest John, a seat on his back under such circumstances was by no means a desirable position. He might get into a flurry and slip off, in which case I preferred to have him go it alone. Releasing my feet from the stirrups and placing my hands behind me, I raised myself from the saddle to the mule's back and slid off over his stern.

Once more on terra firma, the question arose, how was I to get the mule out of the scrape? It was eight or ten rods from where I took the trail. There was not room to pass to the mule's head except by crawling beneath him. This I succeeded in doing, but when I took hold of the bit, I had little faith that I would be able to back the animal along that narrow ledge to the starting point. Whatever his faults, Honest John was no fool, and despite his natural disposition to cussedness, showed himself competent to look after Number One.

Apparently conscious of his danger, the mule kept three feet constantly on the ground and used the fourth exclusively for prospecting. He would feel around with his off hind foot which was nearest the edge of the shelf until, satisfied where to place it, he would put it down, and resting on that would withdraw the others a step backwards. Thus he proceeded without any attempt on my part to guide him till he reached the junction of the two trails, where, much relieved, I remounted and continued my journey.

A mule never gets flurried on a mountain trail when it perceives danger, and therein consists its superiority over a horse for mountain travel. Had I been caught with a horse on that narrow shelf, he would have never extricated himself, therefore I say, in all mountain excursions give me a good mule to carry me.

Bob and I were again delegates to the county convention in 1854. He was a candidate for county clerk that year, and we had both done some canvassing in his interest. When on the morning of the convention I rode up to his door, Bob gave me a supercilious glance and remarked, "Why the devil don't you dress up and be somebody?"

As I had taken extraordinary pains with my toilet that morning, had bathed in the river and put on the best I had, which though coarse was whole and clean, and moreover had purchased a new hat expressly for the occasion, I was somewhat taken aback by his observation. Considerably nettled, I replied, "I reckon I'll pass in the crowd, and it sounds rather ungenerous for you, who have just returned from home with a whole outfit of fashionable harness, to criticize my wardrobe and put on airs on the strength of your good clothes, and by [God] I believe you would stand a better chance in the convention dressed as I am, than if you were arrayed like Solomon in purple and fine linen."

Rather surprised that I should show resentment at a remark that was not intended to be offensive, Bob explained that he had no intention of criticizing my raiment, which he admitted would accord better with that of our fellow delegates than would finer apparel, but as he had harness enough for both of us, which was so seldom used that it would be out of fashion long before it was worn out, he had proposed to himself to lend me an outfit so that there would be less disparity in our appearance.

Mollified by his expression of good intention, after some argument I consented to change my rig and temporarily adopt his. For the first time in years I arrayed myself in a white shirt and starched collar with clothing to match, so that, when dressed, I was tempted to doubt my own identity. I insisted, however, on wearing my boots outside my trousers, as I had lost all faith in pockets. It was an ordinary thing to see a man feel in his pocket, find nothing but a hole, and then take off his boots and pour his money and whatever had escaped from the leaky pocket therefrom. I myself had lost $40 only a few weeks before by over-confidence in the pockets of a pair of new trousers, which I disliked to wrinkle by stowing the legs inside my boots, hence my caution.

"Dress makes the man, the want of it the fellow." When we got away that morning with good clothes on, and good horses under us, our own dogs would not have known us. The fact is, we were so dressed up it caused remark. Our best friends failed to recognize us and took us for tenderfoots. Old Mrs. McClung, who kept a hotel on the road, peered at us with her hand shading her eyes, and failed to identify us till we saluted her, when she threw up her arms and exclaimed, "Why, boys, is it you! I declare I didn't know you; I thought it was a couple of gentlemen." Rather an equivocal compliment, we thought. We refused her invitation to "light," and after gossiping a few minutes with the old lady and her daughters Margaret and Dorinda, continued on our way. We called on Bob McGarvey at Belvidere, and "took something" with Pete Snyder at Wood's Crossing, reaching Sonora before noon.

The delegates came in from all quarters—Democratic in sentiment, Democratic in dress, Democratic in the matter of drinks; every man of them could truthfully and consistently endorse David B. Hill's well-known avowal and exclaim exultantly, "I am a Democrat." The clans gathered from the mountains, the flats, the rivers, and the valleys. Big Oak Flat, the Garotes, Rattlesnake, Jacksonville, Wood's Creek, Chinese Camp, Green Springs, Black Springs, Belvidere, Jamestown, Tuttletown, Columbia, Shaw's Flat, the river Bars and all other precincts were represented. [Henry J.] Barber was there, Jim Coffroth, Judge [Leander] Quint, Charley Scott, Jim Mandeville, Major [P. L.] Solomon, Captain [T. N.] Cazneau, Captain Amy [C. B. Amy or Fleming Amyx?], Jim McLean, Harry Worthington, and A. M. Francisco were all present. In fact, the prominent politicians came, not single spies but in battalions, all prepared to have a good time.[36]

We registered at the Placer Hotel, a fine new hostelry lately opened, and left our horses at Cooper & McCarthy's livery stable. The convention was organized at 2 o'clock, P.M., and after the appointment of committees, adjourned till the following day.

The Palace Saloon was the chief rendezvous for citizens and visitors. The proprietor, under the pseudonym of John Smith, was known by everybody and popular with the multitude. He was pleasant, accommodating, and always treated the boys to the matutinal cocktail. He accumulated a large fortune and disappeared. None knew whence he came or whither he went; even his name was unknown by those among whom he resided for years.

The saloon was gorgeously furnished, and money was freely lavished to make the place attractive. Gold pitcher, gold spoons, gold muddlers, mirrors, easy chairs, settees, etc., no end. Though the establishment was a combination of saloon and bagnio, none seemed to consider that he lost caste by patronizing the bar, which was always stocked with the best of liquors. Judges of the courts, governors, Senators, Congressmen, candidates for office and all officials high and low, drank with the proletariat at the Palace Saloon, where the man in broadcloth hobnobbed with him of the flannel shirt.

When the delegates assembled next day, there was less friction than in the convention of the year before, though the machine which had its headquarters in Sonora was still powerful. The contest over the nomination for county clerk was a hot one. Bob had the delegates from the river Bars and the outlying districts, but the machine controlled those from the large towns. The vote was close, but Bob was defeated for the nomination. A few years after, however, he was nominated and elected, and held the office for several successive terms. The Democratic candidates were all elected that year, and Major Solomon, who was again chosen sheriff, appointed Tom [Gardiner] collector of foreign licenses.[37]

Hitherto I have said little about lynchings, shooting scrapes, and public executions, as the subject is distasteful. Though a witness to eight cases of deliberate homicide while in California, the details, except in the instances recorded, are too revolting for publication, even if I had space to spare.

All executions of those who were tried, convicted, and sentenced by the judge, were public. When a criminal was hanged, a morbid curiosity to witness the performance drew crowds to the county seat. Such exhibitions were repugnant to me, and I persistently avoided them except in one instance, when I happened in Sonora on the day of execution.

A man named [Robert] Bruce had been convicted and sentenced for the murder and robbery of an inoffensive Chinaman [Mexican]. Justice viewed with a lenient eye homicides committed in hot blood, but where robbery was the incentive, the criminal had the sympathy of neither the court nor the jury, and in case of conviction was strung up in the presence of the multitude. The man Bruce was found guilty of flagrant, unjustifiable, deliberate murder for the purpose of gain, and I decided for once [December 8, 1854] to see a criminal "worked off."

Major Solomon, the sheriff, gave me a position in rear of the drop, which, when it fell, hid the body from view of those in front of the scaffold. The condemned was brought to the place of execution and mounted the platform attended by a clergyman, the sheriff, and his deputies. Major Solomon, who was naturally kind-hearted, disliked the performance, and would have gladly delegated his duty to another, but the law was explicit and he was compelled to act as hangman.

The prisoner, who seemed resigned, evinced no show of weakness. He coolly took hold of the rope, measured the slack, and suggested that the fall was insufficient, which at his instigation was increased to six feet. The prisoner asked for a glass of brandy, which was brought by a deputy sheriff, drank it, and said he was ready. The clergyman made a few remarks, in which were included a portion of the burial service, ending with a short prayer.

The condemned shook hands and bade goodbye to those who were about him; his arms and legs were pinioned, the black cap was drawn over his head, the rope was placed around his neck, the bolt was released, the drop fell, and the doomed man shot downward to eternity while the solemn words of the preacher were still lingering in my ear. "I am the resurrection and the life, saith our Lord; he that believeth in me though he were dead, yet shall he live; and whosoever liveth and believeth in me shall never die."

The fall apparently broke the man's neck, as aside from one spasmodic contraction of the lower limbs, there was no struggle. Immediately after it was straightened out, the rope, a new one, began untwisting, spinning its burden around to and fro for some minutes ere it came to rest. Soon afterward, the heart had ceased to beat, and the physicians pronounced life extinct. The remains were placed in a coffin and carried away for burial, and the vast crowd of spectators soon dispersed.[38]

When homicides were committed in hot blood without malice prepense, the perpetrators usually escaped scot-free. Sometimes, however, one would be sentenced to imprisonment for a short term, but the law was construed so liberally and public opinion was so averse to its strict construction, that occasionally one was acquitted who should have been convicted. A case in point occurs to me, which I will relate.

One, Billy W. [William H. Werth or Worth], a Virginian, was on trial for murder. He was charged with killing an old man named Kitterage [George Kittering], from Pennsylvania. Kitterage, who was a blacksmith, plied his calling at Campo Seco [Algerine Camp] and was well-known in that vicinity. He was a Democrat politically, free and outspoken in his advocacy of men and measures, and when excited never stopped to chew his words. In some canvassing tour, W. visited Campo Seco, where he met Kitterage, who opposed him. They got into an altercation and W. shot the old man. The unwarranted assassination of Kitterage, who had many friends, caused a tremendous sensation throughout the county, and W. was arrested and held to bail.[39]

At the next session of the Circuit Court [Fifth District Court], in which Judge Cramer [Charles Creanor] presided, W. appeared for trial. Both the slain and the slayer had powerful friends. The trial was conducted with much acrimony, and assumed a sectional aspect ere its conclusion.

The greatest difficulty was experienced in choosing a jury. The panel was soon exhausted, and with few exceptions all were excused and talesmen were brought in. Having reached the limit of peremptory challenges, the attorneys exercised their right to challenge for cause.

An illustration of the manner of questioning adopted by the counsel and sanctioned by the court will give the reader an idea how the choice of jurymen was made. A man was sworn to answer questions, and the following is about the style of interrogatory to which he was subjected:

"What is your name?"

"John Smith."

"What is your occupation?"

"I am a miner."

"Do you know the prisoner at the bar?"

"I do not."

"Did you know the man Kitterage who was killed?"

"I did not."

"Do you read the newspapers?"

"Sometimes."

"Have you read about this case?"

"Yes."

"Have you talked about it?"

"Yes, it has been a common topic throughout the county."

"Have you ever expressed an opinion regarding the guilt or innocence of the prisoner?

"I have not."

"Do you think that in case you should be accepted as a juryman you would judge dispassionately and render a fair and impartial verdict in accordance with the law and the evidence?"

"I see no reason why I should not."

"What is your nationality?"

"I am an American citizen."

"Native or foreign-born?"

"I am a native-born citizen."

"What State are you from?"

"Vermont.'

"What!!?"

"Vermont."

"Ah! We'll excuse you, Mr. Smith."

And the court ruled accordingly. The prejudice against a New England man sometimes almost amounted to social ostracism in that community.

A man from a Middle, Western, or Southern State could not be ruled out on account of his former residence, but in criminal cases Southerners were preferred by the defendant's counsel. As one lawyer remarked sententiously, "A Yankee is apt to be too d— pious and cold-blooded to give a prisoner a fair show." As a result of this prejudice, it was as hard for a New Englander to get on a jury in Tuolumne County in those days as for a rich man to get into the Kingdom of Heaven.

It was a long trial, in which eminent counsel were engaged on both sides, and it is probable that some of the old residents of Tuolumne County speak of it to this day. W. was acquitted, and, I think, removed to San Francisco.[40]

Bob and I returned home after the convention adjourned and on our way made several calls. We knew everybody that lived on the road, and being old residents, most everybody knew us. Wherever we stopped, we were welcomed, and if at mealtime were expected to join the family at table.

Shortly after returning from convention, I was subjected to a serious affliction which eventually necessitated a surgical operation. The pain I suffered for two or three weeks was so excruciating that at times it actually drove me crazy. The doctor came, pronounced my case an inflammation of the prostate gland, prescribed, and went home. The prescription did no good, the pain was incessant night and day, and the only way in which I could obtain relief was in the use of powerful narcotics. For a week or two I swallowed opium no end. A piece as big as a marble was requisite to kill the pain and put me to sleep for an hour or so. The cool water of the river seemed to afford relief, and a dozen times a day I would stand for a while in the current, but the relief was temporary and unsatisfactory. Disgusted with the doctors, I procured a copy of Grinn's *Domestic Medicine* and diagnosed my own case. Suppuration finally supervened, and as Doctor Grinn discussed the symptoms thoroughly, I was convinced that mine was a case of "fistula in ano," which conviction proved to be correct.

As the physician who came from Sonora charged $20 for each visit, I concluded it was cheaper for Mahomet to go to the mountain, so sent to Chinese Camp for a conveyance.

Angelina had come in with a calf a few weeks previous, which, remembering my experience with Oliver, I had tied up to wean it. Before leaving, I arranged to have it run with the cow while I was away.

When the carriage reported at the top of the hill, a donkey packed with a mattress served as an ambulance to carry me up the mountain. I was driven first to Sonora, but Doctor Claiborne hesitated about performing an operation, and advised me to go home where I could have proper attention. This advice did not accord with my ideas at all, so I was driven back to Jamestown, sent the carriage home, and put up at the hotel kept by Matchin & Streeter.[41]

Dr. John W. Dodge was at that time practicing in Jamestown. He had been a surgeon in the Navy, and when called in promised to "fix me out all right!" He was a jolly fellow whose confidence in his ability to cure me so encouraged me that I felt safe in following his advice.[42] He dieted me for several days, and when the time for the operation came, Bob and Jack Ward, another friend, were present. Chloroform was administered, and Bob afterward told me that when I passed from a conscious to a comatose state my last words were, "You can't have bread with one fish ball."

The operation though serious, was successful. When awakened and told that all was over, I was surprised, as I had felt no pain, but a casual glance at the knives and hooks on the table convinced me.

What a luxury it was to feel for the first time in weeks free from pain! How pleasing to look forward to the not-distant future when I should be restored to health! My friends congratulated me, and I was happy. The doctor administered a powerful astringent, had me removed to another bed, handed me a cigar, and told me to lie down and make myself comfortable. Bob remained for an hour or two, when satisfied that I was all right he returned home.

I remained at the hotel a month, but was confined to the bed only two or three days, during which there was no lack of company, which with an exuberance of books and cigars enabled me to pass the time comfortably. Mrs. Matchin, a very entertaining and agreeable young lady, occasionally came in for a chat, and her husband and Streeter were both sympathetic and attentive.

After a few days, I was able to go downstairs to the office, where I met old acquaintances, played euchre, and enjoyed myself hugely. The doctor had enjoined me from participating in vinous beverages, but the weather was hot and the temptation strong to indulge in a sherry cobbler sub rosa now and then despite his injunction. Notwithstanding his prohibition, the doctor frequently came to my room with a bottle, and, pouring out a drink, would hand it to me with the remark, "This is good, it will do you no harm, but beware of the rotgut down stairs."

Matchin, who was subsequently lieutenant governor of the State, was an old-line Whig, who swore by Henry Clay. One day Senator [William McKendree] Gwin, who was "looking after his fences," took dinner at the hotel and went away without paying for it. It was customary to deadhead prominent officials at all hotels, as it was considered that their presence drew enough extra customers to warrant so doing. Matchin, who did not subscribe to that doctrine, especially where a Democrat was concerned, was much disgruntled at what he termed "Gwin's cheek," and swore by the "great hook block" that if he ever came again, he should account for that dinner.[43]

During my period of convalescence, a shooting scrape occurred in Jamestown and a remarkable incident connected therewith induces me to refer to it here. A difficulty arose between the collector for the water company and a miner who disputed the correctness of his charges. The difficulty culminated in open hostilities; both parties drew their weapons, and a general bombardment ensued, wherein the miner was wounded and his adversary unharmed. The miner was shot in the leg and his thigh bone was broken. In his fall the bone was again fractured. Doctor Dodge was called, and the wounded man removed to the physician's office. The miner was a stalwart young fellow six feet high and about 30 years old. An attempt to find the bullet was unsuccessful, and the doctor decided that amputation was necessary in order to save the man's life. The miner objected to losing his limb, and though the surgeon assured him his only salvation was in amputation, he refused to have the operation performed. In a short time gangrene supervened, when the miner, compelled to choose between loss of limb and loss of life, consented to amputation.

A table was prepared in the office, the patient extended thereon, and an anesthetic administered. When the subject was reduced to insensibility, the doctor, assisted by his brother Mark, commenced operations. He first raised the skin and laid it back in sections, then cut the flesh, taking up and tying the arteries as he proceeded, till he came to the bone, which was quickly severed by the saw. Replacing the flaps of skin over the trunk, they were secured by stitches. The stump was bandaged, and the patient awakened. The surgeon gave him a huge pill of opium, which had the effect of putting him to sleep again.

"Now," said the doctor, when all was quiet, "I'm going to find that bullet." Taking the dissevered member, he removed the flesh from the thigh bone and disconnected it at the knee joint, placing the balance of the leg beneath a counter in a corner of the office. Investigation disclosed that the bone had been cut off about half an inch above the upper fracture caused by the fall. Some three inches below was the bullet hole. The ball had struck the bone fair and square, penetrating one side only. It then followed the pith and lodged in the knee joint.

While the surgeon was engaged in tracing the course of the bullet, the patient suddenly awoke and gave vent to the most heart-rending screams. "Turn my leg over, turn my leg over," he shouted. Amazed at the outburst, we listened for a moment, but the persistent cries and evident agony which induced them impelled compliance with the seemingly absurd request. Mark, the doctor's brother, discovered that the portion of the leg beneath the counter was reversed, so that the heel was where the toes should have been to correspond with the man's position on the table. The limb was turned over, when immediately the cries ceased and the patient relapsed into insensibility.

Whether it was imagination that caused the outcry, or whether a sympathy existed between the stump and the leg beneath the counter, is a question for scientists. The doctor confessed his inability to account for the incident, which I have represented briefly but faithfully in every respect.

After a month's sojourn at the hotel, the memory of which has always been a pleasant one, the doctor pronounced me sufficiently restored to return to the river. The night before my departure, he gave a champagne party, where, though present, I was a mere "looker on in Vienna," as stimulants were forbidden me.

Though still far from well, I was free from pain, but it was a year before my health was completely re-established. Immediately after my return to the Bar, I began to look after matters personal to myself, and discovered that in one instance at least, my instructions had not been carried out. The calf had not been returned to its mother, for in some way it had managed to slip its halter and had unaccountably disappeared. Of course, the cow was ruined for milking purposes, and my expectations of a milk diet were dissipated.

As the calf was less than a month old when lost, there seemed little hope of its survival, but considering there was possibility of it, I one day hailed Yong Lun, a vagabond China-man, and offered him fifty cents to find it. He started out, and in less than half an hour returned, shouting, "Ba-a ba-a," as he pointed to the mountainside. A couple of the boys went with him and soon returned with what was left of Barnaby Rudge, as the calf was called, which I do not believe weighed fifteen pounds. There must be a good deal of vitality in a calf, for how the deuce that animal managed to sustain life for a month with-out teeth, without water, and without sustenance of any kind except such as was afforded by the sparse shrubbery on the hillside in the midst of the dry season, was a mystery to all. With proper nourishment and care, the calf soon recuperated, and for a while was a sort of pet with the boys, but as he grew older, he grew mischievous, and I was com-pelled to banish him from camp.

XXIII

AT INDIAN BAR

Soon after my return from Jamestown, as I was incapacitated for active exertion, I started a store at Indian Bar, two miles below Swett's Bar. The population was not large and consisted mainly of Chinese. Mike [Keogh] hauled the materials of the building, which Bob [Gardiner] had occupied, from Campo Seco. This was, I think, the first wooden store building on the river below Jacksonville. Tom [Gardiner], who at that time made his headquarters at the Golden Ranch three miles away,[1] of which he owned a part, was interested in the store at Indian Bar.

At the place where the building was located, the mountain was steep, and its base bordered the river. This necessitated grading a site for the store, which was about fifty feet above the level of the stream ordinarily, and when finished, it was quite an imposing structure. The store was soon stocked with pork, beans, bacon, whiskey, rice, and such articles as go to make up the miner's commissariat.

As the Chinese trade was desirable, I employed a Celestial who acted as cook, drummer, and interpreter. His name was Incut, but it was abbreviated to "Cut," who understood but little English when he came, but was bright and quick to learn. There was a good deal of cardplaying in the store at night, and the Chinaman's sleep was often disturbed by the ejaculation of some impatient player when he requested an inattentive comrade to "cut," which exclamation aroused the cook, who thinking his name was called responded promptly, much to the amusement of the boys. He soon caught on, however, and the players' calls passed unnoticed. At first Cut was a great disappointment as a cook. He provided boiled pork and cabbage for breakfast one morning, at which I was so provoked that I made him sit down and eat the whole of it, though there was enough for six, and even now as I write, I can see his imploring eyes asking for a respite.

Though I sold whiskey, I kept no bar. A half-dozen tumblers on the head of a barrel were at the disposal of customers who came in, helped themselves from the faucet, and, as they passed out, held up one or more fingers to designate the number of drinks. Taken altogether, they were a bibulous crowd, and the whiskey barrel was frequently drained. They were the most inveterate cardplayers I ever encountered. For a while it was so that I could not sell a thing to a white man unless I played a game of "seven-up" to decide whether I should give the article or receive double-price.

One night, just as I was going to bed, a fellow came in and wanted a pair of shoes, price $4, and proposed to play cards for them. Rather reluctantly I sat down; fortune favored me and I beat him out of a dozen pairs of shoes. He refused to quit, I got sleepy, and the result was that at daylight we quit even, when he bought his shoes and went home. I, who had lost a night's rest, made a resolution which was strictly observed, that from that time I would play no more cards for dry goods, groceries, or clothing, limiting the stake to drinks or some trifling article.

It was a rule with me never to drink with the boys in my own place, who, when they found me inflexible, ceased to urge me. Thus was I able to control them. Sometimes a rough crowd gathered and there were disagreeable proceedings. The store roof was full of bullet holes, the result of sundry hilarious displays on the part of my customers. Though surrounded by a reckless, unscrupulous set, yet with the exception of the Sam McL[ean] episode, I was never assaulted or threatened with violence during all the years passed in California.

Having occasion to go away one day, I left Blanchard, the man who made the involuntary trip from San Francisco to Oregon,[2] in charge. I was away all night, and while I was gone, the boys kept Blanchard busy. They played cards all the time. The stock was low, and bacon, beans, and whiskey were the staple commodities. When Blanchard made his report, I discovered he had won about $200 worth of bacon from A., B., and C., which he considered ought to belong to him. Inasmuch as he represented me during my absence, and I paid him for it, his assumption seemed rather unreasonable. "Reverse the case," I said. "Suppose you had lost that amount, who would have suffered?" To this he had no answer.

The fact is, those boys could play cards for anything, and it was usually the "hard cases" who won. It was a good thing for the store, nevertheless, as I will explain.

Take for instance "A.," who is a mighty uncertain quantity, reckless, extravagant, and always in debt, the collection of which is at least questionable. He inveigles "B.," a steady, hard-working, forehanded fellow, into a game at cards and beats him out of, say, $50 worth of bacon. "A." goes to the grocer and says, "I don't want that bacon, if you will charge it to "B." and credit me $25 on my account, you may have it."

As "B." is perfectly good pay, and "A." both morally and financially shaky, his proposition is accepted as a matter of course. "A." is credited and "B." debited, in which transaction the grocer gets $25 on account of a bad debt and makes $25 on the charge to "B."

When the boys had money, they would play poker. When I retired at night while a game was in progress, a man was left to look after things and particularly charged to keep run of the "doubleheaders" which went to pay for the candles, and see that they were deposited in the candlestick. After going to bed, I was lulled to sleep by the monotonous expressions incident to the game and the constant chink of money as it was manipulated by the players.

They played the old-fashioned game. "Jack pots" were not in vogue then; neither was "draw poker." Sometimes, when one "passed out" on a good hand, he would show his anger by tearing his cards and calling for a new deck. Often in the morning the floor was littered with new cards, which the Chinaman would pick up, assort, replace what full decks he could make out of the lot in their covers, and put them on the shelf to be sold again.

The necessities of trade induced the purchase of a jackass for the transportation of merchandise to far-away cabins. The miners would drive him to their quarters, unpack him, and let him go, when he was sure to return home, where he invariably received a few handfuls of barley after making a trip. I called him "Alborak," after Mahomet's mule, which he rode to Paradise. Someone attached a card with a motto to the ass's neck, and I have seen strangers chase him half an hour to read the legend, "When shall we two meet again?" and then look all around to see if anybody was watching them.

Dick Clamp, a typical Irishman who had come out with Stevenson's Regiment,[3] attached himself to me as a sort of majordomo. Like all of his class, he was fond of whiskey, a jovial, good-natured fellow full of fun and frolic. Dick was heir to all the heel taps and lees in the liquor barrels, which he saved carefully, mixing whiskey, cherry brandy, port wine, and whatever else there might be in the line of stimulants indiscriminately in one cask. There was more drunk and headache in a quart of his mixture than in a barrel of Mexican pulque, which bears the palm in that respect.

One morning I was called away and left Dick in charge. The day previous some empty casks had been cleaned of their lees, and Dick had secured several gallons of "Clamp's cordial," as the boys called it. In the afternoon, when I returned, I was surprised to see two or three drunken men stretched out before the store door, and though Dick was comparatively sober, it was evident he had been no idle spectator of the debauch.

"Dick," I asked, "what the devil does all this mean?"

"It's Saint Patrick's Day, and we've been having a blow out."

"Ah! that accounts for it. Who are these men?"

"Irishmen from the crown of their heads to the sole of their feet."

"Do you know them?"

"Old friends, old friends, we've lived and loved together through many a changing year. This big fellow is John Dering, he's drunk as a biled owl now; that other is Reuben, you ought to hear him sing 'Norah Creina' once."

"I cannot understand why these men are in such a condition, both dead-drunk while you are able to get about."

"You see, they aren't used to mixed liquors, and that cordial of mine kind 'er surprised 'em. They'll be all right tomorrow."

"You have no business to give that stuff to white men, you'll poison somebody yet."

"They'll be all right tomorrow; you can't poison those fellows with liquor."

The two men were not all right next day. They lay in a stupor for twenty-four hours. The drink came near killing them, and it was a week before they were sufficiently restored to go to work again, but when they did come round, they steered clear of Dick's mixture and took their whiskey straight.

Miller, the newsman from Chinese Camp, made semi-monthly trips to all the river bars and distributed his magazines and newspapers.[4] Thus we were enabled to learn what was doing in the outside world.

The action of the Vigilance Committee in San Francisco excited a good deal of comment, and opinions were divided as to its expedience. The law and order men ranged themselves on one side, and the advocates of summary punishment on the other, and for a while it looked as if we might have a civil war in the State. The Governor called out the militia, the Vigilantes entrenched themselves, bade the State defiance and maintained their organization despite the law. [Charles] Cora, [James] Casey, and others of a class that for a time flourished unpunished, were captured, tried, condemned, and hanged. The organization finally disbanded voluntarily, but while it existed, it was a terror to evildoers, and made it exceedingly warm for the criminal element, many of whom fled from the State to avoid arrest.[5]

Though the Vigilantes carried things with a high hand, popular opinion sustained them, and there is no doubt that society was greatly benefited by their illegal acts.

During the period of quiescence necessitated by my physical condition, I used to sit in the store door and watch the grand old mountains in the distance whose peaks were covered with eternal snow. Though the thermometer sometimes stood at 100 on the river, and very seldom receded to the freezing point, a few hours' ride would carry one to where the snow was fifty feet deep. I do not believe there is another country in the world that within the same area exhibits such a diversity of surface, soil, and climate, as California. The mountain snow was conveyed by pack trains to Sonora and other large towns, where it was used by the saloonkeepers to concoct iced drinks.

The hill where the store stood ran down abruptly to the river. There was no gold in the bed of the stream, and the flat on the opposite side was by no means rich. In view of this fact, I conceived the idea that there had been a landslide which had covered the original bed of the river and diverted the water from its course.

Acting on this theory, I determined to run a tunnel into the hill beneath the store, hoping to strike the bed of the ancient stream, which I believed was not far away. In excavating for the foundation of the building, I had discovered that the debris from the mountainside was composed of a sort of sandstone easily penetrated by a hand drill. I did not believe that the sandstone extended far, and once through it, thought that the ledge would pitch downward to the bed of the old river. All this was mere hypothesis, however, and I dared not undertake the work at my own expense, so I arranged with an impecunious miner to provide a grubstake and furnish tools.

After working a while and running the tunnel about ten feet, the man was discouraged and quit work. A second and third man tried it, but got tired and jumped the job. The tunnel was now in twenty feet when I induced a man named William Pray from Quincy, Massachusetts, to go in on the same terms as his predecessors. Pray carried the tunnel ten feet farther when he too lost heart and would work no longer. These frequent disappointments, together with more pressing business, caused me to abandon the project, but subsequent events proved that my theory was correct. A hydraulic company who were washing the bank above, reached the locality of the tunnel a few years later, and I was notified that ten feet further would have pierced the sandstone and struck the gravel in the old river bed, which was rich in gold and paid many thousands in dividends to the fortunate miners who discovered it.

There was another store on the bar, the proprietor of which had a license to run a ferryboat. One day Ezekiel Jones, a customer of mine, advised me that Peck had promulgated a new rule that prohibited the free use of his boat except to his own patrons, all others being taxed twenty-five cents for passage and the same amount for every hundredweight of freight. This was rather arbitrary, and as nine-tenths of the people lived on the flat across the river, the rule, if enforced, would deprive me of most all my trade. So there seemed no way out of the dilemma except to provide a boat.

Bob owned an excellent boat about twenty feet long, flat-bottomed, with a square stern and sharp prow. He did not need it, as there were several other boats at Swett's Bar, so I purchased it. The expense of transporting the boat by land would have been considerable; therefore I resolved to run it through the canyon between the two points.

Thoroughly accustomed to handling the boat, I decided to take charge myself. As the canyon was beset with rocks, whirlpools, and eddies, I chose one Louis Chapman, a plucky youngster from Maine, to accompany me.

Waiting for a good stage of water that would carry the boat over the worst obstructions, I made preparation for the trip by providing extra paddles for use in case of emergency, put the craft in good shape, and when the time came, started to make the run. Chapman on his knees in the bow acted as pilot, and as the roar of the waters drowned his voice, he was instructed to raise his right or left hand when necessary to steer to starboard or port and keep a sharp lookout for rocks.

The rapids were quickly passed, but when we entered the thunderous current of the canyon, it required constant vigilance to avoid disaster. It was necessary to urge the boat in order to maintain steerage way, [and] watch the rocks and other obstructions; and as we swished past the dangerous points, two or three times narrowly escaping shipwreck, and shot out of the gorge into the smoother water below, there was cause for relief. The whole time of the passage did not exceed six minutes, but they were long, long, minutes to the passengers in that boat.

We hauled up in front of the store and proceeded to stretch a two-inch manila line across the river. The boat was attached to a patent block that traveled on the rope and was impelled to and fro by the current. The law of the State prohibited the establishment of a ferry within a mile of one that was licensed, but as I made no charge, there seemed no reason why I should not be permitted to use the boat.

Nevertheless my neighbor sued me, and the case was tried at the next term of the Circuit court. The fact that I charged no ferriage, and that the plaintiff had virtually compelled me to procure a boat by his rule discriminating against me, was pled in justification, and he was non-suited.

My neighbor owned a grindstone, the use of which was denied to my customers. On the strength of the successful defense in the ferry suit I bought a stone with patent rollers to run on. The boys set it up, and thereafter the sign "Free Ferry and Free Grindstone" attracted no little attention.

In the spring a company was formed to flume five hundred feet of the canyon between Indian and Morgan's bars—the same one into which the mule fell some years before. It was a rough, impracticable spot, but there was a good fall from the rapids above, which would give a strong current in the flume. The rapid could be dammed without much trouble, but the problem was how to find a foundation for the flume. The water in the canyon was very deep, and even at a low stage there was but little room between the precipitous wall and the river.

After a careful survey, we concluded that by blasting a few obstructions and building substantial abutments on the river side for the sleepers where there was a good rock bottom, the enterprise was feasible. The main difficulty was the fool dam which had to be constructed in twelve feet of water. There was one place, however, where two immense rocks stood within twelve feet of each other in the middle of the stream, between which was deep water. To put in a dam there with the appliances we had was no small contract; nevertheless, we resolved to try it and take the chances.

It was decided to build a crib of timber and sink it between the two rocks, loading the crib as we proceeded till it stood on the bottom. The outside was banked with sand after planking it. The head dam was built in the shoal water of the rapid and had four piers or cribs of timber, which faced the current at an angle of 45 degrees. Timbers were secured to the top, bottom, and midway of the cribs, and planked. In building the dam at that angle, it was considered that the weight of water in case of a freshet would tend to hold it more firmly in place, which indeed proved to be correct. The dam stopped the silt and gravel that came down, which gradually filled the stream above and strengthened the work, which stood firm as bilsa rock when the fall freshet came.

What prompted the undertaking was the fact that the ground near the head of the canyon had been immensely rich, and grew richer as it pitched into the deep water where it had been impracticable to follow the lead. It was simply that knowledge alone that induced us to risk our money in the enterprise, which was under the circumstances a formidable one.

There were eight in the company. Bob and I each owned a share, which was worked by substitution. The plan of operations was decided on, the boys went into the hills, chopped pine trees, and hewed them for the stringers and crossties. Bob and myself bought the lumber for the flume and became responsible for the payment therefor.

We engaged two excellent mechanics to boss the job, and work proceeded without intermission till the flume was completed. The fall from the rapids gave a strong current to turn two big water-wheels which operated four immense lift pumps that stood in a hole twenty feet deep. Taken altogether, the carpenters made a first-class job.

When all was ready, the pumps were started and the wheels went round merrily without a single hitch. They were connected with the pumps by a rope band with a "flemish eye" in either end, through which a lacing passed to take up the slack when necessary.

The water was lowered two feet the first day, which showed that there was very little leak in the dams. But the lower it got, the greater the strain on wheels and pumps, and the slower they moved. It is astonishing what a pressure there is in a column of water ten or twelve feet high. Those pumps, constructed of three-inch plank bound strongly with iron bands, carefully made and closely jointed, streamed water from every pore. The streams were infinitesimal, indeed, but it actually seemed as if the enormous pressure forced the water through the wood itself. As the water went down, the labor of the wheels was so increased that the friction of the wooden gudgeons was tremendous. We modified this to a great extent by placing "pork rinds" in the blocks. The strain was excessive, but nothing broke. The lower the water got, the less the area, and though the pumps worked more slowly, they gained steadily till at the expiration of ten days the water in the claim was nearly exhausted.

About this time, I was called away to attend the county convention as a delegate from Indian Bar. Horseback exercise was forbidden, so a carriage met me at the top of the hill, in which I rode to Sonora. Bob was also a delegate. We met many old acquaintances and the reunion was a pleasant one.[6]

I was away three days, and as I had left no word when I would return, there was no horse sent to meet me, so I left the buggy at the summit and started to walk down the mountain. Before I had gone far, an enormous bear track confronted me right in the middle of the road. The trail was a warm one, and it was evident that the bear had preceded me only a few minutes. Bear tracks were common enough not to create any surprise, especially in that neighborhood, and when on horseback no one noticed them. In the vicinity of the Golden Ranch, where cattle were slaughtered for market, bear tracks were as thick as sheep tracks in a farmyard. Grizzly bears, cinnamon bears, young bears, and old bears were constantly prowling round. They sometimes caught two or three in a night in traps at the slaughter pen.

Had I been on horseback, the sight of the big track in the road would have caused no alarm, but on foot the case was different. The Bar was a mile and a half away, the road ran through chamisal bushes, not a tree to flee to, and that track freshly made loomed up before me like a seventy-four gun ship as I followed it. The bear kept the middle of the road till near the base of the mountain, when it sheered off into the bushes, much to my relief, and I passed onward without stopping to investigate.

Dick met me as I approached the store, and his lengthened visage warned me that he had bad tidings.

"What is it, Dick? Spit it out," I said.

"Bad news, bad news," he replied.

"What is it? What is it? Don't keep me in suspense."

"The dam bursted yesterday and the claim is full of water."

"That is bad news, indeed; where are the boys?"

"All down there waiting for you."

This was perfectly awful. The boys were owing me, Bob and I were holden for lumber and materials, and unless the money therefor came out of the claim, it must come out of our pockets, which was by no means a consoling thought.

Without going to the store, I hastened to the claim, where I found the boys sitting around smoking their pipes and looking gloomy. They were all despondent, down-hearted and discouraged. Explanation showed that the cause of the disaster was a small sandbar on which the crib between the two rocks had rested at one end. The claim had been pumped out, and the leakage was so small that one pump easily kept it free. The immense pressure from without had forced the sand bar inwards, and as a natural result inundated the claim. The trifling cause of the calamity once ascertained, the remedy was not difficult.

"Now, boys," I said, "this disaster is through no fault of yours or mine. It was an accident which no human foresight could foresee. When the sandbar was forced inwards, the crib settled down on the solid rock and there is nothing to do but renew the embankment outside and try it again. So far as the claim itself is concerned, my interest is the same as each of yours, no more, no less. But there are other things to be considered. You must remember that I am at the rowing oar and stand by me as I have stood by you. I have the boarding house for you and the mechanics; I am bounden for the lumber and materials, and each of you owe me more or less on private account. I cannot believe that you will leave me in the lurch at this stage of the game. The pumps are here, the wheels are in good order, there are no leaks to contend against, we have seen the bottom once and we shall see it again if we go to work in earnest. There are yet two months and perhaps three before the rains come, and we can dry this claim and work it out long before then if we start in again."

After some discussion, the boys agreed to turn on again. Next morning they were at work; the break was repaired, and the pumps set going at noon, but the previous work had so worn them that from time to time they gave out. The rope was weakened, broke, and had to be spliced. The flemish eyes pulled out and had to be renewed. All these breakages delayed matters and caused a heap of trouble.

Though the boys worked, they lacked the ardor that characterized them at the commencement, and labored in a perfunctory way that showed little interest in the enterprise. The machinery frequently broke down at night, when they refused to respond to the call of the watchman, who came to me and I was compelled to turn out, go down, and dive to clear a choked pump or turn in a flemish eye that had drawn out. Yet I made no complaint and did what I could to encourage the others.

We did not wait to dry the claims thoroughly the second time before prospecting. As soon as the water was low enough to reach it, we began where we knew the rich dirt was, and in two days took out 144 ounces of gold dust. This good haul so encouraged us that things went better for a while, and the claim after many breakdowns and repairs was drained a second time.

At this period Joaquin, the notorious Mexican bandit with his gang of cutthroats, was committing murder and robbery throughout the whole vicinity. Only a few miles away, a merchant was killed and robbed, as was supposed, by the Mexican outlaw. Parties were out in pursuit of the highwaymen, and the whole county was excited over their repeated raids.[7]

It was while this excitement existed that our company made the strike, and the dust was in my charge. My sleeping room was separated from the storeroom by a cloth partition, and the treasure was placed in the bed for safe keeping. When I retired at night, it was customary to place my pistol, not under the pillow, but in the bed with me, where it was ready to grasp at short notice, and could not be abstracted without awakening me.

Of course, Joaquin's outrages were a common theme, and the murder of the neighboring merchant frequently discussed. These facts, together with the knowledge that everybody was aware that I was the custodian of the company's gold, made it very unpleasant for me, and for a few days my nerves were subjected to a constant strain, especially at night, and I was anxious to get rid of the treasure as soon as possible, but was compelled to hold it several days before it could be shipped safely.

While in this nervous condition, I was awakened one night by a noise in the store. Naturally my first thought was of Joaquin and his band, and my heart's pulsations responded to the idea. After listening for a while and hearing no further disturbance, I lit a candle and went out to investigate. As soon as I entered the store, the cause of the clatter was apparent. The rats, which were plentiful, had dislodged half a dozen cans of oysters from the top shelf, and it was their fall that had startled me. Provoked at the false alarm, yet thankful that matters were no worse, I blazed away at a big rat and shot his tail off close to his body. He survived, however, and for months afterward the short-tail rat was often seen about the premises. After that night's experience, I arranged with Frank Casey to sleep in the store till the exigency had passed.

Aside from the rich strike, which was soon exhausted, there was not much pay dirt in the canyon. The smooth rock was scoured by the floods, and except in a few crevices and sheltered places, there was nothing to be found. When we had thoroughly prospected and convinced ourselves that there was nothing more, the pump was stopped and the claim abandoned.

As the company was still indebted to me, I made a proposition to square the account, release all claims, and take the assets, provided they would remove the flume and pile the materials above high-water mark. This they agreed to do. The mechanics also agreed to a compromise, and their claims were settled. It was pretty rough on all concerned. The boys had lost their summer's work, and all hands felt blue. Nevertheless, they turned courageously and proceeded to take out the flume and machinery, which was all saved and piled beyond reach of the floods. I can hear them now as they swayed away on the long timbers and sang at their work of how

"There was a rich merchant in London did dwell"

and joined unanimously in the chorus:

"Ri tural, ri ural, ri ural, ri ee"

by which they timed their heaves at the fall.

When the work of taking out the flume and machinery was completed, the boarding house was discontinued, and the Chinese cook, whom the boys had christened "Bully Waterman," as he prided himself on having sailed as cook on the ship which that notorious skipper commanded,[8] was discharged, and with the donkey Alborack, which he had purchased, sought fresh fields.

Thus ended the season's work of the company. The experience was divided among all its members, and I had the assets to provide for the liabilities. These were subsequently sold to a company at Don Pedro's Bar, and in the spring floated down the river to that point. The proceeds remunerated me for the company's indebtedness with a surplus, which was applied pro rata on the individual debts of its members. All bills against the company were paid. Bob and I got out even, except the loss of labor in the claim, performed principally on account of "dead horses," which would have never been paid for otherwise.

There were a few boys on the Bar, reckless, free-hearted fellows, who accumulated debts thoughtlessly without adequate prospects or means of paying. They seemed to consider the grocer a sort of a public milch cow and his establishment an eleemosynary institution. They were honest, and would pay when they had the money, but were inconsiderate. They would play cards and in the event of losing would expect to have the amount chalked up as a matter of course.

Tom Severns, of Texas, was a boy of this stripe, a first-rate fellow but careless and inconsiderate beyond measure. I got out of patience with him one day and said, "Look here, Tom, you've got to wake up and go to work, you owe me $50 now and the debt is increasing daily."

"Do I owe you as much as that?"

"Yes, you do, and I don't propose that you shall make it any more."

"By thunder! I've prospected all over the neighborhood and couldn't find anything worth working. Only a few of the boys are making grub, and even the Chinamen are leaving. What the devil to do, I don't know. I thought of going to work for that ditch company that is taking the water from Six Bit Gulch to Don Pedro's, but they pay in scrip, and I can't use scrip or sell it."

"I tell you what I'll do, Tom. You go to work for the ditch company and I'll take your scrip and allow you par for it and furnish you with grub while you are at work for them. I think I can get rid of the scrip by and bye when the ditch is finished. You give me your note for what is already due and pay for your grub in scrip hereafter as you need it."

"That's fair, I'll do that. You write the note and I'll sign it and go to work on the ditch tomorrow morning."

I proceeded to write the note, when Tom stopped me and asked, "What is the price of that hat?"

"Five dollars," I replied.

"Well, I need a new hat bad; I'll take it and you can add it to the note."

Somewhat surprised at his innocent assurance, I was about to refuse, but a single glance at his dilapidated old tile convinced me it was time to "shoot it," and the price of the hat was embodied in the note. Severns went to work next day and stuck to his job till the note was paid, faithfully handing me all his scrip.

One night he came in from work and exclaimed excitedly, "Hell to pay up at Peck's."

Peck kept a boarding house. The tent stood beside his store with its gable end to the mountain. The kitchen was in the rear, and the long table ran lengthwise in front. There was a path on the hillside back of the tent, which Tom followed in going to and from his work on the ditch.

That night, while pursuing his usual route, Tom inadvertently stepped on a huge boulder weighing several hundred pounds, which his weight dislodged, and it went crashing down the declivity immediately in rear of Peck's cook house, which it struck with tremendous force and cleaned out fore and aft. The cook stove was demolished, the table and dishes smashed, and but for the temporary absence of the cook, he would have perhaps been killed. The stone made a straight wake through the whole length of the boarding house, and rolled down to the river in front.

The accident created great consternation on the premises, and next day the hillside in the rear was critically examined to ascertain whether there were any more loose rocks that might "fetch away" and do more damage. None ever suspected the cause of the accident. Severns kept shady, and I held his communication as confidential.

With that year the glory of Indian Bar departed. The miners deserted the place until there were not more than a dozen or so left. These had comfortable cabins, but little ambition. They had seen their hopes grow dim and die, and were content to remain as long as they could eke out a subsistence. Even the Chinese became disgusted, and sought other localities. My competitor on the Bar failed, and his creditors took possession of his store. My stock was suffered to run down till there was but little left. I closed up and returned to the old tent beneath the evergreen tree near the garden site. My health was now completely re-established, and I was fit to rough it as of old.

Tom [Gardiner], who had been in San Francisco for some weeks under the doctor's care, camped with me. Hydraulic mining had lately been introduced in the vicinity, by which method old abandoned claims were made to pay well by reason of the vast quantity of dirt put through the sluices. In my peregrinations among the surrounding mountains, I had discovered a stream which, though not perennial, carried a good deal of water during the rainy season, and sufficient for hydraulic purposes up to midsummer. The elevation was such that the water could be conveyed by means of a ditch to the adjacent river bars.

There was a flat half a mile above our cabin called Chambers' Bar, which was entirely deserted.[9] This Bar was some three acres in area and contained a very large supply of inferior gravel. There was a fine, large cabin on the flat which had been constructed by one Jonathan George, who had located a ranch there and claimed title to 160 acres of farming land. The flat was bounded by a bluff eighty feet high, from which a valley extended to the mountains half a mile distant. All was smooth greensward, shaded at intervals by evergreen oaks, and was the most delightful place imaginable for a residence.

The chief objection was its isolation. I have often thought of the locality in years since, and sometimes regretted that I ever left it, for the sun never shone on a lovelier spot.

George, while he occupied the cabin on Chambers' Bar, met with a queer experience. First his dog and then his cat suddenly and unaccountably disappeared. He procured another dog, which soon turned up missing. A third dog was tied in the rear of his cabin, a yelp from which awakened his master during the night, who turned over, took a fresh start, and went to sleep again. In the morning the third dog was gone. These successive disappearances, taken in connection with the yelp of the preceding night, excited a suspicion that the animals had been carried off by Chinamen for food. George resolved to watch. He procured a fourth canine, which he tied in a conspicuous spot, and armed with an old army musket "loaded for bear," Jonathan stationed himself by a small window in the cabin and awaited developments.

After a vigil of some hours, a whine from the dog notified him that business was about to commence. Presently he saw a dark form emerge from the gloom, aimed at it, and let fly. The responsive growl notified him that no Chinaman was interested in that affair, and as he was disinclined to gratify his curiosity at the moment, he turned in and slept till morning. When daylight came, George was out bright and early to see what he had shot. The dog was safe, but a bloody trail marked plainly the line of retreat adopted by the nocturnal visitor. Following the trail, it led him to a small gully, where he came upon the defunct remains of an enormous California lion. Thus was the mystery solved. It was the lion which had devoured the cat and three dogs, and would doubtless have got away with the fourth but for the intervention of the old musket. The carcass was given to the Chinamen, who held high carnival at the dinner table that day.

After figuring the thing out, I suggested to Tom that we should purchase George's cabin and ranch, construct a conduit from the mountain stream and try the hydraulic process at Chambers' Bar. Tom thought well of the proposition, and we decided to go in. He was delegated to secure title, while I explored the route of the proposed ditch. After a thorough examination, I found the project feasible, counted the number of flumes necessary, estimated the quantity of lumber required, and the probable expense of excavation.

Tom had no difficulty in arranging with George, and we purchased his interest for a nominal consideration. Having secured title, there was nothing to prevent proceeding with the enterprise. The first thing in order was to survey a route for the ditch, which was over a difficult country beset with chaparral and chamisal; and as the line followed the mountainside, it was tedious traveling.

I devised a simple instrument to mark the line of survey. This was nothing more than a straight-edge strip six feet long, to which was attached at right angles another strip five feet long. A plumb bob in the center of the straight-edge fell along the upright leg, which had a hole for the bob to rest when the leg stood perpendicular, and when it did so, the straight-edge was of course perfectly level. A pole five feet one inch long was prepared, and sights were taken every two rods. When this pole stood on the ground so that a sight along the level straight-edge struck its top, its bottom was just one inch lower than the bottom of the leg of the straight-edge; a stake was driven to mark the spot, and the level was moved up to the stake for another sight. This gave the ditch a fall of half an inch to the rod. This fall afforded a good current, and enabled the conduit, which was two-and-one-half feet at top, eighteen inches at bottom, and twenty inches deep, to carry an ample supply of water. The flumes, which were made of sluice lumber, were given a good deal bigger fall than the ditch, and though smaller had a greater capacity. Any old miner will understand this; the details are given for the general reader.

When arrangements were perfected, I proceeded to survey the line, beginning at the point where it was decided to dam the creek and take the water. The line was along the precipitous mountainsides, whose sinuosities were followed so as to maintain a proper level, and when a ravine intervened, it was left to be flumed and the ditch was continued on the opposite side. There were many difficulties to contend with, one of which was to get a man to hold the pole and drive the stakes, as the chaparral was so annoying that the stake-holder soon got disgusted.

It required about two days to do the surveying, after which I went over the line a second time to satisfy myself that the stakes were properly placed. There were no very bad places to flume. One length of twelve feet was generally sufficient. There was one bad gorge which, though but one hundred and twenty feet across where the flume spanned it, was a hundred feet deep.

When the survey was completed and verified, we proceeded to contract with some Chinese for the grading and excavation of the water course. The Celestials were paid one dollar and a quarter per rod for construction. The grubbing and grading on the steep mountainside was more laborious than the excavation, and at certain points the solid rock cropped out, necessitating the building of a stone wall where practicable, or the construction of a flume. The whole length of the ditch was three-and-one-half miles.

Some thirty Chinamen were engaged on the ditch, and established their quarters on the mountain. After a little preliminary instruction the work proceeded satisfactorily. The Mongolians were faithful, and showed considerable gumption in getting around bad spots. Their camp was quite an institution, and was visited daily by the meat peddlers and other itinerant merchants. The fact that while at work on the ditch they were exempted from the payment of the license tax was quite a consideration with the workmen.

The buckskin horse that I had received in exchange for the white mule had been broken to harness and was still in my possession. A teamster who desired to buy him agreed to deliver 2,500 feet of sluice lumber in payment, which I accepted. Thus the lumber for the flumes was provided. It was hauled as near as possible to where it was to be used, and carried on men's shoulders up the mountain to the ditch.

As the work proceeded, the necessary connections were made, but the deep gorge taxed my mechanical ingenuity. The gulch, which in time of rains was a raging torrent, required a substantial substructure for the flume, and when the trestle work was completed, it was really a creditable piece of engineering. The conduit across the ravine had a fall of twelve inches in its length of 120 feet, so that when the ditch was running full, the water in the flume did not exceed three inches in depth. The flume in the center was 100 feet above the bottom of the gorge, and it may be taken for granted that when working at that height, I assured myself that everything was secure below me. I was my own engineer, cut the trees, and placed the timbers, with the assistance of one man and a horse.

Between the gorge and the place of debouchment, there was a ridge to cross which required some fine figuring to graduate the fall. Though the ridge was narrow, not exceeding five or six rods in width, it was solid rock just beneath the surface, so that when I reached it, I was gratified to find that without an inch to spare my calculation was correct. From that point, all was downhill and plain sailing.

The rains held off that year till late in November, so that everything was finished before they came. I was much disturbed, however, by the fear that I had made some blunder in the survey, and looked forward anxiously to the time when I should be able to test its accuracy by actual demonstration.

When at length the rain did come, it came in the night. There was no cessation in the deluge next morning when I climbed the mountain on a tour of investigation. The rain was pouring down when I reached the head of the ditch, where the ravine was foaming, splashing, and roaring like a diminutive Niagara. The first sight of the ditch satisfied me that it had fall enough at the head, as the current was swifter than I anticipated, though not rapid enough to do any harm. I followed the water course along the mountain and was gratified to see that the uniformity of the current proved the correctness of the survey.

The water ran swiftly through the chute at the big gorge, which carried it easily, though not half full. But at one place the Chinamen had shirked. They had avoided a big rock that rested in the line of the ditch and passed below it. They had shifted the stakes to save labor. Here the water stopped and poured over the side of the ditch. With this exception the work had been properly done. The Chinamen were required to move the rock and reconstruct the ditch at that point, and in due time the water from the mountain was pouring over the eighty-foot bluff at Chambers' Bar.

XXIV

AT CHAMBERS' BAR

DECEMBER, 1855–APRIL, 1857

The successful introduction of water accomplished, we proceeded to set the sluices and begin washing. For several days the work continued, but though we tried different places, the yield was not half enough to cover the expense of wages. After consultation with Tom [Gardiner], who spent most of his time at the Golden Ranch, we decided to quit prospecting and discharge the crew.

The failure of the enterprise was soon bruited, and the quid nuncs found a fruitful subject of discussion. I was denounced as a visionary fool, and at times felt that the denunciation was deserved. We had expended $2,500, taken the chances, and lost. Without pay dirt to wash, the water was useless. "I knew it would be a failure" was the universal comment, and though some sympathized with us, others declared that "the whole enterprise was a Utopian scheme from its first inception, that the Bar had been worked out years before, and there was not gold enough in it to tempt even a Chinaman, that Cal, though a sensible man in some respects, was a speculative cuss whom it was not safe to tie to."

As the reader may easily conceive, it was not exactly easy to listen to these comments, and it was very hard to give up the idea which had so long possessed me regarding Chambers' Bar. Though I had not succeeded in finding the deposit, a latent conviction still existed that it was there somewhere.

About a week after the discharge of the crew, I resolved to make another effort to find something, and requested a young Englishman to take a pick, pan, and shovel and go with me to Chambers' Bar. During the time of abandonment, the water had continued to flow over the bluff, and as we approached, we discovered it had cut a deep ditch in the flat below, which on examination showed yellow gravel at the bottom beneath about eight feet of sand and soil.

As soon as I discovered the substream, I cried out, "jump in, Ned, and try a panful of that gravel." He did so, and panned out about fifteen cents. This seemed too good to be true, and we tried another and another panful, but all yielded about the same.

"Eureka, Glory Halleluiah! We've struck it; who would have dreamed of finding pay-dirt away back here under the bluff? Drum up a crew, Ned, and we'll go to work after dinner."

Ned went for men, and I remained washing panful after panful to convince myself that it was no delusion. Providence had so ordered that the ditch debouched immediately above the Bar. It was the water, not man's perspicacity, to which I was indebted for the find. Falling perpendicularly a distance of eighty feet, its resistless force tore up sod, roots, and all obstructions and found its way to the auriferous deposit where no man would have ever dreamed that it existed. It was a piece of sheer good luck that one sel-

243

dom encounters, and the reaction from despondency to hope was so sudden that it almost took away my breath.

After dinner, we hurriedly set the sluices and with five men took out fifteen ounces that afternoon. The next day we began systematically, and cut a tail race six hundred feet to the river. I put on a gang of eight Chinamen, and brought Ephraim Williams from Indian Bar to boss them.

The bar which was covered by the sand bank lay parallel with the river, and the gravel grew deeper as we went back, its color changing from yellow to gray underneath the bluff, where it was four or five feet deep. It was an easy matter with the stream of water to remove the sand from the surface, which was washed through the tail race to the river, and the bar exposed as the work progressed. One day, while clearing off the sand, we washed out two human skeletons, which, as soon as exposed to the air, crumbled to dust. How they came there was a question, as the California Indians cremated their dead. They may have lain there for eons and belonged to some prehistoric race, the traces of whose existence are lost beyond the reach of human ken.

That Tom and I were rejoiced at the changed condition may be readily understood. I was especially pleased, as it was at my instigation the scheme was inaugurated.

After matters were systematized, work proceeded regularly and the ditch soon stood on its own bottom. I removed my quarters to the cabin at Chambers' Bar, which was large and convenient, and Williams lived with me. Ephraim was a farmer's boy from Ohio, who had been one of my customers at Indian Bar. He was one of the reckless, rollicking boys who had a penchant for fun and cards, though he played only at night, for he was a steady worker. His habits and love of cards were such that his usual condition was that of impecuniosity. He was an all-around good fellow, energetic and reliable. It was for that reason that before all others I chose him to take charge of my crew. He was the best axeman I ever knew. It was amusing to see him tackle a big tree, as he often did, for mere recreation. The cabin had a huge fireplace that would take in sticks six feet long. In the chilly, rainy evenings he would pile it high with body wood, then light his pipe and sit down and watch the cheerful blaze as he smoked contentedly. Inordinately fond of beans and bean soup, he could cook them to perfection, and I ate more beans while he lived with me than ever before or since, in the same space of time. They always tasted good, and we did not tire of them. Day after day for breakfast, dinner and supper it was beans or bean soup.

Williams, though generally good-natured, was at times impatient and irascible. He had no more regard for a Chinaman than for an ox, although he would not hurt one maliciously. It was customary, when the sluices were cleaned, to remove the slats that held the sides together and replace them after washing down. Williams frequently missed them and had to provide others, which so incensed him that when one night he caught an outside Chinaman gathering them up for firewood, he seized a slat and struck the Mongolian as he stooped, a tremendous blow across the posteriors. Giving a fearful yell, the

Chinaman dropped the sticks and fled for dear life. Examination showed that the slat which Williams held contained a tenpenny nail, the protruding point of which had severely wounded the stricken thief.

During the winter I had occasion to visit Maxwell's Creek to collect some debts from delinquent Chinamen. It was in February, on the anniversary of their New Year's Day. Proceeding to Coulterville, which is located on the creek, I collected the money and started next morning on my return. There were several other delinquents at Moccasin Creek, and it occurred to me that I might interview them on my way home and save a second journey.

Stopping at a place called Pino [Peñon] Blanco,[1] I asked the proprietor if there was a trail from that point to Moccasin Creek. He said "no," but pointing to a white quartz peak about five miles distant, told me to keep it in view and on the further side I would strike a trail leading from Moccasin to Big Oak Flat. As I knew that trail, I decided to try the short-cut with the quartz peak for my guide.

I was riding Honest John. The day was damp and drizzly; there was no path, and I was compelled to pick my way as best I could, sometimes following the course of a dry ravine, at others forcing a passage through the chaparral, keeping my landmark constantly in view. When within two miles of the peak, the course was intersected by a gulch which was too precipitous to cross, so I coasted it till I found a trail that apparently crossed it.

Turning into the path, I had proceeded but a few rods when Honest John pricked up his ears, snorted, and refused to go farther. Thinking it was perhaps a bear that frightened him, I shouted, as a bear will usually avoid a man. After waiting a while I concluded to ride on, but the mule concluded otherwise, and would not budge, so I decided to get off and explore.

Securing the mule firmly to a clump of chaparral, I started, pistol in hand, to investigate. The bushes grew close to the trail, which had evidently been made by wild animals in pursuit of water, and was very steep. Parting the bushes before me and peering cautiously as I descended, I had not gone far when I espied a pair of boots beneath the chaparral beside the trail. This sight was so unexpected, and so startled me, that I retreated incontinently, and in half a dozen strides was once more beside the mule with my heart pounding like a trip hammer.

A little consideration, however, convinced me that there was no cause for alarm, as, judging from the position of the boots, the wearer was lying with his head downhill, and was probably drunk. So believing, I approached the boots a second time, and discovered when I opened the bushes that partially concealed them, not a sleeping man, as expected, but a hideous skeleton, which confronted me with exposed teeth and orbless eye sockets. Though greatly surprised, curiosity impelled me to make a thorough examination of the remains, so that I might account for their presence in that lonesome spot.

The whole skeleton was lying intact, and with the exception of the leg bones, which were disconnected at the knee joint, and protruded from the boot legs, was in perfect condition. The bones were denuded of every particle of flesh, which was probably the work of insects. The skeleton lay in the position in which the body fell, and the bones, from which the tattered clothing had fallen away, were white as ivory.

The deceased must have been a man six feet high. A hole in the forehead just above the eye explained the manner of his death, and the spurs still attached to the long riding boots showed that he had been killed while on horseback. The clothing still covered a portion of the bones, and from its appearance I judged that the man had been assassinated not long before.

Having made these observations, I returned to the mule, but all my attempts to induce him to proceed were futile. A mule is proverbial for its obstinacy, and Honest John possessed more than an average share of that quality. Like Baker's cat, "Tom Quartz," when he was once sot, he was sot for good, and all the whipping, spurring, and coaxing in creation wouldn't [dis]lodge him an inch.

It was evident that the mule was afraid. He trembled in every limb, and the sweat poured off him like rain. Fright, sheer fright, was the cause of his obstinacy on that occasion, but what frightened him I could not understand. The bones were out of sight, and were so dry that they exhaled no odor. I tried to drive him, tried to lead him, and tried to back him, but after working an hour was forced to give up.

I sought to find another pass, but though I coasted the gulch up and down, was unable to discover one. It came on to rain, it was getting late in the day, the mist hid the quartz peak from view, so that even if the gulch were passed, it would be difficult to direct my course. These considerations impelled me reluctantly to turn back and go home by the road.

Honest John needed no urging on the return trip. His very soul seemed to be in his heels, and ere long I pulled up at Pino Blanco with the mule actually white with perspiration. Wet and uncomfortable, I went in and called for a glass of whiskey, and as I drank it told the saloonkeeper of my remarkable find. He listened attentively, and when my tale was ended, proceeded to tell the following story:

"Nearly a year ago, a man came in from Coulterville and asked as you did, for a trail to Big Oak Flat. I gave him the same directions I gave you. He left to follow the course pointed out and from that time was never heard of. Your description of the skeleton, the locality where you found it, and the fact of the spurs on the boots convinces me that you have found that man's bones. He was a drover, on his way from Mariposa to Big Oak Flat. He had been out collecting, and as I afterward learned, had about $6,000 with him when he rode up and asked me the way. His non-appearance at Big Oak Flat, where it was known he carried a good deal of money with him, excited suspicion of foul play, and a search was instituted. The man was traced to my place by parties who informed me of these details, and here the trace ended. You have found what is doubtless the drover's skeleton, who was probably followed, waylaid, and murdered in that gulch."

After my return home, I had an interview with Doctor Dodge and we arranged to go and get the skeleton, which he proposed to articulate, but for some reason the plan was never carried out. The discovery of those bones was a gruesome episode, and I would have liked well to rescue them from their lonely resting place, from whence they were probably never removed.

The claim at Chambers' Bar continued to pay well while the water lasted and honors were easy for Tom and myself. I sold the store building at Indian Bar with its contents to Edwards & Co., who succeeded Peck. They bought to prevent another from buying, and I traded out the purchase price by giving orders for supplies to the Chinese employes.

The Chinamen were faithful workers, obedient and tractable, always ready to respond when called on for service, no matter how disagreeable such service might be. I recall one instance where their fidelity to orders was severely tested.

The ravine which fed the ditch was difficult to dam, as it was full of crevices through which the water escaped. As the water decreased in volume, these crevices were carefully stopped with sand bags, which rotted in a few days and had to be replaced. As this was annoying, it occurred to me to substitute bags made of rawhide, which I thought would be more durable. Accordingly the rawhide bags were provided, but as they lay some days before it was necessary to use them, when the time did come for their removal to the dam, they distilled odors not at all calculated to remind one of "Araby the Blessed."

One morning, when two of the Chinamen were directed to transport the bags to the dam, they approached the steaming pile, smelled and retreated holding their noses in their fingers, and for once it looked as if they were about to refuse duty. This did not prove to be the case, as after a brief conference, they started away and presently returned with two long poles, to the ends of which they attached the bags. They shouldered the poles that sustained the burden and marched off complacently with the bags ten feet from their noses. An American would never have thought of that device to avoid the propinquity of the repulsive freight. The hides were no improvement, as they rotted quicker than the cloth bags, and were superseded by a dam of plank cut in profile to fit the inequalities of the rocky bottom.

On one occasion our attention was attracted by the continuous barking of a dog on the mountain, and when noon came, Williams, who was quite a sportsman, went up to see what the dog had treed. He soon returned and stated that the canine had a big wildcat corralled in a pine tree half a mile away. He loaded a shotgun and I took my revolver, and together we proceeded to assist the dog and, if possible, slaughter the cat. When we reached the tree, the cat was crouched comfortably on a limb, which was so situated that the range was a long one for a pistol, as the tree stood on a steep mountain. We could only see the cat from the lower side. The limb, a hundred feet above us, so shielded the animal that nothing but its head was visible.

Arranging that one piece should remain loaded ready for action in case the cat charged on us, I took position immediately below it and blazed away with the pistol. When the pistol was again loaded, Williams let fly with the gun. Thus we continued the bombardment for fifteen minutes, with the dog as an interested spectator. The mark was a small one, and the cat was tough. With a bullet through its head, it still clung to the branch with wonderful vitality. Finally, however, the cat, exhausted by loss of blood, let go, and came down with a rush. The dog, which was a pointer, was game, for no sooner had the cat struck the ground than he tackled it. The contest between canine and feline would no doubt have been disastrous to the dog, for the cat was twice his weight, but the fight was all out of it when it struck terra firma, and it soon gave up the ghost. It was a male, and weighed perhaps fifty pounds. We hooked a stick to the animal's jaw and dragged it to camp, where I took off the hide and gave the carcass to the Chinamen, who cooked and ate it. I do not think the cat panned out equal to their expectations, for the next day a Celestial remarked lugubriously, "Cat no good, John, too muchee strong," which was doubtless the case, as he was evidently an old stager.

The water failed in June, and operations were suspended till the rains came again. Experience had taught the necessity of economizing the water by saving what ran nights, so I resolved to build a reservoir. Back of the bluff, there was a depression between two mounds, across which I threw up an embankment ten feet high in the center, with a sluice gate to let off the water when needed. This reservoir formed quite a lake when full, and served an excellent purpose the next season.

Everybody respected our rights, for though we held more than the mining law entitled us to, we had expended our money and taken the chances. The discovery was owing to the introduction of water, without which the bar would have not been found. This fact was recognized by all, and during the interregnum between seasons, no one encroached on our claim at Chambers' Bar.

Bob, who the year previous had opened a store at Belvidere Flat near Chinese Camp,[2] came back to Swett's Bar about this time, leaving the place at Belvidere in charge of a deputy who had rather a rough experience.

There was a small safe in the Belvidere store, in which the miners deposited their savings. Soon after Bob left, this safe, with its contents, some $1,500, all belonging to outsiders, was carried off bodily. Some of those who had deposits in the safe suspected the clerk was concerned in the robbery. They caught him one night as he was going home from Chinese Camp, charged him with the theft, put a rope round his neck, and strung him up to a tree. He was a heavy man, advanced in years, and the torture he endured was frightful. All attempts to induce a confession were failures. Twice he was hanged till he was almost suffocated. As they were about to suspend him a third time, he protested his innocence, refused to confess, and told his captors that if they were determined to hang him he would not die with a lie on his lips. Finally they desisted, and the clerk, who was undoubtedly innocent, was suffered to depart. The safe was found a few weeks later in an abandoned shaft, where it had been thrown after it was blown open and rifled.

Bob proposed to me that summer to make an excursion to the Chowchilla River in the southern part of the State.[3] It was reported that there were many Chinese there whose trade was very desirable, as they were generally prompt in payment. He intended if the conditions warranted, to remove from Swett's Bar and open a store on the Chowchilla.

After discussing the probabilities we decided to make a tour of investigation. He rode a bay mare of mine called Topsy and I rode the buggy horse, which was used in the carriage purchased while horseback exercise was forbidden me. Topsy was a good saddle horse, but she had no slow gait to correspond with [that] of mine, which had a pace between a trot and a walk. When my horse paced slowly, Bob's trotted, and shook him up so lively that he remonstrated and insisted on going faster. The difference in the gait of the animals resulted in a separation before we returned home.

Crossing at Don Pedro's Bar, we stopped the first night at Coulterville, proceeded next day to Split Rock Ferry, passed through Bear Valley and hung up the second night at Mariposa. From there we reached our destination the same day. There were many Chinese on the Chowchilla, but there was also a multiplicity of stores. Moreover, the dust on the river bars was not so valuable as that on the Tuolumne, being alloyed with silver or some other metal that reduced its value to $14 an ounce. This was three dollars less than the average price. The prospect on the Chowchilla was not satisfactory, so the idea of locating there was abandoned.

Every trader was necessarily a judge of gold dust. There is a great difference in the looks of dust taken from different localities. An expert could tell at a glance just where the gold was taken from, if mined anywhere in his vicinity. The dust on the Chowchilla looked precisely like that on the Tuolumne, which was worth three dollars an ounce more. The difference in value could not be detected unless an assay was made. A dealer buys gold dust the same as he buys wheat, corn, or any other commodity, and if he loses, his judgment is alone to blame.

The fact of the difference in value between the Chowchilla and Tuolumne gold had been hitherto unknown to either of us, and the resemblance was so perfect that neither would have hesitated to pay the same price for the former as the latter. This suggested an idea which was discussed on our journey home, that one of us might locate on the Chowchilla, where he could doubtless buy 200 ounces a week, and meet the other at the Merced River, who would dispose of it at the current price of Tuolumne gold, thus realizing the difference in price of $600 weekly. Either of us could have easily sold the dust, as we were well known in Tuolumne County, but finally decided that it would not be a straight legitimate transaction and dismissed the idea.

We stopped at the new hotel in Mariposa on our return trip, where the cups and saucers were of a new-fangled pattern, the latter being merely receptacles for the cups and unfit to drink from. Bob, whose coffee was hot, was disgusted to find he could not pour it into his saucer and cool it, and demanded an old-style saucer, which was brought him. We had been accustomed as boys to pour from cup to saucer as was the universal usage, and to drink from the saucer, a cup plate being provided for every guest. This custom had become obsolete and unfashionable, and though I took kindly to the new style, Bob clung to that of his boyhood.

We pursued our journey together until we left the mountains, when my companion, tired of Topsy's jogtrot, decided to leave me behind and started off on a lope. I, who had been cautioned against undue exercise on horseback, rode slowly and maintained a steady gait, as it would carry me home by night, which was all I desired.

An hour or two after we parted, I discovered a huge watermelon under a tree by the roadside, which, as I approached it, I discovered was half-eaten. A big knife sticking in the melon was recognized as Bob's, and indicated that the half had been left for me. The day was sultry, and the melon was duly dispatched with thanks to the considerate provider.

During the interval between quitting work on the claim and the advent of the rainy season, I took matters easy, enjoyed myself as best I could, and had all sorts of adventures.

There was a strange horse in the drove which I had noticed several months before, and as he belonged to no one in the neighborhood, I resolved to catch him, advertise him, and in the event of no claimant appearing, appropriate him as treasure trove. He was an iron-gray, rough and untamed, and it took two days to get him into the corral where I lassoed him and tied him up. He broke his halter in the night and got away again. I caught him a second time, and as I was going to Sonora next day, resolved to ride him. It was very evident that he had been ridden, as his back was covered with saddle marks, so I had no hesitation in trying him.

In the morning I led the horse across the river and made him presentable by combing his mane and tail. It was very difficult to saddle him, but by covering his eyes I finally got the saddle on, and as he was full of grass, cinched the girth so tight that he resembled an "hour glass," as the cowboys say.

When all was ready, I jumped into the saddle and told the Chinaman who was holding the horse to cast off the halter and blinder. Immediately this was done, and before I had fairly found the stirrups, down went the animal's head, his four feet were drawn together, there was a sudden and violent spinal curvature, and the mustang executed a series of the most remarkable bucks imaginable. Before he had grunted twice, I was flying through space with the velocity of Halley's Comet, and landed on a sand bank about thirty feet away. The Chinaman grabbed the bridle, and I, though somewhat astonished, was not injured in the least.

Changing the snaffle bit for a cruel Mexican curb, I remounted, and without giving the horse time to think, socked the wicked spurs into his flanks and breasted the mountain, pushing him to the utmost till we reached the summit, when the animal was thoroughly winded and the starch pretty effectually taken out of him. From that time he went quietly and showed no temper. I passed through Chinese Camp and stopped for dinner at Bob's store in Belvidere. Here a very singular incident happened that was so much out of the ordinary it is worth telling.

While at Indian Bar I was robbed of a number of small gold specimens which had been preserved for keepsakes, together with a few trinkets that were in a tin box in my bedroom. No clue to the thief had ever been discovered. The box was emptied with the exception of a finger ring that belonged to Tom [Gardiner], in which was a small daguerreotype encased in glass.

I was sitting on a sack of barley reading a newspaper when Spooner, the clerk, called to me from an adjoining room saying he had something to show me. When I went to him, he handed me a peculiar gold coin that was minted by a Mormon company in California in 1849.[4] I remarked that it was a rarity, as the coins, being pure gold without alloy, had been retired from circulation, the metal being worth more than the face value. Just here it occurred to me that there was a similar coin in the box that was rifled at Indian Bar, and asked, "Where did you get this? I believe it belongs to me."

Spooner pointed to a Chinaman from whom he had just received it. The man kept a small store at Chinese Camp, and remembered from whom he got it. I resolved to follow the clue and ferret out the thief if possible. Retaining the coin with a promise to redeem it later, I started immediately after dinner with the man who bought it, and soon discovered from whom he received it. The piece was so uncommon that all remembered it, and as I held each man responsible till he pointed out who paid it to him, it was easily traced from hand to hand. I remained at Belvidere that night.

I went to bed early, rose with the lark next morning, and discovered the horse standing the whole length of the riata away from the barley provided the previous night. He had eaten nothing, and was evidently afraid of the bucket, which showed that he was unaccustomed to grain. I had some trouble in saddling him, which I finally accomplished, and was just going to breakfast when a teamster came along and desired to borrow the horse to look for his cattle, which were grazing in the vicinity. To this I readily assented, as I was confident the horse would buck at the start, and had no desire for another tumble.

The teamster untied the horse, jumped on, and the circus began just as I anticipated. Away went the teamster like a stone from a catapult; I grasped the bit, held on, and laughed, while the unfortunate swore and accused me of "putting up a job" on him. He felt of his bones to see how many were broken, but had sustained no harm. I explained that the animal was apt to give a little exhibition of that kind as a sort of prelude to the day's exercise, but after his little flurry would go quiet as a lamb. The teamster refused to trust him, and remarked sententiously that he "didn't want any more of it in his." Despite my assurance that the horse would go all right, he sought his cattle on foot.

After breakfast I mounted the mustang, which showed no further inclination to "cut up," and proceeded to follow the clue which eventually led to the thief. The coin had passed through a dozen hands, all within a circuit of a few miles, each man explaining how it came into his possession.

The thief was dumbfounded, and had no reasonable excuse to offer. It was proven that he was mining at Indian Bar when the coin was stolen, and there was no doubt that it was he who stole it.

It was only a couple of miles from where the thief was caught, to the store at Belvidere. I tied his hands, and placing the riata around his body, started to lead him there. The capture created a tremendous sensation among the Chinese, who gathered about me thick as leaves in Vallambrose, and by the time I reached the store, they mustered at least three hundred strong. There was no attempt to release the prisoner, neither was there any hostile demonstration whatever.

While I had the Mongolian in tow, it occurred to me to hold him to ransom, as that would be more satisfactory than condign punishment. This course was adopted, and his compatriots were given to understand that $200 would redeem the prisoner and save his life. They were allowed one hour to raise the money, in default of which the thief would be strung up right there in the presence of the multitude. The Chinese discussed the matter, and after much talk and many gesticulations the money was paid, and the prisoner released.

The recovery of the coin and the detection of the thief was an exceptional instance of good luck. I had merely stopped at the place for dinner. The visit was a casual one, and had not Spooner called me when the piece was tendered, I would have eaten my dinner and departed. There seemed to be a special providence attending the transaction. The coin has ever since been retained by me, and is now in the house where I am writing. After my return home, I had it converted into a watch key, and carried it attached to my fob ribbon for many years, but it was so heavy it wore out the ring sustaining it, when for fear of losing it I consigned it to the care of my wife, who placed it among her valuables.

Without giving details of operation at Chambers' Bar in the fall and winter of 1856 and 1857, it is sufficient to state that when the rains came, the work proceeded. The claim continued to pay well, and our good fortune was a subject of general comment. In the spring of '57 I prospected quietly and satisfied myself that we had already secured the cream, and before the end of the season were likely to come to skim milk. The bar beneath the bluff was about 200 feet long. The main thing that puzzled me was the character of the gravel under the 80-foot bluff. If the ledge pitched, the dirt was likely to grow richer as we went in. But there was no way to ascertain except to run a tunnel which I dared not do for fear of unpleasant disclosures.

The claim bore a good reputation, and an opportunity occurred to dispose of it at a good, round figure. The question was whether to accept the offer or follow the lead under the bluff, where it would be very expensive to work it even if it yielded well. If, on the other hand, the claim ran out, $3,000 invested in the ditch and appurtenances would be inevitably lost.

In April Bob came from Belvidere and advised me that a syndicate of Chinese traders desired to buy the claim. They were reliable, and had ample means to purchase. We canvassed the matter, and after careful consideration I decided to sell out. Tom was consulted, and was of course governed by our judgment. Bob returned home, had a conference with the syndicate, my proposition was accepted, and $2,000 paid on account, the balance to be paid when the papers were executed.

The documents were ready a few days later, and the claim with all its crooks, angles, dips, and sinuosities, together with the water right, ditch, flumes, reservoir, and all other property appertaining or belonging thereto was transferred to the syndicate.

The sale, which had been quietly made, excited a terrible commotion among my employes, who, when they heard of it, held an all-night session and denounced several of their comrades for depriving them of their job. Charges and recriminations were freely bandied, and from their actions I divined that some of their number had given the syndicate a cue and were interested in the transaction, while their co-mates were left out in the wet.

When the sale of the property at Chambers' Bar was consummated, I decided to go East. After many years I had accumulated a few thousands and felt that I could afford the trip. It was my intention to make a visit of a few months and return to the State of my adoption, but circumstances not foreseen prevented. The enterprise at Chambers' Bar was the last of my mining experience in California.

After my removal from the river, my headquarters were at Belvidere. Bob had sold out to Spooner, with whom I boarded till I took my departure for the East.

XXV

AT BELVIDERE FLAT

During the summer I was occupied in settling up outside matters, which, though not of vast importance, entailed no little trouble. Among other property, I owned half a dozen horses that were running out and scattered all over the country. Only one horse was kept up for use. The fall previous, Tom [Gardiner] had unfortunately foundered a fine saddle mare, and as he needed a horse, I exchanged Topsy for his animal and took the chances of her recovery. Taking the shoes from her feet, I turned her out, and when I removed to Belvidere, she had been running at large for six months.

When the mare was brought from the ranch to Belvidere, she was poor as a crow, but had entirely recovered the use of her limbs and was in high feather. Proper food and care soon brought her up, and in six weeks she was as fat and sleek as a mole. The mare was a roan, with four white feet and black mane, and tail fine and silky as a woman's hair. She was a splendid traveler, and would not break her gait for an obstruction three or four feet high or a ditch as wide. I enjoyed taking care of that animal, and spent hours under the big oaks in front of the store currying, washing her feet, and greasing her hoofs. And she repaid me for it. No man ever bestrode a finer saddle horse. I kept the mare blanketed in the stable, and whenever I went away, a crazy Chinaman who lived nearby would wash the blanket and hang it on a bush, where I always found it clean and ready for use on my return. With that animal to carry me, I took frequent trips that summer to every part of the county.

The buggy which I had purchased during my season of disability was seldom needed, as I preferred to travel on horseback. The women in the neighborhood made common stock of the vehicle, which was constantly on the go. On one occasion, when I wanted it for some purpose, I discovered it was gone. Sam, the cook, informed me that Mrs. McClung had taken it several days before. Rather provoked, I sent the cook with my compliments to Mrs. McClung and instructed him to tell her to "keep the buggy; I would make her a present of it."

A few days later Billy McClung came over and said his mother had a horse she would give me for the buggy and harness. I told him to send the horse over, and the next day it came. It was a stout, chunky sorrel mare, which the woman had ridden across the plains. I sold it a few days after to a butcher and guaranteed it would work in harness, as it was an American animal, which of course I considered had been properly broken. But the butcher brought the mare back, said he had hitched her to his wagon, when she balked and defied all his efforts to move her.

Surprised at the butcher's statement, I concluded that the animal had been spoiled by the women. Confident that she would work if properly handled, I one day hailed Jim Armstrong, who was passing with a four-mule team, and requested him to put the mare in the off wheel and drive her to Sonora. Jim hitched her up but she set back and held his whole team.

A few days afterward, Mike [Keogh] came from Stockton with a load for Spooner. When he departed on his return trip, he at my request hitched the mare at the wheel and started his big, heavy mules. They towed the recalcitrant animal along despite her opposition, and dragged her through the dirt like a plaything. A quarter of a mile of that treatment took the obstinacy all out of the balky quadruped, which regained its feet, took the collar, and from that time there was no further trouble. Mike drove her a second trip to Stockton, where he sold her for a good price.

I had some difficulty in recovering my stray horses, though I eventually found all but one, which I could get no trace of and finally abandoned the search. An old Spaniard, Don Pedro, who resided at Chinese Camp,[1] called on me one morning with testimonials from Snyder, who kept a hotel and livery stable. He was about to leave for the plains after stray horses belonging to people in the neighborhood. Snyder had sent him to me, knowing that I had some out. I had recovered all my animals with the exception of two, whose marks, brands, and general description I gave the Mexican with written authority to catch them and bring them in.

The old man went his way, and I heard no more of him till some weeks later, when a message came from Snyder stating that Don Pedro had been arrested and was in custody charged with horse-stealing. Snyder was sick and unable to go to the assistance of the prisoner, who had appealed to him for protection. He requested me to go and look after the matter, as the man was in a bad fix, and unless some friend interfered in his behalf, would undoubtedly be hanged next morning.

As the old Mexican was an honest, inoffensive citizen well-known in Chinese Camp and vicinity, my sympathies were awakened, and I determined to go to the rescue. Before daylight next day, I was in the saddle en route to the ranch on the Stanislaus, some forty miles distant, where the prisoner was held. I rode briskly, and Kate soon carried me to my destination, which I reached before nine o'clock. A group of ranchmen standing about the premises notified me that Judge Lynch's court was in session,[2] and hurriedly dismounting, I pushed my way through the assemblage and entered the house.

There were fifteen or twenty men inside, some of whom I knew and greeted. In a corner of the room sat the Mexican with his head bowed in his hands, who had apparently given up all hope of rescue. The stern, uncompromising attitude of his captors boded ill for the prisoner, who had been caught "in flagrante delicto" with their horses in his possession. He had been granted a short respite to enable him to bring evidence of his innocence of intentional criminality, and the time would expire in an hour. A sympathetic cowboy had voluntarily carried the news of the man's arrest to Snyder, at whose instance he had started on his mission.

I walked over to the Mexican and placed my hand on his shoulder. He raised his head at the touch, and the instantaneous change from despair to hope that transfigured his countenance as he recognized me will never be forgotten. All alone and friendless, unable to understand the language, ignorant of the specific charges against him, with only a vague and indistinct perception of why he had been arrested, the old man was tonguetied and incompetent to defend himself. My presence, and the touch on the shoulder convinced him that I was there in his interest, and he watched the proceedings with a hopeful but anxious expression.

A long discussion ensued. The ranchmen who had lost horses before made common cause with those whose animals had been found in the prisoner's possession, and demanded summary punishment. I apprised them of the estimation in which the prisoner was held by his neighbors at home, dwelt on the old man's character for honesty and integrity, related the circumstances under which he had started in pursuit of horses for myself and others, exhibited his authority from the owners, showed the marks and brands as set forth therein, and asked comparison with those on the horses the prisoner was driving when arrested.

An adjournment was had to the stock yard, where the horses were confined. I identified a gray mustang as my property and compared the brands with those depicted in the written description I had given the Spaniard. Snyder's brands were easily recognized on several animals. Even the brands, color, and other marks on the ranchmen's horses corresponded so closely with the written documents that the prisoner was excusable if not justified in assuming that they were the animals described.

All these facts were duly set forth, and the further fact that the man had driven the horses along the public highway was dwelt on to establish his innocence of criminal intent.

Some of the farmers sided with me, and some opposed me, but the consensus of opinion was favorable to the prisoner, who was discharged from custody, much to my relief and also much to the chagrin of those who had insisted on extreme measures. The ranchmen's horses were detained and the old man was permitted to go on with the others. I returned home pleased with the consciousness of having performed a generous action, which had probably saved an innocent man from the gallows tree.

There was a western boy mining at Montezuma Flat, a short distance from Spooner's store, who was quite a character. If in describing an event with which he was connected, the writer for once, like Mr. Wegg, "drops into poetry," let us trust the reader will excuse him, as there is no "extra charge":

> William Gost of Montezuma crossed the plains in '49,
> William was an early comer by the prairie schooner line;
> William's State was old Missouri, and his native county Pike
> He's my hero, and my story tells you how he made a strike.

> William Gost of Montezuma heard the wondrous tidings told
> By the hundred tongues of Rumor, all about the land of gold,
> And like Putnam, in the furrow left his plow and left his team,
> Longer disinclined to burrow, or to pull against the stream.

Bill was used to driving cattle, knew the nature of a mule,
Knew that that was half the battle in the struggle for the goal,
So, lit out for Independence, then the starting point for trains
Of Argonauts and their attendants on their trip across the plains.

'Twas a long and toilsome journey ere he reached the far frontier,
He was mighty short of money, and found transportation dear,
But he never once lost courage, for he kept his end in view,
Though at times hard up for forage, somehow managed to pull through.

He reached Fort Independence on a "sheeny April morn"
All alone, without attendance, worn with travel and forlorn,
Though at times within his bosom hope had struggled with despair,
He had feet, and pluck to use 'em, and his feet had brought him there.

Colonel Stubblefield's attention was attracted to the boy,
And when he heard him mention he was seeking for employ,
He made a proposition, which to William seemed a dream,
Based on one reserved condition, "Could he drive a six-mule team?"

"Can I drive six mules in harness! Why, sir, I was raised in Pike,
And we drove for old man Varness, me and my twin brother Ike,
I ain't much on education, such as people get in schools,
But, by gosh and thunderation! I know how to handle mules."

As metrical composition is rather a tax on the intellect, we will drop versification and leave Bill to find his way across the plains, the Rockies, the alkaline desert, the snow-clad Sierras, and once more introduce him at Belvidere. He had mined for a long time in the vicinity, but his penchant for fighting the tiger and attending fandangos kept him in a chronic state of hardupitiveness, no matter how well his claim paid.

It was customary with the Chinese to gather up the remains of their departed brethren at certain seasons and ship them home to the Flowery Kingdom for interment. It came to pass in the summer of 1857 that a box of bones that had been exhumed in the Tuttletown district[3] was brought to Belvidere for shipment. The wagon in which the remains were to be transported had not arrived when the box came, so those in charge applied for permission to deposit it temporarily in my stable, which was readily accorded.

That afternoon Bill Gost was in the store and remarked that there was to be a masquerade ball at Chinese Camp that night, and sorely bemoaned his impecuniosity, which prevented enjoyment of the festivities. He had heard of the deposit of bones in the stable and wondered what would happen in case they were not forthcoming when the wagon called.

I told him that Char Fung Mow, the dead Chinaman, had been a prominent character among his countrymen, and should anything happen to prevent shipment of his bones it would probably create an immense sensation in the Celestial ranks.

Bill whistled and withdrew. I dismissed the subject from mind and thought no more of it till a few hours later, when the wagon came. About seven o'clock that evening, there was a fearful outcry among the Chinamen. The wagon had come, but the bones were gone. Here was a pretty kettle of fish. My mind instantly reverted to the conversation with Bill Gost a few hours before. Though I said nothing, I was convinced that Bill, who was present, knew where the bones were.

The case was a serious one. The Chinese were excited, the wagon was waiting, and the devil was to pay generally. The Chinamen, who doubtless suspected that the box had been abstracted with speculative motives, after some discussion offered a reward of $25 for its recovery. As I anticipated, Bill Gost earned the reward. He came in a half an hour later with the bone box on his shoulder and made some explanation respecting its discovery that was not at all satisfactory to the Chinamen, who paid over the money with many a grimace.

Bill Gost attended the masquerade ball that night and no doubt enjoyed himself hugely. But if the disembodied spirit of Char Fung Mow was ever permitted to take a ghostly tour through that region, it is highly probable that it sought out the dormitory of William Gost and reproached him for his wicked and inexcusable act of gratifying his taste for dissipation in raising a stake by the abstraction of a dead man's bones.

During all the summer of 1857, I was out of business and had nothing to do except to collect debts and arrange for my departure in the early fall. Therefore I had plenty of time for recreation and enjoyed myself as best I could.

There were frequent raids on the Chinese quarters in the neighborhood of Belvidere, and numerous petty thefts were committed. The Chinamen complained of these larcenies, but took no action to abate them, as Mongolians had no standing in court and dared not resort to the "lex talionis." One day the Chinese cook informed me of these depredations, and I instructed him to tell his countrymen to capture the next intruder and I would try and have him punished.

A few nights afterward, I was aroused from sleep by the cook, who exclaimed excitedly, "Misser Cal, Misser Cal, get up, Chinamen catch um lobber." I arose and dressed myself, and went to where they had the man, whom I discovered was a diminutive Greaser that had been captured in one of their tents. He was such an insignificant specimen of humanity that I was disposed to let him go, as he was apparently half-witted; moreover, so far as it appeared, he had stolen nothing and there was no evidence to convict him.

Nevertheless, the Chinese reminded me of my promise and insisted that the Greaser should be punished, so I resolved to gratify them and have some fun myself. There were about five hundred Chinamen in attendance, and the shouting, noise, and confusion were simply deafening. In the midst of the crowd stood the lone Mexican, trembling like an aspen leaf and half frightened out of his life.

I decided to take the prisoner to Chinese Camp and surrender him to the constable, and in order to make the procession as imposing as possible, directed every man to provide himself with a candle and follow me.

The Greaser's hands were tied behind him, and the line was held by one of his captors. When the preparations were completed, I mounted my horse and led the procession. Immediately behind followed the prisoner, and the multitude, marching three abreast, each bearing a lighted candle, brought up the rear. The ranks extended half a mile and every man was shouting excitedly. Talk about Babel, it wasn't in it with that crowd. As we proceeded, the Mongolians on the route were awakened and joined the revel. I rode in front like Genghis Khan at the head of his Tartar hordes, and our descent on Chinese Camp was like that of the barbarians of the north on ancient Rome.

It was midnight when we reached the Camp. The noise and unusual illumination awakened everybody. A deputation of citizens came out to meet us and ascertain whether we came in peace or in war. I soon satisfied them on that point, and sent for the constable to take charge of the prisoner. He was in bed and refused to turn out, saying it was one of my larks, and he did not propose to be fooled. Nevertheless, he came finally, when I surrendered the prisoner and he was placed in the "lock up."

The next morning the Greaser was arraigned before the justice to answer the charge of robbery. The Chinese cook, who spoke English, was present as a witness, but was ruled out as the statutes provided that no Chinaman could testify in a case to which a white man was a party. I was called to the stand, but as I knew nothing except what I had heard from others, my testimony was worthless, and the prisoner was discharged.

The discharge of the Mexican caused consternation in the ranks of the Chinamen. They were unable to account for it, and concluded that I had been bribed by the Greaser's friends. Sam, the cook, came and asked, "How muchee that Gleaser give you let him go? S'pose Gleaser give you $50 let him go, Chinaman give you $100 to shut him up. Chinaman velly muchee scared. They say now Gleaser gone he get his friends and raise melly hell with the Chinamen."

The Chinese cooks and waiters sometimes mingled slang terms with their pigeon English, which they picked up in their intercourse with the whites. Jack Keeler, who kept a saloon in Stockton, had a bright Chinaman in his employ who was often called upon to act as interpreter in the courts. On one occasion a Chinese servant had been arrested charged with larceny from a compatriot. After having interpreted the evidence, Jack's Chinaman was himself called to the stand to testify in behalf of the defendant, and the judge proceeded to question him.

"John," queried the judge, "do you know this prisoner at the bar?"

"You bet."

"Do you consider him an honest man?"

"Straight as a string."

"Does he stand well among his countrymen?"

"High, low, jack and the game."

"Do you mean to say that his character is good?"

"Bully."

"Then from your own knowledge you believe he is a good man?"

"Bully, by G—d, Judge."

These replies were received without comment by the court, and as they were thoroughly intelligible and given without any consciousness of a breach of decorum on the part of the witness, who answered in accordance with his lights, they elicited no smiles from the spectators.

I tried in vain to quiet the fears of the Chinamen over the release of the Mexican, and endeavored to explain why the cook's testimony had been rejected as well as my own. They could not comprehend my explanation, and some of them packed up and went elsewhere.

As the day of my departure for home drew near, I determined to make a final effort to collect something on account of what was due from the boys on the river. I knew they would pay if they could, but as they were mostly "hard up," there was but little probability of extensive collections. Nevertheless, though it was a forlorn hope, I resolved to go and see them and say goodbye before I left the State. So one August morning I saddled my horse and started for the river.

The manner of collection was unique, but was characteristic of the times. As I met one after the other, I accosted them somewhat as follows:

"I am going home and have come down to say goodbye. You are owing me, and I would like to have you pay me. If you can't pay all, pay half. If you can't pay half, pay what you can. If you can't pay anything, come in and take a drink and we will call it square."

This mode of address was far more effective than one would suppose. Some who had a little paid a little, some who had nothing borrowed what they could and paid that, and some who could not raise anything frankly confessed, and were excused.

This was my last visit to Indian Bar. As I shook hands with the boys, they wished me well and bade me godspeed.

Tom [Gardiner] met me at Swett's Bar, and we adjourned to the shade of a tree on the hillside for what proved our final interview. We sat for an hour and discussed my departure. I knew while we talked that he would have liked to go with me. But as it was my intention to return in a few months, the thought never presented itself that I should see him no more forever. Though but 25 years old, the seeds of a mortal disease were in his system, and he had long been subjected to some chronic ailment that eventually carried him off. Though he had never while in California been physically capable of hard labor, his native courage never deserted him, and despite his valetudinarianism he was constantly on the move. What seemed singular, walking did not fatigue him, and as collector of foreign taxes, he would often trudge from camp to camp while his horse was idle at home. Unlike many of his contemporaries, he was never unduly harsh with the Chinese while in the execution of his official duties. Patient and considerate, the destitute Mongolian never appealed to his sympathies in vain.

That this forbearance was appreciated by the recipients was demonstrated when he died a few years later, when delegations of Chinese from Mariposa, Merced, Calaveras, and Stanislaus counties joined their countrymen of Tuolumne in paying respect to his memory by attending his funeral at Sonora and following his remains to their last resting place. For years afterward, the name of "Ah Tom" was a household word with the Celestials, and whenever mentioned awakened emotions of gratitude in many a Chinese heart. [He died October 1, 1862.]

The time was now at hand when I was to leave for the East. My business had been settled and closed up, and there was nothing to detain me. I had resolved to wait till the last minute before leaving for San Francisco, and tarry the shortest possible time in that city. It was now August, 1857, and since my departure in the spring of 1851, I had not visited the seacoast.

During the fortnight that intervened before steamer day I called on my friends in the vicinity. Among others of my old acquaintances was Mrs. McClung, to whom I paid my devoirs before leaving.

The old lady had heard of my intended departure, and as I entered the sitting room and established myself in a comfortable chair, she saluted me by saying,

"I understand you are going home to get married."

"That does not necessarily follow, Mrs. McClung, I have been a long time separated from my people and naturally desire to see them. The marriage question is altogether a secondary consideration, and I can assure you I have given the matter very little thought."

"Don't tell me! I know what you boys are, and at your age they are always thinking about getting married. Now you are coming back again, of course, and when you do come, don't for heaven's sake bring one of those hi-falutin,' nambypamby, stuck-up eastern girls with you. They ain't no earthly account in this country, and one of them would just wear your life out in six months. Now you just listen to me. In the first place, it would cost you $2,000 to go home and bring one of those girls from the East, and suppose you did bring one, what would she be good for up here in the mountains? She would soon get homesick and discontented, and would give you no peace of your life till you carried her back again. One of those girls may be well enough in the city, where she could drum the piano and go shopping every day, but what would she amount to cooped up in a log cabin with a dirt floor, or cooking at a campfire? What you want for a wife is one of our western girls who is accustomed to rough it, and ain't so gall-darned particular about where they live, what they eat, or how they are dressed. There are plenty of that kind hereabout who have crossed the plains, are strong and healthy, and not eternally sitting alongside a pillbox. Some of them are mighty good-looking girls, too. To be sure, they are not educated; they can't play the piano or talk what is called "society talk," but they can cook, wash, and mend, and milk cows if necessary, and that's the kind of a wife you want for this country."

"Ah! Mrs. McClung, you take a practical view of it, and no doubt you are right to a certain extent, but there are other things to be considered besides cooking, washing, and mending. I know a number of these western girls, and they are mighty nice girls, too, and would unquestionably make excellent wives, but I am at present inclined to believe with Saint Paul, who advises us that 'he who weddeth doeth well, but he who weds not doeth better.' My present idea is to steer clear of all conjugal entanglements and live a bachelor for a while longer and be my own master with none to question 'where goest thou? or whence comest thou?' "

"Well, well, well; I suppose you know best. I was only giving you some good, sound advice and thinking of you know whom. He is all tangled up with some girl down east, and fretting his life out because he can't bring her here. He knows that this is no place for her, and though she would probably come if he asked her, he is too proud to have her come. He knows that the society here would never suit her. She has been tenderly reared and thoroughly educated, but her rearing and education would only tend to make her more dissatisfied with her surroundings, where she would be like a lily-of-the-valley in the midst of a potato patch, out of character with everything. He can't go where she is, and he will not ask her to come where he is. So there you are. The result will be a fizzle. The match will be broken off and two lives will be spoiled. We all know he is a splendid fellow, and we all like him. It's too bad."

"Yes, it is disagreeable, that's a fact. But what can he do? Man proposes and God disposes. He made the proposition and God made the disposition. They are probably only one of hundreds of young couples in the same fix. Providence has so ordered that their lives are cast in different places. He is fishing in troubled waters, and has no desire to subject her to the same ordeal. When I go East, I may possibly call on the young lady and explain matters, but it is very questionable whether I do so, as I have no inclination to put my spoon in another man's dish. Well, I must be going. I'll think of your advice, and if when I return I can find some nice western girl to say 'yes' when I ask her, I'll freeze to her like a chicken to a hot johnnycake. Goodbye!"

"Goodbye! Be sure and come and see me when you come back, and tell me all about your visit."

A few days before leaving Belvidere, as I stood in the door at Spooner's place one afternoon, a young man came up and accosted me, inquiring if my name was G[ardiner].

"That is what folks call me hereabouts," I replied, "and I usually answer when so hailed."

"Don't you know me?" he asked.

"No, I do not, come nearer and let [me] have a look at you. You are so disguised with dust and dirt that even if I did know you, it would be difficult to identify you till you are cleaned up."

As he came nearer, I raised the hat from his head and exposed his auburn locks, which as soon as I saw them, gave me a clue to his identity.

"Art thou Prentice, the son of Ezekiel and Eliza?" I asked.

"Ecce Homo!" he replied.

"My stars! Is it possible! I never should have recognized you but for that red head. Where are you from?"

"From San Francisco. I reached Chinese Camp by stage and walked over from there."

"How did you find my whereabouts?"

"The simplest matter in the world. There was not a place I stopped at on the road but what somebody knew you. The stage driver and half the passengers knew you also, and told me just where to find you."

"It must be ten years since I saw you; you were only a boy when sauntering about the Mansion House. Come inside; the son of your father shall not lack hospitality in this ranch."

Such was my introduction to Prentice Mulford in California. He was some years my junior, and at the time I met him, was in about the same condition financially that I was when I made my advent at Horse Shoe Bar. This was his first visit to the mines, where he remained for many years. Though not successful as a gold-digger, he saw all the different phases of a miner's life. He was a man of more than average intelligence, and in after days gained considerable celebrity as a newspaper correspondent and as an author.

The first thing in order was a bath. I had rigged up a shower bath near the store, using a barrel secured to the limb of an oak tree as a reservoir, which the Chinaman kept constantly full. A valve in the bottom of the barrel covered an orifice which was covered below by a piece of tin pierced with small holes. There was a string attached to the valve by which it could be opened and closed at pleasure by one standing beneath. As the fall was about ten feet, when the valve was raised it gave the bather a generous douche.

That Prentice appreciated the bath goes without saying, as he was much soiled with the dust of the road. A thorough application of soap and water soon relieved him of the accumulated dirt and enabled him to enjoy the hearty meal which followed, with better appetite.

It was only two or three days previous to my departure that Prentice came, and I had but little time to attend to him. That night we went over to Chinese Camp, where I introduced him to the boys, and the next day he proceeded to the river, where Bob gave him a job.[4]

The evening before I took the stage for Stockton, I sent my saddle mare, Kate, to the livery stable. I had, months previous, arranged for her sale, with the understanding that I should retain possession to the time of my departure. That time had now come, and as I handed the bridle rein to Captain Covington, a neighbor, who volunteered to deliver the animal at the stable, I did so with a heavy heart, as it seemed like wrenching the last link that bound me to California. She had carried me many a weary mile by mountain gorge and arid plain, and had never failed me in an emergency.

> "Farewell! Farewell, my bonnie steed that standest meekly by,
> With proudly arched and glossy neck, and dark and fiery eye,
> Some other hand, less fond, must now thy corn and bed prepare,
> Thy silky mane, I braided once, must be another's care!

The morning sun shall dawn again, but never more with thee
Shall I gallop through the desert paths where we were wont to be."

Bob came up from the river, and we passed the night previous to my exit at Chinese Camp. Like myself, he considered that my visit would not extend over any great space of time, and confidently expected my return after a few months. Providence, however, had ordered otherwise, and we were destined to meet no more.

The great monetary crisis of '57 was at its height when I reached New York City, and the whole business world was in a state of effervescence. The banks had suspended, trade was demoralized, stocks were away down, money was scarce, business was virtually dead, and mercantile failures were numerous. Before a month had passed after my arrival, I became so involved while trying to assist others that a permanent stay was unavoidable. These unforeseen complications changed the whole tenor of my life.

Bob remained on the Pacific Coast and never again visited the East. He married a year or two later, was elected county clerk of Tuolumne, abandoned merchandising, and made his home in Sonora. He was re-elected to the office several times and was subsequently deputy State Comptroller. As years passed, we became so interested in our private affairs that correspondence virtually ceased. He raised a family in California who, strangers to their eastern kin, reside in their native State. Their father died in 1883 [1886].[5]

It was on a Thursday morning in September [the 17th] that I left Chinese Camp for San Francisco. The six horses attached to the stage hustled us along at a tremendous gait, and the driver, like Jehu, the grandson of Nimshi, drove furiously. Up hill and down dale, past dikes and ditches, past the Black Springs, past Green Springs, we soon left the mountains behind and in a few hours reached the Stanislaus at Knight's Ferry. Here we changed horses, and then away again to the next station, the horses traveling at a gallop throughout their ten-mile course.

Things had changed since when, eight years before, we had trudged beside Peck's wagon over this same road on our way to the mines; when, beneath a boiling August sun, [we had been] tortured with thirst and worn with travel, yet with hearts unbent and spirits brave, hopefully anticipating a successful future, with little idea of the toils and disappointments to which we were to be subjected. These illusions were dispelled after a few months' experience of the stern realities of a miner's life and the uncertainty attending the search for gold, a pursuit in which "few could reach the purposed aim, and thousands daily were undone."

As I write, my memory reverts to that toilsome journey, and in imagination I see the seven who constituted our coterie as they then appeared. All young and in possession of robust health, all free from any responsibility except for their own maintenance, and all confident of the good fortune which the future held in store. A few months later the scene changed, and the group was scattered, nevermore to be reassembled. Since then nearly fifty years have passed, and one by one, death has claimed them for his own.

Like bubble on the fountain, like spray upon the river,
Like dew upon the mountain, they have passed away forever

and now, weary and old with service, the writer alone is left to make this sad record.

[Napoleon] Griffing succumbed early, and was buried at Hawkins' Bar; Ed Howell returned to the East and has long slept with his fathers. Absy [Griffing] if still in the flesh, I know not of. Will Huntting returned home in '55. He engaged in business in a western State, accumulated a competency and died suddenly in 1892. After my return, our former intimate social relations were re-established, and I often visited him in his pleasant western home. Stephen [French], who is mentioned at length elsewhere, died in New York City in February, 1896.

Robert [Gardiner] was the only one who remained permanently in California, where his marriage and the advent of children detained him and hampered his movements. Well and favorably known throughout the southern part of the State, he was popular with all classes. Generous and free-hearted, too confident in the honesty of humankind, he was often victimized by his fellows, and that to an extent that forbade the accumulation of wealth. A prominent member of the society of Odd Fellows, at his death the brethren of his Lodge took charge of the funeral ceremonies. His remains were interred in the cemetery at Sonora, where a noble monument erected by the association marks his resting place, and shows in what esteem he was held by his contemporaries.

There, "each in his narrow cell forever laid," the brothers sleep side-by-side. Far away from their Island home, where the ceaseless waves of the broad Atlantic have for generations tolled the funeral dirge of their ancestors, may they rest peacefully, where the breezes from the Sierras fan the flowers upon their graves, and the resounding crash of avalanches peals their requiem.

The stage reached Stockton in due time, and on Friday evening I took passage on the steamboat for San Francisco. Just before the boat left, Mike [Keogh] came on board with letters from home, which had come in that day.

Mike was an excellent, reliable, thoughtful fellow, who had driven the team for years and was well-known from Stockton to Sonora. He was a great beau and very popular with the girls. When the opportunity occurred, he attended every ball within a radius of twenty miles. On one occasion he invited a girl to go with him to a cotillion party at Rattlesnake Creek. The young lady was anxious to go, but she unfortunately had no riding skirt, and the time was too short to procure one. Mike promised to remedy that objection, so it was waived, and when the appointed hour came, he was on hand with a saddle horse. There were a half-dozen couples at the start, which number was increased by accessions on the way. Mike's girl extemporized a skirt from a shawl, which answered the purpose till they reached Jacksonville, where all dismounted. The boys went in to "take something," and the girls sought a store, where they procured the material from which their nimble fingers soon manufactured a proper skirt, when all went on their way rejoicing. Thus it was always. No false delicacy interfered to prevent having a good time. If, when invited to attend a party, a girl lacked shoes proper to appear in, she would say so without hesitation, and when her beau came, he would bring the shoes with him. Living isolated as they did, there was no opportunity for shopping at short notice, and the young ladies were compelled at times to depend on their escort to supply slight deficiencies in their wardrobes.

Mike was out of the swim now, however, as he had taken a wife two years before, and as a result had abandoned the "colts" to train with the "work horses." He had become a staid married man and a father, hence he eschewed balls and like frivolities in favor of domestic life. He was always a hard worker, and teaming in the '50's was a killing business. The hill at Swett's Bar was an ugly one, and very difficult to descend. To Mike the very thought of the mountain was a bugbear, whenever he approached it with a loaded wagon carrying a freight of 16,000 pounds. He had so trained his mules that in descending the mountain they co-operated with almost human intelligence in overcoming the difficulties of the road. Most of the teamsters drove with a single line. Mike always used two lines, and had his team under perfect control, as was evident to whoever saw him make his way from the summit of the mountain to the river at its base. Every wheel was locked, and heavy iron shoes beneath acted as drags and prevented the wear of tires. The grade was so steep that every effort of the wheel mules was in the way of resistance to the impetus of the wagon. All their weight was on the breeching as the animals slid down the declivity and exerted their strength to resist the impulse of the vehicle. For a mile this strain continued, and when at last the descent was safely made, it was a cause of congratulation to all concerned.

Mike died only a year or two after I bade him goodbye on the boat at Stockton, and the co-partnership which had so long existed between him and Bob was dissolved by his demise. Among all my California friends, the names are few that are held in greater estimation than that of Michael Keogh.

I reached San Francisco on Saturday morning [September 19] and registered at the Palace Hotel. After breakfast, I made my way to the "market" on Long Wharf, where I recognized Luther H.—and hailed him by his patronymic, "Squire."[6] He had come out subsequent to my departure from the city, and at first was puzzled to account for the familiarity of my address.

He soon caught on, however, and shouted my name to his brother, who was asleep in the room above. John soon made his appearance on the stairs, half-dressed, and greeted me cordially. We had not met in many years. It was he with whom I made the rounds in New York City while waiting for the departure of the schooner *Ann D* for Norfolk, Va., in 1848. He was the "young man of the commercial marine" who saw me off at the wharf. He was older now. Ten years had changed his appearance. He was a man of fine bearing and distinguished presence. To the figure of a Hercules was joined the attractiveness of an Apollo.

After partaking of a hasty breakfast, John joined me, and together we proceeded to look about the city and note the changes that had taken place during my absence. San Francisco had grown amazingly, and the appearance of the town was greatly improved. The tents had been relegated to the outskirts, and fine buildings now occupied their former sites. The sand hills at Happy Valley had disappeared. The bay along the city front had been filled in, and Battery Street, that formerly ended at Broadway, had been extended to Long Wharf. Battery was no longer a frontier street, as others outside of it had been constructed with dirt from the sand hills. I have forgotten the names of these streets, as I was not familiar with the new district. That old landmark, the *Niantic* warehouse, had entirely disappeared.[7] The simple footpaths which I followed when I landed from the *Sylph* had been superseded by broad streets lined with imposing structures. Horse railways had been introduced, and we took a car for the Mission Dolores, which was now suburban, and a favorite resort of the populace. There we saw many fine cottages and other improvements that had worked a great transformation in the valley, which little resembled the locality as it appeared when Stephen and I first visited it in pursuit of oxen.

We spent the day in sightseeing, and met many old acquaintances who had taken up their residence in San Francisco, though most of the Argonauts from our vicinity had long before returned to their eastern homes.

The next day, Sunday, John, Luther, and myself took dinner with their sister, Mrs. Ayres, whose husband was a prominent physician in San Francisco.[8] In the evening we went downtown, where in company with several fellow townsmen, we sat talking till a late hour.

When Monday morning [September 21] came, there was but little margin between breakfast and the hour set for the steamer's sailing. Thus far I had made no arrangements for my passage. After purchasing a few articles necessary for the voyage, I proceeded to the steamship office to buy my ticket. As the vessel was to depart in an hour, I had no time to spare when I entered the office. Addressing the ticket agent, I requested him to select the most eligible vacant stateroom, stating that I would leave the selection to him, and asking that he would use his best judgment and act the same as he would for himself.

He smilingly assented, looked over the diagram, and chose a room midway of the steamer on the starboard side. As there were many passengers, I was rather surprised that such a room had been left vacant, but without asking questions accepted the ticket and started for the vessel.

On my way I stopped at the "Market," from whence a number of my acquaintances accompanied me to the wharf. A few minutes later the lines were cast off, and the steamer *Golden Gate* [*John L. Stephens*] proceeded on her voyage to Panama.[9]

XXVI

HOMEWARD BOUND

As the steamer pursued its course towards the Golden Gate, the harbor presented a different appearance from what it did when the good ship *Sylph* dropped her anchor in the bay on the 26th day of July, 1849. The chaotic fleet of abandoned vessels which then greeted our vision no longer existed. Their crews had been to the mines, had seen the elephant, and a majority of them had returned to the coast prepared to resume their calling. Seamen were no longer scarce in San Francisco, and no difficulty was experienced by shipmasters in getting full complements of men. Such of the derelict vessels as had not been dismantled and moored or beached on the city front for storeships, had been gotten away and were once more ploughing the ocean.

Matters in and about the harbor had assumed a more systematic appearance. Wharves had been constructed for the accommodation of vessels, which now loaded and discharged thereat, and lighters had become things of the past. The excessive charges for transportation from ship to shore which formerly obtained, now no longer prevailed, and were only spoken of in a reminiscent way by such as bewailed the departure of the "good old times." The old lightermen had made their fortunes, and such as had not killed themselves by undue labor and exposure had returned to their eastern homes to enjoy the fruits of their enterprise. The boatmen's occupation was now virtually ended, and their miniature flotilla which formerly blocked the landing in the vicinity of Clark's Point had disappeared with the advent of wharves.

Swept seaward by the receding tide, we rounded North Point and soon lost sight of Mount Diablo and other well-known landmarks. We passed the Presidio, passed the well-remembered rock with a hole through it, which had excited so much comment among the passengers as they observed it from the deck of the *Sylph* as she entered the harbor.

Thus far I had remained on deck and viewed with no little interest the changes which a few years had wrought. The entrance at the Golden Gate was no longer a matter of speculation to the bewildered mariner. That rugged headland which Captain G[ardiner] and I scanned so closely from the foretop of the *Sylph* while attempting to locate the passage to the harbor was now surmounted by a light house, which obviated all uncertainty regarding the entrance to the port. Twenty miles away, another light gleamed nightly from the Farallones, a beacon surer than quadrant, chronometer, or compass, which told the storm-tossed sailor that his voyage was nearly ended.[1] Pilot boats, easily distinguishable by the figures emblazoned on their sails and the characteristic lack of a fore topmast, rode lazily over the ocean swell, and everything indicated that California was no longer an unknown land. While these thoughts occupied my mind, the steamer passed outside the heads and met the perennial roll of the broad Pacific.

Once more upon the waters, and once more
The good ship bounds beneath me
as a steed that knows its rider.

Exhilarated with the thought that neither calms nor adverse breezes would delay our passage, I now for the first time sought my stateroom, which I had not yet visited. On boarding the steamer, I had handed my luggage to a porter and requested him to carry it to my berth. It had puzzled me to divine how it happened that a room had been reserved in what seemed to me such a desirable locality, and I desired to solve the mystery.

When I reached the stateroom, I discovered that the berth opposite mine was occupied by a young man who was evidently an invalid. With a natural repugnance to consorting with a sick man, I was at first disposed to regard his presence as an unmitigated nuisance, which had probably influenced others to avoid his company.

A few words, however, satisfied me that there was no cause for alarm, as the young man was not afflicted with any contagious complaint. He was a pleasant-spoken young fellow, and informed me that his was an internal trouble that necessitated perfect rest. He at times suffered great pain, but the spasms were brief and occurred infrequently. That he was a gentleman was apparent after a short conversation, and as we became better acquainted, I came to like him exceedingly, and during his intervals of freedom from bodily suffering, we enjoyed many hours of pleasant converse.

The returning Californians were nearly all strangers to one another, but were homogeneous, and with that spirit of bonhomie generated by consorting with the Argonauts, affiliated kindly and soon became familiar in their intercourse. Of course, there were cliques, as is always the case on ocean steamers, and these drank, smoked, and played cards together, excluding all outsiders from intimacy.

The *Golden Gate* [*John L. Stephens*] had a full complement of passengers, both in cabin and steerage. There were none among them, however, whom I had met previous to going on board. The fare was good, and the tables plentifully supplied with delicacies as well as substantials. Three regular meals were provided daily, to which the passengers, with appetites sharpened by the sea air, did ample justice. There were very few who suffered from sea-sickness, and the quota at meal-times was always full.

There were many women and children on board, and a number of the latter attached themselves to me, to whom I acted as a sort of dry nurse. The water tank in the saloon was taboo to the young ones, and it somehow became a part of my duty to see that they had their regular drinks. Every day at eleven o'clock I was accustomed to visit the water can, where, attended by a bevy of thirsty children, I dispensed the potable element, very much to their gratification. Their mothers seemed to take it as a matter of course that I should look after the kids, and from time to time would come to me to ascertain their whereabouts.

Maggie Barr, a young miss of seven or eight years, ruled the roost. Full of vitality, she took the lead in all the sports, and never hesitated to punish a youthful recalcitrant when occasion required. Like Shakespeare's soldier, "sudden and quick in quarrel," with her it was a word and a blow, and woe to the young one who excited her ire. Boys as well as girls succumbed to her authority, which was universally acknowledged, for she was as full of fight as a Comanche Indian, and would "pitch in" on the least provocation.

On one occasion, when tired of play, she came to me and, climbing on my knee, said, "Now Mr. G., let us talk sense."

"Very well," I replied, "what shall be talk about?"

"Have you ever read the *Swiss Family Robinson?*"

"Yes, I have; have you read it?"

"I read some of it, and Mama read the rest to me."

"Do you remember Fritz, and Jack, and Ernest?"

"Oh, yes, yes, and Francis, and the monkey, and the dogs, and the ostrich, and—and the, Oh, isn't it a nice story?"

Thus the discourse went on, till finally the little head fell back, the eyes closed, and the weary child dropped asleep in my arms. Her mother, ever watchful, came and carried her still sleeping to her stateroom. Forty years have passed since then, and the child that was, if still in the flesh, is now a mature woman. I wonder if she still remembered her trip from California! Should her eye ever fall on this page, it may be that the incident above narrated will awaken her recollection of "auld lang syne."

The steamer stopped at Manzanillo, a Mexican port, to take in treasure. Here we encountered a tremendous thunderstorm as we were leaving the roadstead just at suppertime, which created no little consternation among the women passengers. A violent gale of wind succeeded the storm, and during the night, which was dark as Erebus, the ship's officers displayed a good deal of anxiety, as we were on a lee shore.

The heavy rollers tossed the steamer about as if she were a mere chip in the ocean, and from time to time a sea boarded us and swept the deck fore and aft. Had ours been a sailing vessel, we never could have clawed off, but the engines contended successfully against old Boreas, and ere morning, the ship had secured a safe offing. The gale broke soon after daylight, and by the time breakfast was ready, all was serene.

That morning, as with visions of shipwreck in my mind I stood on the upper deck taking a general survey, I discovered what at first I took to be a boat immediately ahead, but as we approached it, it proved to be a tree. Anything that breaks the monotony of an ocean view has an attraction for the voyager, so I kept an eye on the object, which we passed only a few rods away. As we came near it, I saw something moving, which convinced me that the log had at least one passenger, which closer inspection showed was an immense turtle. It had probably been feeding on the barnacles with which the tree was covered. Frightened by the swish of the steamer, the reptile slid from its perch into the ocean depths, perhaps to return later and regale itself on the crustaceans which regard for its own safety had induced it temporarily to abandon.

The trip from San Francisco to Panama passed without special incident worthy of notice. Wagers were made on the day's run, card-playing went on in the saloon, constitutional walks fore and aft the deck after meals, smoking, drinking, and story-telling were the order of the day. In due time we made the land a little to the northward of Panama Bay, and in the course of the succeeding night the anchor was dropped in the roadstead at Panama.[2]

When I came on deck next morning, the rays of the sun glinting on the pearl-clad spires of the old cathedrals reminded me forcibly of the weary waiting of weeks and the uncertainty attending my departure while domiciled in the ancient city. There was no waiting now. Immediately after breakfast the passengers were transferred to the landing, where a train was ready to transport them to Aspinwall.[3]

As there was no great quantity of luggage, it was soon stowed in the baggage car, and the train moved away on its journey to the Atlantic seaboard. The few stations along the route had each its full quota of spectators, to whom the sight of a railroad train was still a matter of interest. The shrubbery along the line of the road exhibited a luxuriance that is astonishing to one unaccustomed to the rapid growth of vegetation in the torrid zone. The railroad authorities are compelled to keep a force constantly at work to prevent the shrubbery from overgrowing the track.

The original wooden bridge across the ravines and water courses had been long before superseded by iron ones, as it required but a few months in that climate with its humid atmosphere, aided by the millions of indigenous worms and borers, to destroy the most substantial wooden structure.

Though the train ran slowly, a few hours sufficed for the trip to Aspinwall, where there was a tremendous rush to secure berths on the steamer *Northern Light,* commanded by Captain Tinklepaugh, an experienced and competent seaman.[4] Though the heat was oppressive, the transfer of the baggage and treasure was soon accomplished, and late in the afternoon, the steamer proceeded on her voyage, which though comparatively a short one, was destined to be an eventful one.

The heat was almost insufferable for twenty-four hours after leaving Aspinwall, as there was no wind, and the vertical sun beat down unmercifully on the passengers, and for the time being made life a burden. They could find no relief above or between decks, as there was not sufficient air stirring to fill the wind-sails which hung slack and limp in the saloon.

My sympathies were excited by one sea-sick woman who was apparently traveling un-attended by either husband or nurse. There is no more pitiable spectacle than that of a lone woman suffering from "mal de mer." The lady in question was accompanied by three small children, the oldest of whom was not more than five years of age. She seemed to be neglected by everybody, as she reclined on a sofa in the torrid cabin. From time to time the stewardess would answer her call, but she was too busy to remain long, as her services were in constant demand. There was no one but the mother to attend to the little ones, who clustered around her, and she so sick she could hardly raise her head. Had I dared, I would have offered my assistance to care for the children, but was restrained by a fear that she might consider it an impertinence.

It is customary with those who are accustomed to the sea to make sport of such as are suffering from sea-sickness. They pass jokes and suggest all sorts of repulsive remedies. Some manage to take these jokes in good part despite their disquietude, as in the case of a passenger who was one of a half-dozen leaning over the lee rail and sacrificing to Neptune.

"Jim," said his friend, as he came and stood beside him, "are you sea-sick?"

"Yes, I am; do you suppose I am doing this for fun?"

"I think you must have a weak stomach."

"You think so, do you? Well, you just watch and see if I don't throw as far as any of 'em."

That man was like "Mark Tapley," capable of coming out strong under adverse circumstances, and exhibited a degree of jolliness which the occasion hardly warranted.

The living on board the *Northern Light* was excellent, and the tables were well provided. The steward was a stickler for ceremony, and saw that everything pertaining to table service was conducted secundum artem. All the waiters were Negroes. They were dressed in uniform and had evidently been well-drilled. Each waiter had his own bailiwick, which he retained during the voyage. At meal-times the steward would take his stand where he could overlook the table, and at the pressure of his bell, his dusky satellites would march in from the kitchen in Indian file, and, each carrying his plate of provisions, would seek his proper station. When all were in place, a second ring of the bell would cause them to raise the dishes in their hands and lean forward ready to deposit them on the table, and at the third ring, every dish struck the board simultaneously. The charge of that Negro brigade was always a source of amusement to the passengers.

There was an exuberance of wine at dinner. The passengers did not stint themselves in that respect; there were

> Bottles to the right of them, bottles to the left of them,
> Bottles all 'round them labeled and numbered

and all hands did justice to the vinous beverage. It was a common remark that one could track a California steamer by the "dead marines" floating in her wake.

The second day out was as hot as the preceding one, and the consumption of ice-water and the resultant perspiration were enormous. After supper that day, I lit a cigar and ascended to the upper deck, where, seated on a coil of rope in the very eyes of the vessel, I whistled for a breeze. There was not a breath of air stirring, and aside from the ever-present swell, the ocean was as smooth as a mill-pond.

There is very little twilight in that latitude, and the shades of night soon closed around me. As I sat in the darkness watching the phosphorescent waters of the Caribbean Sea, I was startled by a sudden jar which shook the vessel from stem to stern. This was succeeded by a second and third, when the steamer fetched up hard and fast on what my judgment told me was a reef. Hastening to the captain's room, whom I found with his chart before him, where he had been engaged pricking off his course, I asked,

"How is this, Captain? We seem to be aground."

"I do not understand it," he replied, "the chart gives us plenty of water here."

By this time, a vast crowd had collected about the office, and all was confusion and dismay. A moment's consideration convinced me that there was no immediate danger, as the ocean was smooth and the vessel rested easily upon the rocks. She appeared to have slid up on the reef without any violent concussion. Old Providence Island bore N.E. from us about five or six miles distant. Our position was not far from where the *U.S. Kearsarge* was wrecked two years ago. I am under the impression that the reefs are constantly growing in that vicinity, which fact makes old charts unreliable and necessitates frequent surveys. The sailing master of the *Kearsarge* was probably caught like Captain Tinklepaugh by relying too implicitly on his chart.

The scene on board the *Northern Light* that night was an impressive one, never to be forgotten by those who witnessed it. Women, who only a few minutes before had been full of life and gaiety in joyful anticipation of soon rejoining loved ones at home, wandered about the deck wringing their hands in dread of immediate dissolution. Strong men, who should have set a better example, let selfishness prevail over generosity and appeared arrayed in life preservers, the sight of which added confusion to the already frightened passengers. One after another, mothers with pale lips and disheveled hair, holding their children by the hand, appealed to me to tell them whether there was any danger.

What I could do, I did to allay their fears, and assured them that under present conditions they were perfectly safe, as the vessel had sustained no material damage and was resting quietly, with the probability of an early release. The steerage passengers were wild, and insisted that the boats should be lowered, and they set ashore on Old Providence Island. Their demand was complied with, and many were landed. I took an early occasion to visit my friend the invalid, in his stateroom, who was naturally much discomposed, as he was unable to help himself should the emergency require. Advising him to lie quiet and telling him that there was no immediate cause for alarm, I left him much relieved by my assurance, and with a promise to look after him in case of imminent danger, I returned to the deck.

Meanwhile, the ship's officers had not been idle. Immediately after the vessel struck, a boat was lowered and soundings taken, which showed more water ahead than astern. The pumps were sounded and gave no indication of a leak. An attempt was made to force the steamer over the reef. The engines were started with a full head of steam, but the attempt was abortive. Thinking perhaps the vessel had caught on a point of rock, which if broken off would release her, the mate came aft and requested the passengers to walk all to one side of the ship. This gave the steamer a tremendous list as she heeled over. Thus we walked from starboard to port and from port to starboard, careening the big vessel with our weight, but the mate's experiment was a failure. What the state of the tide was when we struck, I do not remember, but as the rise and fall in that quarter is only a few inches, it was perhaps disregarded.

While the mate was engaged in walking us to and fro, his colleagues were also busy. The flare of burning blue lights illumined the ship, and rockets shot skyward to attract the notice of passing vessels. These signals were answered both from the north and from the south, and we were relieved by the thought that in case we should require it, assistance was at hand.

All efforts to force the vessel over the reef having proved unavailing, it was decided to lighten the ship by discharging water from the boilers. This, however, failed to release us, and our supply of coal was mostly jettisoned, which so lessened the draft that just before daylight the steamer slipped off into deep water. The boats were dispatched for those passengers who had been landed, who, when they returned, were rather chagrined at their want of faith in the ship's officers, despite whose remonstrances they had deserted the vessel.

When daylight came, we discovered that in the event of need, help would have been extended. To windward was a bark bearing down to us with studding sails set to catch the light breeze that wafted her on her errand of mercy. It was she that had answered our signals the night previous. To leeward was the U.S.S. *Wabash*, steaming towards us with all sails furled.[5]

As they were yet some miles distant, we did not speak them. The *Northern Light* proceeded on her way, but as the remaining fuel was insufficient to carry us to New York, we were compelled to make for Havana to coal up.[6] This diversion from our course was a gratification rather than an annoyance to our passengers, as it gave them an opportunity to visit the "Queen of the Antilles" and acquaint themselves with the appearance and topography of its far-famed city.

It was night when we approached the island, and the light at Cape San Antonio shone resplendently, illuminating the waters far around. It was, I think, the most brilliant light I ever beheld. As our vessel was restrained by the port regulations from entering the harbor during the night, we lay off until daylight, and then proceeded to the anchorage.

The Morro Castle, which we passed as we entered the harbor, is very eligibly situated for protecting the port. The channel runs close under the walls of the fort, and the passage at the entrance is very narrow. The harbor itself is a fine one, land-locked, and protected from the ocean storms.

If I remember correctly, Spain was at that time engaged in a dispute with Mexico. Quite a large fleet of war vessels had made a rendezvous at Havana, and their flags and bands of music, with their boats plying to and fro, gave the port a joyous and attractive appearance.

As our steamer would be detained twenty-four hours while coaling, it gave the passengers a chance for a run on shore, which they were not slow to take advantage of. But certain formalities had to be attended to before they were permitted to land. Every passenger who went ashore was required to procure a passport, which was good only up to the time of the steamer's departure. This precaution seemed rather strange to us Yankees, accustomed to come and go without question, but as it was the law of the port, we of course complied with it. To show the formalities which hedge in a stranger, I give a copy of the permit issued to our passengers:

Jurisdiccion De la Habana   Registrado Cil Nº 2'687
El Brig Gobernador De Este Jurisdiccion
Concede permiso para disembarcar y pernoctar en este cuidad y sus barrios bajo las reglas que se expresan al respaldo a John Smith pasajero de transito Elegado a este puerto en-cloop Northern Light procedente de Aspinwall.

                                        Habana 10th de October 1857
                                        El Brigr Gobernador
                                          E Chavarria

El Sub Com—de policia encargado
del reconocimiento de buques—
Vale 8 rs. fs—Ho Averela—

On the back of this permit was endorsed the following warning in several languages:

WARNING

Transient passengers must present this permit on landing; and failing therein become liable to a fine of ten dollars or fifteen days imprisonment.

This permit authorizes them to stay in town or its suburbs for the time necessary to leave by the first opportunity for their ultimate destination.

Any transient passenger staying longer without previous authority from the Government, will be arrested until his departure from the island.

If on account of sickness or any important business he should wish to remain, he can obtain the necessary permit from the Government thro' the Commissary of the Ward.

In Havana passengers are allowed to land only at the special wharf designated for that purpose alongside the Derrick, where these permits will be distributed and the baggage be examined.

No passenger will be allowed to enter the city without subjecting to these requisites, and will be obliged to justify its fulfillment by presenting the permit and mark or sign which the Custom House agents put on the respective packages after inspection to the officer at the door of said landing office.

Passengers wishing to sleep on board will have to be there before eleven o'clock at night after which hour no boats are allowed to cross the harbor.

The landing or carrying arms of all sorts, is strictly prohibited by the police regulations to which infractors will be subjected.

For each of the above permits there was a charge of one dollar. So it seems that the city treasury or somebody was enriched to the extent of several hundred dollars by the disembarkation of our passengers.

Having complied with the forms of law, we landed; our permits were distributed; and our passengers were soon scattered about the city. About every other person we met was a hawker of lottery tickets, the peddling of which seemed to be confined to slaves and coolies. They were very respectful, however, and the simple negative, "No," went every time.

The sidewalks in Havana are an abomination, as they are not more than two feet wide. The ladies in our crowd, with their expansive crinolines, which were then the fashion, found locomotion difficult, and a majority of them chartered volantes and sought the suburbs, or confined their promenades to the park.

Those volantes are an institution peculiar to Havana. They have but two wheels and are similar to an old-fashioned one-horse gig. The shafts of the vehicles are about ten feet long, and the horse or mule which draws them is hitched at the extreme end of the thills. The driver, a Negro dressed in a shabby livery, sits on his horse beyond hearing or smelling distance of the occupants of the carriage. These vehicles seemed to be in great demand, but their passengers were mainly of the female sex.

The streets are very narrow, with the gutter in the middle of the roadway. About every other shop is occupied as a cigar factory. Some of the cigars are excellent, and some are execrable. I was fortunate enough after some search to strike a respectable shop, where I procured several hundred cigars, which though not much to look at, as they were three-cornered in shape, possessed a delicious flavor.

During their short stay in Havana, our passengers explored the town pretty thoroughly. With a friend I boarded a volante, and we were driven about the outskirts of the city. We visited the fish market, where we saw many specimens of the finny tribe which we were unable to classify. Like the vegetation of the island, the tenants of the waters are gorgeously colored, and their prismatic scales presented all the hues of the rainbow. If as attractive to the palate as to the sight, the fish must prove very acceptable in a first course at dinner.

At the hotel we discovered that the barkeeper was well up in the preparation of American drinks. He understood the mystery of a "sherry cobbler," and concocted several to our entire satisfaction. Ice, though out of character with the climate, was plentiful, and the cooling beverage, served in tall glasses emblazoned with grotesque figures, was exceedingly refreshing. That the cobblers were appreciated was evidenced by the frequent calls of our countrymen, who occupied seats at the tables scattered about the saloon.

The day was passed in sightseeing, and at night we were treated to an unexpected exhibition which was indeed an agreeable surprise. It happened to be the anniversary of the Queen's birthday, and a great demonstration was made in honor thereof. The splendid park opposite the Governor's palace was illuminated, and from the fleet in the harbor came numerous martial bands, which enlivened the scene with their dulcet strains.

The streets outside the park were crowded with public and private vehicles, each filled with joyous occupants. The dark-eyed senoritas seemed the very embodiment of careless languor, as they lazily reclined on the cushions of the carriages and puffed their cigarettes complacently. From time to time their dark eyes flashed as they recognized some acquaintance in the crowd, and their musical cachinnations mingled pleasantly with the diapason of the bands. Bareheaded and arrayed in their gaudy costumes, they reminded me of butterflies, or as my friend remarked, they resembled "sections of a rainbow." It is undeniable, that the Cubans, however much they may lack in energy and enterprise, get the utmost out of life in the way of enjoyment.

The musicians, each band of whom was under the direction of a drum major, were stationed at intervals beside the fence that enclosed the park, and were so placed that they entirely surrounded it. At a signal, a tune was started and continued till, at a second signal, the performers stopped short and the refrain was taken up by the next in turn, and thus passed from band to band, completely encircling the park with one unbroken strain of music.

"Oh! Isn't it heavenly!!" exclaimed a lady in my vicinity.

"Yes, indeed!" replied her companion, "it really makes me wish that I were an angel."

The plaza was thronged with an appreciative audience that wandered to and fro along the sinuous walks. The multitude were decorous and well-behaved. There was no loud talking or interruption of any kind. All seemed bent on pleasure, and all apparently enjoyed the concert. Everybody smoked. Twenty times that night, I was asked for a light by strangers, and my cigar was invariably returned with the conventional salute, accompanied with the single word, "gracias!"

The steamer was to sail early next morning, and as the regulations of the port required that we should be on board by eleven o'clock, we were reluctantly compelled to conform thereto and seek the landing, from whence a boat soon transported us to the vessel.

What injury the *Northern Light* might have sustained by her unfortunate collision with the reef it was impossible to determine till the ship was placed in drydock; therefore, it was arranged that the steamship *Daniel Webster* should accompany us on the trip to New York. Accordingly the two steamers left Havana together, and were in close proximity during the voyage.

It was amusing to note the interest manifested by the inexpert ones among our passengers regarding the comparative speed of the two vessels. Whenever the helm was changed on board our ship, it of course changed the bearing of the attendant steamer. The *Daniel Webster* was sometimes seen over the bow, sometimes abeam, and occasionally astern, but never more than four or five miles away. Though the ships maintained the same relative position by compass, the bearings changed frequently, and the exclamation was often heard, "we are leaving her behind," or "she is leaving us behind," as the case might appear.

Off Charleston, S. C., we sighted a water-logged ship. We ran down to her, but there was no one on board, and the absence of the boats indicated that the crew had taken them, to escape in. There was quite a sea on, and the vessel was submerged to her deck. As we ran under her stern I discovered that she was from Kennebunk, Maine, but have forgotten her name. The ship was timber-laden, and as she was right in the route of vessels coming from the Gulf, was a very dangerous obstruction to navigation, as a collision with the derelict would have been almost as certain destruction as if she were a rock or an iceberg.

There is something in connection with an abandoned vessel as she is tossed about at the will of the winds and waves, that seems almost sentient. The deserted wheel, no longer efficacious in directing the ship's course, revolves to and fro under the impulse of the sea. The cracking blocks and yards, and the groaning bowsprit, the stoven bulwarks, the loose and broken ropes, the rent sails, the empty davits with their falls sweeping the water, the great hull itself, struggling against the impetuous assaults of the tireless surges, now rising to the summit of some tall wave and again sinking to the hollow as if to seek shelter from the persistent battery to which it is subjected, all seem to make a dumb appeal for assistance in their unequal combat with the resistless powers of the ocean.

We passed Cape Hatteras in the night. A dense fog prevailed, and as I watched the man on lookout peering into the Cimmerian waste, I wondered what he expected to see in that Egyptian darkness. It is perhaps possible that a vessel's lights might have pierced the fog, which enveloped us like a funeral pall, but I do not believe so. The darkness was such that one could almost feel it, and had we chanced to encounter a ship in our course, not Briareus with his hundred eyes could have discovered her in time to avoid a collision. It caused me more anxiety as the steamer plunged on amid the obscurity, than when she was piled up on the reef in the Caribbean Sea. The passengers were all asleep in their berths, apparently unconscious of any unusual risk. Not so the ship's officers. I know they felt nervous. The engines were slowed down, and our speed materially decreased. Fortune favored us, however, and we passed out of the fog unscathed.

Late in the afternoon, two days after passing Hatteras, we made the land off Barnegat and took a pilot. I strained my eyes to catch a glimpse of "Old Long Island's sea girt shore," but night closed in before the low coast was visible. After supper I lighted a cigar (forerunner of several that were consumed ere I sought my berth), and walked the deck in a reminiscent mood.

As night deepened, the light at Sandy Hook gleamed brightly in the distance. Long years had passed since I watched its receding rays from the deck of the *Crescent City*. Since then my experience had been a varied one. I had witnessed life in many different phases. Sometimes in sunshine, and sometimes in shadow, I had enjoyed the one, and endured the other. Though California had proved a Canaan to many an exile, and Ararat to many a shattered Ark, not all who sought its shores realized the hopes that impelled them to forsake friends, home, and kindred in pursuit of fickle Fortune.

Types of a restless class whose numbers are daily increasing in the inevitable progress of modern civilization, it is by such that new lands are settled. It is to such that California, Australia, and southern Africa owe their wondrous development.

In this inventive age, when through the agency of steam and electricity distance is virtually annihilated, a journey of a thousand miles is nothing. The circumnavigation of our Globe is a mere pleasure trip. The transit from Chicago to San Francisco occupies but a hundred hours, and the passenger who boards the steamer at Southampton on Monday can count confidently on eating his dinner in New York on Saturday.

It is this facility of communication that has militated to the advantage of new and remote settlements. The world owes much to the inventors of the steam engine and the electric telegraph. Watt and Stevenson by their wonderful ingenuity and perseverance, found the "weak side of nature and vanquished her." The very lightnings of heaven were made subservient to mankind, and yielded obedience to the philosophy of Morse.

The students of electricity are as yet in the Freshman Class. Who knows what possibilities may be connected with the esoteric powers of that tremendous natural agent! Who can say what thoughts may be today fermenting in the fecund brain of Edison! The savants in every department of knowledge and research are all alert. Every day some wonderful scientific discovery is promulgated as the result of their indefatigable experiments. In the colleges, the laboratories, the observatories, and dissecting rooms, scientists are industriously striving to lift the veil which conceals the occult laws of Nature.

Even the heavens have been photographed outside our immediate solar system, and mapped as intelligently to the astronomer as are the charts of ocean to the master mariner. Galileo, Herschel, and Isaac Newton, though they furnished clues, had no conception of the possibilities of human progress. Franklin, when he drew sparks from the key hanging to his kite-string, had little thought that those sparks would eventually kindle a flame that would illuminate cities, and awaken a power that would carry messages to the Antipodes and speed railroad trains across the continent from ocean to ocean.

Who can measure the boundless enterprise of man! Who can estimate the wonderful capacity of the human brain! On, on, on, upward, ever upward in the intellectual sphere, he who was created in the image of his Maker grows nearer to his Creator day by day. The hidden properties of earth, air, and water are gradually but certainly being disclosed. Though the Arctic and Antarctic Poles have thus far baffled his pursuit, man will yet surmount the icy barriers that guard them and place his foot on the Ultima Thule of the frozen zones.

Not content with his dominion over land and sea, man is today seriously considering the possibilities of aerial navigation. Already thousands of devices have been suggested, which though thus far failures, are premonitory of ultimate success. Philosophers no longer view ethereal voyages as beyond the scope of human ability; agreeing in the belief that it is only a question of time when man will follow the birds in their flight and vie with the eagle for supremacy in the realms of air.

What then? It may be that the Almighty, jealous of human enterprise, will decide that the utmost limit has been attained. He may then pronounce His fiat, and say, "Thus far shalt thou go, but no further, for I, the Lord thy God, am a jealous God, and will brook no joint jurisdiction in my peculiar domain." The Grand Circle is rounded! The hour has come when in the Homestead of Eternity, man's past and man's future must meet where Time disappeared!

From the rhapsodic digression let us return to my story, which is now almost ended. Too restless and excited for sleep, I remained on deck long after the other passengers had retired to their berths. The night was clear and starlit, the ocean was smooth, and the steamer rapidly made her way along the coast. Soon after midnight, we passed Sandy

Hook, entered the Narrows, and glided swiftly to the anchorage. Presently the lights of the vast city shining near and far assured me that the voyage was completed. Steam was shut off, the engines ceased to vibrate, the anchor was dropped, and[on October 16, 1857] the huge vessel swung to the tide off Staten Island.

Four decades have passed since then, and the writer who was at that period in the first flush of manhood, looks back to his last six years in California as the happiest in the whole course of his experience. No one can tell how dear the memory of that wild life is to him who has enjoyed it. How often his thoughts recur to it in the commonplace of civilized surroundings! Its freedom from anxiety, its dangers, its risks, its sense of animal health, its constant series of adventures; the exciting gallop over hill and plain, the thrilling explorations amid mountain gorges, all come back to me as I write this, and I lay aside my pen with a sigh as I bid my reader farewell and close my narrative.

NOTES

1. James W. Marshall made the epochal California find at Coloma, on the South Fork of the American River, January 24, 1848. For an analysis of the event, and all the known source documents, see Rodman W. Paul, *The California Gold Discovery* (Georgetown, Calif., 1966); and for a comprehensive biography of Marshall, see Theressa Gay, *James Wilson Marshall: Discoverer of California Gold* (Georgetown, Calif., 1967). Ralph P. Bieber, *Southern Trails to California in 1849* (Glendale, Calif., 1937), pp. 63–131, traces the spread of the news to the East Coast; generalized reports began to appear in mid-August, 1848, and detailed accounts a month later. Symptoms of gold fever were discernible by the end of November, and it became epidemic after President Polk's message to Congress, with supporting documents, on December 5.

2. The books referred to are Richard Henry Dana, *Two Years Before the Mast* (New York, 1840); Charles Wilkes, *Narrative of the United States Exploring Expedition. During the Years 1838, 1839, 1840, 1841, 1842* (Philadelphia, 1844, 5 vols.); and John Charles Frémont, *Report of the Exploring Expedition to the Rocky Mountains in the Year 1842 and to Oregon and North California in the Years 1843–'44* (Washington, 1845). Not specifically recalled by Gardiner but available late in 1848 was Frémont's *Geographical Memoir upon Upper California* (Washington, 1848), with its useful map by Charles Preuss.

3. For this history see John Haskell Kemble, *The Panama Route, 1848–1869* (Berkeley and Los Angeles, 1943).

4. See F. N. Otis, *Illustrated History of the Panama Railroad* (New York, 1861).

5. These remarks are somewhat misleading, in that the Panama Railroad was projected before the Gold Rush began. Surveys for the road began early in 1849, but there was no idea of completing it as soon as Gardiner implies. Difficulties were many, and it was not until January, 1855, that the first train ran from ocean to ocean.

6. For some of these routes, see Bieber's work cited in Note 1; and compare Dale L. Morgan and James R. Scobie, eds., *Three Years in California: William Perkins' Journal of Life at Sonora, 1849–1852* (Berkeley and Los Angeles, 1964), for the experiences of some who crossed Mexico to Mazatlan.

7. Not having traveled overland, Gardiner exaggerates the harassment by Indians; and lack of knowledge of the route was not in most instances a material factor in the experiences of such Forty-niners. (Trouble followed upon divergence from known routes.)

8. These sage remarks on the experiences of the organized companies who traveled by sea (and land) are fully borne out by the record.

9. See Note 1.

10. A chronological list of the early sailings for California, beginning December 14, 1848, is printed in the New York *Herald*, April 19, 1849. Up to that time 14,191 individuals had sailed in 226 vessels via Cape Horn, while 3,547 had sailed in 52 vessels for

Chagres. The list was purportedly complete for all sailings from eastern ports. By all routes, 19,717 passengers had sailed in 300 vessels.

11. The *Balance* sailed from New York April 1, 1849, and reached San Francisco the following November 24. Gardiner must have seen this ship in March, 1849. The Bancroft Library has an extensive series of letters written en route by a passenger, John McCrackan.

12. The *Brooklyn*, which had made a famous voyage to California early in 1846, again sailed from New York jammed with 171 gold-seekers, on January 12, 1849, to reach San Francisco on August 12. A journal of the voyage by Stephen L. Fowler, of which the Bancroft Library has a transcript, is given attention hereafter.

13. The great days of the clipper ships are described in Arthur H. Clark, *The Clipper Ship Era . . . 1843–1869* (New York and London, 1910), in which is printed excerpts from the log of the *Flying Cloud* on her record voyage (the 89-day passage was equaled, once by herself, but never surpassed). Another interesting study is Carl C. Cutler, *Greyhounds of the Sea; the Story of the American Clipper Ships* (New York and London, 1930). A more general work, touching upon many other aspects of Pacific maritime history, is Raymond A. Rydell, *Cape Horn to the Pacific, The Rise and Decline of an Ocean Highway* (Berkeley and Los Angeles, 1952).

14. The *Contest* was not launched till 1852, after Gardiner left San Francisco for the interior; and none of the other vessels is listed by Arthur H. Clark among the clippers.

15. This voyage of the *Challenge* occurred in 1851, described at length in Arthur H. Clark, *The Clipper Ship Era*, pp. 181–189. Clark vigorously defends the captain, Robert H. Waterman, and his handling of "a large but very poor crew—incompetent and mutinous," while noting, "Off Cape Horn three men fell from aloft, one of whom was drowned while two struck the deck and were killed." Gardiner's account reflects some of the tales told by crew members after reaching San Francisco, which stirred up mob violence against the Captain, a chapter in the history of the Vigilance Committee of 1851.

CHAPTER II. *A Winter in the South* (pp. 5–10)

1. Lovejoy's Hotel, of which J. S. Libbey was proprietor, was a celebrated hostelry at the corner of Beekman Street and Park Row.

2. As reported by the New York *Herald* next day, the *Ann D.*, Bedell, finally sailed for Norfolk on November 11, 1848.

3. The phrase, "seeing the elephant," came to signify the facing of hardships; here Gardiner uses it in its original sense, seeing the primary sights, as in a circus. Something of the history of the phrase is developed by George P. Hammond, *Who Saw the Elephant?* (San Francisco, 1964).

4. Gardiner provides enough information in Chapter XXV for his friend to be identified as John D. Hildreth. He followed Gardiner to California a few years later.

5. These theatrical memories are confused. George Barrett appeared at the Park Thea-

tre on Saturday, November 5, 1848, in the farce, "Founded on Facts," and gave place next week to H. Placide, performing in various comedies in the same theater. Charles Kean was not showing in New York this week. Chanfrau was holding forth in "Chanfrau's New National Theatre, formerly Chatham." The Bowery Theatre was featuring the New Orleans Serenaders, and different comedies each night. Mitchell's Olympic Theatre, the Broadway Theatre, and Burton's Theatre in Chambers Street also advertised in the *Herald*.

6. Fortress Monroe, begun on Point Comfort, Va., in 1819, was more substantial by 1848 than Gardiner implies. In Union hands throughout the Civil War, it was the base from which McClellan launched his Peninsular Campaign of 1862. The celebrated action between the *Monitor* and the *Merrimack*, March 9, 1862, was fought just off the fort. Here, too, Jefferson Davis was confined from 1865 to 1867. See Robert Arthur, *History of Fort Monroe* (Fort Monroe, Va., 1930). In 1946 it became headquarters for U.S. Army field forces, after serving for many years as a coast artillery post.

7. Edênton, seat of Chowan County, is a town on an inlet of Albemarle Sound in northeastern North Carolina, settled about 1658 and incorporated in 1722. Today it is the State's largest peanut market, and an agricultural trade center, with cotton-yarn factories, lumber mills, and shad and herring fisheries.

8. Winton is now the small seat of Hertford County, North Carolina, on the Chowan River southeast of Murfreesboro. Sawmilling is its principal industry.

9. As appears later, Gardiner refers to the ship *Sabina*, which sailed from Sag Harbor February 7, 1849.

10. Plymouth is the seat of Washington County, 28 miles northeast of Washington, North Carolina, situated on the Roanoke River. Founded late in the 18th century, and incorporated in 1800, it is now supported largely by food-canning, lumber-processing, and paperbox manufacturing.

11. Seat of Beaufort County, North Carolina, Washington is today a small city at the head of the estuary of the Pamlico (Tar) River estuary, a shipping center for a farming, fishing, and timber area, the chief industries lumber milling and fertilizer manufacturing. The town was founded prior to the American Revolution.

12. The celebrated fight between Tom Hyer and James ("Yankee") Sullivan was staged February 7 at a farm on Roaches' Point, Kent County, Maryland, some 40 miles from Baltimore. It was won by Hyer in 15 rounds, as described in the New York *Herald*, February 9–10, 1849. Both Hyer and Sullivan came to California soon after.

13. One might infer from Gardiner's comment that there was only one Chagres steamer, the *Crescent City*, which sailed from New York on her second voyage February 5, described in Dale L. Morgan's edition of William McCollum's *California As I Saw It* (Los Gatos, 1960). A tabular appendix of Chagres sailings printed in that work (pp. 188–192) shows that several other steamers were on this run, including the *Northerner* and the *Falcon*, which began their first and third voyages on March 1 and March 5. Gardiner waited for the third sailing of the *Crescent City*, March 15, 1849.

CHAPTER III. *Our Village: Sag Harbor* (pp. 11–14)

1. Sag Harbor sent thirteen whalers to sea in 1846, described as the "boom" year by John R. Spears, *The Story of the New England Whalers* (New York, 1910), p. 323. Contrary to the impression Gardiner gives, whaling continued to be a remunerative occupation beyond the era of the California Gold Rush. A. H. Clark, as cited in Chapter I, Note 15, observes: "The fishery reached high water in Buzzard's Bay in 1857, when New Bedford owned 329 whale ships, and those owned at the other ports of the bay, including Fairhaven, Dartmouth, Westport, Mattapoisett, and Sippican, brought the Bay fleet up to 426 vessels." The San Francisco *Alta California*, November 12, 1850, reported no less than 50 American whalers at Lahaina in September and early October, each "loaded to its utmost capacity with oil and bone. . . . At Honolulu the same influx of whalers is observed, though our reports from that port are not so complete as those from Lahaina."

2. An account of "Yankee" Sullivan, clipped from an unidentified source for H. H. Bancroft's California Biography file (MS., Bancroft Library) says that he was born in Ireland, transported to Sydney for felony, "and escaped thence, leaving his true name, Francis Murray, behind him, but bringing to Sag Harbor, Long Island, the reputation of a prize-fighter. Very soon Sullivan removed to New York, where he kept, on Division Street, the 'Sawdust House,' and extended his fighting fame. He got the name of 'Yankee' from the fact that he went into the ring, at one of his fights, with the American flag wrapped about his loins. . . . In 1850 he came to California, but tarried only a short time. In 1854 he came again to the State, and plunged into the career of vice for which his previous life had educated him." Imprisoned by the 1856 San Francisco Vigilance Committee for ballot stuffing, he being one of the judges of election, Sullivan begged to be spared, and "wrote a long confession, chiefly regarding his election frauds, which implicated many parties." After eight nights of confinement, on the morning of May 31, 1856, he awoke sweating from a dream in which he had envisioned himself hanged, as he told his guard. Shortly after, with a dull case-knife he sawed "a terrible gash in his arm, and thus severed an artery, from which he bled to death." His grave is still to be seen in the Mission Dolores cemetery.

3. The arrival of the *Sabina* at San Francisco on August 9, 1849, is noted in Chapter VIII. Her sailing was reported in the New York *Herald*, February 11, 1849: "Passengers in the ship *Sabina*, sailed from Sag-harbor, L. I., for San Francisco, on the 7th inst.—C. A. Hatch, Chs. Seeley, J. K. Mills, T. J. Wood, Geo. Howell, N. B. Rogers, Horatio Rogers, C. W. Howell. Names of the stockholders who go out in her.—Hy. Green, David Hand, James Parker, S. B. Halsey, Doyle Sweeney, Hy. Webb, Wm. Post, J. McCue, Daniel B. Glober, Wm. White, A. H. Sandard, Edw. W. White, Thos. E. Warren, Sam'l Ludlow, Geo. Herrick, Thos. J. Glover, Chas. Howell, Albert Rogers, Edw. W. Halsey, L. Ludlow, Nathan Dimen, Jno. Vanvechten, Peter H. Howell, J. K. Field, John H. Green, Edwin S. Isham, Jedediah Conklin, S. S. Van Scoy, Henry Rhoades, Austin Jagger, Albert W. Hildreth, Wm. W. Timeker, Thos. P. Ripley, Jr., Wm. W. Parker, Andrew Ed-

wards, John L. Dodge, M.D., D. B. Green, Wm. C. Haines, Jno.Woodward, Jos. Case, Albert Jagger, Wm.W. Post, David H. Hand, Lewis Jagger, Jetur Reeves, Thos. L. Mc-Elrath, Lewis Sandford, Wm. Halsey, Walter S. Horton, John H. Cook, David F. Parker, John Ludlow. Total, 67." St. Catherines, more properly Santa Catarina, where the *Sabina* put in for repairs, is an island off the coast of southern Brazil.

4. The wanderer eventually told his own story, edited by William S. Lewis and Nao-jiro Murakami as *Ranald MacDonald, The Narrative of his early life on the Columbia under the Hudson's Bay Company's regime; of his experiences in the Pacific Whale Fishery; and of his great Adventure to Japan; with a sketch of his later life on the Western Frontier, 1824–1894* (Spokane, 1923). Gardiner's account must be corrected in some particulars. MacDonald was born at Astoria, Oregon, in 1824, and after various wanderings, on December 6, 1845, sailed from the United States in the *Plymouth* under Captain Lawrence B. Edwards. (The *Plymouth* was gone three years, returning home April 30, 1849, six weeks after Gardiner himself departed for California.) At Lahaina, in the Hawaiian Islands, MacDonald re-shipped aboard the *Plymouth,* "but with the special stipulation on my part, that I was to be free to leave the ship off the coast of Japan wherever and whenever I should desire. . . . At length, on June 27th, 1848, the ship then full and lying off the coast of Japan, about five miles from the nearest Island, I asked the Captain to let me leave the ship. With much reluctance, he consented—according to our bargain. I then bought from him a small boat, specially made for himself, rigged for sailing, a quadrant—for I could take an 'Observation' for latitude and longitude—provisions for thirty six days &c. I also assigned to him, in trust, the balance of my share in the whaling adventure, say about six hundred dollars."

Against "the strong and earnest remonstrances of the Captain and crew," MacDonald then "stepped into my boat, taking with him his "box of books and stationery, a few clothes, quadrant, &c.," but not chart. His fellow crew members refused to unloose the knot which held the boat, and he had to cut the rope himself. The fog was dense, with no land in sight, but he made his way to Yankeshiri, off Yezo, Japan, and was subsequently taken to Soya, then to Nagasaki, where he remained a prisoner until Commander James Glynn in the U. S. S. *Preble* effected his release (with others) in April, 1849. MacDonald eventually settled near Toroda, Washington, where he died August 5, 1894. Gardiner probably first read of his adventures in an account of the *Preble's* voyage in the *China Mail,* May 31, 1849, reprinted in the San Francisco *Alta California,* August 2, 1849. He could have obtained fuller details from *The Friend* of Honolulu, December 1, 1848, October 1, 1849. Supplementary to the above, see Ralph P. Edgerton, "Ranald MacDonald, A[d]venturer," *The Pacific Northwesterner,* Winter, 1969, vol. 13, pp. 1–12.

CHAPTER IV. *In New York City* (pp. 15–19)

1. These "lines" by the senior Gardiner are placed in the text here, though in his manuscript they are copied at the front of the volume. Gardiner's memory is somewhat at fault,

in that the "lines," signed "J.D.G." and dated March 1st, 1849, were published in the *Journal of Commerce* on Friday, March 9, 1849. There are variations in punctuation, capitalization, and (in a few instances) wording between the two versions.

2. The *Crescent City* had been built in 1847 for the New York-New Orleans run. At the outbreak of the California Gold Rush, her owners extended her range to Chagres, and this was to be her third voyage. (She returned from her second voyage on March 3.) For detailed information on Chagres sailings from December, 1848, to April, 1849, see Dale L. Morgan's work on McCollum, cited in Chapter II, Note 13. There also it is noted that the Captain of the *Crescent City*, Charles Stoddard, got a generally favorable press in 1849.

CHAPTER V. *On Board the* Crescent City (pp. 21–31)

1. Paul Boynton, an aquatic acrobat who flourished in the 1880's, is not mentioned in the contemporary accounts of the sailing of the *Crescent City*. It is unlikely that he was seen by Gardiner in 1849.

2. The New York *Herald* reported on Friday, March 16, 1849: "The noble steamship *Crescent City*, Capt. Stoddard, sailed yesterday afternoon, at half-past one o'clock, for Chagres. Among her passengers will be seen Mrs. Col. J. C. Fremont and child, Mr. Jacobs [Richard Taylor Jacob], son-in-law of Hon. T. H. Benton, Col. C. W. Hughes, who goes to the Isthmus as Engineer-in-chief on the Panama Railroad, for Messrs. Howland & Aspinwall, and a number of other distinguished personages. The annexed list exhibits a larger number than has heretofore gone in any steamer for Chagres:—

"Mrs. Colonel J. C. Fremont, child and servant, Col. G. W. Hughes, engineer-in-chief on Panama Railroad, Mr. Jacobs, Samuel C. Gray and lady, Jos. Bell and lady, Rev. T. Seldines, H. A. Whitney, Charles H. Peter, H. S. Cushing, James R. Dow, J. H. Chittenden, M. Loughnane, H. I. Richmond, D. D. Hammond, E. Taggart, A. W. Frick, Francis Arent, A. Winants, E. M. Howison, George Furguson, J. H. Dall, C. Williams, H. N. Dillon, T. A. Warboss, James Gordon, Jos. S. Beemer, Wm. H. Simpson, D. J. Goshine, T. S. Brewster, Edgar Camp, Charles J. Rockwell, H. Hutchinson, Nicholas Rector, N. Woodward, C. D. Gibbs, D. Diderer, T. S. Thompson, L. M. Thompson, J. C. Reidman, E. W. Hopkins, H. C. Bosworth, F. W. Hopkins, Theo. Mills, M. Smith, E. Barry, H. Smith, J. Sullivan, D. T. and W. W. Trimble, C. H. McIntosh, D. J. Adams, G. Hawley, J. Dillon, John Clark, William Johnson, J. G. Carpenter, W. H. Chandler, D. T. Giffith, T. Burns, C. Collins, Julius Smith, S. W. Hastings, E. Tuttle, H. S. Chapman, E. Tuttle, J. B. Chapman, — Ford, G. Copeland, J. Lampier, P. R. W. Prime, J. Sullivan, S. Wallis, S. P. Carmichael, O. Santill, J. G. Dow, M. M. Burtill, T. H. Jefferson, D. Hubbell, W. Weed, Isaac Foote, P. Rector, Thomas Dix, I. B. Raymond, A. Whitney, B. P. Hutchinson, John Harris, E. G. Waite, S. Clute, S. A. Hartness, J. Pope, D. Ray, A. Campbell, W. Cass, J. H. Williams, J. Haggart, T. T. Rice, Abm. Wiley, R. G. Burrell, N. Comra, — Pendleton, J. McCall, L. J. Studley, W. H. Holden, J. Scott, G. Hulem, M. Thompson, R. R. Starr, J. M. Richardson, W. W. Upham, R. Quick, W. Wilson, James Beel, Dr.

Payne, I. Westfall, — Austin, C. H. Westfall, M. H. Lincoln, Edgar Smith, R. Walker, Wm. Russ, T. B. Tyler, J. Bartlett, G. R. Barbour, J. W. Goster, M. D. Mapes, C. Weber, L. Proper, W. S. Gibson, S. T. Walker, B. Billings, J. Wells, R. S. Wolverton, J. C. Mc-Geven, F. W. Collins, H. S. Putney, M. B. Clark, W. L. Kemp, H. E. Tooker, J. Swift, P. A. Whitmore, S. Jones, F. Ballard, J. Merrihew, E. L. Winslow, B. W. Clark, J. C. Lawrence, A. Cornish, H. Taylor, S. Davis, J. Thomas Mulholland, F. B. Hitchcock, W. H. Allen, A. W. Geer, C. J. Watkins, C. Adams, W. Hodgekins, N. G. Field, J. Bass, W. M. Shearer, W. Colburn, P. Shaw, M. Grannils, G. Geer, B. Ishain, F. E. Westbrook, M. Callahan, T. Irvine, A. Hammond, E. C. Joslin, J. Allen, C. P. Huntington, E. R. Sabine, L. Chamberlin, G. W. Murray, C. Carpenter, D. Parkhurst, S. Dunnelle, C. Fuller, S. Shufelt, J. Miller, J. Cornell, H. R. Robins, S. L. Hays, F. Allerton, J. Chapman, W. Ramsdell, A. Cook, W. Sutherland, L. Alden, C. Bentsell, F. Noble, R. Taylor, C. Vanderburgh, J. R. Merrell, F. S. Boyd, W. R. Sutton, T. N. Wilcox, W. B. White, H. Tidman, S. Swart, R. B. Archer, J. F. Randall, Snow, T. Kinna, J. Gridley, jr., W. H. Thomas, Ira Hotchkiss, J. Molioney, J. Lufkin, S. McClun, W. H. Shipperd and four friends, G. Hale, A. Hale, C. H. Worden, J. Hanford, L. C. Drummond, M. Barkalou, C. W. Latonville, D. Mack, T. Andrews, D. H. Ferguson, M. Patrick, H. Ashley, J. E. Stearns, R. James, W. Trout, W. Trout jr., R. Jones, J. Flain, J. W. Jordon, W. Barner, M. Speer, F. L. Foot, H. A. Barnes, C. W. Paul, J. R. Lanfair, M. R. Blair, D. W. Cud, J. Malby, S. Gane, J. Colby, W. H. Bennett and son, L. Cross, B. Hunt, J. Simpson, N. Coffrey, J. S. Beckwith, J. S. Hopper, S. Vlinn, R. Rees, M. D. Fairchild, W. H. McKinster, J. Runyon, D. A. Runyon, A. Hosmer, M. Culver, D. Fairchild, M. S. Norton, S. Thornton, E. C. Spooner, T. A. Skinner, A. E. Hutchinson, J. Kittridge, O. Crocker, W. Metcalf, J. P. Gruley, C. De Gram, W. Bercham, J. McManie, J. S. Talbot, L. Belin, S. Parnish, W. E. Lewis, H. Mires, A. Broman, A. Mattier, L. M. Mattier, H. C. Gardner, W. K. Morris, J. Bullock, D. Hammond, C. R. Sanders, H. M. Robinson, S. W. Preble, J. A. Throckmorton, S. Patton, L. B. Gilkey, W. E. Lewis—Total, 838[!]."

Jessie Benton Frémont, en route to join her husband in California, has a personal account of the voyage in her *A Year of American Travel* (New York, 1878), pp. 20–45. (She remembered Captain Stoddard's name as Schenck.) Her brother-in-law, who accompanied her only as far as the Isthmus, was lieutenant governor of Kentucky during the Civil War. Among the other passengers, C. D. Gibbes became a celebrated California cartographer; and we are struck by the possibility that T. H. Jefferson is the man who published at New York this year an important *Map of the Emigrant Road from Independence, Mo., to St. Francisco, California,* based on his overland journey of 1846; nothing has been known of his later life.

3. Gardiner later gives Allen's first name as Will. All the men now mentioned were his boon companions until he reached San Francisco. Pollard is not in the *Crescent City's* passenger list (unless as "F. Ballard"), but there is sufficient record of him.

4. Worthington does not appear in the *Crescent City's* passenger list, nor afterward aboard the *Sylph*.

5. A brief account of John Conness is found in *Biographical Directory of the American Congress, 1774–1961* (Washington, 1961), p. 730. He was born in Ireland in 1821, immigrated to the United States in 1833, and after coming to California in 1849, engaged in mining and mercantile pursuits. He was several times elected to the California legislature, and in 1861 was an unsuccessful candidate for governor. He was subsequently elected to the U.S. Senate as a Douglas Democrat (becoming a Union Republican), and served from March 4, 1863, to March 3, 1869. He then settled in Boston and died in Jamaica Plain, Mass., January 10, 1909.

6. For experiences of earlier arrivals at Chagres, see Morgan's edition of William McCollum, cited in Chapter II, Note 13; and for "bungoes," see next chapter, Note 4.

7. The *Crescent City* arrived off Chagres at 8:15 A.M. on March 24, as recorded in a letter of that date signed "G," reprinted in the Mobile, Miss., *Daily Advertiser,* April 18, 1849, from the Baltimore *American.* This letter says the *Crescent City* brought 349 passengers, including Mrs. Frémont, who was accompanied by a Mrs. Robinson, from Baltimore, as attendant, besides the latter's husband, a carpenter. A sedate-looking Irishwoman (with husband) completed the female contingent, the writer said. He lavished praise on the excellent stewardess, Mrs. Young, "whose kind attention and motherly care of the sea-sick passengers, made her appear really a ministering angel."

Many Forty-niners set down vivid impressions of Chagres at this time, including William McCollum, Theodore T. Johnson, and John M. Letts. Gardiner does not mention the principal point of interest, ruined Fort San Lorenzo, atop its 150-foot-high rock on the right bank of the Chagres River at its mouth, which dated from the late 16th century.

8. The little river steamboat mentioned by Gardiner, the *Orus*, had reached Chagres January 14, having sailed from New York December 21, 1848. According to Jessie Frémont, "The little tender on which the passengers and mails were landed was as small as a craft could well be to hold an engine, and was intended to go as high as possible up the Chagres River. It seemed like stepping down upon a toy. But even this had to be exchanged, after the first eight miles, for dug-out canoes, the shallows and obstructions of every kind making it impossible to use the little steamboat." The *Orus* afterward came to grief in the rapids of the San Juan River in Nicaragua; Oliver Goldsmith, *Overland in Forty-Nine* (Detroit, 1896), p. 128, saw her wreckage early in 1851.

CHAPTER VI. *On the Isthmus of Panama* (pp. 33–44)

1. In 1849 it was believed that fevers were occasioned by "miasmatic" air. The agency of the mosquito in yellow fever and malaria was established soon after Gardiner set down his recollections.

2. Most of those who had reached Chagres on the second voyage of the *Crescent City,* to say nothing of those who had come on other vessels, were still waiting in Panama for transportation to California.

3. The New York *Herald,* April 8, 1849, reported as follows on the return of the *Crescent City* the previous morning: "She arrived at Havana on the morning of the 30th, after

a passage of four days and a half, and sailed for New York on Monday, April 2d, at half-past five, P.M., and has thus made the passage in four days and nine hours.

"She arrived at Chagres on Saturday morning, the 24th of March, making the passage from New York in eight days and eighteen hours. After landing 350 passengers, she sailed for Havana on Sunday, March 25th, at six P.M., with twenty passengers.

"The *Oregon* sailed from Panama on the 15th of March, at six o'clock in the morning, for San Francisco, with two hundred and fifty passengers, leaving about eight hundred at Panama. Since that time to the 25th ult., about five hundred and thirty more had arrived at Chagres.

"The health of both places is very good—only a few cases of intermittent fever, brought on by exposure, existed.

"There were only two vessels at Panama on the 23d—the ship *Humboldt*, with coal; the other a small brig, called the *Eterline*, bound up, with passengers.

"The whale bark *Equator*, of New Bedford, sailed on the 21st March, with one hundred and thirty passengers for San Francisco. Several other whalers were expected soon.

"An English ship, the *Col[lo]ony*, sailed on the 20th, with two hundred and one passengers, for the same place.

"The latest news from San Francisco, at Panama, was by the *Belfast*. It was to the 9th of December only.

"The passengers by the *Crescent City* chartered canoes to take them up to Gorgona, for nine dollars each, with all their baggage, a distance of forty-five miles. The road from Gorgona to Panama is in very good order, a distance of twenty-one miles; baggage is taken over at six dollars per hundred pounds; have heard of no accident on the road; provisions are plenty at Panama, and board can be had at $1.20 to $1.50 per day, and persons can live at fifty cents per day, with a little management; marketing and cooking for themselves.

"American eagles at Panama, were worth eight dollars in change, half eagles four dollars, half dollars forty cents, five franc pieces pass for ten one dime pieces, a dime passing for one-eighth of a dollar. Doubloons are worth seventeen dollars.

"The English steamer *Eudora*, had arrived from Valparaiso at Panama, on the 23d, at 5 A.M., with few passengers, and one million in gold bars, on English account."

4. Gardiner presumably left Chagres the day before his future shipmate Hiram Dwight Pierce arrived there on the *Falcon*, which departed New York March 8, but stopped en route at Havana and New Orleans, thus reaching Chagres at 1:30 A.M. on March 28. Later that day Pierce observed: "Chagres & its environs, with the old Spanish fort is a romantic looking place & in dry weather passable. The village which contains perhaps 100 huts, lies on the east side of a small bay or cove. The huts are built by setting posts in the ground & lashing poles to them, & weaveing in grass or coco leaves or flags, & covering them with the same. The inhabitants are a mixture of Indian & Negro. Spanish of course." See his MS. diary in the Bancroft Library, or a published version: *A Forty-niner Speaks* (Oakland, 1930), p. 12.

The dugout canoes used on the Isthmus were universally known to the Forty-niners as "bungoes," though the large freight canoes were more properly called "cayucas." Theodore T. Johnson, some weeks earlier, described a bungo as a 'species of roof made of the branches of leaves of the palmetto, extending some six or eight feet in length, and just high enough to creep under upon our hands and knees; leaving space enough at the stern for the seat of the patron, or captain, who, with a short broad paddle, both aided to propel and steer the canoe." For their passage, in small canoes, Johnson's party of four paid $8 each, plus $4 per hundred pounds for their baggage. William McCollum's party of eight, after taking in six more passengers, and bringing along six or seven tons of baggage, paid $80 toward the expense of the river voyage.

5. At Gatun Gardiner intersected the route of the subsequent Panama Canal, which from the celebrated Gatun Locks veers off toward Navy Bay (Bahia de Limon) in preference to following the lower course of the Chagres River.

6. Gorgona, "place of rocks," was in the dry season the principal terminus on the upper Chagres River, though in the rainy season Cruces, ten miles higher up, was the head of navigation. Roads went off to Panama from each village. Knowing of the continuing "blockade" in Panama, many travelers at this time chose to pause at Gorgona, with its higher and "healthier" situation; one such was Hiram D. Pierce, who remained at Gorgona from March 30 to April 4. Jessie Frémont also paused there a few days, owing to the illness of her brother-in-law. As will be seen a few paragraphs farther on, Gardiner favorably recalled the Alcalde of Gorgona; in contrast, Theodore T. Johnson remarked astringently that "besides being the richest man, [he] was notorious as the greatest rascal and cheat in Gorgona. [The Alcalde] was a mixture of Spanish and negro, wore spectacles for dignity, and was deaf for convenience."

7. Vasco Nuñez de Balboa crossed the Isthmus to "discover" the Pacific Ocean in 1513.

8. Jessie Frémont retained a forbidding recollection of this stage of her journey across the Isthmus: "The distance from Gorgona to Panama was about twenty-one miles. It was *distance*, not a *road*; there was only a mule track—rather a trough than track in most places, and mule staircases with occasional steps of at least four feet, and only wide enough for a single animal—the same trail that had been followed since the early day of Spanish conquest; and this trail followed the face of the country as it presented itself—straight up the sides of the steepest heights to the summit, then straight down them again to the base. No bridges across the rapid streams. These had to be forded by the mules, or, when narrow, the mule would gather his legs under him and leap it. If one could sit him, so much the better; if not, one fell into the water; and in this way many emigrants got broken bones, and many more bruises and thorough wettings. There was no system about the baggage; people generally had taken the largest trunk they could find, because the journey was to be a long one; there was no provision for taking these across other than by hand; and when the trunk was absolutely too large, mules and cows were pressed into the service. . . . The slender Indians bending under the weight of a trunk carried between them on poles, and the thin, ill-fed little mules which almost disappeared under the load

of trunks, valises, and bags, both got rid of their load when tired of it. There were very narrow defiles worn through the rock where we could only go in single file, and even the men sat sidewise, because there was not room to sit as usual . . ." (*A Year of American Travel,* pp. 53–55).

Many other accounts might be cited. It may be more useful to note what is said in the prefatory Remarks accompanying E. L. Autenrieth's *A Topographical Map of the Isthmus of Panama* (New York, 1851), pp. 10–11: "The first rancho is about three miles from Gorgona, but it requires nearly three hours walk to reach it; good oranges are commonly found there. Further on, you meet another rancho before you arrive at the *Half-way-House,* which is about two hours-and-a-half walk from the first. This place is situated close to the *Cerro Rayo,* and the country presents a fine view. A great many stop here during the night. There is a fine brook with clear water, and a pretty good bathing place a little to the right. During the dry season, two large tents are commonly erected here; kept by Americans, for the entertainment of passers by. [William Penn Abrams, MS. diary, Bancroft Library, remarked on April 20, 1849, that the owner was an accommodating New Hampshireman.] On the top and foot of the hill are some Indian huts.

"From this you must walk three hours and a half to reach the junction of the Gorgona and Cruces road, where you find several houses, and may get some refreshments. A quarter of a mile further on, you cross the River Cardenas, which during the dry months contains hardly any water, but swells in the rainy season, after a heavy rain, so much, that travellers have sometimes to wait for five or six hours, before they can cross with safety.

"From here to Panama the road is good even in the rainy season.

"Arriving on the height of the Cerro Juan Diaz, we would advise every one to be on the look out for the Pacific Ocean, and the Cathedral of Panama, which will be seen a little to the right at the foot of a fine mountain. The view is beautiful. . . ."

Autenrieth's interesting and detailed map, "The Isthmus of Panama and Darien," is conveniently reproduced on the end pages of Morgan's edition of William McCollum's book. This shows the road to Gorgona, but not the branch road to Cruces.

9. "Stout Cortez," the poet Keats notwithstanding, never set foot on the Isthmus. The paved (Cruces) road dated from after the conquest of Peru, when treasure shipments destined for Spain made use of the Isthmus route.

10. Perhaps the proprietor of the American Hotel was William Hollenbeck, who advertised it in the *Panama Star,* November 10, 1849. Editorially, that issue of the paper noted: "This hotel is owned by an American citizen and is kept in the real American style. It is the largest, most commodious and airy Hotel in the city. The gentlemanly proprietor is ever most ready to accommodate his American friends, and is sure to give satisfaction. Give him a call." Dr. Gaius L. Halsey, who reached the Isthmus about two weeks before Gardiner, recalled in his own reminiscences that a "large three story building standing on the main street was bought that spring for 300 dollars and opened as the 'American Hotel.' It is still [1890] run as a hotel as I have noticed in the news from there." See Francis Whiting Halsey, *The Pioneers of Unadilla Village . . . [and] Reminiscences of*

Village Life and of Panama and California from 1840 to 1850 by Gaius Leonard Halsey M. D. (Unadilla, N.Y., 1902), pp. 229–230. The French Hotel, which is pictured in *Century Magazine*, April, 1891, p. 914, was reported by the Panama *Star* of November 10, 1849, to have comparable attractions. It was operated by J. Mattossy & Co. near the Gate of the City of Panama: "For neat rooms and clean bedding it surpasses any Hotel in the city, and its table is always supplied with the best that the market can afford." A third establishment advertised at this time—six months after Gardiner departed Panama—was J. J. Landerer's Oregon Hotel.

11. Old Panama, five miles to the east, had been founded in 1519. Only its romantic ruins were to be seen in 1849, for after its capture by Henry Morgan in 1671 the city was rebuilt, nearer the port, as a walled town. (Thus old and new Panama, considered together, comprise the oldest city of European origin on the American mainland.)

"Viator," a correspondent writing in the New York *Herald*, December 18, 1848, presented this interesting picture of the place on the eve of its transformation: "The city of Panama is situated on the shores of the bay of that name, and a most beautiful bay it is, too. What is the number of the present population, I cannot say, as it is doubtless filled with strangers—it formerly contained from 5,000 to 7,000 inhabitants, and was a quiet, still city, where, during the day, nought but the sounds of the convent and church bells disturbed the horses of the citizens in their grazings in the public squares, which were all overgrown with grass. The trade carried on consisted in importing dry goods from Jamaica, for the supply of the Isthmenians, the neighboring province of Veragua, the pearl islands, the towns of Chiriqui, David and their vicinities, and the various little inland towns. Goods also were sent down to the ports of Payta, in Peru, and Guayaquil, in the Equador. The returns made for these goods consisted in the produce of the Isthmus such as gold dust, hides, India rubber, pearl of oyster shells (from which the mother of pearl of commerce is made) sarsaparilla, &c. Agriculture is at a low point on the Isthmus, as not enough sugar was raised to supply the city of Panama, and they depended for their supplies of wheat, flour, salt, sugar and groceries, on Peru or Jamaica, on the Atlantic side. The climate is warm, say from 80 to 85 degrees, all the year round—the rainy season long and severe [May to December]. The nights in Panama, however, are much cooler than usual in tropical climates. Its market and accommodations are poor. . . . It is only within a few years that a public hotel has been established; previous to that, travellers had to depend on the hospitality of those to whom they carried letters of introduction. If there is any extraordinary influx of strangers to Panama, of course prices for accommodations will rise."

12. The "blockade" was occasioned by the disruption of transportation on the Pacific side, no vessels arriving to carry on to California those who kept streaming across the Isthmus from Chagres. Gardiner exaggerates the number of those hung up at Panama. The New York *Herald*, May 13, 1849, based on reports brought the day before by the *Crescent City*, commented: "The number of persons awaiting passage for San Francisco

at Panama, on the 28th [of April], was estimated at 2,500; but of this number 1,280 had engaged passage in the vessels to sail that week."

13. The *Oregon* finally got back to Panama on May 5, her captain (notwithstanding Gardiner's comment) having managed to keep his crew on board. The *Panama* arrived soon after; see Note 22. The Bremen bark *Humboldt,* loaded with coal for the use of the *Oregon,* had been at Panama as early as January, expected then to return home with a cargo of guano. Eventually she was sold, for $60,000, to sail for San Francisco shortly after Gardiner left Panama. A graphic account of her voyage is given by Julius H. Pratt, "To California by Panama in '49," *Century Magazine,* April, 1891, pp. 901–917 (this article has interesting illustrations "by Gilbert Gaul after drawings made by the late Charles Nahl, in 1850"); in slightly altered form reprinted in Pratt's *Reminiscences . . .* [1910].)

14. Gardiner's recollection was faulty. Jessie Frémont and a few other American women had voyaged with him to Chagres on the *Crescent City,* and two would sail with him from Panama in the *Sylph*. William Penn Abrams, on April 22, "Met Mrs. Fremont in the streets this eve and find there are many American Ladies in the place." They were not numerous, however.

15. British mail steamers ran between Panama and various South American ports, as far as Valparaiso. Some of the Forty-niners detained at Panama took passage on one of these steamers, expecting to transfer to a ship bound for San Francisco. Others, as Gardiner says, hoped to make arrangements by which whalers or other vessels would sail to Panama to pick up their stranded fellows. The American consul at Panama also dispatched word south respecting the opportunities available to shipmasters.

16. John M. Letts, *California Illustrated,* p. 40, similarly relates: "In the anxiety to get off, a party purchased an iron boat on the Chagres River, carried it across to Panama on their shoulders, fitted it out, and sailed for California. The first 'bungo' that sailed, after getting out into the bay some three or four miles, was struck by a slight flaw of wind, dismasted, and obliged to put back for repairs. This caused a very perceptible decline in 'bungo' stocks."

Incredible as it seems, at least one of these bungoes made it through to California. Isaac Wistar mentions in his *Autobiography,* p. 175, having seen at Nye's Ranch (Marysville) on the Feather River "a Central American pongy or 'dug-out,' with raised sides, canvas half-deck, and two masts with small lug sails, which had safely brought six men from Panama, a voyage of 3500 miles, involving constant landings on a surf-bound shore for water and provisions."

Others had a still rougher time. Hiram Dwight Pierce, subsequently Gardiner's shipmate in the *Sylph,* made a diary entry at Panama which he elaborated after reaching San Francisco, as follows: "2 Ships arived in the offing [on April 28] making 4 Brigs & 5 Schooners & some Bunges that are beeing fitted up. One Co. is fitting up a life boat to make a passage in to Cal. The history of the Life boat I have since learned. that after beeing out some 2 months & beeing wet all the time they had got some 500 miles above

Acapulco & were obliged to put back. They there abandoned their boat & took passage on a French vesel & she was wrecked while lying at Anchor before leaveing port. She draged her anchor & was driven on the rocks, & some 20 lives lost, among the number 2 of the boats co. I saw one of the men just before I left S. Francisco [August 1]. He had Just got in. He looked like a used up specimin of Humanity."

17. Panama had many churches and convents, but only one cathedral, with the twin towers that denote an archbishop's seat. From the contemporary viewpoint of John M. Letts (p. 34): "There are numerous extensive churches, the principal one being the cathedral [a sketch of which he reproduces]. This is a magnificent structure, and of colossal dimensions. In the end fronting the plaza are three niches, in which are life-size statues of the twelve Apostles, of marble. It has two towers, the upper sections of which are finished with pearl. The interior was furnished without regard to expense. It is now somewhat dilapidated, but still has a fine organ. The convent, 'La Mugher,' is an extensive edifice, being 300 feet in length. The roof of most parts has fallen in, and the walls are fast falling to decay. The only tenant is a colored woman who has a hammock slung in the main entrance. She has converted the convent into a stable, charging a *real* a night for a horse or mule—they board themselves; they, however, have the privilege of selecting their own apartments. It encloses a large court, in which there are two immense wells, and numerous fig, and other fruit trees. There is a tower still standing on one end of the building, without roof or window; it has, however, several bells still hanging. The convent of 'San Francisco,' is also an extensive structure, in a dilapidated state; one part of it is still tenanted by nuns. It has a tower with bells still hanging. These buildings, as well as all the buildings of Panama, are inhabited by innumerable lizards, a peculiarity of the city that first strikes the stranger. They are harmless, but to one unaccustomed to seeing them, are an unpleasant sight.

"The people here, as in all catholic countries, are very attentive to religious rites and ceremonies, and almost every day of the week is ushered in by the ringing of church and convent bells. The ringing is constant during the day; and people are seen passing to and from church, the more wealthy classes accompanied by their servants, bearing mats, upon which they kneel on their arrival. Almost every day is a saint's day, when all business is suspended to attend its celebration."

18. Easter in 1849 came on April 8, and Gardiner is describing the characteristic rites attendant on Good Friday. John M. Letts offers a vivid description of the Panama scene, and Hiram Dwight Pierce supplies these piquant details: "Sat [April] 7th. . . . The Catholics last evening had a great turnout. They had in the procession 4 cars, there beeing a frame with bars or poles projecting, by which they were bourn on the shoulders of the Natives, one of them I should think emplying as many as 60 men. On these frames were built Pirimids coverd with wax candels enclosed in large vases or bell glasses, of various coullors beautifully lashed on with robbins. Those Pirimids were from 12 to 20 feet high Surmounted, one by the Virgin Mary, one by the Risen Saviour, one by Peter, &c. There was a long procession, each one carrying a candle. There was many Ladys, some Spanish,

the Elite of the Town. Many Americans joined the procession, beeing desirous to see the whole. The van was led by a Monk completely veiled, who with a sort of a bell kept up a clanking, & by dropping on his knees in front of the car every few rods indicated the Stopping & Starting periods. Following him was some half dozen Negroes with violins, who seemed to vie with some dozen Priests behind them, that were chanting, to see which could make the most noise. Thus the whole cavelcade moved through the principal Streets untill a late hour, amid the din of some 50 Bells, many of them cracked. There beeing 4 bells to a tower & sometimes Cathedrals & Churches formeing nearly whole streets, long before day the next morning, I was awakened by their noise, & looking out I saw them paraded on the palaza, with their cars & lights still burning. The day was celebrated by the fireing of heavy guns & ringing of Bells. . . ."

19. Gardiner enlarges our Spanish vocabulary with the names for beer, bread, fish, and chocolate.

20. Tobago is one of the principal islands in the Bay of Panama. Ships watered there, the Pacific Mail Steamship Company had a station on it, and excursion parties of Forty-niners came out in bungoes to break the monotony of their stay in Panama.

21. The *Humboldt,* advertised to sail May 10, the day after Gardiner left Panama, was noted by the San Francisco *Alta California,* August 31, 1849, to have had a 101-day voyage to reach San Francisco on August 30, which would make the date of departure May 22. Julius H. Pratt (see Note 13) says she took 48 days to reach Acapulco on July 7, which would make the date May 21. Originally she had upwards of 400 passengers, but some, like Pratt, left her at Acapulco where others boarded her. She reported 325 passengers on arrival at San Francisco.

22. Gardiner's memories became mixed, in that the *Oregon* reached Panama from California before the *Panama* got there around South America, and this just before he himself left the Isthmus. Hiram Dwight Pierce wrote in his diary on May 5: "At ½ past 8 in the evening the Steamer *Oregon* came to Anchor. There was a great rush & tremendous excitement. In the morng we recieved most flattering reports." (The *Oregon* had sailed from San Francisco April 12 with 19 passengers and $160,000 in gold dust, as reported in the *Alta California,* April 14, 1849.) William Penn Abrams wrote in his own diary on May 6: "Great excitement last night. was arroused with firing of guns and soon after heard the shout Steamer in sight. Steped into my Pants and went out on the Batery and learned that the *Oregon* has indeed returned from San Francisco which revives the drooping spirits of hundreds that hold her tickets in this place Not able to learn until today of her news Am rejoiced to hear that all reports hitherto are confirmed—She brings about one million dollars[!] We are again surprised to see another Steamer come into port, and learn that the *Panama* is here also and the City is perfectly enraptured at the prospect of a speedy departure to the golden regions." (Pierce agrees that the *Panama* came to anchor at 2 P.M. on May 6.)

With 290 passengers, the *Panama* reached San Francisco June 4, 17 days from Panama. The *Oregon,* with 323 passengers, arrived June 12, 20 days from Panama via Monterey.

The *California,* meanwhile, detained at San Francisco since February 28, finally got off May 1 with 51 passengers and $300,000 in gold dust. She returned to Panama May 23, and got back to San Francisco July 15, 22 days from Panama via Acapulco, San Blas, and San Diego; she brought 242 male and 11 female passengers, and the report that at the time of her departure there were very few on the Isthmus bound for California. (However, the flow of emigration via the Isthmus built up again in the fall.)

23. This recollection is incorrect; as seen by the preceding note, Gardiner departed Panama before either the *Oregon* or the *Panama* got under way. Nor is this a recollection of the *Oregon's* departure on her first voyage, which was March 13, two days before he left New York. Gardiner did not see a steamer leave during his stay in Panama; and he had arranged passage in the *Sylph* before either steamer reached Panama.

24. Mark Tapley, several times referred to by Gardiner, is a character in Charles Dickens' *Martin Chuzzlewit,* renowned for his irrepressible jollity and optimism.

25. Fortunately Hiram Dwight Pierce's diary gives us a contemporary daily record of the voyage of the *Sylph*. A few extracts chronicle the preliminaries:

"Monday [April] 23d. This morning a ship is comeing in said to be the *Sylph*. The Dr has gone to see about getting passage [for Pierce's company, from Troy, N.Y.]. . . . At night our names were given in for passage on the *Sylph* which is said to be provisioned & waterd & will sail in a few days. . . .

"Wensday 25th . . . The bargain was concluded & receit obtained for I think $2955. . . .

"Friday [May] 4th . . . Great anxiety is felt to leave this place. . . . The *Sylph* droped down to Teboga for water. . . .

"Monday 7th . . . We now expect to go on Shipboard tomorow. . . .

"Tuesday 8th. All well. Made preperations for a move. During the day got our baggage on board in the midst of a violent rain storm. The natives had to wade in the water up to their sholders freequently as the boats were toss about by the surf. At night we borrowed some beds & a tent & slept on the flouer.

"Wensday 9th. Went on the Ship, & at 5 P M Waid Anchor, fair wind & Tide. We steered South S.W. The *Sophia* mad sail at the same time."

26. A complete list of the *Sylph's* passengers was printed in George R. Parburt, *Oration: Delivered on Board the Ship Sylph* . . . (Geneva, N.Y., 1849), a work more fully described in the next chapter. The following is derived from that list:

MAINE: C. C. Emory and E. R. Waterman, *Saco*; G.W. Foster, *Machias*; S. Emory, *Biddleford*; L. B. Gilkey, *Unity*; Capt. Osgood, P. S. Peters, and G. W. Ray, *Blue Hill*.

NEW HAMPSHIRE: Cyrus B. Walker, *Hanover*.

RHODE ISLAND: George H. T. Cole and T. S. Hiscow, *Wickford*; E. V. Hathaway, J. Cushing, T. G. Howland, John B. Luther, Jason White, and George Steere, *Providence*.

MASSACHUSETTS: F. A. Gushee, Joseph Crackbon, Edward Wilder, H. A. Whiting, Romulus Norwood, Roland H. Macey, Irving Lawton, Orlando Lawton, A. D. Hatch, and Edward Saunderson, *Boston*; V. Hathaway and E. D. Hathaway, *Freetown*; Charles Butler, David D. Hammond, James Merrihew, Jr., and A. M. Swift, *Fairhaven*; James E.

Eddy, Richard Murphy, and B. W. Hathaway, *Fall River;* Dwight R. Perry, Edward Pollard, J. S. Richardson, and F. P. Shaw, *New Bedford*; Alfred Clifford, *Martha's Vineyard*; S. T. Hathaway, *Freetown*; A. Hutchinson, *Mid[d]letown*; T. S. Kinton, *Gloucester*; C. H. Porter, *Newburyport*; Stephen Potter, *Dartmouth*; B. Stetson, *Bridgewater*; S. F. Torrey, *Quincy*; H. H. Jones and C. B. Macey, *Nantucket*; S. Kent and E. C. Skinner, *Lynn*; T. B. Robinson, *North Chelmsford*; T. A. Skinner, *Woburn*.

NEW YORK: Dr. N. Nininger, M. Morse, A. G. Grant, E. Greenwood, John Conness, R. P. Lee, Jr., and John E. Hazleton, *New York City*; A. B. Haskins, L. W. Haskins, and D. Newcomb, *Pittstown*; George Eddy, *Union Village*; D. M. Holding, *Covington*; J. E. Fuller, J. M. Taylor, P. Tinker, W. Torrence, Kingsbury Root, J. Stone, H. D. Pierce, Dr. Wesley Newcomb, Lady, son, daughter and servant, A. M. Comstock, John Cramer, and Corydon Bristol [who died on the voyage], *Troy*; T. A. Sherwood, *Fort Edward*; L. Southard, *Essex*; M. Kenyon, *Cambridge*; George R. Parburt, *Geneva*; Henry Putney, *Rushville*; John D. Lynde, *Willsborough*; J. H. Milligan, Yates Harold, E. S. Youmans, J. Tilfair, Wm. Turner, Daniel Stewart, R. Stafford, G. Purdy, James W. Cramer, and Seneca Daniels, *Saratoga*; W. Hodgkins, *Plattsville*; T. Gregory, *Salem*; William Burling, Z. Clements, and B. Tabor, *Schuylerville*; J. Mott Smith, *Albany*; Elos L. Winslow and E. W. Clarke, *Malone*; Charles C. D. Glasford, *Morrison*; H. C. Gardiner, *Sag Harbor*; W. H. Allen, *South Hampton*; S. Davis and John S. Thomas, *Bangor*; L. Wyman, S. H. Paine, and John Pardee, *Fort Covington*; C. R. Saunders, *Burnt Hills*; David Fairchild and Mahlon D. Fairchild, *Newark*; George Batchelder, *Westford*.

PENNSYLVANIA: J. E. Taggart and G. S. Marks, *Philadelphia*; H. Bicknell, W. Bicknell, and J. A. Blake, *Pleasant Grove*.

MARYLAND: James H. Browne, G. Sharp Oldfield, Haskins Bowie, Wm. C. Beach, J. F. Spence, J. H. Sherley, H. Ray Bowie, Miss Ann Gruber, and Hamilton Bowie, *Baltimore*.

GEORGIA: J. Lockaby and Luther Phenizie, *Columbus*.

MISSISSIPPI: L. Soher, D. Pinson, J. B. Therrill, J. M. Hill, and James Hill, *Woodville*; C. Frazee and B. C. Hunt, *Columbus*; B. F. Hastings and R. P. Wilson, *Vicksburg*.

ARKANSAS: Maj. John S. Houston, *Clarksville*; Thomas Parcel and M. Abagge, *Little Rock*.

FLORIDA: Col. Thomas Hayward and Thomas Howard [Hayward?], Jr., *Tallahasse[e]*.

LOUISIANA: Thomas Bodley, J. A. Read, J. P. Waddell, Joshua Lipman, and J. McVea, *New Orleans*; J. L. Chapline, B. Ray, Peter Jarvis, and Henry King, *Monroe*; Wm. Akenhead and T. H. Scribner, *Bayou Chicot*; Z. L. Dickson, *Bayou Sara*; J. Dickinson and D. Dickinson, *Red River Landing*; J. Norwood, *Clinton*; O. W. Flinker, *Darlington*.

OHIO: James Miller, O. P. Cheney, B. H. Cramer, W. F. Furguson, and W. P. Rice, *Lancaster*; J. A. Moody, W. H. Heath, E. D. Young, and B. Young, *Belville*; S. B. Kinton, *Mt. Vernon*.

INDIANA: Alpha Frisby and Moses Clark, *Frisby's Mills*.

ILLINOIS: J. Evans, *Ottoway*; J. H. White, *Carthage*.

KENTUCKY: W. H. Small, *Mayslick*; Thomas M. Reed, *Henner*.
MISSOURI: J. L. Howard and J. Heatherington, *St. Louis*.
Washington, D.C.: S.W. Langton.
Caracas [VENEZUELA]: Samuel Van Pragg.
Lima, PERU: William Watson Brand.

Thus the *Sylph* had 191 passengers, including two women and two children (?). Her officers were: Francis M. Gardner, *Nantucket, Mass.*, Master; Thomas Hussey, *Nantucket*, Chief Mate; Dr. Edward Dorgriffin Bumstead, *Boston*, Surgeon; Thomas R. Anthony, *New Bedford, Mass.*, Clerk; Wm. H. Dunham, *Nantucket*, 2d Officer; James F. Cathcart, *Nantucket*, 3d Officer; petty officers were Samuel Allen and Henry Eastham, *New Bedford*; W. Worth and John Chase, *Nantucket*; A. Rowe, *Boston*; and Jabez Chandler.

CHAPTER VII. *On Board the* Sylph (pp. 45–63)

1. Hiram D. Pierce's diary fixes the date of departure as May 9. His date and time are confirmed by an "Outline of Voyage of Ship *Sylph*, from Panama to San Francisco," printed as an appendix to George R. Parburt's *Oration*, pp. 25–29: "At 5 P.M. on Wednesday, May 9th, 1849, the ship *Sylph* of Fair Haven, Mass., commanded by Francis M. Gardiner, of Nantucket, Mass., with a company of nearly 200 passengers, weighed anchor, and with a fair westerly breeze, glided out of the harbor of Panama. . . ."

2. Hiram Pierce shows that living arrangements aboard the *Sylph* began to be regularized only on the third day out:

"Thursday 10. a fair wind all night & by 12 to day we had made 160 miles. In the afternoon a calm. I was Sea Sick. Our fare was wretched, & I cast up all that I had eaten. The Ship was wretched dirty & we were crowded in a sad plight. I confess that I wished myself in Troy.

"Friday 11th. I felt some better, eat for breckfast, a small piece of Sea bread & 1 cup of coffey. Continued sick through the day. have not yet kept any thing on my stomach that I have taken on the Ship. At noon it rained hard. So that those who went on deck for dinner got drenched unless protected by oil cloth.

"Saturday 12th. 3d day out. I felt some better in the morning. Cast up some bile & felt better through the day. It was quite calm, not making over 2 or 3 knots. A meeting was held & means taken to better the condition of the Passengers. The passengers were divided into 3 messes called 1st, 2d & 3d mess, to take their turns in beeing served. At evening a shower & good breeze for an hour or two & then lulled all knight."

Later, on May 20, Pierce added: "Our mode of liveing is truly brutish. Our Company is now divided into 2 messes, Starbord & Larbord. One mess first one day & the other the next. We form ourselves in two lines when we can, on that small part of the deck that is left clear. And a man passes through with the Coffey. Another with the Sugar. Another with a basket of bread. Another with a pan of Boiled meat. Another with a bottle of vinegar & malases. & then the grabbing commenses. we ketch a piece of meat in the fingers &

crowd like a lot of Swine. The ship perhaps so careened that you will need to hold on or stagger & pitch like a Drunken man. Many behave so swineish that I prefer to stay a way unless driven to it by hunger. Often we get a lurch & go Scating across deck on back or belley, Coffey Sugar & Bread scattered in wild profusion."

Concerning the food, he observed on May 16: "Our fare for breckfast Coffy & hard bread & molases. For Dinner Pork Corned beef, & beans or rice some times. Supper Bred and sugar. Butter is served but the sight is sufficient without the smell. Meals taken in hand, standing when we can & when we cannot we go down."

3. The *Sylph* sailed south, down the coast of South America, May 9–23, then put in at the small Ecuadorian port Atecames (13 miles southwest of present Esmeraldas), which survives today in a tropical forest from which balsa wood, tagua nuts, mangrove, bananas, and coco are exported. The "Outline" says of this stage of the voyage: "The *Sylph* proceeded on to the southward, beating against head winds, until Wednesday the 23d of May she came to anchor in the Bay of Tacames, or Attacames, in the Republic of Ecuador. After remaining several days to procure wood and water, the *Sylph* weighed anchor on Sunday morning, the 27th day of May, and stood out to sea in a westerly course." Hiram D. Pierce is much more informative:

"Wensday 23d. 14 D[ay]. O[ut]. Wind fresh W. S. quite cool so that I needed an overcoat. Making preperations to Anchor & land. At 4 P. M. Came to Anchor 3 miles from the village of Tecamos 40 miles North of the Equator. 12 of our co went a shore in our boat. One other boat landed a few. That was all that landed the first day. They brought off a quantity of Fruit. There is a small River comes in 2 miles from the Vilage & whalers frequent it for water. It is situated about 4 [40?] miles I think North of the Equator on the North Side of Cape San Francisco, & something 70 miles from the Famous Citty of Queto [Quito] & near the same distance from the famous burning mountains of Cotopaxi & Chimborazo, which may be seen & heard from the Sea in clear weather. But it beeing thick, we Saw nor heard nothing of them.

"Thursday 24. 15. D. O. I went on shore after breckfast at Tecamas, 3 miles from the Ship. It is a small village of about 300 Inhabitants nine tenths of which I judge are pure Indians. They live in Bamboo or Reed Houses, about 10 feet from the ground. The houses beeing built on posts. They are built of split reeds or bamboo poles & thatched with flag or coco leaves, with floors beds & tabels where they have these luxuries, of split reeds. Their Ladder, by which they go up, the take up nights, the object being protection against Wild beasts, Sand flies & creeping things, & I think perhaps the water, as the surf rolls on the beach tremendiously & I think in a gale with the wind in the right direction it must be horible. In many cases they ascend to their rooms by means of a notched Stick. Scare a board is seen in the village. The inhabitants appear quite nice & compared with the inhabitants of the Isthmus tidy. They seem a much better race. do not seem to be so mixed up with the Negro & Spanish. They seem to have no trade with any boddy. I judge there is not a Mechanic in the place, except it be Segar makers. I saw some of them. I could not buy a pound of sugar or pint of malases in the place, & yet there are groceries where Liquor & some few articles are sold. There seemed a great Scarcity of what we would call provisions. After great effort & 3 hours delay I got some Dinner such as it was. It Consisted of Stewed Monkey Boiled plantain, hard bread & plaintain, & peppers. I supposed the meat to be wild hog untill after I had eaten. It was not the most savory dish & I ate but litle. Their meat consist entirely I learned of Wild Hogs, Monkeys Peacocks, & perhaps some fish. all game. But the great Sight & attraction & on which they live is Fruit. Such as Coco nuts Bananas Plaintains Yucas, or Yams. Oranges, Lemons, Limes, Mellons, Coffey &c &c. All these things seem to gro spontaneously. I saw allso Sugar cane of an extreordinary size. Cloves Peppers Coffey Ginger & many other things grow wild. But the Oranges took the lead. I stood in groves where they seemed to form all-most a perfect sheet over my head & they were of an extreordinary size. We had them picked at 50 cts the hundred & picked them ourselves at 20 cts. I helped bring a bundel of Bananas to the Boat that cost 2 rials, as much as 2 could carry handily on a pole. It was like the cluster of Escol. Game is said to be plenty a litle back. There is said to be a small species of Elephant [!]. Lions Tigers &c. W snakes of all descriptions. Such as Boacon-strictors Bush masters, &c, the latter of which grow to a great size. & are said to be the worst snake there is. After spending most of the day we started for the Ship with our fruit & several hundred Oranges. The Tide was rolling in & the Surf was tremendous. We had a good man at the steering oar or I think we should have got swamped. as it was we got safe on board.

"Friday 25th. 16 D. O. My Birth day. I had an oppertunity to go on shore again, but as there was a ship here about to sail for some port on the Coast, I chose to spend my birth day in Wrighting to my Wife & family & did so verry hapily. But I suppose they have never get the letter which was put into the hand of the Captain about to sail. Some of our boys fried some cakes, such as they were. On the whole I enjoyed my birth day quite well.

"Saturday 26. 17. D. O. The Dr & party went a Shore on a pleasure excursion. They invited me but I chose to stay on board. They had quite a flurry in landing & broke 2 oars & got wet.

"Sunday 27. 18. D. O. Got under way at daylight. Wind W. S. W. Beautifull morning. During the day & night a stiff breeze. Ship lay over so that it was dificult to stand. Had no service.

"Monday 28. 19. D. O. Runnig S. W. Wind strong, sea in great Commotion. All feeling rather down. In the afternoon the capt of the New Bedford [ship?], that had taken my letters & that started with us came aboard & then stood for Mazatlan, intending to get a load of Passengers for Cala. Wind fresh & we made good time."

4. It will be seen from the preceding note, and especially Pierce's entries for April 25 and 28, that Gardiner's memory respecting the *New Bedford* was not entirely correct. If, as he and Pierce intimate, she did go on to San Francisco, I have not been able to establish the fact, even allowing for the possibility that *New Bedford* was not her correct name. The Hamburg ship *Sophia,* which Pierce says sailed from Panama at the same time as the

Sylph, reached San Francisco on August 9, 90 days from Panama, with 124 passengers, her captain's name Miller, as reported by the *Alta California.*

5. The *Sylph* took her roundabout course, first south and then west, in consequence of the prevailing winds, and as a means of finding the northeast trade winds, the key to reaching San Francisco. The ship continued on its generally western course, and on July 11 Pierce observed gloomily, "There is some talk about going to the Sandwich Islands, as it seems impossible to get to San Francisco"; nobody hoped to reach San Francisco inside three weeks. According to the "Outline of Voyage of Ship *Sylph,*" on Friday, July 13, "the *Sylph* was in longitude 136. 93 West, her farthest westing during the voyage."

6. Concerning the water rationing, Hiram D. Pierce provides the following information: On July 8: "At 10 Service was held, after which we were put on allowance of one quart of water per day, or 1 pint of water & 1 pint of coffee." On July 12: "Cold & looks gloomey. Our bread is miserable & the meat seems likely to make us Sick, & there appears at least 3 weeks betwene us & S F, & 1 quart of water per day." On July 15: "Our course is rather more favourable. The butt was opend to us again this afternoon & another pint delt to each man, which seemed to spread joy through all our ranks as if we had found treasures."

7. It does not appear that very many signed on as nominal hands. When the *Sylph* reached San Francisco, she officially reported 180 passengers (if this figure was correctly printed in the *Alta California*). On leaving Panama, she had 191 named passengers, of whom one died en route.

8. Dolphin steaks were indeed regarded as a delicacy, and are so viewed in the Hawaiian Islands today, called mahimahi. Hiram D. Pierce, casting some doubt on the dolphin angle, tells of the event as follows: "Two Porpoises & a Cowfish were caught & taken on board [June 14]. they were harpooned. the cowfish would weigh about 500 lb. I think the porpois has the nicest shaped head & jaws & finest set of teeth that I ever saw. The head is shaped like the Pikes only it comes narrower forward, & is armed with 80 beautifull round teeth & Shut so close as to nearly form a water joint. Roasted a litle on the coals & it tasted well, but at home it would have ben rather dark." Next day: "There was quite an excitement about dinner. Capt. Butler, a passenger, made a cowfish chowder, putting in pork & crust. About two Barrels were made. As it was a fresh dish each one watched the pots with eagle eye untill about 2 P. M. when it was brought forth, their stomachs refusing to be comforted or fed on expectation any longer. Capt. B. meantime had crowded the fires out of pure compassion & nearly smoked his eyes out, & there beeing such a mass in the kettle, it was badly burned. Each in the exercise of his selfishness, loaded his plate, when on taisting, spitting & spewing & dumping of plates overboard commenced, & for a time it was a wrathy sene. Capt. B. shrunk from view, & was no wither. He never got over that chowder during the voyage."

9. This incident is not discussed at any length by Hiram D. Pierce. He had noted on May 31 that the *New Bedford* kept alongside at a distance of 5 miles. This was three days after he made the diary entry quoted in Note 4. Seven weeks passed, to July 21 (one day

prior to sighting the California coast), before he could write, "Saw a sail in the morning to Leward."

10. Asa D. Hatch established himself as a commission merchant in San Francisco soon after reaching there, and continued in the business at least as late as 1877–1878, by which time his residence was noted by the San Francisco directory to be Oakland. He had other occupations along the way; in 1852–1853 a grocer; in 1861–1862 an inspector for the Customs House; in 1863–1864 secretary of the Front Street, Mission & Ocean R. R.; in 1868 in mining stocks, and in 1869 a mining agent.

11. Fairchild's son, Mahlon D., wrote some "Reminiscences of a 'Forty-Niner," including an account of their voyage to Chagres on the *Crescent City* (with Gardiner), and on to San Francisco in the *Sylph*, printed in California Historical Society *Quarterly*, March, 1934, vol. XIII, pp. 3–33.

12. Perhaps Gardiner has reference to "Captain Osgood," as listed among the passengers. For other possibilities in respect of a "Captain K.," see the names listed under Massachusetts, New York, Louisiana, and Ohio, Chapter VI, Note 26.

13. Hiram D. Pierce wrote on July 3, "Today a dozen or more were engaged in making & frying donuts." Next day: "Independance. I reckon I thought of Home. The morning verry cool & unpleasant, & I was quite sick. I ate no supper or breckfast. At 10 the Passengers assembeld & comenced the Celebration of the day. Prair was offerd by Mr. Fairchild & a National Song was sung, after which the Decleration was red by Judge Buoy, followed by a most Eloquent Oration from Mr. Parbert of Geneva, Ny. It was recieved with enthuseas followed by another Song & closed by the Benediction. After which Rice Donuts Honey & Panama Molases were served out, & we all enjoyed the day as well as we could under the circumstances. No liquor or gunpowder were used during the day."

14. Again Gardiner's memories must be corrected by reference to a contemporary source, the pamphlet: *Oration Delivered on Board the Ship Sylph in the Pacific Ocean, July 4, 1849. Latitude 25°28' N.: Longitude 131° 00' W. Together with a Brief Account of her Voyage from Panama to San Francisco. By George R. Parburt, Esq.* Geneva, N. Y.: I. & S. H. Parker, Printers. 1849. (The printed paper wrapper on the copy in the California Historical Society library is dated 1850: in any case, this is a very early Gold Rush item.) Officers of the Day are listed as follows: Col. Thomas Hayward, President. Capt. Francis M. Gardner, John A. Reed, esq., Vice Presidents. Reader of Declaration, H. Ray Bowie, of Baltimore. Orator, George R. Parburt, of Geneva, Chaplain, David Fairchild. Music conducted by Jason White, of Providence, R. I. Marshal, Major John S. Houston. As shown by correspondence of that date having a view to publication, the Committee of Arrangements were F. M. Gardner, D. R. Perry, Wm. Akenhead, R. P. Wilson, G. S. Oldfield, Jr., Dan'l Newcomb.

The oration itself is lengthy, running to 16 printed pages. Howard Gardiner's written recollection is also very long, but bears small resemblance to the original. This recollection may have some value, as a composite of all the Fourth of July orations heard over a lifetime; but, it clearly has no documentary value for Gold Rush history, and I excise it from his text.

George R. Parburt was also the author of *Anselmo: A Poem* (San Francisco, 1865). He eventually followed Gardiner to Tuolumne County, becoming editor of the Columbia *Gazette* near the end of 1857. He purchased the paper on March 18, 1858, but it expired on July 29. Mrs. Barbara Eastman tells me he was something of a blackguard, and cites the Sonora *Tuolumne Courier,* May 8 and 22, 1858.

15. The heavy gale Gardiner describes occurred much earlier, on June 21, while on the westerly leg of the course from Atecames. Mahlon D. Fairchild, the "Outline of Voyage of Ship *Sylph,*" and Hiram D. Pierce all provide graphic accounts of this storm. The "Outline" says:

"On Thursday, June 21st, she was in lat. 15 deg. 55 min. North, and longitude 216 deg. 16 min. West by observation. Soon after mid-day the winds increased, and the showers were very heavy and abundant. By 4 P. M. all the miz[z]en sails were furled, and the topsails double reefed. The dark, leaden clouds at sunset, gave indications of a storm—the swift flying scuds, obedient, were gathering into dense clouds, preparatory to an onset in the war of elements. At 11 P. M. the storm began to rage with much violence. The intense darkness of the night, the shrill whistling of the winds, the deafening roar of the waves, broken occasionally by the earnest and loud voice of the officer of the deck, as he moved from one part of the deck to another, gave assurances that a much more serious storm was upon the wings of the wind than any the *Sylph* had before experienced on the voyage. Sail after sail was shortened, until 1 A. M. every sail was furled except the double reefed maintopsail, which was swinging finely before the increasing gale, and seemed almost like a spirit of life, playing about the mainmast, as the guiding and guardian angel of the ship. Soon after the main spanker was shivering in the breeze, and the *Sylph* was 'lying to,' in order to ride out the gale. The surges swept over the darkness like huge winrows of light, rolling far up from the black abyss below, and towering above, broke far away and sank as vast sheets of liquid fire upon the dark velvet of the sea.

"At dawn on Friday, the 22d, the sea presented a scene of wild and glorious magnificence. The tempest swept fearfully along upon its outstretched wings—far as the eye could reach the mountain billows were rolling and dashing fearfully against each other, covering the sea with angry foam, and breaking around the *Sylph* in wildest revelry; still she rode magnificently in the gale, leaping the giant surges like a thing of life. At six o'clock the wind veered more westerly, and in half an hour after, the jib, jib-boom and flying jib-boom were carried away, and the foretop-gallant-mast hung dangling in the shrouds. In the course of the forenoon the stern boat was stove in and one of the side boats injured. The storm continued throughout the day, and was broken about midnight, and by 9 A. M., on Saturday the 23d, the reefs were shaken out, and the *Sylph* bounding on westward over the subsiding billows."

Hiram D. Pierce provides a more personal note: "It was said by the Capt who had followed the sea 24 years that he had never seen but one Storm so severe & that of but few hours duration. And it was generally said that a vesel never lived through a harder one to tell the story. Eating was given up. All sat or lay in mute astonishment, & some at least who at other times would curse their Maker were willing afterwards to thank Him, & say that nothing but the tender Mercies of Allmighty God had spared them, & to confess that they Praid, but they soon forgat their vows. . . ."

16. Compare Note 8. Was a sail really seen at this time?

17. As reported in the San Francisco *Alta California*, August 2, 1849, the Boston ships *Capitol* and *Pharsalia* reached that port July 20 and 23, with 210 and 135 passengers. (The *Sylph* arrived July 26.) Nothing was said by the *Alta* about damage sustained. For further information on both vessels, see Octavius Thorndike, *Argonauts of '49* (Cambridge, Mass., 1923), pp. 202, 210–211, 220–221.

18. The "Outline of Voyage" remarks: "on Saturday, the 21st day of July, at 6 P. M. made the highlands a little southward of Monterey, having been but 55 days out of sight of land." Hiram D. Pierce, on the 22nd, says: "Land was seen last evening. Wind strong all Knight. This morning verry cool. Thermometor 55 degrees. At ¼ before 10 the coast of California was in Sight before us. We stood on our course running sharp on the wind untill within 2 miles & then tacked & ran 2 hours & tacked again & ran into the coast having made but 5 miles, & at 4 tacked & ran 9 hours, & then tacked in until 12 having made 13 miles. Tacked West again the wind blowing quite a gale the whole time. Lat. 37 deg. 9 min." On July 23 Pierce adds: "Cold & cloudy. We found that we had made land in the gulf of Monteray. At 12 came near land 43 miles South of San Francisco by observation. Then tacked W. S. W. 10 hours, then tacked N. E. & stood on the course."

19. Hiram D. Pierce journalizes: "Tuesday [July] 24th. 76. D. O. Still cold, during yesterday & last night it blew allmost a gale. At 12 came in sight of land again running nearly paralell with the Coast. Breakers were seen along the coast at the distance of 10 miles. At Sundown in 10 miles of the coast off & on during the night. The hills at a distance look red like burnt clay. At 3 A. M. I heard as I supposed sticks or kelp scrape the sides or bottom of the Ship & feeling a little uneasy got up & went on deck. The mate was throwing the lead. It had Shoaled to 7 fathom. The sails were immediately clued up & all hands called. The Captain came on deck in his shirt flaps & orderd the Anchor droped in 6½ fathom. During the afternoon we saw a Whale close along Side. One throwed himself out of water finely. His flukes presented a formidable appearance.

"Wensday 25th. 77. D. O. Laying at anchor Somewhere in the neighborhood of the entrance to S. F. but none can tell where, as the whether is thick & foggy. We knew we were near Shore but could see but a few rods. There was a current running some 4 or 5 knot. The Capt thought our situation unsafe as it blew fresh & at 6 got up the Anchor & stood out & ran up the coast. At 10 saw a sail & boarded it & learned that we had anchord at the entrance. We were now some 12 miles above. Bout ship & the wind lulled & at sundown came to anchor 4 miles abrest the entrance."

The "Outline of Voyage" says corroboratively: "On Wednesday morning, at 3 A.M.

July 25th, anchored on the bar of San Francisco, and being a very dense fog, at 6 A.M. stood out to sea. Having learned from a Captain of the ship which was boarded during the forenoon our position, the *Sylph* stood in again for the harbor, and at 9 P.M. anchored off the mouth of the Bay." We infer that the vessel from which information was obtained was the American brig *Henry,* Bray, which sailed for the Columbia River from San Francisco July 24. No other sailings were recorded by the *Alta California* after July 20; and no vessels seem to have cleared for the Hawaiian Islands this week, Gardiner's subsequent comment notwithstanding.

20. There is some confusion of memory here. Charles Wilkes, *Narrative of the United States Exploring Expedition . . . ,* vol. V, pp. 41–42, says only: "On approaching the coast in the neighborhood of San Francisco, the country has by no means an inviting aspect. To the north [of the Golden Gate], it rises in a lofty range, whose highest point is known as the Table Hill, and forms an iron-bound coast from Punto de los Reyes to the mouth of the harbour.

"To the south, there is an extended sandy beach, behind which rise the sand-hills of San Bruno, to a moderate height. There are no symptoms of cultivation, nor is the land on either side fit for it; for in the former direction it is mountainous, in the latter sandy, and in both barren. The entrance to the harbour is striking: bold and rocky shores confine the rush of the tide, which bore us on and through a narrow passage into a large estuary: in this, several islands and rocks lie scattered around: some of the islands are clothed with vegetation to their very tops; others are barren and covered with guano, having an immense number of sea-fowls hovering over, around, and alighting upon them. The distant shores of the bay extend north and south far beyond the visible horizon, exhibiting one of the most spacious, and at the same time safest ports in the world. . . ."

21. News of the Astor Place Riot in New York on May 10, 1849, reached San Francisco by the *California* July 15, printed four days later in the *Alta California.* The riot, a venting of anti-British feeling, grew out of professional jealousy between the American actor, Edwin Forrest, and the English tragedian, William Charles Macready. There was a preliminary riot at the Astor Place Theatre on May 6, and a disastrous sequel four days later, when Macready appeared in *Macbeth.* Police not having succeeded in dispersing a mob, the militia was called out, and in the attendant violence some 22 were killed and upwards of 30 wounded. Detailed reports may be found in the New York *Herald,* May 11–15, 1849.

22. Gardiner evidently refers to Arch or Bird Rock, a mile west of Alcatraz, which was blown up as a menace to navigation in 1901.

23. By Presidio Gardiner means more precisely Fort Point, where the south end of the Golden Gate Bridge now stands. The name Washerwoman's Bay, applied to the cove inside Fort Point, seems to have fallen into disuse, after originating, evidently, in 1849. The *Alta California,* March 20, 1850, recounts a meeting of washerwomen there to fix price scales. Presumably they resorted to the fresh water at what became known as Washerwoman's Lagoon, and by extension the name was applied to the Bay shore beyond.

24. As reported by the *Alta California,* the American ship *Thames,* Payne, master, arrived in San Francisco May 27, 1849, with 116 passengers, 75 days from "Takahuana" (Talcahuano, Chile).

25. By Telegraph Point Gardiner evidently means North Point, at the base of Telegraph Hill, from the top of which, beginning April 19, 1850, the arrival of inbound ships was signaled to "The City." The *Sylph* swept around to Yerba Buena Cove, soon to be filled in as San Francisco expanded.

26. The *Alta California,* August 2, 1849, reported the arrival on July 26: "Am ship *Sylph,* Gardner, 76 days from Panama, cargo to order, 180 passengers." The "Outline of Voyage" comments almost as tersely: "On Thursday, June [July] 26, 1849, at 2 P. M., the *Sylph* dropped anchor in the Bay of San Francisco, opposite the city, having completed her voyage from Panama to San Francisco in 78 days, and run during that time more than 8000 miles." Hiram D. Pierce does rather better: "Thursday 26th. 78t. D. O. Morning thick & foggy not able to see a mile. At ½ past 12 raised Anchor & got underway for the harbour. Wind & tide in favour. The senery was most wild & desolate. Large naked rocks some of them covered with guana projecting out & towering up, the entrance beeing about one mile wide & tide running through 6 miles. A great abundance of fowls covered the water. At 2 P. M. droped anchor 3 miles from the landing, the wind blowing a gale. The bay stretches in one direction 60 miles & the other 10, & in clear weather we can easily see across it. It is interspersed with islands. At 4 miles from town we passed Guana [Alcatraz] Island, perhaps of 2 acres. It towers up some 50 feet & looks like a great Snow bank, beeing perfectly white with guana. There is said to be 175 Sail in the Harbour. All is life & bustle."

27. Corydon Bristol, a member of Hiram D. Pierce's company from Troy, New York, died July 16, 1849. On June 27 Pierce noted that in the evening he gave his berth to "Mr. Bristol who was sick," taking his place in a boat on deck. On July 7 he observed that during the past few days "Mr Bristol has been failing verry much," and on July 15, "Mr. Bristel is verry feeble." Next day: "This morning at 6 Mr Bristel Expired after a few weeks of most intense Suffering, brought on I think by scalding his fingers at the galley & taking cold in his hand. And notwithstanding it is the blasting of all his worldly hopes & prospects, yet in view of his sufferings it seemed a sweet relief. His request was that his boddy might be sent home, & we comenced to make preperations accordingly. We asertained that spirits could be obtain at about $2. per gallon. We got a cask of the Capt. It would take about 40 gallons. A meeting of the pasengers was called & it appointed a comity composed of the Phisicians on board, to concider & report the best mode of preservation. They reported it could best be done in spirits & then it was decided by the Surgon of the Ship & other Phisicians that his heart & vitals must be taken out, otherwise it would burst the cask. To this his friends objected & a majority of our company voted against opening him, & that rather than have him cut to pieces we would bury him in the deep. So a comity was appointed to make the nessesary preperations, & at 6 P M, he was brought to the waist of the Ship sewed up in canvass with his face exposed while the

English Service was gone through in a Solom maner, after which all was sewed up & he was committed to the deep. The Ship passed on & in one moment he was hid from mortal eyes untill the morning of the Resurection. The sene was a Salom one & many eyes were sufused with tears. Thus perished one of our most active & usefull members before we had reached the field of opperation. It took place in Lat. 33. 33. L 130. 28."

The "Outline of Voyage" prints a report of proceedings on July 16, 1849, whereby the passengers of the *Sylph* expressed regret and commiseration to Mrs. Frances Bristol, the afflicted widow, and her two orphan children. This source gives the place as "Lat. 33 31 North, Long. 130 18 West."

28. The issue of the *Alta California* that recorded the arrival of the *Sylph*, August 2, 1849, printed a report by the harbormaster listing ships then in the port of San Francisco; 116 were named as having arrived between April 2 and July 24, 1849, besides 7 U.S. ships, 8 vessels at Sacramento, 8 at Stockton, and one at Sausalito, a total of 140 vessels exclusive of 43 that were plying the rivers San Joaquin and Sacramento. Arrivals prior to April 2 were not listed. There were more clearances all year than Gardiner's remarks would lead one to suppose, and not only for coastal or near-coastal shipping. Also, contrary to his recollection, no Chinese junks had reached San Francisco.

29. Happy Valley lay immediately south of what was then the town of San Francisco, extending several blocks back from the waterfront, at First Street, diagonally between present Market and Howard streets (the locality of the future Palace Hotel). By 1852 it was built up, but in 1849–50, as Gardiner says, it afforded a convenient camping place for new arrivals (and the indigent). The *Alta California*, March 19, 1850, provides this tidbit: "Our cotemporary of the [*Pacific*] *News* is mistaken in giving Commodore Martin the credit of naming Happy Valley. . . . Two great minds frequently hit upon the same idea, and it is not by any means improbable that the Commodore may have given the locality alluded to the name of 'Happy Valley' without the knowledge that it had previously received the same appel[l]ation. Certain it is that Happy Valley was known as such long and long before the arrival of Mr. Martin—many months. . . ."

30. Clark's Point, at the foot of present Broadway, was named for William Squire Clark, an overland emigrant of 1846; it marked the northern limits of Yerba Buena Cove, which extended southward to Rincon Point. The arrival of the American whaling bark *Romulus*, Cartwright, at Honolulu on March 28, 1849, was noted in *The Friend*, April, 1849, vol. 7, p. 32. Nothing was said of her condemnation, but neither is she reported to have sailed. In September *The Friend* reported the arrival of "Mr. Cartwright" among the passengers in the *Pacifico*, 14 days from San Francisco. Was this the same man?

31. San Francisco was much more built up by midsummer of 1849 than most Forty-niners afterward remembered; there were even some houses of brick, besides those of adobe. A building of the latter type was the post office, situated at the corner of Pike and Clay streets, of which a representation is published in Frank Soulé, *et al., Annals of San Francisco* (New York, 1855), p. 260.

32. Gardiner gives us the impression that all the passengers of the *Sylph* departed im-

mediately on arrival at San Francisco, but Hiram D. Pierce's diary is a healthy corrective. As quoted in Note 24, Pierce's entry for July 26 affords us no reason to think anybody landed that afternoon. His record continues:

"Friday 27th. Went ashore & found such a wild state of things as allmost to intoxicate a person without giveing 50 cts a glass. Money seemed of no act. Houses that would not cost over $100 in Troy rents for $300 per month. Others of the commonest class & cheapest construction rent for $800. per month. One house that might be rented in Troy for $200. rents as I am informed for $180,000 [per year]. Lumber is worth $450. per M. Brick $100 per M. Wages from 12 to $16 per day, & yet provisions & clothing in particular is comparitively cheap. Yet some articles is high enough to make up. Flour 6 to $12 per bbl. Choice Cheese 6/per lb. Salaratus $12. per lb. Eggs $12 per doz. I paid $1.50 for breckfast. Reports from the mines are verry encourageing. Men are coming in, some of them loaded with the dust. In the forenoon there is a thick cold fog, & about noon the Sea breeze begins to blow a gale untill in the evening. S Fro is a miserable dusty dirty town of some 5000, out of every kindred tongue & people under Heaven.

"Sat 28th. Morning bright & clear. The anchor was raised to run in nearer shore. I feel quite well. Rose & took notes, went ashore at 9, looked round, bought a chest of Tea at 40 cts, one cheese of 43 lb. 55 cts, bread 25 cts per loaf, mince pies 4/. Returned to the Ship after a hard strugle. Wood is from 40 to $60. per cord.

"Sunday 29.—Staid a board & wrote home. A pleasant day but windy & cold. 2 Ships Came in, one that Started the midle of Jan.

"Monday 30th. Still at anchor. today wrote three letters. . . . Mr Bills came a board & took dinner with us today, & spent the afternoon.

"Aug 1st This morning we are verry buisy in packing up & getting readdy for a start up the rivers. We have decided to form 2 parties. One to go up the Sanjoaquin & one up the Sacramento. I go up the Sacramento with the Dr [Comstock]. We got our things aboard a Schooner Comanded by Capt Macy one of our pasengers. . . ."

CHAPTER VIII. *In San Francisco* (pp. 65–73)

1. This acquaintance would appear to have been Phineas Hudson, though Gardiner is soon saying that Hudson came out in the *Daniel Webster,* and as will be seen in the next note, only a G. B. and an R. Hudson appear in the passenger list for that vessel. Stephen Fowler, one of Gardiner's fellow Long Islanders, in his MS. journal on October 7, 1849, writes at San Francisco: "To day I had quite a long chat with Mr Phineas Hudson. He formerly resided in Sag Harbor." Caspar T. Hopkins, in his "California Recollections," mentions Phineas as a San Francisco shipwright in 1850 (California Historical Society *Quarterly,* September, 1946, vol. 25, p. 259).

2. The *Daniel Webster* sailed from New York Saturday, February 3, 1849, Pierce, master, and reached San Francisco July 21. The New York *Herald,* February 6, 1849, listed as her passengers: "Dr. John Gunn, C. D. Elliott, A. McKendry, G. F. Archibald, W. J. Stoutenborough, D. F. Finley, Wm. Merry, George Sealy, Henry W. Watts, Leander

McLoughlin, E. P. Howell, Thomas Steers, M. F. Coon, E. B. Newcomb, J. Hammer, A. Thompson, G. B. Hudson, William Gray, L. Reinhold, Henry F. Green, A. Hollingsworth, C. Rathaway, John S. Tileston, Caleb Hyatt, O. W. Sheffield, J. F. Ryer, William McGarry, James R. Walters, Theo Bernard, L. B. Rogers, J. Shepard, N. B. Coon, A. Lamb, R. Crawford, E. Allen, E. Fenno, J. H. Cook, F. Steinbergan, O. P. Chapan, J. Steward, E. K. Kernell, J. Clark, D. Cook, J. C. Whitlock, John R. Russell, A. S. Dickerson, William McCabberly, H. V. L. Vandhoef, Foster N. Mott, John J. Bertholf, Luther Hill, A. Lockwood, P. Hammer, B. Prou, R. Hudson, M. Campbell, W. H. Brown, John P. Staats." (Thus 58 men were named.)

3. E. P. Howell appears in the passenger list of the *Daniel Webster,* and so does G. B. Hudson. Presumably these were two of the three young men mentioned. Was Henry or Phineas the "R. Hudson" of the passenger list?

4. The *Sylph* was still in the port of San Francisco August 29, 1849. Her sailing went unrecorded by the *Alta California,* but *The Friend,* November 1 and 15, 1849, vol. 7, pp. 72, 80, noted her arrival at Hilo September 23 and at Lahaina October 8, "Clean, from California, taking in cargo for the United States."

5. Angel Island is a principal feature of San Francisco Bay. I have not established the circumstances of Captain Payne's death. A Captain John Payne is listed in San Francisco directories for 1852 and 1854 in connection with a saloon. Was this the same man?

6. Dr. J. B. D. Stillman, who landed at Happy Valley from the ship *Pacific* August 5, 1849, expressed the opinion in a report published in 1851 that almost none of those who passed through Happy Valley that summer escaped dysentery; the cause, he suggested, was that the emigrants relied for water on hundreds of brackish little seep-hole wells, from two to three feet deep. See George W. Groh, *Gold Fever* (New York, 1966), for this and other aspects of the medical history of the California Gold Rush.

7. As seen in Chapter III, Note 3, the *Sabina* sailed from Sag Harbor February 7. In noting her arrival on August 9, the *Alta California* gave as her place of departure Greenport, also on eastern Long Island. Gardiner does not mention at this point the arrival of the ship *Brooklyn* three days later, but Stephen Fowler, who landed from that vessel on August 15, does us the service of recording on the 16th: "Robert and Howard Gardiner and Stephen French called on us to day. Davis Osborn is to the Mines. The Ship *Sabina* of Sag Harbour is up to New York a town some distance about [above] this."

8. For comment on Peter Smith, see Chapter XVI, Note 5. It may be that he had not yet reached California.

9. The Southern Mines were understood to be those drained by the San Joaquin or its tributaries, or those still farther south. The Northern Mines were those in the valley of the Sacramento. Stockton was the entrepôt for the former, Sacramento for the latter.

10. Gardiner may refer to the fire of May 4, 1850, with its estimated losses of $4,000,-000. A description of this fire, from the *Alta California,* May 6, 1850, is reprinted in Dale L. Morgan and James R. Scobie, eds., *Three Years in California, William Perkins' Journal.* . . . , pp. 149–150.

CHAPTER IX. *From San Francisco to Stockton* (pp. 75–78)

1. I have not found a record of the schooner *Favorite* on inland waters. The reports by the San Francisco harbormaster concerning ships in port and plying the rivers, printed in the *Alta California*, August 2 and August 31, 1849, named the following as vessels "plying up the rivers of San Joaquin and Sacramento": *Kauai, Odd Fellow, Placer, Rialto, Olivia, Constellation, Feliz, Carolina, Iowa, San Blassina, Adelia, Mazatlan, Empire, Eclipse, Velasco, Phoenix, Sagadahock, Elbe, Liberto, Chance, Spry, Rainbow, Adee, Veloz, Lola, 6th June, Zack Johnson, Laura, Emily Jane, Nuevo Hermanos, Union, Milman, Plymouth, Star, Mary, Louisa, Charles and Edward, Diana, Sophia, Roe, Sea Witch, Patuxent, Ann, Enterprise.* All were sailing craft.

That there was such a vessel as the schooner *Favorite* is, however, shown by later records. She is mentioned in Matthews' list (see Chapter XIX, Note 3) as present in San Francisco Bay on September 2, 1850. Next winter and spring the *Alta* has frequent notations on her clearances to and arrival from Santa Cruz or Monterey, usually with cargoes of redwood lumber, one Brown then her master; see *e.g.*, the issue for April 23.

2. The Sisters, still so known, are two islets off Point San Pedro. Their counterparts, The Brothers, one of which is occupied by a lighthouse, stand opposite, off Point San Pablo. For a well-written and well-informed book about this watery world, see Harold Gilliam, *San Francisco Bay* (Garden City, N.Y., 1957).

3. The projectors of Benicia (at first called Francisca) were Robert Semple and Commodore Thomas ap Catesby Jones. The townsite was purchased from Mariano G. Vallejo in 1847 by Semple and Thomas O. Larkin; Jones made it the headquarters for the Pacific Squadron; and a determined though unavailing effort was launched to establish Benicia rather than San Francisco as the great seaport and metropolis of northern California.

4. New York of the Pacific, founded by J. D. Stevenson, G. McDougall, W. C. Parker, and Samuel Norris, was alluringly described by the proprietors in the *Alta California*, May 17, 1849, and thereafter. They had the townsite surveyed by R. P. Hammond, William Tecumseh Sherman, and James Blair; some of their maps may be seen in the Weber Family Collection in the Bancroft Library. New York of the Pacific did not catch on, and Pittsburg, in Contra Costa County, occupies the site today. For further information see Ernest A. Wiltsee, "The City of the New York of the Pacific," California Historical Society *Quarterly*, March, 1933, vol. 12, pp. 25–34. A useful footnote to the history of both New York of the Pacific and the *Sabina* is provided by some correspondence printed in the *Alta California For the Steamer*, August 31, 1849:

SAN FRANCISCO, AUG. 15, 1849.

Messrs. Editors.—When the survey of the Bay of Suisun was made known, and the site of New York of the Pacific selected, you very kindly noticed the survey of the Bay and the site for the town in a most liberal manner. Your remarks were at that time, and have frequently since been, the subject of censure by many persons interested in other towns, and more especially by some persons occupying high official stations in this country. A subsequent survey of the Bay of Suisun by a distinguished naval officer, Capt. [Cadwalader] Ring[g]old,) has confirmed the first survey, as to the capacity of the channel; and the annexed letter from the gentleman (W. H. Fauntleroy, U. S. N.,) who piloted the first ship from this town to New York, more than confirms all you said of its advantages for a great city at the head of ship navigation.

Very respectfully your obed't sevts.,
STEVENSON, PARKER & CO.

NEW YORK OF THE PACIFIC, CAL.,
AUGUST 11, 1849.

Dear Sir,—I have taken the vessel (the ship *Sabina,* with cargo and 16 feet draught), from San Francisco to this place, in seven hours, a distance of 43 miles, during low tide, and had not less than four and a half fathoms water during the run, except over 100 yards of ground, upon which I had 18 feet; but, by avoiding that channel and taking another, 27 feet water can be carried from the ocean to this place, with perfect safety. I would have no hesitation in beating a merchant ship, with cargo, of the largest class, from this place to sea. Off New York there is excellent anchorage ground for five times the number of vessels now lying at San Francisco. I am much gratified by my visit to this place; I drank the water from the river with others, and all pronounced it excellent; and I am not alone in opinion here that the site for a city and other facilities afforded for convenience hereafter, is unequalled by any other that I have seen in California. Your ob't sev't,

WM. H. FAUNTLEROY, U.S.N.

COL. STEVENSON, *San Francisco.*

5. This locality was famous—or infamous—for the ferocity of its mosquitoes all through the Gold Rush period; it is not impossible that the failure of New York of the Pacific to take hold reflected this circumstance.

6. Even today, the Delta region has an intricate pattern of channels, as may be seen by air travelers. The first detailed map of this region was Charles D. Gibbes, "Map of San Joaquin River" (San Francisco, 1850), reproduced in George P. Hammond and Dale L. Morgan, *Captain Charles M. Weber, Pioneer of the San Joaquin and Founder of Stockton, California* (Berkeley, 1966).

7. Stockton Slough is still so known. Modern dredging has made Stockton a continued shipping point for ocean commerce.

8. Some things are unexplained about the *Mazeppa* at Stockton. An American bark *Mazeppa,* Girlder, master, reached San Francisco December 2, 1849, 224 days from New York, but cleared for the Sandwich Islands January 12, 1850. An English ship of the same name arrived from Port Adelaide, Australia, October 14, and sailed for Sydney December 24, 1849. No other vessel with such a name seems to have been recorded among ship arrivals of 1849. Wherever she came from, there was a *Mazeppa* at Stockton, for in the

Times of that city, April 6–May 4, 1850, Starbuck & Spencer offered the storeship *Mazeppa* for sale, inquiry to be made on board. On January 15, 1851, in the same paper, Starbuck & Spencer gave notice to all persons having trunks or other properties on storage, on board the storeship *Mazeppa,* that unless the same were taken away on or before March 15, they would be sold to pay expenses.

H. H. Spencer and S. Starbuck were listed in the first census for San Joaquin County, each 23 years old as of November, 1850, the former from New York, the latter from New Hampshire. On May 14, 1851, the Stockton *San Joaquin Republican* published a notice by Stephen Starbuck and Harvey H. Spencer that their partnership was dissolved by mutual consent on April 26, 1851. Presumably Spencer went elsewhere but Starbuck remained in Stockton for some time.

CHAPTER X. *From Stockton to Hawkins' Bar* (pp. 79–80)

1. Charles M. Weber, an overland emigrant of 1841, acquired title in 1845 to the Mexican grant El Campo de los Franceses, and on a part of this grant, in 1847, he founded the town he named for Commodore Robert F. Stockton. Weber was a town-builder and community planner of the first order, his talents amply demonstrated before he died in 1881 at the age of 67. For details, see the work by Hammond and Morgan cited in Chapter IX, Note 6, in which his papers are calendared. The same work contains a reproduction in color of a painting of Stockton made in 1849, before the late December fire there. A statement by Weber, setting forth the advantages of Stockton, was published weekly in the *Alta California* through the summer of 1849, commencing June 14.

2. Gardiner never gives Peck's first name, but the man crossed his path intermittently for some years.

3. The road to the Stanislaus River via Lone Tree kept to the east of French Camp, which lies about five miles south of Stockton. Lewis C. Gunn, who crossed this same plain on August 14, 1849, journalized: "Started at sunrise to make the twelve miles to the next watering place. Not a tree during the whole distance—one vast parched plain, and the sand and clay had not fairly recovered from yesterday's heating. In two hours the heat was oppressive. With our heavy packs, and our feet tender after the long sea voyage, we could not endure the additional bounce received from the pack, and our feet blistered most shockingly. I could scarcely reach the end of the twelve miles, and there were thirteen more before us. We stopped many times, and did not reach the well until eleven o'clock. We bathed our feet and rested till two o'clock under the Lone Tree, for so the place was designated, there being but one tree. A tent with stores was here, as also at the place where we stopped last night. Our afternoon's walk was very severe and we did not reach the river till dusk." See Anna Lee Marston, ed., *Record of a California Family. Journals and Letters of Lewis C. Gunn and Elizabeth Le Breton Gunn* (San Diego, 1928), p. 62.

4. Although his name appears familiarly in the record of 1849–1850, little seems to be known about the Texan, Colonel Alden Apollo Moore Jackson. Heckendorn & Wilson's

Miners & Business Men's Directory, from the near perspective of January 1, 1856, comments that the thriving town of Jacksonville was "one of the oldest in the Southern mines. The first store was put up by Col. Jackson, in June '49, and from its favorable location, being situated at the junction of Wood's creek with the Tuolumne river, it possesses advantages which are not enjoyed by most river towns." Herbert O. Lang, *A History of Tuolumne County*, pp. 17, 50–51, observes that "In the month of June [1849] Jacksonville was founded, Colonel Jackson having discovered gold-bearing gravel at the junction of Wood's creek and the Tuolumne river. These diggings are said to have sustained for many years their reputation of moderate richness, other more pretentious camps having died in the interim. . . . [But Colonel Jackson] does not possess the distinction of being the first settler, for that honor belongs to a Mr. Smart, who located there a few weeks previously and engaged in agricultural pursuits. His property was known as 'Spring Garden,' which acquired celebrity as being the first fruit garden in this portion of the State.

"The new town grew but slowly, as compared with the rate of increase of other locations. Its growth, however, was permanent. From the time when Col. Jackson erected the first store until the middle of the Summer of 1851, there had been a steady enlargement, sufficient to place it second only to Sonora in point of population. And in later years, although Jacksonville suffered the inevitable decline that has attended all the mining towns of that era, still she sank into insignificance but slowly. . . ."

Colonel Jackson had mercantile interests in Stockton during 1850, but is not listed in the U.S. census made there that fall.

5. Gardiner says that his party reached the Stanislaus at Knight's Ferry, but he appears to have traveled via Taylor's Ferry, at present Oakdale, soon to be renamed Heath and Emory's Ferry. Gardiner returned from the foothill country in December via Knight's Ferry, as seen on a later page. At this season—late summer—the river was low, and the Stanislaus could be forded with little difficulty.

6. Green Springs, a double spring, still flows near the present Keystone, Tuolumne County. A drawing of the locality as of April 5, 1850, is reproduced in Carl Schaefer Dentzel, ed., *The Drawings of John Woodhouse Audubon . . .* (San Francisco, 1957).

CHAPTER XI. *Life at Hawkins' Bar* (pp. 81–86)

1. Hawkins' Bar, now drowned by the waters impounded by Don Pedro Dam, was situated on the Tuolumne River below its confluence with Woods Creek. John Woodhouse Audubon noted on March 29, 1850, that the Tuolumne came out of a gorge in the steep and rocky hills a mile above Hawkins' Bar, "and sends forth the troubled stream to be tossed and dashed over rocks and shallow bars, for miles through hills and chasms until it reaches the plains, when it moves quietly, but still rapidly at this season, as it makes its way to the San Joaquin, ninety or a hundred miles from the mouth of that stream." (Frank Heywood Hodder, ed., *Audubon's Western Journal: 1849–1850*, Cleveland, 1906,

pp. 218–221.) This son of the famous naturalist made two drawings of Hawkins' Bar, one reproduced in Hodder's work, and both in the book edited by Dentzel cited in the previous note. They are again reproduced herein.

Lewis Richard Price, who reached Hawkins' Bar on October 22, 1849, some weeks after Gardiner, thought the place had "a much neater, and more comfortable appearance than the camp at Woods' diggings, but the amount of suffering, I should suppose is much the same, & that its superiority is confined to its appearance.

"The hills that shut in the river Tahualame at this point are very high and exceedingly steep. I remained here the greater part of the day—saw some of the diggings—the people were doing well—and generally seemed satisfied with their proceedings. Some regularity appeared to have been established in the workings—the place being parcelled out into small patches of which one is assigned to anyone who wishes it but he cannot encroach on his neighbour. The washing was done here in common rockers—the gold got out was small, like bran, but of a very good quality. No quicksilver was used—and I believe it has been used hitherto up at the north in the Mormon diggings, &c." See W. Turrentine Jackson, ed., "Mazatlan to the Estanislao, The Narrative of Lewis Richard Price's Journey to California in 1849," California Historical Society *Quarterly*, March, 1960, vol. 39, p. 47.

The identity of the man for whom the Bar was named is one of the trophies awaiting future scholarship relating to the Mother Lode country. Herbert O. Lang, *A History of Tuolumne County, California*, p. 52, says that Hawkins' Bar "was the site of the first river-bed workings on the Tuolumne. Its name was derived from one Hawkins, who kept a trading tent, the first in the place. In April, 1849, there were fifteen or twenty miners working on the banks with pans and rockers, in the primitive mode of mining. By September of the same year, the population had increased to seven hundred men, who, at the first legislative election, cast five hundred votes. . . ."

2. By the time Gardiner reached Hawkins' Bar, the overland emigrants had begun to arrive in California in numbers. The Sonorans who had come to the Tuolumne area early in the year tended to bring their women with them, with the result that what became Tuolumne County, particularly the Sonora area, had an entirely different type of society than the diggings elsewhere, well pictured by William Perkins in Morgan and Scobie, eds., *Three Years in California . . .*, as previously cited.

3. For an account of the various modes of placer mining, see Rodman W. Paul, *California Gold* (Cambridge, 1947), pp. 50–66, and sources therein cited, especially John S. Hittell, *Mining in the Pacific States of North America* (San Francisco, 1861), pp. 127–153. Most of the devices employed had been seen earlier in Georgia or North Carolina; in the "dry diggings," prior Mexican experience made a useful contribution to California mining technology.

4. *Prentice Mulford's Story*, Chapter XI, preserves this anecdote of Gauley (or Gawley): "[Alex] Smith was one of the first settlers at Hawkins' Bar; Smith could remember when it contained a voting population of nearly eight hundred souls; Smith knew every point

on the river which had yielded richly; Smith could show you Gawley's Point, where Gawley pitched his tent in '49 and buried under it his pickle jars of gold dust. The tradition of Hawkins was that Gawley used to keep a barrel of whisky on free tap in his tent. And that in the fall of 1850 Gawley, warned by the experience of the previous rainy season, determined to lay in a winter's stock of provisions. But Gawley's ideas as to the proper quantities of food were vague. He had never before been a purveyor or provider on a larger scale than that of buying a week's 'grub' at the Bar store. He went to the trader and told him what he wanted. 'Make out your order,' said the merchant. Gawley gave it to him verbally. 'I guess,' said he, 'I'll have a sack of flour, ten pounds of bacon, ten of sugar, five of coffee, three of tea, a peck of beans, a bag of salt and—and—a barrel of whiskey!' "

CHAPTER XII. *The Trip to Sullivan's Creek* (pp. 87–94)

1. Sullivans Creek is a southern affluent of Woods Creek, entering that stream some distance above Jacksonville. The creek took its name from John Sullivan, who made a rich strike there in the late summer or early fall of 1848. Subsequently he was a successful San Francisco banker, as set forth in San Jose *Pioneer,* August 5, 1882. Big nuggets were a recurrent source of astonishment in the Southern Mines; John S. Hittell, *Mining in the Pacific States of North America,* p. 48, lists some of the better-publicized finds made between 1850 and 1858, particularly in the Sonora area.

2. The development of local law in the various California mining districts is abundantly illustrated by Gardiner later in his narrative. For an over-all view of the phenomenon, see Rodman W. Paul, *California Gold,* Chapter XIII. This local law went far beyond lynch law in the one direction, or adjudication of claims in the other, instanced in Gardiner's text here and later.

3. Woods Creek was one of the earliest affluents of the Tuolumne to be exploited, in the fall of 1848, and proved to be one of the richest. A conclusive case has not yet been made for the identity of the man Wood from whom the name derived—possibly Benjamin, an Oregonian who came to California in 1848 and was one of those killed by Indians at Murderer's Bar on the Middle Fork of the American River in 1849. He was not "the Rev. Jas. Woods of Philadelphia," as the early county histories say; see Morgan and Scobie, eds., *Three Years in California, William Perkins' Journal of Life at Sonora,* p. 15.

4. The Spanish word "rodeo" was used in earlier days in the sense we now employ the term "round-up" in the West; it now usually refers to a spectacle or public performance of the cowboy skills—riding, roping, bull-dogging, etc.

5. Curtis Creek is the major affluent of Sullivans Creek. Again, the circumstances of its naming needs investigation—and luck in finding sources.

6. This dire punishment for horse-stealing was the spontaneous law of the mining region. After the State of California began to legislate on the subject, it provided on April 22, 1851, not merely for imprisonment but "death, in the discretion of the jury," for this form of grand larceny. See *California Statutes,* 2d Session, 1850–1851, pp. 406–407.

CHAPTER XIII. *At Sullivan's Creek* (pp. 95–99)

1. The rainy season had commenced late in 1848, not until the third week of December, but in 1849 L. C. Gunn, near Jamestown, recorded rain on the nights of October 9, 10, and 30, all day on October 31, on alternate days from November 3 to 9, soaking rains on November 13–14, and intermittent rain from then on. The Sacramento *Daily Union,* September 18, 1851, offers this useful information on "California Winters," which may be serviceable to students:

"The *Alta* of the 16th has an interesting article on the above subject compiled from the records of a journal kept during the winters of 1847, 1848, and 1849. This record refers to the weather in San Francisco, and is scarcely a correct criterion by which to judge of the climate in this city and vicinity.

"By referring to a Diary which we [John F. Morse, Editor?] kept during the fall and winter of 1849, we find that the weather during the latter part of November, and the greater part of December, was most delightful, but that the month of January 1850, was terribly stormy. Snow, sleet and hail, accompanied with high winds, prevailed also throughout the month of March in Placer and El Dorado counties. The *Alta* gives the following information relative to the winters of 1846, '47 and '48:

" 'The first showers of the fall season of 1846 were felt in this place in the latter part of the month of October. The rains began during the first week in November quite severely. March, 1847, was a dry month. April 1st heavy showers set in—latter part of the month dry. Last showers fell about the 20th May.

" 'Aug. 28th, 1847, first rains fell. A few slight showers visited various parts of the country, accompanied by thunder and lightning. Nov. 1st, rains commenced with great severity. During January [1848], weather extremely mild, for over three weeks. Feb. 16th, heavy Norther in this bay. Light showers in May closed the rainy season for 1847 [–1848].

" 'The opening showers of the succeeding winter came on Sept. 28th, with thunder and lightning. The season began late—as late as Dec. 20th, and was quite severe. Jan. 12, 1849, very heavy showers, with snow storms and harsh weather. Feb. 1st, winter commenced "breaking up." Feb. 8th, a fierce Norther at this port. Rain ceased during the latter part of the month.' "

2. Irene D. Paden uses this image forcibly in her *Wake of the Prairie Schooner* (New York, 1943), p. 308. Supposedly an Indian in present Idaho illustrated the difference between alternate roads by showing emigrant women a bucket. "He ran his finger around half of the circumference, supposed to be the Fort Hall route, and showed them that it was longer than the diameter, representing the cutoff. Then he raised the bail in his slender (and very dirty) brown fingers and said 'This—road.' When the bail lay down along the rim it was flat, but when he raised it over the diameter it arched up in the middle. 'All same,' he said earnestly. . . ."

CHAPTER XIV. *Back at Hawkins' Bar* (pp. 101–107)

1. It seems pertinent here to continue the quotation from Lang's *A History of Tuolumne County*, pp. 52–53, from where we left off in Chapter XI, Note 7. At Hawkins' Bar, says Lang: "The hillsides were covered with tents, and all the bustle characteristic of some old market town was exhibited. Large operations were commenced, but the rise of the water interfered disastrously with them, as had been the case at Jacksonville. Consequent upon this, large numbers left the camp, while the remainder gave themselves to the digging of an immense canal for the complete drainage of the bar in the coming season. Again fortune frowned upon their efforts, for in the summer of 1850 a sudden rise of the water drove out of their respective claims the various companies, who had just commenced to extract gold. At that time the number of miners was six hundred. By the next year the number had dwindled to one hundred and fifty, with perhaps one hundred on the opposite side of the river, and half as many more scattered along the river, from Red Mountain Bar to Swett's Bar. The latter worked either alone, or with two or three in company. The average daily product of these river miners, in the year 1851, was stated at eight dollars per day.

"Of the claims at Hawkins' Bar, that of Captain Lutter was worked by coffer damming, as was also that of Armstrong. These two claims employed fourteen men. The McAvoy Company consisted of sixty men, who, for a time, averaged twenty dollars per day each. The original company, consisting of one hundred and thirteen men, known as the Hawkins' Bar Company, after two years of persistent efforts, finally abandoned their attempts to work the bed of the river by damming."

2. These were camps located, for the most part, on the heads of Woods Creek.

3. It will be a point of honor with the editor to find out hereafter how Morgan's Bar acquired its name. Like Texas, Hawkins', Indian, and Red Mountain bars, it is now drowned by the Don Pedro Reservoir.

4. Gardiner has previously mentioned John Mills, at the close of Chapter IX. His name appears as J. K. Mills in the *Sabina's* passenger list, Chapter III, Note 3.

5. It seems unlikely that any Texas steers had yet reached the Southern Mines. Gardiner probably refers to a California steer or bullock, which had plenty in common with the Texas variety.

6. Indian Bar was about midway between Don Pedro Bar and Red Mountain Bar.

7. California was never a "territory" in U.S. terminology. After its capture by U.S. forces in 1846–1847, the area continued for a time under military rule, though locally under Mexican law, as Gardiner says. California attained Statehood on September 9, 1850, but meanwhile the California legislature met, following elections in November, 1849, and set up a system of county government. Tuolumne County was created as one of the original California counties in an act signed February 18, 1850.

CHAPTER XV. *En Route to San Francisco* (pp. 109–113)

1. Gardiner and his companions may have left Hawkins' Bar on December 19. That was a clear day, but it rained heavily after nightfall, the rain continuing over the next two days, as recorded in his diary by Lewis C. Gunn.

2. It would be useful if we could establish beyond all question the date Gardiner reached Knight's Ferry, for here we find him recording William Knight's death, hitherto known only to have occurred sometime in the winter of 1849–1850. According to notes in H. H. Bancroft's California Biography (MS., Bancroft Library), Knight was a Missourian who went out to New Mexico as early as 1830. He was naturalized there, but came on to California in 1841 with the Workman-Rowland party. Subsequently he was one of Sutter's volunteers on the side of Micheltorena in the Micheltorena War of 1844–1845, and obtained from Sutter a grant in the Sacramento Valley later declared invalid. He established Knight's Landing on the Sacramento River, and in 1849 located Knight's Ferry on the Stanislaus River. Inexplicably, Bayard Taylor, who met him at Stockton in the late summer of 1849, called him "the first man who followed in the track of Lewis and Clark, on the Columbia River." He had a Mexican wife and several children. His ferry was taken over by John and Lewis Dent, who later associated James Vantine with them as Dent, Vantine & Co. The name Knight's Ferry, however, persists to this day.

3. French Camp, so known since the 1830's because the area was used as a rendezvous point by French-Canadian trappers of the Hudson's Bay Company, also known for a time as Castoria, is about five miles south of Stockton.

4. For the *Mazeppa* and its owners, Stephen Starbuck & Harvey H. Spencer, see Chapter IX, Note 8. George H. Tinkham, *A History of Stockton* (San Francisco, 1880), p. 307, relates: "Store ships were sailing vessels, which came to Stockton from all parts of the world, and were anchored in the stream or moored to the bank. Each of these vessels had a history that would, if known, be of great interest. So many of these ships were anchored in the slough, that they were a detriment to navigation, and in February, 1850, five months before the city was organized, the merchants sent a petition to Captain Weber, requesting him to cause to be removed any vessel lying at anchor in the slough.

"This petition was signed by 107 citizens representing 21 different occupations, including 36 merchants. Of these signers, Wm. G. Phelps and Thomas Sedgwick are still residents of this county.

"Weber requested the owners of the vessels to leave, but they did not all of them comply with his request. We find the Council in 1851 ordering S. Starbuck to remove his brig from the stream. The brigs were used for store ships in which to store goods, as they were much safer than in the tents on the land. Finally many of them were taken to Mormon Slough and burned."

CHAPTER XVI. *Once More in San Francisco* (pp. 115–135)

1. For an account of the early gold-buying business in California, see Ira B. Cross: *Financing an Empire: History of Banking in California,* (Chicago, 1927), 4 vols., vol. 1, pp. 40–44; and for a concrete example of such gold-seeking, George P. Hammond, ed. *Digging for Gold—Without a Shovel, The Letters of Daniel Wadsworth Coit . . .* (Denver, 1967). Coit came to San Francisco from Mexico City with the express purpose of buying gold dust for a firm having connections with the Rothschilds.

2. The story of the *Niantic* is told in considerable detail in Dale L. Morgan's edition of William McCollum's *California As I Saw It* (Los Gatos, 1960). The site where the *Niantic* became a store ship, now well back from the Bay shore at Clay and Sansome streets, is marked by a bronze tablet on the (third) Niantic Building. A picturesque view of the *Niantic* before she burned in the great fire of May 4, 1851, is found in Frank Marryat, *Mountains and Molehills* (London, 1855), opp. p. 37.

3. California lice have never had their dues from historians, but with considerable sprightliness, Douglas S. Watson discoursed in the California Historical Society *Quarterly,* December, 1936, vol. 15, pp. 329–337, on "The Flea in California History and Literature." This is admittedly a mere introduction to the subject. Further researches might take off from the remarks on fleas offered during 1850–1851 by the San Francisco *Evening Picayune;* see Kenneth M. Johnson, *San Francisco As It Is, Being Gleanings from the Picayune, 1850–1852* (Los Gatos, 1964), pp. 52, 196–198.

4. William B. Almond was an original, fondly recollected in many a reminiscence of 1849–1850. For a brief biography, see W. M. Paxton, *Annals of Platte County, Missouri* (Kansas City, Mo., 1897), p. 110; and the much more extended account by Clyde Arbuckle, "His Honor Judge William B. Almond," *Pony Express Courier,* June–November, 1942. Almond was born in Virginia, October 25, 1808, and after a varied career, including a year as clerk for Sublette & Campbell on the Yellowstone, 1833–1834, came overland to California at the head of a company of Forty-niners from Platte County, Mo., reaching Sacramento on July 30, 1849, as shown by a letter he wrote next day. The following December he was named judge of a Court of First Instance set up in San Francisco, a court having civil jurisdiction only. Anecdotes of the judge and his court are related in Soulé, *Annals of San Francisco,* pp. 238–241, and H. H. Bancroft, *California Inter Pocula* (San Francisco, 1888), pp. 591–600. His tenure lasted only seven months, district courts in California's emerging judicial system by then having replaced the stopgap Court of First Instance. Almond moved to San Jose, where he had a prominent role in organizing the city's first Masonic lodge, but late in 1850 returned to Missouri. He revisited California briefly in 1852, but soon went back to Missouri, a prominent citizen of Platte City with strong pro-slavery inclinations. Almond died of a heart attack at Leavenworth, Kansas, March 4, 1860.

5. In view of his ultimately destructive impact on San Francisco—comparable to the great fires of 1849–1851—it is surprising how little is known of the personal history of

Peter Smith. When he reached San Francisco is not certain—perhaps not until late 1849. In the *Alta California*, April 19, 1850, we find him joining other physicians in signing a memorial against a medical law under consideration by the legislature, and he there signs himself, "P. Smith, M. D. Philadelphia and Pennsylvania." From the *Proceedings of the Town Council of San Francisco, Upper California* (San Francisco, 1850), pp. 58, 69, we learn that on January 30, 1850, he forthrightly petitioned (while two other doctors only applied) for the lately vacated office of City Physician. The matter was referred to the Committee on Health and Police, and on February 5 the council resolved simply "that Dr. Smith be employed to attend the public patients in his private hospital, at the rate of $4 per day, under the supervision of the committee on Health and Police, until such time as the Council shall see fit to make other arrangements." After an ordinance was passed by the newly organized San Francisco Board of Aldermen providing for the creation of a city hospital, May 30, 1850, a group of local physicians petitioned the Board that Smith be named City Physician. This document, printed in the *Alta California*, June 15, 1850, says in part:

"It is well known to us that Dr. Smith is fully competent in every respect, to represent well in that office our profession, and to give satisfaction to the community.

"It is also well known, that Dr. Smith has been at great expense in fitting up a Hospital —and its healthy location, and its appliances for the care of the sick, render it superior to any similar establishment now in the city, and as good as can be afforded from the private means of any individual. It is also well known that Dr. Smith received from the late Ayuntamiento but a few months ago, the office of City Physician, and the improvement that has since taken place in care of the sick poor, is highly creditable to the selection made of him for that office. We have reason to believe that should another than Dr. Smith be appointed to City Physician for this year, that Dr. Smith would be a severe loser by ever having held the office, and that no corresponding benefit would accrue to the city."

The desired appointment was made by the Board of Aldermen on June 24, Dr. Smith being allowed "$4 per diem for board, lodging and medical attendance for each patient," as reported by the *Alta* next day. Some account of the functioning of his hospital is provided by Sophia A. Eastman, who reached San Francisco in July, 1850, and worked for him until November; she also remarks that Dr. Smith and lady boarded at the St. Francis Hotel. (See her MS. letters in the Bancroft Library.) Smith's hospital was periodically attacked, and regularly defended by his friends (as in the *Alta* for June 29 and July 12). He offered to sell his establishment to the city, an offer which was declined— unfortunately, as can now be seen. The last week of October, he was active with other doctors in combating the cholera which had reached San Francisco; and on October 31 the *Alta* printed a 3 A. M. bulletin: "We stop the press to announce the total destruction of Dr. Smith's City Hospital [by fire]. We have only room or time to say the sick were removed in season." (The incident is graphically described by Daniel W. Coit.) The Waverly House on Pacific Street was pressed into service as a temporary hospital; Smith's establishment had stood on Clay Street. In the wake of the fire, Smith resigned as city physician; and thereafter began the disastrous litigation to which Gardiner refers, described in detail by Soulé, *Annals of San Francisco*, pp. 370–377.

Altogether, the city owed Smith $64,431, which he had been paid in scrip. The city was in no shape to settle with him in cash and sought to have him accept city bonds—in effect, paying off one set of promissory notes with another. He declined, brought suit for his money, and on February 25, 1851, obtained judgment for a part of it, $19,239. A second judgment was handed down March 4, 1851, for $45,538. On July 8 the sheriff began to sell as much of the city property as might be necessary to settle the judgments, including various wharves, the old city hall lot, and the city hospital and buildings. Counsel for the city—Gardiner mentions Solomon Heydenfeldt—did not serve the municipality well; the city officials cried down the validity of Smith's titles, so that selling prices for property were poor, and ever more property had to be sold to make up the amount. In the end, the California Supreme Court upheld most of the "Peter Smith titles." Soulé remarks: "There is still, as there has long been, much bitter and angry feeling existing in the city respecting the 'Peter Smith Titles.' San Francisco has somehow lost its best and most valuable property, and individual citizens have gained immense fortunes by the loss. . . ." Smith was in San Francisco in 1854, when he had a settlement with Sophia Eastman and was listed in the city directory (as he had not been in 1852), but I am not informed as to his subsequent history.

6. Soulé, *Annals of San Francisco*, p. 306, reproduces a likeness of the medal, which bore the legend, "California Admitted Sep. 9, 1850. Presented to Memb'r Board of Ass't Aldermen by the City of San Francisco, Oct. 19, 1850."

7. For corrective information on the newspapers of San Francisco, see Helen Harding Bretnor, ed., *A History of California Newspapers, 1846–1858, by Edward C. Kemble* (Los Gatos, 1962). At the end of 1849 San Francisco had two tri-weeklies, the *Alta California* (which became a daily January 22, 1850), and the *Pacific News* (which became a daily March 4, 1850). Many other papers began publication in 1850, including the *Journal of Commerce, Evening Picayune*, and *Herald*. The *Alta California* had commenced publication January 4, 1849, as the successor to the *California Star & Californian*; one of the proprietors, as Gardiner says, was Edward Gilbert, who was subsequently elected to Congress only to be killed in an August, 1852, duel by J. W. Denver. Benjamin R. Buckelew had nothing to do with the *Pacific News*, which survived till late May, 1851, but he did found the San Francisco *Public Balance* on December 8, 1850, as a rival to the *Alta*. Kemble says nothing about Sam Brannan in connection with *The Hombre*, which he describes as a weekly satirical paper of quarto size . . . commenced by Dr. William Rabe, in April, 1851, but soon abandoned." Kemble's own text needs correction, however, for T. W. Streeter had the first three issues (February 2–16, all published) and George L. Harding has shown me the issue for February 9—modeled on *Punch*. On March 19, 1851, the Sacramento *Union* reported that "Dr. Rabe, the facetious editor of that unique and humorous sheet, the *Hombre*," was a candidate for Recorder of San Francisco, because "at present he has 'nothing to do.' "

8. Gardiner must have spent more of his time in the gambling houses (if only as a spectator) than in the churches, for the San Francisco ecclesiastical scene at this time was not so desolate as he intimates. William Taylor, *California Life Illustrated* (New York, 1858), pp. 56–72, gives an interesting over-all view of the San Francisco denominational activity in 1849–1850. The Baptists and Methodists (to say nothing of the Catholics) both had church buildings by the end of 1849. The Episcopalians dedicated a church in January, 1850; the Congregationalists did as well a month later; and the Presbyterians, after a year and a half of convening in a large tent, by January, 1851, had the satisfaction of meeting in their own building. The faithful church-goer Daniel W. Coit, admirably reflects the San Francisco religious scene in his letters for this period, and George P. Hammond's introduction develops much of the background; see *Digging for Gold—Without a Shovel.*

9. These celebrated gambling houses figure in many of the reminiscences, to say nothing of the letters and diaries, of the time. In January, 1848, the San Francisco Ayuntamiento, or Town Council, had passed stringent resolutions against gambling, only to repeal them at its next meeting (see Soulé, *Annals of San Francisco,* p. 199). Consequently public gambling was legal in California until outlawed by an act of the legislature approved April 17, 1855—a date which from one point of view marks the end of California's frontier era, Frederick J. Turner to the contrary notwithstanding. Subsequently, silver having been discovered in Nevada, legal gambling tended to assume the more sophisticated guise of speculation in mining shares.

Of the proprietors of the three gambling saloons Gardiner refers to, nothing was said in the first (1850) San Francisco city directory, but the contemporary newspapers are more informative.

In the aftermath of the first major San Francisco fire, December 24, 1849, which occurred just prior to Gardiner's return to the city, the *Alta California* noted on January 7, 1850, the rebuilding of Dennison's Exchange by Curtis, Battelle & Co., who had purchased the establishment "only a few weeks previous to the fire;" for their energy praise was lavished upon "the Col." and "Corinthian Tom." (The first reports of the fire gave the names of the owners as Baker, Curtis & Battelle.) Also destroyed in that conflagration was the El Dorado, which, at the corner of Washington and Kearny streets, was next door to the famous Parker House. (Dennison's Exchange was on the other side of the Parker House, on the east side of Kearny.) Chambers & McCabe were named as the owners of the El Dorado, and they too were prompt in rebuilding. The Bella Union was located on Washington Street at Kearny. These establishments regularly burned down in the great San Francisco fires, and were as regularly rebuilt.

10. Catherine Coffin Phillips has devoted an entire book to *Portsmouth Plaza, The Cradle of San Francisco* (San Francisco, 1932). What was originally called the Plaza became known as Portsmouth Square, but the early name was restored in January, 1928. It is a municipal disgrace that the City of San Francisco eventually converted Portsmouth Plaza into a four-story underground parking garage, not without strong objections from the community.

11. The motley patronage of the saloons is wonderfully expressed in a lithograph by Frank Marryat, "The Bar of a Gambling Saloon," in his *Mountains and Molehills* (London, 1855), opp. p. 224.

12. Mission Dolores was founded in 1776, at the time of the first settlement of the San Francisco region by the Spaniards. It still stands, on Dolores Street between 16th and 17th streets.

13. This casual appropriation of other men's property, or public property, was eminently characteristic of behavior in the West by men who at home were models of honesty.

14. Gardiner exaggerates the age of Mission Dolores, as seen by Note 12. The mission fathers held sway from 1776 to 1833, when the California missions were secularized by the Mexican government. The property was restored to the Roman Catholic diocese in 1857. In 1849–1850 the area was sadly disordered, and by 1851 it had become an amusement area, with race tracks and other divertissements of the kind.

15. The New York Regiment of Volunteers was created in 1846, and came around the Horn next winter under Colonel Jonathan D. Stevenson. A good many toughs were numbered in its ranks, and after they were mustered out, they contributed to the reckless disregard of law and equity which was one aspect of the California scene after 1848. For additional details and a muster roll, see Guy J. Giffen, *California Expedition, Stevenson's Regiment of First New York Volunteers* (Oakland, 1951).

16. Mission Creek, which takes its name from Mission Dolores, flows into Mission Bay between Rincon Point and Point San Quentin.

17. Jay Monaghan, *Australians and the Gold Rush* (Berkeley and Los Angeles, 1966), a lively account of the impact of the California Gold Rush on "down under," 1849–1854, includes information (pp. 94–95, 103) on the shipment of draft horses and carts to San Francisco in the fall of 1849. Charles Bateson, *Gold Fleet for California* (Sydney, 1963), provides data on the vessels sailing to and from Australian and New Zealand ports.

18. This picture of the travail of women who reached California overland is not without some truth, but sentimentalized and exaggerated.

19. Don Pedro's Bar has outlived other placenames on the Tuolumne River owing to construction of a reservoir bearing the same name. Pierre Sainsevain, a carpenter, came to California in 1839 at the age of 20, and became known as Don Pedro. He went to the mines in 1848, and the name of Don Pedro's Bar must date from that fall, or the very early spring of 1849. Sainsevain was a member of the 1849 Constitutional Convention, and later a prominent vineyardist and vintner.

20. "T. P. R." plainly is Thomas P. Ripley, Jr., one of the Long Island contingent who came out in the *Sabina*. His father was a substantial merchant at Sag Harbor. Gardiner was reluctant to name him, for reasons implicit in his previous paragraph.

21. John S. Powers was listed as a deputy sheriff in the 1850 San Francisco directory. The "sculptor Powers" presumably was Hiram Powers (July 29, 1805–June 27, 1873), though he died of infirmity brought on by a violent fall, at Florence, Italy. Powers'

"Greek Slave" (1843) has been called the most celebrated statue of its day (one marble copy is in the Corcoran Gallery at Washington, D.C.); he also made many notable portrait busts.

22. I have not conclusively identified the Dennison whom Gardiner calls "a fellow townsman." As seen by Note 9, no one named Dennison appears in the winter of 1849–1850 as proprietor of the Exchange which bore his name. Could he have been Samuel Dennison? A letter by William Dennison, San Francisco, January 14, 1850, printed as *The Letter of a '49er now first printed from the original with foreword by Oscar Wegelin* (New York, 1919) appears to speak of a brother in saying, "you of course knew that Sam was here, he is well & report says rich, he has made me a number of fine offers if I would send for my family, but that I will not do, for California is not the place for more than one in a family, therefore he & myself steer different courses." He himself arrived in San Francisco the last of October. "I see Sam he owned a Brig which was soon expected which he wished me to take, & I agreed to do so, but in the meantime a Gentleman from Illinois whom I become acquainted with, had purchased the Schooner *Jacob M Ryerson* of N York & said if I would take charge of her he would let me have a third of her & let her earnings pay for her without any interest for the money, so here I am Skipper of a fine New Schooner." He hoped to be again on "old Long Islands Sea Girt Shore," and acknowledged papers received "through Mr N Miller who appears to be doing very well."

23. A sketch of Edward Chauncey Marshall is printed in Herbert O. Lang, *A History of Tuolumne County*, Appendix, p. 36; a condensed account may be found in *Biographical Directory of Congress*, 1961, p. 1264. Born in Kentucky June 29, 1821, Marshall reached California by the Gila route in November, 1849, and practiced law in San Francisco until May, 1850, when he established himself at Sonora, Tuolumne County. In 1851 he was elected to Congress, and in 1856 failed by a narrow margin of election to the U.S. Senate. Later he practiced law in Kentucky, but returned to San Francisco in 1877 and was elected Attorney General of California, 1883–1886. He died July 9, 1893. One reminiscent recalled that when elected to Congress, Marshall set out for Washington via the Isthmus with no baggage but an old leather satchel and a bottle of whiskey.

24. Jesse B. Hart published at New York in 1853 a substantial *Treatise on the Practice of the Courts of California*. For Jonathan Drake Stevenson, who became a substantial business man and land speculator after the New York Regiment was mustered out, see Giffen's work cited in Note 15.

25. It must have been not May, but about the first of April, that Gardiner left San Francisco for the interior, as brought out in the next chapter. A corroborating circumstance is that he clearly preserved no memory of the devastating fire of May 4, 1850.

26. John Satterlee, a native of Cayuga County, N.Y., who had studied law in Buffalo with Millard Fillmore, came to California in 1849 and was elected judge of the superior court for the County of San Francisco in September, 1851. Before and after his judicial career, he practiced law and engaged successfully in real estate speculations. He died un-

married at the age of 60 in January, 1876; see a brief obituary in *Alta California*, January 21, 1876.

27. Gardiner means to say that he and his friends won the suit for the value of the boat, but got nothing additional in the way of damages for detention of their property.

28. Ira B. Cross writes in *Financing an Empire*, vol. I, pp. 47–48: "Some claim [though there are other claims] that Dr. Stephen A. Wright's 'Miner's Bank,' established presumably towards the close of 1848, was the first banking house to enter the field [in San Francisco]. It was the outcome of the exchange brokerage business started by Wright & Company some time, so it is surmised, during 1848. We know that in September, 1849, this firm was located at the corner of Kearney and Washington streets, Portsmouth Square, paying a rental of $6,000 a month for a little wooden cottage. In the early part of the following November the partners, Stephen A. Wright, John Thompson, Samuel W. Haight and J. C. L. Wadsworth, definitely organized as bankers with an announced capital stock of $200,000. In 1854 Wright's bank changed its name to 'Miners' Exchange and Savings Bank' with offices in the old Armory Hall on the northeast corner of Sacramento and Montgomery streets. . . . In December, 1854, it moved into spacious new quarters at the northwest corner of Montgomery and Jackson streets. . . . This concern at first was successful and profitable, and remained solvent throughout all the uncertain days of the gold rush, only to succumb in the disastrous Black Friday of February 23, 1855, at which time three other banking firms closed their doors."

Black Friday was occasioned by the failure of Page, Bacon & Co. on February 22, 1855. Adams & Co., Wells Fargo & Co., Robinson & Co., and the Miners' Exchange all came to grief next day. On March 3 Wright published a statement in the *Herald* showing an excess of assets over liabilities amounting to $41,020.78; and four days later the depositors agreed to submit a proposition to Dr. Wright authorizing him to resume business on condition that he agree to pay twenty-five per cent. on his deposits every other month until the whole was paid. (See California Historical Society *Quarterly*, June, 1936, vol. XV, pp. 268, 272–274.)

All this is somewhat afield from the present allusion to the Miners' Bank. More to the point is it that this bank was one of several which during 1849–1850 issued its own coins, including a ten dollar gold piece that was intrinsically worth $9.87. See Cross, *op. cit.*, pp. 127–131, which also notes that gold coins made in Utah fell into disrepute, and "the Miners' Bank gold next came into disfavor, and was only accepted at twenty per cent discount. Both issues were soon driven from circulation, and those who owned them were forced to sell them at their bullion value and pocket the loss." Further information is given by Edgar H. Adams, *Private Gold Coinage of California, 1849–55, Its History and Its Issues* (Brooklyn, 1913), pp. 69–70. Only a $10 denomination bore the impress of the Miners' Bank. Adams quotes a letter in the *Alta California*, April 11, 1850: "The issue of the Miners' Bank is a drug on the market. Brokers refuse to touch it at less than 20 per cent discount. Moffat's issue will probably soon be no better; he already refuses to redeem it in American gold. . . ." On March 29 the *Alta* had observed: "We understand that a respectable mercantile firm in this city, having a considerable quantity of California gold coins, issued by various establishments in this country, preferred having them melted down to paying the discount now demanded. The gold was found to be only 21 carats fine."

CHAPTER XVII. *A Second Trip to the Mines* (pp. 137–141)

1. As will be seen hereafter, there is good reason to think it was about the first of April, 1850, that Gardiner parted from Steve French in San Francisco. The two did not get together again until 1852; see Chapter XXII, Note 1.

2. Mariposa is situated in the foothill country at the head of the Mariposa River, the name of which derives from butterflies seen by an expedition under Gabriel Moraga which explored the south San Joaquin in 1806. For an extended history of the area, see Charles Gregory Crampton, *The Opening of the Mariposa Mining Region, 1849–1859, with Particular Reference to the Mexican Land Grant of John Charles Frémont* (Berkeley, Ph.D. thesis, 1941).

3. The most celebrated of these grants were Charles M. Weber's El Campo de los Franceses, on which Stockton was founded, and John Charles Frémont's Las Mariposas—each purchased from the original Mexican grantee. All through the 1850's, such grants were being litigated—some confirmed, others rejected. The Bancroft Library has, on deposit from the U.S. District Court, California (Northern District) an extensive file of records relating to the claims litigated between 1850 and 1860.

4. Grayson, on the west bank of the San Joaquin above the mouth of the Tuolumne River, in present Stanislaus County, was originally promoted by Andrew Jackson Grayson, an 1846 overland emigrant from Missouri, later a notable ornithological artist, of whom a biography is in preparation by Lois C. Stone. Advertisements concerning the Grayson townsite appeared in the Stockton *Times* through the summer of 1850, commencing June 15, and in the *Alta California* commencing May 17, with separate promotion of the Grayson Ferry across the San Joaquin. For the later history of Grayson, see *History of Stanislaus County, California* (San Francisco, 1881), pp. 123–124.

5. On March 18, 1850, Enos Christman crossed the Merced River by "the New York Company's Ferry," ferriage $5 per team; but this seems to have been some distance up the Merced, not at its mouth (*One Man's Gold*, p. 121). A sketch of William C. Turner in *History of Merced County* (San Francisco, 1881), pp. 142–143, incidentally mentions the camp of a New York company on the Merced in the fall of 1849.

6. As recorded by the *Alta California,* the ship *Senator,* Coffin, master, cleared San Francisco for the Sandwich Islands June 25, 1850, consigned to Charles Minturn.

7. Gardiner has clearly said that this theft occurred in the camp on the Merced; but compare next Chapter, Note 3.

CHAPTER XVIII. *Mining at Mariposa* (pp. 143–147)

1. The Mariposa diggings had their unique aspect, in that the first gold discovery was made within the bounds (or was made to be within the bounds) of a Mexican land grant that had been acquired by John Charles Frémont. Most other land grants, as it turned out, were for areas marginal to the gold-bearing localities. Frémont had sent a party of Sonoran miners to Mariposa under Alex Godey in the spring of 1849, and it was they who made the first strike. Gregory Crampton surmises that the initial find was on Godey Gulch, one of the tributaries of Agua Frio Creek; but neighboring Mariposa Creek proved more productive. Crampton points out, "The Mariposa vein, called for a short time the Frémont vein, was the first gold-bearing formation with the metal in place to be opened in California" (*The Opening of the Mariposa Mining Region*, p. 50). Mariposa became the principal town of the locality, and eventual county seat. Mariposa County (embracing all or parts of nine other modern counties, the whole south end of the San Joaquin Valley), was created February 18, 1850.

2. Memory has betrayed Gardiner; there was no newspaper at Mariposa until the *Chronicle* was founded, January 20, 1854. A successor, the *Gazette*, entered upon the scene July 1, 1855, and still survives. See Helen H. Bretnor's edition of E. C. Kemble's *History of California Newspapers*, pp. 189–190.

3. I have found no record of this shooting in a contemporary newspaper, but a reliable diarist fills in the gap, incidentally requiring correction of Gardiner's chronology over the past several chapters. Enos Christman wrote in his journal at Mariposa on April 17, 1850: "Yesterday afternoon a bloody tragedy was enacted in the town, resulting in the death of a young man named Marcey, of Massachusetts. A man named Messick accused Marcey of robbing him of seven hundred dollars while on a drunken frolic together last winter, and it is said had sworn to shoot Marcey the first time he saw him. He had armed himself early in the morning with a double-barrelled shot gun heavily charged with buckshot, and lay in wait until the afternoon, expecting Marcey to pass that way. By and by Marcey made his appearance, only armed with a sheath knife and revolver, as is usual in this country, and an altercation took place, in which Marcey endeavored to clear himself of the charges brought against him. He was about going away when Messick cocked both barrels of his gun and asked the other if he was armed, and he replied that he was, and that he would fight him in a fair fight but he would not fight in that way. Messick then told him to defend himself, to which he replied that he might fire if he would. At this he fired one barrel which the other received principally in the right arm, and instantly turned with his back towards the man with the gun, who seeing that the other did not fall, immediately fired the other barrel which took effect through the lungs and heart. Marcey fell, uttered a few words and was a corpse in a few minutes. Messick, with a companion, left at once for parts unknown. The deceased has a number of mules and for some time had been engaged in the packing trade. Of him all speak favorably." (*One Man's Gold*, pp. 140–141.)

4. I have not identified this alcalde. Hiram D. Pierce, Gardiner's fellow passenger of the *Sylph,* was at Mariposa from November 21, 1849, through April 1, 1850, without mentioning such a dignitary. On March 31 he recorded, "A caucus was held to day by the miners to nominate candidates for the diferent offices to be voted for tomorow." (A week later, on the Merced River, Pierce remarked, "In the afternoon we had an election of Alcalda & Sherif.") Enos Christman, who reached Mariposa March 26, 1850, similarly recorded on the 31st: "Tomorrow an election takes place for judge, sheriff, and other county officers, and today a meeting was held at one of the drinking and gambling establishments for the purpose of forming a ticket to be voted for. . . . I heard one Captain Miller, who was a candidate, swear he had fought the guerillas in the Mexican War, and upon one occasion he said he had saved the United States five millions of dollars, when it was near being lost at the National Bridge. To add to his other qualifications he was then gambling and pretty well overcome by red-eye." On April 1 Christman "passed the election ground twice but seeing no voting done did not stop." Eventually, on Tuesday, May 14, Christman noted that on the 12th a political meeting was held in the forenoon "to nominate candidates for constable and alcalde, the election taking place on Monday." But he furnished no details. Newell D. Chamberlain's entertaining *The Call of Gold, True Tales on the Gold Road to Yosemite* (Mariposa, 1936), p. 9, does not list the alcaldes (justices of the peace) but says: "The first officers of the County were: County Judge, James M. Bondurant; Sheriff, James Burney; County Clerk, Samuel A. Merritt (afterwards Chief Justice of Utah); Recorder, J. C. Bland; Treasurer, Edward Beasley; District Attorney, Orrin A. Munn; Assessor, Thomas K. Munk; Coroner, B. S. Scriven. In the early days, officials were hard to keep, the ever-festive nuggets alluring them from their political aspirations and honors."

5. Enos Christman similarly remarked on May 14, the day before he headed for the Tuolumne Diggings: "About four weeks since, this valley was crowded with gold seekers and every foot of ground on the creek was taken up for three miles, and lots were selling at from an ounce to $200; but now how changed the scene! The valley is nearly deserted and hundreds of claims are abandoned after many days' labor upon them, mine among the rest. Storekeepers are selling out and the place will soon be forsaken until fall, when the river bed can be worked . . ." (*One Man's Gold*, p. 148).

Agua Frio, "cold water," was the originally designated seat of Mariposa County, but gave place to the town of Mariposa in 1852. Hornitos, "little ovens," was started on Burns Creek in 1850, Newell Chamberlain says, "by some Mexican miners, gamblers and dance-hall women" who had been expelled from Quartzburgh, two miles higher up the creek, "by a well-armed 'Law and Order Committee.' The name . . . was given to this settlement because of the presence of some odd Mexican graves, built of stone on top of the ground, and shaped like bake-ovens. Several of these can still be seen in the little cemetery on the hill." The town soon became an important way-point on the road between Stockton and Los Angeles. For Sherlock's Creek, see Chapter XXII, Note 34.

6. Many miners to their sorrow learned of the malevolence of poison oak. Its disposition has not improved since 1850.

7. Many Sonorans and native Californians had come to the Southern Mines, beginning in late 1848. Frequently their women accompanied them, giving rise to a major distinguishing feature between the society of the Northern and Southern Mines. They were victimized by anti-foreign agitation in the spring of 1850 and thereafter, which had much to do with the appearance of marauding bands like that led by Joaquin Murrieta a few years later. For fuller information, see Morgan and Scobie, eds., *Three Years in California: William Perkins' Journal of Life at Sonora, 1849–1852.*

8. Rattlesnake Creek is an eastern affluent of Moccasin Creek, a southern tributary of the Tuolumne. The settlement of the same name flourished only briefly, during the 1850's. For information on the area, see Irene D. Paden and Margaret E. Schlichtmann, *The Big Oak Flat Road, an account of freighting from Stockton to Yosemite Valley* (San Francisco, 1955); and see Chapter XXII, Note 3.

9. The English bark *Vicar of Bray,* Duggan, master, had cleared for Valparaiso March 10, 1850, not long before Gardiner set out for Mariposa. I find no record of a return voyage to San Francisco this year. She had reached San Francisco from Valparaiso November 3, 1849.

CHAPTER XIX. *Life in San Francisco* (pp. 149–162)

1. The 1850 San Francisco directory lists Mosley E. Miller, a member of the firm of Hutton & Miller, as located on Broadway at Clark's Point; but there is also a listing for Nath. Miller, grocer, on Battery between Broadway and Vallejo. In September, 1850. Stephen Fowler had business relations with N. Miller, which may indicate who Gardiner's Miller was. (See also Chapter XVI, Note 22.) The 1850 directory additionally lists "Howard C. Gardiner, merch't, Batt. b B'way and Vallejo," almost certainly our Forty-niner. The entry is the more interesting in that Charles P. Kimball dated the title-page of his directory September 1, 1850, only a few weeks after Gardiner's return to San Francisco.

2. According to Kimball's 1850 San Francisco directory, Lovejoy's Hotel, operated by J. H. Brown, was situated on Broadway between Sansome and Battery streets.

3. The *Alta California* did not record the *Huron's* arrival, but a list by F. C. Matthews of vessels in San Francisco Bay, September 9, 1850, printed in *Pacific Marine Review,* September 1921, records her as an American ship of 290 tons which arrived March —, 1850.

4. The ship *Haidee,* Soule, master, reached San Francisco December 12, 1850, 187 days from New York via Valparaiso.

5. The Pacific Mail Steamship Company first brought to San Francisco the *California,* the *Oregon,* and the *Panama,* all in 1849. These were not ideally suited to the work, and better vessels were added as soon as possible, including the *Tennessee* in 1850, the *Golden Gate* in 1851, the *John L. Stephens* in 1853, and the *Golden Age* in 1854. See John Haskell Kemble, *The Panama Route, 1848–1869, passim.*

6. However plausible the details, I have found no record of the arrival or departure of the ships *John* and *Edward* in 1850–1851. The idea of iron warehouses attracted many, including Daniel W. Coit, who wrote his wife from San Francisco as late as March 15, 1851: "I am now daily looking for the arrival of certain iron warehouses, which were ordered from England more than a year ago. They were planned by me for certain friends of mine who propose to erect them as soon as they arrive. They are very large, entirely of iron, and of course fireproof, and when put up will be the most extensive and commodious buildings for the storage of entire cargoes of any that exist here . . ." (*Digging for Gold—Without a Shovel*, p. 104). Coit's project went awry when the bluffs above his warehouse slid down, damaging buildings and contents. (*Ibid.*, p. 16.)

7. The ship *Caroline Read*, Read, master, reached San Francisco November 23, 1850, 142 days from New York, consigned to Cooke Brothers & Co. She cleared for Calcutta January 11, 1851.

8. Kenneth M. Johnson provides an interesting note on the "Dramatic Museum" in editing *San Francisco As It Is*, p. 34: "Dr. D. G. Robinson was one of the best liked, and today is one of the best remembered men of the period. He was called 'doctor' because when he first arrived in San Francisco he operated a drug store. On July 4, 1850, he and one James Ev[r]ard opened a little theater on California Street near Montgomery; it was called the Dramatic Museum and was a great success from the start. Robinson was deeply in the theater as owner, composer, actor, comedian, and promoter. Later Robinson built the well known American Theater in direct competition with Thomas Maguire who had the Jenny Lind. Because of his popularity, stemming from his theatrical activities, he was elected Alderman and proposed as a candidate for Mayor.

"Robinson's strong forte was the composing of satirical verse about the men and events of the time; these would be sung to the tune of some current popular song, and the audience would join in. An evening at the Dramatic Museum seems to have been a lot of fun. In 1853 some of these verses were collected and printed in what has been termed California's first song book. The title page reads as follows: '*Comic Songs; or, Hits at San Francisco. By D. G. Robinson, and sung by him at the San Francisco Theater.* San Francisco: Commercial book and job office, 1851.'" (A copy of this 59-page work may be seen in the Bancroft Library.)

Johnson also observes (p. 132) that Evrard was afterward a sergeant of police in San Francisco. The *Alta California* on February 4, 1850, noted his arrival in California from New York, identifying him as "the Comedian from Mitchell's Olympic Theatre"; soon after he was mentioned as English director at that theater; and by March 23, when the Phoenix Exchange opened, he and one Curtis appeared as stage managers. On June 15, reporting the great fire of the day before, the *Alta* observed that the building in which Dr. Robinson intended to locate his Dramatic Museum was entirely destroyed. Notwithstanding this hard luck, on July 4 Robinson and Evrard (the former mentioned as late of the Boston theatres) advertised the opening of their New Dramatic Museum; they had rebuilt and redecorated their building. Appropriately, one of the features of opening night was "Seeing the Elephant." It may also be noted that the *Alta* on January 10, 1851, referred to the first appearance of Mrs. Evrard at the Dramatic Museum. It appears that the two men closed their theater February 16, 1851, to inaugurate a more imposing New Dramatic Museum, which was opened April 7 only to be destroyed in the disastrous fire of May 4, 1851. In October following, the persistent Robinson swung wide the doors of his yet finer theater, The American.

9. There was no Fort Independence; Gardiner means Independence, Missouri, one of the jumping-off places for the overland emigration.

10. The American ship *Deucalion,* Cole, master, had cleared San Francisco for the Sandwich Islands February 6, 1850. She extended her voyage to Australia, and returned to San Francisco October 11, 1850, 78 days from Hobart Town, 8 passengers, Green, master. (The *Deucalion* reached San Francisco originally, from Boston, November 10, 1849.)

11. The hometown clubbiness of the miners, instanced in Gardiner's narrative by the tendency of Long Islanders to flock together, is also well attested by Stephen Fowler in his MS. journal, both when visiting San Francisco (January-February, and September, 1850, February, 1851) and when laboring in the mines. Fowler had cordial relations with David L. Gardiner of Easthampton, he and his associates leaving their gold dust on deposit with him in San Francisco.

12. Gardiner's political discussion is imprecise, in that from the outset California sought admission as a State, not Territorial status. Utah ("Deseret") and New Mexico also sought Statehood, but with insufficient population could expect nothing so gratifying at the hands of Congress. The bill in question became law September 9, 1850, a date since celebrated in California as Admission Day. We should also note that California's constitutional convention, which met at Monterey in September, 1849, completed its work before the U.S. Congress convened in December to struggle with the political problems consequent upon the Mexican cession.

13. News of California's admission to the Union was brought to San Francisco on October 18, 1850, by the mail steamer *Oregon,* which arrived with masts bedecked with flags and signals, and with signal guns firing. The occasion was more festive than one would infer from Gardiner's recollection.

14. It so happened that Gardiner was not in San Francisco when most of the six great early fires occurred—December 24, 1849, May 4, June 14, and September 17, 1850, May 3–4, and June 22, 1851. The one exception, perhaps, was the fire of September 17, 1850, which started on Jackson Street and made havoc of the area between Dupont and Montgomery streets bounded by Washington and Pacific streets. For the *Evening Picayune's* account of the following day, see Kenneth M. Johnson, ed., *San Francisco As It Is,* pp. 47–51. There were lesser fires, short of general conflagrations, and Gardiner may be recalling one of these. See H. H. Bancroft, *History of California* (San Francisco, 1888), vol. VI, pp. 201–207.

15. The wild-goose chase to Gold Bluff (on the California coast south of the Klamath River) began in December, 1850, and continued for some weeks. For a brief account, see

John S. Hittell, *Mining in the Pacific States of North America*, pp. 23–24, and for further comment, H. H. Bancroft, *History of California*, vol. VI, pp. 364–365.

16. Long (or Central) Wharf, an extension of Commercial Street into the Bay, just south of Clay Street, was begun as early as May, 1849. For an account of this and other early wharves, see Soulé, *Annals of San Francisco*, pp. 291–292; and for interesting contemporary comment of 1850–1852, see Kenneth M. Johnson, ed. *San Francisco As It is*, index.

17. Gardiner got these details from Blanchard some years later, as may be inferred from Chapter XXIII, Note 2.

18. Several Ryders appear as masters of vessels arriving at or departing from San Francisco in 1850–1851—evidently they were a seafaring clan. Perhaps Gardiner has reference to the bark *Ann Walsh*, Ryder, master, which reached San Francisco October 13, 1850, 56 days from Hong Kong, and cleared for the same port December 4. But he could also have referred to the bark *Eureka*, Ryder, master, which reached San Francisco August 23, 1850, and cleared for China October 23 with $23,000 aboard. The latter vessel got back March 15, 1851, 63 days from Hong Kong.

19. Steamboat navigation on the interior waters of California merits booklength treatment, beyond the interesting discussions by Soulé, *Annals of San Francisco*, pp. 235–236, H. H. Bancroft, *History of California*, vol. VI, pp. 450–451, and Win. J. Davis, *An Illustrated History of Sacramento County, California* (Chicago, 1890), pp. 107–112. John Haskell Kemble has published two limited monographs, "The First Steam Vessel to Navigate San Francisco Bay," California Historical Society *Quarterly*, June, 1945, vol. 14, pp. 143–146, and "The 'Senator,' The Biography of a Pioneer Steamship," *ibid.*, March, 1937, vol. 16, pp. 61–70 (with a painting of the *Senator* reproduced opp. p. 61), besides scattered notes in his *The Panama Route*.

The first effort at steamboat navigation was by William A. Leidesdorff, who in 1847 acquired a 37-foot steam launch from the Russian American Company at Sitka, made it ready for service under the lee of Yerba Buena Island, and on November 15, 1847, used her for a gala cruise around the island from San Francisco. Next month she ran up the Sacramento River to Sacramento, but on February 12, 1848, this "first steamer on the Bay, a mere toy, and a most dangerous one too," in the words of the San Francisco *Californian* of February 16, sank in a norther blowing itself out on the Bay. Her hull was afterwards rigged as a schooner, *Rainbow*, and her engine reportedly put to use powering a coffee grinder. It is doubtful that the vessel ever was formally christened, but she may have borne the name *Sitka*, or *Little Sitka*.

With the onset of the Gold Rush, speculators sent out from the Atlantic States vessels better suited to the work. Davis and Bancroft tell of one such craft, the *George Washington*, put together at Benicia, which completed her first trip to Sacramento on August 17, 1849, and Davis adds that the first boat advertised for regular trips between Sacramento and San Francisco appears to have been the *Sacramento*, in September, 1849. Commanded by Captain John Van Pelt, she had "two engines of sixteen horsepower, could carry about

100 passengers, besides freight. She was built about where Washington now stands, opposite the northern portion of Sacramento City, and the captain . . . . made successful and regular trips with this vessel as far down as 'New York of the Pacific,' . . . where passengers and freight had to be transferred." Soulé relates: "The *Pioneer*, a little iron steamer, brought out in pieces from Boston, sailed upon the waters of the Sacramento River about [September, 1849]; and, being the first that had penetrated so far into the interior, deserves the title she had assumed. On [October 9, as reported in the *Alta California* two days later], the small iron steamer *Mint* had a trial trip, which was highly satisfactory. She was intended to ply between San Francisco and the towns on the upper waters." Davis also remarks upon the *Mint,* "really the first steamboat to make successful trips with passengers and freight all the way between that city and Sacramento, beginning in the middle of October, 1849."

Soulé and Davis agree that the steam-propeller *McKim,* which reached San Francisco around the Horn on October 3, 1849, was the first large vessel to navigate the Sacramento River by steam. She set out on her first voyage October 26, as recorded in the *Alta California.* "Before this time," Soulé observes, "voyages across the bay and up the Sacramento and San Joaquin Rivers were made in schooners and launches. These vessels were often detained a week or ten days in sailing that distance, which a steamer now accomplishes in half a day. Both the steamers mentioned sailed every alternate day from San Francisco, and on the intervening days left Sacramento for the return passage. The fares at first were thirty dollars cabin, and twenty dollars deck. If berths were used, five dollars *extra.* Meals on board, two dollars each. The well known Steamer *Senator* was shortly afterwards placed on the same station, and the little *Mint* withdrawn and placed on another [the Stockton run]."

Some further notes may be serviceable. The *Alta California,* November 1, 1849, reported that the long-expected *Senator* had arrived on Friday, October 27, 22 days from Panama, which was the day after the *McKim* set out on her first voyage to Sacramento. An advertisement noted that after this first voyage the *McKim* would sail each Monday and Thursday at 5 P. M., leaving Sacramento at 7 A. M. on Wednesday and Saturdays. Another advertisement advised that the *Mint* would run to Sacramento on Mondays, Wednesdays, and Fridays, returning on the succeeding days. The *Alta* did not report in detail the first river voyage of the *Senator,* but on November 22 had an advertisement that she would sail that day for Sacramento. The *Senator* was a fabulous financial success, with her size, speed, and comfort eclipsing all rival craft during the earliest period. Kemble discusses rates charged for passage on her at different times.

By the time of Gardiner's recollection, March, 1851, a considerable steamboat fleet was operating on the Sacramento. In the *Alta* of March 1, the Union line advertised that its steamboat *Confidence,* Capt. J. P. Gannett, would leave Long Wharf for Sacramento every Tuesday, Thursday, and Saturday at 4 P. M., while the "People's Line" advertised its steamers *New World,* Captain Hutchins, and *Senator,* Captain John Van Pelt, which connected at Sacramento with the steamers *Gov. Dana* and *Fashion* for Marysville. A third company promoted the steamer *H. T. Clay*, and a fourth concern the steamer *West Point*; there were also advertisements for the steam packet *Mariposa* and the steamer *Santa Clara*, which sailed for Stockton on alternate days. The standard time for leaving San Francisco was 4 P. M. According to a notice in the *Alta* of March 15, 1851, the cabin fare from San Francisco to Sacramento on the *New World* and *Senator* was $12. On April 1, 1851, the *Alta* ran advertisements for the *New World* and *Senator*, the *Confidence* and *Wilson G. Hunt*, and the *H. T. Clay*, all running to Sacramento, and the *Jenny Lind* and *Boston*, running to Stockton. All this adds up to a more complex picture of river navigation in 1851 than one might infer from Gardiner's text. His memory may have been at fault about the *Fashion* running to Stockton at this time, but there were frequent shifts in the assignments of steamboats. On July 3, 1851, the Sacramento *Union* reported that the *Fashion* had been auctioned off yesterday for $9,555 to Capt. Jno. Bensley, and by August 16 the *San Joaquin Republican* was mentioning her as one of four steamboats on the Stockton-San Francisco run. She was again listed as one of the steamboats on this run March 16, 1853, J. Chapman then her master.

20. By the spring of 1851, Sacramento was more built-up than Gardiner remembered, despite the great flood of January, 1850.

21. Sutter's Fort was then on the eastern outskirts of Sacramento, but the city has since expanded around it, the restored fort now a museum and a state historical monument—a municipal treasure. John A. Sutter established himself here in 1839.

22. Folsom is on the south bank of the American River, so unless Gardiner recrossed that stream, he did not encamp on the actual townsite. The place is named for Captain Joseph L. Folsom of Stevenson's Regiment, and was laid out in 1855 on the land grant acquired by William A. Leidesdorff. At the time Gardiner passed by, the locality was known as Negro Bar, "from the circumstance of negroes being the first men to do any mining at that point. This was in 1849." The quotation is from Win. J. Davis, *An Illustrated History of Sacramento County*, pp. 227–229, who summarizes the history of the town to 1890. The Sacramento Valley Railroad, the first in the State, was completed from Sacramento to Folsom on February 22, 1856. Folsom is now better known as the name of a nearby dam on the American River, and as that of the State Penitentiary, 2 miles away.

23. These celebrated lines were penned by Joaquin Miller.

24. Horse Shoe Bar and Whiskey Bar were located on the North Fork of the American River. Myron Angel, *History of Placer County* (Oakland, 1882), pp. 400–401, notes that Beal's Bar was the first upon the North Fork, just above the confluence with the South Fork, in the southeast corner of the county. "Following up the stream from Beal's Bar, are Condemned, Doton's, Long, Horseshoe, Rattlesnake, Whisky, Milk Punch, Deadman's, Smith's, Lacy's, Granite, Manhattan, Oregon, and Tamaroo Bars, before arriving at the point where the Middle Fork joins, the names of which are suggestive, which have at one time been densely peopled, and each has an interesting history if pains were taken in rescuing it from a fast-concealing oblivion." Concerning Horseshoe Bar, Angel adds: "Situated about seven miles above Beal's and about two miles south of the old '49 Sacra-

mento road, was first worked by Mormons in 1848. In the four or five following years it had quite a population, and was a trading center for the following named adjacent bars: Whisky, Beaver, Deadman's, Milk Punch and, until 1853, Rattlesnake Bar. In 1852 there were four hotels and stores there, owned by the following firms: Harrub & Manseur, Sweet & Barney, Clark & Canfield, and George W. Martin & Co. That year it was estimated that there were three hundred voters at Horseshoe, and that the gold product was one hundred thousand dollars."

CHAPTER XX. *Horse Shoe Bar, American River* (pp. 163–176)

1. See the last note in the preceding chapter concerning these and other productive bars of the North Fork of the American River. Murderer's Bar was located on the Middle Fork, above its confluence with the North Fork, so named because six Oregon miners were killed there by Indians in the spring of 1849. Mormon Bar has rather sunk from sight, not even mentioned in Angel's summary of the North Fork diggings, but it is frequently noticed in the contemporary press, for example in the "Notes of a Late Tour through the Mines by a Sacramentan," published in the Sacramento *Daily Union*, August 28, 1851:

"The Manhattan Company, situated about one mile above Mormon Bar, are beginning to pocket some of the 'shining, yellow earth,' which they so well deserve, after the laborious prosecution of their race, which was opened, one month ago. It cost five months' hard work. . . .

"MORMON BAR RACE COMPANY.—This company, who have taken up the famous Mormon Bar, which yielded some $60,000 two years ago to a party of Mormons, from whom it derived its name [not to be confused with Mormon Island on the South Fork of the American River, the first really rich find, made in 1848], have just completed a race which, for beauty of finish and substantiality of structure, is unprecedented in the annals of mining in this country. It was opened on Saturday week past, and a large number of the workmen on the dams and races above and below Mormon Bar, flocked during the last week to witness the passage of the river through its infant bed. The race was commenced on the 25th May last. It measures 1,000 feet long, 24 feet deep, and 22 ft. wide. Towards the head of the race, the company had to dig through four feet of granite. The old bed has been effectually drained for upwards of an eighth of a mile, and no dam has been required. Instead of backing water upon the upper companies, as is too often done by parties who forget the interests of their neighbors in their anxiety for what they suppose their own—the evil effects of which have been seen to result in crimination, recrimination and finally bloodshed—this company have actually reduced the water two feet at Mr. McGrath's wing-dam, and one foot at Lacy's Bar, the former about a quarter of a mile, and the latter half a mile above Mormon Bar. The work has been carried on under the superintendence of Mr. Allen Tucker, of Greenville, N. C., and Mr. Even, of St. Louis [16 members altogether in the company]. . . ."

2. The legend that California was settled up by the hardy Forty-niners will bear re-

examination, as shown by the fact that none of the men Gardiner names is listed as a resident of Placer County in the *Great Register* of 1867. One man did acquire a celebrity in county annals. Angel's *History of Placer County*, p. 102, says: "Abram Bronk, one of the pioneers of California, and one of the first and most respected officers, politicians, and public-spirited men of Placer County, died at Manchester, Ontario County, New York, May 17, 1870. Mr. Bronk was a native of Rotterdam, New York, and spent the most of his life in that State, with the exception of about six years' residence in Placer County. On arrival in Placer, in the summer of 1849, Mr. Bronk settled at Lower Horseshoe Bar, on the north fork of the American River, where he engaged in mining, which pursuit he followed until May, 1851, when he was elected Treasurer of the county, and held the position until June, 1853. During his official term he performed much of the work of Recorder and Auditor, in aid of the Clerk who then filled these positions *ex officio*. In 1854 he became the candidate of the Gwin faction of the Democratic party for County Judge, but the division of that party, and the nomination of a ticket by the Broderick wing, caused the election of the Whig ticket, and James E. Hale was the successful candidate. The following year, 1855, Mr. Bronk was the Democratic candidate for State Senator, but the Know-Nothing furor then prevailing, he was defeated by Charles Westmoreland. After his retirement from office he still continued mining at Horseshoe, but subsequently became a member of the company which constructed the Whisky Bar Turnpike road and wire suspension bridge—a work costing $50,000. He superintended the construction of the bridge, which was the first wire suspension bridge erected in Placer County. After the completion of this work, he erected the first suspension bridge across the main American River at Folsom, either as superintendent or by contract. Returning to his native State late in 1855, he there purchased a farm, married and settled down; but several years later he again thought of returning to Placer, and but a few months before his death, corresponded with his acquaintances in this county, making inquiry as to prices, etc., of certain foot-hill lands he desired to make his future home upon, with which he had been familiar in former years. At the time of his death, he still owned a considerable interest in the North Fork bridge and toll-road. Abram Bronk was possessed of a mind far above ordinary, stored with information and acquired knowledge rarely to be found among men in common walks of life, to which were added pure moral courage, rectitude of daily life, an honest heart and a conscience void of offense. Those who knew him best in Placer County, appreciated the honest, intellectual man most, with his modest, retiring worth."

3. The Klondike Gold Rush of 1896–1898 gave much wider currency to the term "Sourdough," for it was applied to miners who had wintered in the Far North (and knew something of the intricacies of bread-making) as distinguished from the Cheechakos or new-comers.

4. Salmon are still caught in the Sacramento River and its tributaries.

5. The evolution of the express companies in the California mines has given rise to an interesting monographic literature; see, *e. g.,* the series of twelve Keepsakes edited for the

Book Club of California in 1960 by Edgar B. Jessup, M. C. Nathan, and Henry H. Clifford, with the general title, *Early California Mail Bag*. For an overall history, see Oscar Osburn Winther, *Express and Stagecoach Days in California, from the Gold Rush to the Civil War* (Stanford, 1936), or his more popularized *Via Western Express and Stagecoach* (Stanford, 1945).

6. The introduction of the "long tom" into California during the winter of 1849–1850, is described by Rodman W. Paul, *California Gold*, pp. 61–62. It had been used in Georgia and North Carolina, and Paul remarks that "one of the machines described by Agricola sounds singularly like it." An outgrowth of the cradle, it was built in two sections. "The top section was an open-ended box or trough, usually about twelve feet long and always mounted in a down-sloping position. This trough was shaped like an inverse funnel: starting with a width of one or two feet at the higher end, it increased to double that width at the middle. At the middle the sides straightened out and ran parallel until they reached the lower end. In this broad, straight part the bottom was made of perforated sheet iron, with the sheet iron bent up into a gradual curve as it approached the lower end.

"The bottom section of the long tom was placed beneath the perforated sheet iron. It was called a riffle box, and was simply a wooden box with cleats ('riffle' or 'ripple' bars) across its bottom. To operate the machine water was piped into the high, narrow end of the trough. As this stream cascaded down the inverse funnel, two men continuously shoveled dirt into it, while a third man stood by the perforated sheet iron portion to stir the mixture as it piled against the up-curving strainer. In this way the coarser parts of the debris were retained in the top section of the long tom, while the finer material plunged through into the riffle box, where the gold was separated from the rest of the debris in precisely the same fashion as in the bottom of the cradle.

"Obviously the long tom was simply an adaptation of the cradle to the needs of large-scale production. The top section, or trough, of the long tom was the hopper of the cradle enlarged so as to permit the use of a continuous current of water instead of bailing by hand. So much larger a volume of dirt could be handled that two or more men could be uninterruptedly employed in shoveling and a third in stirring. The bottom section, or riffle box, was essentially the cradle with the hopper removed. . . ."

7. The Indians hereabouts belonged to the southern division of the Maidu, who occupied the country from the Cosumnes River to Mount Lassen, between the Sacramento River and the Sierra divide. South of the Maidu, to the Kern River, lived the Miwok. For these peoples, see A. L. Kroeber, *Handbook of the Indians of California* (Bureau of American Ethnology Bulletin 78, Washington, 1925), Chapters 27–30.

8. Again Gardiner has given us a graphic example of self-government by the miners, outside the formal juridical system.

9. The area embraced by modern Placer County was, when the first counties were organized in 1850, placed partly in Yuba County, partly in Sutter County, with Auburn the seat of the latter. Placer County was created by an act of the legislature approved April 25, 1851. Myron Angel, *History of Placer County*, p. 97, notes that an act organizing

the county, passed the same day, provided for an election to be held in Placer and Nevada counties, for county and township officers, on the fourth Monday of May. "The election occurred on the 26th of May, two days before the approval of the bill by the Governor, resulting in the choice of the following gentlemen to fill the various offices: Hugh Fitz-simmons, County Judge; Samuel C. Austin, Sheriff; R. D. Hopkins, District Attorney; James T. Stewart, Clerk; Alfred Lewis, Assessor; Douglas Bingham, Treasurer; Abram Bronk, Public Administrator; John C. Montgomery, Coroner. The total number of votes cast, or allowed, was 2,792." Irregularities in the election resulted in abortive court action. Bingham died, and Bronk was appointed Treasurer by the Court of Sessions. Angel says further that the general election of 1851 was held September 3, when "Gen. Jacob Fry was elected Senator; Patrick Canney and J. H. Gibson, Assemblymen; Abram Bronk, Treasurer; Jonathan Roberts, Public Administrator, and S. B. Farwell, District Judge, for the Eleventh Judicial District, comprising the counties of Placer, Yolo and El Dorado." No party lines had been drawn in the May election, but in the fall election for members of the legislature "conventions were held and party nominations made. The Democratic ticket was successful by majorities ranging from 400 to 500, in a total vote of 1,968."

10. The Democratic convention which led to the results described in the preceding note was held in Auburn, probably about the middle of June, 1851, but I have not found a newspaper notice.

11. Gardiner refers to Thomas Ewbank's *A Descriptive and Historical Account of Hydraulic and Other Machines for Raising Water, Ancient and Modern. . . .* (New York, 1842). Eleven editions of an enlarged version were published between 1846 and 1851.

12. The sheriff was Samuel C. Astin; see Note 10. He was re-elected in 1852.

13. Grizzly Bear Pavilion was the name applied to Bob Gardiner's store at Swett's Bar.

14. The Rio Chico, an eastern affluent of the Sacramento River, has given name to present Chico. Much of the area was embraced within a Mexican land grant obtained by William Dickey in 1843, and bought by John Bidwell in 1849–1852. Colusa is on the west bank of the Sacramento above the mouth of Butte Creek, seat of the county of the same name. Bidwell got a grant for this area in 1845, but sold it in 1849 without ever settling on it.

CHAPTER XXI. *At Secret Ravine* (pp. 177–183)

1. Secret Ravine is a long, northwesterly-trending valley which heads just south of Newcastle, Placer County, and drains finally into Dry Creek, south of Roseville. Supposedly it was so named because one Gibson, who discovered a rich placer there, sought to keep it a secret. Evidently Gardiner established himself in Secret Ravine about northeast of Horse Shoe Bar.

2. Hawes's Ranch may have had some tie-in with one of the express companies, but at this time and until August 29, 1854, there was no Secret Ravine Postoffice. The earliest U.S. Postoffice in Placer County was Yankee Jim's, established September 3, 1852. Oro

City had a postoffice from January 6 to December 20, 1853, Auburn from July 21, 1853, and Illinois Town (the modern Colfax) from November 22, 1853. See Walter N. Frickstad, *A Century of California Post Offices* (Oakland, 1955), p. 121.

3. The kangaroo rat is described by Webster's Dictionary as "Any of numerous pouched, nocturnal, jerboalike, burrowing rodents (genus *Dipodomys*) of arid parts of the western United States."

4. An account of Elkhorn Township in F. T. Gilbert, *History of San Joaquin County* (Oakland, 1879), pp. 113–114, says, "J. C. White settled, in 1850, on the Elkhorn ranch, from which the Township takes its name. He has paid for his ranch three times, and has not yet a title that is free from dispute." Perhaps the Elk Horn Inn to which Gardiner alludes was on this ranch. In the first issue of the Stockton *Times*, March 16, 1850, A. M. McCoffey advertised the "well known Elk Horn Inn," but this establishment was located on the road leading from Stockton to San Jose, 5 miles west of Bonsell & Doaks's Ferry on the San Joaquin River.

5. These bear-baitings, or "bull and bear fights," were regular features of the California scene in the 1850's. William Perkins in his *Life in California*, pp. 273–277, and Enos Christman, *One Man's Gold*, pp. 198–200, describe an affair of this kind at Sonora in September, 1851.

6. Only in Chapter XXV does Gardiner identify Bob Gardiner's partner as Michael Keogh.

CHAPTER XXII. *At Swett's Bar* (pp. 185–228)

1. Stephen Fowler in his MS. journal gives us a single glimpse of Steve French during this period of vagabondage. On September 15, 1850, while at Plumas, on the Feather River, Fowler wrote: "Mr Hatch went to Marysville to day, this afternoon French, Tinker and [Samuel Cook] of Sag Harbor come down with him to stay with us to night. Mr French stated to me that a lot well situated in Marysville, which last spring was sold for $1000, was again sold last week at auction for $60. . . ."

2. The "Gold Lake" excitement was one of the notable events of May, 1850. See the account in George and Bliss Hinkle, *Sierra Nevada Lakes* (Indianapolis, 1949), pp. 89–109, and that in John S. Hittell, *Mining in the Pacific States of North America*, pp. 22–23. Hittell also tells (pp. 25–26) of a second Gold Lake hunt in the summer of 1851, a side effect of which was the finding of rich diggings at what became Forest City, Sierra County.

3. An account of the more southerly diggings of Tuolumne County contributed by "Mountaineer" at Big Oak Flat, December 16, 1851, to the Stockton *San Joaquin Republican*, December 20, 1851, merits quotation at length: "As we follow the winding course of the Tuolumne up from the plains for about fifteen miles, it rushes through deep canons, and over piles of rocks, making in many places beautiful falls. Scattered along at intervals of from one to three miles there are bars or points left in the high stages of the stream. Passing up on the left or southern bank, the first water we find emptying into it is Moccasin Creek. The mouth of this creek is at Lewis' ferry, about three miles above

Jacksonville, where Wood's Creek empties, which is the first creek upon the northern bank of the river.

"Moccasin Creek takes its rise upon the high lands between the two rivers [Merced and Tuolumne]—one branch starting from this place—Oak Flat. This creek has never been found to be very rich, although there are and have been, for the last year and a half, a considerable number of men at work upon it; it will doubtless pay well to work in 'sluices,' when the wages of labor are lower, as there are *acres* of two cent dirt, from the surface down.

"Quartz Gulch, which comes down from Quartz Mountain, has been as rich as any in the country; it was discovered and worked by a Mexican, in the spring of 1850, and before he was discovered by the Americans he had taken out seventy pounds of gold, part of which was very coarse. He was then called upon for the 'Foreign Miners' Tax,' when he left; the place was afterwards worked with considerable success by Americans until the water gave out, which was in that summer; and, owing to the scarcity of that indispensable agent, the place has been but little worked since. It is singular that, although the gulches upon each side of this hill, or mountain, as it is called, have been found to contain gold, none as yet has been found in the ledge, notwithstanding there have been many there 'prospecting' quartz. Rattlesnake Creek, another fork of this (Moccasin) creek, has been extremely rich; one claim in particular, was taken up by a party of men, and worked early in the spring of '50, from which they averaged over fifty dollars per day to the hand for several weeks, when they abandoned it, supposing it worked out. Another party went in, and made from one to two ounces per day, by widening out or working further into the banks; *they* then left it, and another party commenced, and by working over the old dirt with cradles, made from twelve dollars to an ounce per day. Yet again, last winter, a party went to work upon it with a 'long tom,' and made from an ounce to twenty dollars per day, for some time. This was only on one claim. I have heard it asserted by those who have worked long upon this creek, that in its whole length—upwards of three miles—there was not a single claim of fifty yards but would have yielded a moderate fortune, if it had been thoroughly worked; and any one who was about there in June, 1850, will say the same. At present there are quite a number of long toms running, making, as their owners say, '*grub,*' which I will state, for the benefit of those who have never traveled through the mines, is the usual answer a person will get to the oft repeated question by Mr. Greenhorn—'How are you making it here?' Cobb's Creek is another branch of Moccasin, and has proved very rich. I notice several who wintered there last season have returned to their old quarters. Beyond this is another large creek, which, as yet, has never proved very rich, although gold has been found in small quantities—while most of the gulches emptying into it contain more or less of the precious metal. Maxwell's Creek takes its rise at the head of this creek, and, flowing towards the south, empties into the Merced. This creek was first worked by Major [James] Savage, with a party of Indians, in the winter of '48, but was soon abandoned because they could not make over an *ounce* per day, which was small pay at that time. . . .

"But to return. . . . As we pass up Rattlesnake, the first creek of note we meet is 'Slate Gulch,' which has been worked but little since the spring of '50, when they made an average of two ounces per day to the hand. There is considerable dirt thrown up on this gulch, and a fine chance to run toms when we get plenty of water. We next reach Garote Creek, so named because there was a Mexican hung here for theft, soon after its discovery. There were nearly two thousand Mexicans in this vicinity in June, 1850, when a difficulty occurred between the Indians and whites, which resulted in the death of one white man and several Indians. This occurrence so frightened the Mexicans that most of them left. There have been many thousands of dollars taken out of this creek, and there is more left, which will be extracted if we get a little more water, that article being short at present. This creek enters into what is called Big Creek, as also does the creek of Garote No. 2.

"Big Creek rises upon what is called 'Savage's Flat,' which is the finest piece of ground I have ever seen in the country, being upwards of a mile wide by two miles in length, without a tree or shrub. The grass here has been green all summer, and I am told that there has been frost nearly every week during the same time, which fact proves that it can never be cultivated; but there has been a large amount of hay cut and hauled to this place. Big Creek flows through a flat country, until within a few miles of the Tuolumne, when it enters a canon, which it follows until it empties into the river. This creek has been worked to a considerable extent, from the mouth of Garote Creek, to where it enters the canon, a distance of about four miles. This work was done last spring, when the water suddenly dried up, and labor was suspended. The average yield, with long toms, was from eight to twenty-four dollars per day to the hand. Two miles beyond this is 'Humbug,' so called from the gold being found in spots—one hole paying very well, while the one next to it pays nothing. There is a large number of Mexicans at work at this place at present. This is the extreme of the diggings in this direction, being not more than three or four miles from the south fork of the Tuolumne, and but a short distance above the forks. Besides these creeks and innumerable gulches known to contain gold, there is 'Deer Flat,' situate three fourths of a mile to the north of this place. Upon this flat gold has been found in several places in great abundance, but it has been but little more than prospected, as there was not water to work there last winter. . . .

"The town [Big Oak Flat] at this place contains eight stores for the sale of general merchandise, three boarding houses, two blacksmiths' shops, and a *postoffice* [actually established January 21, 1852, Flemming Amyx, P.M.]; while at Garrote there are two stores, blacksmith shop, boarding house, etc, and about the same at Garote No. 2. These stores are supplied with every description of goods, and unless we get a good supply of water, will not be used for several months. With plenty of rain there would be a rush of miners, and the stock would rapidly diminish. . . ."

4. For Sherlocks Creek, a tributary of the Merced, see Note 34. I do not find any account in the Stockton or Sonora papers of the incident which follows.

5. Prentice Mulford is more fully discussed in Chapter XXV, Note 4. In *Prentice Mul-*

ford's Story (New York, 1889), toward the end of Chapter XII, he says: "Generally speaking, Swett's [Bar] was divided in two portions. There was the old bar on the right bank of the river, settled in ''49,' and there was the flat on the other side, whose golden store was not discovered until 1859. . . . When first we struck the diggings at Swett's left bank we had great expectations. It was a later discovery, a 'back river channel.' Consequent on the discovery of pay-ground one thousand feet back of the river, and the definite fixing of the boundary lines between the various claimants, there ensued the usual series of disputes, rows, bad blood, assaults, and threatened shootings. Nobody was shot—not even a mining lawsuit came of it. . . . [They obtained water by fluming and commenced washing] but the dirt did not pay as we expected. We averaged—week in and week out— some three dollars per day, and one dollar of this went for water money."

6. French Bar, on the lower Tuolumne River, eventually was renamed La Grange. At this time it was a part of Tuolumne County, but when Stanislaus County was created out of the western part of Tuolumne in 1854, its history took another course. La Grange was the county seat from late 1855 to 1862. French Bar was one of the lowest diggings on the Tuolumne River. The *History of Stanislaus County, California* (San Francisco, 1881), pp. 114–116, intimates that the name French Bar became current only during or after 1852, but surely this is a mistake.

7. Split Rock Ferry was located on the Merced River in Mariposa County, near present Kittridge. Bear Valley reaches the Merced from the south at present Bagby, and is traversed today by the highway from Coulterville to Mariposa.

8. Flemming (or Fleming) Amyx was appointed first postmaster at Big Oak Flat in 1852. Although never sheriff of Tuolumne County, he was a deputy sheriff in 1854. Amyx was an Assemblyman from 1855 until his death at Stockton, November 4, 1861; up to the time Gardiner left California, he still lived at Big Oak Flat.

9. The early discrimination against the Chinese in California is discussed by H. H. Bancroft, *History of California*, vol. VII, pp. 336–348. By August, 1852, no less than 18,026 men and 14 women had voyaged to California from China, principally sailing from Hong Kong in British ships. The first Chinese emigrants, two men and a woman, arrived by the clipper bark *Eagle* in 1848. Bancroft further notes: "The placers the white miners had abandoned were usually occupied by Chinese who were content with five or eight dollars a day, while a white man wanted sixteen or twenty. When such returns failed, the Mongolians were often assailed by other miners with no better rights, and driven away from the diggings heretofore despised by these men, who complained to the legislature, which at every session endeavored to make the laws so oppressive to the detested race that they should cease to immigrate."

10. Brief biographical sketches of most of these politically prominent men may be found in Herbert O. Lang, *History of Tuolumne County, passim*. Albert N. Francisco was not yet proprietor of the Sonora *Union Democrat*; this paper commenced publication a year later, on July 1, 1854.

11. The election took place on Thursday, September 8, 1853, a sweeping success for the

Democratic ticket despite valiant campaigning by the Whigs. The prior convention Gardiner describes met at Jamestown on June 15–16. The proceedings were described in a Sonora *Herald Extra,* reprinted in the Stockton *San Joaquin Republican,* June 18, 1853. This account corrects Gardiner's in small particulars; the two should be read together:

"The democratic convention for the county of Tuolumne met at Jamestown on Wednesday, June 15th. Every precinct was represented, and it was one of the largest and most enthusiastic conventions ever convened in the county.

"The convention was called to order at 10 o'clock, A. M., and adjourned *sine die* on Thursday at midnight.

"Hon. James W. Coffroth was unanimously called upon to preside over the deliberations, and Mr. Thomas A. Palmer, Thomas N. Cazneau and Mr. Peter Mehen were appointed vice presidents. Wm. Aspenall and Fred'k B. Latimer were appointed Secretaries.

"A committee of five was then appointed to examine credentials consisting of Messrs. Lane, Otis, Vincent, Harris and Keyes. An adjournment then took place until 1 o'clock.

Re-assembled, and after transacting necessary preliminary matters the following County ticket was duly nominated as Democratic candidates at the coming election.

"*For County Judge.*—Leander Quint.
"*For State Senator.*—Dr. Thomas Kendall.
"*For Representatives.*—J. J. Hoff, J. W. Mandeville, J. T. Hoyt, Dr. Walker, H. B. Goddard.
"*For Sheriff.*—P. A. [P. L.] Solomon.
"*For County Clerk.*—George S. Evans.
"*For County Recorder.*—James Letford.
"*For County Assessor.*—T. A. Fields.
"*For Public Administrator.*—Judge Brunton.
"*For County Treasurer.*—P. O. Bertine.
"*For District Attorney.*—H. P. Barber.
"*For County Surveyor.*—W. H. Richardson.
"*For Coroner.*—Dr. Van Dusen.

"The following delegates were selected to represent the county in the State Convention.

"Paul K. Hubbs,
J. H. Deering,
Samuel McLean,
D. A. Enyart,
James M. Wilson,
H. P. Barber,
M. J. Smith,
J. J. Hoff,
James O'Sullivan,

James W. Coffroth,
Ethan Allen
Jesse Brush,
T. W. Martin
W. S. Tarbox,
Caleb Dorsey,
W. S. Throckmorton,
E. C. Dowidigan,
A. F. Calkins.

"The following are to constitute the Democratic County Committee for the ensuing year.

G. W. Patrick,   D. Fletcher,
Major Kelley,   J. M. Anderson,
James Lane,   N. Francisco,
E. B. Stewart,   Mr. Bryan,
Caleb Dorsey,   J. W. Coffroth.

"The following resolutions were offered by different members of the Convention and severally adopted, after which the Convention adjourned:

"*Resolved,* That the Democracy of Tuolumne county recognise in John Bigler, the present Chief Magistrate of the State, a firm and consistent Democrat, a true friend to the People, a faithful and fearless public servant, and that they look forward with confidence and satisfaction for his re-nomination, and triumphant election.

"*Resolved,* That the County Democratic Committee, be instructed, in the call of a convention hereafter, to call the primary meetings at all the precincts in the county on the Saturday evening immediately preceding the Convention; and the election at all such precincts shall be by ballot cast by democratic voters of the precinct; that the polls shall be kept open at least one hour; that public notices of each primary meeting shall be posted in the precinct for at least one week previous; and that the basis of representation shall be one delegate for the precinct, and an additional delegate for every fifty democratic votes cast at the previous general election, and one for every fraction over 25 votes—the highest democratic vote cast for any State officer being taken as the basis.

"*Resolved,* That the thanks of this convention be tendered to the Hon. Jas. W. Coffroth for the patient, faithful and dignified manner in which he has presided over this convention.

"*Resolved,* That the services rendered to the State by our present Senator, Paul K. Hubbs, eminently entitle him to the confidence of the Democracy of California; and the delegation from this county are hereby instructed to demand of the Benicia Convention, and by all honorable means to sustain, his nomination to the office of *Superintendent of Public Instruction,* or to some high office. [He was so nominated, and was elected in September.]"

12. Campo Seco stood immediately south of Jamestown. It should not be confused with another Campo Seco in Calaveras County. Santiago, sometimes also referred to as Santa Iago or San Diego, was about a mile northeast of the site of Columbia; Mexican miners labored there in 1849, before the rich strike at Columbia in March, 1850. Columbia itself has been restored as a California State Park.

13. Turnback Creek is still so named; it enters the Tuolumne from the right bank below the mouth of the North Fork, not so close to the headwaters of the Tuolumne as Gardiner implies.

14. "Creasing" involved stunning an animal by shooting it through the nape of the neck; delicate skills were involved, as the spinal column could be destroyed by even slightly errant aim.

15. The Calaveras grove of "Big Trees" (Sequoia Gigantea) in 1853 emerged as one of

the wonders of the world. These trees had been seen as early as 1833 by members of Joseph Reddeford Walker's detachment of Captain Bonneville's men, and just possibly in 1841 by John Bidwell of the Bartleson Party. Miners who had gone hunting rediscovered them in 1850, but the discovery that counted, which made the giant sequoias known to the world, was that by Alexander T. Dowd supposedly in the spring of 1852 (actually, 1853?). This interesting history is well developed by Rodney Sydes Ellsworth, *The Discovery of the Big Trees of California, 1833–1852* (Berkeley, M.A. Thesis, 1933). The Stockton *San Joaquin Republican,* May 25, 1853, picked up a notice of the big trees from the *Sonora Herald,* and on June 11 had this to say about "The Largest Tree in the World":

"Capt. W. H. Hanford, of Murphy's Diggings, has presented us with a handsome lithographed view of the mammoth tree, about which so much has lately been said in the up-country journals. Capt. Hanford, the discoverer [!], assures us that there are some fifty other trees in the neighborhood, of enormous dimensions. The bark has been stripped from the largest, and will be sent in sections to New York. There are some fifty cords of this bark.—As a friend says, Capt. Hanford did not 'bark up the wrong tree that time.'

"The tree is standing on the head-waters of the Stanislaus and San Antoine rivers, in Calaveras county. Its diameter is thirty-one feet at the base, its height is two hundred and ninety feet, and it is supposed to be three thousand years old."

For other references, see the *Republican,* June 28, September 17, 1853; and for a general history of the Big Trees, Francis P. Farquhar, *History of the Sierra Nevada* (Berkeley and Los Angeles, 1965), pp. 83–92.

16. An extended account of the operations of water companies in Tuolumne County is found in Herbert O. Lang, *A History of Tuolumne County,* pp. 100, 115–128, 162–178; and see also Edna Bryan Buckbee, *The Saga of Old Tuolumne,* pp. 265–281. Apparently Gardiner labored on the canal built by the Tuolumne Hydraulic Association, which tapped the Tuolumne River some 25 miles southeast of Sonora, and carried water to the Montezuma flats, southeast of Table Mountain.

17. Table Mountain was then, and still remains, a prominent physiographic feature of Tuolumne County, north and east of Jamestown. Edna Bryan Buckbee, *The Saga of Old Tuolumne,* pp. 49–50, says of it:

"Table Mountain, the most remarkable peak of its kind in the West, was formed as the result of a volcanic eruption of molten lava. It has an average height of five hundred feet, an average width of four hundred yards, a length of thirty miles, and an almost flat surface that descends ever so slightly toward the west. The sides near the top are perpendicular walls of solid basalt, farther down they are sloping, being composed of dirt and fragments of basalt that have fallen from above. Under the basalt lie the gravel and sand of the ancient river bed, enclosed at the sides by ridges of rock, which rise majestically above the level of the plain below. When, therefore, the miners first reached the auriferous deposits under the mountain, it was necessary for them to cut tunnels through a rim of rock.

"The tunnels they cut finally drained away all the water, but it was established beyond all reasonable doubt that the auriferous deposit under the basalt was once the bed of some prehistoric river. Every mark indicated it—the wide water-worn bed, the bends, the bars, the deposits of gravel in eddies, the collection of coarse gold in the center, the position of the large flat stones, all pointing downstream and the remains of fresh-water mollusks.

"The pay dirt, filled with large stones, was tough. The distance from the outside of the mountain to pay dirt varied from six to twelve hundred feet. One of the richest claims, only one hundred feet square, yielded $75,000 to its owners. In 1856, an American mining company, while driving a tunnel under Table Mountain, took seventeen pounds of gold from the ancient channel."

18. Gardiner exaggerates, for erosion over long periods of geological time would make impossible any such neat dovetailing of the sides of any chasm.

19. Hugh Miller (1802–1856) was a prominent early writer on geology, whose *The Old Red Sandstone* and *The Testimony of the Rocks* (to name just two works) ran through many editions.

20. Regrettably, these vast gold deposits have never yet been found.

21. Mrs. Barbara Eastman gives me a note from the Tuolumne County Supervisors' Book I, p. 28, with election returns for November 6, 1852, showing that H. C. Gardiner and J. P. Ward were elected justices of the Peace in Township 5; they took office December 1, 1852, to serve until the first Wednesday in October, 1853. Lang, *A History of Tuolumne County*, pp. 303–308, provides in tabular form a list of officers of the county, 1849–1881, displaying the fact that there were seven townships in 1853, that the justices of the peace for Township 5 were Gardiner and Ward, and that the constables were S. B. French and Joel Bass. For 1854 S. McCurdy and M. J. Davis were the justices of the peace, J. Epperson and S. B. French the constables. Thus Gardiner and his friend Steve French took office earlier than he recalled, and well ahead of James Wylie Mandeville's election to the Assembly on September 8, 1853 (so Gardiner may have been indebted to someone other than Mandeville for his copy of the California Statutes). For Mandeville (1824–1876) see in particular Albert Dressler, ed., *Letters to a Pioneer Senator* (San Francisco, 1925), made up of communications addressed to Mandeville between 1853 and 1857.

22. A search of the *San Joaquin Republican* has turned up no reference during 1853–1854 to an occurrence of this kind.

23. H. K. Swope was sheriff in 1852–1853, successor to the first incumbent, George Work. He gave way in 1854 to P. L. Solomon, of whom Albert Dressler says in editing *Letters to a Pioneer Senator*, p. 31: "Known also as 'King Solomon.' Came from Tennessee. He was a hatter at first, then Mexican war soldier, rising to the rank of major. Democrat in politics. Did excellently well as sheriff of Tuolumne County. Quiet, far-seeing and energetic. He afterwards became U. S. marshal. Died in 1863."

24. The Foreign Miner's Tax was first imposed by the California legislature in 1850, as discussed in Morgan and Scobie, eds., *Three Years in California, William Perkins' Journal of Life at Sonora, 1849–1852*, pp. 36–45, 155–156, 397–400. H. H. Bancroft, *History of California*, vol. VII, p. 337, adds a relevant note: "The legislature of 1850 enacted a law

against all foreigners—Mexicans and Indians not included—which required a license to be taken out at $20 per month. This tax, together with the uncertainties of mining was equivalent to a prohibition, and the law became to a considerable extent inoperative, and was repealed in 1851. In 1852 the cost of a foreign miner's license was fixed at $3 a month, but the act was repealed in 1853, when it was raised to $4. An appropriation of $600 was made for translating the law into Chinese and printing 4,000 copies. In 1855 the law excluding from the courts negro and Indian evidence, was amended to include Chinese, and obstructions were thrown in the way of procuring bondsmen, so as to make it difficult for Asiatics charged with crime to procure bail." This was not a pretty chapter in California legislative history.

25. According to *The Friend*, April, 1854, p. 20, the Danish bark *Concordia*, Broderson, reached Honolulu March 7, 1854, in 17 days from San Francisco. With the same master she cleared for Hong Kong on April 24 (*ibid.*, May, 1854, p. 40). She had not returned to Honolulu by the close of 1856. I find no record of another *Concordia* in the Islands at this time.

26. Benjamin Franklin Moore was one of the notable Tuolumne personalities of this decade, strikingly characterized by Lang, *A History of Tuolumne County*, pp. 182–186: "Colonel Moore owed nothing of his phenomenal success to his learning, for even upon legal points that was of the slimmest possible character; and in general matters his illiteracy was profound. Neither did he make any attempt to conceal his want of knowledge. He rather gloried in it. And the want of erudition . . . oftentimes proved a powerful aid before a jury, who felt themselves, as it were, 'in the same boat,' and allowed their feelings to be won by sloppy eloquence, rather than by the more polished and learned efforts of rival attorneys. . . .

"Railing against books and book-learning, sneering when other forms of attack were impossible, domineering over Judge[s] (excepting always Judge Creaner), deriding Northern men and the principles commonly supposed to have been theirs, upholding the superiority of the chivalrous people of the South, bursting into furious eloquence at any and all times, and taking the lead when more modest and perhaps abler men would have hesitated, the Colonel lived throughout the lively 'flush times' without a peer or a dangerous rival in his peculiar province." Carlo M. De Ferrari, who reproduced a portrait in his edition of Thomas Robertson Stoddart's *Annals of Tuolumne County* (Sonora, 1963), p. 73, says that Moore was born in Choore's Bluff, Alabama, about 1823, but spent much of his early life in Florida and was usually supposed to be a Floridan, a heavy drinker and "quick tempered in classical southern style." He was a member of the convention which framed the State Constitution in 1849 without making any notable contribution, "although at one point during its deliberations he broke a seemingly habitual silence to defend the right of gentlemen to engage in duels." Moore afterward served in the legislature and died at Stockton January 1, 1866. (*Ibid.*, pp. 79, 100.)

27. A sketch of C. W. H. Solinsky is printed in Lang, *A History of Tuolumne County*, p. 315. Born in Poland August 14, 1814, he came to the United States in 1840, served in

the Mexican War, 1846–1848, and came to California in the ship *Osceola*. After engaging in mining for several years in Calaveras and Mariposa counties, and near Sonora, he became a member of the firm of Miller & Co., and afterward agent for Adams & Co.'s Express. When that company dissolved, in 1857, he became agent for Wells, Fargo & Co., so continuing "until the present time. During these years Mr. Solinsky has also engaged in several mining operations; nor is this all that is within the scope of his business activity. One of the best appointed and well managed hotels in the foothills has been under his proprietorship for a number of years." Further details are provided by Edna Bryan Buckbee, *The Saga of Old Tuolumne*, pp. 464–465, the date of his death there given as April 5, 1896, and that of his coming to the United States as 1836. He lived for some time in Chinese Camp, where he began his career as a miner.

28. Chinese Camp, also known as Chinese Diggings, sprang up several miles northeast of Jacksonville. An undated letter by "Mountaineer" in the Stockton *San Joaquin Republican*, June 11, 1853, said that the Chinese Diggings were "so called from being first worked by a company of Chinamen, who were hired and brought to this country by an Englishman, some time early in the year 1849. The house put up by this Englishman is still standing but it is so surrounded by improvements, that it would hardly now be recognized by its former proprietor. At this place there is a large number of miners hauling dirt to be washed, most of the mining here being done in that manner."

29. Heckendorn & Wilson's *Miners & Business Men's Directory [of Tuolumne County] for the Year Commencing January 1st, 1856* (Columbia, 1856), pp. 84–85, lists several of these men as residing at Chinese Camp: J. W. Gashwiler, Miner, Missouri; M. R. Graham, Postmaster, Indiana; John S. Payne, Butcher, New York; and A. Stair, "Salloon," Pennsylvania. Douglas and Saunders by then apparently had departed Chinese Camp.

30. "Mountaineer's" letter cited in Note 28 speaks of McLean's Ferry on the Stanislaus, and adds: "Capt. McLean is one of the few who are now left in our midst, who prospected through our hills and ravines before the swarms of 1849, poured into them, and many are the tales he will tell of gold hunting when it was new. He has a fine two story house and he lives like a lord. There is some mining done just below, upon the river, but nothing very extensive." (McLean's Ferry was on the road to [or from] Melones.) Was this the man to whom Gardiner refers?

31. The circulating library at Hawkins' Bar has come to have a certain celebrity, thanks to Prentice Mulford. In the reminiscences printed in Lang's *A History of Tuolumne County* (Appendix, p. 30), Mulford spoke of Morgan Davis as a "prominent inhabitant of Hawkins'. He was for years the custodian of the Hawkins' Bar Library, which had been purchased by the 'Boys' in San Francisco—and a very creditable library it was. Often have I, at the East, cited this as a proof of the character of the early Californians. The prevalent idea in the States is that the Californian of that time was a rough, uncouth, whiskyguzzling semi-outlaw, when in fact those who came from 1849 to 1852 were the very pick of the energy, enterprise and intelligence, not only of the States but of other countries." *Prentice Mulford's Story*, Chapter XI, tells of a visit to Hawkins' Bar as late as 1870,

when but one house was standing, "the cabin wherein had lived Morgan Davis, the former custodian of the Hawkins' Bar library. As early as 1854 or '55 the Hawkins' Bar 'boys' had clubbed their funds, sent down to San Francisco, and there purchased a very respectable library. It was a good solid library, too, based on a full set of American Encyclopedias, Humboldt, Lyell, and the like dispensers of heavy and nutritious mental food, rising into the lighter desserts of poetry and novels. As late as 1858 the 'boys' were in the habit of replenishing their library with the newest scientific works, novels and magazines.

"But in '70, on my last visit, the library was gone. Morgan was dead. His cabin door had fallen from its hinges; a young oak tree had sprung up and blocked the entrance; the flooring had been torn up, the window sashes taken out; a dinner-pot and broken stove were all that remained of Morgan's cooking utensils. Some of the roofing had disappeared. It was a ghostly place. . . ."

32. In his contribution to Lang's *History* cited in Note 31, Prentice Mulford remarked: "At Hawkins' Bar, Munson Van Riper, of the New York Knickerbocker stock, was voted 'our oldest and most respected citizen.' Munse, in the early days, was counted the best cook and housekeeper on the Bar. He used to wash his own shirts and sheets. He slept in sheets, which at that time was deemed ultra-luxurious."

33. Compare Note 31. Mulford was a prolific writer, and Gardiner may have seen another account of Morgan Davis and his library; more likely, despite the quotation marks, Gardiner is summarizing his recollection of what Mulford said in his book. Franklin Walker gathered up *Prentice Mulford's California Sketches* for the Book Club of California (San Francisco, 1935), but his gleanings from the *Californian* and *Overland Monthly* include nothing here relevant.

34. Gardiner has the saving grace to say that the Merced above the mouth of Sherlock Creek was only "comparatively" unknown. The river above, all the way into Yosemite, had been reconnoitered by miners at least as early as October, 1849, as we may infer from the MS. diary of William Penn Abrams in the Bancroft Library (see Note 35). Sherlock Creek flows into the Merced from the south above Bear Valley, separated from that valley by Bullion Mountain. A letter dated Sherlock's Diggings, Mariposa, Sept. 27, printed in the *Alta California*, October 25, 1849, says that the diggings "were discovered two or three months since by a man named Sherlock, who with a company of seventy Mexicans worked these deposits on shares. . . . Sherlock has gone into the mountains, no one knows where, and we have elected a new Alcalde, who, the day of his installation into office, issued an order for all Mexicans to decamp, which they did forthwith. We all intend to winter here, as we can easily make comfortable quarters. This place is distant 11 miles from Fremont's discovery. Many large pieces have been recently found here, averaging from one to eight pounds, pure gold. The finest pieces usually are worth about fifty cents, so you perceive this is the region of 'big lumps.' " C. Gregory Crampton, *The Opening of the Mariposa Mining Region, 1849–1859*, pp. 70–72, gives many citations to newspaper and other accounts relative to the inception of mining in this area. In this work

and in his *The Mariposa Indian War, 1850–1851* (Salt Lake City, 1957) Crampton details at length the Indian campaigns which made Yosemite more generally known.

35. Joseph R. Walker, leading a detachment of Captain Bonneville's trappers to California in 1833, is believed to have been the first white man to see Yosemite from above, but William Penn Abrams, as mentioned in the preceding note, gives the first account of the famous falls that has yet come to light. Abrams wrote in his diary at San Francisco under date of October 18, 1849: "Returned to S. F. after visit to Savages property on Merced R. prospects none too good for a mill Savage is a blaspheming fellow who has five squaws for wives for which he takes his authority from the Scriptures While at Savages Reamer and I saw grizzly bear tracks and went out to hunt him down getting lost in the mountains and not returning until the following evening found our way to camp over an Indian trail that led past a valley enclosed by stupendous cliffs rising perhaps 3000 feet from their base and which gave us cause for wonder. Not far off a water fall drops from a cliff below three jagged peaks into the valley while farther beyond a rounded mountain stood, the valley side of which looked as though it has been sliced with a knife as one would slice a loaf of bread and which Reamer and I called the Rock of Ages." See Francis P. Farquhar, *History of the Sierra Nevada*, pp. 74–81, for a discussion of this diary entry and subsequent events. Farquhar also traces the later history of Yosemite as State and National Park (pp. 201–216).

36. The Tuolumne County Democratic Convention of 1854 was held not in Sonora but in Jamestown, June 17, as reported in the Stockton *San Joaquin Republican* two days later. The 1855 convention was also held in Jamestown, on June 16, as reported in the *Republican* eight days later. However it happened that Gardiner got his recollections mixed, the details he supplies certainly reflect a visit to Sonora made at some time or other. The Placer Hotel (Adams & Bemiss, proprietors) and John C. Smith's Saloon at Sonora both had full-page ads in Heckendorn & Wilson's *Miners & Business Men's Directory* for 1856, which also listed as livery stable operators W. H. Cooper of Indiana and D. O. McCarthy of Massachusetts. (There was no personal listing of John C. Smith, so this source sheds no light on his origins.)

37. The election was held September 6, 1854. Major Solomon at this time was first elected sheriff, succeeding H. K. Swope. The internal fighting in the Democratic party this year was primarily an aspect of the statewide conflict between the Broderick and Gwin factions. The successful Democratic candidate for county clerk was George S. Evans; not until 1862 was Robert E. Gardiner first elected to this office. The political struggle H. C. Gardiner relates went on into the next year, for the Stockton *San Joaquin Republican*, June 24, 1855, has the following report on the Jamestown Democratic convention of the 16th which nominated as its ticket:

"State Senator, Chas. L. Scott; Assembly, Caleb Gilman, Singleton J. Cooke, Thomas Maxey and L. T. Jarvis; Sheriff, P. L. Solomon; Clerk, George S. Evans; District Attorney, Otis Greenwood; Recorder, J. D. Darden; Assessor; M. R. Graham; Supervisors, John N. Stone, — Hall, — Kerrick, E. Linoberg and R. A. Molyneux.

"The following gentlemen were then elected delegates to the State Convention [at Sacramento on June 27], with power to fill vacancies in their number: G. W. Patrick, C. L. Scott, J. W. Mandeville, J. A. Lank, Caleb Gilman, S. L. Conner, R. Thompson, R. Hickey, A. A. Mack, F. Amyx, J. McGlenchy, W. G. Heslep, Geo. Kittering.

"On the adoption of a resolution denunciatory of know nothingism, twenty-nine delegates withdrew from the convention, organized, and nominated the following ticket:

"Senate, Thos. C. Brunton; Assembly, J. T. Van Dusen, Chas. Tupper, R. H. Towle, Dr. Cook; Sheriff, James McLean; County Clerk, R. E. Gardiner; Recorder, M. Walworth; Assessor, F. E. Dreyfous; District Attorney, Caleb Dorsey; Public Administrator, Wm. Brown; Surveyor, John A. Davis; Coroner, Dr. Moss; Supervisors, J. Wilson, S. H. Moss, Chas. C. Parker, Wm. Carroll, — McBarton.

"The members of the party who style themselves the 'True Democracy' also assembled at Sonora, on the 16th inst., and made the following nominations:

"Senate, J. W. Coffroth; Assembly, H. G. Worthington, Uriah Miller, J. B. Bronson and S. V. Frazier; Sheriff, James O'Sullivan; Assessor, Isaac A. Stevens; Treasurer, Thos. C. Brunton; County Attorney, E. A. Rogers; Recorder, Dr. L. C. Gunn; Surveyor, B. G. Liscomb; Public Administrator, Calvin Honey; Coroner, Dr. A. Moss; Supervisors, P. Lynch, D. B. Demming, Joseph Coombs, Wm. Donovan and D. Van Vechten.

"Three delegations were also elected to the State Convention."

38. An account of Bruce's execution, only the second by legal process in the county, is given by Lang, *A History of Tuolumne County*, pp. 147–149. Lang says Bruce died "for the murder of a Mexican Indian boy, of sixteen. The murder took place in Sonora the previous year, and was committed during a brawl in a fandango house. Bruce was immediately arrested, tried and convicted, but owing to the law's delays, more than a year passed before his execution." At one time Bruce broke jail, but was pursued, wounded, and recaptured near Burn's Ferry. Lang briefly relates the hanging, but it may be more useful to quote the report by "Pegleg" dated Sonora, December 8, 1854, printed in the Stockton *San Joaquin Republican*, December 11, 1854:

"This day will be long remembered by the citizens of this city and county. We have just witnessed a most terrible and shocking spectacle; within the last hour Robert Bruce has suffered the awful penalty which our laws attach to the crime of murder. Accustomed as we have been to scenes of blood, hardened as we may have become by a long residence in the mines of California, yet we have never been so profoundly agitated, never experienced such indescribable emotions, as we have this day, in beholding the execution of the death penalty.

"The demeanor of the prisoner, his whole bearing, from the time he left the jail to the last act in the dreadful tragedy, was firm, dignified and manly, and in other circumstances would have been called heroic. We do not mean that he was reckless, or indifferent to his fate, or that he manifested the sullen spirit of a hardened and depraved criminal; on the contrary, his appearance was that of a naturally brave man, possessed of extraordinary nerve, and fully determined to meet a fate which he could not avoid with courage and coolness. I am sure he had the sympathies of the immense crowd of people by whom he was surrounded, and I cannot believe that there was a single person on the ground who did not in his heart pity the fate of this unfortunate young man, or one who did not most sincerely regret the combination of circumstances which had brought one in the prime of manhood, so prepossessing in his appearance, and possessed of manly, noble and re-deeming qualities, to an untimely and dishonorable grave.

"Our Sheriff, Major Solomon, is deserving of much credit for the manner in which the affair was conducted, and for the order and decorum which prevailed throughout the vast assemblage.

"The prisoner was taken from the jail to the gallows in a carriage, which contained also his spiritual adviser, the Rev. Mr. Evans, and the Sheriff. The 'Columbia Fusileers' marched in front, and the 'Sonora Greys' surrounded the carriage. The drums beat the 'Dead March,' and at 12 M. the solemn procession moved slowly on to the place of execution.

"People from all parts of the county and from the adjoining counties had been collect-ing for several hours previous around the gallows and on the surrounding hills. The num-ber who witnessed the execution is variously estimated from 5,000 to 8,000 persons. It was undoubtedly the largest crowd that has ever assembled in this county. The military companies surrounded the gallows and presented a very formidable appearance.

"At a quarter past twelve o'clock, the prisoner descended from the carriage and mounted the stairs with a firm step, and seated himself on the scaffold, with the clergy-man on his right side and Marshal McFarland and the Sheriff on his left. The death war-rant was then read, after which the Sheriff asked him if he desired to make any remarks. The prisoner then arose, laid aside his cloak, and after drinking a glass of water, he bowed gracefully to the audience, and in a perfectly calm and clear voice said: 'Gentlemen, I am innocent of the crime of murder. Judge Carley has sworn away my life; had it not been for him, I should not be where I now am. I have nothing more to say.' Mr. Evans then read a chapter from the Bible, and gave out the hymn commencing, 'Hark, from the tombs,' &c., which was sung by a few persons who ascended the scaffold for that pur-pose. The Reverend gentleman then offered a very appropriate prayer, which was lis-tened to with profound attention and perfect silence. He was then invited by the Sheriff to address the crowd, which he did in a most forcible and eloquent manner. He censured in the strongest terms the 'morbid curiosity' which had brought so many people, far and near, from their homes and business, to witness the dying struggles and ignoble fate of a fellow man.

"I would that I were able to wipe from my recollection the scene which followed; but it is too vividly impressed to be ever forgotten. The rope was now let down from the cross beam, and the prisoner, after looking at it, told the Sheriff that it was too short and would not give him sufficient fall. The rope was then lowered some two or three feet, by his direction, and after it was again fastened, he measured its length by standing up against it, and tried its strength. He then took off his neck-handkerchief, shook hands with the minister, the City Marshal, the Sheriff, and two of his friends whom he called on the scaffold; and turning to the crowd, he said: 'Farewell, friends—*adios mi amigos*.' His hands and feet were then tied, the rope adjusted around his neck, the black cap drawn over his face, the scaffold was cleared, and the next instant the drop fell, and after a few hard struggles, the spirit of the unfortunate and misguided Robert Bruce passed from the jurisdiction of earthly courts to be tried before the Supreme Court of the universe. He was 24 years of age, and was born in Scotland."

For the only previous execution of the kind, that of the Mexican horsethief José Corrales at Sonora on January 7, 1852, see William Perkins' account in *Three Years in California*, pp. 293–294.

39. The circumstances of the killing of George Kittering were more complicated than Gardiner gives us to believe, detailed in Lang, *A History of Tuolumne County*, pp. 178–187; with additional details to be had from the Stockton *San Joaquin Republican*, July 8, 12, and 22, 1855, March 12, 1856. On June 30, 1855, four robbers broke into the home of Judge Thomas C. Brunton and robbed him of $12,000, also knocking the judge down and knifing him before departing. This was immediately after the political events described in Note 37, and passions were high. Kittering accused Werth of being concerned in the robbery, refused to make a retraction, and was shot several times, dying immediately. Werth gave himself up to the authorities, and was committed for trial, which came off in Sonora on March 6, 1856. Lang gives an entertaining account of the proceedings, similar to Gardiner's. The case went to the jury late on the evening of March 10, and after four hours a verdict of not guilty resulted. "An unusual degree of interest was manifested in the case," said the *Republican*, "as the defendant was much esteemed and respectably connected."

40. Lang's version, cited in the previous note, is that by the jury verdict "W. H. Worth was set free, soon to shake the dust of Tuolumne from his feet. His subsequent history is unknown, but there is good evidence for believing that he became an Episcopal clergyman at a later period, and that he made his habitation in Virginia during the great Civil War."

41. Dr. J. W. Claiborne, from Virginia, was practicing not at Sonora but at Jamestown according to Heckendorn & Wilson's directory, his headquarters as of January 1, 1856, being Claiborne's Drug Store. No Matchin was then listed either in Sonora or in Jamestown, but see Note 43. A New Yorker, S. D. Streeter, was listed as a miner in the latter place.

42. Edna Bryan Buckbee, *The Saga of Old Tuolumne*, pp. 478–479, tells us: "Jamestown's first medical men were Doctors James W. Claiborne, Mark T. and J. W. Dodge. The first drug store in the town was opened by Dr. Claiborne."

43. Evidently Gardiner has reference to Thomas N. Machin, of whom a brief biography, clipped from a newspaper of 1864 or 1865, may be found in the Benjamin Hayes Scrapbooks, California Notes, vol. III, p. 49, in the Bancroft Library. Machin was born in New York in 1824, emigrated to Wisconsin and thence to California in 1852, and

eventually settled in Mono County. A practicing lawyer, he was elected to the Assembly from Tuolumne and Mono counties in 1861, and was reelected next year, when he was chosen speaker. In 1863 he was elected lieutenant governor on the Union ticket, running with F. F. Low. Then single, he married a San Francisco widow in 1864; either Gardiner's memory was faulty, or a first wife died.

CHAPTER XXIII. *At Indian Bar* (pp. 229–242)

1. Concerning this ranch, Prentice Mulford recalled in the recollections he wrote for Lang's *A History of Tuolumne County*, Appendix, p. 21: "My first service to the community in Tuolumne was rendered at the Golden Ranch, a locality three miles from Don Pedro's Bar and three from Hawkins', where the life was knocked out of Mexican cows a year old, called calves, and other septuagenarian, long-horned cattle, whose flesh was termed beef. For a few weeks I peddled this beef to the miners of Tuolumne. One day the horse ran away and discharged the entire freight of beef in the panniers on the golden sands of California. I picked the steaks up as they fell, stacked them in piles on the road, caught the horse, reloaded him, led him to the muddy river, washed the beef, and left it, per custom, at the miners' cabins. Next day I was discharged." The locality, as "Golden City," is shown on J. P. Dart, "Map of the Principal Quartz and Gravel Mines in Tuolumne County (Sonora, 1879).

3. Guy J. Giffen, *California Expedition*, p. 35, lists Richard Clamp as a member of Company A in Stevenson's New York Regiment; he "Added one to the population of Chinese Camp. He was there in 1871 and also 1882."

4. Evidently this was S. M. Miller, a Pennsylvanian who as of January 1, 1856, was agent for the Pacific Express in Chinese Camp.

5. Gardiner refers to the San Francisco Vigilance Committee of 1856, organized after James Casey shot the editor of the San Francisco *Evening Bulletin*, James King of William. Casey and another alleged murderer, Charles Cora, were hanged on May 22, eight days after the shooting. For an extended account, see H. H. Bancroft, *Popular Tribunals* (San Francisco, 1887), 2 vols., vol. II. Bancroft upholds the vigilance committee; an opposite viewpoint is taken by John Myers Myers, *San Francisco's Reign of Terror* (Garden City, N.Y., 1966).

6. For this convention, again held at Jamestown (not Sonora) on June 16, 1855, see Chapter XXII, Note 37. Apparently this, more than 1854, was the fractious political year in Tuolumne County.

7. Gardiner is writing in a context of 1855, but Joaquin Murrieta's celebrated incursions were made prior to and in 1853. He was hunted down by Captain Harry Love, after which his severed head was widely exhibited in California. At least, that is the accepted story, though as Francis P. Farquhar has sagely observed, "When a bandit attains the celebrity of a Joaquin Murieta it becomes almost impossible to distinguish the actualities of his life from the legend that grows up around him." There were those who denied that

the man killed in 1853 was actually "Joaquin," and robberies kept on being attributed to "Joaquin." See the note by Morgan and Scobie in William Perkins, *Three Years in California*, pp. 326–327.

8. See Chapter I, Note 15; and for further information on Robert H. Waterman, with a reproduction of an attractive painting of him, see David Andrew Weir, *That Fabulous Captain Waterman* (New York, 1957).

9. The history of Chambers' Bar is regrettably obscure; Gardiner tells us more than I have found anywhere else. Even its existence goes unmentioned in Heckendorn & Wilson's *Miners & Business Men's Directory*, which for example says in respect of "Small Camps or Districts": "Stevens', Red Mountain, Hawkins', Indian, Texas, Morgan's, Don Pedro's, Rodgers' and many other Bars on the Tuolumne river, are all in Tuolumne county, and are places of considerable note. In 1850 they were the largest camps in the county—thousands of miners were engaged in attempting to turn the river, the bed of which they imagined contained millions of treasure; but few companies succeeded in diverting the channel from its course, and what few did were disappointed in its supposed richness. Some few companies done well, but as a general thing the river turning that year was a failure—since then the mode of operating has been very different, and the bed of the stream in a number of places has paid well for the expense of fluming, which is the only mode by which it can be successfully worked. The River will furnish profitable employment for many years to come" (p. 89).

CHAPTER XXIV. *At Chambers' Bar* (pp. 243–253)

1. Peñon Blanco, about 2 miles northwest of Coulterville on Blacks Creek, is shown along the road to Jacksonville via Moccasin Creek on a 1914 "Map of Mariposa County California." The Spanish name *peñon blanco*, "large white rock," was applied to a ridge about three miles west of the place, perhaps the "white quartz peak" Gardiner mentions.

2. Heckendorn & Wilson say in their *Miners & Business Men's Directory*, p. 89: "The Camps of Belvidere Flat, Quartz Mountain, Humbug Hill, Amazon Gulch, Ohio Diggings, Loves' Bar, (on Wood's creek,) Campo Seco, Kincaid's Flat, Cooper's Flat, Half oz Gulch, Roache's Camp, Sullivan's Creek, are all south-east of Sonora, and the farthest not over fifteen miles distant. Most of them are small though promising places, and have more or less mining ground in their vicinity, and so soon as they can get a supply of water, the entire season, they will be able to give a good account of their receipts of Gold, as many others of a larger territory, and greater facilities." Twenty-two residents of Belvidere Flat are listed, all miners except H. Mattison, Hotel Keeper, and C. L. White, Merchant. Gardiner better locates Belvidere Flat, which was between Chinese Camp and Montezuma, west and somewhat north of Sonora.

3. The Chowchilla River, named in Mexican times for Miwok Indians, rises in southern Mariposa County, then flows northwesterly toward the San Joaquin in Madera County, just south of the Mariposa line.

4. I am not aware of any Mormon coins minted in California. Surely Gardiner must refer to one of those minted in 1849 at Great Salt Lake City. See Reva Holdaway Stanley, "The First Utah Coins Minted from California Gold," California Historical Society Quarterly, September, 1936, vol. 15, pp. 244–246, with photographs of the coins. Jacob R. Eckfeldt and William E. DuBois, New Varieties of Gold and Silver Coins, Counterfeit Coins and Bullion; with Mint Values (Philadelphia, 1850), p. 61, comments: "The Mormon Coins have just been received [January 10, 1850], through a gentleman who came overland from Great Salt Lake in eighty-one days. They consist of 20, 10, 5, and 2½ dollar pieces. In fineness they are about 899 thous., with little variations; and they contain only the native silver alloy. The weights are more irregular, and the values very deficient. The 20 dollar piece weighs from 436 to 453 grains, value $16.90 to $17.53. The 10 dollar, 219 to 224 grains, $8.50 to $8.70. The 5 dollar, about 111 grains; $4.30. The 2½ dollar, about 58 grains, $2.25.

"On one side of the coins is HOLINESS TO THE LORD, with a large eye [the All-Seeing Eye], and something like a mitre; on the other, two hands in friendly grasp, with the date 1849, and a legend containing the alleged value, and the initials G. S. L. C. P. G., meaning GREAT SALT LAKE CITY, PURE GOLD. The ten dollar piece has PURE GOLD, in full."

CHAPTER XXV. At Belvidere Flat (pp. 255–268)

1. This "old Spaniard, Don Pedro," was not the early French settler, Pierre Sainsevain ("Don Pedro") who gave name to Don Pedro's Bar; see Chapter XVI, Note 19.

2. That is, a lynching bee was in progress.

3. Tuttletown was north and slightly east of Sonora, situated on a branch of Mormon Gulch. Heckendorn & Wilson, Miners & Business Men's Directory, p. 79, said of it: "Gold was struck on mormon gulch in '48, by a company of miners, and in the summer and fall of '49, large quantities of gold was taken from it, and its limits. It was a flourishing camp in '49, and '50, but there are but few persons there at present, although it is said that those who work there still realize good wages on an average.— Tuttletown received its name from Judge [A. A. H.] Tuttle, the first county Judge of this county, who built and occupied the first cabin at that place."

4. This entertaining account of Prentice Mulford's advent upon the Tuolumne County scene is considerably more detailed than any provided by Mulford himself. The son of Ezekiel Mulford, born at Sag Harbor April 5, 1834, he shipped before the mast in 1856, and after various adventures wound up in San Francisco all but broke, so that he made for Hawkins' Bar. In his book Mulford gives the year as 1858, but Franklin Walker more correctly says that it was in 1857 that Mulford "turned up at Hawkins' Bar on the Tuolumne with $7 in cash and a trunk containing several vests, all that remained of the clothes he had brought from the East." (In his contribution to Lang's A History of Tuolumne County, Mulford says he landed in Tuolumne County with $18 in his pocket "and a sailor's bag of clothing, which, among other things, contained seven vests," since a

single vest would outlive five pairs of pantaloons. We have previously quoted his remarks on his first job, at the Golden Ranch (see Chapter XXIII, Note 1). He went on to say "that he then "served a short time at the grocery and boarding-house of my esteemed friend, Robert E. Gardiner, at Hawkins' Bar. After allowing another horse, packed with provisions for a mining company, to get away from me and wreck the entire load, I sought other fields of labor I worked a bank or surface mining claim for two years, at Swett's Bar. It did not pay regularly, perhaps owing to my own irregularities." Beginning in 1860, he taught school in Jamestown for a time, then engaged in a copper mining venture, after which he "Arrived in Sonora, profoundly 'busted,'" and "set to work digging post-holes for my old and faithful friend Robert E. Gardiner, then County Clerk of Tuolumne. I don't think he was very anxious to have post-holes dug on his premises, but I do think he allowed me to imagine I was earning something in this way out of charity for my condition."

Mulford took up lecturing, ran unsuccessfully for the legislature, and drifted into journalism, commencing with some contributions to the Sonora *Union Democrat* under the pseudonym "Dogberry." In 1866 he was invited to join the *Golden Era* in San Francisco, and except for rare visits, Tuolumne County saw him no more. All this is set forth at length, and very entertainingly, in his book. Most of his later life, after sixteen years in California, was spent on the East Coast and in Europe. Franklin Walker, in his introduction to Mulford's *California Sketches,* says that Mulford "brought an English wife with him when he recrossed the Atlantic in 1874. Tales of his courtship have probably been much romanticized. Rumor has it that he and Joaquin Miller found Josie Allen starving on the London streets and practically adopted her; that Miller, [Charles Warren] Stoddard, and Mulford fell successive victims of her charms, and that Mulford won the prize before he realized it; and that he educated her, introduced her into society, and took her with him on his travels to Paris and Vienna. Even wilder stories circulated about the reason for their separation some years after returning to America. It was said that Josie, dissatisfied with Prentice's meager income as a columnist on *The New York Graphic,* resorted to an old practice of posing in the nude for pin-money, and that her husband first became aware of her folly when he found her picture on the back of a pack of cigarettes. Whatever the cause may have been, Mulford and his young wife agreed to go their separate ways, she to another marriage and he to a hermit's hut in the New Jersey swamps."

Walker further relates that on May 31, 1891, the 57-year-old Mulford "was found dead in his small boat on Sheepshead Bay. A few days before, he had set out to cruise alone from Hoboken to Sag Harbor. He had taken with him provisions, his blankets, some writing pads, and his banjo, his inseparable companion; on the night of May 27th he had rolled himself in his blankets to sleep under the stars; and for some reason never satisfactorily explained he had not awakened."

5. Mrs. Barbara Eastman gives me these additional notes on Howard Gardiner's cousin and long-time friend: "Robert Emmet Gardiner on September 4, 1861, was elected Tuolumne County Clerk and ex-officio School Superintendent, to take office March 3, 1862.

On August 15, 1862, under a new Act, John H. Stone was appointed School Superintendent. The 1863 election returns were challenged and Gardiner served until August 1, 1864. He was defeated in 1863 and 1865, but elected again in 1867 and 1869 as County Clerk, as shown by County Supervisors' Records. When he went out of office in 1872, he became a partner of Donald McLean in the Livery business. In September, 1874, his signature appears on an affidavit he signed for Mrs. Margaret Mehen as Secretary of the Pioneer Society of Tuolumne County. In 1876, when James Mandeville became State Controller, he appointed Gardiner as his Clerk. He remained to serve the full term, although Mandeville had died in office. Apparently Gardiner returned to Sonora, but in 1883 was given an appointment under the State Harbor Commission and moved to San Francisco, where he died. He had five children; one son, a lawyer, remained in Sonora." Robert E. Gardiner was married twice. He died February 3, 1886, aged 59 years, 3 months, and 5 days.

6. See Chapter II, Note 4. The San Francisco city directory for 1852–1853 first lists L. S. Hildreth and S. T. Hildreth as butchers at 24 Commercial Street. In 1854 S. T. Hildreth & Co., Contra Costa Market, was listed at 24 Commercial Street, and so were John D. and Luther S. Hildreth, butchers at the same address. In 1856 J. D., L. S., and S. F. Hildreth, of Hildreth & Co., appear as proprietors of the Contra Costa Market, Commercial near Front Street. In 1858 John D. and Luther S. Hildreth were listed as members of S. T. Hildreth & Co., Contra Costa Market, 104 Davis Street. In 1859 only Luther S. Hildreth was recorded, but a new member of the family was evidently on hand, for Henry P. as well as Luther was located at 211 Stockton Street. In 1860 there was a listing only for Luther Hildreth, "bds with Doctor Wm. Ayres." By 1861 Luther too had vanished from the city directory.

7. The *Niantic*, as a store ship or warehouse, burned in the San Francisco fire of May 4, 1851. By this time a Niantic Building occupied the site.

8. William O. Ayres, M.D., was recorded in the San Francisco directories from 1856, when his office was given as Washington above Dupont, his residence, corner of Powell and Sacramento. By 1858 he had established himself at 211 Stockton Street, for which see Note 6. He maintained himself there through 1860, but in 1861 was living at 815 Stockton Street. The directories continued to list him through 1874. In August, 1886, the *Overland Monthly* published his "Personal Recollections of the Vigilance Committee [of 1856]."

9. As the next chapter makes fully evident, Gardiner sailed from San Francisco on the *John L. Stephens,* not the *Golden Gate.* The latter vessel at this time was being refitted at Benicia, and did not sail for Panama until October 5. On that southward voyage she broke her center shaft and had to put in at Monterey; her run was completed by her sister ship, the *Golden Age.* The normal sailing dates from San Francisco for Pacific Mail Steamship vessels were the 5th and 20th, but as September 20 came on a Sunday, the *John L. Stephens* sailed one day later. At this period no opposition lines were running between San Francisco and Panama. P. M. S. sailings through the late summer of 1857 were the

Golden Gate, August 5, *Sonora,* August 20, and *California,* September 5. The *Alta California* noted on Monday, September 21: "The mail steamship *J. L. Stephens* leaves punctually this morning, at the hour of 9 o'clock, from her berth, foot of Vallejo street. She takes down few passengers and but a moderate amount of treasure. [On arrival, the Panama *Star & Herald* gave the total as $2,000,000.] Captain Pearson having gone down in command of the *California,* which left two weeks since, Commodore [James T.] Watkins will have charge of the *Stephens* on this trip." The *John L. Stephens* had last returned from Panama on August 30. (For the history of this vessel, a side-wheeler, see J. H. Kemble, *The Panama Route, 1848–1869,* p. 233.)

CHAPTER XXVI. *Homeward Bound* (pp. 269–281)

1. The lighthouse on the southernmost of the Farallon Islands was noted as under construction in the Stockton *San Joaquin Republican,* April 14, 1854.

2. According to a notice printed weekly in the Panama *Star & Herald* at this period, the Pacific Mail Steamers from San Francisco were expected at that port about the 3rd and 18th of each month, and sailed about the 15th and 30th. U.S. Mail Steamers from New York normally reached Aspinwall about the 15th and 30th of each month, and sailed about the 4th and 19th. The publisher's file of the *Star & Herald,* of which the Bancroft Library has a microfilm, is in rather fragmentary condition through 1857, and the story on the arrival of the *John L. Stephens* has almost entirely disappeared from the issue of October 6. We infer from Gardiner's account that she arrived late on the 3rd.

3. As seen in Chapter I, Note 5, the Panama Railroad was completed in January, 1855. At the time Gardiner reached Panama, the prevailing fares as published by the company in the *Star & Herald* were $25 for adults, children under 12 half price, children under 6 quarter price. The trains ran daily (except on Sundays and American steamer days), departing Panama at 9:15 A. M., and Aspinwall at 8:30 A. M. According to Gardiner's recollections, which seems entirely accurate, his was an almost continuous passage from arrival at Panama to departure from Aspinwall. Therefore his second stay on the Isthmus was brief, from the morning of October 4 to the afternoon of October 5.

4. That the side-wheeler *Northern Light* was on hand to meet the passengers from the *John L. Stephens* was in itself a story. The previous San Francisco steamer, the *Sonora,* had through-connections with the *Central America.* On September 12 this vessel foundered in a gale after leaving Havana, and of her 550 passengers, some 400 were drowned. The *Northern Light* was sent off to Aspinwall in her place, and arrived with news of the tragedy October 2. This news largely filled the columns of the Panama *Star & Herald* the day Gardiner arrived, October 3. (For a condensed history of the *Northern Light,* see J. H. Kemble, *The Panama Route, 1848–1869,* pp. 237–238, or his contribution to the Book Club of California's Keepsake Series of 1958, *Gold Rush Steamers,* which has a spirited lithograph of her at sea.)

5. Reports of the *Northern Light's* misadventure were promptly published in the Pan-

ama *Star & Herald*. On October 15 a telegraphic dispatch from Aspinwall dated the 13th reported: "The U. S. steam frigate *Wabash* returned here this morning after a cruize of a few days. At Old Providence Island she met the U.S. Mail steamer *Northern Light*, which had just got off the reefs surrounding that Island, where it had been aground for about twelve (12) hours. The *Northern Light* had to land a considerable number of her passengers to enable her to float off, and apparently sustained no damage." The vessel had sailed, the *Star & Herald* added, with 800 passengers from California.

A fuller account was reprinted in the *Star & Herald* on November 5, 1857, from the Boston *Evening Traveller* of October 19: "Steamer *Northern Light*, which arrived at New York on Friday morning [October 16], was in a dangerous situation, shortly after leaving Aspinwall. When about 23 hours out she ran on a coral reef three miles from Old Providence, (a small island in the Carribean Sea, in lat 13 21 N., and about a hundred miles east of the Mosquito [Nicaragua] coast,) where she remained some eight or nine hours. The sea was calm, and the shore was nigh, but the passengers who had just before heard of the loss of the *Central America*, could not but contemplate with some apprehensions, the contingency, should a storm arise, of a similar fate. The following account is furnished by one of the passengers:

"We left Aspinwall at 8 o'clock P.M., on Monday, Oct. 8[5], having just heard the news of the loss of the *Central America*. We had beautiful weather, and at noon on Tuesday had made 180 miles on our way to Havana. We were then in lat. 12 15 North, long. 80 46 West.

"The afternoon passed off pleasantly, and we were making twelve knots an hour, when at a few minutes before 7 in the evening we were startled by the ship's thumping five distinct times on what proved to be a coral reef. The engines were immediately stopped, and the sounding lines thrown over. A boat was soon lowered away, and we found but 14 feet of water all around the ship.

"Rockets were thrown up, and were answered by the arrival from the Island of Old Providence, about three miles distant, of two dug-outs, manned by the inhabitants, but having with them the captain of a coal ship in the Company's service, which had been wrecked near the same place some eight weeks previously. His men went to Aspinwall in open boats, took passage in the *Central America* home, and were lost in that unfortunate steamer.

"He informed us that there was plenty of water and provisions on the island, and a good harbor on the opposite side, where three five-ton schooners were lying. We then sent the second officer with a boat to induce the schooners to come to the steamer; but there was no wind, and one only reached us about 7 o'clock the next morning.

"In the meantime, the engines were started every few minutes, and the passengers sent from stem to stern, and from larboard to starboard, that their weight might assist in moving her. At midnight an anchor was dropped ahead, which, by the help of the windlass, caused the ship to swing almost round. The bows were clear, but she still seemed to be fast from midship to stern.

"About three o'clock in the morning four boat loads of passengers were sent on shore, and thirty tons of water discharged from the boiler. The tide had now risen. A strong pull was made upon the anchor, both wheels were put in motion, and at 4 o'clock the steamer went off into deeper water, having been on the reef all night."

Having come to no harm from this misadventure, the *Northern Light* was back at Aspinwall November 15 with 1,270 California-bound passengers and the U.S. mail.

6. Havana was a regular port of call for the steamer from Aspinwall. Gardiner had forgotten by 1896 that the passengers must have had misgivings about stopping at Cuba in 1857, for yellow fever was then reported to be causing great havoc at Havana. See the Panama *Star & Herald*, September 19, 1857. In the San Francisco *Alta California*, September 15, 1857, a Havana letter of August 26 says, "The yellow fever is raging all over the Island, and great consternation prevails on account of it. . . ."

Acknowledgments and Some After-Thoughts

Having at length reached the point where I must part company with this rather formidable book, one which has both enlightened and bedeviled me for some years now, I welcome the opportunity to express appreciation to those who have accompanied me through all the ups and downs, frequently with that most indispensable kind of help, the things you cannot do for yourself.

First of all, then, I am indebted to Eugene L. Schwaab and Michael Ginsberg, who in themselves *are* Western Hemisphere, booksellers and now publishers. When Howard Gardiner's manuscript reminiscences and some collateral papers came into their hands, they immediately recognized their potential, and resolved to have them edited and printed in fitting style. Thus I and the distinguished printers Lawton and Alfred Kennedy entered the picture, as the latest of many fruitful collaborations. Messrs. Schwaab and Ginsberg have given me an absolutely free hand with the manuscript, asking only that I be pleased with the final result; and similarly they have given the Kennedys, father and son, full liberty in the design and printing of the book. Would that all authors had such publishers to back them up!

It will be seen that after much reflection, and in view of the signal stature of the Gardiner reminiscences in the literature of the Gold Rush, I thought it desirable to preface Gardiner's story with a general survey of this literature, from 1860 to the present day. Or, at least, so much of that literature as has been published, or republished, in book form. The Bancroft Library is an extraordinary good base for a wide-ranging survey of this kind; I learned of few significant titles not in the Bancroft collections, and was thus enabled to examine personally almost everything described. Thus I have a very large indebtedness also to the Bancroft Library and to members of the staff who have given me help along the way: Director Emeritus George P. Hammond, Assistant Director Robert H. Becker, John Barr Tompkins, Miss Estelle Rebec, Miss Marie Byrne, Mrs. Vivian Fisher, and Miss Irene Moran.

Farther afield, Archibald Hanna, Curator of the Western Americana Collection, and Miss Dorothy Bridgewater of the Yale University Library befriended this book as they have so many past books of mine; in particular Miss Bridgewater enabled me to make my first real headway in establishing just who Howard C. Gardiner was, beyond the limits of the California frame of reference. Other valuable institutional assistance was provided by James de T. Abajian, former librarian of the California Historical Society, by Allan R. Ottley, head of the California section of the California State Library, and by staff members of the State Historical Society of Wisconsin, the New York Public Library, the Green Bay Public Library, and the Library of Congress.

The once-baffling question of Howard C. Gardiner's posterity was answered at last with the help of various family members, especially Mrs. John Urquhart Gardiner of Hyattsville, Maryland, Mrs. John L. Gardiner of Arlington, Virginia, Mrs. Harley C. Warner of Wallingford, Connecticut, and by Howard Stanley Judd, Jr., and Mrs. John

V. Silcox, Jr. They have generously and happily cooperated in this publication of Howard C. Gardiner's book.

Before the manuscript could be edited, it had to be transcribed, and this job was efficiently done by Mrs. Marguerite Reusser, with the assistance of Leonard Incledon. Help on knotty points was given by Mrs. Louise C. North, Mrs. Barbara Eastman, Doyce R. Nunis, George L. Harding, Reginald Bretnor, and Miss Mildred O. Browning. The map was especially prepared for this work by Mrs. Lois C. Stone, who even went to the trouble of making a track-chart for Gardiner's voyage from Panama to San Francisco in the *Sylph*. Except for the portrait of Howard Gardiner, which was kindly furnished by Mrs. John L. Gardiner, all the illustrations come from the pictorial collections of the Bancroft Library. I had anticipated that two drawings of Hawkins' Bar by John W. Audubon would be made available for use in this work (see p. 316), but in the event, the Southwest Museum declined its cooperation, and other subjects have been substituted.

Most of the book had been printed when I embarked upon the index, so I am able only to point out, not effectively to correct, certain errata that crept in, additional to that just mentioned. At p. x, line 17, for "discoveriest" read "discoveries." At p. xxvii, line 4, for "Nicolet's" read "Perlot's." At p. 46, line 2, omit "out." And at p. 272, line 3, for "Bar" read "Bay."

Thus it profited me, doing the index. A few more positive merits of the index might be dwelt upon, though at first glance it may seem almost excessively detailed. The index serves some of the usual function of a bibliography, in that the literature comprised of California Gold Rush reminiscences is here listed alphabetically, keyed to the generally chronological discussion in the introduction. Again in this book I have carried out a practice inaugurated in earlier works pertaining to the Gold Rush, in that I have listed states, foreign countries, and even cities and counties from which 49ers came. Some day, in my view, we must have a state-by-state history of the California Gold Rush, and the indexes of my books are intended to be a contribution toward that end. For this same reason, names are consistently reported in the index from text and notes. Names derived from passenger lists in contemporary newspapers may sometimes be misprinted, and I have had strong misgivings about some of the names I have included in such lists; but it has been necessary for the most part to follow copy and hope for the best. In any case, the index may well be regarded as one of the most signal features of this book, an organizing and identifying scholarly device which may prove useful far beyond the apparent limits of the volume now at hand. And this, I think, is a good point for me to part company with Howard C. Gardiner and his reminiscences of the California Gold Rush.

DALE L. MORGAN

INDEX

NOTE: *The Gardiner Genealogy, pp. xliii–xlv, lxi–lxii, is indexed only insofar as members of the family figure in Howard C. Gardiner's correspondence and California reminiscences.*

367